PROBLEMS AND MATERIALS ON
BANKRUPTCY LAW AND PRACTICE

By

Stephen L. Sepinuck
Professor of Law
Gonzaga University School of Law

Linda J. Rusch
Frederick N. and Barbara T. Curley
Professor of Commercial Law
Gonzaga University School of Law

AMERICAN CASEBOOK SERIES®

THOMSON
WEST

Mat #40516343

American Casebook Series and West Group are trademarks
registered in the U.S. Patent and Trademark Office.

© 2007 Thomson/West
    610 Opperman Drive
    St. Paul, MN 55123
    1–800–328–9352

Printed in the United States of America

ISBN: 978–0–314–17174–0

TEXT IS PRINTED ON 10% POST CONSUMER RECYCLED PAPER

To Doug, Kari, and Anna

    LJR

To Sandra, Ben, and Jacob, who make life worth living.

    SLS

PREFACE

This book is designed for an introductory, three-credit course on bankruptcy. In creating it, we have drawn on our three decades of collective experience in teaching this course, our experience teaching other commercial law and statutory courses, as well as our work in private practice and in various commercial law reform projects.

Our general approach to teaching code-based subjects is to focus on problems, rather than cases. However, because this course is typically populated by students who have already had one or more other commercial-law, statutory courses, we do not focus heavily on imparting the skills necessary for statutory construction. We expect students to come into this course having experience with reading statutory text in order to identify ambiguities and construct possible interpretations. Instead, we concentrate on the substance of bankruptcy law and its effect on bankruptcy and commercial practice. There is more than enough there to fill many books.

We love this area of law. Bankruptcy cases directly or indirectly affect tens of millions of Americans every year and employ thousands of attorneys. The law governing them is extraordinarily dynamic, as a result of both thousand of judicial decisions each year and frequent legislative tinkering. Bankruptcy law also has a profoundly broad impact: affecting commercial activity at virtually every level, from structuring a transaction to collecting a debt. And it is filled with fascinating policy issues. We hope that our affection is evident, at least occasionally, in the pages that follow and that some of our affection for this area might even be infectious as you work your way through these materials.

We invite all who use this book – teachers and students alike – to send us their comments about this book. Only with them can we possibly improve it.

ACKNOWLEDGMENTS

A book such as this, which is intended not as a treatise but as a teaching tool, needs input from a variety of people with different levels of experience and different learning styles. We are therefore deeply grateful to all our students who provided suggestions and noted errors on earlier drafts of this book. We also appreciate their willingness to be the test subjects of a work in progress.

SUMMARY OF CONTENTS

TABLE OF CONTENTS

TABLE OF CASES

TABLE OF FEDERAL STATUTES, RULES & FORMS

TABLE OF UNIFORM STATUTES

Problems and Materials on Bankruptcy Law and Practice

PART I

AN INTRODUCTION TO BANKRUPTCY LAW AND PRACTICE

CHAPTER ONE
BACKGROUND ON STATE LAW & DEBT COLLECTION
_____

The bulk of this book focuses on the federal Bankruptcy Code (codified in Title 11 of the United States Code) and how it modifies the rights of creditors and debtors. However, it is important to remember that bankruptcy law is built on a large foundation of non-bankruptcy law. A working knowledge of what rights the parties have under non-bankruptcy law is a prerequisite to understanding bankruptcy. This is because, as a general matter, the Bankruptcy Code does not create creditors' rights; instead, it limits some of the rights of creditors, eliminates others, and provides a mechanism to enforce those rights that remain. For example, the Bankruptcy Code may temporarily enjoin a creditor's efforts to collect the debt owed to it, may discharge the debtor's obligation to the creditor entirely, or it may alter a creditor's claim to specific assets of the debtor. Yet in all cases, the analysis begins with whatever non-bankruptcy rights exist.

Whether a person owes an obligation to another is usually not determined by bankruptcy law. For example, the Uniform Commercial Code (U.C.C.), which is enacted at the state level, and the general law of contract and tort, will have much to say about what obligations the debtor owes to another individual or entity. Bankruptcy is a process for dealing with obligations created under that other law.

Creditors also come to bankruptcy armed with a wide array of property rights in the debtor's assets. The local real property law (often codified in part in state statutes) and the rules governing the creation, perfection, and enforcement of security interests in personal property (governed in large part by U.C.C. Article 9) form a critical part of the edifice of property rights upon which bankruptcy is built. Both a mortgage and an Article 9 security interest are created as a matter of contract between the debtor and creditor. The debtor in consideration for a loan or other value from the creditor grants the creditor an interest in the property (a mortgage if in real property, a security interest if in personal property) to secure the repayment of the loan or other debt to the creditor. These consensual arrangements give the creditor a property interest (called a "lien") in the debtor's real property identified in the mortgage and the debtor's personal property identified in the Article 9 security agreement.

Sometimes, a state statute or common-law rule will give a creditor a lien on property to secure an obligation. Common examples of such nonconsensual liens are a mechanic's lien to secure payment due for improvements to real estate, an artisan's lien to secure payment due for repairs of personal property, and a landlord's lien on personal property located on the leased premises to secure payment of the rent. Another, perhaps more ubiquitous example, is a tax lien: a lien on a taxpayer's property in favor of the taxing authority to secure the taxes due. The number and types of statutory and common-law liens varies widely from state to state.

A lien, whether contractual or nonconsensual, is very important because it greatly enhances the lienholder's ability to collect the obligation owed to it. Although the enforcement mechanisms vary,[1] the lienholder is typically entitled to seize the property, sell it, and use the sale proceeds to pay the debt owed, returning any surplus to the debtor.

Creditors without a lien have far fewer rights and often far fewer options for collecting the debts rightfully due them. Various laws, such as the Fair Debt Collection Practices Act, may prevent the creditor from harassing the debtor for payment.[2] Unless the debtor is cooperative, a creditor's best option may be to bring a civil action in the hope of obtaining a judgment against the debtor. Of course, entry of a judgment may not enhance the debtor's eagerness or ability to pay. The debtor may continue to ignore the creditor's demands for payment and may even take steps to avoid the creditor's efforts to extract payment. However, a judgment does entitle the creditor to use various additional collection mechanisms.

Before discussing those mechanisms, a word of warning is in order. What follows is a broad outline of the judgment collection process. This summary is exceedingly generic because the judgment collection process varies both in substance and in terminology from state to state. It is offered merely to provide a foundation for the study of bankruptcy law and should not – must not – substitute for a thorough understanding of the relevant state rules in the event you later represent either a creditor trying to collect on a judgment or a debtor trying to resist such efforts.

The process of collecting on a judgment involves seizing some of the debtor's assets, selling them, and then applying the proceeds of sale against the amount of the judgment debt owed. The first step in this process is, of course, to identify and locate the debtor's assets. Finding the judgment debtor's real estate is often not difficult because the debtor's ownership will likely be a matter of public record. In most states, the judgment creditor can then record the judgment and that act gives the judgment creditor a lien on whatever real estate the defendant owns in the county in which the lien is recorded.

Locating the judgment debtor's personal property is often more challenging. Fortunately, most states permit the judgment creditor to question the debtor under oath about what assets the debtor has and where they are located. Such questions are posed during a post-judgment deposition or through post-judgment interrogatories. The problem with this discovery-like process is that by the time the creditor learns what

---

[1]   If the debtor has granted a mortgage on real estate to secure a loan, the process the mortgagee (the creditor) uses to enforce the mortgage will be governed by the applicable foreclosure statutes in the relevant state. If the creditor has a U.C.C. Article 9 security interest in the debtor's personal property, Article 9 details the processes available to the creditor to extract value from the collateral to satisfy the debt owed.

[2]   15 U.S.C §§ 1692–1692o.

assets the debtor has and where they are located, and the creditor completes the paperwork and obtains the authorization necessary to actually seize the assets, the debtor may have moved the assets or otherwise put them beyond the creditor's reach.

If a judgment creditor does successfully identify and locate personal property of the debtor, the creditor typically has two options on how to proceed: execution and garnishment. A writ of execution is generally used against the debtor's tangible assets. The creditor obtains a writ of execution from the court clerk (typically the court that entered the judgment) and delivers that writ to the sheriff (or other law enforcement officer). The writ directs the sheriff to seize and sell whatever assets of the debtor it specifies. The seizure process is called a "levy." A levy is ordinarily effected by the sheriff actually taking possession of the property. However, if the property is too large to move (such as factory equipment), state law may authorize a levy to occur by posting a notice on the property or by filing notice of the levy in the applicable public record.

A writ of garnishment is typically to collect on intangible assets, particularly obligations owed to the debtor by a third party. For example, if an employer or bank owes money to the debtor, the creditor may obtain a writ of garnishment from the court clerk and serve that writ on the employer or bank (the garnishee). The writ directs the garnishee to pay the obligation either to the creditor or to the court, rather than to the debtor.

Generally, a levy pursuant to a writ of execution creates a judicial lien on the assets seized. Similarly, the service of a writ of garnishment creates a judicial lien on the obligation garnished. In other words, the judgment creditor can obtain an interest in the debtor's property through judicial process

Once an asset is levied on, the asset is then sold pursuant to a process prescribed by state statute. Typically, the sale is conducted as an auction by the sheriff after public notice is given. The proceeds of the sale are used to satisfy the costs of execution (*i.e.,* the levy and the sale) and then applied to the judgment debt. Prices obtained at execution sales are usually quite low in comparison to the value of the asset. Most courts, however, will not invalidate an otherwise properly conducted execution sale on the basis of low price alone. However, if there was some irregularity in the sale process and a shockingly low price was obtained, the court may set aside the sale and require that the sale be conducted again. The judgment creditor may continue to levy on and garnish personal property of the debtor until the debtor runs out of assets or the judgment debt is paid.

Some judgment debtors have the ability to "exempt" – *i.e.,* to shield – some of their real and personal property from execution and garnishment. Generally, exemptions are available only to debtors who are human beings, not to other types of entities (such as partnerships, trusts, corporations, or limited liability companies). Exemptions are considered necessary for three reasons. First, exemptions prevent the debtor from becoming impoverished. After all, if a creditor could use judicial process to impoverish the debtor, the law would be elevating the creditor's interest over the public interest. As a result, most states exempt some basic "life necessities," such as food up to a certain value or a homestead. In addition, federal law restricts the amount of a debtor's wages that may be garnished.[3] Second, some of the debtor's exempt property may have no meaningful resale value even though it would be difficult or costly for the debtor to replace. Seizure of such assets – family photographs or used clothes, for example – would be counter-utilitarian. Third, some property is exempt for spiritual or humanitarian reasons. Thus, items such as family bibles and inexpensive wedding rings are often exempt.

Despite the various rationales for exemptions, some states are rather miserly in what they permit a debtor to protect from creditors. In contrast, some states have very generous exemptions (such as an unlimited value for a homestead). Some states exempt odd things, such as a pew in the church, a burial plot, or ten chickens. The type of property, the value of property, and the types of debtors that may use the exemptions vary widely from state to state.

On some occasions, a creditor may be able to go after the debtor's assets even prior to judgment. Most states permit issuance of a pre-judgment writ of attachment (similar to a post-judgment writ of execution) or a pre-judgment writ of garnishment. Using these processes, a creditor may have the sheriff seize the debtor's asset or may require an obligor to pay the amount owed to the debtor into court before judgment is rendered against the debtor. Such pre-judgment processes are generally available only if the creditor can demonstrate to the court that the debtor is trying to hide assets in anticipation of an adverse judgment. In addition, state statutes may require that the debtor be provided notice and opportunity for a hearing prior to issuance of the writ and may require that the creditor post a bond to protect the debtor from damages in the event that judgment is not entered against the debtor. Like their post-judgment counterparts, though, these pre-judgment processes create a lien on the assets of the debtor that are levied on or garnished. Because these processes can interfere with the debtor's property rights even though there has been no judgment of liability to the creditor, they are subject to scrutiny as a potential violation of the debtor's constitutional protections against unlawful seizure or denial of due process.[4] In analyzing these issues, courts generally balance the fairness and efficacy of the procedures available to protect the debtor's property interest against the creditor's interest in eventually collecting on the judgment.

There are two other state-law processes that are occasionally available to creditors and which are worthy of note: an assignment for benefit of creditors and a receivership. In an assignment for benefit of creditors, a debtor voluntarily turns over all of its property to an assignee. The assignee receives creditors claims against the debtor and

---

[3]   *See* 15 U.S.C. §§ 1671–1677.

[4]   *Connecticut v. Doehr*, 501 U.S. 1 (1991) (procedural due process); *Soldal v. Cook County, Illinois*, 506 U.S. 56 (1992) (search and seizure).

uses the assigned property value to pay those claims as well as the cost of administering the assignment. Unlike a bankruptcy proceeding, however, an assignment for benefit of creditors does not result in a discharge of the debtor's obligations to the extent those obligations are not satisfied through the assignment and distribution process. While some or all of the debtor's creditors may agree to regard their distribution as terminating the debtor's remaining liability,[5] such an agreement would be voluntary, and not, as in bankruptcy, imposed by operation of law.

A receivership is an equitable device courts use to protect creditors with interests in the debtor's property. Prior to the availability of a federal bankruptcy process, receiverships were often used to keep the debtor's business operating. This allowed assets to be liquidated in an orderly fashion, rather than in a rushed sale, and on occasion for the business to be sold as a going concern. Even today, creditors seek the appointment of receivers, typically to take charge of real property that is subject to a mortgage. The main reason for doing this is to protect the creditor from depreciation that may result from the debtor's misuse of the property. Indeed, many mortgages of commercial property expressly authorize the creditor to seek appointment of a receiver. Not surprisingly, receivers are subject to court supervision and bonding requirements.

Both an assignee for benefit of creditors and a receiver are trustees of the debtor's property and subject to the fiduciary obligations of a trustee. Both of these devices have more limited utility given the wide availability of the bankruptcy process. As you study the bankruptcy process, you will see similarities to the assignment for benefit of creditors process in the bankruptcy liquidation process and to the receivership process in the bankruptcy reorganization process.

---

[5]   At common law, this process of multiple creditors' compromise of debts owed is called a composition agreement. Each creditor's agreement to compromise the debt it is owed provides consideration for the promises of the other creditors to compromise the debts they are owed. The assignment for benefit of creditors process may use this common-law method of getting agreement of creditors to accept less than full satisfaction of debts.

CHAPTER TWO
BANKRUPTCY BASICS

———————

Bankruptcy law has tremendous impact on our society. For the last decade, more than one million individuals have filed for bankruptcy protection each year.[1] That figure does not include the corporations and partnerships that also filed or the millions of creditors of all the bankruptcy debtors. In short, bankruptcy directly affects a large segment of the individual and business populations each year.

From the lawyer's perspective, bankruptcy is even more important. It permeates almost all areas of legal practice, from family law and personal injury, to almost any type of commercial work. It is particularly significant in transactional work, because almost all commercial planning is done against the backdrop of a possible bankruptcy.

Bankruptcy law provides a process for dealing with a debtor whose financial obligations have become overly burdensome. Before getting into the specifics of how bankruptcy law attempts to solve debtors' financial problems, however, it is useful to have a better understanding of what those problems are.

A. DEBTORS AND THE PROBLEMS THEY FACE

We are all debtors. Almost all individuals owe utility bills and taxes. Most adults have obligations on a mortgage or for rent. Many also owe on student loans and for credit card charges. Businesses typically owe for many of the same things – utilities, taxes, rent – but also for supplies and labor. Many businesses also borrow to obtain the finances necessary to start up, to fund their operations, or to expand their operations.

If everyone is a debtor, what prompts only a small percentage – a large number but a small percentage – to seek relief from their debts? Well, while the causes that impel debtors to seek protection from their creditors are legion, there are several recurring reasons. Individuals who get into financial trouble typically have faced a major

———————

[1] For statistics on filings organized by year, bankruptcy chapter, judicial district, and state, see www.abiworld.org/Content/NavigationMenu/NewsRoom/BankruptcyStatistics/Bankruptcy_Filings_1.htm

calamity, such as a job loss,[2] a divorce,[3] a personal injury to – and resulting medical bills for – themselves or one of their dependents,[4] or an uninsured casualty to their property. Indeed, even credit card companies, who lobbied strongly to make bankruptcy relief more difficult for individuals to obtain, acknowledge that unemployment and divorce are major contributors to the large number of bankruptcy filings.[5]

Businesses also occasionally suffer a calamity, such as a strike (as with Eastern Airlines and Greyhound Bus Lines) or a product failure (as with asbestos for Johns Manville and the Dalkon Shield for A.H. Robins). More commonly, their financial problems are attributable to inadequate capitalization, poor business planning, an economic recession, negative cash flow, or some combination of these things.

While a few individuals and businesses who file for bankruptcy protection may be seeking relief from only minor or short-term financial difficulties, that is not the typical scenario. Most bankruptcy debtors are facing significant financial problems. Some of these problems may be of the debtor's own making. Other debtors bear no blame for the predicaments in which they find themselves. Whether any bankruptcy system can adequately account for the different causes of bankruptcy and provide an appropriate response for each is highly questionable. Whether our current system comes anywhere close to striking the proper balance will be a question we consider throughout this book.

Problem 2-1

Identify all the things the government could do with, to, and for individuals and businesses who lack the ability to pay their debts. Which of them, if any, should the government do? Should the legal system get involved at all in a systemic way or merely leave the debtor and the debtor's creditors with their normal legal and contractual rights?

---

[2]   A study of individuals who filed no-asset Chapter 7 bankruptcy petitions in 2000 revealed that 19% were unemployed at the time of filing, compared with a general unemployment rate of about 4%. Perhaps more interesting was the job tenure of the 81% who were employed: 30% of them had been employed for only one year or less and their median job tenure – 2.0 years – was only 43% of the national median of 4.7 years. *See* Gordon Bermant & Ed Flynn, *Just Recently Hired: Job Tenure Among No-Asset Chapter 7 Debtors*, 21 A.B.I. J.22 (2002).

[3]   While divorce affects all socio-economic classes – the rich as well as the poor – it almost invariably causes financial loss for at least one party to the marriage. This is because a divorced couple typically will try to maintain two separate households whereas before divorce they kept only one. Even for the affluent, the sudden rise in expenses is often unmanageable.

[4]   *See* David Himmelstein, Elizabeth Warren, Deborah Thorn & Steffi Woolhandler, 24 HEALTH AFFAIRS W5-63 (2005) (concluding that medical problems – which generate bills and reduce the ability to earn income – contributed to almost half the personal bankruptcies in 2001).

[5]   *See* Visa U.S.A., Inc., *Consumer Bankruptcy: Causes and Implications* (July 1996).

Most would probably agree that the law's general response to people with serious financial problems should depend on how and why those problems arose. Many would also agree that most bankruptcy debtors fall into at least one of three *nonexclusive* groups: the unlucky, the foolish, and the dishonest.[6] It is probably fair to say that the Bankruptcy Code, as enacted in 1978, was premised on the assumption that most bankruptcy debtors had simply been unlucky but that luck tends to even out over time. In other words, the Code regarded a debtor's massive debt not as a symptom of some other problem, but as the problem itself. Accordingly, simply relieving the debtor of most or all debts would solve the problem and enable the debtor to return to the economic community as a productive participant.

Since 1978, the almost endless stream of amendments to the Bankruptcy Code have been premised on the assumption that many debtors are or were dishonest; indeed, that the mere act of filing for bankruptcy protection and seeking to escape from their lawful debts was itself deceitful or improper. As a result, these amendments placed more and more hurdles for debtors to climb in order to receive a discharge and left those who did get past them with more and more of their debts intact.

In fact, there is a great deal of statistical information available about the individuals and businesses that seek bankruptcy protection. In spite of that, there is little reliable information about the percentages of them that are unlucky, foolish, or dishonest. This may be because a debtor's financial misfortunes are rarely attributable to a single event and, even when they are, that event may in turn be explained by bad luck, a poor choice or careless action, or dishonesty. For example, consider an individual who has been fired from a job and is unable to find another. The job loss may have resulted from: (i) the employer's decision to downsize (the debtor's bad luck); (ii) the debtor's poor job performance (foolishness or carelessness); or (iii) discovery of the debtor's embezzlement (dishonesty). Similarly, extensive medical bills for the debtor or a dependant of the debtor may have been caused by: (i) a sudden and unavoidable illness (bad luck); (ii) risky behavior, such as drunk driving or cigarette smoking (foolishness); or (iii) a beating after being caught cheating at poker (dishonesty). The same holds true for businesses. Their financial collapse could be caused by: (i) a general economic downturn or a competitor's development of a better product (bad luck); (ii) operating under a poor business plan or with inadequate capitalization (foolishness); or (iii) using company assets in a scheme to defraud investors (dishonesty).

Added to all this is the fact that it is probably too difficult and costly to ascertain the underlying causes in each individual case. As a result, bankruptcy policy must be

---

[6]   For those familiar with Yiddish, the terms schlimazel, schlemiel, and gahniff can be substituted. A gahniff is a thief. Schlemiels and schlimazels are closely related terms. The classic distinction is that a schlemiel is someone who goes to a fancy dinner party and spills the soup. A schlimazel is the person the schlemiel spills it on. *See* LEO ROSTEN, THE JOYS OF YIDDISH 343-46 (1968).

premised on assumptions about the characteristics of bankruptcy debtors in the aggregate.

Problem 2-2

The calamities and poor financial planning that set the stage for most bankruptcies can be years in the making. The debtor may have tried for a long time to cope with them and their effects. What events, then, do you think actually trigger most bankruptcy filings? In contemplating this, review the short summary of creditor collection activity in chapter one.

B. THE COUNSELING SOLUTION

In recent years, there was a growing call to deal with the increasing number of individuals in dire financial straits through consumer credit counseling. These calls were premised on the belief that consumers' misuse and abuse of credit cards is what causes many or most of their financial problems. In fact, a fairly recent statistical analysis of whether mandatory credit counseling helps Chapter 13 debtors actually showed a slight negative correlation: debtors who were counseled were actually less likely to complete their payment plan.[7] Beyond that, the consumer credit counseling industry has come under widespread attack. While some counseling agencies provide truly valuable guidance to debtors for little or no fee, others are profit-making or fee-generating enterprises that provide little assistance to debtors. Some are even financed by creditors and purposefully refrain from advising debtors about ways to reduce their obligations.[8]

Nevertheless, the recent bankruptcy reform legislation made credit counseling a prerequisite to filing for bankruptcy protection for most individuals. Read 11 U.S.C. § 109(h).[9] The legislation did, however, implicitly acknowledge some of these problems

---

[7]   *See* Jean Braucher, *An Empirical Study of Debtor Education in Bankruptcy: Impact on Chapter 13 Completion Not Shown*, 9 AM. BANKR. INST. L. REV. 557, 578 (2002).

[8]   *See, e.g.,* David A. Lander, *Recent Developments in Consumer Debt Counseling Agencies: The Need for Reform*, AM. BANKR. INST. J. (Feb. 2002).

More recently, in May, 2006, the Internal Revenue Service revoked the tax exempt status of the nation's largest educational credit counseling services, representing 41% of the $1 billion credit counseling industry, after IRS audits revealed that the credit counseling agencies "exist mainly to prey on debt-ridden customers." *I.R.S. Ends Tax Exempt Status For Some Credit Counselors,* N.Y. TIMES, May 16, 2006, at C6.

[9]   From here on, citations to section numbers refer to sections of the Bankruptcy Code unless otherwise indicated.

because it placed some substantial restrictions on the agencies that may provide them and it permits an individual debtor to forego credit counseling if the U.S. Trustee for the district in which the debtor resides determines that approved budget and credit counseling services are not reasonably available. *See* §§ 109(h)(2), 111.

Still, from a policy perspective, the decision to impose the credit counseling requirement is questionable. One Bankruptcy Court recently summed up the situation in this manner:

> Credit counseling was a significant aspect of the new bankruptcy legislation because the requirement was intended to provide debtors with education as to all of their options when experiencing financial difficulty, *before* a resort to bankruptcy protection was necessary. Congress envisioned that credit counseling would provide individuals with the skills necessary to lead financially responsible lives. This facially well-intentioned section of the BAPCPA has evolved into an expensive, draconian gate-keeping requirement that has prevented many deserving individuals from qualifying for bankruptcy relief. The credit counseling requirement has not proven to be of assistance to debtors in seeking relief outside of the bankruptcy context, as shown by a recent survey of credit counseling agencies performed by the National Association of Consumer Bankruptcy Attorneys. That study determined that of 66,335 consumers served by the participating credit counseling agencies, a paltry 3.3 percent qualified for alternative (*i.e.,* non-bankruptcy) debt management treatment. Additionally, many of these same credit-counseling agencies have come under fire for fraudulent practices; some have lost their not-for-profit status. The requirement that a debtor seek "credit counseling" before being eligible for bankruptcy relief is quickly becoming the most outrageous fleecing of consumer debtors in this Court's memory – a perfunctory exercise with little or no substance which leaves a putative debtor $50-$100 the poorer.[10]

Irrespective of its wisdom, the counseling requirement now exists and, as the following case demonstrates, can present a significant impediment to obtaining immediate bankruptcy relief.

---

[10]   *In re Elmendorf,* 345 B.R. 486, 490 (Bankr. S.D.N.Y. 2006).

IN RE TALIB
335 B.R. 417 (Bankr. W.D. Mo. 2005)

Dow, Bankruptcy Judge.

The issue before the Court is * * * whether a debtor who waits until the afternoon prior to the day of a scheduled foreclosure sale to seek credit counseling and is told by the credit counseling service that the required counseling can be provided within two days – less than five days subsequent to her request, but after the scheduled foreclosure sale – is eligible for a waiver of the prepetition credit counseling requirement. For all the reasons set forth below, this Court holds that * * * the Debtor is not eligible to be a debtor and that the case must be dismissed.

I. FACTUAL BACKGROUND

Debtor filed a petition initiating a case under Chapter 13 of the Bankruptcy Code on November 18, 2005. In lieu of a certificate evidencing her having obtained the briefing required by § 109(h)(1), Debtor filed a Certification of Exigent Circumstances and Motion to Waive Debt Counseling Prior to Filing ("Certification"), seeking, pursuant to § 109(h)(3), a waiver of the requirement of prepetition credit counseling. The Certification, which was submitted by her counsel, was accompanied by a separate statement signed by the Debtor attesting to the facts alleged in the Certification. In the Certification, Debtor asserted that a foreclosure sale of her residence was scheduled to occur sometime between the hours of 9:00 a.m. and 5:00 p.m. on November 18, 2005 and that she first contacted counsel about the possibility of filing a Chapter 13 proceeding to halt the foreclosure at 4:45 p.m. on November 17. According to the Certification, the Debtor was immediately instructed to contact Consumer Credit Counseling of Springfield, Missouri ("CCC"). Debtor reported back to her counsel that she had contacted someone at CCC who suggested that she download and complete forms for the required credit counseling on the CCC website and advised that she would be contacted by a counselor soon thereafter. Apparently anxious about the completion of her credit counseling, Debtor contacted CCC at 8:00 the following morning to determine when her counseling might be completed. She was told that the counseling could be completed within approximately two days, but not by noon on November 18, 2005 (apparently the precise time at which the foreclosure sale was scheduled to be conducted). The Certification then asserts that counsel could not be assured of obtaining a certificate of completion before filing the petition in time to halt the scheduled foreclosure sale and requests that the Court consider the cited circumstances to be exigent, grant a waiver of the prepetition credit counseling requirement and authorize Debtor to submit the certificate within 30 days.

II. DISCUSSION AND ANALYSIS
A. Applicable Law

Added to the Bankruptcy Code by the Bankruptcy Abuse Prevention and Consumer Protection Act of 2005 ("Act"), § 109(h)(1) requires that an individual debtor receive, prior to the filing of the petition, certain counseling from an approved credit counseling agency during the 180-day period prior to the filing in order to be eligible for relief under any chapter of Title 11.[11] Section 521(b)(1) implements this provision by adding to the list of documents required to be filed at the commencement of a case a certificate from the agency providing those services. Proposed amendments to the Federal Rules of Bankruptcy Procedure (adopted as local rules) require that document to be filed "with the petition in a voluntary case." Interim Bank. R. 1007(b)(3) and 1007(c). A debtor may obtain an exemption from the requirement of receiving those services prior to the filing of the petition under the exigent circumstances exemption contained in § 109(h)(3). In order to qualify for that waiver, the debtor must file a "certification" which must: (1) describe exigent circumstances that merit a waiver of the requirement of prepetition credit counseling; (2) state that the debtor requested credit counseling services from an approved agency, but was not able to obtain the services during the five-day period beginning on the date of the debtor's request; and (3) be satisfactory to the court. § 109(h)(3)(A). This certification must be filed "with the petition in a voluntary case." Interim Bank. R. 1007(b)(3) and 1007(c). Because the requirements are stated in the conjunctive, each of the three requirements must be satisfied for the debtor to qualify for the described exemption.

* * *

B. Adequacy of the Debtor's Certification

* * * Here, the Debtor alleges that she first consulted counsel and sought credit counseling at approximately 5:00 p.m. on the afternoon prior to the date of the scheduled foreclosure sale on her residence. At first blush, the imminence of the proposed sale would appear to satisfy the exigent circumstances requirement. Upon closer examination, this Court has some doubt on the issue. The statute requires that the Court find that there are exigent circumstances that "merit a waiver" of the requirement that the debtor obtain counseling services prior to filing. This suggests that the Court should consider all the facts and circumstances relating to the debtor's alleged inability to obtain credit counseling prior to filing a petition for relief. In other words, the focus should be not so much on the imminence of the event that threatens the debtor with loss of property and requires filing of the petition for relief in order to invoke the automatic

---

[11] The requirement is referred to in subsection (h)(1) as a "briefing" that "outlined" opportunities for credit counseling and included assistance in performing a budget analysis. In paragraph (3) of that same subsection, the reference is to "credit counseling services." Given the context, the Court will assume that the same requirement is being addressed and will simply refer to it for purposes of convenience in this opinion as "credit counseling."

stay, but on the reasons why the debtor was unable to obtain the required credit counseling prior to having to file for relief.

In this instance, when the Debtor first turned her attention to the credit counseling requirement, she was less than 24 hours away from a foreclosure sale. Obviously, invoking the automatic stay by filing for relief was necessary in order for the Debtor to prevent a foreclosure sale on her home. The Debtor offers no explanation, however, as to why it would not have been possible for her to request the required credit counseling well in advance of the scheduled foreclosure sale. In the absence of such an explanation, the Court finds it difficult to determine whether the circumstances are such that a waiver of the prepetition credit counseling requirement is merited. Assuming the holder of the deed of trust on Debtor's residence complied with Missouri law (and its publication and notice requirements) the Debtor has been apprised of the date of the pending foreclosure sale for several weeks. In addition, this case was not filed immediately after the effective date of the Act, but more than 30 days after the new requirement had become effective and was widely known. Based on the Certification submitted, the Court would be justified in finding that the exigent circumstances which make it necessary for the Debtor to request authorization to file without having first obtained credit counseling were of the Debtor's own making and that no case has been made as to why they "merit" a waiver. Put another way, the Certification would not be "satisfactory to the Court." The Court recognizes that procrastination in arranging a bankruptcy filing is commonplace and may occur for a variety of reasons, some justifiable, some not, ranging from inability to muster the funds necessary to compensate bankruptcy counsel to unwillingness to come to terms with the debtor's financial difficulties. No justifications for the delay in this case are set forth in the Certification. The Court is not saying that a debtor who waits until the eleventh hour may never satisfy the exigent circumstances exception, but only that a certification requesting a waiver in such a situation must not only address the imminence of the event which requires the debtor to file by a particular time, but also provide an explanation as to why the required credit counseling services were not or could not have been obtained prior to the filing. Exigent circumstances must be considered in conjunction with the objective requirement regarding the availability of credit counseling services after request, to which the Court now turns. The existence of this objective requirement is a restraint on the ability of debtors to obtain a waiver in circumstances such as this and may obviate the need for the Court to engage in second guessing the reasons for the debtor's procrastination. Because the Court has not previously expressed its views on the scope of the exigent circumstances waiver and because, for the reasons set forth below, it finds the Debtor has failed to satisfy the objective requirement set forth in § 109(h)(3)(A)(ii), it does not reject the Certification in this case for an inadequate description of exigent circumstances.

* * * In this case, the Debtor alleges specifically that she sought credit counseling on the afternoon before the day of the scheduled foreclosure sale and was told that she could not obtain the required counseling for a period of approximately two days. It thus poses the specific question of whether a debtor who can obtain the required credit counseling within the five-day period, but subsequent to the event which creates the need to file, is eligible for an exigent circumstances waiver.

A similar scenario was recently presented to the court in *In re Wallert,* 332 B.R. 884 (Bankr. D. Minn. 2005). In that case, although the facts are not entirely clear, the debtor apparently consulted counsel for the first time on the day before the scheduled foreclosure sale. She then consulted two credit counseling agencies, both of which advised that it would not be possible to conduct the credit counseling on such short notice. She then elected to file the case because of the imminence of the pending sale. The court denied the request for a waiver, holding that the debtor's failure to allege that she had been unable to obtain the counseling services during the five-day period beginning with the date of her request rendered her ineligible to be a debtor. The Court observed that this objective requirement appears to constitute a congressional determination that providing services within five days after request is a reasonable response on the part of the credit counseling agency and offers the debtor a reasonable opportunity to obtain the services prior to filing. In this case, the Debtor also sought credit counseling services for the first time only the day prior to the scheduled foreclosure sale. The Debtor was told that she could obtain credit counseling within two days from the date of her request, well within the five-day window established by the statute. Accordingly, her Certification fails to comply with the objective requirement for a waiver contained in § 109(h)(3)(A)(ii).

The statutory language is clear and the Court's obligation is to apply it according to its terms, unless such a literal application would produce an absurd result or one demonstrably at odds with the intent of the drafters.[12] As the court noted in *Wallert,* Congress may have imposed this requirement specifically to discourage the practice of hastily filing for relief. *Wallert,* 332 B.R. 884, 888-89. Whether that is a wise policy decision is not a determination for this Court to make. In this case, the Debtor could not reasonably have expected the credit counseling service to accommodate her need for counseling given the time allowed between her request and the time of the pending foreclosure sale. The response she received was well within the parameters set by Congress and apparently consistent with voluntary industry standards on best practices. The seemingly harsh effect of the literal application of the statutory requirement is ameliorated in part as well by the opportunity, sanctioned by the terms of the statute, to obtain the required counseling via the internet or by telephone.

---

[12]   Concededly, a literal application of the statute may lead to anomalous results. For example, in this case, had the Debtor consulted a different credit counseling service which had advised her that she could obtain the required credit counseling services no sooner than seven days after the date of her request, she would have satisfied the requirements of § 109(h)(3)(A)(ii). Whether this Court would also find under that set of facts that the Debtor had established exigent circumstances that merited a waiver of the prepetition credit counseling requirement is not an issue this Court needs to decide here.

Because the Debtor did not obtain the credit counseling prior to the filing of the petition, and because she does not qualify for an exigent circumstances waiver, she is not eligible to be a debtor under § 109(h). Under these circumstances, the Court may not grant the requested extension to obtain the credit counseling postpetition. The Debtor's ineligibility for relief constitutes cause for dismissal of the case under § 707(a). Dismissal of the case, although harsh, is the only appropriate remedy given that the Debtor's failure to comply with the provisions of § 109(h) cannot be cured subsequent to the filing.

For all the reasons cited above, the Debtor's Motion to Waive Debt Counseling Prior to Filing is denied and the case is dismissed.

NOTE

Section 109(h) requires that the debtor receive credit counseling "during the 180-day period preceding the date of filing." This phrasing suggests that the counseling must be completed not merely before the petition is filed, but before *the date* on which the petition is filed, and courts are divided on how to apply this rule if the debtor completes counseling on the same day as the petition but a few hours or minutes before filing it.[13]

C. THE BANKRUPTCY SOLUTION

1. *The Governing Law*

To some extent, "bankruptcy law" is a meaningless term. Virtually any source of law – constitution, statute, regulation or rule – on virtually any subject – torts, contracts, property, taxation, antitrust, *etc.* – can be relevant to a bankruptcy proceeding. However, certain legal sources relate solely to bankruptcy, and these are what most lawyers mean when referring to "bankruptcy law." Most of this bankruptcy law is federal, and is codified in three places in the United States Code. Title 28 – the Judicial Code – contains the provisions on the bankruptcy court system and its jurisdiction, bankruptcy judges, and the structure of the United States trustee system. Title 18 – the Criminal Code – defines the criminal conduct relating to bankruptcy. Title 11 – the Bankruptcy Code – contains both the substantive and procedural law governing bankruptcy liquidation and reorganization cases. Learning bankruptcy law is a matter of learning both a set of substantive rules that alter the relationship between a

---

[13]   *See In re Gossett*, 2007 WL 1226629 (Bankr. N.D. Ill. 2007) (discussing the split in authority).

bankruptcy debtor and its creditors and a set of procedural rules that dictate how that alteration will or may occur. Of course, a full understanding requires not merely knowledge of the rules themselves, but also an appreciation for how the rules affect people's behavior and expectations.

(a) The Bankruptcy Code

The Bankruptcy Code is divided into nine main chapters (numbered 1, 3, 5, 7, 9, 11, 12, 13 & 15). The first three chapters cover general material applicable, for the most part, to all bankruptcy cases. More specifically:

> Chapter 1 contains, among other things, the definition section (§ 101), various rules of construction (§ 102), a general grant of power to bankruptcy courts (§ 105), and rules on the tolling of various time limits (§ 108). It also specifies who may be a debtor under each of the different kinds of bankruptcy cases (§ 109).
>
> Chapter 3, entitled "Case Administration," covers how a case is begun and deals with the players in a bankruptcy proceeding by detailing their powers and providing for their compensation. The chapter also contains various administrative provisions and the very important "Administrative Powers" subchapter, which includes the automatic stay (§ 362), limitations on the use, sale, and lease of property (§ 363), rules for obtaining credit (§ 364), and rules regarding the assumption or rejection of certain contracts and leases (§ 365).
>
> Chapter 5 contains much of the substantive law of bankruptcy, including rules regarding creditors' claims (§§ 502–507), the debtor's duties (§ 521), what property constitutes the bankruptcy estate and will thereby be available to pay creditors' claims (§ 541), and the trustee's extremely important avoiding powers (§§ 544–549).

Each of the final six chapters governs a particular type of bankruptcy proceeding (commonly referred to by the number of the governing chapter, *i.e.*, "a Chapter 7 case"), or type of relief. The availability of these six chapters depends on the debtor's eligibility, *see* § 109, and on what the debtor or other person filing the bankruptcy petition seeks to accomplish.

Students should always bear in mind that under section 103, the provisions of Chapters 1, 3, and 5 apply in any kind of case brought under the Bankruptcy Code, whether it be liquidation under Chapter 7 or reorganization under Chapter 11, 12, or 13. In contrast, the provisions found in Chapters 7, 9, 11, 12, 13, and 15 are not generally applicable; they apply only to cases brought under their particular chapter.

(b) The Bankruptcy Rules

In bankruptcy, as in federal practice generally, matters of procedure are, for the most part, governed by rules promulgated by the Supreme Court rather than by provisions of the United States Code. The rule-making enabling statute for bankruptcy is 28 U.S.C. § 2075. It authorizes the Supreme Court to prescribe rules for practice and procedure in bankruptcy. If, within 90 days after such rules are submitted to Congress, Congress fails to pass a law amending the rules or preventing them from becoming effective, they take effect and have the force of law so long as they are not inconsistent with the Bankruptcy Code or with other statutes. There is relatively little of a procedural nature in the Bankruptcy Code or in Title 28; Congress purposely left a wide field for the Court to occupy by exercising its rule-making power. And, at present, there are 209 different Bankruptcy Rules (compared to only 191 sections in the six chapters covered in these materials – don't worry, we will not cover all 191 sections), and 25 Official Forms.

We will cover only a few of these Rules, but that does not mean that the remainder are unimportant. Rule 2004, for example, authorizes any interested party to conduct an examination of anyone else and to require the person examined to produce relevant documents, in an effort to learn information about the debtor's financial condition. This authorization can be an extremely valuable and powerful tool for creditors.

Most bankruptcy courts also have their own local rules, including model Chapter 13 plans. Practitioners need to be well versed in these local rules because failure to comply with them can lead to sanctions.

2. *The Leading Players*

To understand the drama of bankruptcy, one needs to know both who the players are and what they do. Unfortunately, it is all but impossible to separate these two issues; many of the players are identified by what they do. For lack of a better alternative, we will begin by identifying the leading members of the cast and briefly describing their roles. From there, we will explore the drama itself: what happens in a typical bankruptcy case. Then we will return to the supporting cast and other actors who may make a cameo appearance. As you read this material, bear in mind that it is merely an overview of what will be covered in the remainder of the book.

(a) The Bankruptcy Court

All bankruptcy cases are filed in federal court and each is – at a fundamental level – a judicial process. Most of what occurs does so with either the express approval or at least under the direct or indirect supervision of the court. Unfortunately, the existing bankruptcy court system, enacted by the Bankruptcy Amendments and Federal Judgeship Act of 1984 ("BAFJA"),[14] is a mixture of compromises and is both confusing and possibly unconstitutional. To understand it, one must examine its tortuous history.

The 1978 Bankruptcy Reform Act, which brought us the Bankruptcy Code, greatly upgraded the status and powers of bankruptcy courts and bankruptcy judges. It did not, however, establish Article III bankruptcy courts with judges who enjoyed the full powers of a federal trial court.[15] It created bankruptcy courts that were nominally referred to as adjuncts of the federal district courts but were in fact virtually independent of them. Judges were to be appointed by the President, with the advice and consent of the Senate, to serve 14-year terms. Bankruptcy judges were given broad powers to hear all Title 11 bankruptcy cases and all proceedings "arising under title 11 or arising in or related to cases under title 11."[16] They thus could decide matters involving either federal or state law, hold jury trials, and issue declaratory judgments.[17] The only limitation on their power was that bankruptcy judges could not punish a criminal contempt committed outside the presence of the court and could not enjoin other courts.[18]

In 1982, the Supreme Court invalidated the entire grant of jurisdiction to bankruptcy courts in *Northern Pipeline Constr. Co. v. Marathon Pipe Line Co.*[19] The Court's decision did not produce a majority opinion, and that has resulted in some uncertainty about the case's full import. Justice Brennan, writing for a plurality of four Justices, ruled broadly that the creation of non-Article III courts to handle the wide range of matters authorized by the jurisdictional grant of authority to them was unconstitutional. He concluded that the grant of authority went well beyond previously recognized exceptions to the requirement that judges be given life tenure and that,

---

[14]   Pub. L. No. 98-353, 98 Stat. 333 (1984).

[15]   Article III of the Constitution requires judges exercising the judicial power of the United States to be appointed to serve during good behavior, sometimes referred to as life tenure, and to be protected against salary diminution. Because the 1978 Act provided for 14-year terms rather than life tenure, bankruptcy judges were not Article III judges. Presumably, Congress created and staffed the courts under its Article I powers to create uniform laws on bankruptcy and to regulate interstate commerce.

[16]   28 U.S.C. § 1471(b) (repealed).

[17]   28 U.S.C. §§ 1481, 2201, 2256 (repealed).

[18]   28 U.S.C. § 1481 (repealed).

[19]   458 U.S. 50 (1982).

although labeled as adjuncts to the district courts, bankruptcy courts were actually quite independent.

Justice Rehnquist, writing for himself and Justice O'Connor, concurred on a narrower ground. They believed that non-Article III courts were prohibited from deciding only those traditional common-law issues having little direct relationship to the bankruptcy case, such as Marathon's state-law contract action against a defendant who had no other connection to the bankruptcy proceeding. Three Justices dissented, including Chief Justice Burger. He then took the unusual action of writing a separate opinion explaining the narrow limits of the *Marathon* holding and advising Congress that the best way to solve the problem *(i.e.,* the easiest way to get a majority of the Court to uphold a jurisdictional grant similar to the one made) was to address the concerns of Justices Rehnquist and O'Connor by rerouting traditional common-law matters to the federal district courts, leaving everything else within the jurisdiction of the bankruptcy courts. Justice Brennan's opinion sharply disagreed with Chief Justice Burger's suggestion, but Justice Rehnquist's opinion did not.

The Court twice stayed its decision in *Marathon* to give Congress time to act. When Congress failed to respond, the Court established emergency rules of action along the lines of the Chief Justice's suggestions. Finally, in July, 1984, Congress passed the BAFJA, which created a court system closely modeled on the emergency rules and Justice Burger's suggestions.

Under the current system, the federal district courts are vested with primary bankruptcy jurisdiction. 28 U.S.C. § 1334. Bankruptcy judges are appointed for each judicial district. They are appointed by the circuit courts of appeal for 14-year terms and may be removed only by the judicial council for the circuit and "only for incompetence, misconduct, neglect of duty, or physical or mental disability." 28 U.S.C. § 152. They "constitute a unit of the district court to be known as the bankruptcy court for that district." 28 U.S.C. § 151. The exact meaning of this statement and the exact nature of the relationship between district courts and bankruptcy courts remains somewhat unclear.

What is clear is that Congress has authorized district courts to "refer" to the bankruptcy judges all cases and proceedings within the district court's bankruptcy jurisdiction. 28 U.S.C. § 157(a). And, in fact, every district court in the country has adopted a policy of virtually always making such a complete reference. Thus, bankruptcy courts are now performing the trial court function except when the law specifically limits that role and reserves certain powers to the district courts.

The extent of the bankruptcy judges' power to act in referred matters depends on whether the matter is classified as a "core" proceeding. In core proceedings, bankruptcy judges may "hear and determine" the matter, that is they may conduct the entire proceeding and may enter a final judgment, subject only to timely appeal.[20] The district court's role in such matters is as one of two possible appellate tribunals:

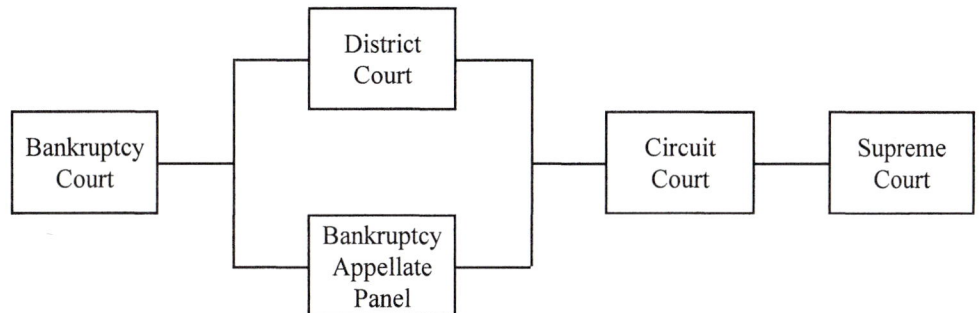

The district court's decisions on appeal from the bankruptcy court are of course binding on the bankruptcy court in that case. Whether they are binding precedent in future bankruptcy court cases is unclear, particularly if the district court has more than one judge who decides bankruptcy appeals and who might decide the same issue differently.[21]

Alternatively, the parties may – and frequently do – choose to litigate an appeal before a Bankruptcy Appellate Panel ("BAP"), a group of three bankruptcy judges from the judicial circuit (if a BAP is established for the relevant federal circuit).[22] Here too,

---

[20]　28 U.S.C. § 157(b)(1).

It remains somewhat unsettled whether bankruptcy courts have civil contempt powers, even in core proceedings. *Compare In re Sequoia Auto Brokers, Ltd.,* 827 F.2d 1281 (9th Cir. 1987) (no) *with In re Skinner,* 917 F.2d 444 (10th Cir. 1990); *In re Walters,* 868 F.2d 665 (4th Cir. 1989) (yes). *See also In re Ragar,* 3 F.3d 1174 (8th Cir. 1993) (bankruptcy courts have criminal contempt power); *In re Hipp, Inc.,* 895 F.2d 1503 (5th Cir. 1990) (bankruptcy courts lack criminal contempt power).

[21]　Bankruptcy courts disagree about the *stare decisis* effect of district court decisions. *Compare In re Baker,* 264 B.R. 759 (Bankr. S.D. Fla. 2001); *In re Shattuc Cable Corp.,* 138 B.R. 557 (Bankr. N.D. Ill. 1992) (both ruling that district court decisions are not binding precedent), *with In re Rand Energy Co.,* 259 B.R. 274 (Bankr. N.D. Tex. 2001) (ruling that they are); *In re Phipps,* 217 B.R. 427 (Bankr. W.D.N.Y. 1998) (ruling that they are if the district court decision is published). District courts too disagree about whether their rulings bind the bankruptcy courts within the district. *Compare In re Shunnarah,* 273 B.R. 671 (M.D. Fla. 2001) (ruling that bankruptcy courts are bound by district court decisions); *with In re Raphael,* 238 B.R. 69 (D.N.J. 1999) (ruling that they are not).

[22]　*See* 28 U.S.C. § 158(b), (c)(1). Each of the First, Sixth, Eighth, Ninth, and Tenth Circuits has a BAP.

There is now a third appeals path. The Bankruptcy Abuse Prevention and Consumer Protection Act of 2005, Pub. L. 109-8, § 1233(a)(2), 119 Stat. 23, 202 (2005), created a direct appeal from a bankruptcy court to a circuit court, if the bankruptcy court certifies the issue as needing immediate review at that level. *See* 28 U.S.C. § 158(d)(2).

there is disagreement about whether bankruptcy courts are bound by decisions of the BAP from that circuit, in part because panel decisions clearly do not bind the district courts (because it occupies an equal place in the appellate hierarchy) and thus a bankruptcy court could face conflicting rulings from the panel and the district court from the district in which it sits.[23]

In noncore proceedings (which are "otherwise related" to cases under Title 11), bankruptcy judges may issue final orders only with the parties' consent. Their function is similar to that of special masters or magistrates: they submit proposed findings of fact and conclusions of law to the district court, which reviews *de novo* any "matters to which any party has timely and specifically objected."[24]

Most important matters in a bankruptcy case constitute core proceedings. A nonexclusive list of fifteen core matters appears in 28 U.S.C. § 157(b)(2). These include: all matters concerning the administration of the bankruptcy estate or affecting the liquidation of the assets of the estate; the validity and amount of claims against the estate and of exemptions from the estate; proceedings to recover preferential and fraudulent transfers; motions for relief from the automatic stay; proceedings to determine the availability of a discharge or the dischargeability of certain debts; and determinations regarding the validity, extent, and priority of liens. Very few matters that arise in a typical bankruptcy case are noncore. These expressly include only the liquidation of personal injury and wrongful death claims against the estate.[25] They apparently also include *Marathon*-type proceedings, involving a non-bankruptcy claim that the debtor possessed at the time the bankruptcy case began against someone who otherwise does not participate in the bankruptcy proceeding, and certain suits between

---

[23]   *Compare In re Muskin, Inc.*, 151 B.R. 252 (Bankr. N.D. Cal. 1993) (ruling that they are bound), *with In re Vessey*, 2003 WL 1533445 (Bankr. D. Id. 2003) (ruling they are not). *See also Philadelphia Life Ins. Co. v. Proudfoot*, 144 B.R. 876 (9th Cir. BAP 1992) (declaring that its decisions are indeed binding on bankruptcy judges). *Compare Bank of Maui v. Estate Analysis, Inc.*, 904 F.2d 470 (9th Cir. 1990) (BAP decisions not binding on district courts); *In re SF Drake Hotel Assocs.*, 147 B.R. 538 (N.D. Cal. 1992) (same). For a thorough and scholarly discussion of these issues, see Bryan T. Camp, *Bound by the BAP: The* Stare Decisis *Effects of BAP Decisions*, 34 SAN DIEGO L. REV. 1643 (1997). *See also* Thalia L. Downing Carroll, *Why Practicality Should Trump Technicality: A Brief Argument for the Precedential Value of Bankruptcy Appellate Panel Decisions*, 33 CREIGHTON L. REV. 565 (2000) (arguing that BAP decisions should be binding within their respective circuits).

[24]   28 U.S.C. § 157(c).
Note that when acting as an appellate tribunal with respect to core matters, the district court reviews facts on a "clearly erroneous" standard. Rule 8013. When reviewing noncore matters, the district court uses a "*de novo*" standard. This does not mean that the district court must conduct a new trial or receive further evidence; it need only make an independent judgment and it may, if it chooses, rely on the record before the bankruptcy judge. *Moody v. Amoco Oil Co.*, 734 F.2d 1200 (7th Cir. 1984) (decided under the emergency rules). *See also* Rule 9033(d).

[25]   *See* 28 U.S.C. § 157(b)(2)(O).

third parties, such as a suit by a creditor against a guarantor of the debtor's obligations, which might indirectly affect the bankruptcy estate.

Bankruptcy court proceedings are generally conducted without a jury. Normally this is not a problem; the Seventh Amendment guarantees a jury trial only in those types of traditional common-law actions in existence at the time the Amendment was ratified, and thus is inapplicable to most bankruptcy matters. However, in 1989, the Supreme Court ruled that a person who has not filed a claim in bankruptcy court – and thereby become voluntarily involved in the case – has a Seventh Amendment right to a jury trial when sued by the bankruptcy trustee to recover a fraudulent transfer.[26] The Court expressly refused to decide whether the United States Code permitted bankruptcy courts to conduct jury trials in fraudulent transfer actions and, more importantly, refused to decide whether the Seventh Amendment or Article III permits jury trials of such actions to be held before non-Article III bankruptcy judges.[27] Congress has since expressly authorized bankruptcy courts to conduct jury trials, but only "if specially designated to exercise such jurisdiction by the district court and with the express consent of all the parties."[28] The consensual nature of this authorization should insulate it from constitutional attack. Nevertheless, should the Court ever rule that one or more parties have a right to a jury trial in other core proceedings, and that non-Article III courts cannot conduct such trials, the whole bankruptcy court structure could come tumbling down.

The intricacies of bankruptcy court jurisdiction and power are beyond the scope of this book. For our purposes, you should assume that the bankruptcy judge will decide all contested issues just as any Article III judge would decide them (albeit without a jury). For the most part, this reflects the reality of how bankruptcy cases really do proceed.

Nevertheless, there is something worth noting about bankruptcy courts: they produce a staggering, almost overwhelming, number of decisions, both published and unpublished. If you think about it, this should not be surprising for several reasons. First, a very large number of bankruptcy cases are filed each year. Second, by their very nature, bankruptcy proceedings are judicial and many of the disputes that arise in them must be resolved by the court. Consequently, there is simply a tremendous amount of bankruptcy litigation and judicial decision making. That sometimes makes researching bankruptcy law issues an exhausting endeavor. On the other hand, it can also make for fun lawyering. There are so many decisions that, on almost every issue, you can find some authority for whatever position you want to argue. That means the lawyer who can

---

[26] *Granfinanciera, S.A. v. Nordberg*, 492 U.S. 33 (1989).

[27] *Id.* at 64.

[28] 28 U.S.C. § 157(e) (added by § 112 of the Bankruptcy Reform Act of 1994, Pub. L. 103-394, 108 Stat. 4106, 4117).

argue the point most persuasively – whether based on the statutory text, policy, or the structure and operation of the Bankruptcy Code – will often win.

(b) The Trustee

All Chapter 7 cases are administered by a "trustee." The moment a bankruptcy petition is filed, an "estate" is created consisting of most of the debtor's prepetition assets. § 541(a). The trustee represents and administers the bankruptcy estate. § 323(a). In essence, this means that the Chapter 7 trustee represents the debtors' creditors, at least those with unsecured claims. The trustee protects their interests by: gathering, managing, and maintaining the debtor's property (which, of course, means insuring it too),[29] selling the property for as much as can reasonably be obtained, and distributing the proceeds to the claimants according to the priorities established by the Code. The trustee is also responsible for: (i) scrutinizing the claims filed, to make sure none are illegitimate or inflated; (ii) examining the exemptions claimed by the debtor, to make sure none are improper; and (iii) objecting to the debtor's discharge, if grounds therefor exist. In performing these tasks, the trustee is empowered to investigate the debtor's financial affairs. § 704(a).

In Chapter 7 cases, promptly after entry of the "order for relief," which is usually the filing of the bankruptcy petition,[30] the United States Trustee appoints an interim trustee from a panel of private trustees. At the first meeting of creditors (which typically occurs within 20 to 40 days after the order for relief), the unsecured creditors have the right to replace the interim trustee and elect a qualified trustee of their own choosing by a majority vote. To do this, creditors holding at least 20% of the total amount of the unsecured claims against the debtor must call for the election. § 702(c). An elected trustee need not be a member of the panel. However, trustees are rarely elected, primarily because of the substantial creditor effort needed to meet the statutory requirements for an election and because there is usually little reason to do so. If no election takes place, the interim trustee continues to serve as the trustee for the remainder of the case. § 702(d). The trustee is paid from the proceeds of the estate. §§ 330, 326.

Chapter 13 cases are also administered by a trustee, but a Chapter 13 trustee's duties are generally more limited than those of a Chapter 7 trustee. This is because usually there will be no liquidation of the debtor's assets or significant investigation of the debtor's financial affairs in a Chapter 13 case. Instead, the trustee reviews the

---

[29] *See* § 704. This duty also includes recovering property which the debtor transferred before the bankruptcy case was filed but which the Bankruptcy Code nevertheless makes available to the debtor's creditors. *See* § 541(a)(3).

[30] *See* §§ 301, 303.

debtor's payment plan to ensure that it complies with the Code's requirements and then acts as a conduit through which payments are made to creditors.

For Chapter 13 cases, there is ordinarily at least one standing trustee in each district to whom all the cases under that chapter are assigned as the petitions are filed; the creditors have no opportunity to elect someone else. § 1302.

In most Chapter 11 reorganizations, there is no trustee. Although the court may order the appointment of a trustee for cause, § 1104(a), this rarely occurs. Instead, the debtor becomes a "debtor in possession" and is normally given most of the powers of a trustee. *See* §§ 1101(1), 1107(a).

(c) The Debtor

No cast roster would be complete without the debtor. Still, while the debtor can play an important role, it would be a mistake to assume that the debtor is the star of the show. Particularly in Chapter 7 cases, where the trustee takes charge of and liquidates the bankruptcy estate, reviews claims and exemptions, and makes distributions to creditors, the debtor's role may be fairly limited. A consumer debtor must file a statement indicating what the debtor intends to do with the collateral for any secured claim and must perform that stated intention within a fairly short time frame. § 521(a)(2). The debtor must also be prepared to respond to any objection to a claimed exemption or to any complaint attacking the debtor's discharge. In most cases, however, no such objection or complaint is ever filed. Business entities in Chapter 7 have even less of a role. Because they can receive no discharge and are generally entitled to no exemptions, and because the trustee is the one administering the estate, they have virtually no lines to speak at all.

In Chapter 13 cases, the debtor is a more central player. The creditors are typically paid out of the debtor's postpetition earnings, and those earnings in turn are dependent on the debtor remaining gainfully employed or otherwise financially productive. A Chapter 13 debtor who suffers a postpetition job loss or income-reducing injury will often default on the repayment plan, which often leads to a dismissal of the Chapter 13 case.

3. The Processes

As indicated above, there are six main types of bankruptcy proceedings, each governed by a different chapter of the Bankruptcy Code (Chapters 7, 9, 11, 12, 13, and 15). This book covers only three of them: Chapters 7, 11, and 13.[31]

(a) Chapter 7

Chapter 7 governs "liquidations," sometimes colloquially referred to as "straight bankruptcies." Its purpose is to achieve a fair distribution to creditors of whatever nonexempt property the debtor has and to give the individual debtor a fresh start by discharging the debtor's obligation to pay the unpaid portion of most debts.

Chapter 7 liquidations are used both by individuals and businesses and in most routine cases take three to six months. The case is commenced when the debtor files a petition for bankruptcy relief and pays the appropriate filing fee, or when creditors take the procedural initiative to file what is referred to as an "involuntary petition." §§ 301, 302, 303.

Filing the petition invokes one of the most important attributes of the bankruptcy process: the automatic stay. *See* § 362(a). The stay is an injunction against virtually all creditor collection activity, whether targeted at the debtor or at the debtor's property. The stay's prohibition on collection efforts frequently provides an immediate benefit to the debtor by preventing, among other things, the commencement or continuation of lawsuits, mortgage foreclosures, garnishments, executions, and repossessions. The stay also benefits creditors, at least in theory, by preserving the status quo. Each creditor can relax, assured that all the other creditors of the debtor are similarly enjoined and that an orderly and reasonably fair process will be used to identify, sell, and distribute the debtor's assets.

Despite its broad scope, the stay does not normally prohibit creditors from seeking payment from co-obligors or guarantors. Moreover, secured creditors may be able to have the stay lifted under certain circumstances in order to repossess and sell collateral, *see* § 362(d), and they may begin litigation immediately after the bankruptcy filing to

---

[31]   Chapter 9 governs the bankruptcies of municipalities. Chapter 15 deals with cross-border cases. Both are too specialized to be covered in this book.

     Chapter 12 is designed to give special relief to a "family farmer with regular annual income," and a "family fisherman with regular income," both of which are defined terms. *See* § 101(18), (19), (19A), (19B), (20), (21). Individuals, partnerships, and corporations are potentially eligible so long as the debtor's total indebtedness does not exceed specified limits: $3.237 million for family farmers, $1.5 million for family fishermen. These amounts are adjusted every three years to reflect inflation. § 104. Because of its specialized nature, and the fact that its provisions closely resemble those in Chapter 13, Chapter 12 is also not covered in this book.

have the stay lifted. Nevertheless, the stay gives the debtor at least a brief respite during which the debtor may be able to refinance secured obligations or arrange for a more orderly sale of the encumbered property with the expectation of realizing a better price.

Shortly after the filing there will be a "first meeting of the creditors." *See* § 341. This meeting is likely to be attended by the debtor, the debtor's lawyer, and the trustee. In the typical consumer Chapter 7 case, however, no members of the class after whom the meeting is named will attend; no creditors will come to the meeting of the creditors. Knowing that the typical consumer debtor has no assets available for distribution, these creditors do not find it productive to attend the meeting, particularly given that the trustee essentially represents their interests. During this meeting, the trustee will ask the debtor questions in an effort to locate missing property or uncover fraudulent transfers.

Much of the activity in a typical Chapter 7 case will center around the trustee's primary responsibilities of collecting the debtor's property, turning it into cash, and distributing it to creditors. *See* §§ 701, 702, 704, 726(a). The property subject to the bankruptcy process in a Chapter 7 case – collectively known as the "bankruptcy estate" or simply as the "estate" – includes:

1. All the debtor's legal and equitable interests when the case begins. § 541(a)(1). For individual debtors, these typically include: the debtor's ownership or equity in a house, furniture, and other household goods; clothing; a car; and deposit accounts at a bank, savings & loan association, or credit union. The legal and equitable interests of corporate and other business debtors include the debtor's interest in its business equipment, inventory, fixtures, accounts receivable, any real estate, and bank accounts.

2. Property that the debtor transferred prior to the commencement of the case that the trustee is able to recover for the benefit of creditors. §§ 541(a)(3), 550(a). These include: gifts to the friends and relatives of individual debtors; certain payments or grants of security interests to unsecured creditors which "prefer" them over other creditors; and fraudulent transfers.

3. Certain limited property that the debtor acquires after the commencement of the case. This includes bequests and inheritances that the debtor receives or becomes entitled to receive within 180 days after the commencement of the case. § 541(a)(5).

4. Most anything else acquired with property of the estate, including the earnings and sale proceeds of a business debtor. § 541(a)(6), (7).

Despite the broad scope of the forgoing, there are two main limits on its reach. First, the list of estate property does not include an individual debtor's future wages or salary. Postpetition earnings from personal services are not part of the bankruptcy estate. § 541(a)(6). Second, when the debtor is an individual, the debtor may exempt certain property from the estate, and thereby from distribution to unsecured creditors. § 522(b). The types and value of property that the debtor may exempt varies significantly from state to state. Typical examples of exemptible property are the debtor's clothes, household goods, and all or a portion of any equity that the debtor has in a principal residence. At the beginning of the case, a debtor entitled to exemptions files a list of all property claimed as exempt. The trustee or any creditor may object to any exemption so claimed, § 522(l); Rule 4003, and if such an objection is timely filed, the bankruptcy court will decide whether the exemption is valid.

After the exemptions are claimed and, if necessary, disputes about them resolved, the trustee sells the remaining assets to generate cash for distribution to creditors. Ordinarily, to share in the distribution of assets from the bankruptcy estate, a creditor must file what is known as a "proof of claim." *See* § 501; Rules 3002, 3003; Official Form 10. This essentially consists of whatever documentation is necessary for the creditor to demonstrate the validity, nature, and amount of its claim. At or about the time the petition is filed, debtors provide the court with a list of creditor claims. The court then mails the creditors a notice of the bankruptcy case along with instruction on filing proofs of claim. In general, creditors must file their proof of claim within 90 days after the first date set for a meeting of creditors. Rule 3002. Once a proof of claim has been timely filed, the claim will be "allowed" (and thereby entitle the creditor to share in distributions from the estate) unless a party in interest objects. § 502. Objections to claims are resolved by the court.

Of course, having an allowed claim does not guarantee that the claimant will be paid in full or even in part. In a Chapter 7 case, the percentage of payment depends largely on how much, in money and other assets, the trustee is able to bring into the estate and what the total amount of all the allowed claims are. However, other factors also affect the amount paid on a given claim. For example, the claims of secured creditors are generally ignored in a Chapter 7 proceeding. They are not paid by the trustee but the creditor retains its interest in the collateral. The secured creditor then extracts value from the collateral, such as by foreclosing on it, either after the case is closed or when the creditor is otherwise granted relief from the automatic stay. Moreover, while the Code itself, at least in a Chapter 7 case, is designed to distribute the bankruptcy estate to unsecured creditors on a pro rata basis, certain claims are accorded a priority position in the distribution scheme. *See* §§ 726, 507, 503. For example, claims for taxes and child support take precedence over most other claims. So too does an employee's claim for wages against a business debtor. Not surprisingly, the trustee's fees, along with the other the costs of administering the estate, are also accorded priority treatment. All priority claims must be paid in full before general claimants receive any distributions. Throughout the case, the court may be called on to resolve a dispute about the priority of any given claim.

To the extent an individual debtor's debts remain unpaid after the trustee's distributions, the debts may be "discharged." That is, creditors are enjoined from seeking to extract repayment of the debt from the debtor. § 727(a). However, not all claims are dischargeable and not all individual debtors are entitled to a discharge. Claims for taxes and child support, as well as for certain torts and educational loans, are nondischargeable. §§ 523(a), 727(b). That is, to the extent they are unpaid by the trustee, they will survive the bankruptcy process. Debtors who misbehave, such as by lying to the court, destroying records, or concealing assets, get no discharge at all. § 727(a)(2)–(6). Neither do corporations, § 727(a)(1), persons who received a discharge in a Chapter 7 or 11 proceeding commenced within the previous eight years, § 727(a)(8), or some debtors who received a Chapter 12 or 13 discharge in a case commenced within the previous six years, § 727(a)(9).

Disputes about the debtor's right to a discharge must be resolved during the bankruptcy case by the bankruptcy court. In contrast, disputes about the dischargeability of a specific debt may be litigated in bankruptcy court any time during the bankruptcy proceeding, or may be resolved by any other federal or state court after the case is over if the creditor seeks to enforce the debt despite the debtor's general discharge. *Cf.* § 523(c); Rule 4007.

With all this said, it is important to note that not all debtors are permitted to be in Chapter 7. Beginning with the most recent amendments to the Bankruptcy Code, debtors whose monthly household income exceeds the median income in that state for a household of the same size are subject to a means test. Those who fail the test are presumptively ineligible for Chapter 7 relief. § 707(b).[32] They are relegated to the relief available under other chapters, typically Chapter 13 but also possibly Chapter 11.

(b) Chapter 13

Chapter 13 cases are quite different. They are essentially a rehabilitation vehicle for individuals with regular income:[33] The debtor's postpetition wages or salary are included in the bankruptcy estate, § 1306(a)(2), and the debtor is put on a budget. In essence, whatever postpetition income is left over after paying the debtor's reasonable

---

[32] Banks, railroads, insurance companies, and municipalities are also ineligible for Chapter 7 relief. *See* § 109.

[33] Chapter 13 is available only to individuals. Corporations and partnerships are not eligible for Chapter 13 relief. *See* §§ 101(30), 109(e).

living expenses is used to pay creditors' claims in whole or in part. In exchange for making future income available to creditors – something that does not happen in Chapter 7 – the debtor generally is permitted to retain his or her assets. Thus, in Chapter 13 the debtor keeps assets and gives up future income to creditors, whereas in Chapter 7 the debtor keeps future income but gives up existing, nonexempt assets. Approximately 32% of individuals who file for bankruptcy protection do so under Chapter 13; almost all the rest do so under Chapter 7.[34]

Payments to creditors in Chapter 13 are funneled through a trustee. Typically, the payment plan lasts for three years, but it may extend to five years either for cause or if the debtor's monthly household income exceeds the median monthly income for the same size household in that state. § 1322(d). Unless creditors will be paid in full, the debtor must transfer all disposable income (income less reasonable and necessary living expenses) to the trustee. The trustee takes a percentage and distributes the rest to creditors according to the priority of their claims. At the end of the payment plan, the debtor receives a discharge of most unpaid debts. In fact, Congress used to entice debtors into Chapter 13 by giving them a larger discharge; several debts that are nondischargeable in Chapter 7 were dischargeable in Chapter 13. Now, the differences between the scope of a Chapter 7 discharge and a Chapter 13 discharge are minor. *See* § 1328(a). Chapter 13 remains an enticement for debtors, however, because debtors can use its provisions to keep their homes and other nonexempt assets.

From a creditor's standpoint, payment may take a lot longer in Chapter 13 than in Chapter 7. However, they are compensated for this. Each creditor must receive – in present value terms – at least what that creditor would receive if the debtor went into Chapter 7. § 1325(a)(4). Moreover, most individuals in Chapter 7 have no nonexempt assets, and thus in most Chapter 7 cases, the creditors get nothing.

To be eligible for relief under Chapter 13, the debtor must generally have unsecured debts totaling less than $336,900 and secured debts less than $1,010,650. § 109(e). These amounts are adjusted for inflation every three years. *See* § 104. A debtor whose debts exceed either or both of these limits may be limited to relief under Chapter 11.

(c) Chapter 11

Chapter 11 is a unified set of provisions for all kinds of "reorganizations." It is used most often by those engaged in business, whether doing so as an individual or through a partnership, limited liability company, or corporation. It applies to corporations whose shares are publicly traded as well as to those whose stock is closely held. However, it

---

[34]   *See* Visa U.S.A., Inc., *Consumer Bankruptcy: Causes and Implications* (July 1996).

is also available to individuals without a business and may be desirable to those who have too much debt to be eligible for Chapter 13.

Congress favors reorganizations over liquidations for a variety of reasons. They get debtors and creditors to work together, rather than merely operate under some arbitrarily imposed scheme. They presumably lead to a greater percentage of recovery for creditors, although this is by no means certain. And they allow a floundering business the chance to stay afloat and thus remain a contributing part of the economy and a source of employment.

To make reorganization proceedings attractive to debtors, debtors in Chapter 11 are empowered to remain in control of their financial affairs, rather than have a trustee come in and take over. §§ 1107, 1108 They also have the exclusive right to file a "plan of reorganization" – their blueprint for dealing with their financial affairs and for paying their creditors – for the first 120 days after the filing. § 1121(b).[35] They can even continue to incur new debts, albeit in many cases only with the consent of their creditors or with the court.

The rules governing plans of reorganization are few, largely because Chapter 11 is fundamentally a consensual process. The plan will typically organize creditors into groups – called "classes" – and detail how each class will be treated. In other words, it will specify when and to what extent the creditors in each class will be paid. The creditors are then entitled to vote on the plan. Unless a majority of the voting claimants in each class, and two-thirds of the amount of the voted claims in each class, approves the plan, the plan will not generally be confirmed. *See* §§ 1126(c), 1129(a)(8), (b). One other notable requirement is that each claimant must either accept the plan or be paid, in present value terms, at least the amount the creditor would recover in Chapter 7. § 1129(a)(7).

If the plan complies with the Code's other requirements, if creditors approve it, and if the court determines that the plan is feasible, it is "confirmed" (*i.e.*, put into effect). Typically, plans provide for payment of only a small portion of nonpriority debts, and even that may be postponed for many months or several years. The remainder of the debtor's obligations are discharged. In short, the debtor is given a fresh start through the binding effect on all concerned of what must be essentially a consensual plan of reorganization.

As this brief explanation suggests, reorganization proceedings require a great deal of negotiation. Because of that, they can also generate a lot of animosity and litigation. Issues likely to be disputed include: what the debtor may do with available cash, particularly how much of it may be used to pay the salaries of officers, directors, and other upper-level management of corporate debtors; which employees should be laid off; which unperformed contracts and unexpired leases of the debtor should be assumed and

---

[35] In large bankruptcy cases, courts routinely extend this exclusive period.

which rejected, and by when such decisions must be made; and what protection the debtor must offer to secured creditors for its continuing use of the collateral. *See* §§ 361, 362(d), 363.

Throughout the potentially hostile exchanges over these issues, the debtor in possession will negotiate with its various creditors, and the creditors will negotiate among themselves, to determine whether or not a plan that satisfies the requirements of the Code can be agreed to. Ultimately these negotiations may bear fruit in the form of a plan agreed to by all. More likely, they will produce a partial agreement, and the debtor will then ask the court to impose the plan on the remaining creditors. At that point the parties will argue about, and possibly litigate, whether the plan complies with the requirements of the Code and can be confirmed. *See* § 1129. Although statistics are surprisingly meager, most cases never make it to the confirmation stage.

For these reasons, the Chapter 11 process has been likened to bargaining over a dish of ice cream in a warm room. The debtor's business is frequently losing money – sometimes hemorrhaging it – during the bankruptcy process. If the parties fail to reach prompt agreement on a plan of reorganization, they may find themselves with little left to divvy up. When this happens, the debtor may simply dismiss the case or, more likely, convert the case to a Chapter 7 liquidation. *See* § 1112. Indeed, folklore has it that most business bankruptcies wind up in Chapter 7 even though many, and perhaps most, begin life as a Chapter 11.

4.   *The Supporting Cast*

(a) The United States Trustee

To separate the judicial and administrative roles in bankruptcy proceedings, Congress created the United States Trustee system. Under this system, responsibility for supervising most of the administration of bankruptcy estates was given to the applicable United States Trustee. There are 21 United States Trustees, each overseeing a group of federal judicial districts. 28 U.S.C. § 581(a). The Attorney General appoints a United States Trustee for each region for a five-year term and has general supervisory power over the person appointed. 28 U.S.C. §§ 581(a)-(c), 586(c). The Attorney General may also appoint (and remove) assistant United States Trustees. 28 U.S.C. § 582.

The United States Trustee appoints the members of a panel of trustees for each judicial district. 28 U.S.C. § 586(a)(1). *See also* § 1302(a). Qualifications for membership on these panels are prescribed by the Attorney General. 28 U.S.C. § 586(d). In each Chapter 7 case, the United States Trustee appoints a person from the panel to serve as the trustee in that case (unless creditors elect someone else pursuant to section 702). § 701(a)(1).

In Chapter 11 cases, the United States Trustee also appoints a private trustee, but only if the court orders that there should be one in the case. The person appointed need not be a member of the standing panel. § 1104(c). In Chapter 13 cases, the United States Trustee may act as trustee but, more typically, leaves this role to the standing trustee who oversees all the Chapter 13 cases in a particular judicial district. §§ 1202(a), 1302(a); 28 U.S.C. § 586(b).

Most important, the United States Trustee is responsible for generally supervising all Chapter 7, 11 and 13 cases and for supervising the actions of the trustee who may be serving in those cases. *See* 28 U.S.C. § 586(a)(3), (b). To fulfill this responsibility, the United States Trustee is empowered: (i) to monitor applications for employment of professionals and applications for compensation and reimbursement of expenses; (ii) to monitor plans filed in reorganization cases and to monitor creditors' committees in Chapter 11 cases; and (iii) to ensure that all required schedules and other papers and reports are timely and properly filed and that required filing or similar fees are paid. The statute also authorizes the United States Trustee to report to and advise the court concerning all matters of administration and to take any necessary steps to ensure that cases under the Code progress expeditiously. 28 U.S.C. § 586(s)(3)(A)-(H).

It should be emphasized that the United States Trustee is not an official with enforcement powers and cannot make orders in the sense that a court or even an administrative agency makes orders that require compliance with prescribed regulations. Rather, the influence of the United States Trustee is exercised through his or her standing to file an appropriate motion, complaint, or objection that seeks a ruling by the bankruptcy court on a matter of administration as to which there has been no voluntary compliance. *See* § 307.

The United States Trustee system is funded out of filing fees and other assessments made in bankruptcy cases. *See* 28 U.S.C. § 1930(a)(6).

(b) The Debtor's Attorney

While the trustee in a Chapter 7 case is concerned about gathering and liquidating all the debtor's nonexempt assets and paying legitimate claims out of those proceeds, the debtor's attorney is concerned with helping the debtor through the bankruptcy process and with protecting the debtor's post-bankruptcy life. The debtor's attorney therefore typically helps the debtor fill out and file the petition and accompanying forms (such as the schedules of assets and liabilities). The debtor's attorney may also be needed to assist the debtor if creditors object to any exemptions the debtor has claimed, to the dischargeability of a particular debt, or to the debtor's discharge in general. The debtor's attorney is also involved in any negotiations concerning the debtor reaffirming a debt that would otherwise be discharged. While the debtor's attorney must disclose to the bankruptcy court any compensation received from the debtor in the year prior to the bankruptcy filing, so that the court can evaluate the reasonableness of that compensation, *see* § 329, the debtor's attorney in a Chapter 7 case is not compensated from the estate property. Instead, the debtor must use exempt assets or postpetition earnings to compensate his or her attorney.

(c) Secured Creditors

To use a metaphor, secured creditors – those with a lien on some property of the debtor – are the brats of bankruptcy. They want what is theirs, they want it now, and they often threaten to throw a fit if they don't get it. This is of course an unflattering and probably unfair generalization, but it nevertheless reflects the general way the Bankruptcy Code treats them. Secured creditors generally retain their interest in the debtor's property. Beyond that, many provisions of the Bankruptcy Code seek to ensure that the secured creditor's interest in the collateral does not diminish in value. Put simply, bankruptcy operates principally on the debtor's *in personam* obligations, not on the *in rem* liability of any collateral. In Chapter 7 cases, this typically means that the secured creditors will eventually foreclose on the collateral, even though the bankruptcy process may delay that eventual outcome. In Chapter 13 cases, secured creditors typically continue to receive payment on the secured obligation according to the original payment schedule. In Chapter 11 cases, their consent to a plan of reorganization is often critical and the debtor must often agree to the secured creditor's terms in order to obtain that consent.

5. *Bit Players*

(a) Unsecured Creditors

Unsecured creditors are like young children during the era when tykes were to be seen and not heard. If you think about it, at least in the context of a Chapter 7 case, this makes some sense. After all, the trustee represents the interests of the unsecured creditors. Thus, there is little need for individual creditors to become involved and most of the other players regard any attempted involvement by unsecured creditors as a nuisance. In addition, many Chapter 7 consumer bankruptcies are "no asset" cases. That is, after accounting for the costs of administering the estate, the secured creditors' liens on the property, and the debtor's allowable exemptions, there are no assets remaining to liquidate and distribute to the unsecured creditors. In such cases, the unsecured creditors really have very little at stake. Admittedly, though, they can raise some problems for the debtor by objecting to the debtor's discharge or seeking to have the debt due them declared nondischargeable.

In Chapter 11 cases, where the debtor is generally permitted to continue operating its business, things are a bit different. There, much of the oversight of the debtor is left to a committee comprised of the creditors with the largest unsecured claims. Such creditors will have much to say in how the debtor in possession conducts its affairs and will often play a significant role in negotiating the plan of reorganization.

(b) Co-Owners

Sometimes a bankruptcy debtor will own only some of the "sticks" representing the ownership rights in a particular piece of property. For example, the debtor may own some real estate as tenants in common, joint tenants, or tenants by the entirety with someone else. Similarly, the debtor may lease real or personal property, leaving the reversionary interest with the lessor. In general, only the debtor's rights to property are dealt with in bankruptcy. However, it is often not possible to deal with the debtor's interests without having some affect on the rights of any co-owners. This is particularly true with respect to community property. We will encounter several of the many ways the Bankruptcy Code deals with issues that arise because of co-ownership.

(c) Co-Debtors

Sometimes two or more people will be responsible for a single debt but only one of them will file for bankruptcy protection. The nonfiling co-debtor may be someone jointly and severally liable for the whole debt, a guarantor who is secondarily liable, or the principal obligor whose debt was guaranteed by the bankruptcy filer. In general, bankruptcy has no affect on the liability of co-debtors. The principal exception is that, in Chapter 13 cases, efforts to collect from some co-debtors are stayed during the case. § 1301.

(d) Prepetition Transferees

For the most part, the bankruptcy process deals with the debtor's assets and liabilities as they exist on the date the bankruptcy petition is filed. In the weeks and months prior to that filing, the debtor is likely to have made payments to creditors and possibly even given some property away. These transfers can significantly deplete the debtor's assets and thus potentially disrupt the bankruptcy distribution scheme. To prevent that disruption, the Bankruptcy Code includes some very important provisions for recovering these transfers. §§ 544–549. We will study these provisions in chapter three of this book.

(e) Equity Interest Holders

A corporation or other business entity that files for bankruptcy protection is usually insolvent. Its stockholders or other owners are therefore likely to receive very little back on their initial investment. In other words, their ownership interest is no longer likely to have any value. Occasionally, however, the debtor has the prospect of earning enough money to pay off its creditors over time. When that prospect exists and the debtor is undergoing a Chapter 11 reorganization, the owners of the debtor – denominated as interest holders – have a limited role to play. They remain in control of the debtor in possession, at least indirectly, and typically try to negotiate a plan of reorganization that will allow them to retain all or a portion of their equitable stake in the debtor. Particularly in large bankruptcy cases, there is some evidence that they are able to do just that.[36]

(f) Employed Professionals

Trustees, debtors in possession, and certain creditors' committees may, with court authorization, employ attorneys, accountants, and other professionals at the expense of the estate. §§ 327(a), 1103(a), 1107(a). Indeed, the court may authorize a trustee to act as the estate's attorney or accountant and to be compensated for both types of services if this authorization is in the best interests of the estate. § 327(d).

A court order authorizing the employment must be obtained before services are rendered for compensation to come from the estate, although occasionally some courts will enter such an order nunc pro tunc. In addition, professional persons employed by the trustee or debtor in possession must generally be "disinterested," as defined in section 101(13), and free from adverse interests. § 327(a), (e). An attorney or accountant employed by a creditors' committee also may not hold or represent any adverse interest; although the statute does not expressly require disinterestedness for them, *see* § 1103(b), disinterestedness is a practical necessity because lack of it is a

---

[36] *See*, Lynn M. LoPucki, *Patterns in the Bankruptcy Reorganization of Large, Publicly Held Companies*, 78 CORNELL L. REV. 597 (1993).

ground for denying all compensation to someone so employed. § 328(c). Courts enforce the requirement of disinterestedness with some rigor, and attorneys who fail to disclose conflicts of interest are regularly denied compensation for their services.[37]

Employed professionals can have many and varied duties. Typically, though, accountants are used to reconstruct the debtor's books and records so as to ascertain what assets the debtor has, to whom assets may have been transferred or where assets may have been hidden away, and who has valid claims. Attorneys are employed to litigate actions filed by or against the trustee, most commonly actions to bring assets into the estate or to determine the validity or liquidate the amount of a creditor's claim against the estate.

D. THE POLICIES

There are two principal policies underlying current bankruptcy law: (1) the fresh start; and (2) providing for a fair and orderly distribution to creditors. The fresh start is grounded in the notion that a debtor should not be forever indentured by debts. At some point, after repayment efforts have been made, debtors should be granted relief from their debts and be allowed to start their life over. In a nation founded largely by debtors, the idea of a fresh start should not be surprising.

A fair and orderly distribution to creditors is the quid pro quo for the fresh start. Debtors are expected to make their nonessential assets available to creditors through a process that treats the creditors fairly. This means that creditors generally stand on equal footing and share on a pro rata basis, unless some other policy intervenes and warrants granting one creditor or type of creditor priority over others. It also means that the process should be quick, inexpensive, and require a minimum of effort by creditors.

The tension between these two policies underlies virtually all of bankruptcy law and practice. The National Bankruptcy Review Commission expressed it well when it wrote in 1997:

> This year, more than a million American families will declare themselves bankrupt. They are bookkeepers, truck drivers, computer programmers, managers, department store clerks, loggers, executives, secretaries, accountants, plumbers' assistants, consultants, postal workers, machinists, day care workers, flight attendants, dentists, steelworkers, teachers, and waitresses. They work for large companies, for small companies, for the government, for themselves, and for no one. They are single mothers, single fathers, married couples, big families, and small families. What they have in common is that

---

[37] *See, e.g., In re Granite Partners, L.P.*, 219 B.R. 22 (Bankr. S.D.N.Y. 1998) (denying $2.4 million in fees).

each one of them has filled out forms under penalty of perjury about their finances, walked into a courthouse, been sworn in for examination by a trustee, and waited for questions from their creditors. For nearly 1.3 million American families, the most important event of 1997 will be the public declaration that they are bankrupt.

Consumer bankruptcy has become part of America's economic landscape. Once regarded as an unlikely legal alternative chosen by only a few desperate families, bankruptcy had become a refuge for one in every 96 American families by the time the National Bankruptcy Review Commission filed its report. Journalists, academics, and lobbyists trained their sights on the bankruptcy system. Bankruptcy, a centuries-old phenomenon, has become a part of the changing world of consumer credit.

As bankruptcy filings increase, creditors justifiably worry whether a promise to repay has any meaning, while consumer advocates express concern that the financial distress of more than a million American families each year foreshadows a larger economic problem. The inherent conflict between the twin goals of bankruptcy – appropriate relief for those in trouble and equitable treatment for their creditors – ensures that it always will be an area of contention. To deal with financial loss, the bankruptcy system necessarily embraces competing interests. Recommendations fully endorsed by either debtors or by creditors would not maintain the balance essential to any consumer bankruptcy system. Bankruptcy is a system born of conflict and competing values. To function well, it must remain unpopular and controversial.[38]

Problem 2-3

Which of the following is the best candidate for bankruptcy and why? What benefits, if any, might the other two obtain by seeking bankruptcy protection?

(a) Astute is a computer programmer who lives in Silicon Valley. Over the last several years, while the economy was booming, Astute ran up large bills to purchase various luxury items (a Porsche, a major home video system, etc.). A few months ago, with the economy lagging, Astute's employer laid Astute off. Astute found substitute employment, but now earns only $65,000 per year instead of $125,000. Astute's unsecured debts total $30,000 (mostly on credit cards) and Astute owes about $25,000 on the Porsche (which is worth

---

[38] National Bankruptcy Review Commission, *Bankruptcy: The Next Twenty Years* 77-78 (October 20, 1997).

about that amount). Astute pays $2,400 per month in rent on a very nice apartment.

(b) Baker is a single parent whose child had a major medical ailment last year. The child is now cured but Baker's outstanding medical bills exceed $60,000. Baker is employed at a local pastry shop, which pays Baker $28,000 per year but provides no health insurance. Baker owns a home valued at about $100,000 but is two months in arrears on the $95,000 home mortgage. Baker also owes about $2,000 on credit cards and to utility companies.

(c) Couch is an auto mechanic who was laid off three years ago and has been unable to find or keep steady employment. Couch's unemployment benefits expired some time ago. Couch owes $2,600 on various credit cards, and has no more available credit. Couch also owes several hundred dollars for utility services, and both the phone company and the cable company have already discontinued service. Couch lives in an apartment that has one old and worn sofa, no bed, a small TV, one lamp, one plate, one fork, one knife, no spoons, and several beers. Couch is behind on the $300/month rent and the landlord is threatening eviction.

E. STARTING THE CASE

1. The Petition and Schedules

A bankruptcy case begins with the filing of a petition, a relatively simple document that identifies the debtor's name, address, approximate number of creditors and the estimated amount due them, the total value of the debtor's assets, and the chapter of the Bankruptcy Code under which the petition is filed. *See* Official Form 1. The filing fee (and associated fees and surcharges) is currently $299 for a petition under Chapter 7, $274 for a petition under Chapter 13, and $1,000 for a petition under Chapter 11. 28 U.S.C. § 1930(a), (b). An individual debtor (not corporations or partnerships) may pay the fee in up to four installments, with the final payment due no later than 180 days after the petition is filed. 28 U.S.C. § 1930(b); Rule 1006(b); Official Form 3A. Alternatively, an individual debtor may now obtain a waiver of fee entirely if the debtor's income is less than 150% of the "income official poverty line," as determined annually by the Office of Management and Budget. 28 U.S.C. § 1930(f).

Venue may be in any U.S. district in which the debtor's domicile, residence, principal place of business, or principal assets have been located for the previous 180 days (or the longest part of such 180 days if more than one district). 28 U.S.C. § 1408(1). Thus, some debtors may have a choice of jurisdiction in which to file.

The vast majority of bankruptcy cases are voluntary – that is, the debtor is the person who files the petition. A voluntary petition constitutes the "order for relief." §§ 301(b), 302(a). In other words, the petition qualifies as a sort of court order approving the exercise of jurisdiction to administer the case. A tiny fraction of bankruptcy cases – less than 1% – are begun not by the debtor but with a petition filed by one or more creditors. In such involuntary cases, the court enters an order for relief only if it determines that (i) the debtor qualifies for relief under the chapter under which the case is commenced; (ii) the debtor is not paying debts as they become due; and (iii) the petitioning creditors qualify in number and in the amount and type of claims they hold. § 303(a)–(h). The distinction between the petition and the order for relief can be important. Some provisions of the Bankruptcy Code and the Bankruptcy Rules are based on and some time periods commence when the petition is filed,[39] while others are based on or commence when the order for relief is entered.[40] For example, in voluntary cases the debtor must file a list of creditors with the petition,[41] and must also file, either with the petition or within 15 days thereafter, fairly detailed schedules of assets, liabilities, and exemptions.[42] In contrast, the debtor need file those schedule in an involuntary case only after the court enters an order for relief.[43]

The requirements for filing an involuntary petition are fairly detailed. Read § 303(b). The dollar amounts in this statute are adjusted every three years. § 104. Normally, at least three creditors holding claims that are both noncontingent and undisputed must join in the petition.

Problem 2-4

Dougherty owns and operates a house painting business. The business, which is unincorporated, has for years been late paying its bills. Several of Dougherty's creditors, who happened to be lunching together yesterday, discussed their frustration with Dougherty's business practices. They are considering filing an involuntary Chapter 7 bankruptcy petition against Dougherty and have asked you to ascertain whether they may. Given the

---

[39] *See, e.g.*, §§ 362 (governing the automatic stay); 547(b)(4) (providing for the avoidance of certain prepetition preferential transfers).

[40] *See, e.g.*, §§ 108(a)(2), (b)(2) (extending certain non-bankruptcy statutes of limitation and time periods to file pleadings in pending non-bankruptcy litigation); 546(a)(1)(A) (placing a time limit on when the debtor or trustee may exercise certain bankruptcy avoiding powers).

[41] *See* Rule 1007(a).

[42] *See* Rule 1007(a), (c); Official Form 6.

[43] *See* Rule 1007(c).

description of Dougherty's debts below, is there a group of Dougherty creditors who collectively satisfy the § 303(b) requirements? If so, which of them must join the petition?

1. $8,000 on a guaranty of Daughter's college loan from Banker. Payment is not yet due from Daughter.
2. $7,000 to Supplier for paint delivered.
3. $40,000 to Mortgagee whose debt is secured by Dougherty's $50,000 home.
4. $10,000 to Brother-in-Law for a loan made seven months ago.
5. $5,000 to Former Employee for back pay and the subject of a currently pending wrongful discharge action in state court.
6. Various amounts to more than 20 other institutional creditors (*e.g.*, utility providers, credit card issuers), none of whom is likely to join the petition.

Might there be any other impediment to the petition? *See* §§ 109(h), 303(a).

After the involuntary petition is filed, but before an order for relief is entered, the debtor remains authorized to operate its business and to use, acquire, and dispose of property. § 303(f). However, the court may impose restrictions on that authority if necessary to preserve the estate. § 303(g). On the other hand, the court may require the petitioners to post a bond to compensate the debtor for any damages caused by the petition if the court declines to order relief. § 303(e), (i).

The standard for ordering relief in an involuntary case normally requires that the debtor is generally not paying debts as they become due. § 303(h). This is different from being insolvent, which is defined as having a negative net worth. § 101(32). Courts have developed a variety of tests for determining whether a debtor is generally not paying debts as they mature,[44] but unquestionably the most important factors are: (i) the number of debts unpaid each month compared to those paid; and (ii) the amount of the debts unpaid compared to the amount paid.[45] As a result, a small number of delinquencies will be more significant for a debtor with only a small number of debts than for a debtor with many.

---

[44] *See, e.g., In re Harmsen*, 320 B.R. 188, 201-03 (10th Cir. BAP 2005) (identifying several tests).

[45] *See General Trading Inc. v. Yale Materials Handling Corp.*, 119 F.3d 1485, 1504 n.41 (11th Cir.1997); *In re WLB-RSK Venture*, 320 B.R. 221 (9th Cir. BAP 2004).

2. *Attorney Liability Issues*

The 2005 amendments to the Bankruptcy Code include several provisions that can subject attorneys to liability or sanctions.[46] While a detailed discussion of all these provisions is beyond the scope of this book, four deserve some attention.

First, if an attorney signs the debtor's Chapter 7 petition, that signature constitutes a certification that the attorney has conducted a reasonable investigation and that the petition is well grounded in fact and existing law. § 707(b)(4)(C). If the debtor's petition is later dismissed because it constitutes an abuse of the Bankruptcy Code – as it would, for example, if the debtor failed to satisfy the Chapter 7 means test – the attorney can be liable to the trustee for costs and attorneys' fees associated with obtaining that dismissal. § 707(b)(4)(A).

Second, if an attorney signs the debtor's Chapter 7 petition, that signature constitutes a certification that the attorney has no knowledge, after conducting an inquiry, that the information in the schedules is incorrect. § 707(b)(4)(D). If this certification later proves to be untrue, the court may assess a civil penalty against the attorney. § 707(b)(4)(B). It remains unclear what kind of investigation will insulate the attorney from liability. Not surprisingly, few debtors' attorneys now sign the petition, choosing instead to end the representation before the filing is made. *Cf.* Rule 9011.

The remaining rules apply to "debt relief agencies," a term that apparently includes lawyers who provide bankruptcy assistance for a fee to anyone whose debts consist mostly of consumer debts and whose nonexempt assets are worth less than $150,000.[47] Such attorneys must include the following disclosure in all their advertisements of bankruptcy and debt-relief services: "We are a debt relief agency. We help people file for bankruptcy relief under the Bankruptcy Code." § 528(b). They must also provide to their debtor clients certain written notifications about the various forms of bankruptcy relief. §§ 342(b), 527(a). More significant – and problematic – are two other requirements: (i) they must provide some advice that is slightly inconsistent with the law; and (ii) they must refrain from providing some advice that may be in their clients' best interests.

---

[46] *See* Catherine E. Vance & Corinne Cooper, *Nine Traps and One Slap: Attorney Liability under the New Bankruptcy Law, in* BANKRUPTCY ABUSE PREVENTION AND CONSUMER PROTECTION ACT OF 2005 137-87 (ALI-ABA 2005).

[47] *See* § 101(3), (12A). Note, the assisted person need not be a debtor. The provision is intended to reach those who counsel debtors but is phrased broadly enough to reach those who counsel creditors who are individuals with mostly consumer debts. Thus, for example, an attorney assisting a person trying to collect support from a former spouse would seemingly qualify as a debt relief agency. Moreover, there is apparently no *de minimis* exception or time limit, so that an attorney who only rarely or once represents consumers on bankruptcy matters qualifies as a "debt relief agency" forever.

The required advice pertains to the process for exempting assets, a subject explored more fully in chapter four of this book. Section 527 seems to require that attorneys advise their debtor clients in writing that all assets must be valued at replacement value. § 527(a)(1)(B), (c)(1), (3). However, while replacement value is clearly the standard to be used for valuing consumer goods subject to a lien, *see* § 506(a)(2), it is far from clear that replacement value is the appropriate standard for valuing unencumbered goods or other assets.[48]

The advice that attorneys are prohibited to give is even more of a problem. Section 526(a)(4) prohibits debt relief agencies from advising a person to incur more debt in contemplation of bankruptcy.[49] However, borrowing money on the eve of bankruptcy is not necessarily illegal or improper, and is often in the client's best interests. For example, it may be wise for the client to refinance a mortgage at lower interest rates. Perhaps the client needs to borrow funds to purchase needed medicines. Maybe the client needs money to purchase airline tickets to fly a child home from a foreign country where war has just erupted. Okay, that last one might be a rare occurrence, but the larger point is that none of these borrowings would be illegal, none would make a subsequent bankruptcy an abuse, and none would be grounds for denying the bankruptcy discharge or declaring the particular debt nondischargeable. Nevertheless, this rule prohibits attorneys from advising their clients to acquire such debt, even if the debtor intends to reaffirm the obligation. The rule even prohibits the attorney from advising the client to borrow the funds necessary to pay the costs associated with the bankruptcy filing. Apparently, therefore, attorneys for bankruptcy debtors can no longer accept payment of their fees by credit card.

Not surprisingly, these restrictions on attorneys are being challenged on First Amendment grounds. To date, only a few courts have rendered a decision on the merits. All have ruled that § 526(a)(4) is unconstitutional but reached varying decisions on the constitutionality of § 527.[50]

---

[48]   *See infra* chapter six, § D.2.

[49]   The clause is rather cumbersome and there are at least four different ways to read its provisions. *See* Vance & Cooper, *supra* note 46, at 165-66.

[50]   *See Milavtez, Gallop & Milavetz v. United States*, 355 B.R. 758 (D. Minn. 2006) (also ruling that provisions of § 528 are unconstitutional and that § 527 does not – and constitutionally could not – apply to attorneys); *Zelotes v. Martini*, 352 B.R. 17 (D. Conn. 2006); *Olsen v. Gonzales*, 350 B.R. 906 (D. Or. 2006) (also holding that § 527 is constitutional); *Hersch v. United States*, 347 B.R. 19 (N.D. Tex. 2006) (also ruling that § 527 is constitutional).

PART II

THE BANKRUPTCY PROCESS

CHAPTER THREE
THE BANKRUPTCY ESTATE

_____

At the moment a bankruptcy petition is filed, an "estate" is created by operation of law. It is as if a new corporation or trust had been formed and the debtor's assets deposited into it. Perhaps the best analogy is to a decedent's estate, which is created by law upon someone's death. Bankruptcy is essentially a financial demise, which creates an estate consisting of all the debtor's interests in property at the time the petition was filed.

A. PREPETITION PROPERTY INCLUDED IN THE ESTATE

Property of the estate is a deliberately expansive concept. Review § 541(a). It includes in the estate:

(1) . . . all legal or equitable interests of the debtor in property as of the commencement of the case.

If a visual metaphor helps, we like to think of the estate as a vat into which the debtor's prepetition assets are poured:

As the empty space in the vat suggests, we will add to the image as we explore more about bankruptcy. For now, though, it is important not to take the metaphor of assets as a liquid too literally. Some assets that are poured into the estate are quite illiquid – interests in real estate, for example – and selling them may be difficult, expensive, and time consuming. One of us used to own an undivided, one-quarter share of a remainder interest in some residential property (in which a step-mother held a life estate). Try liquidating that!

The point is, that even when looking only at this single provision, the scope of the estate is very broad. In another sense, however, this provision is also restrictive. If the debtor has a limited interest in a piece of property, then only that limited interest comes into the estate. For example, if the debtor leases a piece of property, only the leasehold comes into the estate, not the whole property. This of course makes sense. Inclusion of more would make being a landlord a very risky and unprofitable business. Similarly, if the debtor has a lien on some item of property, then only the lien comes into the estate.

What if the debtor owns property subject to a lien? Consider the following case. In doing so, think about what rights in the property the debtor had the moment before the bankruptcy petition was filed.

UNITED STATES V. WHITING POOLS, INC.
462 U.S. 198 (1983)

Justice Blackmun delivered the opinion of the Court.

Promptly after the Internal Revenue Service (IRS or Service) seized respondent's property to satisfy a tax lien, respondent filed a petition for reorganization under the Bankruptcy Reform Act of 1978, hereinafter referred to as the "Bankruptcy Code." The issue before us is whether § 542(a) of that Code authorized the Bankruptcy Court to subject the IRS to a turnover order with respect to the seized property.

I

Respondent Whiting Pools, Inc., a corporation, sells, installs, and services swimming pools and related equipment and supplies. As of January 1981, Whiting owed approximately $92,000 in Federal Insurance Contribution Act taxes and federal taxes withheld from its employees, but had failed to respond to assessments and demands for payment by the IRS. As a consequence, a tax lien in that amount attached to all of Whiting's property.

On January 14, 1981, the Service seized Whiting's tangible personal property – equipment, vehicles, inventory, and office supplies – pursuant to the levy and distraint provision of the Internal Revenue Code of 1954. According to uncontroverted findings, the estimated liquidation value of the property seized was, at most, $35,000, but its estimated going-concern value in Whiting's hands was $162,876. The very next day, January 15, Whiting filed a petition for reorganization, under the Bankruptcy Code's Chapter 11 in the United States Bankruptcy Court for the Western District of New York. Whiting was continued as debtor-in-possession.[1]

The United States, intending to proceed with a tax sale of the property, moved in the Bankruptcy Court for a declaration that the automatic stay provision of the Bankruptcy Code, § 362(a), is inapplicable to the IRS or, in the alternative, for relief from the stay. Whiting counterclaimed for an order requiring the Service to turn the seized property over to the bankruptcy estate pursuant to § 542(a) of the Bankruptcy Code. Whiting intended to use the property in its reorganized business.

---

[1]   With certain exceptions not relevant here, a debtor-in-possession, such as Whiting, performs the same functions as a trustee in a reorganization. § 1107(a).

The Bankruptcy Court determined that the IRS was bound by the automatic stay provision. Because it found that the seized property was essential to Whiting's reorganization effort, it refused to lift the stay. * * * [T]he court directed the IRS to turn the property over to Whiting on the condition that Whiting provide the Service with specified protection for its interests.

The United States District Court reversed, holding that a turnover order against the Service was not authorized by either § 542(a) or § 543(b)(1). The United States Court of Appeals for the Second Circuit, in turn, reversed the District Court. It held that a turnover order could issue against the Service under § 542(a), and it remanded the case for reconsideration of the adequacy of the Bankruptcy Court's protection conditions. The Court of Appeals acknowledged that its ruling was contrary to that reached by the United States Court of Appeals for the Fourth Circuit in *Cross Electric Co. v. United States*, 664 F.2d 1218 (1981), and noted confusion on the issue among bankruptcy and district courts. We granted certiorari to resolve this conflict in an important area of the law under the new Bankruptcy Code.

II

By virtue of its tax lien, the Service holds a secured interest in Whiting's property. We first examine whether § 542(a) of the Bankruptcy Code generally authorizes the turnover of a debtor's property seized by a secured creditor prior to the commencement of reorganization proceedings. Section 542(a) requires an entity in possession of "property that the trustee may use, sell, or lease under § 363" to deliver that property to the trustee. Subsections (b) and (c) of § 363 authorize the trustee to use, sell, or lease any "property of the estate," subject to certain conditions for the protection of creditors with an interest in the property. Section 541(a)(1) defines the "estate" as "comprised of all the following property, wherever located: (1) . . . all legal or equitable interests of the debtor in property as of the commencement of the case." Although these statutes could be read to limit the estate to those "interests of the debtor in property" at the time of the filing of the petition, we view them as a definition of what is included in the estate, rather than as a limitation.

In proceedings under the reorganization provisions of the Bankruptcy Code, a troubled enterprise may be restructured to enable it to operate successfully in the future. Until the business can be reorganized pursuant to a plan under §§ 1121-1129, the trustee or debtor-in-possession is authorized to manage the property of the estate and to continue the operation of the business. *See* § 1108. By permitting reorganization, Congress anticipated that the business would continue to provide jobs, to satisfy creditors' claims, and to produce a return for its owners. Congress presumed that the assets of the debtor would be more valuable if used in a rehabilitated business than if "sold for scrap." The reorganization effort would have small chance of success, however, if property essential to running the business were excluded from the estate.

Thus, to facilitate the rehabilitation of the debtor's business, all the debtor's property must be included in the reorganization estate.

This authorization extends even to property of the estate in which a creditor has a secured interest. § 363(b) & (c). Although Congress might have safeguarded the interests of secured creditors outright by excluding from the estate any property subject to a secured interest, it chose instead to include such property in the estate and to provide secured creditors with "adequate protection" for their interests. § 363(e). At the secured creditor's insistence, the bankruptcy court must place such limits or conditions on the trustee's power to sell, use, or lease property as are necessary to protect the creditor. The creditor with a secured interest in property included in the estate must look to this provision for protection, rather than to the nonbankruptcy remedy of possession.

Both the congressional goal of encouraging reorganizations and Congress' choice of methods to protect secured creditors suggest that Congress intended a broad range of property to be included in the estate.

The statutory language reflects this view of the scope of the estate. As noted above, § 541(a) provides that the "estate is comprised of all the following property, wherever located: . . . all legal or equitable interests of the debtor in property as of the commencement of the case." § 541(a)(1).[2] The House and Senate Reports on the Bankruptcy Code indicate that § 541(a)(1)'s scope is broad. Most important, in the context of this case, § 541(a)(1) is intended to include in the estate any property made available to the estate by other provisions of the Bankruptcy Code. Several of these provisions bring into the estate property in which the debtor did not have a possessory interest at the time the bankruptcy proceedings commenced.[3]

---

[2]   Section 541(a)(1) speaks in terms of the debtor's "interests . . . in property," rather than property in which the debtor has an interest, but this choice of language was not meant to limit the expansive scope of the section. The legislative history indicates that Congress intended to exclude from the estate property of others in which the debtor had some minor interest such as a lien or bare legal title. Cf. § 541(d) (property in which debtor holds legal but not equitable title, such as a mortgage in which debtor retained legal title to service or to supervise servicing of mortgage, becomes part of estate only to extent of legal title); 124 Cong. Rec. 33999 (1978) (remarks of Sen. DeConcini) (§ 541(d) "reiterates the general principle that where the debtor holds bare legal title without any equitable interest, . . . the estate acquires bare legal title without any equitable interest in the property"). Similar statements to the effect that § 541(a)(1) does not expand the rights of the debtor in the hands of the estate were made in the context of describing the principle that the estate succeeds to no more or greater causes of action against third parties than those held by the debtor. These statements do not limit the ability of a trustee to regain possession of property in which the debtor had equitable as well as legal title.

[3]   See, e.g., §§ 543, 547, and 548. These sections permit the trustee to demand the turnover of property that is in the possession of others if that possession is due to a custodial arrangement, § 543, to a preferential transfer, § 547, or to a fraudulent transfer, § 548.

Section 542(a) is such a provision. It requires an entity (other than a custodian) holding any property of the debtor that the trustee can use under § 363 to turn that property over to the trustee.[4] Given the broad scope of the reorganization estate, property of the debtor repossessed by a secured creditor falls within this rule, and therefore may be drawn into the estate. While there are explicit limitations on the reach of § 542(a), none requires that the debtor hold a possessory interest in the property at the commencement of the reorganization proceedings.

As does all bankruptcy law, § 542(a) modifies the procedural rights available to creditors to protect and satisfy their liens. In effect, § 542(a) grants to the estate a possessory interest in certain property of the debtor that was not held by the debtor at the commencement of reorganization proceedings.[5] The Bankruptcy Code provides secured creditors various rights, including the right to adequate protection, and these rights replace the protection afforded by possession.

This interpretation of § 542(a) is supported by the section's legislative history. Although the legislative reports are silent on the precise issue before us, the House and Senate hearings from which § 542(a) emerged provide guidance. Several witnesses at those hearings noted, without contradiction, the need for a provision authorizing the turnover of property of the debtor in the possession of secured creditors. Section 542(a) first appeared in the proposed legislation shortly after these hearings. The section remained unchanged through subsequent versions of the legislation.

Moreover, this interpretation of § 542 in the reorganization context is consistent with judicial precedent predating the Bankruptcy Code. Under Chapter X, the reorganization chapter of the Bankruptcy Act of 1878, the bankruptcy court could order the turnover of collateral in the hands of a secured creditor. Nothing in the legislative history evinces a congressional intent to depart from that practice. Any other interpretation of § 542(a) would deprive the bankruptcy estate of the assets and property essential to its rehabilitation effort and thereby would frustrate the congressional purpose behind the reorganization provisions.[6]

---

[4] The House Report expressly includes property of the debtor recovered under § 542(a) in the estate: the estate includes "property recovered by the trustee under section 542 . . . , if the property recovered was merely out of the possession of the debtor, yet remained 'property of the debtor.' "

[5] Indeed, if this were not the effect, § 542(a) would be largely superfluous in light of § 541(a)(1). * * * The fact that § 542(a) grants the trustee greater rights than those held by the debtor prior to the filing of the petition is consistent with other provisions of the Bankruptcy Code that address the scope of the estate. *See, e.g.,* § 544 (trustee has rights of lien creditor); § 545 (trustee has power to avoid statutory liens); § 549 (trustee has power to avoid certain postpetition transactions).

[6] Section 542(a) also governs turnovers in liquidation and individual adjustment of debt proceedings under Chapters 7 and 13 of the Bankruptcy Code. Our analysis in this case depends in part on the reorganization context in which the turnover order is sought. We express no view on the issue whether § 542(a) has the same broad effect in liquidation or adjustment of debt proceedings.

We conclude that the reorganization estate includes property of the debtor that has been seized by a creditor prior to the filing of a petition for reorganization.

III

We see no reason why a different result should obtain when the IRS is the creditor. The Service is bound by § 542(a) to the same extent as any other secured creditor. * * *

Of course, if a tax levy or seizure transfers to the IRS ownership of the property seized, § 542(a) may not apply. The enforcement provisions of the Internal Revenue Code of 1954, 26 U.S.C. §§ 6321-6326, do grant to the Service powers to enforce its tax liens that are greater than those possessed by private secured creditors under state law. But those provisions do not transfer ownership of the property to the IRS.

The Service's interest in seized property is its lien on that property. The Internal Revenue Code's levy and seizure provisions, 26 U.S.C. §§ 6331 and 6332, are special procedural devices available to the IRS to protect and satisfy its liens, and are analogous to the remedies available to private secured creditors. See Uniform Commercial Code [§ 9-609]. They are provisional remedies that do not determine the Service's rights to the seized property, but merely bring the property into the Service's legal custody. At no point does the Service's interest in the property exceed the value of the lien. The IRS is obligated to return to the debtor any surplus from a sale. 26 U.S.C. § 6342(b). Ownership of the property is transferred only when the property is sold to a bona fide purchaser at a tax sale. In fact, the tax sale provision itself refers to the debtor as the owner of the property after the seizure but prior to the sale. Until such a sale takes place, the property remains the debtor's and thus is subject to the turnover requirement of § 542(a).

IV

When property seized prior to the filing of a petition is drawn into the Chapter 11 reorganization estate, the Service's tax lien is not dissolved; nor is its status as a secured creditor destroyed. The IRS, under § 363(e), remains entitled to adequate protection for its interests, to other rights enjoyed by secured creditors, and to the specific privileges accorded tax collectors. Section 542(a) simply requires the Service to seek protection of its interest according to the congressionally established bankruptcy procedures, rather than by withholding the seized property from the debtor's efforts to reorganize.

The judgment of the Court of Appeals is affirmed.

NOTE

The phrase "and by whomever held" was added to the end of the introductory paragraph of § 541 in 1984, in an apparent effort to codify the result in *Whiting Pools*. The Bankruptcy Amendments and Federal Judgeship Act of 1984, Pub. L. No. 98-353, § 456, 98 Stat. 333, 376. For a provocative analysis of whether *Whiting Pools* is still (or ever was) good law, see Thomas E. Plank, *The Creditor in Possession under the Bankruptcy Code: History, Text, and Policy*, 59 MD. L. REV. 253 (2000). *See also In re Lewis*, 137 F.3d 1280 (11th Cir. 1998) (collateral repossessed prepetition held not to be property of the estate).

Whiting Pools dealt with what qualifies as a "legal or equitable interest[] of the debtor in property" under § 541(a)(1). Although the Court interpreted that language quite broadly, the fact remains that for something to become property of the estate, it must first of all be "property." Not every expectancy a debtor has qualifies as a property right. Consider a debtor who has season tickets to a professional sports team's home games. Teams routinely allow season ticket holders to buy season tickets for the next year, even though there may be quite a lengthy waiting list for others who want them. Is this expectancy a property right includable in the bankruptcy estate?

As is common in the bankruptcy arena, courts are split. Several have ruled that the debtor's renewal option is really just the expectation of receiving an offer, and thus is not a property right to be included in the estate.[7] Other courts have ruled to the contrary.[8] As is often the case, though, the split in authorities may be less a reflection of disagreement and more attributable to differences in the underlying facts or the applicable state property law.[9] Remember, bankruptcy is built upon an edifice of state property and debt-collection law. Thus, there necessarily will be significant variations in how debtors from different jurisdictions are treated.

Moreover distinguishing property from nonproperty is often difficult. Consider a debtor's driver's license. It represents a very valuable legal right, but one that is of no value to anyone else. It does not become property of the estate. On the other hand, a

---

[7]   *E.g., In re Harrell*, 73 F.3d 218 (9th Cir. 1996) (interest in Phoenix Suns season tickets not property of the estate); *In re Liebman*, 208 B.R. 38 (Bankr. N.D. Ill. 1997) (option to renew Chicago Bulls season tickets was not an interest in property).

[8]   *E.g., In re I.D. Craig Services Corp.*, 138 B.R. 490 (Bankr. W.D. Pa. 1992) (renewal right to Pittsburgh Steelers season tickets is property of the estate).

[9]   *See In re Walsh*, 28 F.3d 1212 (4th Cir. 1994) (right to buy season tickets to Charlotte Hornets is property of the estate because the debtor had paid a $10,000 deposit for the right to buy up to 100 tickets each year).

taxicab license or permit to operate a television station may be technically nontransferable, but may in reality be bought and sold all the time. If that is true, the license may well be property and become part of the estate.

Now consider whether a restriction on transfer of the debtor's interest in property should be respected when the debtor files for bankruptcy protection. For example, assume a court determines that the debtor's prior purchase of tickets for a local team's current season gives the debtor a contractual right – rather than merely a hope – to buy season tickets for next year, and that this contractual right constitutes a legal or equitable interest in that property. Indeed, assume that the right to purchase tickets is a valuable one, something for which people without tickets would gladly pay. However, the contract between the debtor and the ticket issuing entity expressly declares that the debtor's right to purchase those tickets is not transferrable. If that contractual restriction were respected, the bankruptcy estate – and, therefore, the debtor's creditors – would not be able to benefit from this property right of the debtor. Indeed, crafty debtors, through careful contract drafting, might be able to shield much of their property from their creditors.

Now read § 541(c)(1). This is a remarkable provision. It overrides contractual and legal rules that prohibit the debtor from transferring particular property, to ensure that the estate acquires the debtor's rights in that property. It also overrides certain contractual provisions and legal rules that treat the debtor's insolvency or a bankruptcy filing as triggering a forfeiture. For example, if the debtor had a fee determinable in real property subject to a possibility of reverter triggered by bankruptcy, the debtor's bankruptcy would not in fact cause the debtor's fee interest to revert and it would instead pass to the bankruptcy estate. Be careful, though. While § 541(c)(1) renders restrictions on transfer and forfeiture-on-bankruptcy clauses unenforceable, it does not transform nonproperty into property. Whether something constitutes an interest in property at all is a separate, predicate issue determined by nonbankruptcy law.

One anti-alienation restriction remains effective. Read § 541(c)(2). This provision effectively excludes "spendthrift trusts" from the bankruptcy estate. A spendthrift trust is a device typically used to redistribute wealth within a family. Its purpose is to assure that the beneficiary will be the exclusive recipient of distributions from the trust. It does this by providing that the beneficiary's right to receive distributions cannot be voluntarily assigned or involuntarily transferred by judicial process to the beneficiary's creditors. This remarkable legal invention allows the beneficiary to continue to enjoy the fruits of the trust while the beneficiary's creditors go unpaid.

One might question why an interest in such a trust should be excluded from the bankruptcy estate. Indeed, the Commission on Bankruptcy Laws which reported to Congress in 1973 recommended that they be excluded only to the extent necessary to support the debtor and the debtor's dependents. However, Congress rejected this recommendation when it enacted the Bankruptcy Code.

Bear in mind, however, that there is one widespread limitation on the efficacy of spendthrift trusts: most states do not permit a person to create a valid spendthrift trust for himself or herself.[10]

Although the legislative history of § 541(c)(2) indicates that it was aimed at spendthrift trusts, it is not so limited. One of the principal uses of this provision now is to exclude the debtor's pension plan benefits from the bankruptcy estate. If the pension plan is "ERISA-qualified," then anti-alienation rules will apply. *See* 29 U.S.C. § 1056(d)(1); 26 U.S.C. § 401(a)(13). Such benefits will therefore be excluded from the estate.[11] However, if the plan is not ERISA-qualified because its anti-alienation provision is for some reason unenforceable, the debtor's interest in the plan will become property of the estate.[12] Note, individual retirement accounts ("IRAs") need not and typically do not have restrictions on alienation. If they have one, however, then the § 541(c)(2) exclusion will apply.[13]

The bottom line on all this is that most restrictions on alienation will not prevent the debtor's interest in property from becoming part of the bankruptcy estate. An exception exists for the debtor's beneficial interest in the types of trusts specified in § 541(c)(2).[14]

---

[10]   *See, e.g., In re Brown*, 303 F.3d 1261, 1266-67 (11th Cir. 2002) (based on Florida law); *In re Kincaid*, 917 F.2d 1162, 1166-67 (9th Cir. 1990) (discussing Oregon and Massachusetts law); *In re Jordan*, 914 F.2d 197, 199-200 (9th Cir. 1990) (based on Washington law). *See also* RESTATEMENT (SECOND) OF TRUSTS § 156(1) (1959).

Five states apparently do permit self-settled spendthrift trusts. *See* Alaska Stat. § 34.40.110; Del. Code Ann. tit. 12, §§ 3570–3573, Nev Rev. Stat. §§ 166.040–166.050; R.I. Gen. Laws §§ 18-9.2-1–18-9.2-7. Colorado also permits self-settled spendthrift trusts but such a trust is void as against existing creditors. *See* Colo. Rev. Stat. § 38-10-111. Section 548(e) of the Bankruptcy Code, added by the 2005 amendments, permits the trustee to avoid transfers to a self-settled spendthrift trust within ten years prior to the bankruptcy filing if made with intent to hinder, delay, or defraud a creditor.

[11]   *Patterson v. Shumate*, 504 U.S. 753 (1992).

[12]   *Compare In re Watson*, 214 B.R. 597 (9th Cir. BAP 1997), *with In re Moses*, 167 F.3d 470 (9th Cir. 1999). *Cf. In re Sewell*, 180 F.3d 707 (5th Cir. 1999); *In re Baker*, 114 F.3d 636 (7th Cir. 1997) (both ruling that even though a pension plan was taxable under ERISA, its anti-alienation provision was still valid and the debtor's interest was not part of the bankruptcy estate).

[13]   *See, e.g., In re Yuhas*, 104 F.3d 612 (3d Cir. 1997) (based on NJ law).

In any event, after the 2005 amendments to the Bankruptcy Code, IRAs that are initially included in the bankruptcy estate under § 541 are nevertheless likely to be exemptible. *See infra* Chapter Three, Section B.

[14]   The § 541c)(2) exclusion applies only to a beneficial interest in a trust. Thus, if the debtor has an asset – such as an annuity – that does not qualify as a trust, the asset will be included in the bankruptcy estate even if it contains a restriction on transfer. *See Hill v. Dobin*, 358 B.R. 130 (D.N.J. 2006).

B.   POSTPETITION PROPERTY INCLUDED IN THE ESTATE

The estate is comprised mainly of property rights that the debtor owns when the petition is filed. Property that the *debtor* acquires postpetition is generally excluded from the estate. In particular, earnings from services performed by an individual debtor after the commencement of a Chapter 7 case are not included in the estate. § 541(a)(6). *Cf.* § 1115, 1306. Thus, it is useful to think of two vats: one containing the estate and one containing property that remains the debtor's:

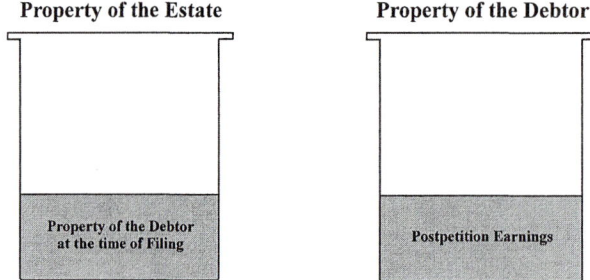

Nevertheless, certain rights arising postpetition are also included in the estate. These include any interest in property that the *estate* acquires postpetition. § 541(a)(7). They also include "[p]roceeds, products, offspring, rents, or profits of or from property of the estate." § 541(a)(6). Thus, if the estate includes some Microsoft stock, any stock dividends declared and paid postpetition would be included in the estate. Similarly, if the trustee sells the stock, the sale proceeds are part of the estate.

There is one big exception to the distinction between what the *debtor* acquires postpetition and what the *estate* acquires postpetition. Read § 541(a)(5). This provision includes in the estate all property acquired by bequest, inheritance, settlement incident to divorce, or life insurance, to which the debtor becomes entitled within the 180 days after the petition date.[15] This provision prevents a debtor who expects to receive such an infusion of capital from strategically declaring bankruptcy and discharging debts shortly before acquiring such assets.

---

[15] The debtor is required to disclose any receipt or entitlement to such property within ten days of learning of it. Rule 1007(h).

Thus, at this point, our estate vat looks like this:

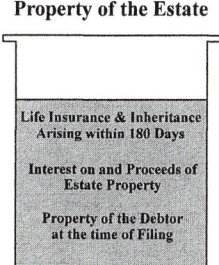

Property of the Estate

C. **PROPERTY EXCLUDED FROM THE ESTATE**

1. Property Held in Trust

Read § 541(d). The application of § 541(c)(2) to spendthrift trusts is very different from the application of § 541(d) to other trusts. Although both provisions effectively keep property out of the bankruptcy estate, they do so for different reasons and act on very different types of property interests. A debtor whose interest in a spendthrift trust is kept out of the estate by § 541(c)(2) is the *beneficiary* of the trust. In contrast, § 541(d) keeps out of the estate any property in which the debtor has bare legal title but no equitable interest: in other words, trust property which the debtor administers as *trustee*. The underlying principle is fairly obvious: the trustee of a trust (if not also one of the beneficiaries) has legal title to the trust corpus merely to facilitate administration of the trust agreement. To nevertheless treat the trust corpus as property of the estate, thereby making it available to the debtor's creditors, would in essence require a defalcation and breach of the debtor's fiduciary duty. Moreover, it would do so when the creditors had no real expectation of going after such assets and would seriously undermine the utility of trust arrangements by imposing a significant impediment to the use of individuals as trustees. Accordingly, only the debtor's bare legal title, without any equitable interest, comes into the estate. § 541(d).

While the underlying principle is obvious, sometimes application of the rule is difficult. Consider, for example, a trustee who embezzles from the trust, say by using trust funds to buy assets for personal use. The trust certainly has a cause of action against the trustee for breach of fiduciary duties. Less clear is whether the assets purchased with the embezzled funds will be included in the bankruptcy estate of the trustee. Nonbankruptcy law would likely impose a "constructive trust"[16] on all proceeds

---

[16]   In law, "constructive" is a euphemism for fictional.

of the stolen funds to protect the victims of the theft. Should the proceeds therefore be excluded from the bankruptcy estate under § 541(d), and thus made available to the victims rather than to creditors? The intuitive answer to this question for most people is probably yes. However, what if the constructive trust arose in a different context? Consider an employee who embezzles money from an employer or a thief who steals money from people's homes, and who buys assets with the stolen loot. The law would likely impose a constructive trust in that situation too, but should the victim of the theft necessarily be preferred over other creditors of the criminal, bearing in mind that they may include other tort victims who cannot so readily trace down the proceeds of their property? Put another way, how much should bankruptcy law respect this constructive trust remedy, given that it completely alters the bankruptcy priority and distribution schemes? Should it matter whether a court imposes the constructive trust prepetition or whether it is sought postpetition from the bankruptcy court?[17] Consider the following case, involving a constructive trust created by statute.

IN RE MEGAFOODS STORES, INC.
163 F.3d 1063 (9th Cir. 1998)

Harlington Wood, Jr., Circuit Judge:

STATEMENT OF FACTS

Handy Andy, Inc., a wholly owned subsidiary of Megafoods Stores, Inc. (referred to collectively as "Debtors"), operated a chain of grocery stores in Texas. In the course of business, Debtors collected Texas state and local sales taxes from their customers and deposited the tax funds into Debtors' bank accounts, along with proceeds from the sale of Debtors' general merchandise. Under Texas law, on the 20th day of each month, Debtors were required to pay to the Texas Comptroller of Public Accounts ("Comptroller") the sales taxes collected during the prior calendar month. *See* Texas Tax Code Ann. § 151.401(a) (West 1992).

During July and August of 1994, Debtors collected Texas state and local sales taxes as part of their retail sales. On August 17, 1994, Debtors filed voluntary Chapter 11 bankruptcy petitions. Debtors failed to pay Texas sales taxes on August 20, 1994 (when sales taxes collected from July were due) and on September 20, 1994 (when sales taxes collected from August 1 to August 16 were due).

After attempts to persuade Debtors to voluntarily turn over the sales taxes failed, the Comptroller filed a motion with the bankruptcy court for adequate protection of the sales taxes on an interim basis. The Comptroller sought to compel the Debtors to establish a segregated interest-bearing bank account for the sales taxes, which, according

---

[17]　*See In re Newpower*, 233 F.3d 922, 932 (6th Cir. 2000) (indicating that timing does matter).

to the Comptroller, were recognized under Texas law as being held in trust by the Debtors. After filing an initial motion for adequate protection, the Comptroller filed an adversary proceeding on October 21, 1994, seeking payment of the sales tax trust funds and postpetition interest. The Comptroller asserted that the monies were held in a statutory trust for the Comptroller, despite the fact that all of the tax monies collected had been commingled with the Debtors' general funds. To date, Debtors have not yet paid these taxes, arguing that because the tax monies collected were commingled with the Debtors' general funds, no trust ever existed. The only way to identify the trust funds, according to Debtors, would have been by voluntary payment, citing *Begier v. IRS*, 496 U.S. 53 (1990). Debtors maintain that the sales tax revenues collected are part of the bankruptcy estate.

The court issued an order of protection on June 15, 1995, which designated one of Debtors' bank accounts to be considered as the one holding the alleged tax trust funds and required that Debtors not allow the balance in that account to fall below the amount of tax trust funds claimed by the Comptroller pending resolution of the Comptroller's adversary proceeding. Although the Debtors complied, this account was then claimed by one of the Debtors' secured creditors as its cash collateral and continues to be used as such by the Debtors.

A one-day trial was held on September 26, 1995. On November 24, 1995, the bankruptcy court issued a minute entry/order which held that when the Debtors collected sales taxes, a statutory tax trust arose in favor of the Comptroller by operation of Texas Tax Code § 111.016. Although no identifiable trust fund existed, the court found that, using the "lowest intermediate balance test" ("LIBT") applicable to common law trusts, evidence established that $319,877.90 of Texas sales tax trust funds could be traced into the Debtors' general account. The court ordered Debtors to transfer that amount plus any accrued interest into a segregated interest-bearing account. The parties stipulated that the actual earned interest on the funds was four percent per annum.

* * *

Debtors appealed the bankruptcy court's finding as to the principal amount of traced funds, arguing that commingling of the monies in Debtors' accounts prevented the creation of a trust and that the only tracing test allowed was through voluntary pre-petition payments. * * * On April 30, 1997, the bankruptcy appellate panel ("BAP") affirmed the lower court's findings as to the tax trust funds * * *.

ANALYSIS

* * * [W]e must first deal with Debtors' challenge to the validity of recognizing the sales tax monies as trust funds and the legitimacy of having traced those trust funds using the LIBT. We adopt that portion of the BAP's holding which finds that a statutory trust was created under the substantive laws of Texas and that the sales taxes owed to Texas were merely collected by Debtors in trust for the benefit of the State. We agree with the BAP that commingling of the sales taxes and general funds does not prevent the creation of the trust nor tracing of the trust funds. In addition, we concur that a sufficient nexus was established between the commingled statutory sales tax trust funds and the general funds through the use of the LIBT.

Debtors argue that a statutory tax trust fund was never created but instead the tax monies comprised part of the bankruptcy estate. We disagree. In *Begier v. IRS*, the Supreme Court found that a trustee in bankruptcy may not recover payments of certain withholding and excise taxes previously made to the IRS. 496 U.S. at 55. The Court stated that those payments were not preferential payments which could be avoided if made ninety days prior to the bankruptcy filing under § 547(b) of the Bankruptcy Code. *Id.* at 58-60. It held that the tax monies were never property of the debtor but that a trust was created at the moment the taxes were collected or withheld. *Id.* at 60-62. In examining 26 U.S.C. § 7501, the Internal Revenue Code's trust-fund tax provision, the Court found that § 7501 did not mandate segregation and that an employer cannot avoid the creation of a trust simply by refusing to segregate. *Id.* at 61. "The mere fact that [the debtor] neither placed the taxes it collected in a segregated fund nor paid them to the IRS does not somehow mean that [the debtor] never collected the taxes in the first place." *Id.* at 60.

Under Texas Tax Code § 111.016, "[a]ny person who receives or collects a tax or any money represented to be a tax from another person holds the amount so collected in trust for the benefit of the state." A sales tax trust in which the debtor holds only legal title and not an equitable interest, is not property of the bankruptcy estate. § 541(d); *see also Begier*, 496 U.S. at 59 ("Because the debtor does not own an equitable interest in property he holds in trust for another, that interest is not 'property of the estate.' "). In addition, under Texas law, state sales taxes that are statutorily designated as being held in trust for the state are not the "property" of the debtor.

Debtors argue that the Court in *Begier* "mandated" that "the methods allowed to trace funds into a common law trust cannot be applied to trace statutory trust funds." The language in *Begier* contradicts Debtors' assertions:

> Unlike a common-law trust, in which the settlor sets aside particular property as the trust res, § 7501 creates a trust in an abstract "amount" – a dollar figure not tied to any particular assets – rather than in the actual dollars withheld. Common-law tracing rules, designed for a system in which particular property is identified as the trust res, are thus unhelpful in this special context.

Begier, 496 U.S. at 62-63. The Court further explained the fact that "Congress expected that the IRS would have to show some connection between the § 7501 trust and the assets sought to be applied to a debtor's trust-fund tax obligations." *Id.* at 65-66. This required nexus involves the tracing of the trust funds.

In the absence of any suggestion in the Bankruptcy Code about what tracing rules to apply, we are relegated to the legislative history. The courts are directed to apply "reasonable assumptions" to govern the tracing of funds, and . . . one such assumption [is] that any voluntary prepetition payment of trust-fund taxes out of the debtor's assets is not a transfer of the debtor's property. . . . Other rules might be reasonable.

Id. at 67.

The BAP's opinion states, "The facts, issues, arguments and case authorities cited in [*In re Al Copeland Enterprises, Inc.*, 133 B.R. 837 (W.D. Tex. 1991), *aff'd*, 991 F.2d 233 (5th Cir. 1993)] are virtually identical in this appeal." In *In re Copeland*, payment was withheld of sales taxes which had been collected by the debtor prior to debtor's filing of bankruptcy. The State identified the debtor's bank accounts into which the sales taxes were deposited and then traced them to an ultimate concentration bank account.[18] The State showed that from the date of collection of the taxes to the date of the bankruptcy petition, the debtor's daily combined cash balances never fell below the amount of the State's sales tax trust fund claims. The court held that the lowest intermediate balance rule was satisfied and that the State, therefore, had sustained its burden of proof. The issues of the trust fund claim and the tracing of the funds by application of the LIBT were not appealed.

Debtors argue that the debtor in *In re Copeland* "ha[d] not resist[ed] payment of the principal amount of the tax claims themselves but ha[d] only requested that the State obtain authority from this Court for it to pay the same." Debtors maintain that this "lack of resistance" is the equivalent of a voluntary payment, which they contend is the only way to satisfy the Supreme Court's requirement to identify funds as tax trust funds. As previously discussed, the Supreme Court noted that voluntary payment was but one method of identifying tax trust funds. *See Begier*, 496 U.S. at 67. Texas has simplified this problem by statutorily creating a tax trust fund at the time the taxes are collected. *See* Tex. Tax Code Ann. § 111.016. The debtors in both *Copeland* and the instant case did not take any affirmative steps on their own to pay the sales tax claims on a timely basis. Therefore, both cases are identical in that the debtors withheld payment of a sales tax trust fund.

Following the Supreme Court's reasoning, we find that the tracing of commingled trust funds using the LIBT is allowed and uphold the lower court's findings as to the recovery of the trust fund claim.

---

[18]   In its review of the facts, the Fifth Circuit noted that "the State's tax revenues were never commingled with Copeland's." *Matter of Copeland*, 991 F.2d at 235. Because the bankruptcy court's treatment of this issue was much more detailed, and due to the fact that the tracing issue was not on appeal to the Fifth Circuit, we rely on the facts as presented in *In re Copeland*, 133 B.R. 837, 838, which indicate that Copeland did commingle funds * * *.

NOTE

The use of constructive trusts in bankruptcy remains quite controversial.[19] Nevertheless, implied and constructive trusts continue to be recognized, even in favor of members of the debtor's family.[20] Creditors seeking repayment – or defending against a preference action – are well advised to consider whether such an equitable remedy would be available outside of bankruptcy. If so, raising a trust argument may make the difference between no recovery and full recovery.

The rationale underlying the § 541(d) exclusion of assets the debtor is holding in trust for others also supports § 541(b)(7). That provision excludes from the estate wage deductions and employee contributions that are intended to be placed in employee benefit plans, deferred compensation plans, or other types of retirement plans. Once these funds are turned over to a plan administrator, they are likely to qualify as trust funds and therefore fall under the § 541(d) exclusion. Before then – that is, after they have been withheld from employees' pay but before they have been transferred to the plan administrator – they may not qualify as trust funds under nonbankruptcy law. This is particularly likely if the funds have not been segregated from the employer's other assets. Section 541(b)(7) apparently protects employees if the employer files for bankruptcy while such funds are in this state of limbo.[21]

2. Certain Education Savings

In 2005, Congress decided to exclude from the bankruptcy funds contributed to educational IRAs and qualified state tuition programs (*e.g.*, 26 U.S.C. § 529 plans). *See* § 541(b)(5), (6). To qualify for the exclusion, the funds must have been contributed at least 365 days before the petition. Moreover, there is a $5,475 limit – calculated

---

[19]   *See* Andrew Kull, *Restitution in Bankruptcy: Reclamation and Constructive Trust*, 72 AM. BANKR. L.J. 265 (1998); Emily Sherwin, *Constructive Trusts in Bankruptcy*, 1989 U. ILL. L. REV. 297.

[20]   *See, e.g., In re McDowell*, 258 B.R. 296 (Bankr. M.D. Ga. 2001).

[21]   The provisions also applies in a completely different context: if the employee is the bankruptcy debtor. A Chapter 13 debtor's postpetition earnings from personal services are included in the bankruptcy estate. § 1306(a)(2). Section 541(b)(7) restricts the scope of that rule by making clear that the amounts the employer withholds from the debtor's pay for contribution to an employee benefit plan or deferred compensation plan is not property of the estate. *See, e.g., In re Johnson*, 346 B.R. 256 (Bankr. S.D. Ga. 2006) (also ruling that amounts withheld to repay a loan the employee/debtor took out from the retirement plan were not property of the estate).

separately for each designated beneficiary – for funds contributed less than 720 days before the bankruptcy filing.

As a result of this exclusion, along with that for spendthrift trusts and interests in ERISA-qualified pension plans, the debtor's vat of assets is a bit larger than previously indicated. At this point, it can be depicted as follows:

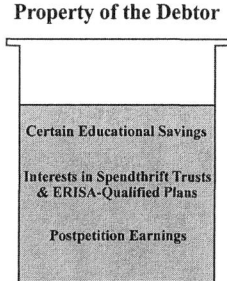

3. Other Exclusions

No single, coherent theory explains the other paragraphs of § 541(b). Instead, the various other exclusions from the bankruptcy estate for which they provide appear to represent successful lobbying efforts of various industries: real estate lessors, § 541(b)(2); the oil and gas industry, § 541(b)(4); pawnbrokers, § 541(b)(8); and money order sellers, § 541(b)(9). This is not the last time that we will see the intermixing of some statutory rules supported by a unifying rationale with others designed to benefit a special interest group.

D. ALLOCATION PROBLEMS

Because the bankruptcy estate contains the property rights that the debtor had at the moment the bankruptcy petition was filed – but not most assets that the debtor acquires postpetition – it is occasionally necessary to determine when the debtor acquired certain rights. For most property rights this is not difficult. For example, it is easy to determine when the debtor bought a car or received a gift. For some property rights, particularly intangible rights, the determination is more difficult.

Consider, for example, a debtor who is employed at the minimum wage and who is paid weekly on Friday afternoons. The debtor files for bankruptcy protection at 12:00 pm on Wednesday. At that time, the debtor had no immediate right to receive payment for the work already done that week. The debtor's right to payment for 2½ days had accrued but had not yet matured, given the nature of the employment relationship.

Nevertheless, it is fairly easy to see that when the debtor is paid on Friday, the payment is partially allocable to the pre-bankruptcy past and partially allocable to the postpetition period. Moreover, it is also easy to see that the allocation should be based on the proportion of the pay period that fell prepetition. Unfortunately, not all rights are so easily divisible into pre- and post-bankruptcy periods. Nevertheless, because bankruptcy is by necessity a finite process – indeed, it is supposed to be a short and efficient one – allocations will have to be made.

1. *Tax Refunds*

Consider the following problem.

> Debtor is employed at a salary of $2,000 per month. Debtor's employer withheld income tax at the rate of $400 per month. Debtor filed a Chapter 7 petition on August 1 and continued employment at the same salary and with the same withholding for the remainder of the year. Debtor filed a tax return in March of the following year. Debtor had no income other than the $24,000 in salary, and therefore incurred an income tax liability of $4,500. Since Debtor's employer has withheld $4,800, debtor received a $300 tax refund in May. What part of the refund is property of the estate?

Some courts, perhaps most, simply allocate the refund based on the proportion of the taxable year that fell prepetition.[22] That may work adequately in a simple scenario, such as when income is earned and deductible expenditures are made evenly over the tax year, but in many cases it will be arbitrary. Nevertheless, many courts stick to this simple formula. As one court noted:

> Thus far, courts have prorated refunds solely on the basis of the number of calendar days before and after the petition, rather than in the ratio of actual excessive withholding before and after the petition. * * *
> The debtors herein argue that a calendar day proration could result in an inequitable division of the refund. A calendar day formula is based on the premise that excessive withholding is proportional per day. Yet a change in income, marital status, or number of dependents would result in unproportional withholding. For example, where a debtor works only the first 6 months of the

---

[22] *See, e.g., In re Lambert*, 283 B.R. 16 (9th Cir. BAP 2002) (allocating on such a basis a $600 early refund resulting from a lowering of the tax rate on the first $12,000 of income).

year, all of the excessive withholding would occur during those months. A debtor who filed a petition during the latter six months of the year would not be entitled to any of the refund, if the refund were proportioned on a calendar day basis. Thus, calendar day prorationing can result in a windfall to the trustee or the debtor, depending on the circumstances of the case.

The Court finds merit in the debtors' objection to a strict calendar day prorationing. However, as a practical matter, calendar day prorationing is the most efficient method to determine how much the estate is entitled.[23]

2. *Contingent Rights*

Allocation becomes even more problematic when the debtor's rights are not only unmatured and unliquidated, but also contingent. Consider the case of an employee whose employer routinely distributes significant bonuses at the end of each year. Is all or a portion of the year's bonus property of the estate? What if the employer decides not to award bonuses this year or to award much smaller bonuses? How is the debtor's expectancy to be measured as of the petition date?

If the debtor does not have a contractual right to the bonus, most courts will exclude the entire bonus from the estate on the grounds that the hope of receiving it was not a property right on the date of the petition.[24] When the debtor does have a right to the bonus, however, most courts will include the prepetition portion in the estate. Making the allocation between the prepetition and postpetition periods is often simply a matter of calculating the percentage of the working year that fell before the petition and multiplying that number by the amount of the bonus.[25] However, the allocation can sometimes be very difficult, depending on how the amount of the bonus is calculated. Consider the following case involving a payment due upon termination of employment. Then compare it to the subsequent case involving another contingent right.

---

[23]   *In re Rash*, 22 B.R. 323 (Bankr. D. Kan. 1982).

[24]   *See, e.g., In re Palmer*, 57 B.R. 332 (Bankr. W.D. Va. 1986). *See also In re Bracewell*, 454 F.3d 1234 (11th Cir. 2006) (farmer's right to federal crop disaster funds for prepetition crop failures was not estate property because federal program was not authorized or funded until after the petition was filed); *In re Burgess*, 438 F.3d 493 (5th Cir. 2006) (same).

[25]   *See, e.g., In re Soboslai*, 263 B.R. 700 (Bankr. D. Conn. 2001).

IN RE RYERSON
739 F.2d 1423 (9th Cir. 1984)

Canby, Circuit Judge:

Ryerson appeals from a decision of the Bankruptcy Appellate Panel. The panel determined that money to which Ryerson became entitled upon the termination of his employment, some eight months following the filing of his petition in bankruptcy, should be included with the bankruptcy estate.

On January 12, 1977, Ryerson entered into an Appointment Agreement with the Farmers Insurance Company of Arizona appointing him to the position of District Manager for District 25. The Agreement provided that in the event of cancellation or other termination of the appointment "the Companies may at their option elect to pay 'contract value,' as hereinafter defined, to the District Manager." "Contract value" was defined as the service commission overwrite paid to the District Manager during the six months immediately preceding termination times a factor determined by the number of years of service as District Manager. Nothing was payable until the District Manager had served one full year. The Agreement further provided that as a condition precedent to the District Manager's right to receive "contract value" he must be in good standing with the Companies on the date of his termination and that he not have been guilty of certain specified forms of misconduct. Termination occurred upon the death of the District Manager, and the contract could be cancelled by either party without cause upon 30 days written notice.

Ryerson filed a chapter 7 bankruptcy proceeding on February 10, 1981. His appointment as District Manager for the Farmers Insurance Group terminated on November 1, 1981. The "contract value" on the date of termination was determined to be $18,588, which has not yet been paid to the debtor. Ryerson sought a declaratory judgment from the bankruptcy court declaring that this sum was not property of the bankruptcy estate.

The old Bankruptcy Act provided that all "rights of action arising upon contracts" passed to the trustee in bankruptcy. § 110(a)(6) (repealed). The current Bankruptcy Code defines the bankrupt estate as consisting of "all legal or equitable interests of the debtor in property as of the commencement of the case." § 541(a)(1). Among the debtor's legal interests that become a part of the bankruptcy estate under the Code are his choses in action and claims against third parties as of the commencement of the case. These choses in action and claims clearly include rights of action based upon contract.

Under the Appointment Agreement, the contract has value upon termination or cancellation after the District Manager completes one year of service in that position. At the time this case was commenced, Ryerson had served four full years as District Manager. He therefore had accumulated value to which he was entitled upon termination or cancellation of his Appointment Agreement. The debtor nevertheless argues that at the time of the filing of the bankruptcy petition his appointment had not yet been terminated or cancelled and that therefore he had no claim to the "contract value." He asserts that an unvested, contingent interest is not includable within the bankruptcy estate if it cannot be transferred by the debtor or levied upon or otherwise reached by the debtor's creditors. Under the Act, a contingent interest in personal property passed to the trustee only if it was capable of being assigned or was subject to execution, seizure, or sequestration. However, the requirement that the debtor must be able to transfer the interest or that his creditors by some means must be able to reach it has been eliminated under the Code. By including all legal interests without exception, Congress indicated its intention to include all legally recognizable interests although they may be contingent and not subject to possession until some future time. We therefore conclude that Ryerson's interest in the "contract value," albeit contingent at the time of filing and not payable until such time as his appointment is terminated or cancelled, is includable within the bankruptcy estate pursuant to section 541(a)(1).[26]

Having concluded that Ryerson's right to "contract value" is property of the bankruptcy estate, we have no difficulty concluding that any payments paid upon termination of Ryerson's appointment are also property of the bankruptcy estate although paid after commencement of the case, at least to the extent the payments are related to prebankruptcy services. Section 541(a)(6) of the Code includes in the bankruptcy estate after-acquired property consisting of "[p]roceeds, product, offspring, rents, and profits of or from property of the estate, except such as are earnings from services performed by an individual debtor after the commencement of the case." § 541(a)(6). It follows therefore that earnings from services performed prior to bankruptcy are includable within the bankruptcy estate. Under the Act, the test was whether the after-acquired property was "sufficiently rooted in the prebankruptcy past and so little entangled in the debtor's ability to make a fresh start that it should not be excluded from property of the estate." *Segal v. Rochelle*, 382 U.S. 375, 380 (1966). The Code follows *Segal* insofar as it includes after-acquired property "sufficiently rooted in

---

[26] The debtor makes much of the fact that "contract value" is payable only at the option of the Company. Even if the payment of the "contract value" were truly optional, the fact that the contingency may not occur would not render the debtor's interest unenforceable at common law. It is the nature of a contingent interest that it may never take effect in possession because of the failure of the specified event to occur. However, Ryerson's right to the "contract value" is not truly contingent. First, the termination or cancellation of the appointment is an event certain to occur. Therefore, Ryerson's right to the "contract value" is not made contingent by the fact that the appointment had not yet terminated at the time of bankruptcy filing. Second, the fact that the Company may elect not to pay the "contract value" does not necessarily have the effect of denying him the right to collect it: the Appointment Agreement permits Ryerson to recover the "contract value" from his successor in the event that the Company elects not to pay it. We therefore attach no significance to the fact that payment of the "contract value" is stated to be at the option of the Company.

the prebankruptcy past" but eliminates the requirement that it not be entangled with the debtor's ability to make a fresh start. We think that the termination payments representing value for years of service completed prior to bankruptcy, and not being an arbitrary amount arising after bankruptcy, are "sufficiently rooted in the prebankruptcy past" as to be included within the bankruptcy estate.

Our ruling does not necessarily mean that all of the $18,588 is property of the bankruptcy estate. The Bankruptcy Appellate Panel determined that only the debtor's interest at the time of bankruptcy is property of the estate; any interest attributable to post-filing services was expressly excluded from the estate. We agree. Section 541(a)(6) excludes from the estate "earnings from services performed by an individual debtor after the commencement of the case." Thus any portion of the $18,588 related to services performed after February 10, 1981 are not includable within the bankruptcy estate.

The judgment of the Bankruptcy Appellate Panel is therefore affirmed.

IN RE CLAY
241 B.R. 534 (Bankr. N.D. Tex. 1999)

Akard, Bankruptcy Judge.

Myrtle McDonald, the Trustee-in-Bankruptcy (Trustee) for Paul Clay and Mary Clay (Debtors), seeks to have Farmers Insurance Exchange, Truck Insurance Exchange, Fire Insurance Exchange, Mid-Century Insurance Company, Farmers New World Life Insurance Company, Texas Farmers Insurance, and Farmers Texas County Mutual (Companies) turn over to her the "Contract Value" of Mr. Clay's Agent Appointment Agreement (Agreement). She asserts that the Agreement is property of the bankruptcy estate under § 541 of the Bankruptcy Code and that the Contract Value should be turned over to her pursuant to § 542 of the Bankruptcy Code.

The court finds Contract Value to be part of an unassumable executory contract for personal services under § 365, and thus it is not property of the estate. The court further finds that although the Contract Value might have had value to the estate on the date of filing, any contingent interest the Trustee had in Contract Value expired twelve months following the Debtors' voluntary filing of their bankruptcy petition.

FACTS

Effective October 1, 1984, Mr. Clay entered into a Farmers Insurance Group of Companies Agent Appointment Agreement to serve as an insurance agent for the Companies in Pampa, Texas. On November 24, 1997, the Debtors filed for relief under Chapter 7 of the Bankruptcy Code. They scheduled $190,000 in Contract Value under the Agreement as an asset. The Debtors also scheduled an obligation to the Farmers Insurance Group Federal Credit Union (Credit Union) in the amount of $83,000 secured by a lien on the Contract Value. The schedules showed tax obligations of $137,523.40 and general unsecured debts of $15,024.57.

The Trustee did not assume the Agreement subsequent to the bankruptcy filing. Mr. Clay continued to operate as an agent for the Companies under the Agreement. Neither Mr. Clay nor the Companies terminated the Agreement.

AGREEMENT

The Agreement appointed Mr. Clay as an agent to sell policies issued by the Companies. The Companies agreed to pay him new business and service commissions in accordance with their established schedules, to give him training and advertising assistance, and to make group life and medical insurance available to him. Mr. Clay agreed to sell insurance for the Companies and to submit every request or application for insurance of the type provided by the Companies to them. Mr. Clay was to provide his own office as well as a fidelity bond. The Agreement could be terminated by the mutual consent of the parties or by either party on three months written notice.

Paragraph G of the Agreement provides that in the event of termination of the Agreement, the Companies will pay the Contract Value to Mr. Clay or his heirs, except in the case of embezzlement when there would be no payment. The Contract Value is based upon:

(1) the amount of service commissions paid to the Agent on active policies during either the six month or twelve month period immediately preceding termination; (2) the number of policies in the Agent's active code number; (3) the number of years of continuous service as an Agent for the Companies immediately prior to termination.

The Agreement provides that if an agent has less than fifty policies in an active code number, there will be no Contract Value. Otherwise, the Contract Value will be computed for each company in accordance with a schedule contained in the Agreement.

* * *

POSITIONS OF THE PARTIES

The Trustee asserts that the Agreement is property of the estate under § 541 of the Bankruptcy Code and that the Contract Value (less the amounts owing to the Credit Union) should be paid to the Trustee under § 542 of the Bankruptcy Code. The Companies state that the Contract Value is neither a matured debt nor money owed to Mr. Clay. Thus, it is not subject to turnover under § 542 because it is neither property the Trustee may use, sell, or lease, nor is it property that the Debtor could exempt. The Companies filed a third party action against Mr. Clay asserting that the Trustee's action should be against Mr. Clay instead of against the Companies. Mr. Clay asserts that he has no entitlement to the Contract Value until the Agreement is terminated and that the Contract Value is in the nature of a trust for Mr. Clay's retirement.

ISSUE

The Agreement provides that the Contract Value is to be paid upon termination. The Trustee has no better rights under the Agreement than the Debtor. Consequently, the Trustee cannot force payment of the Contract Value as long as the Agreement remains in force. Therefore, the issue becomes whether the Trustee can terminate the Agreement in order to receive the Contract Value for the benefit of the creditors. The Debtor asserts that if the Agreement is terminated, he would not be given a new agent's appointment by the Companies because of his bankruptcy and the fact that he does not have a college degree. He asserts that the Companies are no longer appointing agents who do not have college degrees.

DISCUSSION
Property of the Estate

The court first determines whether the Agreement, and thus the Contract Value, is property of the estate. All legal and equitable interests of the debtor become property of the estate upon commencement of the case. § 541(a)(1). The Fifth Circuit, however, has stated that, "[u]nlike other assets of the debtor, the interest in an executory contract does not automatically vest in the bankruptcy estate at the time of filing." *In re Tonry*, 724 F.2d 467, 469 (5th Cir. 1984). An executory contract becomes part of the bankruptcy estate when the contract is assumed by the trustee. However, the executory contract is nonassumable if, under applicable law, any party other than the debtor may decline to accept performance by the trustee. § 365(c)(1)(A), (B). If an executory contract is nonassumable, and thus not part of the bankruptcy estate, it may still have value at the date of filing, measured on a quantum meruit basis of the services performed before the bankruptcy filing. *See In re Avery*, 947 F.2d 772, 774 (5th Cir. 1991).

The Agreement fits within the generally accepted definition of an executory contract which states "a contract under which the obligation of both the bankrupt and the other party to the contract are so far unperformed that the failure of either to complete performance would constitute a material breach excusing performance of the other." *In re Cajun Elec. Power Co-op., Inc.*, 230 B.R. 693, 702 (Bankr. M.D. La. 1999). In her trial brief, the Trustee also acknowledges that the Agreement is an executory contract for personal services and cannot be assumed. The Agreement, as an executory contract for personal services, is not part of the bankruptcy estate. However, the analysis does not stop there. Any amounts the Debtor earned under the contract prior to filing his petition are property of the estate. Therefore, the court must determine if Contract Value includes payment for any prepetition services rendered.

Contract Value Attributable to Fees Earned Prepetition

The personal service cases cited by the Trustee dealt with determinable amounts related to prepetition services. *See In re Kemp*, 52 F.3d 546, 554 (5th Cir. 1995) (prepetition earned income withheld by the employer is property of the estate); *In re Avery*, 947 F.2d at 774 (fees earned prepetition under an attorney's executory contracts are property of the estate); *In re Ryerson*, 739 F.2d 1423, 1425 (9th Cir. 1984) (fees related to prebankruptcy services paid through contact value received upon termination of position are property of the estate); *In re Tomer*, 128 B.R. 746, 762 (Bankr. S.D. Ill. 1991) (deferred commissions on prepetition policies are property of the estate). The most factually similar case cited by the Trustee, *Ryerson*, dealt with a trustee seeking turnover of the debtor's interest in "contract value." Ryerson was also an agent working under an agreement with Farmers Insurance. However, Ryerson terminated his agreement eight months after filing his Chapter 7 petition. The court held that any portion of the contract value relating to prepetition services was part of the bankruptcy estate and any postpetition services were not included in the estate. *Ryerson*, 739 F.2d at 1425-26.

Because Ryerson filed his bankruptcy petition within twelve months of termination, prepetition contract value could easily be determined. Contract value was calculated upon Ryerson's termination and Ryerson had a legal right to contract value at that point. The Agreement in this case has not been terminated.

The Agreement provides that the Contract Value is to be determined and paid upon termination and that no Contract Value exists if the agent either embezzles from the company or fails to have at least fifty policies in his active code number at the time of termination. The only way Contract Value can accurately be determined is through the calculation stated in the contract based on "either the six month or twelve month period *immediately preceding termination*" (emphasis added). Contract Value cannot be determined, and thus cannot come into quantifiable existence, until termination. Contract Value, therefore, cannot be apportioned between prepetition and postpetition services until the value is actually determined. If the Agreement were terminated within twelve months of the Clay's filing of their petition, Contract Value could be determined and a portion of that value would clearly be property of the estate. However, neither party to the contract has sought to do so. Both Mr. Clay and Farmers expressed their desire to continue, not terminate, the Agreement.

Forced Termination of the Contract

This court agrees with the conclusions of the *Groves* Court. *In re Groves*, 120 B.R. 956 (Bankr. N.D. Ill. 1990). Ms. Groves was required to make employee contributions to her retirement plan through mandatory wage deductions under her employment agreement with the state. Ms. Groves could only withdraw her contributions upon termination of employment or disability. After filing her Chapter 7 petition, the trustee filed an adversary proceeding to recover the contributions. *Id.* at 958. The court held that although the contributions were property of the estate, the court could not order turnover of the contributions while the debtor was still employed by the state. The court said:

> Nothing in the Bankruptcy Code or Rules gives the bankruptcy court the power to force the debtor to quit her job in order to mature her claim . . . for the benefit of the trustee. . . . It would be antithetical to the fresh start purpose of the Bankruptcy Code for this court to order the debtor to leave her employment. . . . By the same token, however, nothing in the Bankruptcy Code or Rules allows this court to rewrite the agreement between the debtor and [her employer].
>
> [T]he trustee has succeeded to exactly what the debtor had in terms of recovery . . . as of the date of the petition, *i.e.*, a contingent right to the return of the money in the event the debtor's employment by the state is terminated.

Id. at 965-66.

As discussed in *Groves*, a trustee has the same options as with any other property interest. The options are as follows: (1) keep the Chapter 7 case open and see if the contingent interest matures, *i.e.*, if the agreement is terminated within twelve months of filing, so that Contract Value could be determined; (2) sell the contingent right to Contract Value for whatever the market will bid; or, (3) if no buyer exists and it is unreasonably burdensome to keep the estate open, the trustee can seek an order authorizing her to abandon the contingent right.

The Clays filed their petition on November 24, 1997. Clearly, twelve months have passed without termination of the Agreement. Thus, the estimated value of $190,000 never matured into Contract Value that the Debtor could force Farmers to pay. Neither Mr. Clay nor the Trustee is entitled to payment of Contract Value at this time.

CONCLUSION

The court finds Contract Value is not property of the estate and any contingent interest the Trustee had in Contract Value expired twelve months following the Debtors' voluntary filing of their bankruptcy petition.

Problem 3-1

Two days after filing for bankruptcy protection, Diana wins $2,000,000 in the state lottery. Are the winnings property of the estate?

Problem 3-2

As part of her estate planning, Grandmother is contemplating putting $10 million in trust for her grandson, David. Because David is something of a spendthrift, Grandmother wants to limit David's current access to the funds. The most recent draft of the trust agreement provides that David will receive $10,000 each month from the trust's income but none of the remaining income and none of the corpus until David reaches the age of 50.

A. Before Grandmother signs the trust agreement, she wants to know what will happen if, after she signs it, Davis were eligible and filed for Chapter 7 bankruptcy protection. Specifically, what assets, if any, related to the trust would become part of the bankruptcy estate? In answering this, be sure to identify what different property rights David would have.

B. What, if anything, could Grandmother include in the trust agreement that would change the answer to Part A, and how would the answer change?

C. What bankruptcy implications would there by if the trust agreement provided that David was to get the corpus and remaining income upon Grandmother's death, rather than upon reaching the age of 50?

Problem 3-3

Diligent is a real estate broker who contracts with clients wishing to sell their property. These contracts entitle Diligent to a 6% commission whenever Diligent produces a buyer who is ready, willing, and able to purchase the listed property on the terms specified by the seller, regardless of whether the sale is completed. Prior to filing for bankruptcy protection, Diligent had produced willing buyers for thirteen clients who had not yet paid Diligent a commission. Each of the sales was completed postpetition after Diligent worked hard to ensure that the transaction closed. Such labors included scheduling and attending inspections, applying for title insurance, and negotiating modifications to the sales contracts. What portion of the commissions should be included in the estate? *See In re Parsons*, 280 F.3d 1185 (8th Cir. 2002). *Cf. In re Jess*, 169 F.3d 1204 (9th Cir. 1999) (dealing with an attorney's contingent fee).

Problem 3-4

When Dispirited filed for bankruptcy protection, Unreliable, Dispirited's ex-spouse, owed Dispirited $3,000 in past-due child support and $2,000 in past-due alimony, both pursuant to a court order entered in connection with the divorce. Shortly thereafter, Unreliable sent Dispirited a check for $4,000. How much, if any, of the proceeds of that check constitutes property of the estate? *See In re Poffenbarger*, 281 B.R. 379 (Bankr. S.D. Ala. 2002).

Problem 3-5

Six weeks before filing for bankruptcy protection, Disenchanted purchased a new 27" television from Retailer. Pursuant to Retailer's policies, customers may return any defective merchandise for a full refund any time within the first 60 days after purchase. They may also return nondefective goods for any reason within the first 30 days after purchase, but only for a store credit. Eighteen days after buying the television, Disenchanted returned it for a store credit. On the petition date, Disenchanted still owned that credit. May the trustee compel Retailer to issue a refund? What else may the trustee do with the credit?

Problem 3-6

You represent consumers who file for bankruptcy protection. Because they file their bankruptcy schedules under penalty of perjury, you want to help them be sure to list all of their assets. Review the types of personal property listed on Form 6, Schedule B. What other types of personal property – particularly intangible property – will you specifically ask your clients if they own in an effort to jog their memories?

E.   RECOVERED PROPERTY

Section 542(a) gives the trustee broad power to require any entity that possesses property of the estate to turn such property over to the trustee. Of course, as much of the reading so far illustrates, not all of the debtor's assets may be realty or tangible personal property. Some of it is likely to be intangible personal property not capable of possession, such as contract rights, bank deposits, or accounts receivable. Section 542(b) gives the trustee the power to require any entity that owes an obligation constituting property of the estate to make payment to the trustee.

Yet the trustee's powers extend well beyond these rights. Bankruptcy is an equitable proceeding. To do equity, it is occasionally necessary to reach back in time – to before the bankruptcy petition was filed – and recapture property that the debtor previously transferred away or which a creditor previously seized, and make that recovered property available to creditors. Section 541 includes such recovered property in the estate. *See* §§ 541(a)(3), (4), 550, 551. In essence, these assets are poured into the vat comprising the estate:

Property of the Estate

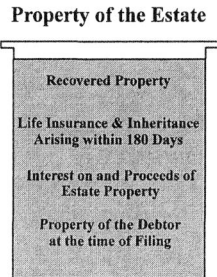

Two of the most important types of transfers that the bankruptcy trustee is empowered to avoid are preferences and fraudulent transfers. They are discussed below. We will encounter other avoiding powers of the trustee and the debtor in chapter six.

1. *Preferences*

Outside the bankruptcy process, debt collection from an insolvent debtor is a cross between a wedding banquet and a feeding frenzy. On the one hand, creditors whom the debtor favors – whether through familial affection or commercial need – are apt to receive a disproportionate share of the debtor's available assets. On the other hand, creditors who seek to compel payment through legal process or other means operate in a first-come-first-served world, where only those who diligently fight for a share of the debtor's wealth will get anything. In short, the ones who are fed from the debtor's wealth are those whom the debtor invites to the table and those pesky few who grab an uninvited chair. The patient creditors, those who try to accommodate the debtor but who do not become one of the debtor's favorites, are left hungry and angry.

One of the principal tenets of bankruptcy is that the process should be fair to creditors. This normally means that, absent some policy warranting favored treatment for some claimants, creditors should share ratably in the debtor's available assets. Clearly, there is a tension between this tenet and pre-bankruptcy practice. If, shortly before bankruptcy, a debtor were permitted to pay a favored creditor or a shark-like creditor were able to extract payment, then the principle of creditor equality inside bankruptcy would become meaningless. The bankruptcy estate would often contain only the crumbs left after selected creditors had their fill.

Preference law is an attempt to deal with this problem. It is designed to undo certain pre-bankruptcy transactions that frustrate the bankruptcy distribution scheme. Thus, if the bankruptcy estate has only enough assets to pay unsecured creditors ten cents on the dollar, and shortly before bankruptcy the debtor paid one unsecured creditor in full, preference law would "avoid" the "transfer" and compel the creditor to return the money received. The formerly preferred creditor would then stand in line with the other unsecured creditors hoping for payment in the bankruptcy proceeding. In short, preference law is an effort to deal with the fact that the bankruptcy process occupies just a small part of the time line of the debtor's financial affairs, and it allows the bankruptcy court to go back in time, before the bankruptcy petition was filed, and unwind certain transactions that frustrate bankruptcy policy. In effect, the law puts the debtor and the unsecured creditor back in the relative positions they occupied before the avoidable transfer was made. Assets removed from the debtor are recovered, and the debt that was paid is revived. In a few bankruptcy cases, the only significant assets in the estate are preference claims against certain creditors.

What has been written so far makes preference law seem perfectly reasonable and appropriate. That is because it was written from the bankruptcy lawyer's perspective (or perhaps from the unpaid creditor's perspective). From the preferred creditor's perspective, preferences are monstrous. The very idea that, after a lawfully created debt has been properly paid, the creditor may have to disgorge the money seems to them preposterous. Why, they ask, should a diligent creditor who compelled payment have to return it so that slothful creditors may share in those assets?

A traditional response to this question notes that preference law encourages creditor restraint, which helps debtors with cash flow problems get through difficult times, and thereby helps save businesses and jobs. You should question that response, however, for two reasons. First, it is far from clear that the economy truly benefits from creditor restraint. Perhaps the economy would benefit more if creditors diligently pursued their debtors and got money out of doomed enterprises and into more productive uses. Unless and until empirical research can tell us which approach produces the most social utility, we should not jump to any conclusions. Second, it is not at all clear that preference law really promotes creditor restraint. A diligent creditor who extracts a preferential payment may have to return the money, but otherwise suffers no penalty. In short, creditors have everything to gain by seeking payment (perhaps they will get it and get to keep it, either because the debtor never files for bankruptcy protection or does so after enough time has passed to insulate the payment from avoidance) and nothing to lose except the costs of enforcement, which may be fairly minimal.

Nevertheless, despite creditor criticism, preference law does further the bankruptcy policy of fair and equal treatment of creditors.

(a) The Six Elements

Section 547(b) outlines the elements of an avoidable preference. Most books on bankruptcy indicate that there are five elements to an avoidable preference, one in each of the five paragraphs within § 547(b). However, the flush language of § 547(b) also has an important element, so it is more useful to think of there being six elements. They are:
  (1) A transfer of an interest in the debtor's property – § 547(b)
  (2) To or for the benefit of a creditor – § 547(b)(1)
  (3) Made on account of an antecedent debt – § 547(b)(2)
  (4) Made while the debtor was insolvent – § 547(b)(3)
  (5) Made within the 90 days preceding the bankruptcy petition, or within one year if made to or for the benefit of an insider – § 547(b)(4)
  (6) That enables the creditor to receive more than if the transfer had not been made and the debtor's assets are liquidated under Chapter 7 – § 547(b)(5).

The first thing to notice about these elements is that no particular state of mind is required for either the creditor or the debtor. In other words, there need be no intent to prefer or to be preferred. Because of this, there is no blame associated with making or receiving a transfer that later proves to be preferential. While that may seem strange, it is countered, as we will see, by numerous affirmative defenses that insulate many ordinary transfers from avoidance.

Let's explore the elements that do exist in a bit more detail.

(i) A Transfer of an Interest of the Debtor in Property

There are at least three things worth noting about this element. First, "transfer" is defined very broadly in § 101(54). It may be by any method, and may be direct or indirect, absolute or conditional, voluntary or involuntary. The major implication of this is that it does not matter whether the debtor pays the creditor by check or the creditor has the sheriff levy upon property pursuant to a writ of execution. Both are a type of transfer that is potentially avoidable as a preference.

Second, the transfer need not involve all the rights to a particular piece of property; it need only concern "an interest . . . in property." Consequently, transferring an easement or life estate can be preferential. So too, as we will see in chapter six, can transferring a security interest.

Third, and most important, the interest in property transferred must have been the debtor's. Consider the following hypothetical.

To start up a new business, Debtor borrows money from Creditor. One of Debtor's relatives, Guarantor, guaranteed this obligation. The contract of guaranty allows Guarantor to seek reimbursement from Debtor for any payments Guarantor makes to Creditor on Debtor's behalf. Debtor later defaults on the obligation and Guarantor pays Creditor. Two weeks later, Debtor files for bankruptcy protection. May the bankruptcy trustee recover the payment from Creditor?

The answer is no. Because the payment was not made out of the debtor's property, the transfer is not avoidable.[27] Does this make sense? Well, yes. Sure Creditor was preferred over Debtor's other creditors, but not out of assets that would have become part of the bankruptcy estate. All that really happened when Guarantor paid Creditor, from the trustee's perspective, was that Guarantor was substituted for Creditor on Debtor's list of creditors.[28] Debtor's total assets and total liabilities, however, remain unchanged. Put another way, none of Debtor's other creditors were affected. Perhaps this can best be illustrated by looking at Debtor's balance sheet.

Assume that before Guarantor's payment, Debtor had $20,000 in nonexempt assets, and owed each of four entities, including Creditor, $10,000. Debtor's balance sheet might have looked like this:

Assets		Liabilities	
Various	$20,000	Creditor	$10,000
		Bank A	$10,000
		Bank B	$10,000
		Bank C	$10,000
Total	$20,000	Total	$40,000

Clearly, Debtor was insolvent and, if each claimant were entitled to the same priority, each would expect to receive 50¢ on the dollar in bankruptcy.

After the payment by Guarantor, Creditor is no longer owed any money but, by virtue of the right of reimbursement, Guarantor is. Otherwise, everything else is the same. Debtor's balance sheet thus now looks like this:

---

[27] *See In re Corland Corp.*, 967 F.2d 1069 (5th Cir. 1992).

[28] This is because a guarantor normally has the right to be reimbursed from the debtor if the guarantor makes good on its guaranty by paying the debtor's creditor. *See* Restatement (Third) of Suretyship and Guaranty § 26 (1996).

Assets		Liabilities	
Various	$20,000	*Guarantor*	$10,000
		Bank A	$10,000
		Bank B	$10,000
		Bank C	$10,000
Total	$20,000	Total	$40,000

Debtor's other creditors – the three banks – were totally unaffected by Guarantor's payment of creditor. Although Creditor received payment in full, the principle of creditor equality was not really compromised because none of the other creditors was hurt. More significantly, a contrary result would greatly undermine the efficacy of guarantees and thus potentially have serious adverse consequences on the availability of credit in our economy. So, the transfer is not avoidable. Put another way: no harm, no foul.

One corollary to the requirement that the property transferred be the debtor's is the so-called "earmarking" doctrine. Suppose, shortly before bankruptcy, the debtor borrows money from A for the express purpose of paying a debt to B (perhaps because A was willing to provide better credit terms). The "earmarking" doctrine essentially treats the loan from A as never having been an asset of the debtor. It applies when: (1) there was an agreement between the new lender and the debtor that the funds would be used to pay a specified existing creditor; (2) that agreement was performed according to its terms; and (3) the transaction as a whole does not diminish the estate.[29] Essentially, as long as the debtor's access to the funds is restricted, payment of the old creditor will not be avoidable.[30] Although the doctrine has been criticized,[31] it

---

[29]   *In re Bohlen Enterprises, Ltd.*, 859 F.2d 561, 566 (8th Cir. 1988). Note, if the debt to the new creditor is secured and the debt paid off was not, then the estate has been diminished and the doctrine does not apply. *E.g., Caillouet v. First Bank & Trust*, 2007 WL 1302523 (E.D. La. 2007); *The Cadle Co. v. Mangan*, 316 B.R. 11 (D. Conn. 2004).

[30]   While no longer so limited, the doctrine arose out of cases in which the new creditor providing funds was itself obligated to pay the prior debt as a guarantor. In other words, the guarantor gave the debtor money with instructions to pay the creditor, which the debtor did. If the transfer to the creditor were avoided as preferential, the creditor would seek repayment from the guarantor, who would then have to pay a second time. This result was thought to be highly inequitable. *See In re Moses*, 256 B.R. 641, 645-47 (10th Cir. BAP 2000) (ruling that the doctrine should be limited to such co-debtor situations).

[31]   *See In re Kemp Pac. Fisheries, Inc.*, 16 F.3d 313, 316 n.2 (9th Cir. 1994); *Bohlen Enterprises*, 859 F.2d at 566.

nevertheless survives.[32] Perhaps this is because an earmarked transaction is functionally the same as having the new lender deal directly with the old creditor, buying the old creditor's rights against the debtor. That certainly involves no asset of the debtor and is not an avoidable transfer.

(ii) To or for the Benefit of a Creditor

Only transfers that benefit creditors can be preferential. Giving assets away to friends, family, or charitable organizations cannot be preferential. Such transfers may be avoidable for other reasons – they may, for example, be fraudulent transfers, *see* § 548 – but only creditors can receive a preference.

(iii) On Account of an Antecedent Debt

The Code does not define what an "antecedent debt" is, but there is rarely any dispute over its meaning. All this requirement means is that the debt must have arisen prior to the preferential payment.[33] For the most part, this element adds little to the previous requirement that the transfer be to or for the benefit of a creditor. If the transferee qualified as a creditor, then there necessarily was a debt.

When does a debt arise? That is a question of nonbankruptcy law. Consider the following two examples:

1. A goes to a grocery store and selects an item for purchase. A brings it to the checkout counter and pays for it.
2. B contracts to buy goods. The contract calls for payment within 30 days after delivery. The goods are delivered and 28 days later B pays.

In the first example, there was no antecedent debt. Indeed, there was no contract at all until payment was made. Put another way, the debt was created and payment was made simultaneously. In contrast, the second example does involve an antecedent debt. Although the obligation may not have matured, it did exist and predate the payment.[34] Indeed, in that fact pattern the creditor actually intended to extend credit.

---

[32] *See, e.g., In re Superior Stamp & Coin Co.*, 223 F.3d 1004 (9th Cir. 2000); *In re Green Valentine, Inc.*, 330 B.R. 880 (6th Cir. BAP 2005).

[33] *See In re Barefoot*, 952 F.2d 795 (4th Cir. 1991) (debt arises when debtor first became legally obligated to pay).

[34] Unmatured debts are still debts and can create a valid claim. *See* § 101(5) & (12).

This is not to say that there must have been a voluntary extension of credit for an antecedent debt to arise. Consider an accident between a driver and a bicyclist. Even if, immediately upon exiting the car, the driver hands the cyclist a check in settlement of any resulting injury claim, it would still be payment of an antecedent debt. An antecedent debt can be contingent or disputed and still form the basis of an avoidable preference.[35]

(iv) While Insolvent

The debtor is presumed to have been insolvent for the 90 days preceding the bankruptcy filing. § 547(f). Although the ultimate burden of proof on this point remains with the trustee, the preference defendant must produce some evidence to rebut the presumption before the trustee is required to address the issue.[36]

The Bankruptcy Code defines "insolvent" as having a sum of all liabilities that exceeds the value of all nonexempt assets owned; in other words, as having a negative net worth. § 101(32).[37] This is an easy test to state, but often difficult to apply. Valuing assets is often difficult and subject to much speculation. Beyond that, there is not complete agreement on what the proper valuation standard should be. The Code requires a "fair" valuation, *see* § 101(32), but that vague standard leaves open the question of whether the assets should be valued at liquidation value, at replacement cost, as a going concern, or in some other manner. As we will see, such valuation problems permeate much of bankruptcy practice. They arise in many different contexts and often require different answers. For preference purposes, however, the following case illustrates the prevailing approach.

---

[35] *See In re Enron*, 357 B.R. 32 (Bankr. S.D.N.Y. 2006).

[36] *See* S. Rep. 95-595 at 178-179; *In re Sierra Steel, Inc.*, 96 B.R. 275, 277 (9th Cir. BAP 1989).

[37] Note, this is different from the definition in the Uniform Commercial Code, under which either having a negative net worth (while still counting exempt assets) *or* not being able to pay debts as they become due makes a person insolvent. *See* U.C.C. § 1-201(b)(23). Under the Uniform Fraudulent Transfer Act, insolvency is defined as having liabilities that exceed assets, but a person not able to pay debts as they become due is presumed to be insolvent. U.F.T.A. § 2(a), (b).

IN RE DAK INDUSTRIES, INC.
170 F.3d 1197 (9th Cir. 1999)

Per curiam.

The Trustee of the bankruptcy proceedings of DAK Industries, Inc. ("DAK") sued certain creditors to recover payments made to them by DAK during the 90 days preceding the bankruptcy petition. The bankruptcy court found that the Trustee had not established that DAK was insolvent during the preference period, as required by § 547(b), and, therefore, granted judgment in favor of the creditors. The district court affirmed the ruling of the bankruptcy court. We . . . affirm the judgment.

FACTS

DAK Industries was engaged in direct marketing of consumer electronics, and owed much of its 30-year success to the unique catalogue selections and style created by its founder, Drew Alan Kaplan. After many successful years of operation, DAK began to experience financial problems and sought bankruptcy protection under Chapter 11 in the spring of 1992. DAK operated as a debtor-in-possession for two and one-half years (June 1992 to October 1994). However, DAK was not able to regain its financial health, and lost approximately $14 million during those years. Ultimately, DAK's Chapter 11 proceeding was converted to one under Chapter 7.

The Trustee initiated the present action to recover allegedly preferential payments made to various suppliers and creditors during the 90-day period preceding DAK's original Chapter 11 petition. A two-week trial followed, during which the parties vigorously contested DAK's solvency during the preference period, and both sides submitted extensive evidence and expert testimony on that issue.

After reviewing the conflicting evidence, the bankruptcy court determined that DAK was, during the time in question, a going concern, and selected as the most appropriate valuation of DAK a report, submitted by one of the creditors' experts, which concluded that DAK was solvent during the preference period. On appeal, the district court affirmed the findings of the bankruptcy court. We review the bankruptcy court's factual findings for clear error, without deference to the decision of the district court.

DISCUSSION

To succeed in a preference action, a trustee must show, inter alia, that the debtor was insolvent at the time of the contested transaction.[38] § 547(b). The Bankruptcy Code defines insolvency, for a corporation, as a "financial condition such that the sum of such

---

[38] In general, the trustee in a preference action is entitled to rely on a presumption that the debtor was insolvent during the preference period. However, if a creditor produces some evidence that the debtor was solvent, as in this case, the trustee bears the burden of proof with respect to the debtor's insolvency.

entity's debts is greater than all of such entity's property, at fair valuation." § 101(32). Although the Code does not define "fair valuation," courts have generally engaged in a two-step process of analysis. *See, e.g., Matter of Taxman Clothing Co.*, 905 F.2d 166, 169-70 (7th Cir. 1990). First, the court must determine whether a debtor was a "going concern" or was "on its deathbed." Second, the court must value the debtor's assets, depending on the status determined in the first part of the inquiry, and apply a simple balance sheet test to determine whether the debtor was solvent.[39] *Id.* at 170. We agree that a "fair valuation" of a debtor's assets must begin with a determination of whether a debtor is "a going concern" and end with the application of a balance sheet test to determine solvency.

In this case, the bankruptcy court determined that DAK was a going concern during the preference period, relying primarily on the fact that DAK continued to conduct business under Chapter 11 protection for two and one-half years. In light of the amount of business transacted by DAK during the preference period and the years that followed, as well as DAK's ability to pay its operating expenses during the same period, this finding was not erroneous.

The bankruptcy court went on to find that DAK was solvent during the preference period. The court came to this conclusion after hearing testimony from numerous expert witnesses and evaluating many reports and exhibits submitted by the parties. As the evidence in this case demonstrates, the precise value of a company as a going concern is far from certain. The bankruptcy court did not err by finding that the creditors' report was the most credible and accurate assessment of DAK's financial status, particularly in light of the fact that the valuation evidence submitted by DAK was based on liquidation values.

* * *

CONCLUSION

The Bankruptcy Court correctly determined that DAK was both a going concern and solvent during the 90-day period preceding its original Chapter 11 petition. The challenged judgment accordingly is affirmed.

---

[39]   If the debtor was a going concern, the court will determine the fair market price of the debtor's assets as if they had been sold as a unit, in a prudent manner, and within a reasonable time. If the company was on its deathbed, *i.e.*, only nominally extant, then the court will determine the liquidation value of the assets, such as a price expected at a foreclosure sale.

Problem 3-7

Daisy Systems, Inc. is a small business in financial difficulty. Within the preference period Daisy pays a favored creditor on an antecedent debt. At the time of payment, Daisy's total liabilities are less than the value of its inventory, equipment, and other assets if those assets are valued at their cost. If, however, past depreciation of assets (particularly the equipment) is taken into account, Daisy's total liabilities exceed the value of those assets. Daisy also has very loyal customers (*i.e.,* goodwill) and carries a positive allocation for this on its balance sheet, so that the current depreciated value of Daisy's total assets exceeds Daisy's total liabilities. Is Daisy insolvent within the meaning of § 547(b)(3)? How should assets be valued for the purposes of analyzing preference actions? *See In re Taxman Clothing Co.*, 905 F.2d 166 (7th Cir. 1990).

(v) Made within 90 Days (or One Year to an Insider)

One might think that this element is so clear, that there could be no issues about how it applies to any particular situation. Nevertheless, while this element is rarely contested, it has raised two interesting questions.

First, is the preference period to be calculated by counting forwards from the date of the transfer or backwards from the date of the petition? This actually can make a difference. Bankruptcy Rule 9006(a), which is based on Federal Rule of Civil Procedure 6(a), provides that the last day in any statutory period is not to be counted if it is a Saturday, Sunday, or legal holiday. Thus, if a petition were filed on a Friday, the 90th day before the petition would be a Saturday. If the period is to be calculated by counting backwards, the preference period would be extended to the previous Friday. On the other hand, if the period is to be calculated by counting forwards from the date of the transfer, any petition filed on a Monday actually generates a preference period of 92 days. The majority of courts that have looked at the issue, including one circuit court, have ruled that the period is to be calculated by counting backwards.[40]

Second, if the debtor pays an obligation by check, when does the transfer occur for the purposes of § 547(b)? Is it when the check is mailed, received, deposited, or when paid by the drawee bank? This issue arises frequently and has made it all the way to

---

[40] *See In re Nelson Co.*, 959 F.2d 1260, 1266-67 (3d Cir. 1992). *But see In re Greene*, 223 F.3d 1064 (9th Cir. 2000); *In re Bergel*, 185 B.R. 338 (9th Cir. BAP 1995) (both ruling that § 547(b) is a substantive rule, not a procedural one, so that Rule 9006 is wholly inapplicable).

Supreme Court, which ruled that the transfer occurs on the date the check is honored.[41] This probably makes sense because this date is (a) consistent with Article 3 of the Uniform Commercial Code; (b) easiest to prove; and (c) less subject to manipulation.[42] Note, however, this rule applies to regular checks. If the check is a cashier's check, the transfer occurs upon delivery.[43]

One other thing to note about this element is its interaction with the presumption of insolvency. Even if the preferred creditor is an insider, *see* § 101(31) (defining "insider"), so that a one-year preference period applies instead of the normal 90-day period, the presumption of insolvency created by § 547(f) extends only to the 90 days preceding the filing. Thus, if the trustee goes after an insider creditor for a transfer made more than 90 days but less than one year before the petition, no presumption of insolvency will apply.

(vi) That Enables the Creditor to Receive More

This element is the heart of preference actions. It requires proof that the creditor really did benefit by the transfer. In most Chapter 7 liquidations, this is easy to determine, once the size of the estate and the priority of the various claimants is determined. In Chapter 11 cases, however, the court must determine what the creditor would have received had the allegedly preferential transfer not been made and the debtor liquidated under Chapter 7. As should be apparent, that may be very difficult to determine with any accuracy, because it presupposes a liquidation of the debtor's assets that is in fact not occurring. As a general rule of thumb, however, and regardless of whether the debtor is in Chapter 7 or Chapter 11, any payment by an insolvent debtor to a non-priority, unsecured creditor will have preferential effect.

---

[41] *Johnson v. Barnhill*, 503 U.S. 393 (1992).

[42] Note, a different rule apparently applies for the purposes of § 547(c)(2) and (4). Circuit courts have unanimously adopted a date-of-delivery rule for those preference defenses. *See, e.g., In re Tennessee Chemical Co.*, 112 F.3d 234, 238 (6th Cir. 1997); *In re Kroh Bros. Dev. Corp.*, 930 F.2d 648, 650-51 (8th Cir. 1991) (citing *In re New York City Shoes*, 880 F.2d 679, 681 n.2 (3d Cir. 1989); *In re White River Corp.*, 799 F.2d 631 (10th Cir. 1986); *In re Gold Coast Seed Co.*, 30 B.R. 551, 553 (9th Cir. BAP 1983); *In re Almarc Mfg.*, 62 B.R. 684, 687 & 689 n.8 (Bankr. N.D. Ill. 1986)). On the other hand, most courts have adopted the date-of-honor rule for § 549 purposes, dealing with postpetition transfers. *See, e.g., In re Oakwood Markets, Inc.*, 203 F.3d 406 (6th Cir. 2000).

[43] *In re Lee*, 179 B.R. 149 (9th Cir. BAP 1995) (concluding delivery, not purchase, is the relevant time). *See also* U.C.C. § 3-310(a).

Problem 3-8

At the beginning of June, Dickinson had $6,000 in nonexempt assets and $10,000 in liabilities, of which $4,000 was owed to Cummings. During that month, Dickinson paid Cummings $2,000, with the understanding that the balance would be paid later. In July, before any additional payments were made, Dickinson filed for bankruptcy protection under Chapter 7.
A.   May the trustee avoid the June payment to Cummings?
B.   How, if at all, would the analysis in Part A change if Dickinson's debt to Cummings was guaranteed by Granger, who has ample assets?

(b) The Nine Defenses

Congress has given creditors nine affirmative defenses to preference actions. *See* § 547(c). For all such defenses, the creditor has the burden of proving their applicability. § 547(g). Three of these defenses, § 547(c)(3), (5) & (6), expressly relate to secured claims, and a fourth, § 547(c)(1), while not referencing secured claims, is in fact used almost exclusively by secured creditors. All of these defenses will be covered in chapter six. The remaining five defenses are discussed below in increasing order of importance.

(i) De Minimis Consumer Transfers – § 547(c)(8)

Section 547(c)(8) provides a defense for reasonably small consumer payments. Only if the aggregate value of all the property transferred is worth $600 or more, is the transfer avoidable.[44] Unfortunately, its wording is a bit ambiguous. Consider the following problem.

Problem 3-9

Eclectic Merchandise, Inc. obtained a $3,000 judgment against DeMinimis for failure to pay for several items DeMinimis purchased on credit. Eclectic then obtained a writ of garnishment against DeMinimis's employer, who, over the next two months, made four $400 payments to Eclectic pursuant to the writ (out of DeMinimis's wages). DeMinimis then filed for Chapter 7 bankruptcy protection and the trustee now seeks to recover the payments from

---

[44]   Note, this is *not* one of the Code's dollar amounts that adjusts with inflation. *See* § 104(b).

Eclectic. Are the payments avoidable? *See In re Hailes*, 77 F.3d 873 (5th Cir. 1996).

(ii) De Minimis Nonconsumer Transfers – § 547(c)(9)

The 2005 amendments to the Bankruptcy Code added a similar defense for nonconsumer transfers, albeit with a much higher dollar amount: $5,000 (which has since been adjusted for inflation to $5,475).[45] While it suffers from the same ambiguity that § 547(c)(8) does, it probably protects a large number of business transfers from avoidance.

(iii) Spousal & Child Support Payments – § 547(c)(7)

This defense is one of many provisions of the Bankruptcy Code designed to protect support claimants. The other protections include: an exception from the discharge, § 523(a)(5); immunity from exemptions, § 523(c); and priority over other claimants, § 507(a)(7). The combined effect of these provisions is to actually encourage the debtor to make preferential payments of support obligations.

(iv) The Net Result Rule – § 547(c)(4)

Some businesses and even a few individuals have a revolving line of credit under which they are constantly making payments to and then borrowing more from (often by purchasing goods on credit) the same creditor. If there were no preference protection at all for such relationships, the creditor would run a severe bankruptcy risk: not only would the creditor stand to lose whatever amount the debtor owed on the date the bankruptcy petition was filed, but might also have to disgorge prior payments that had been followed by extensions of additional credit.

Consider the following example of a debtor who, at the end of April, owed a supplier $10,000 and who on July 21st filed for bankruptcy protection:

---

[45] This was one of three recommendations made in 1997 by the National Bankruptcy Review Commission and relating to preference actions that Congress adopted in 2005. The others were to expand the scope of the defense in § 547(c)(2) for transfers in the ordinary course of business and to amend 28 U.S.C. § 1409 to make the district of the preference defendant's residence the proper venue for any action against a noninsider to avoid a transfer of less than $10,000 on a nonconsumer debt. That amount has since been adjusted for inflation to $10,950.

Date	Payment	New Value
May 1	$10,000	
May 15		$11,000
June 1	$11,000	
June 15		$12,000
July 1	$12,000	
July 15		$13,000

Without the § 547(c)(4) defense, each of the three listed payments would be an avoidable preference. In addition, the supplier would potentially lose all or most of the $13,000 debt outstanding on the date the petition was filed. In sum, the supplier would stand to lose $46,000. In reality, however, the supplier may not have provided goods or services in May, June, or July had not the debtor made the payments listed two weeks before. In other words, each payment the debtor made allowed the debtor to actually borrow more by allowing the debtor to borrow again.

Section 547(c)(4) partially protects the supplier in this example by insulating from preference avoidance each payment to the extent it is followed by a grant of new value. The defense therefore "encourages creditors to continue their revolving credit arrangements with financially troubled debtors, potentially helping the debtor to avoid bankruptcy altogether."[46] Protecting such creditors is thought not to be unfair to other creditors of the debtor because the preferential payments are replenished by the preferred creditor's extension of new value.[47]

Now try the following problem.

Problem 3-10

Which transfers are avoidable and to what extent if, within the preference period, the prepetition transactions were as follows, again assuming the debtor owed the creditor $10,000 at the end of April:

---

[46] *In re Toyota of Jefferson, Inc.*, 14 F.3d 1088 (5th Cir. 1994). *See also In re IRFM, Inc.*, 52 F.3d 228 (9th Cir. 1995).

[47] *See also In re Jones Truck Lines, Inc.*, 130 F.3d 323 (8th Cir. 1997) (employees providing services protected by § 547(c)(4)).

Date	Payment	New Value
May 1	$10,000	
May 15		$41,000
June 1	$10,000	
June 15	$20,000	
July 1		$5,000
July 15		$13,000

(v) Payments in the Ordinary Course – § 547(c)(2)

The classic preference involves a privileged creditor – perhaps an insider – with knowledge of and influence over the affairs of the debtor who, seeing that the debtor is sinking into insolvency, obtains payment from the debtor before the debtor's financial problems become manifest. Indeed, § 60b of the old Bankruptcy Act made avoidable only those preferences received when the creditor had "reasonable cause to believe that the debtor [was] insolvent." Thus, only if the creditor was on notice that receipt of property from the debtor might prejudice the rights of other creditors could the transfer be avoided.

This notice requirement was excluded from the Bankruptcy Code because it was too difficult for trustees to prove. On the other hand, many, if not most, creditors paid shortly before a bankruptcy filing have not taken advantage of any special status that they have and indeed may not be aware that the debtor is in financial trouble. After all, most debtors in financial trouble try to hide their insolvency and often succeed for an extended period of time. Accordingly, some protection was thought necessary for creditors who really did nothing out of the ordinary. This protection is codified in § 547(c)(2). ***Do not read this provision yet.*** It excepts from preference avoidance payments made in the ordinary course of business and it is by far the most important of the preference defenses.

Does this protection undermine the principle of creditor equality? Sure it does. Yet consider this. Normally, in the 90 days preceding bankruptcy, the debtor pays many unsecured debts of a recurring nature as they become due. An individual debtor, for example, pays utility bills and usually at least minimum payments on credit card balances. A business debtor normally purchases both inventory and the services of employees on terms that call for payment within reasonably short time frames, from seven days to as long as six months, and even an insolvent debtor may pay many of these obligations as they become due. Without the § 547(c)(2) defense, such payments would become avoidable preferences if the debtor goes into bankruptcy less than three months later. Such a result may not be appropriate. Some other casebook authors summed it up nicely:

> One vital goal of any commercial law regime is certainty and finality in transactions. If large numbers of ordinary commercial transactions can be unwound in later legal proceedings, all transactions of that type become more expensive. Creditors must then charge for the increased risk. There is general consensus in favor of avoiding preferences made in out-of-the-ordinary transactions in which a creditor seeks, and is given, favored treatment by a debtor in obvious financial difficulty. However, it is not so clear that payments by an insolvent debtor on obligations as they mature should be avoided merely because the incidental result is that the creditor who received payment was preferred over others who did not have the good fortune to be paid before bankruptcy. If a doctrine designed to obtain equality for all creditors interferes with normal commercial practices and significantly adds to the cost of ordinary commercial transactions, the cost of equality may be too high.[48]

To put it simply, bankruptcy law should not impel the typical creditor – such as a utility company or employee – to run a credit check every month or week, or to go through the hassle and expense of taking a security interest. Section 547(c)(2), by immunizing transfers made in the ordinary course of business, makes sure that most creditors do not need to take such precautions.

As originally enacted, § 547(c)(2) protected only those transfers "made not later than 45 days after such debt was incurred," and thus was restricted to short-term trade debt. This 45-day rule caused some problems, though. First, it failed to recognize that a significant portion of short-term financing calls for payment beyond 45 days. Second, it was not always easy to determine when the debt was incurred. For example, suppose a debtor receives an invoice that covers a series of purchases of goods or services, as in the case of a telephone bill covering a series of long distance calls or a credit card bill covering a month of purchases. The debtor sends the creditor a check 25 days later. Some of the underlying charges covered by the bill were likely made more than 45 days before payment. If the debtor paid only a portion of the bill, which of the charges should the payment be deemed to have covered? Similarly, a typical bill for electricity covers a 30-day period. Is such a debt incurred at the time the electricity was provided or when the invoice was sent? In other words, if the debtor paid the bill 25 days after receipt, the payment would cover some electricity received more than 45 days beforehand. Is it worth the time, effort, and expense to figure that out, merely to bring a bit more money into the estate?

---

[48] WILLIAM D. WARREN & DANIEL J. BUSSEL, BANKRUPTCY 359 (7th ed.2006).

In 1984, Congress addressed this problem by repealing the 45-day rule. This action greatly expanded the scope of § 547(c)(2). However, as is often the case, this effort to clarify the law actually raised additional questions. One of these questions was resolved by the Supreme Court in the following case.

UNION BANK V. WOLAS
502 U.S. 151 (1991)

Justice Stevens delivered the opinion of the Court.

Section 547(b) of the Bankruptcy Code authorizes a trustee to avoid certain property transfers made by a debtor within 90 days before bankruptcy. The Code makes an exception, however, for transfers made in the ordinary course of business, § 547(c)(2). The question presented is whether payments on long-term debt may qualify for that exception.

On December 17, 1986, ZZZZ Best Co., Inc. (Debtor), borrowed $7 million from petitioner, Union Bank (Bank).[49] On July 8, 1987, the Debtor filed a voluntary petition under Chapter 7 of the Bankruptcy Code. During the preceding 90-day period, the Debtor had made two interest payments totaling approximately $100,000 and had paid a loan commitment fee of about $2,500 to the Bank. After his appointment as trustee of the Debtor's estate, respondent filed a complaint against the Bank to recover those payments pursuant to § 547(b).

The Bankruptcy Court found that the loans had been made "in the ordinary course of business or financial affairs" of both the Debtor and the Bank, and that both interest payments as well as the payment of the loan commitment fee had been made according to ordinary business terms and in the ordinary course of business. As a matter of law, the Bankruptcy Court concluded that the payments satisfied the requirements of § 547(c)(2) and therefore were not avoidable by the trustee. The District Court affirmed the Bankruptcy Court's summary judgment in favor of the Bank.

Shortly thereafter, in another case, the Court of Appeals held that the ordinary course of business exception to avoidance of preferential transfers was not available to long-term creditors. *In re CHG Int'l, Inc.*, 897 F.2d 1479 (9th Cir. 1990). In reaching that conclusion, the Court of Appeals relied primarily on the policies underlying the voidable preference provisions and the state of the law prior to the enactment of the 1978 Bankruptcy Code and its amendment in 1984. Thus, the Ninth Circuit concluded,

---

[49]   The Bankruptcy Court found that the Bank and Debtor executed a revolving credit agreement on December 16, 1986, in which the Bank agreed to lend the Debtor $7 million in accordance with the terms of a promissory note to be executed and delivered by the Debtor. On December 17, 1986, the Debtor executed and delivered to the Bank a promissory note in the principal sum of $7 million. The promissory note provided that interest would be payable on a monthly basis and would accrue on the principal balance at a rate of 0.65% per annum in excess of the Bank's reference rate.

its holding in *CHG Int'l, Inc.* dictated a reversal in this case.[50] The importance of the question of law decided by the Ninth Circuit, coupled with the fact that the Sixth Circuit had interpreted § 547(c)(2) in a contrary manner, *In re Finn*, 909 F.2d 903 (6th Cir. 1990), persuaded us to grant the Bank's petition for certiorari.

I

We shall discuss the history and policy of § 547 after examining its text. In subsection (b), Congress broadly authorized bankruptcy trustees to "avoid any transfer of an interest of the debtor in property" if five conditions are satisfied and unless one of seven exceptions defined in subsection (c) is applicable. In brief, the five characteristics of a voidable preference are that it (1) benefit a creditor; (2) be on account of antecedent debt; (3) be made while the debtor was insolvent; (4) be made within 90 days before bankruptcy; and (5) enable the creditor to receive a larger share of the estate than if the transfer had not been made. Section 547 also provides that the debtor is presumed to have been insolvent during the 90-day period preceding bankruptcy. § 547(f). In this case, it is undisputed that all five of the foregoing conditions were satisfied and that the interest and loan commitment fee payments were voidable preferences unless excepted by subsection (c)(2).

The most significant feature of subsection (c)(2) that is relevant to this case is the absence of any language distinguishing between long-term debt and short-term debt.

Instead of focusing on the term of the debt for which the transfer was made, subsection (c)(2) focuses on whether the debt was incurred, and payment made, in the "ordinary course of business or financial affairs" of the debtor and transferee. Thus, the text provides no support for respondent's contention that § 547(c)(2)'s coverage is limited to short-term debt, such as commercial paper or trade debt. Given the clarity of the statutory text, respondent's burden of persuading us that Congress intended to create or to preserve a special rule for long-term debt is exceptionally heavy. *United States v. Ron Pair Enterprises, Inc.*, 489 U.S. 235, 241-242 (1989). As did the Ninth Circuit, respondent relies on the history and the policies underlying the preference provision.

II

The relevant history of § 547 contains two chapters, one of which clearly supports, and the second of which is not inconsistent with, the Bank's literal reading of the statute. Section 547 was enacted in 1978 when Congress overhauled the Nation's bankruptcy laws. The section was amended in 1984. For purposes of the question presented in this case, the original version of § 547 differed in one significant respect from the current

---

[50] In so holding, the Ninth Circuit rejected the Bank's argument that the revolving line of credit in this case was not "long-term" because it was for less than one year. Because we hold that the ordinary course of business exception applies to payments on long-term as well as short-term debt, we need not decide whether the revolving line of credit was a "long-term" debt.

version: it contained a provision that the ordinary course of business exception did not apply unless the payment was made within 45 days of the date the debt was incurred. That provision presumably excluded most payments on long-term debt from the exception. In 1984 Congress repealed the 45-day limitation but did not substitute a comparable limitation.[51]

Respondent contends that this amendment was intended to satisfy complaints by issuers of commercial paper[52] and by trade creditors[53] that regularly extended credit for periods of more than 45 days. Furthermore, respondent continues, there is no evidence in the legislative history that Congress intended to make the ordinary course of business exception available to conventional long-term lenders. Therefore, respondent argues, we should follow the analysis of the Ninth Circuit and read § 547(c)(2) as protecting only short-term debt payments.

We need not dispute the accuracy of respondent's description of the legislative history of the 1984 amendment in order to reject his conclusion. For even if Congress adopted the 1984 amendment to redress particular problems of specific short-term creditors, it remains true that Congress redressed those problems by entirely deleting the time limitation in § 547(c)(2). The fact that Congress may not have foreseen all of the consequences of a statutory enactment is not a sufficient reason for refusing to give effect to its plain meaning. *Toibb v. Radloff*, 501 U.S. 157, 164 (1991).

Respondent also relies on the history of voidable preferences prior to the enactment of the 1978 Bankruptcy Code. The text of the preference provision in the earlier Bankruptcy Act did not specifically include an exception for payments made in the ordinary course of business. The courts had, however, developed what is sometimes described as the "current expense" rule to cover situations in which a debtor's payments on the eve of bankruptcy did not diminish the net estate because tangible assets were

---

[51] We use the term "presumably" because it is not necessary in this case to decide whether monthly interest payments on long-term debt were protected by the initial version of § 547(c)(2). *Cf. In re Iowa Premium Serv. Co., Inc.*, 695 F.2d 1109 (8th Cir. 1982) (holding that interest obligations are "incurred" when they become due, rather than when the promissory note is signed). We refer to "most" instead of "all" long-term debt payments because of the possibility that a debtor's otherwise avoidable payment was made within 45 days of the date the long-term loan was made.

[52] Because payments to a commercial paper purchaser within 90 days prior to bankruptcy may be preferential transfers under § 547(b), a purchaser could be assured that the payment would not be avoided under the prior version of § 547(c)(2) only if the commercial paper had a maturity of 45 days or less. Commercial issuers thus complained that the 45-day limitation lowered demand for commercial paper with a maturity in excess of 45 days.

[53] Trade creditors stated that normal payment periods in many industries exceeded 45 days and complained that the arbitrary 45-day limitation in § 547(c)(2) deprived these trade creditors of the protection of the ordinary course of business exception to the trustee's power to avoid preferential transfers.

obtained in exchange for the payment. Without such an exception, trade creditors and other suppliers of necessary goods and services might have been reluctant to extend even short-term credit and might have required advance payment instead, thus making it difficult for many companies in temporary distress to have remained in business. Respondent argues that Congress enacted § 547(c)(2) in 1978 to codify that exception, and therefore the Court should construe § 547(c)(2) as limited to the confines of the current expense rule.

This argument is not compelling for several reasons. First, it is by no means clear that § 547(c)(2) should be construed as the statutory analogue of the judicially crafted current expense rule because there are other exceptions in § 547(c) that explicitly cover contemporaneous exchanges for new value. Those provisions occupy some (if not all) of the territory previously covered by the current expense rule. Nor has respondent directed our attention to any extrinsic evidence suggesting that Congress intended to codify the current expense rule in § 547(c)(2).

The current expense rule developed when the statutory preference provision was significantly narrower than it is today. To establish a preference under the Bankruptcy Act, the trustee had to prove that the challenged payment was made at a time when the creditor had "reasonable cause to believe that the debtor [was] insolvent." § 96(b) (1976 ed.). When Congress rewrote the preference provision in the 1978 Bankruptcy Code, it substantially enlarged the trustee's power to avoid preferential transfers by eliminating the reasonable cause to believe requirement for transfers made within 90 days of bankruptcy and creating a presumption of insolvency during that period. At the same time, Congress created a new exception for transfers made in the ordinary course of business, § 547(c)(2). This exception was intended to "leave undisturbed normal financial relations, because it does not detract from the general policy of the preference section to discourage unusual action by either the debtor or his creditors during the debtor's slide into bankruptcy." H.R. Rep. No. 95-595, at 373.

In light of these substantial changes in the preference provision, there is no reason to assume that the justification for narrowly confining the "current expense" exception to trade creditors before 1978 should apply to the ordinary course of business exception under the 1978 Code. Instead, the fact that Congress carefully reexamined and entirely rewrote the preference provision in 1978 supports the conclusion that the text of § 547(c)(2) as enacted reflects the deliberate choice of Congress.

III

The Bank and the trustee agree that § 547 is intended to serve two basic policies that are fairly described in the House Committee Report. The Committee explained:

> A preference is a transfer that enables a creditor to receive payment of a greater percentage of his claim against the debtor than he would have received if the transfer had not been made and he had participated in the distribution of

the assets of the bankrupt estate. The purpose of the preference section is two-fold. First, by permitting the trustee to avoid prebankruptcy transfers that occur within a short period before bankruptcy, creditors are discouraged from racing to the courthouse to dismember the debtor during his slide into bankruptcy. The protection thus afforded the debtor often enables him to work his way out of a difficult financial situation through cooperation with all of his creditors. Second, and more important, the preference provisions facilitate the prime bankruptcy policy of equality of distribution among creditors of the debtor. Any creditor that received a greater payment than others of his class is required to disgorge so that all may share equally. The operation of the preference section to deter 'the race of diligence' of creditors to dismember the debtor before bankruptcy furthers the second goal of the preference section – that of equality of distribution.

Id. at 177-78. As this comment demonstrates, the two policies are not entirely independent. On the one hand, any exception for a payment on account of an antecedent debt tends to favor the payee over other creditors and therefore may conflict with the policy of equal treatment. On the other hand, the ordinary course of business exception may benefit all creditors by deterring the "race to the courthouse" and enabling the struggling debtor to continue operating its business.

Respondent places primary emphasis, as did the Court of Appeals, on the interest in equal distribution. When a debtor is insolvent, a transfer to one creditor necessarily impairs the claims of the debtor's other unsecured and undersecured creditors. By authorizing the avoidance of such preferential transfers, § 547(b) empowers the trustee to restore equal status to all creditors. Respondent thus contends that the ordinary course of business exception should be limited to short-term debt so the trustee may order that preferential long-term debt payments be returned to the estate to be distributed among all of the creditors.

But the statutory text – which makes no distinction between short-term debt and long-term debt – precludes an analysis that divorces the policy of favoring equal distribution from the policy of discouraging creditors from racing to the courthouse to dismember the debtor. Long-term creditors, as well as trade creditors, may seek a head start in that race. Thus, even if we accept the Court of Appeals' conclusion that the availability of the ordinary business exception to long-term creditors does not directly further the policy of equal treatment, we must recognize that it does further the policy of deterring the race to the courthouse and, as the House Report recognized, may indirectly further the goal of equal distribution as well. Whether Congress has wisely balanced the sometimes conflicting policies underlying § 547 is not a question that we are authorized to decide.

IV

In sum, we hold that payments on long-term debt, as well as payments on short-term debt, may qualify for the ordinary course of business exception to the trustee's power to avoid preferential transfers. We express no opinion, however, on the question whether the Bankruptcy Court correctly concluded that the Debtor's payments of interest and the loan commitment fee qualify for the ordinary course of business exception, § 547(c)(2). In particular, we do not decide whether the loan involved in this case was incurred in the ordinary course of the Debtor's business and of the Bank's business, whether the payments were made in the ordinary course of business, or whether the payments were made according to ordinary business terms. These questions remain open for the Court of Appeals on remand.

The judgment of the Court of Appeals is reversed, and the case is remanded for further proceedings consistent with this opinion.

It is so ordered.

Justice SCALIA, concurring.

I join the opinion of the Court, including Parts II and III, which respond persuasively to legislative-history and policy arguments made by respondent. It is regrettable that we have a legal culture in which such arguments have to be addressed (and are indeed credited by a Court of Appeals), with respect to a statute utterly devoid of language that could remotely be thought to distinguish between long-term and short-term debt. Since there was here no contention of a "scrivener's error" producing an absurd result, the plain text of the statute should have made this litigation unnecessary and unmaintainable.

NOTE

Because long-term capital financing is something debtors may do only once, implicit in the Court's decision is the suggestion that a debt may be incurred in the ordinary course of business of both the debtor and the creditor even though the transaction giving rise to it was their first with each other. Recently, lower courts have expressly so ruled. *See, e.g, In re Ahaza Systems, Inc.*, 482 F.3d 1118 (9th Cir. 2007).

QUESTION

Is the Court's decision consistent with the policy underlying § 547(c)(2)? Did the Court give any guidance on when the debt was incurred in the ordinary course of the debtor's business?

Until the 2005 amendments to the Bankruptcy Code, the § 547(c)(2) defense required proof of three elements:

(A) The debt was incurred in the ordinary course of business or financial affairs of the debtor and the transferee;

(B) The payment was made in the ordinary course of business or financial affairs of the debtor and the transferee; and

(C) The payment was made according to ordinary business terms.

Now read § 547(c)(2). The 2005 amendments restructured and expanded the defense. It retained the first element but moved it to the flush portion of (c)(2). It then re-lettered the latter two elements and made them disjunctive: if either of them is true the payment will not be avoidable. To understand the significance and possible implications of this change, it is necessary to briefly explore how courts had previously interpreted the latter two elements.

In its widely respected decision in *In re Craig Oil Co.,*[54] the Eleventh Circuit greatly restricted the pre-2005 version of the § 547(c)(2) defense through its interpretation of the second element. In that case, one of the debtor's suppliers essentially threatened to join in filing an involuntary bankruptcy petition against the debtor after learning of the debtor's financial difficulties. The supplier requested financial statements and assurance of the debtor's "good faith," mentioning that some of the supplier's customers paid their bills by wire transfer. As a result of the conversation, the debtor began paying its bills to the supplier by cashier's check. The debtor continued to make payments even after it stopped making purchases from the supplier. When bankruptcy ensued, the trustee sued to recover the amount of 14 checks, alleging that they were avoidable preferences. The supplier asserted a § 547(c)(2) defense to this action. The bankruptcy court held that the second and third elements of § 547(c)(2) were not satisfied and the Eleventh Circuit affirmed.

The court quoted legislative history indicating that the purpose of § 547(c)(2) was to "leave undisturbed normal financial relations, because it does not detract from the general policy of the preference section to discourage unusual action by either the debtor or his creditor during the debtor's slide into bankruptcy." The court then drew a distinction between "normal" debt collection and payment practices, which are protected

---

[54] 785 F.2d 1563 (11th Cir. 1986).

by § 547(c)(2), and "unusual" practices which are not. In this case, unusual collection efforts prompted the debtor's payments. The court also found that the payments were not made under normal conditions: the debtor made payment by cashier's checks even though it had never done so before. Furthermore, it continued to make payments after it no longer needed the creditor's supplies, even though it had cash flow problems and was having difficulty paying other creditors. The court concluded that the debtor was favoring the supplier in order to ensure that the supplier would not join in an involuntary petition. This, the court reasoned, is precisely the type of preferential treatment at which § 547 is targeted.

Although *Craig Oil* ruled that neither the second nor third requirement of § 547(c)(2) was satisfied, it appeared to focus principally on the second: that the transfer be in the ordinary course of business or financial affairs of the two parties. It ruled that such a transfer must be consistent with the parties' long-standing relationship and not significantly deviate from the manner in which they have conducted business *with each other*. The third element, in contrast, required that the transfer be made according to ordinary business terms, and thus be consistent with how the parties – and their competitors – deal with others. The following case deals with what the transferee must show to satisfy that requirement.

IN RE TOLONA PIZZA PRODUCTS CORPORATION
3 F.3d 1029 (7th Cir. 1993)

Posner, Circuit Judge.

When, within 90 days before declaring bankruptcy, the debtor makes a payment to an unsecured creditor, the payment is a "preference," and the trustee in bankruptcy can recover it and thus make the creditor take pot luck with the rest of the debtor's unsecured creditors. § 547. But there is an exception if the creditor can show that the debt had been incurred in the ordinary course of the business of both the debtor and the creditor, § 547(c)(2)(A); that the payment, too, had been made and received in the ordinary course of their businesses, § 547(c)(2)(B); and that the payment had been "made according to ordinary business terms." § 547(c)(2)(C). The first two requirements are easy to understand: *of course* to defeat the inference of preferential treatment the debt must have been incurred in the ordinary course of business of both debtor and creditor and the payment on account of the debt must have been in the ordinary course as well. But what does the third requirement – that the payment have been "made according to ordinary business terms" – add? And in particular does it refer to what is "ordinary" between this debtor and this creditor, or what is ordinary in the market or industry in which they operate? The circuits are divided on this question.

Tolona, a maker of pizza, issued eight checks to Rose, its sausage supplier, within 90 days before being thrown into bankruptcy by its creditors. The checks, which totaled a shade under $46,000, cleared and as a result Tolona's debts to Rose were paid in full. Tolona's other major trade creditors stand to receive only 13 cents on the dollar under the plan approved by the bankruptcy court, if the preferential treatment of Rose is allowed to stand. Tolona, as debtor in possession, brought an adversary proceeding against Rose to recover the eight payments as voidable preferences. The bankruptcy judge entered judgment for Tolona. The district judge reversed. He thought that Rose did not, in order to comply with § 547(c)(2)(C), have to prove that the terms on which it had extended credit to Tolona were standard terms in the industry, but that if this was wrong the testimony of Rose's executive vice-president, Stiehl, did prove it. The parties agree that the other requirements of § 547(c)(2) were satisfied.

Rose's invoices recited "net 7 days," meaning that payment was due within seven days. For years preceding the preference period, however, Tolona rarely paid within seven days; nor did Rose's other customers. Most paid within 21 days, and if they paid later than 28 or 30 days Rose would usually withhold future shipments until payment was received. Tolona, however, as an old and valued customer (Rose had been selling to it for fifteen years), was permitted to make payments beyond the 21-day period and even beyond the 28-day or 30-day period. The eight payments at issue were made between 12 and 32 days after Rose had invoiced Tolona, for an average of 22 days; but this actually was an improvement. In the 34 months before the preference period, the average time for which Rose's invoices to Tolona were outstanding was 26 days and the longest time was 46 days. Rose consistently treated Tolona with a degree of leniency that made Tolona (Stiehl conceded on cross- examination) one of a "sort of exceptional group of customers of Rose . . . fall[ing] outside the common industry practice and standards."

It may seem odd that paying a debt late would ever be regarded as a preference to the creditor thus paid belatedly. But it is all relative. A debtor who has entered the preference period – who is therefore only 90 days, or fewer, away from plunging into bankruptcy – is typically unable to pay all his outstanding debts in full as they come due. If he pays one and not the others, as happened here, the payment though late is still a preference to that creditor, and is avoidable unless the conditions of § 547(c)(2) are met. One condition is that payment be in the ordinary course of both the debtor's and the creditor's business. A late payment normally will not be. It will therefore be an avoidable preference.

This is not a dryly syllogistic conclusion. The purpose of the preference statute is to prevent the debtor during his slide toward bankruptcy from trying to stave off the evil day by giving preferential treatment to his most importunate creditors, who may sometimes be those who have been waiting longest to be paid. Unless the favoring of particular creditors is outlawed, the mass of creditors of a shaky firm will be nervous, fearing that one or a few of their number are going to walk away with all the firm's assets; and this fear may precipitate debtors into bankruptcy earlier than is socially desirable.

From this standpoint, however, the most important thing is not that the dealings between the debtor and the allegedly favored creditor conform to some industry norm but that they conform to the norm established by the debtor and the creditor in the period before, preferably well before, the preference period. That condition is satisfied here – if anything, Rose treated Tolona more favorably (and hence Tolona treated Rose less preferentially) before the preference period than during it.

But if this is all that the third subsection of 547(c)(2) requires, it might seem to add nothing to the first two subsections, which require that both the debt and the payment be within the ordinary course of business of both the debtor and the creditor. For, provided these conditions are fulfilled, a "late" payment really isn't late if the parties have established a practice that deviates from the strict terms of their written contract. But we hesitate to conclude that the third subsection, requiring conformity to "ordinary business terms," has no function in the statute. We can think of two functions that it might have. One is evidentiary. If the debtor and creditor dealt on terms that the creditor testifies were normal for them but that are wholly unknown in the industry, this casts some doubt on his (self-serving) testimony. Preferences are disfavored, and subsection C makes them more difficult to prove. The second possible function of the subsection is to allay the concerns of creditors that one or more of their number may have worked out a special deal with the debtor, before the preference period, designed to put that creditor ahead of the others in the event of bankruptcy. It may seem odd that allowing late payments from a debtor would be a way for a creditor to make himself more rather than less assured of repayment. But such a creditor does have an advantage during the preference period, because he can receive late payments then and they will still be in the ordinary course of business for him and his debtor.

The functions that we have identified, combined with a natural reluctance to cut out and throw away one-third of an important provision of the Bankruptcy Code, persuade us that the creditor must show that the payment he received was made in accordance with the ordinary business terms in the industry. But this does not mean that the creditor must establish the existence of some single, uniform set of business terms, as Tolona argues. Not only is it difficult to identify the industry whose norm shall govern (is it, here, the sale of sausages to makers of pizza? The sale of sausages to anyone? The sale of anything to makers of pizza?), but there can be great variance in billing practices within an industry. Apparently there is in this industry, whatever exactly "this industry" is; for while it is plain that neither Rose nor its competitors enforce payment within seven days, it is unclear that there is a standard outer limit of forbearance. It seems that 21 days is a goal but that payment as late as 30 days is generally tolerated and that for good customers even longer delays are allowed. The average period between Rose's invoice and Tolona's payment during the preference period was only 22 days, which seems well within the industry norm, whatever exactly it is. The law should not push businessmen to agree upon a single set of billing practices; antitrust objections to one side, the relevant business and financial considerations vary widely among firms on both the buying and the selling side of the market.

We conclude that "ordinary business terms" refers to the *range* of terms that encompasses the practices in which firms similar in some general way to the creditor in question engage, and that only dealings so idiosyncratic as to fall outside that broad range should be deemed extraordinary and therefore outside the scope of subsection C. Stiehl's testimony brought the case within the scope of "ordinary business terms" as just defined. Rose and its competitors pay little or no attention to the terms stated on their invoices, allow most customers to take up to 30 days to pay, and allow certain favored customers to take even more time. There is no single set of terms on which the members of the industry have coalesced; instead there is a broad range and the district judge plausibly situated the dealings between Rose and Tolona within it. These dealings are conceded to have been within the normal course of dealings between the two firms, a course established long before the preference period, and there is no hint either that the dealings were designed to put Rose ahead of other creditors of Tolona or that other creditors of Tolona would have been surprised to learn that Rose had been so forbearing in its dealings with Tolona. * * *

The judgment reversing the bankruptcy judge and dismissing the adversary proceeding is affirmed.

———

Creditors feared that what was § 547(c)(2)(C) – the requirement that the transfer be according to "ordinary business terms" – would be interpreted as requiring an expensive – perhaps unattainable – showing that there is some single, uniform set of industry-wide credit terms. Judge Posner's opinion in *Tolona* alleviated this somewhat by allowing the creditor to show merely the *range* of terms used by similar businesses. This formulation, which has been adopted in almost every other circuit, gives what is now § 547(c)(2)(B) some independent function without imposing an impossible burden on creditors.[55] Moreover, several courts allow unusual practices to satisfy the

———

[55] *See also In re Jan Weilert RV, Inc.*, 315 F.3d 1192 (9th Cir. 2003) (not only indicating that ordinary course can encompass a fairly wide range of payment practices within an industry, but that the standard must take into account the behavior of similarly situated – *i.e.,* financially distressed – participants within it). *But cf. In re Bridge Information Systems, Inc.*, 460 F.3d 1041 (8th Cir. 2006) (lack of evidence about industry use of admittance advice notations – by which debtor designated to which invoice each payment was directed – took payments outside the § 547(c)(1) defense even though perhaps ordinary in amount and timing); *In re Ramba, Inc.*, 437 F.3d 457 (5th Cir. 2006) (payment 180 days after invoice when industry standard is 120 days is not according to ordinary

§ 547(c)(2)(C) standard if the practices were long-standing and pre-date the debtor's slide into bankruptcy.[56]

Nevertheless, even under this standard, creditors frequently have difficulty providing the requisite proof.[57] This is often because evidence of industry practices – not merely of the debtor's practices with other creditors – is necessary to prove that payments were in the ordinary course of business,[58] and sometimes competitors regard their credit practices as proprietary or, due to antitrust concerns, are unwilling to disclose them.[59] Other times it is because the creditor's evidence is not directed at what the court determines to be the appropriate industry,[60] or because the defendant's own personnel are the only ones testifying about what the industry standard is.[61]

The 2005 amendments to § 547(c)(2) should do much to alleviate these problems. Now a creditor need merely show either that the payment was ordinary between the two parties or that it was made according to ordinary business terms.

Problem 3-11

About six years ago, Digital Enterprises, Inc. borrowed from Bank $750,000 to be used as working capital. The loan was guaranteed by Owner, DEI's principal shareholder. The loan was originally amortized over a 3-year period at 9% interest. However, as was originally anticipated, the parties have

---

business terms).

[56] *See, e.g., In re Molded Acoustical Products, Inc.*, 18 F.3d 217, 225 (3d Cir. 1994).

[57] *See In re Midway Airlines, Inc.*, 69 F.3d 792 (7th Cir. 1995) (testimony that all airlines dealt uniformly with the millwork companies that supplied them was not adequate).

[58] *See, e.g., In re Bridge Information Systems, Inc.,* 460 F.3d 1041 (8th Cir. 2006); *In re Roblin Indus., Inc.*, 78 F.3d 30 (2d Cir. 1996).

[59] *See In re Carled, Inc.*, 91 F.3d 811, 819 (6th Cir. 1996).

[60] *See In re DeMert & Dougherty, Inc.*, 232 B.R. 103 (N.D. Ill. 1999). *See also In re Gulf City Seafoods, Inc.*, 296 F.3d 363, 369 & n.8 (5th Cir. 2002) (indicating that the relevant industry should be defined by both the product and geography but expressing concern that in some instances the relevant industry may be too small for a creditor to present proof about what is ordinary); *In re Molded Acoustical Products*, 18 F.3d at 227 n.12 (suggesting that precepts of antitrust law will often be helpful in defining the relevant industry).

[61] *See In re Bridge Information Systems,* Inc., 460 F.3d 1041 (8th Cir. 2006) (testimony of defendant's own employees can be used to demonstrate industry standards but failed to do so in this case); *In re Toy King*, 256 B.R. 1 (Bankr. M.D. Fla. 2000) (testimony from creditor's own representative was inherently suspect and insufficient); *but cf. In re Kaypro*, 218 F.3d 1070 (9th Cir. 2000) (testimony of defendant's credit manager was sufficient despite self-serving nature).

periodically renegotiated the debt as DEI's need for financing increased. The current note, also guaranteed by Owner, executed about six months ago, is for $1.2 million and requires monthly payments of $21,630 for six years.

Two months ago, a $130,000 judgment was entered against DEI in a patent infringement action. The judgment also enjoins DEI from further infringement. Although DEI is confident that the judgment will be reversed on appeal, the injunction effectively prevents DEI from conducting a major portion of its business. When Bank learned of the judgment, it decided to call in the loan pursuant to a clause in the loan agreement that allows Bank to declare a default and accelerate the debt whenever it reasonably believes the prospect for repayment is impaired. Bank demanded immediate payment in full but DEI was unable to comply. Bank and DEI then negotiated a compromise, pursuant to which DEI made the current monthly payment of $21,630 and paid $700,000 of the $1.1 million principal balance outstanding at the time. DEI then executed a new 1-year note for the remaining unpaid principal amount of $400,000 at 16% interest.

DEI was unable to obtain a stay of the patent judgment pending appeal and a few weeks later filed for bankruptcy protection under Chapter 7. The trustee brought a preference action to recover both the $700,000 principal payment and the $21,630 monthly payment that DEI made when Bank renegotiated the loan. Is the trustee entitled to recover either of these amounts from Bank?

Problem 3-12

Dependable Delivery entered into a written transportation agreement with Careful Carriers under which Careful agreed to pick up and deliver freight for Dependable in the geographical area Careful served. In exchange, Dependable was to pay Careful a percentage of the amounts it billed to shippers. The agreement provided that Dependable would make payment "on or before the 30th day after the shipment" had been delivered. The parties had operated under this agreement for two years, when Dependable filed a bankruptcy petition. In the 12 months preceding the 90 days before the filing of the bankruptcy petition (the 90-day period), Careful received 259 checks from Dependable covering 720 invoices. However, despite the 30-day payment requirement, Careful received these payments, on average, 62 days after the date of invoice. During the 90-day period, Dependable paid Careful $245,000 for services rendered under the agreement.

A. If the payments made during the preference period were, like the ones before, largely made about 60 days after the invoice, and thus after the 30-

day contractual limit, do they nevertheless qualify for the § 547(c)(2) defense?

B.   If about half of the payments during the preference period were made immediately before the filing on invoices that were not overdue, would those be avoidable? *See Lovett v. St. Johnsbury Trucking*, 931 F.2d 494 (8th Cir. 1991). Would it matter if Dependable made such payments only after Careful demanded more prompt payment and threatened to sever their relationship if Dependable did not comply?

(c) Persons Liable

Section 547 by itself merely "avoids" a transfer. Another provision, § 550, actually imposes liability on the preferred creditor to return the property transferred or its value. Note, however, that the preferred creditor need not be the transferee. Recall that § 547(b) covers transfers "to *or for the benefit of* a creditor." Consider the following hypothetical:

> After passing the applicable examinations, Dentist wishes to begin a solo dental practice. To get the funds necessary to open an office, acquire the necessary tools and equipment, and advertise (tastefully), Dentist wants to borrow $75,000 from Bank. Bank is willing, but only if Parents guaranty the debt. Parents do so and the loan is made. Dentist's practice flounders for a while. On May 1, while Dentist is insolvent, Dentist pays Bank $20,000, which is all of Dentist's available cash. Dentist then keeps other creditors at bay for a while, and files for bankruptcy on September 15th.

Although Bank in this hypothetical received preferential treatment, the transfer it received was outside the 90-day preference period, and thus not normally avoidable. However, the payment also benefitted Parents by reducing their liability on the guaranty. Moreover, Parents are creditors of Dentist, because they have a common-law right to be reimbursed by Dentist for any payment they make to Bank on Dentist's behalf.[62] Because Parents are insiders of Dentist, *see* § 101(31)(A), a one-year preference period applies to any transfer to them or for their benefit. Thus, even though they did not receive the transfer, the transfer is nevertheless avoidable under § 547.

The interesting question is who is liable. Certainly Parents should be liable because they are the preferred creditors. And, in fact, § 550(a)(1) makes them liable; it expressly imposes liability on "the entity for whose benefit the transfer was made." Is Bank also liable? As originally enacted, § 550 seemed to say yes. The transfer is avoidable under

---

[62]   *See, e.g.,* RESTATEMENT (THIRD) OF SURETYSHIP AND GUARANTY § 22 (1996).

§ 547 and § 550(a)(1) makes the transferee of an avoidable transfer – in this case, Bank – liable. The Seventh Circuit confirmed this result in *In re V.N. DePrizio Constr. Co.*[63] Five other circuit courts later agreed.[64]

The decision in *DePrizio* sent commercial lenders into a tizzy. They argued that it actually made lenders who received guarantees from an insider of the debtor worse off, because it subjected them to the longer, one-year preference period. Congress addressed their concerns in the Bankruptcy Reform Act of 1994, which added § 550(c) to the Code expressly to overrule *DePrizio*.[65] That amendment prevents the noninsider lender from being liable for a transfer made more than 90 days before the bankruptcy filing that prefers an insider.[66]

It is important to understand what this amendment did not do, however. First, although the amendment overruled the result of *DePrizio* (with respect to transfers made more than 90 days before the filing), it did not overrule the decision's more basic observation that a transfer avoidable under § 547(b) is recoverable from a transferee who was not the preferred creditor. In other words, a transfer made within the 90-day preference period may apparently be recovered from the transferee (*e.g.* Bank) even if it is avoidable only because of its indirect benefit to one or more guarantors (*e.g.* Parents).

Second, the amendment did not in any way lessen the preference liability of the insider guarantor.[67] In short, nothing in the amendment altered the liability of Parents. Because of that, the amendment did not fully satisfy lenders who obtain guarantees. While it did insulate the transferees from preference attack for all transfers made to them more than 90 days before the filing, it left their guarantors vulnerable to such attack, a

---

[63]   874 F.2d 1186 (7th Cir. 1989).

[64]   *See In re Wesley Indus., Inc.*, 30 F.3d 1438 (11th Cir. 1994); *In re Suffola, Inc.*, 2 F.3d 977 (9th Cir. 1993); *In re T.B. Westex Foods, Inc.*, 950 F.2d 1187 (5th Cir. 1992); *In re C-L Cartage Co.*, 899 F.2d 1490 (6th Cir. 1990); *In re Robinson Bros. Drilling, Inc.*, 892 F.2d 850 (10th Cir. 1989).

[65]   *See* Pub. L. 103-394, § 202, 108 Stat. 4106, 4121 (1994).

[66]   A more recent amendment further solidified this result by adding to the Code § 547(i), which makes the transfer avoidable only with respect to the insider. *See* Bankruptcy Abuse Prevention and Consumer Protection Act of 2005, Pub. L. 109-8, § 1213(a)(2), 119 Stat. 23, 194-95 (2005). This change was not necessary to insulate the noninsider from liability for prepetition payments but was necessary to insulate it from avoidance of other types of transfers, notably the grant of a lien on property of the debtor. How preference law affects security interests and secured claims is covered in chapter six.

[67]   *Cf. In re Arkansas Catfish Growers, LLC*, 2007 WL 215815 (E.D. Ark. 2007) (noninsider who received transfer more than 90 days but less than one year before the debtor's bankruptcy petition was not an indispensable party to a preference action against insider guarantors, who could be sued directly).

fact which could weaken the financial position of the guarantors. In other words, if prepetition transfers from Dentist to Bank preferred Parents but, because Bank was not fully paid off, Parents still owed more money on the guaranty, Bank is effectively left competing with the bankruptcy estate for Parents' assets. To resolve this problem, many lenders have required their guarantors to waive all rights to indemnification, contribution, and subrogation from the debtor. This prevents the guarantors from qualifying as "creditors" of the debtor, *see* § 101(10), and therefore any transfers either to them or for their benefit cannot be avoidable preferences.[68]

2.　*Fraudulent Transfers*

An oft-quoted maxim of the law is that "a debtor must be just before being generous." The idea behind this maxim is that before debtor gives property away, the debtor should provide for payment to the debtor's creditors. Since an insolvent debtor by definition cannot pay all creditors, insolvent people should not be permitted to make gifts while leaving their creditors without recourse. An insolvent debtor who does transfer property without getting reasonably equivalent value in exchange has made what the law refers to as a fraudulent transfer.

Fraudulent transfers are not limited to gifts or unequal exchanges. A debtor who makes a transfer in order to conceal assets or remove them from the jurisdiction in an effort to delay, hinder, or defraud one or more creditors has also made a fraudulent transfer. This is true even if the debtor received fair value for the property transferred.

In 1918, the National Conference of Commissioners on Uniform State Laws ("NCCUSL") promulgated the Uniform Fraudulent Conveyance Act ("UFCA"), later adopted by more than half the states, to provide uniform rules on what constitutes a fraudulent transaction. The UFCA allows an aggrieved creditor to sue the recipient of a fraudulent transfer to rescind the transaction. In 1979, NCCUSL appointed a committee to revise the UFCA to harmonize it with the new Bankruptcy Code and with certain other model acts. In 1984, NCCUSL approved a new Uniform Fraudulent Transfer Act ("UFTA") to replace the UFCA. At present, 37 states and the District of Columbia have enacted the UFTA. Five others still have the UFCA and the remainder have nonuniform state statutes or common law that govern fraudulent transfers.

The most important provisions of the UFTA are § 4(a)(1), which covers transactions done with "actual intent to hinder, delay, or defraud" any creditor (sometimes called true

---

[68] *See, e.g, In re Northeastern Contracting Co.*, 187 B.R. 420 (Bankr. D. Conn. 1995); *In re XTI Xonix Technologies, Inc.*, 156 B.R. 821 (Bankr. D. Or. 1993); *In re Fastrans, Inc.*, 142 B.R. 241 (Bankr. E.D. Tenn. 1992) (all upholding the efficacy of this practice). *But see In re Pro Page Partners, LLC.*, 292 B.R. 622 (Bankr. E.D. Tenn 2003) (concluding that such waivers do not solve the preference problem).

fraudulent transfers), and § 5(a), which covers transfers for which an insolvent debtor received less than reasonably equivalent value (sometimes referred to as constructively fraudulent transfers). The former are avoidable by any creditor of the debtor, the latter only by those creditors whose claims arose before the transfer was made. A few more constructively fraudulent transfers are made avoidable by § 4(a)(2). It covers transfers for which the debtor received less than reasonably equivalent value and, although not insolvent at the time, the debtor either: (i) was engaged in a business or transaction for which the debtor's remaining assets are unreasonably small or (ii) intended or should have reasonably believed that the debts were beyond its ability to pay as they came due.

These rules, or whatever analogous rules are in effect in a particular jurisdiction, are given effect in bankruptcy through § 544(b). However, when the bankruptcy trustee uses § 544(b) and state fraudulent transfer law to avoid a transfer, the trustee does so not merely for the benefit of the creditors who could have attacked the transfer, but for all creditors with allowable claims against the debtor.

Aside from § 544(b), which authorizes the trustee to use state law to avoid certain transfers, § 548 of the Bankruptcy Code gives the trustee the express power to avoid certain fraudulent transfers made by the debtor. In fact, as the table after this paragraph shows, § 548 contains two sources of power for the trustee: § 548(a)(1)(A), an analog to UFTA § 4(a)(1), to avoid actually fraudulent transfers; and § 548(a)(1)(B), an analog to UFTA § 4(a)(2) and § 5(a), which covers constructively fraudulent transfers.[69] Perhaps the most critical difference between § 544(b) and § 548 is that § 548 covers only those transfers made within two years before the bankruptcy petition. In contrast, § 544(b), by implicitly referencing the UFTA, generally has a four-year statute of limitations. UFTA § 9(a), (b). Note, however, these two restrictions measure different time frames. Section 548 deals with transfers made within two years before the bankruptcy petition,[70] while § 544(b) and the UFTA generally cover transfers made within four years of when suit is brought to rescind them.

---

[69] Prior to June of 1998, the bankruptcy provisions were numbered § 548(a)(1) and (2), respectively. They were renumbered as part of the Religious Liberty and Charitable Donation Protection Act of 1998. Pub. L. 105-183, 112 Stat. 517. Awareness of this renumbering is particularly important when reviewing cases that predate the change.

[70] Certain transfers to a self-settled trust are avoidable if made within ten years before the petition. § 548(e)(1).

Avoidable Transfer	UFTA combined with § 544(b)	Bankruptcy Code § 548
Made with actual intent to hinder, delay, or defraud	§ 4(a)(1)	§ 548(a)(1)(A)
Received less than reasonably equivalent value and engaged in business when undercapitalized	§ 4(a)(2)	§ 548(a)(1)(B)(i) & (ii)(II)
Received less than reasonably equivalent value and incurred debts beyond ability to pay as they become due	§ 4(a)(2)	§ 548(a)(1)(B)(i) & (ii)(III)
Received less than reasonably equivalent value and was insolvent	§ 5(a)	§ 548(a)(1)(B)(i) & (ii)(I)[71]

(a) Actually Fraudulent Transfers

Proving intent to hinder, delay or defraud can be difficult. Typically, courts rely on objective but indirect evidence, usually referred to as "badges of fraud." These may include:

1. Transfers to a relative, close friend, or other insider.
2. Suspicious timing, such as immediately after a large adverse judgment.
3. Transfers on paper unaccompanied by an actual change of possession.
4. Transfers that put the debtor's assets in a foreign jurisdiction, particularly a jurisdiction that will make seizure through domestic judicial process difficult.
5. Secrecy.

Indeed, UFTA § 4(b) codifies these, as well as a few other things, as badges of fraud.

Problem 3-13

Deceitful, the defendant in a pending lawsuit, sold a parcel of real property to Buyer, who paid full market value of $100,000. Deceitful took the

---

[71]   Under § 548 we need not worry whether any unsecured creditor's claim arose before the fraudulent transfer.

proceeds of the sale and deposited them in an out-of-state bank account under an assumed name. Shortly thereafter, the plaintiff obtained a judgment against Deceitful. Deceitful promptly filed a bankruptcy petition, before the plaintiff could take any action with respect to the real estate sale.

A.   Assume Buyer had no knowledge of Deceitful's intentions at the time of the sale. The real estate is now worth $110,000.

1.   Can the trustee avoid the sale to Buyer under § 548 and, if so, what are Buyer's rights? *See* § 548(c).

2.   What would the result be under § 544(b) and the UFTA? *See* UFTA § 8.

B.   How, if at all, would the answer to Part A differ if, during the sale negotiations, Deceitful had said to Buyer, "I hate to sell this property because I think it will go up in value, but I'm about to lose a lawsuit and I'd rather sell it now than lose it later"?

Problem 3-14

In September, Bank obtained a $480,000 judgment against Devious. Although Devious had substantial assets, this judgment left Devious with a negative net worth. Five months later, Devious became entitled to a $99,500 distribution from a limited partnership in which he had invested. At his request, the distribution to him was made through ten checks of $9,950 each. Devious's two adult daughters, who were also limited partners, each received their distributions in one check. With the Bank pressing for payment on the judgment, Devious endorsed three of the checks to each of his two daughters and asked each to deposit them in their own bank accounts for his benefit. He explained to both daughters that he was unable to open his own bank account. The daughters accepted the money and, over the next several months, used the money to pay some of Devious's living expenses at his direction. After filing for Chapter 7 bankruptcy protection, the trustee sued each of the two daughters for $29,850 under§ 548(a)(1)(A). Does the trustee have a valid cause of action, given that the daughters basically returned the funds by paying Devious's expenses? Are the daughters entitled to a defense under § 548(c)? *See In re Roti*, 271 B.R. 281 (Bankr. N.D. Ill. 2002).

Problem 3-15

Last year, when Descendant was insolvent, Descendant's rich uncle died. The uncle's will bequeathed his entire $400,000 estate to Descendant and Sibling, equally. Not wanting the money to go to creditors, Descendant decided to disclaim the bequest. As a result, under state law the entire estate was distributed as if Descendant predeceased the uncle, and thus went to Sibling. Six months later, Descendant filed for bankruptcy protection. Can the trustee recover the disclaimed bequest? *See In re Atchison*, 925 F.2d 209 (7th Cir.), *cert. denied*, 502 U.S. 860 (1991).

Problem 3-16

Section 548(a)(1) gives the trustee the power to avoid not only transfers of property, but also "obligations . . . incurred by the debtor." When would this apply? Describe a scenario when incurring an obligation would be fraudulent and avoidable. In doing so, consider whether fraudulent transfer law is designed to protect the other party to the transaction or the debtor's unsecured creditors.

(b) Constructively Fraudulent Transfers

Proving that a transfer is constructively fraudulent – that is, that the debtor was insolvent and received less than reasonably equivalent value – is typically much easier. If, as is often the case, no one disputes that the debtor was insolvent at the time of the transfer, then even a very ordinary transfer can become avoidable.

Problem 3-17

A.   Descendant recently completed schooling and has substantial debts for educational loans. As a result, Descendant is insolvent.
1.   In December, Descendant spent $25 to purchase and send to Grandmother a holiday gift. Is the purchase an avoidable fraudulent transfer? Is the gift an avoidable fraudulent transfer?
2.   In January, Descendant purchased and gave to Child a new $115 parka. Child is a dependant of Descendant. Is the purchase an avoidable fraudulent transfer? Is the gift an avoidable fraudulent transfer?
B.   Stockholder owns all the stock of Corporation, which operates a small construction company. Every year for the last two decades Corporation has paid Stockholder a dividend of $1 per share.
1.   If Corporation is insolvent, would it be a fraudulent transfer for it to pay dividends this year?

2.   Stockholder wants to start a second business (not to be affiliated with Corporation) that will do landscaping work, and needs a loan from Bank to get that new business running. Bank demands collateral, so Stockholder has Corporation grant Bank a security interest in its construction equipment to secure Bank's loan to Stockholder. If that transaction leaves Corporation with inadequate capital to conduct its operations, would it be a fraudulent transfer?

C.   Desperate's new business is undercapitalized and insolvent. Beyond that, there is insufficient cash on hand to make next week's payroll. Desperate takes the $2,000 in cash that is available and uses it to play blackjack at the nearest casino. Unfortunately, Desperate loses the whole $2,000. Can the trustee recover the money from the casino? *See In re Chomakos*, 69 F.3d 769 (6th Cir. 1995), *cert. denied*, 517 U.S. 1168 (1996).

Determining whether the debtor is insolvent for the purposes of fraudulent transfer law is much the same as for the purposes of preferential transfers. Accordingly, all the issues about how to value the debtor's assets can arise in this context as well. Note, however, that unlike with preferences, there is no presumption of insolvency during the 90 days preceding bankruptcy.

Often, the parties dispute whether what the debtor received was reasonably equivalent in value to what the debtor transferred away. Unfortunately, cases provide no set rule or clear guidance on how much or what percentage is reasonably equivalent. About the only prediction that can be made safely is that a gross disparity will lead to avoidance.[72]

Reasonable equivalence is, of course, a fact to be determined at the time of the allegedly fraudulent transfer. However, courts and parties examining the issue often have the benefit of 20-20 hindsight. What may have looked like a fair deal at the time may, in retrospect, look very unequal. Some courts do not hesitate to allow the use of subsequent events to demonstrate the gross inequivalence of the bargain. In addition, some types of transactions routinely fail to yield fair market value and thus raise the specter of fraudulent transfer. Consider the Supreme Court's response to one of those typical transactions in the following case.

---

[72]   *See In re Lindell*, 334 B.R. 249 (Bankr. D. Minn. 2005) (payment of $50,000 for notes worth $130,000 was not reasonably equivalent value).

BFP V. RESOLUTION TRUST CORPORATION
511 U.S. 531 (1994)

Justice Scalia delivered the opinion of the Court.

This case presents the question whether the consideration received from a noncollusive, real estate mortgage foreclosure sale conducted in conformance with applicable state law conclusively satisfies the Bankruptcy Code's requirement that transfers of property by insolvent debtors within one year prior to the filing of a bankruptcy petition be in exchange for "a reasonably equivalent value." § 548(a)(2).

I

Petitioner BFP is a partnership, formed by Wayne and Marlene Pedersen and Russell Barton in 1987, for the purpose of buying a home in Newport Beach, California, from Sheldon and Ann Foreman. Petitioner took title subject to a first deed of trust in favor of Imperial Savings Association (Imperial)[73] to secure payment of a loan of $356,250 made to the Pedersens in connection with petitioner's acquisition of the home. Petitioner granted a second deed of trust to the Foremans as security for a $200,000 promissory note. Subsequently, Imperial, whose loan was not being serviced, entered a notice of default under the first deed of trust and scheduled a properly noticed foreclosure sale. The foreclosure proceedings were temporarily delayed by the filing of an involuntary bankruptcy petition on behalf of petitioner. After the dismissal of that petition in June 1989, Imperial's foreclosure proceeding was completed at a foreclosure sale on July 12, 1989. The home was purchased by respondent Paul Osborne for $433,000.

In October 1989, petitioner filed for bankruptcy under Chapter 11 of the Bankruptcy Code. Acting as a debtor in possession, petitioner filed a complaint in Bankruptcy Court seeking to set aside the conveyance of the home to respondent Osborne on the grounds that the foreclosure sale constituted a fraudulent transfer under § 548 of the Code. Petitioner alleged that the home was actually worth over $725,000 at the time of the sale to Osborne. Acting on separate motions, the Bankruptcy Court dismissed the complaint as to the private respondents and granted summary judgment in favor of Imperial. The Bankruptcy Court found, inter alia, that the foreclosure sale had been conducted in compliance with California law and was neither collusive nor fraudulent. In an unpublished opinion, the District Court affirmed the Bankruptcy Court's granting of the private respondents' motion to dismiss. A divided bankruptcy appellate panel affirmed the Bankruptcy Court's entry of summary judgment for Imperial.

---

[73] Respondent Resolution Trust Corporation (RTC) acts in this case as receiver of Imperial. For convenience we refer to all respondents other than RTC and Imperial as the private respondents.

Applying the analysis set forth in *In re Madrid*, 21 B.R. 424 (9th Cir. BAP 1982), *affirmed on other grounds*, 725 F.2d 1197 (9th Cir.), *cert. denied*, 469 U.S. 833 (1984), the panel majority held that a "non-collusive and regularly conducted nonjudicial foreclosure sale . . . cannot be challenged as a fraudulent conveyance because the consideration received in such a sale establishes 'reasonably equivalent value' as a matter of law."

Petitioner sought review of both decisions in the Court of Appeals for the Ninth Circuit, which consolidated the appeals. The Court of Appeals affirmed. BFP filed a petition for certiorari, which we granted.

II

Section 548 of the Bankruptcy Code sets forth the powers of a trustee in bankruptcy (or, in a Chapter 11 case, a debtor in possession) to avoid fraudulent transfers. It permits to be set aside not only transfers infected by actual fraud but certain other transfers as well – so-called constructively fraudulent transfers. The constructive fraud provision at issue in this case applies to transfers by insolvent debtors. It permits avoidance if the trustee can establish (1) that the debtor had an interest in property; (2) that a transfer of that interest occurred within one year of the filing of the bankruptcy petition; (3) that the debtor was insolvent at the time of the transfer or became insolvent as a result thereof; and (4) that the debtor received "less than a reasonably equivalent value in exchange for such transfer." § 548(a)(2)(A). It is the last of these four elements that presents the issue in the case before us.

Section 548 applies to any "transfer," which includes "foreclosure of the debtor's equity of redemption." § 101(54). Of the three critical terms "reasonably equivalent value," only the last is defined: "value" means, for purposes of § 548, "property, or satisfaction or securing of a . . . debt of the debtor," § 548(d)(2)(A). The question presented here, therefore, is whether the amount of debt (to the first and second lienholders) satisfied at the foreclosure sale (a total of $433,000) is "reasonably equivalent" to the worth of the real estate conveyed. The Courts of Appeals have divided on the meaning of those undefined terms. In *Durrett v. Washington National Insurance Co.*, 621 F.2d 201 (1980), the Fifth Circuit, interpreting a provision of the old Bankruptcy Act analogous to § 548(a)(2), held that a foreclosure sale that yielded 57% of the property's fair market value could be set aside, and indicated in dicta that any such sale for less than 70% of fair market value should be invalidated. This "*Durrett* rule" has continued to be applied by some courts under § 548 of the new Bankruptcy Code. *See In re Littleton*, 888 F.2d 90, 92, n.5 (11th Cir. 1989). In *In re Bundles*, 856 F.2d 815, 820 (1988), the Seventh Circuit rejected the *Durrett* rule in favor of a case-by-case, "all facts and circumstances" approach to the question of reasonably equivalent value, with a *rebuttable* presumption that the foreclosure sale price is sufficient to withstand attack under § 548(a)(2). In this case the Ninth Circuit, agreeing with the Sixth Circuit, *see In re Winshall Settlor's Trust*, 758 F.2d 1136, 1139 (6th Cir. 1985), adopted the position first put forward in *Madrid* that the consideration received at a noncollusive, regularly conducted real estate foreclosure sale constitutes a reasonably equivalent value under § 548(a)(2)(A). The Court of Appeals acknowledged that it "necessarily part[ed] from the positions taken by the Fifth Circuit in *Durrett* . . . and the Seventh Circuit in *Bundles*."

In contrast to the approach adopted by the Ninth Circuit in the present case, both *Durrett* and *Bundles* refer to fair market value as the benchmark against which determination of reasonably equivalent value is to be measured. In the context of an otherwise lawful mortgage foreclosure sale of real estate,[74] such reference is in our opinion not consistent with the text of the Bankruptcy Code. The term "fair market value," though it is a well-established concept, does not appear in § 548. In contrast, § 522, dealing with a debtor's exemptions, specifically provides that, for purposes of that section, " 'value' means fair market value as of the date of the filing of the petition." § 522(a)(2). "Fair market value" also appears in the Code provision that defines the extent to which indebtedness with respect to an equity security is not forgiven for the purpose of determining whether the debtor's estate has realized taxable income. § 346(j)(7)(B). Section 548, on the other hand, seemingly goes out of its way to avoid that standard term. It might readily have said "received less than fair market value in exchange for such transfer or obligation," or perhaps "less than a reasonable equivalent of fair market value." Instead, it used the (as far as we are aware) entirely novel phrase "reasonably equivalent value." "[I]t is generally presumed that Congress acts intentionally and purposely when it includes particular language in one section of a statute but omits it in another," *Chicago v. Environmental Defense Fund*, 511 U.S. 328, 338, (1994), and that presumption is even stronger when the omission entails the replacement of standard legal terminology with a neologism. One must suspect the language means that fair market value cannot – or at least cannot *always* – be the benchmark.

That suspicion becomes a certitude when one considers that market value, as it is commonly understood, has no applicability in the forced-sale context; indeed, it is the very *antithesis* of forced-sale value. "The market value of . . . a piece of property is the price which it might be expected to bring if offered for sale in a fair market; not the price which might be obtained on a sale at public auction or a sale forced by the necessities of the owner, but such a price as would be fixed by negotiation and mutual agreement, after ample time to find a purchaser, as between a vendor who is willing (but not compelled) to sell and a purchaser who desires to buy but is not compelled to take the particular . . . piece of property." Black's Law Dictionary 971 (6th ed. 1990). In short,

---

[74] We emphasize that our opinion today covers only mortgage foreclosures of real estate. The considerations bearing upon other foreclosures and forced sales (to satisfy tax liens, for example) may be different.

"fair market value" presumes market conditions that, by definition, simply do not obtain in the context of a forced sale.

Neither petitioner, petitioner's amici, nor any federal court adopting the *Durrett* or the *Bundles* analysis has come to grips with this glaring discrepancy between the factors relevant to an appraisal of a property's market value, on the one hand, and the strictures of the foreclosure process on the other. Market value cannot be the criterion of equivalence in the foreclosure-sale context. The language of § 548(a)(2)(A) ("received less than a reasonably equivalent value in exchange") requires judicial inquiry into whether the foreclosed property was sold for a price that approximated its worth at the time of sale. An appraiser's reconstruction of "fair market value" could show what similar property would be worth if it did not have to be sold within the time and manner strictures of state-prescribed foreclosure. But property that *must* be sold within those strictures is simply *worth less*. No one would pay as much to own such property as he would pay to own real estate that could be sold at leisure and pursuant to normal marketing techniques. And it is no more realistic to ignore that characteristic of the property (the fact that state foreclosure law permits the mortgagee to sell it at forced sale) than it is to ignore other price-affecting characteristics (such as the fact that state zoning law permits the owner of the neighboring lot to open a gas station). Absent a clear statutory requirement to the contrary, we must assume the validity of this state-law regulatory background and take due account of its effect. * * *

There is another artificially constructed criterion we might look to instead of "fair market price." One might judge there to be such a thing as a "reasonable" or "fair" forced-sale price. Such a conviction must lie behind the *Bundles* inquiry into whether the state foreclosure proceedings "were calculated . . . to return to the debtor-mortgagor his equity in the property." 856 F.2d at 824. And perhaps that is what the courts that follow the *Durrett* rule have in mind when they select 70% of fair market value as the outer limit of "reasonably equivalent value" for forecloseable property (we have no idea where else such an arbitrary percentage could have come from). The problem is that such judgments represent policy determinations that the Bankruptcy Code gives us no apparent authority to make. How closely the price received in a forced sale is likely to approximate fair market value depends upon the terms of the forced sale – how quickly it may be made, what sort of public notice must be given, etc. But the terms for foreclosure sale are not *standard*. They vary considerably from State to State, depending upon, among other things, how the particular State values the divergent interests of debtor and creditor. To specify a federal "reasonable" foreclosure-sale price is to extend federal bankruptcy law well beyond the traditional field of fraudulent transfers, into realms of policy where it has not ventured before. * * *

For the reasons described, we decline to read the phrase "reasonably equivalent value" in § 548(a)(2) to mean, in its application to mortgage foreclosure sales, either "fair market value" or "fair foreclosure price" (whether calculated as a percentage of fair market value or otherwise). We deem, as the law has always deemed, that a fair and proper price, or a "reasonably equivalent value," for foreclosed property, is the price in fact received at the foreclosure sale, so long as all the requirements of the State's foreclosure law have been complied with.

This conclusion does not render § 548(a)(2) superfluous, since the "reasonably equivalent value" criterion will continue to have independent meaning (ordinarily a meaning similar to fair market value) outside the foreclosure context. Indeed, § 548(a)(2) will even continue to be an exclusive means of invalidating some foreclosure sales. Although collusive foreclosure sales are likely subject to attack under § 548(a)(1), which authorizes the trustee to avoid transfers "made . . . with actual intent to hinder, delay, or defraud" creditors, that provision may not reach foreclosure sales that, while not intentionally fraudulent, nevertheless fail to comply with all governing state laws. Any irregularity in the conduct of the sale that would permit judicial invalidation of the sale under applicable state law deprives the sale price of its conclusive force under § 548(a)(2)(A), and the transfer may be avoided if the price received was not reasonably equivalent to the property's actual value at the time of the sale (which we think would be the price that would have been received if the foreclosure sale had proceeded according to law).

* * *

For the foregoing reasons, the judgment of the Court of Appeals for the Ninth Circuit is affirmed.

Justices Souter, Blackmun, Stevens, and Ginsburg dissented.

———————

NOTES

1. Although *BFP v. Resolution Trust* technically applies only to § 548 actions, not to those brought under § 544(b) and the Uniform Fraudulent Transfer Act, UFTA § 3(b) expressly provides that a person who buys property at a "regularly conducted, noncollusive foreclosure sale or execution" gives reasonably equivalent value.

2. In a footnote, the Court suggested that a different rule might be applicable to tax sales. Although a few courts have accepted that invitation, and ruled that tax sales are not immune from fraudulent transfer attack,[75] the sale

———————

[75] *In re Sherman*, 223 B.R. 555 (10th Cir. BAP 1998); *In re Murphy*, 331 B.R. 107 (Bankr. S.D.N.Y. 2005).

procedures in those cases did not provide for competitive bidding. When such competition does exist, courts have generally extended the Court's ruling in *BFP* to tax sales.[76]

3.   At least one court has refused to apply *BFP* to a state court judgment of strict foreclosure, which transferred to the creditor all title to the property without requiring a sale.[77] Another distinguished a situation in which there was an impropriety in the foreclosure sale, even though all the statutory requirements had been followed.[78]

Problem 3-18

Demonstrative is a motivational speaker who offers seminars and to business and individuals. In prior years, Demonstrative's services were very popular and generated a lot of income, most of which Demonstrative spent on a lavish lifestyle. More recently, the market for motivational speakers has dried up and Demonstrative has experienced a sharp drop in income. To make matters worse, a recent IRS audit revealed that Demonstrative had significantly understated income for several years and, as a result, owed some $123,000 in back taxes and penalties. The IRS auditor informed Demonstrative that unless the tax liability were paid immediately, the auditor would recommend criminal prosecution.

Desperate for funds, Demonstrative sought to sell an impressionist painting for which Demonstrative had paid $70,000 two years ago and which an appraiser had recently valued at $80,000-$100,000. Demonstrative advertised the property for immediate sale and contacted some art dealers. Only two people responded. One expressed a willingness to pay $90,000 for it in about six weeks but was not willing to purchase at the current time. The other, Broker, offered to buy it immediately for $65,000 in cash. Demonstrative pleaded for more, but Broker said "Your desperation is showing. Take it or leave it." Demonstrative reluctantly agreed, and used the sale proceeds to pay the IRS.

Two months later, Broker resold the painting for $95,000 to Collector, who purchased in good faith. Three months after that, Demonstrative filed a Chapter 7 bankruptcy petition.

---

[76]   *E.g., In re Grandote Country Club Co., Ltd.,* 252 F.3d 1146 (10th Cir. 2001).

[77]   *In re Fitzgerald,* 255 B.R. 807 (Bankr. D. Conn. 2000).

[78]   *In re Ryker,* 272 B.R. 602 (Bankr. D.N.J. 2002) (sale postponed but not re-advertised).

A. Can the bankruptcy trustee avoid the sale to Broker under § 548? If so, what rights does the trustee have against Broker and what rights against Collector? *See* § 550.

B. How, if at all, would the answer to these questions differ if the trustee used § 544(b) and the UFTA?

Problem 3-19

Same facts as in Problem 3-18 except that Broker still owns the painting. In addition, Broker has spent $20,000 for restoration work on the painting, which at the time of Demonstrative's bankruptcy filing was worth $110,000. Assume that Broker purchased the property in good faith but that the transfer is nevertheless avoidable.

A. What may the trustee recover under § 548?

B. What may the trustee recover under § 544(b)?

In 1998, Congress curbed somewhat the scope of fraudulent transfer avoidance in bankruptcy. Consider the following hypothetical:

Mr. & Mrs. Devout, while insolvent, contributed $12,000 (one-tenth of their annual income) to Church in the year preceding their Chapter 7 filing. The bankruptcy trustee sued Church to recover the money on the grounds that it was fraudulent under § 548(a)(1)(B) because the Devouts did not receive reasonably equivalent value for their contributions. At no time did Church require the Devouts to pay a membership or attendance fee, or tie Church counseling services to donations. However, Church doctrine teaches that its members should tithe, that is, give one-tenth of their incomes annually.

Under classical fraudulent transfer principles, the transfers to Church were avoidable. Indeed, even though such tithing might be an expression of the Devouts' faith, the general maxim – that debtors must be just before they are generous – applies.

Throughout the 1990s, as the number of bankruptcy cases rose, fraudulent transfer actions against religious and charitable organizations significantly increased. Some of these organizations tried to defend against such claims by arguing that the donors did receive reasonably equivalent value: some tried to characterize the donor's tax deduction as value, others claimed that the spiritual counseling they provided constituted value, and some argued that the donations allowed the recipient to pay utilities and other expenses of operation, and the donors received the benefit of these while attending services. In general, though, none of these benefits to the donors, even if qualifying as "value," were really "in exchange for" the donation. Accordingly, most courts avoided these types of transfers.[79]

Unhappy with this result, Congress passed, by a large bipartisan margin, the Religious Liberty and Charitable Donation Protection Act of 1998.[80] This act amended both §§ 544 and 548 to define most charitable and religious donations as not being for less than reasonably equivalent value. It was a stunning reversal of hundreds of years of law. Under the new rules, debtors may contribute without fear of later avoidance, up to 15% of their gross annual income – or more, if their practice has been to contribute more – to a religious or charitable organization. *See* §§ 548(a)(2) & 544(b)(2). *See also* § 1325(b)(2) (permitting Chapter 13 debtors to continue to make such contributions). Moreover, these rules appear to be contribution specific, so that a debtor may be able to make several contributions, each up to the maximum permitted.[81]

Problem 3-20

Disingenuous has never contributed to charity. After consulting with a bankruptcy attorney about the relief available under the Code, Disingenuous decides to file for Chapter 7 bankruptcy relief. Before doing so, Disingenuous calculates that there will be slightly more than $2,500 in nonexempt assets available for distribution in the case. Not wanting creditors to receive anything, Disingenuous makes a $2,500 gift to the United Way the day before filing the bankruptcy petition. This amount is less than 15% of Disingenuous' annual income. Is there any way the trustee can avoid that transfer? *See In re Smihula*, 234 B.R. 240, 242-43 (Bankr. D.R.I. 1999).

Problem 3-21

Deflated operates a small business that provides sight-seeing trips in hot air balloons. Because of the seasonal nature of the business, Deflated sometimes has serious cash flow problems. During one of these periods, Creditor repeatedly demands payment for goods provided on credit. Deflated

---

[79] *See, e.g., In re Bloch*, 207 B.R. 944 (D. Colo. 1997); *In re Newman*, 203 B.R. 468 (D. Kan. 1996); *In re Rivera*, 214 B.R. 101 (Bankr. S.D.N.Y. 1997). *But see In re Young*, 141 F.3d 854 (8th Cir.), *cert. denied*, 525 U.S. 811 (1998); *In re Hodge*, 220 B.R. 386 (D. Idaho 1998) (both ruling that the Religious Freedom Restoration Act mandated an exception to fraudulent transfer law for donations to religious organizations).

[80] Pub. L. 105-183, 112 Stat. 517 (1998).

[81] *But cf. In re Zohdi*, 234 B.R. 371 (Bankr. M.D. La. 1999) (single contribution which exceeded the 15% maximum was avoidable in its entirety, not merely the portion exceeding the limit).

owes Creditor $10,000 and offers to transfer one used balloon and gondola to Creditor, for an appropriate credit on the debt. The balloon and gondola are collectively worth $7,000. Assume Creditor accepts this offer and Deflated files for bankruptcy six months later. Does it matter how much Creditor agreed to treat Deflated as having paid in exchange for the property? Put another way, what will happen if Creditor had credited Deflated with paying $7,000 of the debt? What will happen if Creditor had driven a hard bargain and credited Deflated with paying only $5,000 of the debt? *Cf. Universal Computer Consulting, Inc. v. Pitcairn Enterprises, Inc.*, 2005 WL 2077269 (E.D. Pa. 2005).

3.　*Preferences Redux*

Although § 544(b) is used most commonly to avoid fraudulent transfers, it is not in fact so limited. Indeed, its text does not expressly reference fraudulent transfers at all. Instead, it allows the trustee to avoid any transfer that a creditor with an unsecured claim could avoid. If applicable state law provides such creditors with an avoidance action different from a traditional fraudulent transfer action, then the trustee will have such additional rights.

In fact, several states have their own version of a preference avoidance action. Some of these have elements that are slightly different from those in § 547. For example, they may have a longer preference period, a longer statute of limitations, or fewer affirmative defenses. For that reason, trustees are well advised to consider whether state preference law may provide a remedy when § 547 would not.[82]

F.　ADMINISTERING THE ESTATE

1.　*Employing the Trustee and Professionals*

In chapter two, we briefly considered the employment of professionals to administer the estate. In chapter nine, we will consider how those professionals are paid out of the

---

[82]　*See, e.g.,* Wash. Rev. Code §§ 23.72.010–23.72.060 (providing that corporate transfers made any time within four months of the appointment of a receiver that enable the transferee to receive more than it otherwise would have can be avoided if the corporation was insolvent at the time of the transfer and if the transferee knew or had reasonable cause to know that the corporation was insolvent). *But cf. Sherwood Partners, Inc. v. Lycos, Inc.*, 394 F.3d 1198 (9th Cir. 2005) (Bankruptcy Code preempts state law that gives the power to avoid preferences to an assignee for the benefit of creditors).

estate as part of the claims payment process. Here we will briefly consider the process of employing those professionals and the requirements those professionals must meet.

As discussed in chapter two, the trustee is appointed by the United States Trustee. The trustee in a Chapter 7 case will manage the estate property to maximize its value in the liquidation process. A debtor in possession (or a trustee if one is appointed) in a Chapter 11 will be managing the operation of the debtor's business. Section 327 allows the trustee or debtor in possession to hire professionals to help with that process if such help is reasonably necessary. These professionals must not hold an interest adverse to the estate and must be "disinterested." A "disinterested person" is defined in § 101(14). The person must not be a creditor, an interest holder, or an insider. The person cannot have been an employee, director, or officer of the debtor in the two years prior to bankruptcy. Finally, the person must not have "an interest materially adverse to the interest of the estate or of any class of creditors or equity holders, by reason of any direct or indirect relationship to, connection with, or interest in, the debtor." However, if in the operation of the debtor's activities, the debtor had regular professionals, such as accountants, on salary, the trustee or debtor in possession may continue to hire those persons. § 327(b). The disinterested requirement is designed to avoid conflicts of interest and thus prevent situations in which the professional may not be acting solely in the best interests of the debtor. The case law on this requirement is voluminous.[83]

In order for the hired professional to be compensated from the assets of the estate, the employment of that person must be approved by the bankruptcy court prior to the employment. Rule 2014. At the hearing on the whether to approve an employment application, the parties are likely to thoroughly explore whether the person meets the requirements for disinterestedness and whether the services are reasonably necessary.

2.   *First Meeting of Creditors*

Within a short time after the commencement of a case, the United States Trustee will convene a first meeting of creditors. § 341; Rule 2003. The purpose of this meeting is to allow the United States Trustee and the creditors to quiz the debtor regarding its assets, liabilities, transfers of property, and future plans (in the case of a repayment plan or reorganization plan). This is not a court hearing, and in fact, the United States Trustee, not the bankruptcy judge, presides at the meeting. Creditors need not be represented by counsel and can ask questions of the debtor directly. The debtor may be required to answer questions under oath. § 343. While the utility of this first meeting is questioned by some, it may help to give a clearer picture of the debtor's state of financial affairs and identify transfers that may be pursued to add assets to the estate.

---

[83]   *See* COLLIER ON BANKRUPTCY ¶ 327.04 (15th ed. rev. 2006).

CHAPTER FOUR
EXEMPTIONS

The concept that certain property will be immune from creditor attachment – *i.e.*, that it will be exempt from the reach of creditors – is not unique to American law, and in fact, has deep roots. The policy reasons underlying it are basic and threefold. First, individual debtors cannot go to the workplace without clothes, nor can they perform their jobs without the tools of their trades. Exempting such property preserves people's ability to earn a living. Protecting future wages ensures that individuals retain their incentive to continue working and to be productive members of society. Protecting retirement funds and disability payments helps prevent people from becoming public charges when their ability to maintain employment ceases. In short, the main purpose of exemptions is to make sure that people are able – and have the incentive – to be contributing members of society. If the law permitted creditors to make their debtors completely destitute, and thereby a drain on the public purse, the law would effectively be creating a system that indirectly used public funds to pay private debts.

Second, some property exemptions protect items of nominal value that may not be necessary to earn a living, but would do little to satisfy obligations to creditors. For example, used clothes, household goods, and family photographs may have little or no value to a creditor that levies upon and sells them. However, they can be costly or impossible to replace, and a creditor's threat to seize this property can lead a family to liquidate other assets, borrow from other people, or use other means to protect these items from creditors. To curb this leverage, most jurisdictions protect such personal property.

Finally, and for similar reasons, the law protects some property that may have value to creditors but to which the debtor has significant sentimental attachment. Creditor seizure of wedding bands, engagement rings, and family heirlooms is generally regarded as excessive and prohibited through exemption laws, unless of course such property is unusually valuable.

Of course, none of these policies applies to corporations, partnerships, limited liability companies, or any other type of business entity. Accordingly, outside of bankruptcy they generally cannot exempt property from their creditors. Inside the bankruptcy process, only individuals – human beings – are entitled to exemptions. *See* § 522(b)(1).

Outside of bankruptcy, exemptions protect the property from the debt collection processes described in chapter one. In other words, exempt property is immune from execution and garnishment, and from the judicial liens they create. Exemptions do not, however, shield property from statutory liens or consensual liens. Property which is otherwise exempt can still be encumbered by a statutory or consensual lien and any such lien properly created can be enforced. Thus, for example, if a debtor's homestead is otherwise exempt from execution process under the applicable state's law, that exemption does not protect the homestead from the lien created by mortgage. The mortgagee may still foreclose on the mortgage and may sell the homestead pursuant to the foreclosure process. Similarly, in most states a builder is entitled, by statute, to a mechanic's lien on any real property that the builder has improved to cover the unpaid portion of the builder's services. This is true even if the property would otherwise be exempt from judicial process.

Inside of bankruptcy, exemptions operate a bit differently but with largely the same effect. In bankruptcy, exemptions operate to remove the exempt property from the bankruptcy estate. § 522(b)(1). Because the estate is used to pay unsecured creditors in Chapter 7 cases – and used to determine the minimum amount unsecured creditors must receive in Chapter 11 and 13 cases[1] – this means that exempt property will not inure to the benefit of the unsecured creditors in bankruptcy process. Bear in mind, however, the act of exempting property in bankruptcy does not, by itself, affect any otherwise valid lien that has attached to the exempted property. As we will learn in chapter six, there are several bankruptcy provisions that a debtor or trustee may sometimes use to invalidate a lien. Some of these rules operate on exempt property, some on nonexempt property, and some on either. For now, though, you should assume that exempt property will be taken out of the estate, but that any otherwise valid lien on the exempt property will remain.

A. STATE V. FEDERAL

It is important to remember that exemption laws exist outside of bankruptcy. Every state has exempted some property from attachment and execution by creditors. However, the type and value of property that each state has exempted varies significantly. In exercising its constitutional authority to establish "uniform laws on the subject of bankruptcy,"[2] Congress was presented with the difficult question of whether to create its own uniform list of exemptions to be used in bankruptcy proceedings or to simply allow debtors to avail themselves of their state's exemptions. It chose instead a third approach.

The Bankruptcy Code offers debtors a slate of federal exemptions, *see* § 522(d), but also allows *states* to "opt out" of that slate. *See* § 522(b). Through the opt-out mechanism, a state may preclude its own residents from using the federal exemptions

---

[1]   *See* §§ 1129(a)(7), 1325(a)(4).

[2]   U.S. Const. Art. I, § 8.

when they file for bankruptcy.[3] Residents of a state that has not opted out may elect either the state or the federal exemptions. Approximately two-thirds of the states have opted out of the federal slate of exemptions and therefore permit their citizens to claim only state exemptions. Residents of the remaining states may elect either the federal or state exemptions.

The result of this arrangement is that the exemptions available to individual debtors depends significantly on the state in which the debtor resides. Consider the following chart of the various homestead exemptions. Although it deals with only one type of property – homes – it nevertheless illustrates the extreme variation in what states provide by way of exemptions.

State	Exemption Amount	Opted Out of Fed. Exemptions
Florida	Unlimited	✓
Iowa	Unlimited	✓
Kansas	Unlimited	✓
South Dakota	Unlimited	✓
Texas	Unlimited	
Oklahoma	Unlimited ($5,000 if more than 25% is used for business)	✓
Nevada	$550,000	✓
Massachusetts	$500,000	
Minnesota	$300,000 ($750,000 if used primarily for agriculture)	
Rhode Island	$300,000	
Montana	$250,000	✓
Arizona	$150,000	✓
Washington	$125,000	
Idaho	$100,000	✓
New Hampshire	$100,000	

---

[3] Litigants have attacked this scheme as lacking the constitutionally mandated uniformity, as providing an impermissibly broad power delegation to state legislatures, and as a violation of the Supremacy Clause. However, the opt-out clause has uniformly survived such challenges. *See, e.g., In re Storer*, 58 F.3d 1125 (6th Cir.) (the opt-out system does not violate 5th Amendment due process or equal protection rights), *cert. denied*, 516 U.S. 990 (1995); *In re Sullivan*, 680 F.2d 1131 (7th Cir.) (rejecting impermissible delegation argument), *cert. denied*, 459 U.S. 992 (1982).

State	Exemption Amount	Opted Out of Fed. Exemptions
North Dakota	$80,000	✓
Connecticut	$75,000	
Mississippi	$75,000	✓
Vermont	$75,000	
Colorado	$60,000	✓
Nebraska	$60,000	✓
New Mexico	$60,000	
Alaska	$54,000	✓
California	$50,000 ($75,000 for head of household; $150,000 if over 65)	✓
New York	$50,000	✓
South Carolina	$50,000	✓
Wisconsin	$40,000 (per household)	
Maine	$35,000	✓
Oregon	$30,000 ($39,600 for joint debtors)	✓
Michigan	$30,000 (per household; $45,000 if debtor is over 65 or disabled)	
Louisiana	$25,000	✓
Hawaii	$20,000 ($30,000 for head of household or if over 65)	
Utah	$20,000	✓
North Carolina	$18,500 ($37,000 if over 65 and spouse is deceased)	✓
Illinois	$15,000	✓
Indiana	$15,000	✓
Missouri	$15,000	✓
Georgia	$10,000	✓
Wyoming	$10,000 (per "occupant")	✓
Tennessee	$5,000 ($7,500 for couple; $25,000 if minor child resides there)	✓
Virginia	$5,000 (plus $500 for each dependent)	✓

State	Exemption Amount	Opted Out of Fed. Exemptions
Alabama	$5,000	✓
Kentucky	$5,000	✓
Ohio	$5,000	✓
West Virginia	$5,000	✓
Arkansas	$2,500	
Delaware	None (but $50,000 lump sum exemption may be available)	✓
Maryland	None (but $6,000 wildcard exemption for property of any kind)	✓
New Jersey	None	
Pennsylvania	None	

There is great disparity in the types of other property that states permit a debtor to claim as exempt, as well as in the maximum amount of such exemptions. Query whether this level of variation is justifiable.

It arguably would be reasonable to use state law exemptions if they reflected regional variations in cost of living or property use, but they do not. A comparison of state homestead exemptions and the relative cost of living reveals that state homestead exemptions do not reflect a relative cost of living assessment. For example, in 1991, Rhode Island had the fifth highest median home value in the country and yet had a homestead exemption of zero; conversely, Iowa had the third lowest home value in the nation and had an unlimited homestead exemption. No regional cost variation explains why California has very generous exemption laws while New York does not. The lack of rationale extends to personal property as well. For example, compare three states in which a reasonable car might be equally necessary to commute to work: Kansas permits its citizens to exempt up to $20,000 in a vehicle while Missouri exempts only $1,000, and, until recently, Nebraska had no automobile exemption at all.

* * * Debtors with roughly equivalent economic profiles and similar property are receiving vastly dissimilar treatment through the federal bankruptcy system, and correspondingly their creditors do as well. A debtor who cannot save a car, a home, and household furniture under one state's exemption laws may look across the state line to see a similar debtor saving all of those items and more. In addition, although there has been significant revision in state exemption statutes since 1978, state exemption laws are

sometimes a collection of archaic remains. Moreover, some states require a debtor to file a deed of exemption in advance of a bankruptcy filing in order to exempt certain property, a requirement that can become a trap for the poorly informed debtor.[4]

Regardless of whether this variation is good or not, it remains the current law. Moreover, debtors residing in one of the states that permit a choice of state or federal exemptions often need to carefully choose between the different regimes. Mixing and matching both state exemptions and federal bankruptcy exemptions is not permitted. *See* § 522(b). Consider the following chart, which helps compare the exemptions under § 522(d) with those available under Washington law for most common types of property. As you can see, the debtor's choice will often depend on the specific types of property the debtor owns and what the value of such property is. Note, the federal exemption amounts are adjusted every three years to adjust for inflation. § 104.

	Washington Exemption Amount	**Federal Exemption Amount**
Homestead	$125,000	$20,200
Jewelry	$1,000	$1,350
Clothing	No limit	$10,775 aggregate limit; $525 per item limit
Books & Mementoes	$1,500	
Household Goods	$2,700	
Other Property	$2,000 aggregate limit; $200 max. in cash & deposits	$1,075 + $10,125 (of unused homestead)
Motor Vehicle	$2,500	$3,225
Tools of Trade	$5,000	$2,025
Life Insurance Contract	N/A	$10,775
Prescribed Health Aids	No limit	No limit

---

[4]   National Bankruptcy Review Commission, *Bankruptcy: The Next Twenty Years* 122-23 (October 20, 1997).

Problem 4-1

Given the differences between the federal and Washington exemptions depicted above, when are debtors likely to select the federal exemptions and when are they likely to select the Washington exemptions? What is likely to be the biggest consideration in making that decision?

B.   DETERMINING WHICH STATE'S EXEMPTION LAWS APPLY

Because all individual bankruptcy debtors may avail themselves of the exemptions provided by state law and most debtors do not even have the option to use the federal exemptions, it is necessary to make sure you know which state's exemption laws apply. If the debtor has not moved recently, this will not be much of an issue; the law of the jurisdiction in which the debtor resides is the law that governs. If, however, the debtor has moved within the last two years preceding the bankruptcy filing, then a computation based on length of residency in each state during the 180 days prior to the two-year period determines the governing law. Read § 522(b)(1)–(3). In other words, if the debtor moved during the time represented by shaded area in the timeline below, then the jurisdiction in which the debtor lived for the greatest time during the period represented by the lined area is the jurisdiction whose law applies.

Problem 4-2

Dunkirk filed for Chapter 7 bankruptcy protection on April 15, 2006. At that time, Dunkirk owned and lived in a house in Florida. Before moving to Florida, Dunkirk owned and resided in a house in St. Louis, Missouri. Which state's homestead exemption may Dunkirk use:

A.   If Dunkirk moved to Florida on February 1, 2004?

B.   If Dunkirk moved to Florida on June 1, 2004 and had lived in Missouri for 15 years prior to the move?

C.   If Dunkirk grew up in Wisconsin, moved from Wisconsin to Missouri on February 1, 2004, and then moved from Missouri to Florida on November 1, 2005?

D.   What problems for Dunkirk, if any, might the answers to Parts B and C
     pose? *See* § 522(b)(3).

C.   EXEMPTIONS AVAILABLE TO ALL INDIVIDUAL DEBTORS

In 2005, Congress added a very generous exemption for all debtors, whether they
use the state or the federal exemptions. *See* § 522(b)(3)(C), (d)(12). It covers retirement
funds held in IRAs, Roth IRAs, and virtually all types of employer-sponsored retirement
plans, provided the funds are exempt from federal income tax. Unlike § 522(d)(10),
which also exempts IRAs,[5] this new exemption is not limited to the amount "reasonably
necessary for the support of the debtor" and the debtor's dependents. The only
limitation is a $1,095,000, inflation-adjusted cap on IRAs and Roth IRAs (not on other
types of exempt funds). *See* § 522(n). However, this cap can be increased "if the
interests of justice so require" and in any event does not apply to amounts rolled over
from other exempt plans. In short, virtually all of most individual debtors' retirement
savings are likely to be exemptible.

D.   THE PROCESS OF CLAIMING EXEMPTIONS

1.   *In General*

The process of claiming exemptions is fraught with issues about classification,
valuation, timing, and competing claims to the property. Some of these issues are fairly
simple and easy to resolve; others are more complicated and may lack a clear answer.
     The first thing to note is that whether a specific item of property qualifies for a
particular exemption depends first and foremost on what law applies. If the debtor is
claiming the benefit of the federal exemptions, the issue is a matter of federal law. If,
as is more likely, the debtor is seeking to use a state exemption, the issue is one of state
law. Thus, for example, what qualifies as "household goods" or "tools of trade" may
vary from state to state.
     The second thing to note about exemptions is that, as exemptible property
transmutes from one thing to another, the exemption may or may not be lost. For
example, a state law exempting a certain amount or percentage of an individual's wages
is likely to cover the funds upon receipt, but may or may not still exempt them when

---

[5]   *See Rousey v. Jacoway*, 544 U.S. 320 (2005).

deposited into a bank account containing nonexempt funds and is unlikely to cover any nonexempt assets purchased with those funds.[6]

The third thing to bear in mind about exemptions is that they are usually limited in amount. Thus, a debtor is often permitted to claim a car as exempt, but typically only up to a maximum value. This is necessary to prevent debtors from abusing their exemptions (putting $2 million into a custom-made car plated with gold).

What happens to a debtor whose exemptible property has a value in excess of the maximum exemption amount? The short answer is that the debtor would probably not be able to prevent execution, levy, and sale of the property outside of bankruptcy. The same result usually occurs in bankruptcy, at least in Chapter 7 cases. Consider a debtor whose car is worth $6,000 and whose state exemption for automobiles is limited to $2,500. That car is worth $3,500 to the bankruptcy estate:

Property Value		$6,000
Exemption Limit	(goes to debtor)	– $2,500
Residual Value	(goes to estate)	$3,500

In a Chapter 7 case, the trustee will sell the car for $6,000, give the debtor the $2,500 exemption amount, and distribute the remaining $3,500 to creditors. Thus, unless property is worth less than the maximum exemption amount, the debtor will in fact lose the property. Of course, the debtor can use the $2,500 received from the sale to buy a slightly less expensive car, one that will remain exempt. In a Chapter 11 or 13 case, the debtor may be able to keep the car, but only if the debtor has enough other resources – such as postpetition income – to pay creditors the $3,500 excess over the exemption cap.

The fourth thing to note about exemptions is that more than one exemption may be available for a single piece of property. For example, a truck driver may be able to combine an exemption for motor vehicles with an exemption for tools of trade and apply both to a single truck. Such "stacking" of exemptions is common but whether it is available depends on two, independent things: (i) whether the property involved qualifies for each exemption under the applicable law;[7] and (ii) whether the applicable

---

[6]   *See, e.g., In re Christensen*, 149 P.3d 40 (Nev. 2006) (exemptible wages retain their exempt character after payment and commingling in a deposit account, provided they remain traceable under a first-in-first-out approach; assets purchased with those funds are exempt only if they so qualify without regard to the exempt nature of the funds used to acquire them).

[7]   *See, e.g., In re Black*, 280 B.R. 258 (Bankr. D. Colo. 2002) (debtor's truck qualified for tools of trade exemption under Colorado law); *In re Lyall*, 193 B.R. 767 (Bankr. E.D. Va. 1996) (debtor's motor vehicle qualified for tools of trade exemption under Virginia law). *Cf. In re Driscoll*, 179 B.R. 664 (Bankr. D. Or. 1995) (car specially designed for someone with an amputated foot was not a "professional prescribed health aid").

law permits the two (or more) exemptions to be applied to the same piece of property.[8] Most states do permit exemptions to be stacked.

The fifth thing to remember about exemptions is that they typically apply only to the debtor's equity in a piece of property. While our discussion of secured claims is generally put off until chapter six, it is important to understand that if property is subject to a valid and unavoidable lien, then the debtor may exempt only the equity in the property, if any, and in fact need only exempt the equity to prevent the trustee from selling it.

For example, consider that same debtor with a $6,000 car, but this time the car is subject to a properly perfected security interest securing a $4,000 debt. Such a debtor has only $2,000 of equity. The only portion of the car which the debtor may claim as exempt is this equity. Because the maximum exemption amount, $2,500, exceeds the debtor's equity, the debtor can exempt all the equity in the car. If the debtor does so, a Chapter 7 trustee would no longer have an interest in the car ($4,000 in value being allocated to the secured creditor and the $2,000 remainder to the debtor), and therefore would have no incentive to sell it:

Property Value		$6,000
Lien Debt	(value allocated to lienor)	− $4,000
		$2,000
Exemption ($2,500 limit)	(goes to debtor)	− $2,000
Residual Value	(goes to estate)	$0

Indeed, the debtor can probably prevent the trustee from attempting to sell the car. *See* § 554(b). Whether the debtor can prevent the secured party from repossessing and selling the car is another matter, one which will be discussed in chapter six. In a Chapter 11 or 13 case, the exemption again makes the car valueless to the estate, and therefore irrelevant in determining how much unsecured claimants must be paid under the plan.

Given all this, debtors must often engage in a fair amount of planning when deciding how to allocate their exemptions. Try the following problem.

Problem 4-3

Dressage is starting a career as a horse breeder. She owns an Arabian stallion worth $24,000, and plans to sell stud rights to that horse to generate funds to get the business going. She spends much of her time on the internet and phone looking for potential customers. Unfortunately, horses are

---

[8]   *See, e.g, In re Branas*, 143 B.R. 64, 66 (Bankr. W.D. Pa. 1992) (farmers' tractor qualified for both motor vehicle exemption and exemption for tools of trade).

expensive to care for and Dressage and her spouse, Duncan, have run up about $20,000 in debt on their credit cards and in amounts owed the stable for boarding the horse. Last month, Duncan lost his job as a customer service representative for a consumer electronics manufacturer. They own their own home, valued at $82,000, and subject to a $60,000 mortgage. They have household goods and clothes worth $3,000. Because Dressage's horse breeding service is not going well, both Duncan and Dressage are looking for work. They have missed payments on the credit cards and mortgage, and the stable is threatening to evict the horse. They live in a state that has not opted out of the federal bankruptcy exemptions. The state exemptions allow $10,000 for a homestead (one exemption per family), $2,000 for household goods and furnishings per debtor, and an unlimited amount for tools of the trade.

A.   If they file under Chapter 7, what exemption options will they have and what do you advise them to do? *See* § 522(b), (d), (m). Is there any vital information about the horse that you lack but which might significantly affect their decision? *See In re Toland*, 346 B.R. 444 (Bankr. N.D. Ohio 2006).

B.   What if the horse were worth $35,000?

The sixth thing to remember is that the costs of the sale and the trustee's commissions must be factored in before determining what in fact will happen to the property. For example, in *In re Thornton*,[9] the debtors had a home worth $27,000 that was encumbered by a mortgage securing a $14,250 debt. Thus the debtors had $12,750 of equity in the home. The court determined that the trustee would incur $600 in advertising costs and $1,350 in a 5% real estate commission to sell the house, and thus would be able to collect only $10,800 from selling the property. Of this amount, the debtors could exempt $9,275, leaving only $1,525 for the estate. The trustee would then be entitled to a $375 commission on this, *see* § 326, further reducing the amount available to creditors to only $1,150. This amounted to a 1.7% distribution on unsecured claims, which the court characterized as "*de minimis*." It therefore ordered the trustee to abandon the property. The end result was that the debtors got to keep their home (assuming they continued to pay the mortgagee). In short, property has to really be worth going after before Chapter 7 trustees and courts will require debtors to relinquish it.

To claim property as exempt, the debtor needs merely to list it as exempt on the debtor's schedules, which the debtor must file with the petition or shortly thereafter. *See* Official Bankruptcy Form 6, Schedule C. *See also* Rules 1007, 4003. The trustee or a creditor may object to a claimed exemption, but must do so within 30 days of the § 341

---

[9]   269 B.R. 682 (Bankr. W.D. Mo. 2001).

meeting of creditors, which must be held not less than 20, nor more than 40 days after the petition is filed. Rule 2003(a). The objecting party has the burden of proving that the claimed exemption is improper. Rule 4003(c).

In essence, then, exempt assets begin in the estate but are poured back into the debtor's vat if either no one objects or any objections are overruled. Thus, the debtor's vat of assets more accurately looks as follows:

Property of the Debtor

Exempt Assets

Certain Educational Savings

Interests in Spendthrift Trusts
& ERISA-Qualified Plans

Postpetition Earnings

Suppose a debtor lists property as exempt even though there is not even a colorable basis for doing so. An objection is made, but only after expiration of the 30-day period. Should the exemption be allowed? In *Taylor v. Freeland & Kronz*,[10] the debtor claimed an employment discrimination lawsuit and its proceeds as exempt even though there was no basis for the exemption. The Chapter 7 trustee did not timely object. When the debtor ended up recovering $110,000 based on the lawsuit, the trustee sought turnover of the funds, arguing that they remained property of the estate. The Supreme Court ruled otherwise, holding that the debtor's cause of action was exempt once the time for objecting to the claimed exemption had expired. In doing so, the Court rejected the trustee's argument that this would create incentives for a debtor to claim baseless exemptions:

> Deadlines may lead to unwelcome results, but they prompt parties to act and they produce finality. In this case, despite what respondents repeatedly told him, [the trustee] did not object to the claimed exemption. If [the trustee] did not know the value of the potential proceeds of the lawsuit, he could have sought a hearing on the issue, *see* Rule 4003(c), or he could have asked the Bankruptcy Court for an extension of time to object, *see* Rule 4003(b). Having done neither, [the trustee] cannot now seek to deprive Davis and respondents of the exemption.
>
> [The trustee] suggests that our holding will create improper incentives. He asserts that it will lead debtors to claim property exempt on the chance that the trustee and creditors, for whatever reason, will fail to object to the claimed

---

[10]   503 U.S. 638 (1992).

exemption on time. He asserts that only a requirement of good faith can prevent what the Eighth Circuit has termed "exemption by declaration." This concern, however, does not cause us to alter our interpretation of § 522(*l*).

Debtors and their attorneys face penalties under various provisions for engaging in improper conduct in bankruptcy proceedings. *See, e.g.,* § 727(a)(4)(B) (authorizing denial of discharge for presenting fraudulent claims); Rule 1008 (requiring filings to "be verified or contain an unsworn declaration" of truthfulness under penalty of perjury); Rule 9011 (authorizing sanctions for signing certain documents not "well grounded in fact and . . . warranted by existing law or a good faith argument for the extension, modification, or reversal of existing law"); 18 U.S.C. § 152 (imposing criminal penalties for fraud in bankruptcy cases). These provisions may limit bad-faith claims of exemptions by debtors. To the extent that they do not, Congress may enact comparable provisions to address the difficulties that *Taylor* predicts will follow our decision. We have no authority to limit the application of § 522(*l*) to exemptions claimed in good faith.

Justice Stevens in dissent had the following to say about the majority's approach:

The Court states that it has "no authority to limit the application of § 522(*l*) to exemptions claimed in good faith." It does not deny, however, that it has ample authority to hold that the doctrine of equitable tolling applies to the 30-day limitations period in Federal Rule of Bankruptcy Procedure 4003(b). In my view, such a result is supported not only by strong equitable considerations, but also by the common law, the widespread practice of the bankruptcy courts, and the text of § 522(b).

* * * In this case, even if there was no fraud, and even if it is assumed that the trustee failed to exercise due diligence, it remains true that the parties injured by the trustee's failure to object within the 30-day period are innocent creditors. Moreover, it is apparently undisputed that there was no legitimate basis for the claim of an exemption for the entire award. Under these circumstances, unless the debtor could establish some prejudice caused by the trustee's failure to object promptly, I would hold that the filing of a frivolous claim for an exemption is tantamount to fraud for purposes of deciding when the 30-day period begins to run.

Although *Taylor* gives debtors a broad license to exempt property, some lower courts have made sure that debtors who try to be too clever are apt to be sorry. For example, in one post-*Taylor* case the debtor claimed two partnership interests as exempt, and valued each at $1.00. The trustee did not object, but simply found a purchaser more than happy to purchase the partnerships for their market value, which was apparently far in excess of $1.00. The court ruled that while the trustee was barred from objecting to the claimed exemption, the exemption was limited to the amount claimed. The court allowed the trustee to sell the partnership interests, provided the trustee protected the debtor's $1.00 interest in each (presumably by giving the debtor $2.00).[11]

In another post-*Taylor* case, the debtor claimed a judgment for personal injury as exempt. The debtor listed the value of the judgment as $1.00 in his Schedule C and in two other places indicated that he was "unaware of [its] value," even though his state court attorney was already holding over $4,000 in proceeds of the judgment in a trust account, enough to pay all the debtor's unsecured claims. After a *timely* objection was made, the court concluded that the exemption was claimed in bad faith and denied it in its entirety. The court also warned the debtor's counsel that his failure to investigate the true facts was sanctionable under Rule 9011(b), although the court chose not to sanction the attorney for this one impropriety.[12]

If a debtor's exemption claim does not clearly identify the property to which it relates, the 30-day objection period may be tolled while the trustee seeks a clarification from the debtor's counsel.[13]

One way debtors may be able to take fuller advantage of the *Taylor* decision is by filing initially under Chapter 11 or 13 and then converting to Chapter 7. Under the applicable rules, the deadline for objecting to a claimed exemption is 30 days after the § 341 meeting concludes. This time period is apparently not extended upon conversion of the case.[14] Thus, a debtor could file under Chapter 11, claim a spurious exemption, and rely on the likelihood that no creditor will bother to object. Because there is no trustee in Chapter 11, there can also be no objection from that quarter (there could be an objection from the U.S. Trustee, *see* § 307, but that official may not be closely reviewing the exemptions claimed in individual cases). The debtor could then convert to Chapter 7 more than 30 days after the § 341 meeting ends, and effectively foreclose the trustee from ever having the opportunity to object to exemptions. The same tactic could be used by filing initially under Chapter 13. Although the standing trustee assigned to the case might object to a spurious exemption, because exemptions typically do not matter too much in Chapter 13, Chapter 13 trustees may not be closely scrutinizing exemptions claimed by the debtor.

---

[11]   *Addison v. Reavis*, 158 B.R. 53 (E.D. Va. 1993), *aff'd without opinion,* 32 F.3d 562 (4th Cir. 1994). *See also In re Morgan-Busby*, 272 B.R. 257 (9th Cir. BAP 2002); *In re Soost*, 262 B.R. 68 (8th Cir. BAP 2001) (both to the same effect); *In re Wick*, 276 F.3d 412 (8th Cir. 2002) (noting that there was nothing to object to because the exemption claimed was proper, and allowing the trustee to realize the excess value). *Contra In re Green*, 31 F.3d 1098 (11th Cir. 1994).

[12]   *In re Kelley*, 255 B.R. 787 (Bankr. N.D. Ala. 2000).

[13]   *See In re Hendrickson*, 274 B.R. 138 (Bankr. W.D. Pa. 2002).

[14]   *In re Smith*, 235 F.3d 472 (9th Cir. 2000); *In re Bell*, 225 F.3d 203 (2d Cir. 2000). *Contra In re Lang*, 276 B.R. 716 (Bankr. S.D. Fla. 2002).

Whether courts will permit debtors to use this tactic is open to question. It reeks of both bankruptcy fraud and bad faith. Moreover, at least one court has indicated that a new § 341 meeting is necessary after conversion from Chapter 13 to Chapter 7, and that the clock on objections to a claimed exemption starts anew at the conclusion of the new § 341 meeting.[15]

2.   Valuing Property & Calculating Exemptions

There is no doubt that the bankruptcy estate is entitled to all postpetition appreciation in estate property. Therefore, all appreciation of items *partially* claimed as exempt belongs to the estate, except to the extent attributable to postpetition services.[16] Thus, for example, in the situation depicted below, the estate should get all the value above the exemption limit: $1,500.

	Petition Date	Later
Value	$3,000	$3,500
Exemption Limit	$2,000	$2,000
Estate's Equity	$1,000	$1,500

However, if property appreciates postpetition but is still worth less than the total amount the debtor may exempt, the debtor is entitled to that appreciation.

	Petition Date	Later
Value	$3,000	$3,500
Exemption Limit	$4,000	$4,000
Estate's Equity	$0	$0

It remains somewhat unclear how to deal with postpetition appreciation of assets claimed to be *wholly* exempt if the appreciation takes the property's value above the available exemption limit:

	Petition Date	Later
Value	$3,000	$5,000
Exemption Limit	$4,000	?
Estate's Equity	$0	?

---

[15]   *See In re Fish*, 261 B.R. 754 (Bankr. M.D. Fla. 2001).

[16]   *See In re Wick*, 276 F.3d 412 (8th Cir. 2002).

Some courts have held that the debtor's interest is limited to the amount which may be claimed as exempt, and postpetition appreciation above that amount inures to the benefit of the estate.[17] Other courts disagree. As Judge Posner pointed out in *In re Polis*[18]:

> The possibility that the debtor will obtain a windfall as a consequence of the exemptions recognized by the Bankruptcy Code arises from the fact that the date of valuation of an asset for purposes of determining whether it can be exempted is the date on which the petition for bankruptcy is filed; it is not a later date on which the asset may be worth a lot more. Often property appreciates in a wholly unexpected fashion. A lottery ticket that turns out against all odds to be a winner is merely the clearest example. A debtor who exempted a painting thought to be worthless in a market sense, having a purely sentimental value, might discover the day after his discharge from bankruptcy that it had suddenly increased in value because other paintings by the artist had just been bought by the Metropolitan Museum of Art; the creditors could not reach it, provided that until then its fair market value had in fact been slight. Common stock that had traded at $100 a share on the date the petition for bankruptcy was filed might a month later be worth $1,000, and again the creditors would be out of luck if the debtor had exempted her shares by claiming the personal property exemption for them. And so it is with a legal claim. It might when it first accrued have seemed so "far out" that its fair market value would be well within the limits of the exemption, and yet – such are the uncertainties of litigation – it might turn into a huge winner.
>
> This feature of the Code's valuation scheme should not be thought a disreputable loophole. If the assets sought to be exempted by the debtor were not valued at a date early in the bankruptcy proceeding, neither the debtor nor the creditors would know who had the right to them. So long as the property did not appreciate beyond the limit of the exemption, the property would be the debtor's; if it did appreciate beyond that point, the appreciation would belong to the creditors, who thus might – if they still remembered their contingent claim to the property – reclaim it many years after the bankruptcy proceeding had ended. The framers of the Bankruptcy Code could have made ineligible for exemption property that has an unusual propensity to fluctuate in value, thus reserving windfall gains to the creditors; but they did not do so, perhaps because of the difficulty of defining the category or allocating its fruits

---

[17] *E.g., In re Hyman*, 967 F.2d 1316, 1321 (9th Cir. 1992); *In re Heflin*, 215 B.R. 530, 534 (Bankr. W.D. Mich. 1997).

[18] 217 F.3d 899, 902-03 (7th Cir. 2000).

across creditors. An alternative would be to keep the bankruptcy proceeding open indefinitely; the objections are self-evident.

It remains to be seen which view will predominate. For now, trustees need to be somewhat vigilant in protecting the estate by objecting to unwarranted claims of exemptions or, when appropriate, by asking that the debtor clarify the exemption claim by stating an exact numerical value.

Problem 4-4

On line five of Degas' Schedule B, which Degas filed along with a Chapter 7 bankruptcy petition, Degas listed a painting and valued it at $2,000. On Schedule C, Degas claimed the entire value of the painting as exempt. Three months later, the Trustee received an offer to buy the painting for $3,000. Should the trustee's ability to accept that offer – and to bring the resulting $1,000 gain into the bankruptcy estate – depend on whether the "gain" represents true postpetition appreciation or merely an incorrect valuation on Schedule B? In other words, should it matter how much the painting was really worth on the date of the petition if it is worth $3,000 now and the debtor's exemption is limited to $2,000?

Problem 4-5

Determined is filing for Chapter 7 bankruptcy protection in a state that has a $40,000 homestead exemption. Determined's home is worth $100,000 and is subject to a mortgage of $60,000, and thus Determined's equity is fully exempt. Despite being insolvent, Determined has managed to make all mortgage payments on time. The mortgage lender is willing to ignore whatever technical defaults may have occurred and to allow Determined to remain in the home, provided Determined continues to make the required monthly payments (presumably, out of postpetition income). Determined's attorney is concerned, however, that each postpetition mortgage payment that Determined makes will reduce the mortgage debt and thereby increase Determined's equity above the exemption limit. What should the attorney do to protect Determined's home? *See* §§ 362, 554.

Problem 4-6

Destiny, a life-long resident of Wisconsin, is contemplating filing for bankruptcy protection. Destiny owns no home, and therefore plans to use the federal exemptions because they provide more generous allowances for household goods and motor vehicles. Destiny plans to use all but $400 of the § 522(d)(5) catchall exemption to exempt tangible personal property. The only remaining asset Destiny owns is $700 in cash. Destiny could exempt $400 of that cash but first wants to know if there is any way to make use of what Judge Posner said in the *Polis* case (excerpted on page 140) to perhaps parlay the $400 exemption into something much more valuable? *See* Rule 1007(c) & Official Form 6 (Schedule C).

The discussion so far raises the question of how property is to be valued for the purpose of applying exemptions. There are two answers to this, the practical and the legal.

The practical answer is that it rarely matters. For most types of used personal property – clothes, furniture, small appliances, and even jewelry – the debtor will simply assign a value. Rarely will it be worth anyone's time and effort to challenge the valuations of such items.[19] Although the trustee has the duty to investigate and sell any property which would generate value in excess of the claimed exemption amount, *see* § 704(a)(1), (3) & (4), the costs of pursuing such an investigation will often exceed any value the trustee may hope to reap from it.[20] For more valuable property, such as cars and investments, trustees are likely to be more thorough.

The legal answer gets into a recurring theme in bankruptcy: how is property to be valued? Is fair market value the appropriate standard? How about liquidation value? Replacement cost? Retail value? Wholesale value? Does it matter what will happen to the property? Are the costs of any sale to be deducted from the amount assigned? Put another way, is the assessment of value for the purpose of determining what and how much the debtor gets to keep – for which fair market value would seem appropriate – or is it to determine how much would come into the estate if the trustee were to sell it, for which liquidation value might be more appropriate.

If the debtor is using the federal exemptions under § 522(d), subsection (a) would appear to resolve the valuation question. It defines value for the purpose of § 522 as

---

[19] See *In re West*, 328 B.R. 736 (Bankr. S.D. Ohio 2004), in which the debtor had purchased ten items of jewelry for $30,000 but later valued them at only $2,000 on her bankruptcy schedules. The trustee objected to the discharge under § 727(a)(4)(A), arguing that the debtor had made a false statement on the schedules, and submitted an expert appraisal of the jewelry for $8,900. The court overruled the trustee's objection because, following her attorney's advice, the debtor had estimated the jewelry's value as what a pawn shop would pay for it, she had no way of knowing that fair market value was the appropriate standard, and the trustee's expert testified that a pawnshop would pay only $3,860.

[20] On the other hand, some experienced trustees have become quite expert at estimating the value of jewelry, and with loupe in hand have asked to examine the debtor's rings and watches during the debtor's examination at the meeting of creditors.

"fair market value." If, however, the debtor is using state exemptions, the answer is not so clear. Any limitations on the "value" of the property that the debtor may exempt would not necessarily be imbued with the Bankruptcy Code's definition of value. Thus, the result could conceivably vary depending on which state's exemptions the debtor was using. Nevertheless, the few courts to explore this question do not seem to rely on state law and generally agree that fair market value should be used without taking into account the debtor's financial exigencies or any costs of sale.[21] In so concluding, most of these courts have expressly rejected the few earlier decisions suggesting that liquidation value is the appropriate standard.[22]

Problem 4-7

Dorsett has just filed a Chapter 7 bankruptcy petition and has claimed the federal exemptions. Dorsett owns a home with a $40,000 mortgage. Similar homes have sold for about $70,000 after being on the market for two or three months. All the homes that have been sold at this price were listed with a real estate broker who received a six percent commission. Other selling costs, including title insurance and closing fees, have averaged about $1,000. When similar houses have been sold by the sheriff at foreclosure sales, they have brought about $40,000. Dorsett has a 1990 Ford Escort and a small amount of furniture and clothing, collectively worth about $3,000. Dorsett has no other assets.

The trustee asks the judge for permission to sell the house. If the judge grants the request, what will the creditors get? If the judge does not, what is the effective size of Dorsett's exemption? What should the judge do?

3.   *Exemptions in Recovered Property*

What if, shortly before filing for bankruptcy protection and while insolvent, the debtor transfers exempt property to a favored creditor in payment of a debt or to a family member as a gift? In one sense that transfer is preferential or fraudulent. After all, the payment to the creditor had the effect of preferring that creditor. The gift was fraudulent

---

[21]   *See, e.g., Household Finance Corp. III v. Wilk,* 1992 WL 165770 (W.D.N.Y. 1992); *In re West,* 328 B.R. 736, 750 n.8 (Bankr. S.D. Ohio 2004).

[22]   *See In re Walsh,* 5 B.R. 239, 240-41 (Bankr. D.D.C. 1980). *See also In re Blanchard,* 201 B.R. 108, 129-30 (Bankr. E.D. Pa. 1996) (ruling that while fair market value is appropriate for valuable things such as houses, pianos, and jewelry, liquidation value may well be appropriate for general household goods).

because no reasonably equivalent value was received. In another sense, though, the transfer in no way impacted the debtor's creditors: if the transfer had not been made and the property retained, the debtor could have exempted it and creditors would not have had access to it.

Section 522 addresses this situation. If the prepetition transfer was voluntary, and the trustee recovers the property, the debtor will not be permitted to claim an exemption in it. *See* § 522(g)(1)(A). The property will come back into the estate and be available for all general creditors. In effect, the debtor is deemed to have waived the exemption, but that waiver is made to operate for the benefit of all creditors, not merely the prepetition transferee.[23]

If, on the other hand, the prepetition transfer had been involuntary, say perhaps that a creditor had seized property pursuant to a writ of execution and levy,[24] the debtor may still claim the exemption in any property the trustee recovers. § 522(g). If the trustee refuses to go after the property, as the trustee might if any recovery would be wholly exemptible, then the debtor may exercise the trustee's avoiding powers and seek to recover the property. § 522(h).

Problem 4-8

Given that § 522(g) prohibits the debtor from claiming an exemption in recovered property that the debtor transferred away voluntarily, how can a debtor get away with preferring a creditor with exempt property?

Problem 4-9

Section 522(c) provides that exempt property generally retains its status as exempt after bankruptcy. Why is this provision necessary (*i.e.,* for what debts and for what exempt property is the provision needed)?

---

[23] The 30-day limit for objecting to a debtor's claimed exemption, *see* Rule 4003(b) (discussed *supra* at pages 135-138), apparently does not apply to property the trustee recovers using the avoiding powers. Thus, for example, if the debtor voluntarily transferred property prepetition but nevertheless claims it as exempt on his or her schedules, the trustee need not object to the exemption within the 30-day period in order to object to the debtor's attempt to reap the benefit of avoidance under § 522(g). *In re Kuhnel*, 2007 WL 2122062 (10th Cir. 2007).

[24] While creditors cannot normally levy upon exempt property, if the debtor claims the federal exemptions in bankruptcy, some of the exempt property may not have been covered by state exemption laws prepetition. In this sense, § 522(g) and (h) are needed to help give effect to the federal exemptions in those jurisdictions that have not opted out.

E. ABUSING EXEMPTIONS

There is an old maxim that applies in bankruptcy, as in other places: pigs get fat; hogs get slaughtered.[25] The sentiment behind this maxim is that being a little greedy is to be expected and will be winked at. It thus may pay off. Being very greedy, however, is repulsive, will be cause for sanction, and thus may lead to dire consequences.

In the context of exemptions this comes up all the time. Debtors frequently want to preserve whatever assets they have, and take them beyond the reach of creditors. To do this, they frequently convert nonexempt assets into exempt assets shortly before filing for bankruptcy protection. In other words, they sell their nonexempt property to get cash and then use the cash to buy property that is exempt.

This practice smells a lot like a fraudulent transfer: transferring assets in an effort to delay, hinder, or defraud creditors. However, in at least one sense the practice is not only acceptable, but actually encouraged. After all, one of the main purposes of exemptions is to prevent the debtor from becoming a public charge. We therefore want debtors to take advantage of their exemptions.

Nevertheless, excessive conversion of nonexempt assets into exempt assets is just greedy. The pig begins to look a lot like a hog. Drawing the line between acceptable and unacceptable pre-bankruptcy conversions is very difficult. Consider the following two cases decided the same day by the same court. In doing so, pay close attention to the relief requested in each.

HANSON V. FIRST NATIONAL BANK
848 F.2d 866 (8th Cir. 1988)

Timbers, Circuit Judge.

A creditor bank appeals from a district court order * * * affirming the bankruptcy court's order which rejected the creditor's challenge to the debtors' claimed exemptions. On appeal, the creditor asserts that there was extrinsic evidence establishing the debtors' intent to defraud their creditors. We disagree. We hold that the bankruptcy court was not clearly erroneous in finding no fraudulent intent. We affirm.

I

* * * On November 30, 1983 appellees Kenneth Hanson and his wife Lucille Hanson (the "Hansons" or "debtors"), residents of South Dakota, filed a voluntary joint bankruptcy petition pursuant to Chapter 7 of the Bankruptcy Code. Appellant First National Bank in Brookings ("First National") is the principal creditor of appellees. The

---

[25] *See, e.g., In re Bowyer*, 916 F.2d 1056, 1060 (5th Cir. 1990), *rev'd on rehearing*, 932 F.2d 1100 (5th Cir. 1991); Juliet M. Moringiello, *Distinguishing Hogs from Pigs: a Proposal for a Preference Approach to Pre-bankruptcy Planning*, 6 AM. BANKR. INST. L. REV. 103 (1998).

instant appeal arises out of First National's objections to the exemptions claimed by the Hansons.

First National loaned money to the Hansons who were farmers. The Hansons sustained financial problems which led to their default on the loans. Before filing for bankruptcy, the Hansons consulted an attorney. On the advice of counsel, the Hansons had appraised and sold certain of their property which would not be exempt under South Dakota law. They sold to their son, Ronald Hanson, a car, two vans, and a motor home for a total of $27,115, the amount for which the property was appraised. Ronald had purchased the property with money he obtained from a bank loan. The debtors also sold some of their household goods and furnishings to Kenneth's brother, Allen Hanson, for $7,300, the appraised value.

A couple weeks prior to filing their bankruptcy petition, the Hansons used these proceeds to purchase life insurance policies with cash surrender values of $9,977 and $9,978 and, two days before filing their petition, had prepaid $11,033 on their homestead real estate mortgage which was held by First National. This property was exempt from their creditors' reach. Under South Dakota law, a debtor may exempt the proceeds of life insurance policies up to a total of $20,000 and he also may exempt his homestead.

First National objected to these exemptions, claiming that the debtors had converted non-exempt property to exempt property on the eve of bankruptcy with intent to defraud their creditors. At the hearing before the bankruptcy court on September 10, 1984, First National asserted that none of the property allegedly sold ever was transferred to the buyers. The debtors testified that the vehicles sold to their son, Ronald, were stored at their home because Ronald still lived with them while he was working part time and attending school part time. Part of the agreement, the debtors testified, included their permission to store the vehicles on their property. While the debtors said they occasionally used the vehicles, they did so only with express permission of their son. Ronald subsequently sold the motor home to a third party. The household goods and furnishings were stored in the Hansons' home, they said, because Allen Hanson, Kenneth's brother, was then living in Anchorage, Alaska, and could not retrieve the property immediately after the sale. First National did not assert, nor does it assert on appeal before us, that the transfers were for less than fair market value. The bankruptcy court from the bench denied First National's motion which objected to the exemptions. The court found that the Hansons had done what was permissible under the law and that their actions did not constitute extrinsic evidence of fraud.

First National appealed to the federal district court. * * * [T]he district court affirmed the bankruptcy court's order, concluding that it was not clearly erroneous. The instant appeal followed. The sole issue on appeal is whether the Hansons should not be allowed to claim their life insurance and homestead exemption as a product of fraudulent conveyances. We affirm.

II

* * * Under the Bankruptcy Code (the "Code"), a debtor is entitled to exempt certain property from the claims of his creditors. The Code permits a debtor to exempt either under the provisions of the Code itself if not forbidden by state law, § 522(b) & (d), or under the provisions of state law and federal law other than the minimum allowances in the Code. § 522(b)(2). When the debtor claims a state-created exemption, the scope of the claim is determined by state law.

It is well established that under the Code, a debtor's conversion of non-exempt property to exempt property on the eve of bankruptcy for the express purpose of placing that property beyond the reach of creditors, without more, will not deprive the debtor of the exemption to which he otherwise would be entitled. A leading bankruptcy commentator explains that this rule is just because "The result which would obtain if debtors were not allowed to convert property into allowable exempt property would be extremely harsh, especially in those jurisdictions where the exemption allowance is minimal." 3 Collier on Bankruptcy ¶ 522.08[4], at 40 (15th ed. 1984). Nevertheless, this rule is not absolute. Where the debtor acts with actual intent to defraud creditors, his exemptions will be denied. Since fraudulent intent rarely is susceptible of direct proof, courts long have accepted extrinsic evidence of fraud. Absent extrinsic evidence of fraud, however, the debtor's mere conversion of non-exempt property to exempt property, even while insolvent, is not evidence of fraudulent intent as to creditors.

The crux of the issue on the instant appeal is whether there was extrinsic evidence to establish that the Hansons transferred the property with intent to defraud their creditors. We may reverse the bankruptcy court's finding as to the debtors' actual intent only if it is clearly erroneous.

In *In re Olson*, 45 B.R. 501 (1984), debtors with a defunct business had placed non-exempt funds into their homestead asset, which was exempt property, just prior to filing their bankruptcy petition. The debtors, 55 and 56 years old, testified, on the advice of their attorney, that the reason they paid off the mortgages was to protect their homestead and to reduce their monthly living expenses, since they believed they would have difficulty finding employment after terminating their business. The bankruptcy court found that the debtors did not commit a fraudulent conveyance. The court permitted the debtors to exempt their entire homestead after finding that the debtors prior to bankruptcy used their savings to satisfy their mortgages, no business assets having been used and no debts having been incurred.

First National asserts here that the Hansons while insolvent committed a "classic badge of fraud" by transferring their property to family members and at the same time retaining the use and enjoyment of that property. First National asserts that the controlling case is *In re Cadarette*, 601 F.2d 648 (2d Cir. 1979). We disagree.

In *Cadarette*, the debtor, whose business was on the brink of financial collapse, transferred title to his expensive automobile, boat and trailer to his fiancee without consideration three weeks before filing his bankruptcy petition. The district court, reversing the decision of the bankruptcy court, held that the debtor's discharge was denied because of his fraudulent intent to shield his assets from his creditors. The Second Circuit, in affirming the district court, found a number of factors clearly evidencing the debtor's fraudulent intent. The court found significant, among other things, that "someone facing dire financial straits would choose to make a gift of a valuable and highly marketable automobile"; that eight days after the alleged transfer of the car a service charge of $399 was paid not by the alleged new owner but by the debtor, who further depleted his business assets by paying with a company check; that the debtor's fiancee lived only two houses away from him; and that he retained a key to the car and continued to use the car to the same extent as he previously had used it.

We find the instant case quite different from the situation in *Cadarette*. First National does not dispute the fact that the purchasers paid fair market value. The vehicles and household goods were not gifts. Title appears to have been transferred correctly. In the instant case, the debtors had reasonable explanations as to why the property they sold remained on their premises. Of particular significance, their son purchased the vehicles with a bank loan taken in his name and he subsequently resold the motor home to a third party, keeping all of the proceeds himself. The sale to family members, standing on its own, does not establish extrinsic evidence of fraud. * * *

The bankruptcy court found that First National did not establish any indicia of fraud: the Hansons did not borrow money to place into exempt properties; they accounted for the cash they received from the sales; they had a preexisting homestead; and they did not obtain goods on credit, sell them, and then place the money into exempt property. They sold the property for its fair market value and then used this money to take advantage of some of the limited exemptions available under South Dakota law on the advice of counsel.

To summarize: [w]e hold that the bankruptcy court was not clearly erroneous in finding no fraudulent intent by the Hansons and permitting them to claim their full exemptions. We believe that the instant case falls within the myriad of cases which have permitted such a conversion.

Arnold, Circuit Judge, concurring.

I agree with the result reached by the Court and with almost all of its opinion. I write separately to indicate some variation in reasoning and also to compare this case with the companion case of *Norwest Bank Nebraska v. Tveten*, 848 F.2d 871, also decided today by this panel.

* * * The Court is entirely correct in holding that there is no extrinsic fraud here. The money placed into exempt property was not borrowed, the cash received from the sales was accounted for, and the property was sold for fair market value. The fact that

the sale was to family members, "standing on its own, does not establish extrinsic evidence of fraud."

With all of this I agree completely, but exactly the same statements can be made, just as accurately, with respect to Dr. Tveten's case. So far as I can tell, there are only three differences between Dr. Tveten and the Hansons, and all of them are legally irrelevant: (1) Dr. Tveten is a physician, and the Hansons are farmers; (2) Dr. Tveten attempted to claim exempt status for about $700,000 worth of property, while the Hansons are claiming it for about $31,000 worth of property; and (3) the Minnesota exemption statute whose shelter Dr. Tveten sought had no dollar limit, while the South Dakota statute exempting the proceeds of life-insurance policies is limited to $20,000. The first of these three differences – the occupation of the parties – is plainly immaterial, and no one contends otherwise. The second – the amounts of money involved – is also irrelevant, in my view, because the relevant statute contains no dollar limit, and for judges to set one involves essentially a legislative decision not suitable for the judicial branch. The relevant statute for present purposes is § 522(b)(2)(A), which authorizes debtors to claim exemptions available under "State or local law," and says nothing about any dollar limitations, by contrast to § 522(d), the federal schedule of exemptions, which contains a number of dollar limitations. The third difference – that between the Minnesota and South Dakota statutes – is also legally immaterial, and for a closely related reason. The federal exemption statute, just referred to, simply incorporates state and local exemption laws without regard to whether those laws contain dollar limitations of their own.

The Court attempts to reconcile the results in the two cases by characterizing the question presented as one of fact – whether the conversion was undertaken with fraudulent intent, or with an intent to delay or hinder creditors. In *Tveten*, the Bankruptcy Court found fraudulent intent, whereas in *Hanson* it did not. Neither finding is clearly erroneous, the Court says, so both judgments are affirmed. This analysis collapses upon examination. For in *Tveten* the major indicium of fraudulent intent relied on by the Bankruptcy Court was Dr. Tveten's avowed purpose to place the assets in question out of the reach of his creditors, a purpose that, as a matter of law, cannot amount to fraudulent intent, as the Court's opinion in *Hanson* explicitly states. The result, in practice, appears to be this: a debtor will be allowed to convert property into exempt form, or not, depending on findings of fact made in the court of first instance, the Bankruptcy Court, and these findings will turn on whether the Bankruptcy Court regards the amount of money involved as too much. With all deference, that is not a rule of law. It is simply a license to make distinctions among debtors based on subjective considerations that will vary more widely than the length of the chancellor's foot.

NORWEST BANK NEBRASKA V. TVETEN
848 F.2d 871 (8th Cir. 1988)

Timbers, Circuit Judge.

Appellant Omar A. Tveten, a physician who owed creditors almost $19,000,000, mostly in the form of personal guaranties on a number of investments whose value had deteriorated greatly, petitioned for Chapter 11 bankruptcy. He had converted almost all of his non-exempt property, with a value of about $700,000, into exempt property that could not be reached by his creditors. The bankruptcy court, on the basis of its findings of fact and conclusions of law, entered an order on February 27, 1987, denying a discharge in view of its finding that Tveten intended to defraud, delay, and hinder his creditors. The district court * * * affirmed the bankruptcy court's order. On appeal, Tveten asserts that his transfers merely constituted astute pre-bankruptcy planning. We hold that the bankruptcy court was not clearly erroneous in inferring fraudulent intent on the part of Tveten. We affirm.

I

* * * Tveten is a 59 year old physician in general practice. He is the sole shareholder of Omar A. Tveten, P.A., a professional corporation. He has no dependents. He began investing in various real estate developments. These investments initially were quite successful. Various physician friends of Tveten joined him in organizing a corporation to invest in these ventures. These investments were highly leveraged. The physicians, including Tveten, personally had guaranteed the debt arising out of these investments. In mid-1985, Tveten's investments began to sour. He became personally liable for an amount close to $19,000,000 – well beyond his ability to pay. Appellees Norwest Bank Nebraska ("Norwest Bank"), Business Development Corporation of Nebraska ("Business Development"), and Harold J. Panuska ("Panuska") as trustee of the Harold J. Panuska Profit Sharing Trust and the Harold J. Panuska Employee Trust Fund, became creditors of Tveten as a result of his various investment ventures.

Tveten filed a Chapter 11 petition on January 7, 1986. Meanwhile, several creditors already had commenced lawsuits against him. Panuska had obtained a $139,657 judgment against him on October 9, 1985. Norwest Bank and Business Development had commenced an action against him but had not obtained judgment when Tveten filed for bankruptcy. On the date the Chapter 11 petition was filed, Tveten owed his creditors close to $19,000,000.

Before filing for bankruptcy, Tveten consulted counsel. As part of his pre-bankruptcy planning, he liquidated almost all of his non-exempt property, converting it into exempt property worth approximately $700,000. This was accomplished through some seventeen separate transfers. The non-exempt property he liquidated included land sold to his parents and his brother, respectively, for $70,000 and $75,732 in cash; life insurance policies and annuities with a for-profit company with cash values totaling $96,307.58; his net salary and bonuses of $27,820.91; his KEOGH plan and individual retirement fund of $20,487.35; his corporation's profit-sharing plan worth $325,774.51; and a home sold for $50,000.[26] All of the liquidated property was converted into life insurance or annuity contracts with the Lutheran Brotherhood, a fraternal benefit association, which, under Minnesota law, cannot be attached by creditors. Tveten concedes that the purpose of these transfers was to shield his assets from creditors. Minnesota law provides that creditors cannot attach *any* money or other benefits payable by a fraternal benefit association. Unlike most exemption provisions in other states, the Minnesota exemption has no monetary limit. Indeed, under this exemption, Tveten attempted to place $700,000 worth of his property out of his creditors' reach.

Tveten sought a discharge with respect to $18,920,000 of his debts. Appellees objected to Tveten's discharge. In its order of February 27, 1987, the bankruptcy court concluded that, although Tveten's conversion of non-exempt property to exempt property just before petitioning for bankruptcy, standing alone, would not justify denial of a discharge, his inferred intent to defraud would. The bankruptcy court held that, even if the exemptions were permissible, Tveten had abused the protections permitted a debtor under the Bankruptcy Code (the "Code"). His awareness of Panuska's judgment against him and of several pending lawsuits, his rapidly deteriorating business investments, and his exposure to extensive liability well beyond his ability to pay, all were cited by the court in its description of the circumstances under which Tveten converted his property. Moreover, the court concluded that Tveten intended to hinder and delay his creditors. Accordingly, the bankruptcy court denied Tveten a discharge.

Tveten appealed from the bankruptcy court order to the federal district court. In a memorandum opinion and order entered July 10, 1987, the district court affirmed the denial of a discharge, concluding that the bankruptcy court's finding as to Tveten's intent was not clearly erroneous.[27]

The instant appeal followed. Basically, Tveten asserts on appeal that as a matter of law we should reject the factors relied on by the bankruptcy court to infer that Tveten intended to delay, hinder and defraud creditors. We disagree. We affirm.

---

[26] There were no claims that these transfers were for less than market value.

[27] Before the district court entered its order, the Supreme Court of Minnesota held in a decision entered March 27, 1987, that annuities and life insurance contracts issued by a fraternal benefit society were exempt under Minnesota law, but that these statutory provisions violated the Minnesota Constitution. Accordingly, Tveten no longer will be able to claim these exemptions. Following the opinion of the Supreme Court of Minnesota, Tveten claimed an exemption for his pension in the amount of approximately $200,000. He and his creditors settled this issue before the bankruptcy court. He will retain this property as exempt.

II

The sole issue on appeal is whether Tveten properly was denied a discharge in view of the transfers alleged to have been in fraud of creditors.

At the outset, it is necessary to distinguish between (1) a debtor's right to exempt certain property from the claims of his creditors and (2) his right to a discharge of his debts. * * * When the debtor claims a state-created exemption, the scope of the claim is determined by state law. * * *

A debtor's right to a discharge, however, unlike his right to an exemption, is determined by *federal*, not state, law. The Code provides that a debtor may be denied a discharge under Chapter 7 if, among other things, he has transferred property "with intent to hinder, delay, or defraud a creditor" within one year before the date of the filing of the petition. § 727(a)(2). Although Tveten filed for bankruptcy under Chapter 11, the proscription against discharging a debtor with fraudulent intent in a Chapter 7 proceeding is equally applicable against a debtor applying for a Chapter 11 discharge. The reason for this is that the Code provides that confirmation of a plan does not discharge a Chapter 11 debtor if "the debtor would be denied a discharge under section 727(a) of this title if the case were a case under chapter 7 of this title." § 1141(d)(3)(C).

Although the determination as to whether a discharge should be granted or denied is governed by federal law, the standard applied consistently by the courts is the same as that used to determine whether an exemption is permissible, *i.e.* absent extrinsic evidence of fraud, mere conversion of non-exempt property to exempt property is not fraudulent as to creditors even if the motivation behind the conversion is to place those assets beyond the reach of creditors.

As the bankruptcy court correctly found here, therefore, the issue in the instant case revolves around whether there was extrinsic evidence to demonstrate that Tveten transferred his property on the eve of bankruptcy with intent to defraud his creditors. * * *

There are a number of cases in which the debtor converted non-exempt property to exempt property on the eve of bankruptcy and was granted a discharge because there was no extrinsic evidence of the debtor's intent to defraud. In *Forsberg v. Security State Bank*, 15 F.2d 499 (8th Cir. 1926), an old decision of our Court, a debtor was granted a discharge despite his trade of non-exempt cattle for exempt hogs while insolvent and in contemplation of bankruptcy. Although we found that the trade was effected so that the debtor could increase his exemptions, the debtor "should [not] be penalized for merely doing what the law allows him to do." We concluded that "before the existence of such fraudulent purpose can be properly found, there must appear in evidence some facts or circumstances which are extrinsic to the mere facts of conversion of nonexempt assets into exempt and which are indicative of such fraudulent purpose."

There also are a number of cases, however, in which the courts have denied discharges after concluding that there was extrinsic evidence of the debtor's fraudulent intent. In *Ford v. Poston*, 773 F.2d 52 (4th Cir. 1985), the debtor had executed a deed of correction transferring a tract of land to himself and his wife as tenants by the entirety. The debtor had testified that his parents originally had conveyed the land to the debtor alone, and that this was a mistake that he corrected by executing a deed of correction. Under relevant state law, the debtor's action removed the property from the reach of his creditors who were not also creditors of his wife. The Fourth Circuit, in upholding the denial of a discharge, found significant the fact that this "mistake" in the original transfer of the property was "corrected" the day after an unsecured creditor obtained judgment against the debtor. The Fourth Circuit held that the bankruptcy court, in denying a discharge, was not clearly erroneous in finding the requisite intent to defraud, after "[h]aving heard . . . [the debtor's] testimony at trial and having considered the circumstances surrounding the transfer." In *In re Reed*, 700 F.2d 986 (5th Cir. 1983), shortly after the debtor had arranged with his creditors to be free from the payment obligations until the following year, he rapidly had converted non-exempt assets to extinguish one home mortgage and to reduce another four months before bankruptcy, and had diverted receipts from his business into an account not divulged to his creditors. The Fifth Circuit concluded that the debtor's "whole pattern of conduct evinces that intent." The court went further and stated:

> It would constitute a perversion of the purposes of the Bankruptcy Code to permit a debtor earning $180,000 a year to convert every one of his major nonexempt assets into sheltered property on the eve of bankruptcy with actual intent to defraud his creditors and then emerge washed clean of future obligation by carefully concocted immersion in bankruptcy waters.

In most, if not all, cases determining whether discharge was properly granted or denied to a debtor who practiced "pre-bankruptcy planning," the point of reference has been the state exemptions if the debtor was claiming under them. Although discharge was not denied if the debtor merely converted his non-exempt property into exempt property as permitted under state law, the exemptions involved in these cases comported with federal policy to give the debtor a "fresh start" – by limiting the monetary value of the exemptions. This policy has been explicit, or at least implicit, in these cases. In *Forsberg*, for example, we stated that it is not fraudulent for an individual who knows he is insolvent to convert non-exempt property into exempt property, thereby placing the property out of the reach of creditors

> because the statutes granting exemptions have made no such exceptions, and because the policy of such statutes is to favor the debtors, at the expense of the creditors, *in the limited amounts allowed to them, by preventing the forced loss of the home and of the necessities of subsistence*, and because such statutes are construed liberally in favor of the exemption. (emphasis added).

Similarly, in *In re Ellingson*, 63 B.R. 271 (N.D. Iowa 1986), in holding that the debtors' conversion of non-exempt cash and farm machinery did not provide grounds for denial of a discharge, the court relied on the social policies behind the exemptions. The court found that the debtors' improvement of their homestead was consistent with several of these policies, such as protecting the family unit from impoverishment, relieving society from the burden of supplying subsidized housing, and providing the debtors with a means to survive during the period following their bankruptcy filing when they might have little or no income. The court held that exemptions should further one or more of the following social policies:

> (1) To provide the debtor with property necessary for his physical survival; (2) To protect the dignity and the cultural and religious identity of the debtor; (3) To enable the debtor to rehabilitate himself financially and earn income in the future; (4) To protect the debtor's family from the adverse consequences of impoverishment; (5) To shift the burden of providing the debtor and his family with minimal financial support from society to the debtor's creditors.

In the instant case, however, the state exemption relied on by Tveten was unlimited, with the potential for unlimited abuse. Indeed, this case presents a situation in which the debtor liquidated almost his entire net worth of $700,000 and converted it to non-exempt property in seventeen transfers on the eve of bankruptcy while his creditors, to whom he owed close to $19,000,000, would be left to divide the little that remained in his estate. Borrowing the phrase used by another court, Tveten "did not want a mere *fresh* start, he wanted a *head* start." *In re Zouhar*, 10 B.R. 154, 156 (Bankr. D.N.M. 1981) (emphasis in original). His attempt to shield property worth approximately $700,000 goes well beyond the purpose for which exemptions are permitted. Tveten's reliance on his attorney's advice does not protect him here, since that protection applies only to the extent that the reliance was reasonable.

The bankruptcy court, as affirmed by the district court, examined Tveten's entire pattern of conduct and found that he had demonstrated fraudulent intent. We agree. While state law governs the legitimacy of Tveten's exemptions, it is federal law that governs his discharge. Permitting Tveten, who earns over $60,000 annually, to convert all of his major non-exempt assets into sheltered property on the eve of bankruptcy with actual intent to defraud his creditors "would constitute a perversion of the purposes of the Bankruptcy Code." *In re Reed*, 700 F.2d at 992. Tveten still is entitled to retain, free from creditors' claims, property rightfully exempt under relevant state law.

We distinguish our decision in *Hanson v. First National Bank*, decided today. *Hanson* involves a creditor's objection to two of the debtors' claimed exemptions under South Dakota law, a matter governed by state law. The complaint centered on the Hansons' sale, while insolvent, of non-exempt property to family members for fair market value and their use of the proceeds to prepay their preexisting mortgage and to purchase life insurance policies in the limited amounts permissible under relevant state law. The bankruptcy court found no extrinsic evidence of fraud. The district court * * * affirmed. We also affirmed, concluding that the case fell within the myriad of cases which have permitted such a conversion on the eve of bankruptcy.

III

To summarize: [w]e hold that the bankruptcy court was not clearly erroneous in inferring fraudulent intent on the part of the debtor, rather than astute pre-bankruptcy planning, with respect to his transfers on the eve of bankruptcy which were intended to defraud, delay and hinder his creditors.

Arnold, Circuit Judge, dissenting.

The Court reaches a result that appeals to one's general sense of righteousness. I believe, however, that it is contrary to clearly established law, and I therefore respectfully dissent.

Dr. Tveten has never made any bones about what he is doing, or trying to do, in this case. He deliberately set out to convert as much property as possible into a form exempt from attachment by creditors under Minnesota law. Such a design necessarily involves an attempt to delay or hinder creditors, in the ordinary, non-legal sense of those words, but, under long-standing principles embodied both in judicial decisions and in statute, such a purpose is not unlawful. * * *

A debtor's right to make full use of statutory exemptions is fundamental to bankruptcy law. To unsecured creditors, a debtor's conversion of his assets into exempt categories of property will always appear unfair, but this apparent unfairness is simply a consequence of the existence of exemptions under the jurisdiction's bankruptcy law. * * *

To be sure, if there is extrinsic evidence of fraud, or of a purpose to hinder or delay creditors, discharge may and should be denied, but "extrinsic," in this context, must mean something beyond the mere conversion of assets into exempt form for the purpose of putting them out of the reach of one's creditors. If Tveten had lied to his creditors, like the debtor in *McCormick v. Security State Bank*, 822 F.2d 806 (8th Cir. 1987), or misled them in some way, like the debtor in *In re Reed*, 700 F.2d 986 (5th Cir. 1983), or transferred property for less than fair value to a third party, like the debtor in *Ford v. Poston*, 773 F.2d 52 (4th Cir. 1985), we would have a very different case. There is absolutely no evidence of that sort of misconduct in this record, and the Court's opinion filed today cites none.

One is tempted to speculate what the result would have been in this case if the amount of assets converted had been $7,000, instead of $700,000. Indeed, the large amount of money involved is the only difference I can see between this case and *Forsberg v. Security State Bank*, 15 F.2d 499 (8th Cir. 1926). It is true that the *Forsberg* opinion referred to "the limited amounts allowed to" debtors by exemptions, but whether exemptions are limited in amount is a legislative question ordinarily to be decided by the people's elected representatives, in this case the Minnesota Legislature. Where courts punish debtors simply for claiming exemptions within statutory limits, troubling problems arise in separating judicial from legislative power. * * *

If there ought to be a dollar limit, and I am inclined to think that there should be, and if practices such as those engaged in by the debtor here can become abusive, and I admit that they can, the problem is simply not one susceptible of a judicial solution according to manageable objective standards. A good statement of the kind of judicial reasoning that must underlie the result the Court reaches today appears in *In re Zouhar*, 10 B.R. 154 (Bankr. D.N.M. 1981), where the amount of assets converted was $130,000. The Bankruptcy Court denied discharge, stating, among other things, that "there is a principle of too much; phrased colloquially, when a pig becomes a hog it is slaughtered." If I were a member of the Minnesota Legislature, I might well vote in favor of a bill to place an over-all dollar maximum on any exemption.[28] But sitting as a judge, by what criteria do I determine when this pig becomes a hog? If $700,000 is too much, what about $70,000? Would it matter if the debtor were a farmer, as in *Forsberg*, rather than a physician? (I ask the question because the appellee creditor's brief mentions the debtor's profession, which ought to be legally irrelevant, several times.)

Debtors deserve more definite answers to these questions than the Court's opinion provides. In effect, the Court today leaves the distinction between permissible and impermissible claims of exemption to each bankruptcy judge's own sense of proportion. As a result, debtors will be unable to know in advance how far the federal courts will allow them to exercise their rights under state law.

Where state law creates an unlimited exemption, the result may be that wealthy debtors like Tveten enjoy a windfall that appears unconscionable, and contrary to the policy of the bankruptcy law. I fully agree with Judge Kishel, however, that

> [this] result . . . cannot be laid at [the] Debtor's feet; it must be laid at the feet of the state legislature. Debtor did nothing more than exercise a prerogative that was fully his under law. It cannot be said that his actions have so tainted him or his bankruptcy petition as to merit denial of discharge.

I submit that Tveten did nothing more fraudulent than seek to take advantage of a state law of which the federal courts disapprove.

I would reverse this judgment and hold that the debtor's actions in converting property into exempt form do not bar a discharge in bankruptcy.

---

[28]　There is some irony in the fact that the exemption sought by the debtor in this case, that for benefits under annuities or life-insurance policies issued by fraternal associations, has been held unconstitutional under two provisions of the Minnesota Constitution. One such provision, Article 1, Section 12, provides that "[a] reasonable amount of property shall be exempt." The Supreme Court of Minnesota has held that the exemption statute involved in the present case is unconstitutional precisely because it contains no dollar limit. So the principle of limitation has been upheld, the debtor has in any event lost the exemption he sought, but he also loses his discharge under today's decision.

NOTES

1.   A year after these two decisions were reported, the same court tried to reconcile them in a case involving a physician who converted approximately $400,000 in assets into exempt property on the eve of bankruptcy:

> We read *Tveten* and *Hanson* to reaffirm the rule that conduct sufficient to defeat discharge requires indicia of fraud beyond mere use of the exemptions. Under *Tveten, Hanson,* and the cases they discuss, extrinsic evidence can be composed of: further conduct intentionally designed to materially mislead or deceive creditors about the debtor's position; conveyances for less than fair value; or the continued retention, benefit or use of property allegedly conveyed together with evidence that the conveyance was for inadequate consideration.   In addition, *Tveten* establishes that where an exemption, other than a homestead exemption, is not limited in amount, the amount of property converted into exempt forms and the form taken may be considered in determining whether fraudulent intent exists.
>
>   * * * [n]o exemption is more central to the legitimate aims of state lawmakers than a homestead exemption. * * * We hold that *Tveten* does not apply to homestead exemptions absent traditional extrinsic evidence of fraud unrelated to the amount of money involved.   In addition, we remind the lower courts that there is nothing fraudulent per se about making even significant use of other legal exemptions.   Ultimately, fixed dollar limits on the use of exemptions must be set by state legislatures. *Tveten* and *Hanson* sanction an exceptional use of judicial discretion. In light of the danger that judges will inadvertently fix inconsistent or arbitrary limits on statutory exemptions, we must err in favor of the debtor. The power sanctioned in *Tveten* should be reserved for exceptional cases and has no application to homestead exemptions.

In re Johnson, 880 F.2d 78, 82 & 83-84 (8th Cir. 1989).   On remand, Dr. Johnson still lost his discharge. *In re Johnson*, 124 B.R. 290 (Bankr. D. Minn. 1991). The court found extrinsic evidence of fraud in his acquisition of a whole life insurance policy with a cash surrender value just under the $4,000 exemption limit (Dr. Johnson had no dependents and therefore needed no insurance) and in his acquisition of a baby grand piano and harpsichord for about $8,000, both exempt under state law (Dr. Johnson played neither and actually kept the piano in storage).

2.   Several state laws that exempt a debtor's property make express exception for property acquired with nonexempt assets in an effort to defraud creditors. Others make exception for property acquired within a brief, specified period before bankruptcy. To the extent a debtor is relying on state law as the source for the exemption, these limitations may be very important. *See In re Coates*, 242 B.R. 901 (Bankr. N.D. Tex. 2000) (because the state exemption laws had different rules, debtors were denied an exemption in automobiles whose liens they paid off immediately before filing for bankruptcy, but were permitted to exempt their entire homestead despite paying off mortgage at the same time).

In another, more recent venture into fraudulent use of exemptions, the Eighth Circuit again confronted a debtor who sold everything to buy an exempt asset. This time, however, the only asset was a homestead. Nevertheless, the debtor lost the exemption. Can you reconcile this decision with *Hanson*, *Tveten*, and *Johnson*?

IN RE SHOLDAN
217 F.3d 1006 (8th Cir. 2000)

Beam, Circuit Judge.
    Earl Jensen, the personal representative of the probate estate of debtor, Arthur Sholdan, appeals the district court's affirmance of a bankruptcy court order that sustained the bankruptcy trustee's objection to Sholdan's homestead exemption. We affirm.
    Prior to filing for Chapter 7 bankruptcy, Sholdan liquidated almost all of his non-exempt property consisting of bank accounts, certificates of deposit and a mortgage against his former farmstead, and converted it into exempt property in the form of a house worth approximately $135,000. In his Chapter 7 bankruptcy petition, Sholdan listed his new house as an exempt homestead pursuant to Minnesota law. A short while thereafter, Sholdan died. The trustee of his bankruptcy estate (trustee) objects to Sholdan's homestead exemption claim on the grounds that Sholdan acquired title to the property in specific contemplation of filing bankruptcy and with the "intent to defraud" his creditors. Therefore, the trustee maintains that Sholdan and his successors in interest should be denied the benefit of the statutory exemption.
    The Bankruptcy Code permits debtors to exempt property from the bankruptcy estate pursuant to provisions of state law. *See* § 522(b)(2)(A). The scope of a state-created exemption is determined by state law. Minnesota law provides an exemption for an individual's homestead. *See* Minn. Stat. Ann. §§ 510.01-.02 (West 1990). However, under section 513.44 of Minnesota's enactment of the Uniform Fraudulent Transfer Act (UFTA), a debtor may not claim a homestead exemption when he or she transfers the property "with actual intent to hinder, delay, or defraud" creditors.

This same section contains a lengthy list of factors or "badges of fraud" which a court may look to for help in determining actual intent.

* * * the bankruptcy court found that Sholdan had converted non-exempt property to exempt property with the "intent to defraud." Noting that direct evidence of fraudulent intent is rare, the bankruptcy court inferred such intent from applying the "badges of fraud" listed in section 513.44(b). The district court affirmed the bankruptcy court's decision. On appeal, Jensen argues that: (1) the bankruptcy court erred in applying the "badges of fraud" to determine whether Sholdan acted with an "intent to defraud;" and (2) the record does not support a finding of such intent.
* * *

First, we reject the argument that the bankruptcy court erred in applying the badges of fraud set forth in section 513.44(b) of the UFTA. Under Minnesota law, whether fraud exists in a situation involving the conversion of non-exempt to exempt assets is determined by reference to the UFTA. Although Jensen does not dispute that under *Tveten*, an exemption may be denied under section 513.44 of the UFTA if a debtor had the actual intent to defraud, he nevertheless, argues that it was inappropriate for the bankruptcy court to use the "badges of fraud" listed in that section to infer such intent. Specifically, he claims that *Tveten* never took the additional step of sanctioning the use of a "badges of fraud" approach and that such an approach is inappropriate for exemption cases. We find this argument to be without merit.

We find the bankruptcy court's "badges of fraud" approach was appropriate. Although, not specifically referenced by the Minnesota Supreme Court in *Tveten*, we find such an approach to be implicit in *Tveten*'s holding that a court look to the standards governing fraudulent transfers for purposes of determining fraud in the exemption context. Use of the "badges of fraud" to infer fraudulent intent in conveyances and transfers is well settled under Minnesota law. We think the *Tveten* court's omission of a "badges of fraud" reference results from the fact that at the time of the *Tveten* decision there was no codification of specific badges of fraud, as exists currently under the UFTA, rather than from any desire to preclude the use of such badges. Compare UFCA, Minn. Stat. Ann. §§ 513.20-513.32 (West 1986) with UFTA, Minn. Stat. Ann. §§ 513.41-513.51 (West 1990).

That use of the badges of fraud is appropriate for inferring intent in an exemption case, is also dictated by common sense. Badges of fraud represent nothing more than a list of circumstantial factors that a court may use to infer fraudulent intent. Given the fact that direct evidence of fraud is rare, a court in most instances can only infer fraud by considering circumstantial evidence. Furthermore, we note that under section 513.44(b), a court is not limited to only those factors or "badges" enumerated, but is free to consider any other factors bearing upon the issue of fraudulent intent. In sum, we find no error in the bankruptcy court's application of a traditional and well settled approach for determining fraud to a situation involving the conversion of assets from non-exempt to exempt status.[29]

Having decided that the bankruptcy court applied the correct legal standard for inferring whether there was evidence showing an "intent to defraud," we next turn to Jensen's argument that the evidence does not support such a finding. The question of whether an individual acted with intent to defraud in converting non-exempt property into exempt property is a question of fact, on which the bankruptcy court's finding will not be reversed unless clearly erroneous. *See Hanson v. First Nat'l Bank*, 848 F.2d 866, 868 (8th Cir. 1988). It is well settled that the mere conversion of non-exempt assets to exempt assets is not in itself fraudulent. *See id.* Before actual fraudulent intent can be found " 'there must appear in evidence some facts or circumstances which are extrinsic to the mere facts of conversion of non-exempt assets into exempt and which are indicative of such fraudulent purpose.' " *Norwest Bank Nebraska v. Tveten*, 848 F.2d 871, 875 (8th Cir. 1988) (quoting *Forsberg v. Security State Bank*, 15 F.2d 499, 502 (8th Cir. 1926)). Our review of the record convinces us the bankruptcy court was not clearly erroneous in finding there was sufficient extrinsic evidence surrounding Sholdan's conversion of assets from which it could infer that he acted with the "intent to defraud."

The debtor was a retired farmer, ninety years of age and afflicted with serious medical problems. He had been recently named a defendant in a personal injury suit with claimed damages well in excess of his liability insurance coverage. He had no children. He had one nephew, Earl Jensen. Earl had a step-brother, Roger Jensen. In his will, the debtor bequeathed his entire estate to his sister, Earl Jensen's mother. If she predeceased the debtor, Roger Jensen's children were his beneficiaries. At the time of the purchase of the new house, the debtor had been living in an assisted-care facility. Prior to living in the assisted-care facility, he had resided in an apartment for thirteen years.

Then, in what was, as the bankruptcy court noted, a radical departure from his previous lifestyle, the debtor acquired approximately $162,000 by liquidating his bank account and certificates of deposit, and selling his mortgage rights in the farm to Roger Jensen. With the assistance of the Jensens and their attorneys, Sholdan then moved out of the assisted-care facility and purchased with cash a newly-built house worth approximately $135,000. As part of the purchase agreement, the debtor and Jensens asked the builder to add various finishes to the house, such as a deck and landscaping, and specifically inquired as to the amount by which the purchase price of the house would increase. Following the purchase, the debtor's sole source of income was a social security payment of $486 per month, which after covering the costs of his basic living expenses of $435 per month, would leave him with a yearly surplus of approximately

---

[29] We also reject Jensen's argument that the bankruptcy court impermissibly relied on Sholdan's age and the value of his house to infer fraudulent intent.

$600. The property taxes on the new house amounted to $2,000 per year. Following immediately upon the heels of the purchase of the house, the debtor filed for Chapter 7 bankruptcy, listing the house as exempt under Minnesota's homestead exemption.

On these facts, we find the bankruptcy court correctly concluded there was ample evidence extrinsic to the mere conversion of assets that showed fraudulent intent on the part of the debtor. It is one thing to convert non-exempt assets into exempt property for the express purpose of holding it as a homestead and thereby putting the property beyond the reach of creditors. However, it is quite another thing to acquire title to a house for no other reason than to defraud creditors. " 'While the homestead right is a valuable one . . . it was never intended, and it should never be permitted, to operate as a vehicle for fraud and rank injustice.' " *Kangas v. Robie*, 264 F. 92, 94 (8th Cir. 1920) (quoting *Esty v. Cummings*, 78 N.W. 242, 244 (Minn. 1899)).

For the foregoing reasons, the decision of the district court is affirmed.

Arnold, Circuit Judge, dissenting.

I respectfully dissent from the Court's opinion. The Court fails to identify any evidence of fraud extrinsic to Mr. Sholdan's conversion of non-exempt property for the purpose of protecting his assets from creditors. The controlling law in this Circuit is clear:

> [I]t is not a fraudulent act by an individual who knows he is insolvent to convert a part of his property which is not exempt into property which is exempt, for the purpose of claiming his exemptions therein, and of thereby placing it out of the reach of his creditors.

Forsberg v. Security State Bank, 15 F.2d 499, 501 (8th Cir. 1926).

Consistently with our precedent, the Court today acknowledges that "there must appear in evidence some facts or circumstances which are extrinsic to the mere facts of conversion of non-exempt assets into exempt." *Ante* (quoting *Norwest Bank Nebraska N.A. v. Tveten*, 848 F.2d 871, 875 (8th Cir. 1988)). But our rule is broader, including not only the fact of conversion but also the fact that the debtor's purpose in conversion is to evade his creditors. *See, e.g., Tveten*, 848 F.2d at 874 (conversion not fraudulent "even if the motivation behind the conversion is to place those assets beyond the reach of creditors.").[30] I believe that the Court's analysis of this case is flawed because it fails to recognize this principle.

---

[30] Although neither the motive to evade creditors nor the act of conversion itself is extrinsic evidence of fraud, "[e]xtrinsic evidence can be composed [of] further conduct intentionally designed to materially mislead or deceive creditors about the debtor's position; conveyances for less than fair value; or, the continued retention, benefit or use of property allegedly conveyed . . . for inadequate consideration." *In re Johnson*, 880 F.2d 78, 82 (8th Cir. 1989). *See, e.g., McCormick v. Security State Bank*, 822 F.2d 806 (8th Cir. 1987) (extrinsic evidence of fraud where debtor lied to loan officer about the state of his finances to gain time to liquidate non-exempt assets and purchase exempt home).

The facts upon which the Court bases its holding show only that Mr. Sholdan, as allowed by law, purchased his home with the purpose of putting his assets beyond the reach of his creditors. The Court notes that the purchase was "a radical departure" from his previous lifestyle, initiated only in the face of his imminent liability and on the advice of an attorney. A debtor will always make some sort of departure when he converts property to protect his assets, and it is not normally the business of judges to decide what "lifestyle" a citizen should choose. The Court notes that Mr. Sholdan purchased a more expensive home than he needed or could afford; Mr. Sholdan also required the seller to make additions to the home so that its sale price would precisely equal the amount of assets which he sought to protect with his purchase. This simply shows that Mr. Sholdan sought to protect as much of his assets as the law allowed, a practice that we have found is not evidence of fraud. *Forsberg*, 15 F.2d at 502 (no evidence of fraud in converting assets to take maximum advantage of exemptions). None of this is extrinsic to Mr. Sholdan's act of conversion or his motivation to avoid creditors; it is therefore not evidence of fraud.

This Court has in the context of other exemptions considered whether the value of an exemption was so large that it went beyond the social policies justifying the exemption. *See Tveten*, 848 F.2d at 875-76 (8th Cir. 1988) ($700,000 exemption in annuities went beyond the goal of providing debtors with a fresh start). But we have explicitly rejected this practice for homestead exemptions, deferring to the state legislatures to cap the size of these exemptions. *In re Johnson*, 880 F.2d 78, 82 (8th Cir. 1989). Accordingly, the fact that Mr. Sholdan purchased a more expensive house than the Court thinks he needed is legally irrelevant, except to demonstrate that he was seeking to protect all the assets allowed under the exemption.

The Court characterizes Mr. Sholdan's use of the homestead exemption as a "rank injustice." The Supreme Court of Minnesota has itself "deplored the injustices which have arisen from the application of [the homestead exemption]." *O'Brien v. Johnson*, 148 N.W.2d 357, 361 (Minn. 1967). Nevertheless, in the same case, the Court found no fraud where tortfeasors, before judgment could be entered against them, sold their old home and transferred their residence to a much more expensive property. As in this case, the court found that the tortfeasors' purpose was to evade their creditors. As in this case, the new residence, a large commercial property of which living quarters were only a small part, far exceeded the tortfeasors' practical needs for a residence. The Court found no fraud because the tortfeasors' purpose of evading their creditors was not extrinsic to their use of the homestead exemption. *Id.* at 360. As to the injustice of allowing a debtor to escape his creditor so openly, the Court found that it was bound by well settled law to find no fraud without some extrinsic evidence of fraudulent intent. While Mr. Sholdan's case may not be a sympathetic one, his exemption is allowed under Minnesota law, and, like the Supreme Court of Minnesota, we are bound to allow it to him regardless of our sense of its impropriety.

———

NOTE

Other courts are apparently quite permissive in allowing the debtor to convert nonexempt assets into exempt assets on the eve of bankruptcy.[31] For another thoughtful discussion of the issue, see *In re Crater*, 286 B.R. 756 (Bankr. D. Ariz. 2002).

Problem 4-10

Dispirited lives in southern Illinois and is contemplating filing for bankruptcy protection. The bankruptcy court there has previously ruled that a debtor may not use the state motor vehicle exemption to exempt $1,200 in insurance proceeds due for the destruction of his car. *In re Simpson*, 238 B.R. 776 (Bankr. S.D. Ill 1999). Dispirited is expecting a similar recovery because her car was recently "totaled" in an accident. How can she get around this ruling?

Problem 4-11

Several years ago, Designer borrowed $25,000 on an unsecured basis from Parents to start a new interior design business. The business has not prospered and last month, in contemplation of seeking bankruptcy protection, Designer paid Parents the amount remaining due on the loan: $9,000. Designer has come to see you for bankruptcy advice. You believe that Designer is a good candidate for Chapter 7 relief but expect the trustee to pursue a preference action against Parents. What, if anything, can you advise Parents and Designer to do to avoid having that $9,000 recovered for the benefit of all of Designer's creditors? *See* § 547(c)(4); *In re Schabel*, 338 B.R. 376 (Bankr. E.D. Wis. 2006).

Problem 4-12

Dickens is a resident of Arizona who, until recently, had been a partner in an accounting firm with many large, publicly traded, corporate clients. Six months ago, Dickens' firm received several substantial fines from the SEC for improprieties in its accounting practices. At about the same time, it became a defendant in several class-action lawsuits in which the plaintiffs are seeking hundreds of millions of dollars in compensation for alleged malpractice and

---

[31]   *E.g., In re Stern*, 345 F.3d 1036 (9th Cir. 2003), *cert. denied*, 541 U.S. 936 (2004).

fraud. In the last few weeks, it has become evident that the accounting firm's liability insurance is not adequate to cover all these claims and Dickens therefore has substantial personal financial exposure. Because of that, Dickens went to see Friend, an old college buddy who now practices bankruptcy law, for advice.

During their discussions, Friend learned that Dickens owns the following: a $450,000 home in suburban Phoenix subject to a $410,000 mortgage; a $21,000 Acura subject to an $18,000 security interest; $90,000 in mutual funds; and $15,000 in a deposit account. Under Friend's advice, Dickens sold the mutual funds, deposited the proceeds into the deposit account, and then entered into the following transactions:

(1) Used $20,000 to remodel the kitchen, thereby raising the home's property value to $465,000, and used $45,000 to pay down the home mortgage to $365,000. The Arizona homestead exemption limit is $100,000. Ariz. Rev. Stat. Ann. § 33-1101. *See also* § 522(o); *In re Maronde*, 332 B.R. 593 (Bankr. D. Minn. 2005).

(2) Used $2,000 to pay down the car loan. The motor vehicle exemption is limited to $5,000. Ariz. Rev. Stat. Ann. § 33-1125(8).

(3) Used $300 to buy a new flute. In Dickens' hands, the flute is worth about $250. Neither Dickens nor any of Dickens' dependents plays the flute. Musical instruments are exempt up to $250. Ariz. Rev. Stat. Ann. § 33-1125(2).

(4) Used $500 to buy a dairy cow from Cousin who owns a farm about 100 miles away. Pursuant to the agreement, Cousin will board and care for the cow for $35/month. However, Cousin will pay Dickens $35/month for the right to the cow's milk. These two obligations are expressly to be set off against each other. Pets, horses, milk cows, and poultry are exempt up to a maximum value of $500. Ariz. Rev. Stat. Ann. § 33-1125(3).

(5) Used $12,200 to buy enough food to last six months. The food consists largely of frozen meat, fish, and poultry, but also includes a wide selection of canned foods and drinks. It includes some alcohol and some frozen lobster tails. A six-month supply of food and fuel is exempt without regard to dollar limitation. Ariz. Rev. Stat. Ann. § 33-1124.

(6) Used $25,000 to buy a whole life insurance policy with a cash surrender value equal to the purchase price. Such policies are exempt up to a value of $25,000, provided the debtor has owned them for two years. Ariz. Rev. Stat. Ann. § 33-1126(6).

Shortly after engaging in these transactions, Dickens files for Chapter 7 bankruptcy protection. Some creditors object to the debtor's exemptions.

Others object to the debtor's discharge. How should the court rule on those objections? What difference would it make, if any, if Dickens had engaged in some, but not all, of the transactions described?

In the years leading up to the 2005 amendments to the Bankruptcy Code, there was much discussion of one particular perceived abuse of exemption laws: debtors who take advantage of a very high, often unlimited, homestead exemption.

In 1999, the General Accounting Office released a study on the use of unlimited homestead exemptions in the Southern District of Florida and the Northern District of Texas.[32] The study estimated that, of the 34,374 cases closed in 1998 in those districts, 16,531 involved a homestead exemption. It further estimated the average amount of the homestead exemption in those cases to be $15,525. However, it also estimated that in 156 cases the debtor claimed a homestead exemption greater than $100,000.

The study found that in some of these cases people were able to keep homes while writing off over a million dollars in debt. One example cited was a doctor in Texas who wrote off over $7 million in debt he owed when he lost a multimillion dollar lawsuit but was able to keep his $235,000 home. Another example cited was a Texas bankruptcy attorney who wrote off $1.2 million in debt while she continued to own her $400,00 home.

Congress could have limited the homestead exemption for everyone, as many argued it should. Instead, it changed the rules for which state's exemption laws apply, in an effort to crack down on debtors moving from states with little or no homestead exemption to states such as Florida or Texas, with unlimited homestead exemptions. *See* § 522(b)(3) (explored in Problem 4-2).[33] Congress also enacted § 522(o) and (p). Read those provisions. Subsection (o) is aimed at debtors who convert nonexempt assets into an exempt homestead with an intent to hinder, delay, or defraud creditors. It applies to transfers as much as ten years before the petition. Subsection (p) denies any exemption amount in a homestead above $136,875 attributable to an interest acquired within 1,215 days – 3⅓ years – before the petition.[34]

---

[32] *Use of Homestead Exemptions by Chapter 7 Bankruptcy Debtors in the Northern District of Texas and the Southern District of Florida in 1998*, available at www.gao.gov/archive/1999/gg99118r.pdf

[33] Courts have also shown some hostility to this practice and, when so inclined, have found other ways to frustrate it. *See In re Tanzi,* 297 B.R. 607, 612 (9th Cir. BAP 2003) ("debtors do not have an absolute right to change their domicile just to benefit from another state's exemption laws. Such manipulation, intended to preserve assets at the expense of one's creditors, may constitute inappropriate forum shopping.").

[34] *Cf.* § 522(p)(2)(B) (protecting some interests acquired as a result of an intra-state move).

Whether the BAPCA provisions adequately deal with the "abuse" issue is a matter of debate. *See* Juliet M. Moringiello, *Has Congress Slimmed Down the Hogs?: A Look at the BAPCA Approach to Pre-bankruptcy Planning*, 15 WIDENER L. J. 615 (2006).

Problem 4-13

For the last 18 years, Dixon has lived in a suburb of Sarasota, Florida. Seven years ago, Dixon purchased a home for $350,000. Bank provided $300,000 of financing and secured that loan with a mortgage. Last week, Dixon filed for bankruptcy protection. The schedules filed with the bankruptcy petition list the house as worth $600,000 and the mortgage debt as $100,000. Previously, 1,215 days before the petition, the house was worth $400,000 and the mortgage debt was $250,000.

A. How much of a homestead exemption may Dixon claim? *See* § 522(p). *See also In re Virissimo*, 332 B.R. 201 (Bankr. D. Nev. 2005); *In re Blair*, 334 B.R. 374 (Bankr. N.D. Tex. 2005).

B. How, if at all, would the analysis change if, two years before the petition, Dixon had borrowed $50,000 from Bank and used the loan proceeds to build a backyard pool, with the result that the property was worth $650,000 on the date of the petition and the mortgage debt was $150,000?

Problem 4-14

For 15 years, Dillman owned a home in Springfield, Massachusetts. To pursue a new job opportunity, Dillman sold the home for $400,000 and used all the proceeds to purchase a new home in Quincy, Massachusetts. The new job did not work out and Dillman eventually had to file for bankruptcy protection.

A. If Dillman files for bankruptcy protection 700 days after the move, how much of a homestead exemption will Dillman be entitled to claim? *See* § 522(p).

B. How, if at all, would the answer to Part A change if 700 days before filing Dillman had moved from Springfield, Massachusetts to Bristol, Rhode Island?

C. How, if at all, would the answer to Part B change if Dillman filed 800 days after the move?

Do the results in these three scenarios make sense? How would you have dealt with problem that § 522(b)(3), (o), and (p) all address?

CHAPTER FIVE
CLAIMS

————————

In a Chapter 7 case, once the trustee or the court has determined what property is within the bankruptcy estate and what property the debtor may exempt, the trustee begins assembling the non-exempt property for sale. The sale proceeds will eventually be distributed to creditors in the order and to the extent provided for in the Bankruptcy Code. In order to give each creditor the appropriate share, the trustee's attention now turns from the debtor to the creditors. In other words, the trustee determines which creditors have a claim that qualifies for a distribution and how much is owed to each. Similarly, the debtor in a Chapter 13 case and the debtor in possession in a Chapter 11 case will focus on developing a repayment or reorganization plan, each of which requires determining how claims against the estate will be paid.

In connection with this, it is important to understand some basic terminology; in particular, the distinction between debts and claims. In general, "claims" are the rights of a creditor while "debts" are the obligations of a debtor. Thus, distributions from a bankruptcy estate are used to pay those things qualifying as "claims." *See* §§ 726(a), 1129, 1322, 1325. "Debts," in turn, are potentially subject to the discharge. *See* §§ 727(b), 1141, 1328. Not surprisingly, the terms "debt" and "claim" are correlative. Debt is defined in § 101(12) as "liability on a claim." Thus, the debtor cannot be discharged from an obligation unless the obligation is on a claim. Because of this, the definition of "claim" serves the double function of identifying the obligations that will potentially be paid in bankruptcy as well as the obligations that may be discharged.

Section 101(5) defines "claim" very broadly. Read it and then consider the following problem.

Problem 5-1

Section 101(5)(A) uses at least twelve adjectives for different types of claims. The significance of two of these adjectives – "secured" and "unsecured" – will be discussed in chapter six of this book. The remaining ten adjectives represent five dichotomies:

> liquidated v. unliquidated   fixed v. contingent
> matured v. unmatured   disputed v. undisputed
> legal v. equitable

Identify how each of these adjectives is different. For each adjective, describe a debt of that type. Determine what relationship, if any, exists between these five dichotomies.

Not all claims are "allowed." That is, not all claims get a share of the bankruptcy estate. While the saga of the debtor's financial difficulties may encompass an extended period of time, both before and after the bankruptcy petition, the bankruptcy process itself is, and must be, relatively short. Accordingly, that process is concerned primarily with the debtor's prepetition affairs. Just as the bankruptcy estate is comprised principally of the debtor's prepetition assets, the claims that are allowed, and thereby entitled to share in the estate, are generally restricted to those that arose prepetition and are restricted to the amount due as of the petition date. § 502(b).

What about the costs of administering the bankruptcy estate? In a Chapter 7 proceeding, these typically include the costs of maintaining and selling the property of the estate. In a Chapter 11 proceeding, they may include the costs of running the debtor's business and paying its employees while the reorganization plan is formulated. In both Chapter 7 and Chapter 13 cases, these costs include the trustee's fees. All of these postpetition costs are really obligations of the *estate*, not of the *debtor*. Because of the correlative nature of the terms "debt" and "claim," the Bankruptcy Code does not classify these costs as "claims." Instead, they are labeled as "administrative expenses." They are, however, paid out of the bankruptcy estate. Indeed, as we will see in chapter nine, administrative expenses are entitled to priority in the distribution scheme. §§ 503(b), 507(a)(2).

This last point deserves some emphasis. In this chapter we consider what obligations qualify as claims and which claims are allowed. However, not all allowed claims are treated equally. As we will see in chapter six, secured claims fare much better in bankruptcy than do unsecured claims. As we will see in chapter nine, unsecured priority claims fare better than unsecured nonpriority claims. The allowance process we discuss in this chapter is important because it serves as the foundation for a prepetition creditor's rights in the bankruptcy case. However, other rules may have even greater impact on what the creditor's rights are or how much the creditor will ultimately recover.

A. THE FILING & ALLOWANCE PROCESS

A debtor who petitions for bankruptcy protection is required to list all creditors on the schedules filed with or shortly after the petition. *See* Rule 1007(c); Official Form 6, Schedules D, E, F. Ordinarily, a creditor will receive a proof of claim form – Official Form 10 – with the notice of bankruptcy that the court sends. In general, to share in the distribution of assets from the bankruptcy estate, a creditor must file a "proof of claim." *See* § 501; Rules 3002, 3003. This essentially consists of whatever documentation is necessary for the creditor to demonstrate the validity, nature, and amount of its claim.

In Chapter 7 or 13 cases, the creditor must file a proof of claim within 90 days after the first date set for a meeting of creditors. Rule 3002. However, in Chapter 7 "no-asset" cases – those in which there do not appear to be any non-exempt assets for distribution – the court will inform the creditors not to file any proof of claim unless and until otherwise notified. Rule 2002(e). Chapter 7 no-asset cases are so common that many creditors get into the habit of not filing proofs of claim and, inevitably, some creditors neglect to do so even when there will be distributions.

In Chapter 11 cases, the court fixes a date by which proofs of claim must be filed. However, the creditor need not file a proof of claim if the creditor agrees with the amount and nature of the claim as listed on the debtor's schedules and if the claim is not identified as disputed, contingent, or unliquidated on those schedules. Rule 3003. In such circumstances, the proof of claim is "deemed filed." § 1111(a).

Once a proof of claim has been timely filed, the claim will be "allowed" unless a party in interest objects. § 502. Only those claims that are allowed entitle the creditor to share in the assets of the estate. §§ 726(a), 1123, 1322. Objections to claims are resolved by the court. Rule 3007. They are also infrequent. Most claims in a consumer bankruptcy are allowed and share in available estate assets without any objection from the trustee or any other party. Consider how remarkable this is: a number of claims are satisfied, at least in part, without any judicial determination that money was in fact owed. The parties simply agree, either expressly or implicitly through inaction.

In some instances, however, the trustee or some other party may object to one or more claims. When this occurs, the objecting party may argue that there was no valid debt under state law or that the amount of the debt is lower than as claimed. These circumstances are rare,[1] but when they do occur resolution of the dispute requires a sort of evidentiary hearing before the court, much like the trial of a lawsuit. In general, the bankruptcy court will resolve these disputes in a summary hearing and without a jury.[2] Claims for personal injury torts or wrongful death, however, must be tried in a federal district court, rather than in the bankruptcy court, and the right to a jury is preserved.[3]

---

[1]   Because the trustee's compensation is based on the value of the assets distributed, but is unaffected by the number and amount of claims, the trustee has no financial incentive to closely scrutinize all claims.

[2]   By filing a proof of claim in bankruptcy, the claimant brings itself within the equitable jurisdiction of the bankruptcy court and relinquishes a right to trial by jury. *Granfinanciera, S.A. v. Nordberg*, 492 U.S. 33 (1989).

[3]   28 U.S.C. §§ 157(b)(2)(B), (b)(5) & 1411.

In addition, if the claim arises from a contract that includes an arbitration clause, the validity of the claim may have to be resolved by arbitration.[4]

1. Calculating Claims

Perhaps an example of how a claim is calculated would be useful. Assume that Debtor has a charge account with Retailer. The credit terms require payment within 30 days and charge interest at 12% per year on any amounts remaining unpaid after 30 days (this is unrealistic, but let's use it for simplicity). Retailer is also entitled to attorneys' fees and collection costs up to 10% of the amount of the debt if it has to take any legal action to collect (a fairly standard term).

Three months before filing the bankruptcy petition, Debtor made a $100 charge, for which the debtor has since paid nothing. Two weeks before bankruptcy, the debtor made another $50 charge. Retailer would file a proof of claim for the first $100 charge, plus $3 in interest (this assumes simple interest, without compounding; another unrealistic assumption adopted for simplicity), plus $50 for the second charge. The fact that payment is not yet due for the second charge is immaterial. *See* § 101(5) (defining "claim"). If Retailer had incurred prepetition collection expenses it could add that too, but let's assume there were as of yet no collection costs (the costs of completing the proof of claim do not count because they arose postpetition). Thus, retailer has a claim for $153, all of which is allowable under § 502 because it all arose prepetition.

If, after all the estate assets are sold, the trustee has enough to pay unsecured claimants 10% of their claims (10 cents on the dollar), the trustee will send Retailer a check for $15.30. Absent unusual circumstances, the portion of the debt remaining unpaid will be discharged at the conclusion of the case.

If Retailer had made a clerical mistake and filed a claim for $163, it would have been allowed unless someone objected. § 502(a). It would, therefore, have received a slightly higher distribution than appropriate. Of course, a creditor who intentionally files an incorrect claim could be sanctioned.[5] And an attorney that allows its creditor client to file an incorrect claim may also be sanctioned. *See* Rule 9011(b).

2. Disallowed & Revived Claims

Not all claims are allowed. Some are disallowed because a dispute is resolved in favor of the debtor. Using the example above, let's assume the $100 charge was for the

---

[4]   *See In re Transport Assocs., Inc.*, 263 B.R. 531 (Bankr. W.D. Ky. 2001).

[5]   *See In re Sims*, 278 B.R. 457 (Bankr. E.D. Tenn. 2002).

purchase of a small appliance that did not work. If the Chapter 7 trustee objected, the claim would be disallowed because the trustee may assert all defenses to payment that the debtor has including, as in this case, a breach of warranty. § 502(b)(1).

Other claims are disallowed for policy reasons. Read § 502(b)(2)–(9). Again using the example above, assume that it will take five months for the trustee to liquidate Debtor's assets and distribute the proceeds to creditors. Pursuant to its contract, Retailer is entitled to interest on its claim for that period. However, any claim for "unmatured interest," *i.e.,* interest that had not yet accrued by the date the petition was filed, is disallowed. § 502(b)(2). Unsecured creditors get no postpetition interest.[6] As one author has described it, "unmatured interest" is like "unfallen rain." In other words, if you think about it, "unmatured interest" is an oxymoron.

Examine the other grounds for disallowance in § 502(b), particularly § 502(b)(5). It disallows unmatured support obligations.

A new rule added in 2005 allows – but does not require – the bankruptcy court to disallow up to 20% of a claim on an unsecured consumer debt if the creditor "unreasonably refused to negotiate" a reasonable alternative payment schedule proposed by a nonprofit credit counseling service on behalf of the debtor. § 502(k). Presumably this rule is intended to apply some pressure on creditors to cooperate with debtors and agree to nonbankruptcy settlements. Whether it will have much effect is highly questionable. After all, most consumers who file for Chapter 7 bankruptcy relief have no nonexempt assets. Consequently, allowance or disallowance of a creditor's claim is immaterial. Even in Chapter 13, the prospect of payment is often fairly limited. Furthermore, while the provision allows the debtor to move for this partial disallowance, the debtor has no incentive to do so. Think about it, the debtor is generally unconcerned about how the estate assets are distributed; the debtor no longer really owns them. Beyond all this, the phrase "alternative repayment schedule" is undefined and it is unclear whether it relates solely to the timing (schedule) of payment, or also to the amount or percentage of payment. Thus, it is unclear whether it encompasses a proposal to write off a portion of the debt.[7] If not, it has a remarkably limited scope.

While some prepetition claims are disallowed, a very small number of postpetition claims are treated as prepetition, and then allowed or disallowed on that basis. § 502(h). The most common type of this claim is one arising from repayment of a preference. Consider the following scenario:

---

[6]   Except in the highly unusual case where the debtor is actually solvent, and thus can pay postpetition interest on all claims (not merely those based on a contract that provides for interest). *See* § 726(a)(5).

[7]   While § 502(k)(1)(B)(ii) does refer to proposals that call for payment of at least 60% of the debt within a specified period, it does not expressly indicate that the proposal can include writing off the remaining portion.

Before the petition is filed, Debtor owes a debt to Creditor. Shortly before the petition, Debtor pays that obligation in a manner that prefers Creditor. During the bankruptcy case, the trustee sues Creditor for the preference and recovers the payment. At this point, Creditor is still out money. Creditor extended credit, got paid, and then disgorged the payment. Creditor is still owed. However, Debtor's obligation arose, in at least one sense, postpetition, when the preferential transfer was recovered. And, postpetition claims are normally disallowed. However, the whole point of preference law is to unwind the preferential transfer and treat Creditor as if the transfer had not been made. To do that, the revived obligation needs to be treated as having arisen prepetition, and then allowed or disallowed on that basis. Section 502(h) does that. Section 501(d) then permits Creditor to file a proof of claim with respect to the revived claim.

While on the subject of preferences, § 502(d) is another interesting provision. It is a sort of penalty provision: it disallows the claims of a creditor who fails to repay a preferential transfer. Thus, even if the preferential transfer were of minor consequence, say only $100, and the creditor's other claims exceeded $100,000, that entire large sum would be disallowed until the creditor returned the $100.

Although courts are not in total agreement about this, there is apparently another crafty use of § 502(d). Under § 546(a), an avoidance action under § 547 may not be brought more than two years after commencement of the case. In other words, there is a two-year statute of limitations. However, even if a preference action is time-barred, the trustee can apparently still use § 502(d) to avoid the preferred creditor's claim unless that creditor voluntarily returns the preferential transfer.[8]

Another postpetition claim treated as prepetition is a claim that arises in the "gap period" after the filing of an involuntary petition. As you may recall from chapter two, an involuntary petition does not constitute the order for relief. Instead, the court enters an order for relief some time later, only if it first determines that the petition was proper and the applicable conditions were satisfied. Although the automatic stay goes into effect immediately upon the filing of the petition and enjoins all creditor collection activity, it does not necessarily stop the debtor from incurring new debts. As a result, claims may arise after the petition is filed but before the order for relief is entered. Section 502(f) treats such "gap" claims as prepetition.

---

[8]   *See, e.g., In re America West Airlines, Inc.*, 217 F.3d 1161, 1167-68 (9th Cir. 2000).

3. Tardy Claims

What happens if a creditor attempts to file a proof of claim after the time for doing so expires? The answer depends on the type of case. In Chapter 7, late-filed, non-priority unsecured claims are effectively allowable, but subordinated to timely filed claims (unless the creditor had no knowledge of the bankruptcy in time to file on a timely basis but still managed to file before distributions are made). § 726(a)(2) & (3). Tardy priority claims are allowed and retain their priority as long as the proof of claim is filed before the trustee makes distribution to claims of that priority. § 726(a)(1).[9]

In Chapter 12 and 13 cases, tardy claims are simply disallowed. *See* § 502(b)(9). The subordination provisions of § 726(a) do not apply,[10] and the rules do not permit an extension to be granted to most creditors.[11]

In Chapter 11 cases, late filing is governed by Rule 9006(b)(1), which provides that a bankruptcy court may, for cause, on motion made after the bar date, permit a proof of claim to be filed late if the tardiness resulted from "excusable neglect." In *Pioneer Investment Services Co. v. Brunswick Associates Limited Partnership*,[12] the Supreme Court ruled that "excusable neglect" is not limited to things beyond the claimant's control. The Court explained that the rule on late filing in Chapter 7 is strict because of the need to promptly distribute the estate and close the case. In Chapter 11, on the other hand, the goals are to rehabilitate the debtor through a largely consensual process. Hence, an equitable balancing of the interests at stake is more appropriate. The Court indicated that all relevant circumstances should be taken into account in striking this balance but also agreed with several specific factors identified by the lower court: "the danger of prejudice to the debtor, the length of the delay and its potential impact on judicial proceedings, the reason for the delay, including whether it was within the reasonable control of the [claimant], and whether the [claimant] acted in good faith."[13] It expressly rejected the lower court's conclusion, however, that a claimant should not be responsible for the negligence of its attorney. Thus, the proper question in the case before it was whether the neglect of the claimants and their counsel was excusable.

The Court concluded that the claimants and their lawyer were acting in good faith and that there was no prejudice to the debtor or to the interests of efficient judicial

---

[9]   See also § 502(b)(9), added to the Code by the 1994 amendments, which effectively codified the rulings of some courts. *E.g., In re Vecchio*, 20 F.3d 555 (2d Cir. 1994). It remains unclear what happens if a proof of claim is filed after distribution has been made on priority claims.

[10]   *See* § 103(b).

[11]   *See* Rules 3002, 9006(b)(3); *In re Gardenhire*, 209 F.3d 1145, 1147 n.6 (9th Cir. 2000).

[12]   507 U.S. 380 (1993).

[13]   *Id.* at 393.

administration. While the Court refused to treat as relevant any upheaval in the attorney's office, it did regard as significant the fact that notice of the bar date was provided in an unusual manner. Hence, although there was neglect in the sense that the lawyer was remiss in failing to apprehend the notice, the neglect was excusable.

Problem 5-2

The Venn diagram below shows the relationship between those prepetition obligations qualifying as "claims" and those prepetition obligations entitled to share in estate assets (*i.e.,* allowed claims). For each portion of the diagram, identify an example of an obligation that falls within it. Save your work; we will expand upon this diagram in future chapters.

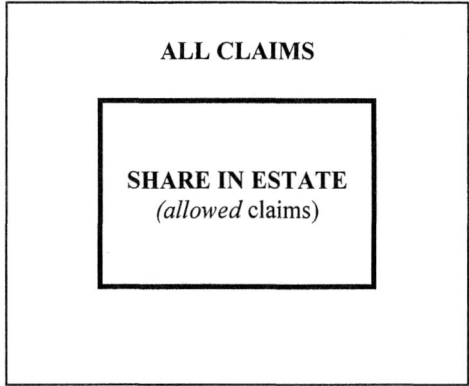

B. Contingent Claims

Not only must the bankruptcy court resolve disputed claims and determine the amount of unliquidated claims, it must also estimate the amount of contingent claims. § 502(c). This can be a very difficult task. By definition, a contingent claim requires that a certain event occur before liability accrues. That means the court must determine the probability that a specified event will happen. This represents a significant change from the law under the old Bankruptcy Act, but is necessary to deal with the fact that bankruptcy proceedings are intended to be of fairly short duration yet permanently affect the rights of creditors, whether they voluntarily participate in it or not. For example, a corporation liquidated in Chapter 7 will be left without any assets after the case is over and, in all likelihood, will be dissolved. A creditor will therefore have no chance to recover post-bankruptcy. The only way the creditor can receive anything is if the creditor's rights qualify as a claim in the bankruptcy proceeding.

Fortunately, the problem of estimating contingent claims does not arise often. When it does, though, the court may be confronted with the problem of deciding whether the claim is sufficiently definite on the date of the petition to merit treatment in the bankruptcy process. This is much like the problem we saw in chapter three of determining whether the debtor's contingent rights should be included in the bankruptcy estate. Here, however, we're focusing on the other side of the bankruptcy balance sheet: whether the debtor's contingent obligations qualify as claims. Consider the following scenarios:

1. Debtor A manufactures building insulation made with asbestos. Many of its employees have begun to suffer the severe effects of asbestosis, resulting from exposure to asbestos. Some of its customers and some end consumers have also become gravely ill. Many of the employees, customers, and consumers have already won products liability actions against Debtor A and the litigation costs for the pending and expected future claims are so substantial that Debtor A files for bankruptcy protection. Do the employees, customers, and consumers who have already been exposed but who have not yet manifested symptoms have a claim? What about the consumers who have not yet been exposed as of the date of the petition but who will later be exposed and who, sometime after that, will become ill? *See In re Waterman S.S. Corp.*, 141 B.R. 552 (Bankr. S.D.N.Y. 1992), *vacated on other grounds*, 157 B.R. 220 (S.D.N.Y. 1993).

2. Debtor B manufactures and sells aircraft. Several aircraft have crashed, resulting in claims against Debtor B. In response, Debtor B filed for bankruptcy protection. Several months before the petition, Baker purchased an aircraft from Debtor B. That aircraft crashes postpetition because of a design or manufacturing defect. Does Baker have a claim on the petition date? What about the people who were passengers on Baker's plane when it crashed? *See In re Piper Aircraft Corp.*, 162 B.R. 619 (Bankr. S.D. Fla.), *aff'd*, 168 B.R. 434 (S.D. Fla.1994), *aff'd*, 58 F.3d 1573 (11th Cir. 1995).

3. Debtor C filed a bankruptcy petition shortly after Spouse filed for divorce. The parties agreed to divide their marital assets equally, with Debtor C retaining sole ownership of the family business (valued at $100,000), Spouse retaining the family home (in which the couple had $50,000 of equity), and Debtor C remaining liable for a $25,000 equalization payment to Spouse. If the divorce is entered and the marital assets divided postpetition, does Spouse have an allowable claim for the equalization payment? *See In re Emelity*, 251 B.R. 151 (Bankr. S.D. Cal. 2000).

To deal with these issues, courts have developed a variety of tests: (1) The Accrued State Law Claim Test; (2) The Conduct Test; and (3) The Prepetition Relationship Test. As the following case indicates, the tests are all similar yet each has a slightly different focus, which can lead to different results in some instances.

IN RE HASSANALLY
208 B.R. 46 (9th Cir. BAP 1997)

Ollason, Bankruptcy Judge:

STATEMENT OF FACTS

On November 13, 1989, Debtors executed a promissory note in favor of Republic Bank ("bank") in the amount of $1,641,500, and entered into a construction loan agreement. The funds were used by Debtors to finance the construction of a 12-unit condominium complex in Gardena, California, completed in 1990. [The Debtors defaulted on the note and filed for bankruptcy protection. The bank obtained stay relief to foreclose upon the property. In taking possession of the property and preparing it for resale, the bank noticed several instances of negligent construction and bank expended funds to make repairs. Bank later purchased the property at the foreclosure sale. Two years later, the bank filed a complaint in state court against the Debtors for negligent construction. The Debtors' bankruptcy case was then reopened to allow them to file a complaint requesting sanctions against the bank for its violation of the discharge injunction.] * * *

ISSUE

The sole issue on appeal is whether the bankruptcy court erred by concluding that § 524 does not enjoin the bank from pursuing its state law cause of action against Debtors for negligent construction because its claim was actually a prepetition claim under federal law that was discharged.

DISCUSSION

* * * Only debts that arise prepetition are dischargeable, and only actions for prepetition claims are enjoined by § 524(a)(2). * * *

Debtors contend that the bank is attempting to hold them personally liable for a prepetition claim. Furthermore, they contend that the bank did not contest the dischargeability of the claim, and there is no category for finding the negligence claim nondischargeable under the Code. On the other hand, the bank contends that its claim, pursuant to state law, did not arise until it acquired the property postdischarge.

Absent an overriding federal interest, the existence of a claim in bankruptcy is generally determined by state law. * * * Claim is defined in § 101(5) as:

(A) right to payment, whether or not such right is reduced to judgment, liquidated, unliquidated, fixed, contingent, matured, unmatured, disputed, undisputed, legal, equitable, secured, or unsecured.

Although the concept of provability was important under the former Bankruptcy Act, it was abandoned in the Bankruptcy Code.

The definition of "claim" was expanded and no longer are claims not fixed as to liability on the date of the filing precluded from participation. The result of the broad definition of "claim" and the abandonment of the concept of provability is that all legal obligations of the debtor, no matter how remote or contingent, will be able to be dealt with in the bankruptcy case.

In re Upstairs Gallery, Inc., 167 B.R. 915, 917-18 (9th Cir. BAP 1994).

In this case it is to the bank's benefit to pursue Debtors' postbankruptcy assets because all debts which would have been dischargeable in a no-asset Chapter 7 case if scheduled, are discharged as if they were scheduled. The bank's claim was based on Debtors' negligent conduct. Thus, if it had been determined to be a prepetition claim, it would have been discharged in the Chapter 7 case. * * *

In California, a civil action ordinarily accrues when the wrongful act is done and liability arises, *i.e.,* upon the occurrence of the last fact essential to the cause of action. The orthodox rule in cases of damage to real property is that the harmful acts occurred, and thus the action accrued, at the time of the construction. This rule is not applied, however, because latent defects are often involved. Instead, the traditional approach of delayed accrual of negligence cases is applied – the statute of limitations does not commence to run until the damage to the plaintiff occurs. Where a construction defect is discovered later, the tortious injury cannot occur until the plaintiff either has actual knowledge of the injury or cause, or could have discovered the injury or cause through reasonable investigation. Thus, the discovery rule dictates when the statute of limitations begins to run. If state law determined when the bank's claim arose, the short answer would be that it arose when the bank discovered or reasonably could have discovered the defects, and the bank averred that it discovered the defects postpetition. State law is predicated not so much on when the claim arose as it is on affording additional time to pursue the claim by a creditor who justifiably did not have knowledge to timely institute action thereon.

While state law determines the existence of a claim based on a cause of action, federal law determines when the claim arises for bankruptcy purposes. *Johnson v. Home State Bank,* 501 U.S. 78, 83 (1991) (holding that the question of whether an interest is a claim for bankruptcy purposes is "to be resolved by reference to 'the text, history, and purpose' of the Bankruptcy Code").

The Code includes contingent and unmatured rights to payment within the definition of claim. By providing for the "broadest definition of claim" Congress intended to ensure that "all legal obligations of the debtor, no matter how remote or contingent, will be able to be dealt with in the bankruptcy case." H.R. Rep. No. 595, 95th Cong., 2d Sess. 1, 309 (1978), *reprinted in* 1978 U.S.C.C.A.N. 5963, 6266. This policy promotes the debtor's fresh start.

A contingent claim is a debt "which the debtor will be called upon to pay only upon the occurrence or happening of an extrinsic event which will trigger the liability of the debtor to the alleged creditor." *In re Fostvedt,* 823 F.2d 305, 306 (9th Cir. 1987). The broad language used to define "claim" "points us in a direction, but provides little indication of how far we should travel." *In re Chateaugay Corp.,* 944 F.2d 997, 1003 (2d Cir. 1991). In other words, courts must decide at what point a contingency is too remote to be called a claim. Bankruptcy courts have applied different tests to determine if a claim arose prepetition.

In this case, the bankruptcy court's legal conclusion was that the debt was not discharged to the extent it was a postpetition cause of action under state law. Under the "right to payment" or "accrued state law claim" test, which the bankruptcy court applied, a claim does not arise in bankruptcy until an action has accrued under relevant substantive nonbankruptcy law. *See In re M. Frenville Co., Inc.,* 744 F.2d 332, 335-37 (3d Cir. 1984), *cert. denied sub nom. M. Frenville Co., Inc. v. Avellino & Bienes,* 469 U.S. 1160 (1985). The Ninth Circuit and other circuits have rejected this test, under a variety of fact patterns, on the grounds that it interprets the term claim more narrowly than Congress intended. *See In re Jensen,* 995 F.2d 925, 929 (9th Cir. 1993) ("[t]o hold that a claim for contribution arises only when there is an enforceable right to payment appears to ignore the breadth of the statutory definition of 'claim' "); *Chateaugay,* 944 F.2d at 1004; *In re A.H. Robins Co.,* 63 B.R. 986, 989-92 (Bankr. E.D. Va. 1986), *aff'd sub nom. Grady v. A.H. Robins Co.,* 839 F.2d 198 (4th Cir.), *cert. dismissed sub nom. Joynes v. A.H. Robins Co., Inc.,* 487 U.S. 1260 (1988). * * * We hold that the bankruptcy court erred as a matter of law by applying this test to grant summary judgment to the bank.

The alleged negligent conduct occurred at the time of the construction, prepetition. Under the "conduct" approach, if a debtor's conduct forming the basis of liability occurred prepetition, a claim arises when that conduct occurs, even though the injury resulting from this conduct was not manifest at the commencement of the case. *In re Jensen,* 127 B.R. 27, 32 (9th Cir. BAP 1991), *aff'd,* 995 F.2d 925 (9th Cir.1993) (affirming, but on the basis of the fair contemplation test); *A.H. Robins,* 839 F.2d at 202-03 (1988) (future uncertain event of manifestation of injury from use of contraceptive device made claim contingent at time the device was implanted); *Edge,* 60 B.R. at 696-705 (court concluding in a tort case that a tort claim arose for purposes of the Code's automatic stay provision at the time the patient received negligent treatment from the debtor dentist).[14] Although the facts of this case fit neatly into a

---

[14]   *Edge* is alternately cited as a conduct or "prepetition relationship" case. The BAP in *Jensen* found

conduct analysis, both parties to this appeal argue that the *Jensen* "fair contemplation" test applies and supports their respective arguments.

The Ninth Circuit Court of Appeals rejected the conduct test as applied to the environmental claims in *Jensen* because it conflicted with CERCLA's goal of cleaning up the environment quickly. In *Jensen,* the California Regional Water Quality Control Board had prepetition knowledge of the presence of toxic chemicals. The California Department of Health Services demanded, postpetition, the cleanup of leakage caused by the chemicals. *Jensen* held that the water board's knowledge could be imputed to the health department. Thus, both the tortious conduct (the threatened leakage) and a fair contemplation of the respective obligations of the parties occurred prepetition.

Jensen concluded that the fair contemplation analysis was the only approach giving "adequate consideration to the policy goals of the environmental laws and the bankruptcy code":

> The only meaningful distinction that can be made regarding CERCLA claims in bankruptcy is one that distinguishes between costs associated with prepetition conduct resulting in a release or threat of release that could have been "fairly" contemplated by the parties; and those that could not have been "fairly" contemplated by the parties.

Jensen, 995 F.2d at 930 (quoting *In re Nat'l Gypsum Co.,* 139 B.R. 397, 407-08 (N.D. Tex.1992)).

Jensen also made a broader criticism of the conduct test:

> The debtor's conduct approach adopted by the BAP in this case is not immune from criticism, either. One commentator has noted that "[d]espite Congress's repeal of the 'provability' requirement and its broad definition of 'claim,' *nothing in the legislative history or the Code suggests that Congress intended to discharge a creditor's rights before the creditor knew or should have known that its rights existed." Discharging CERCLA Liability in Bankruptcy,* 76 Minn. L. Rev. at 348.

Jensen, 995 F.2d at 930 (emphasis added).

Most authorities consider the *Jensen* fair contemplation test equivalent to the "conduct plus," "prepetition relationship" or *Piper* test. *See In re Piper Aircraft Corp.,* 162 B.R. 619, 627 (Bankr. S.D. Fla.), *aff'd,* 168 B.R. 434 (S.D. Fla. 1994), *aff'd,* 58 F.3d 1573 (11th Cir. 1995). The *Piper* test provides:

> [A]n individual has a § 101(5) claim against a debtor manufacturer if (i) events occurring before confirmation create a relationship, such as contact, exposure,

---

Edge persuasive and its holding consistent with the conduct test. *Jensen,* 127 B.R. at 32. *Edge* was cited by the Ninth Circuit *Jensen* case as an example of the prepetition relationship test. In *Edge,* the bankruptcy court held that the tort creditor's claim arose at the earliest point in the relationship between the victim and the wrongdoer-when the dentist performed the negligent act. *Edge,* 60 B.R. at 699.

impact, or privity, between the claimant and the debtor's product; and (ii) the basis for liability is the debtor's prepetition conduct in designing, manufacturing and selling the allegedly defective or dangerous product. The debtor's prepetition conduct gives rise to a claim to be administered in a case only if there is a relationship established before confirmation between an identifiable claimant or group of claimants and that prepetition conduct.

Piper Aircraft, 58 F.3d at 1577.

Recent cases involving future claims have utilized the prepetition relationship test to bring the claims within the bankruptcy proceeding. This appeal does not involve a future claim in the sense of an injury manifesting itself years after the negligent conduct in an unknown claimant. The bank simply discovered original construction defects which it then repaired.

Debtors further contend that the facts of this case are similar to *In re Russell,* 193 B.R. 568 (Bankr. S.D. Cal.1996), where the bankruptcy court applied the prepetition relationship and fair contemplation tests. In *Russell,* the plaintiffs alleged that the debtor sold them certain real property for $715,000 and filed a Chapter 7 bankruptcy 12 days later. The buyers were never listed as creditors because there was no apparent basis for a claim.

Several years later, a plumbing break disclosed that the property had suffered from soil subsidence problems which, according to plaintiffs, were known to the debtors at the time of the sale and not disclosed to the plaintiffs. The plaintiffs sued in state court. The matter was brought back to the bankruptcy court by the debtors' motion to reopen the case to amend the creditor schedules by adding the damage claim and thereby discharge the debt. The plaintiffs in response asserted that theirs was a postpetition claim.

The *Russell* court discussed various aspects of the problem, including the applicability of the prepetition relationship test and *Jensen.* The court first determined that "if the claimant has knowledge (even imputed knowledge) of the existence of the risk or threat of contamination at a particular site, then the claim arose by that point in time for purposes of the Bankruptcy Code." *Id.* at 571. If the claimants, as those in *Russell,* did not have knowledge, then the court next examined the claimants' relationship to the debtor's prepetition act or omission based on factors enumerated in *Piper* to determine if the plaintiffs could have fairly contemplated the claim. The court concluded that the plaintiffs had a prepetition relationship with the debtor:

> After review of the foregoing authorities, and others, this Court concludes that where debtor committed the act or omission complained of prior to filing bankruptcy, and the claimant has a relationship to the act or omission at the time, such as being the patient or a contracting party, the claim arose at that point in time even if there has been no indication or manifestation of the consequences of the act or omission. It is within the fair contemplation of

parties entering into a contract that the other party may breach it, or have made misrepresentations to induce the making of the contract. Thus, a contingent claim arises at that point in time, although it may never mature. The policies of the Bankruptcy Code are best served by an inclusive interpretation of "claim," as § 101(5) contemplates. * * *

Russell, 193 B.R. at 571.

The court then gave the debtor 30 days to add the creditor to an amended creditor's schedule, and the plaintiffs 60 days to file a nondischargeability complaint.

Notice and due process are the fundamental issues affecting the bankruptcy court's ability to discharge future claims of unknown claimants to whom a debtor owes a duty of care based on prepetition conduct. An action for negligent construction may be brought by a downstream purchaser. In addition, state law allows an action to accrue upon discovery of the defect. Nevertheless, the discovery doctrine applied to negligent construction actions implicitly recognizes that the claim's origin was at the time of the wrongful conduct. Unlike the undisclosed subsidence problems in *Russell,* here, it was Debtors' alleged negligent conduct which formed the basis of the contingent claim. The fact that the consequences of the wrongful conduct materialized at a later date does not metamorphose the pre-existing wrongful conduct into future conduct, thereby endowing the results of the wrongful conduct with an independent and unconnected quality. Moreover, the bank in this case was not a classic future claimant.

There is a policy in bankruptcy to deal with any and all claims in the bankruptcy proceeding and to give the debtor a fresh start. Even California imposes a 10-year statute of repose from the completion of construction, in contrast to the indefinite liability exposure under the environmental laws at issue in *Jensen,* or product liability in *Piper.* Such policy considerations to end litigation against the negligent builder are even more acute in a no-asset case such as this one, where the bank – a scheduled creditor – suffered no loss in terms of having access to the estate assets. The bank has not identified any countervailing policy calling for a departure from the conduct test implied from the Code's fresh start policy. On these facts, the determination of when the claim arose under federal law need not be analyzed any further than when the alleged negligent conduct occurred, for a contingent claim arose at that time.[15]

---

[15]   The benefit of looking at it this way is that one does not have to consider what might or might not have been within the parties' fair contemplation. *See Russell,* 193 B.R. at 571. *Russell'*s broad interpretation of a contractual relationship potentially encompasses any possibility including breach, whereas, generally, contracts are written not to be breached but to memorialize an agreement.

Nevertheless, it has been held that the classic conduct cases "presume some prepetition relationship between the debtor's conduct and the claimant." *Piper Aircraft,* 58 F.3d at 1577 (citing *A.H. Robins,* 839 F.2d at 203 and *In re Waterman Steamship Corp.,* 141 B.R. 552, 556 (Bankr.S.D.N.Y.1992), *vacated on other grounds,* 157 B.R. 220 (S.D.N.Y.1993)). It would not be inequitable to apply the conduct test to these facts. The bank was a scheduled creditor based on the loan debt in connection

CONCLUSION

It was undisputed that Debtors' conduct, which allegedly created a construction defect and damaged the property, occurred prepetition. As a matter of law, the bank's negligent construction claim was a prepetition contingent claim which was discharged in Debtors' bankruptcy. Summary judgment in favor of the bank was erroneously granted, and the bankruptcy court's April 18, 1996, order is hereby reversed.

NOTES

1. As the *Hassanally* opinion suggests near the end, one issue often closely related to claim status, particularly when mass torts are involved, is due process. To treat a future injury as a claim and to discharge it without notice to the person who will be injured presents significant constitutional problems. The same types of notice and due process problems arise in class action litigation. For a thoughtful discussion of this, see *Fogel v. Hill*, 221 F.3d 955 (7th Cir. 2000), in which Judge Posner invalidated a settlement between the bankruptcy trustee and the entities that had acquired the debtor's assets. The settlement, which had been approved by the bankruptcy court, barred recovery to anyone whose prepetition purchase of the debtor's defective products resulted in injury (prepetition or postpetition) if they did not file a proof of claim by the bar date, even though some of these potential claimants had no notice or knowledge of the bar date.

2. Despite extensive scholarly and judicial criticism of the Third Circuit's decision in *Frenville*, applying the "accrued state law claim" test, a panel of the Third Circuit reaffirmed it. *Jones v. Chenetron Corp.*, 212 F.3d 199, 206 (3d Cir. 2000). Nevertheless, the court ruled that an individual who was not yet born at the time of confirmation – and for whom the bankruptcy court appointed no representative – would be denied due process of law if barred

---

with the subject real property. Lenders should fairly contemplate the possibility of negligent construction. They have the opportunity to protect against that risk through their inspections which are, presumably, intended to assure the collateral's fair market value and their loan-to-value ratios. At a foreclosure or bankruptcy trustee's sale, what you see is what you get. With the least bit of diligence, even a third party purchaser would know that the defaulting owner was also the builder. The purchaser gets no general warranty of title from the trustee or sheriff, and should not expect a construction warranty from the foreclosed-out owner. That is why, at least in part, foreclosure sales seldom bring fair market value. The purchaser, whether the lender or not, knows that the property is financially troubled, and ought to have constructive notice that there might be defects.

from pressing a claim. It therefore held that that single claim was not discharged. *Id.* at 209-10.

Problem 5-3

Which parties in the bankruptcy proceeding want contingent rights to be treated as a claim and which parties do not? Put another way, is it better for the creditor with contingent rights to have those rights classified as a claim or not?

Problem 5-4

Review the three examples of contingent obligations described beginning on page 175. For each, determine whether it would qualify as a claim under each of the following: (1) The Accrued State Law Claim Test; (2) The Conduct Test; and (3) The Prepetition Relationship Test.

One common type of contingent claim is the claim of the debtor's attorney for legal services contracted for prepetition but rendered postpetition. These are properly allocated to the postpetition period and thus are neither allowable nor dischargeable in a Chapter 7 bankruptcy.[16] The same is largely true in Chapter 13 cases. In Chapter 11 cases, the fees of an attorney employed by the debtor in possession may qualify as an administrative expense and be payable out of the estate, subject to the general requirement that they benefit the estate. §§ 327, 330, 503 1107.

Another common type of contingent claim is that of a person who has guaranteed one of the debtor's obligations. Under the law, most guarantors are entitled to reimbursement from the debtor once they pay the guaranteed obligation.[17] Thus, a guarantor has a contingent claim: a claim contingent on the guarantor paying the creditor. Section 502(e) has special – and important – rules to deal with such claims. After reading that subsection, attempt to answer the problem below.

Problem 5-5

Bank made an unsecured loan to Davenport, and Surety guaranteed payment. When Davenport filed for Chapter 7 bankruptcy protection, the unpaid balance of the loan was $10,000. Assume that distributions in the bankruptcy will pay unsecured creditors 40% of their claims.

---

[16] *See In re Tredinnick*, 264 B.R. 573 (9th Cir. BAP 2001).

[17] *See* RESTATEMENT (THIRD) OF SURETYSHIP AND GUARANTY § 22 (1996).

A. If Bank files a proof of claim in bankruptcy for $10,000 on the loan and Surety files a proof of claim for $6,000 for reimbursement, how much will each receive from the bankruptcy estate? *See* § 502(e)(1)(B). What rights does Bank have against Surety?

B. How, if at all, would the analysis of Part A change if Surety had paid Bank $10,000 on the guaranty before Davenport filed the bankruptcy prepetition?

C. If Bank does not file a proof of claim, does Surety have a claim in bankruptcy? Is it allowable? What should Surety do to protect itself? *See* §§ 501(b) & 502(e)(2).

D. Assume that before the bankruptcy petition Surety paid Bank $4,000 and that on the date of bankruptcy $6,000 remained unpaid. Both Bank and Surety file proofs of claim in bankruptcy. How much will each receive? *See* § 502(e)(1)(B). What rights does Bank have against Surety?

C. EQUITABLE RIGHTS

A "claim" is defined in § 101(5)(B) to include "a right to an equitable remedy for breach of performance if such breach gives rise to a right to payment." What this means is not entirely clear. The structure of this clause – an equitable right is a claim if – strongly suggests that some equitable rights are claims but not all of them. They are claims only if their breach gives rise to a right to payment. However, given that many equitable rights apply only when the right to money damages is inadequate, when does breach of performance give rise to a right to payment? Consider the following three scenarios:

1. Dirtycorp has for years been dumping toxic waste onto several acres of land. The EPA recently secured a court order directing Dirtycorp to clean up the site and to stop all further dumping. Is that order a claim?

2. When Dentist turned 60, Dentist decided to retire. Dentist sold her practice to Purchaser and, as part of the sales agreement, promised not to compete against Purchaser for three years. Dentist entrusted the sales proceeds to Broker, who invested it in high-risk, start-up companies. All the money was lost and Dentist was left with no income or retirement savings. Dentist, who has never had another trade, decides to open a new dental practice in order to generate income. Does Purchaser have a claim against Dentist?

3. Despicable physically abused Spouse during their marriage and stalked Spouse after their divorce. Several months ago, Spouse obtained a court order

enjoining Despicable from coming within 100 yards of Spouse's residence or place of employment. Does Spouse have a claim against Despicable?

Note the implications of these questions. If the equitable right gives rise to a claim, then the holder of the equitable right can potentially share in any distribution from the bankruptcy estate. More significantly, because "debt" is defined as "liability on a claim," § 101(12), if any of these rights qualifies as a claim, the debtor's correlative obligation can potentially be discharged in bankruptcy. Are any of these obligations of a type that a debtor should be able to escape?

The Supreme Court dealt with the first scenario in *Ohio v. Kovacs*.[18] In that case, a state court had issued an injunction ordering the debtor to clean up an environmentally contaminated site. The state court later appointed a receiver to take possession of the property. Cleanup was underway when the debtor filed bankruptcy. After accepting a finding below that all the receiver really wanted was money to defray the cleanup costs, the Supreme Court concluded that the cleanup order had essentially been converted into an obligation to pay money. Accordingly, it qualified as a claim and was dischargeable. The Court emphasized, however, that it was not deciding whether the injunction against further pollution was also a claim.[19]

The third scenario is not the subject of much litigation, probably because most everyone agrees it is not a claim. Violation of the court's no-stalking order will not necessarily give rise to right to payment to the victim, but it will subject the debtor to sanctions for contempt of court.

The second scenario has been the source of some controversy. A few bankruptcy courts have ruled that the right to enforce a covenant not to compete is or at least can be a claim.[20] Consider the following example.

IN RE WARD
194 B.R. 703 (Bankr. D. Mass. 1996)

Queenan, Jr., Bankruptcy Judge.

Seeking to enforce a noncompetition clause in its franchise agreement, The Maids International, Inc. ("Maids") has brought this complaint to enjoin Michael E. Ward and Angela L. Ward (the "Debtors") from owning or operating a maintenance and cleaning service within a fifty mile radius of the franchised territory. Maids contends neither the Debtors' bankruptcy filing nor rejection of their covenant not to compete affects its right to an injunction against the Debtors' competition. I am thus faced with the question of

---

[18]   469 U.S. 274 (1985).

[19]   *Id.* at 284.

[20]   *See, e.g., In re Brown*, 1997 WL 786994 (E.D. Pa. 1997); *In re Ward*, 194 B.R. 703 (Bankr. D. Mass. 1996); *In re Kilpatrick*, 160 B.R. 560 (Bankr. E.D. Mich. 1993).

whether Maids' right to injunctive relief is a "claim" within the meaning of the Bankruptcy Code and hence subject to being discharged. * * *

The Debtors are clearly in breach of their covenant not to compete. Breach of the ordinary contract gives rise only to a claim for damages. Maids, however, has the additional right under state law to obtain an injunction against the Debtors' competition * * *. [B]reach of a covenant not to compete presents a question which has proven difficult for the courts: Do the nondebtor's injunctive rights constitute a "claim" so as to be subject to discharge? The Debtors' discharge hinges upon this issue. A discharge in bankruptcy releases a debtor only as to liability on a "debt," which is defined as "liability on a claim."

The Code defines "claim" as follows:

(A) right to payment, whether or not such right is reduced to judgment, liquidated, unliquidated, fixed, contingent, matured, unmatured, disputed, undisputed, legal, equitable, secured, or unsecured; or

(B) right to an equitable remedy for breach of performance if such breach gives rise to a right to payment, whether or not such right to an equitable remedy is reduced to judgment, fixed, contingent, matured, unmatured, disputed, undisputed, secured, or unsecured.

Maids unquestionably has a "right to an equitable remedy" for breach of the Debtors' covenant. But does the breach also give rise to a "right to payment" within the meaning of the statute? * * *

[One] line of cases holds the other party's right to an injunction against the debtor's competition is not a claim because only monetary rights fall within the statutory definition. These decisions contain no statutory analysis. Some seem largely motivated by facts which evoke no sympathy for the debtor. For example, in *In re Carrere*,[21] the debtor was an actress with a contract to perform in the television series "General Hospital." She filed for bankruptcy in order to reject that contract and be free to perform in another television series for more money. The court was justifiably underwhelmed by her plight.

Focusing more on the statutory definition, some courts hold the nondebtor party's injunctive right is not a claim because it is present only if the remedy at law is "inadequate," or only if the threatened harm is "irreparable," concluding from this that the nondebtor has no right to payment within the meaning of the statutory definition. Although these courts are correct in ruling a right to payment must exist under nonbankruptcy law, their holding that there is no right to payment for breach of a covenant not to compete conflicts with the damage rights of the beneficiary of a covenant as well as with the general standard employed by courts in determining whether a party's remedy at law is adequate. This requires some explanation.

---

[21]   64 B.R. 156 (Bankr. C.D. Cal. 1986).

An injunction against breach of the covenant is a grant of specific performance. As a result of the historical separation of courts of law and equity, such an equitable remedy is available only if the remedy at law, typically damages, is "inadequate." Courts take into account a number of factors in determining whether damages are inadequate. Principal among them are difficulty in proving the existence and amount of damages with reasonable certainty, difficulty in collecting a monetary judgment, and uncertainty that the benefits of a monetary judgment would be equivalent to the promised performance. The rule has been stated as follows: "The adequate remedy at law, which will preclude the grant of specific performance of a contract by a court of equity, must be as certain, prompt, complete, and efficient to attain the ends of justice as a decree of specific performance."[22] Put another way, "the remedy at law, in order to exclude a concurrent remedy at equity, must be as complete, as practical and as efficient to the ends of justice and its prompt administration, as the remedy at equity."[23]

Courts thus compare the remedies at law and equity to see which is more effective in serving the ends of justice. Difficulty in fixing damages is only one factor in that equation. In any event, damages need only be difficult, not impossible, to prove for equitable relief to be available. Comparison of the two remedies usually leads to the grant of equitable relief. Doubts as to the adequacy of the remedy at law are resolved in favor of granting equitable relief. In sum, courts look quite favorably upon equitable relief. This has led one author to conclude that the adequate remedy rule is essentially dead.

Loss of future profits is typically a principal element of damages for breach of a covenant not to compete. The evidentiary problems here for Maids and other covenant beneficiaries are obvious. The proof involves futuristic projections which are especially subject to contest. Courts therefore readily grant an injunction for breach of a covenant not to compete. Indeed, the injured party invariably requests injunctive relief because an injunction gives strong assurance he will receive precisely what was bargained for. This avoids the trauma of future injury, the need to prove damages, and problems in collecting a money judgment. The request for equitable relief has historically been regarded as the election of a preferred remedy.

If the beneficiary of a covenant not to compete elects to receive damages for loss of future profits, he gets the lost profits. Lost profits are a proper element of damages for any breach of contract so long as at the time of the contract the breaching party had reason to know they would be the probable result of breach. The Debtors certainly had that knowledge. The purpose of their covenant was to protect Maids' business. Although damages must be established with reasonable certainty, an approximation rather than mathematical accuracy is all that is required. The perceived difficulty in

---

[22] *National Marking Mach. Co. v. Triumph Mfg. Co.*, 13 F.2d 6, 9 (8th Cir. 1926)

[23] *Walla Walla City v. Walla Walla Water Co.*, 172 U.S. 1, 12 (1898).

proving lost profits is less present today because of the receptive attitude of modern courts toward proof of sophisticated financial data through expert testimony. The award of damages for lost future profits is now a commonplace remedy for breach of all kinds of contracts.

Maids therefore has the right to obtain either damages for the Debtors' future competition or an injunction against the competition. As a result, in the words of the statute, Maids has a "right to an equitable remedy for breach of performance . . . [which] breach gives rise to a right to payment." As an alternative remedy, this right to payment permits a dollar sign to be placed on the equitable remedy, as is done with other claims. Including equitable remedies within the statute's definition of "claim" is therefore supported by a strong bankruptcy policy – equal treatment of similar rights. And because a "claim" is subject to discharge, another important bankruptcy policy is promoted – the policy favoring a debtor's fresh start, unencumbered by past commitments.

In *In re Udell*,[24] the Seventh Circuit came to the opposite conclusion, and in the process added greatly to the confusion in this troubled area of the law. The debtor there had signed an agreement not to compete with his former employer, Standard Carpetland USA, Inc. The covenant was for three years, commencing on termination of employment, and covered a fifty mile radius from the store where the debtor worked. It further provided: "In the event of [the debtor's] actual or threatened breach of the [covenant], Carpetland shall be entitled to an injunction restraining [the debtor] as well as reimbursement for reasonably [sic] attorneys fees incurred in securing said judgment and stipulated damages in the sum of $25,000." Soon after leaving his employment, the debtor purchased a carpet store which he claimed did not compete in the same market as Carpetland's. He sued Carpetland in state court, seeking past due commissions and other compensation. Contending the debtor had breached his agreement not to compete, Carpetland counterclaimed for damages and an injunction against the debtor operating his new store. The state court issued the requested preliminary injunction. The debtor appealed and then filed a chapter 13 petition. Carpetland moved for relief from the automatic stay in order to pursue the state court litigation.

In approving relief from stay as a proper exercise of discretion, the Seventh Circuit in *Udell* held Carpetland's injunctive rights were not a "claim" and hence were not dischargeable in bankruptcy. Although not finding the statutory definition of claim ambiguous, the court nevertheless looked to the legislative history that accompanied the final version of the definition, which reconciled differences in the House and Senate bills. It saw significance in the following statement made on the floors of both houses of Congress:

---

[24] 18 F.3d 403 (7th Cir. 1994).

Section 101(4)(B) [now § 101(5)(B)] represents a modification of the House-passed bill to include [sic] the definition of "claim" a right to an equitable remedy for breach of performance if such breach gives rise to a right to payment. This is intended to cause the liquidation or estimation of contingent rights of payment for which there may be an alternative equitable remedy with the result that the equitable remedy will be susceptible to being discharged in bankruptcy. For example, in some States, a judgment for specific performance may be satisfied by an alternative right to payment, in the event performance is refused; in that event the creditor entitled to specific performance would have a "claim" for purposes of proceeding under title 11.

On the other hand, rights to an equitable remedy for breach of performance with respect to which such breach does not give rise to a right to payment are not "claims" and would therefore not be susceptible to discharge in bankruptcy.[25]

The *Udell* court constructed a confusing alternative test from this floor statement. It seized on the awkward phrase "with respect to which such breach does not give rise to a right to payment" appearing in the last sentence. Because the phrase arguably modifies "equitable remedy" rather than "breach of performance," the court concluded equitable rights are a claim if payment arises from their exercise. This is opposed to the wording of the statute, which clearly requires that the breach, not the equitable remedy, give rise to a right to payment. And the test makes no sense because equitable remedies are typically designed to provide nonmonetary relief. Having thus created a virtually unpassable test, the court ruled it was flunked by the facts before it because the right to obtain liquidated damages arose from the contract, not from an equitable remedy under it.

The *Udell* court also fashioned another test which, if passed, would make an equitable remedy a claim. It here focused on the reference in the floor statement to a right to payment being an "alternative" to the equitable remedy. From this the court concluded *all* right to payment must be an alternative to the equitable remedy. Because state courts would enforce the parties' agreement by granting both damages and an injunction, the court ruled an alternative right to payment was not present, so Carpetland's rights failed this test as well. This reasoning ignores Carpetland's right to damages for future loss, which *is* an alternative to its equitable remedy. The floor statement's reference to a right to payment being an alternative to equitable relief is understandable because the claim for future loss is the monetary equivalent to the right to an injunction against further competition. Nor is there any reason to believe Congress intended that this alternative right to payment be the only right to payment. The statute does not say so. The injured party is obviously entitled to compensation for damages

---

[25] 124 Cong. Rec. H11090 (daily ed. Sept. 28, 1978); S17406 (daily ed. Oct. 6, 1978) (statements of Rep. Edwards and Sen. DeConcini).

already incurred by the time of trial, as well as to an injunction against future competition. The liquidated damage clause before the court was presumably designed to provide this compensation because the parties also agreed upon an injunction to prevent future loss. *Udell* thus commits the double sin of elevating legislative history above the statute's plain wording and then misunderstanding the legislative history.

The real basis for the *Udell* court's holding emerges from the concurring opinion of Judge Raum. He thought the majority opinion "dodges this statute's plain language in an effort to reach a sensible result." To Judge Raum, and one suspects to the other panel members, discharge in bankruptcy of an injunction against competition is like a bankruptcy discharge of an injunction against trespassing, polluting, stalking or battering. Because he thought the debtor's discharge would have similar "patently absurd consequences," Judge Raum believed the plain language of the statute should not be followed.

Judge Raum's reasoning leaves much to be desired as well, quite apart from his willingness to elide what he admits to be the statute's plain wording. The case concerned breach of contract, not trespass, pollution, stalking or battery. Moreover, trespass and the like is prohibited by law, without regard to the existence of an injunction. So a bankruptcy discharge does not terminate the obligation to refrain from such conduct. In the final analysis, the decision in *Udell* comes down to this: The court could not bring itself to equate an injunction against breach of contract with a monetary judgment for breach of contract which is routinely discharged in bankruptcy.

In summary, although the decisions are in disarray, Maids' alternative right to damages from the Debtors' future competition in breach of their covenant not to compete is a "right to payment" within the meaning of the statutory definition of an equitable claim. Hence, under the definition, Maids' injunctive rights constitute a claim. That state courts consider damages inadequate when compared to the equitable remedy of an injunction is beside the point. Although damages for breach of the covenant, particularly damages for lost future profits, are difficult to fix, courts are perfectly capable of doing so. This alternative right to damages fits into the statutory definition of an equitable claim very well. The same breach, a debtor's competition and threat of further competition, "gives rise" to both a damage claim and injunctive rights. The definition imposes no requirement that the claimant elect to receive a monetary payment, that compliance with the injunction require an expenditure of funds, or that the equitable remedy, as opposed to the breach, give rise to a right to payment. Following the statute's plain meaning promotes two fundamental policies of the Bankruptcy Code – the policy favoring a debtor's fresh start and the policy favoring equality among holders of similar rights.

NOTES

1.   After the decision in *Ward*, the Sixth Circuit decided to follow the Seventh Circuit's decision in *In re Udell* and held that the right to injunctive relief for breach of a covenant not to compete is not a claim.[26]

2.   A somewhat related issue regarding non-competition agreements occasionally arises: whether postpetition payments to the debtor pursuant to a prepetition agreement are an asset of the estate. This issue has not generated much disagreement. Most courts addressing the issue have ruled that the payments are estate property.[27] As a result, there is some lack of symmetry: most courts treat the payments to the debtor as sufficiently rooted in the pre-bankruptcy past to be an asset of the estate but the majority treat the debtor's obligation not to compete as something to which the bankruptcy proceeding will not apply. Thus, debtors can neither keep the postpetition money nor discharge the postpetition duty.

Problem 5-6

Duplex owns an unimproved parcel of real estate that is part of a development. All of the lots within the development are subject to restrictions on the size and style of any structure that may be erected. Can Duplex get around those restrictions by declaring bankruptcy and treating the restrictions as equitable rights giving rise to dischargeable claims? Can Duplex discharge the duty to pay dues to the applicable homeowners' association? *See Gouveia v. Tazbir*, 37 F.3d 295 (7th Cir. 1994); *In re Rosenfeld*, 23 F.3d 833 (4th Cir. 1994); *In re Rosteck*, 899 F.2d 694, 697 (7th Cir. 1990). As a matter of policy, what should the answer to these questions be?

One type of equitable right that is clearly not a claim is an ownership interest in the debtor. Thus, the holder of common stock in a corporation that has petitioned for bankruptcy normally has no claim against the estate by virtue of owning that stock.[28] The same is true for those who have invested in a partnership, limited liability company, or other type of entity. Of course, the owners of a business entity may, in addition to contributing assets in exchange for their ownership interest, may have also loaned

---

[26]   *See Kennedy v. Medicap Pharmacies, Inc.*, 267 F.3d 493 (6th Cir. 2001) (injunction is not an alternative to monetary damages because it is available only when money damages are inadequate).

[27]   *See, e.g., In re Alstad*, 265 B.R. 488 (Bankr. M.D. Fla. 2001).

[28]   The stockholder may have a claim if the corporation has declared but not paid a dividend.

money to the entity. In the normal course of affairs, such owners will have a claim for the unpaid balance of the loan but no claim attributable to their ownership interest.

Unfortunately, it is not always easy to distinguish an equity investment from a loan. Several investment structures, such as preferred stock, have elements of both.[29] Beyond that, the parties' behavior may belie whatever the relevant documents would otherwise suggest. In other words, even though an influx of cash or extension of credit to a business entity from its owner is documented as a loan, if the entity never makes payments when they are due and the understanding is that the entity will pay only once it is profitable, the arrangement may be recharacterized by the bankruptcy court as an equity interest rather than a claim.[30]

D.　EXECUTORY CONTRACTS & UNEXPIRED LEASES

Most commercial enterprises and even many consumers enter into various contracts. These include agreements to buy and sell goods, rent real estate, and participate in franchise agreements. It is not uncommon, therefore, for a debtor to have several unperformed contracts when a bankruptcy petition is filed.

If the debtor has fully performed its contractual duties prior to the bankruptcy petition, and thus the other contracting party is the only one whose performance remains due, then the debtor's contractual rights are simply an asset of the bankruptcy estate. Conversely, if the other party has fully performed and only the debtor's performance is due, then the debtor's duties represent a claim against the estate. When neither party has fully performed and some substantial aspect of performance (other than merely the payment of money) remains due from both of them, the contract is labeled "executory" and constitutes both an asset and a liability of the estate.[31]

---

[29] *See, e.g.,* JAMES S. EUSTTICE, FEDERAL INCOME TAXATION OF CORPORATIONS AND SHAREHOLDERS ¶ 4.03 (2007); BORIS I. BITTKER & LAWRENCE LOKKEN, FEDERAL TAXATION OF INCOME, ESTATES AND GIFTS ¶ 91.10 (2003) (both dealing which distinguishing debt from equity for federal tax purposes).

[30] *See In re Official Committee of Unsecured Creditors for Dornier Aviation (North America), Inc.,* 453 F.3d 225 (4th Cir. 2006).

[31] This analysis of what constitutes an executory contract is called the "Countryman" test and is based upon a famous law review article written by law professor Vern Countryman in 1973. Application of the test is often anything but clear. See the discussion in Jay Lawrence Westbrook, *A Functional Analysis of Executory Contracts,* 74 MINN. L. REV. 227 (1989) and Michael T. Andrew, *Executory Contracts Revisited: A Reply to Professor Westbrook,* 62 U. COLO. L. REV. 1 (1991). Moreover, in some settings the result suggested by the Countryman test is generally disregarded because the result is not considered desirable. For example, consider whether a typical security agreement or mortgage is an executory contract. Many times, both the secured party and the debtor have substantial unperformed obligations beyond the payment of money. For example, the debtor often has obligations

In such instances, the other party to the contract has a claim against the estate for the value of the debtor's performance. Yet to reliably value that claim, it is necessary to know whether the trustee (or the debtor in possession in a Chapter 11 case or the debtor in a Chapter 13 case) plans to perform. If the trustee does perform, and does so properly, then nothing else should be owed to the other party. If the trustee instead chooses to breach the contract, then the other party should have a claim that entitles it to share in the assets of the estate.

Section 365 deals with this dilemma by requiring the trustee to assume or reject executory contracts and unexpired leases. § 365(a) & (d). If the trustee rejects the contract or lease, it is treated as a prepetition breach, producing a prepetition claim. § 365(g). If, on the other hand, the trustee assumes the contract or lease, its obligations generally become binding on the bankruptcy estate. However, the trustee is often authorized to assign to another entity the rights and duties of an assumed contract or lease, § 365(f)(1), and if the trustee does so, the bankruptcy estate will have no liability for a future breach by the assignee. § 365(k). The decision to assume or reject must be approved by the bankruptcy court. § 365(a).

There are numerous other rules regarding executory contracts and unexpired leases. Before looking at them, however, it is useful to understand the economic incentives applicable to the decision whether to assume or reject. Consider the following hypothetical:

> Driller, Inc. is an independent oil refinery. Bad market conditions and excessive overhead have caused the company to lose money for the past five consecutive quarters. It has now filed for bankruptcy under Chapter 11. Driller has an outstanding contract with Power Company that requires Driller to furnish 100,000 barrels of oil, a substantial portion of Driller's annual output, to Power Company for $55/barrel. This price seemed lucrative eleven months ago when the contract was negotiated, but now appears to be a disaster. Turmoil in the Middle East has caused the price of oil to rise to $65/barrel. Driller has enough assets to pay unsecured creditors 30 cents on the dollar. What should Driller do?

If Driller assumes the contract, it will have to provide the oil to Power Company at $55/barrel. If Driller rejects the contract, it can sell the oil elsewhere for $65/barrel and Power Company will have a claim for breach of contract. Under general contract principles, Power Company's claim would be for the $10/barrel difference between the

---

to maintain the collateral base and the secured party may have obligations to take reasonable care of collateral in its possession. However, these types of obligations are not considered sufficient to make the mortgage or security agreement an executory contract.

contract price and the prevailing market price.[32] However, as a general, unsecured creditor, Power Company will get only 30 cents on the dollar for that claim.[33] In short, if Driller rejects the contract, it will pay damages to Power Company in "bankruptcy dollars," which are worth far less than real dollars. On these facts, there is an economic incentive to reject (*i.e.,* to breach) the contract.

This example does not mean that rejection is always the better option financially. If, for example, the market price had fallen rather than risen, it would have been in Driller's best interest to assume the contract.

There are two main requirements to assume a contract or lease. First, if the debtor was already in default, the trustee or debtor must promptly cure the default (*e.g.,* pay arrearages), compensate the other party for any resulting loss, and provide adequate assurance of future performance. § 365(b)(1). For this purpose, a contract clause that makes filing bankruptcy or being insolvent a default is ineffective. §§ 365(b)(2), 541(c).

Second, for policy reasons some types of contracts and leases cannot be assumed. These include any contract or lease if applicable nonbankruptcy law excuses the other party from accepting performance from or rendering performance to an entity other than the debtor or debtor in possession. § 365(c)(1). The classic example of this is a personal services contract, such as a contract with an artist to paint a painting.[34] Other agreements that cannot be assumed are contracts to make a loan and nonresidential leases which had been terminated prepetition. § 365(c)(2), (3).

Section 365 also addresses issues of timing. In particular, it contains a variety of rules governing the deadline for the trustee's decision on whether to assume or reject the unexpired lease or executory contract. It also contains rules on whether, before that decision is made, the estate is obligated to perform those duties that become due under the contract or lease. Read § 365(d).

Finally, one of the most controversial issues regarding rejection of executory contracts and unexpired leases is what the consequences are, if any, beyond the creation of a claim for breach that is treated as a prepetition claim. For example, if the estate or the debtor is in possession of leased property, must the property be surrendered to the lessor? If the estate is the lessor, must the lessee give the property to the estate? What if the executory contract is a license of intellectual property, such as a trademark or copyright? If the debtor is the licensor, must the licensor immediately cease using the intellectual property, a consequence that could destroy the licensee's business? Read § 365(d)(4), (h), (i), (j), (n), (p). We will return to some of these issues in chapter twelve.

---

[32] *See* U.C.C. § 2-713(1).

[33] This is no different than if the breach occurred before the bankruptcy petition.

[34] *See* Restatement (Second) of Contracts § 318 comment c.

Problem 5-7

Three years ago, Design Industries ("DI") leased retail space in a building on Main Street in Hicksville. The lease has a 10-year term and calls for rent of $30,000 per year. The lease also provides that each if the following is an event of default: (i) failing to pay rent when due; (ii) the filing of a bankruptcy petition by or against DI; (iii) any assignment by DI of its rights under the lease without the prior consent of Landlord; (iv) DI's failure any time during the term of the lease to provide tax returns and financial statements to Landlord within 30 days after the end of DI's tax year; and (v) DI's failure to maintain an asset-to-liability ratio of at least 1:2 at any time during the term of the lease.

Sixty days ago, DI's tax year ended. Fifteen days ago, because DI had failed to provide Landlord with DI's most current tax return, Landlord sent DI a notice of lease termination. The notice instructed DI to vacate the premises in 20 days. DI has come to you for advice on what, if anything it can do to prevent the Landlord from evicting the DI. Specifically, DI wants to know if filing for bankruptcy would somehow prevent Landlord from terminating the lease. DI also informs you that it has found a sporting goods store that is willing to sublease the space for $40,000 per year. Would entering into a sublease with the sporting goods store and then filing bankruptcy allow DI to capture the $10,000 profit from the sublease? *See* § 365(b)(2), (f).

Problem 5-8

Deanna has a year-to-year lease of an apartment. Two years ago, she entered into a four-year lease of a new car. Both the apartment lease and the car lease make filing for bankruptcy protection a default. Deanna filed for Chapter 7 bankruptcy relief on June 15. On that date, Deanna was current on the apartment rent but six weeks behind on the car lease payments.

A. Is the trustee obligated to make payments to the landlord or the car lessor? *See* § 365(d)(3), (4)?

B. If the trustee fails to act with respect to either lease, what is deemed to happen to them? *See* § 365(d)(1).

C. If the trustee rejects the apartment lease, may Deanna assume it? May Deanna assume the car lease? *See* § 365(p). If not, is the default-on-bankruptcy clause enforceable? *See* § 541(c). Upon rejection, must Deanna give up the apartment and the car?

D. Is the postpetition rent on the apartment an allowable claim? What about the postpetition lease payment on the car?

CHAPTER SIX
SECURED CLAIMS

A. IN GENERAL

The Bankruptcy Code tries to treat claimants equitably, not equally. As a result, and as we will see, the Code distinguishes among claims, such as by giving a select few priority in the bankruptcy distribution scheme and making others exempt from the discharge. By far the most significant distinction the Code makes is the one between secured and unsecured claims. This distinction affects the entire manner in which the claim is handled in bankruptcy and greatly impacts the claimant's recovery. To illustrate this, take a quick look ahead at the bankruptcy distribution scheme under §§ 503(b), 507(a) and 726(a) (see the chart on page 314). Notice what is conspicuously absent from the list: secured claims. This is because *unsecured* claims are treated as general claims against the bankruptcy estate, for which they are generally entitled to their pro rata share. In contrast, *secured* claims are treated as claims to specific property – the collateral – and they extract value directly from that property. Put another way, even though property of the debtor that is subject to a lien will come into the estate – recall the Supreme Court's decision in *Whiting Pools*, excerpted in chapter three – it is really only the debtor's equity in that property that is available for distribution to unsecured claimants. The value of the property encumbered by the lien is reserved for the secured claimant.

Returning to our visual metaphor, whereas most claimants line up for a distribution – administered by the trustee – from the spigot on the right side of the estate vat depicted below, secured claimants syphon off their collateral from the left spigot.

Property of the Estate

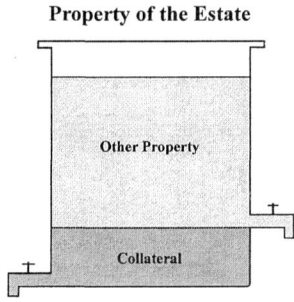

Note, however, that despite the metaphor of assets mixed as a liquid, each secured claimant extracts value from its own collateral, not out of some cocktail formed from all the estate property collateralizing obligations owed to claimants.

Two things follow from this approach to the treatment of secured claims. First, because the Chapter 7 trustee makes distributions only to unsecured claimants, no proof of claim need be filed in Chapter 7 cases for a secured claim. *See* Rule 3002. Second, because secured claims are paid out of the collateral subject to the lien, they are, by definition, satisfied in full. This is so regardless of how the lien was created and even though – as is often the case – little or nothing is paid on nonpriority, unsecured claims.

A corollary to this second point is that a claim is *not* classified as a "secured claim" merely because the creditor has a lien on some of the debtor's property. Instead, it is a secured claim only if and to the extent the claimant has an equitable interest in the debtor's property. The authority for this proposition is in § 506(a), which provides that "[a]n allowed claim of a creditor secured by a lien on property in which the estate has an interest . . . is a secured claim to the extent of the value of such creditor's interest in the estate's interest in such property." This rather cryptic language is really fairly simple to understand: the amount of a secured claim is limited by the value of the collateral. For example, a creditor owed $1,000 who has the only lien on property worth $1,000 or more has a $1,000 claim that is fully secured. However, if the collateral were worth only $800, then the secured claim would be limited to $800, and the creditor would have an unsecured claim for the $200 balance due. In short, creditors with undersecured claims have both a secured claim and an unsecured claim.

The arithmetic gets a bit more complicated – but not much more – if there are multiple liens on the same property. Now, in addition to knowing the amount due to each lienor and the value of the collateral, we also need to know the relative priorities of the liens. Consider the following:

Property Value	$1,000
Debt to Lienor A	$800
Debt to Lienor B	$3,000

If Lien A has priority over Lien B, then Lienor A has an $800 secured claim. That leaves only $200 of value in the collateral left for Lienor B, who therefore has a $200 secured claim and a $2,800 unsecured claim:

Property Value	$1,000
Debt to Lienor A	– $800
Residual Property Value	$200
Debt to Lienor B	$3,000

If Lien B had priority, the result would be substantially different: Lienor B would have a $1,000 secured claim and a $2,000 unsecured claim; Lienor A would have an $800 wholly unsecured claim.

Because secured claims are essentially paid out of the collateral, they are unaffected by the debtor's discharge. This is because a discharge affects only the personal liability of the debtor. It does not affect or cancel the debt itself.[1] If third parties are liable on the debt, they remain liable. For example, a guarantor or other surety remains liable even though the debtor is released as a result of the discharge. A contrary rule would, of course, significantly impair the usefulness of a guaranty. Similarly, if the debt is secured by property of a third party, that property can be reached to the full extent permitted outside of bankruptcy. § 524(e).

The same rule applies if the discharged obligation is secured by a lien on the debtor's property. The debt and the lien continue to exist even after the bankruptcy court has discharged the debtor from personal liability. The Supreme Court recognized this rule more than a century ago in *Long v. Bullard,*[2] and even though the rule is not expressly codified in the current Bankruptcy Code, it is generally understood to survive and several Code provisions imply its continuing vitality. *See, e.g.,* § 506(d). Indeed, a contrary rule would completely undermine the benefit of security agreements and mortgages.

So, to put it succinctly, although the debtor's personal liability may be discharged, the *in rem* liability of any collateral remains unaffected by the bankruptcy discharge.[3]

B.   LIEN STRIPPING

From the brief discussion above, we know that the court must ascertain the value of the collateral to determine whether and to what extent a creditor has a secured claim. Valuation is a recurring issue in bankruptcy. We encountered some of the different standards for valuation in chapter four when we talked about exemptions. The same issue arises in this context, but here there is some statutory guidance. Some, but not much. Section 506(a)(1) instructs that value "shall be determined in light of the purpose of the valuation and the proposed disposition or use of such property."[4]

---

[1]   *See* § 524(a)(2) (providing that a discharge operates as an injunction against efforts to collect a debt "as a personal liability of the debtor").

[2]   117 U.S. 617 (1886).

[3]   Similarly, charges against the debtor's property for which the debtor has no personal liability are still "claims" cognizable in bankruptcy. *Johnson v. Home State Bank*, 501 U.S. 78 (1991) (dealing with an obligation discharged in a previous bankruptcy but secured by a lien on the debtor's home). Thus, a mortgagee has a claim in any bankruptcy case of a co-owner or transferee who did not sign the note or mortgage. *In re Flores*, 345 B.R. 615 (Bankr. N.D. Ill. 2006); *In re Curinton*, 300 B.R. 78 (Bankr. M.D. Fla. 2003); *In re Garcia*, 276 B.R. 627 (Bankr. D. Ariz. 2002).

[4]   More specific guidance is provided in § 506(a)(2) if the debtor is an individual in Chapter 7 or Chapter 13 and the collateral is personal property. In such cases, the collateral is to be valued at its "replacement value" on the petition date.

Assuming there is no valuation problem, are there limitations on the basic concept regarding calculation of the secured claim? Consider the following scenario:

> Shortly before filing for Chapter 7 bankruptcy protection, Despondent inherits the family homestead, which is subject to a mortgage securing a $120,000 debt to Mortgagee. The property, which is not in very good condition, is worth only $39,000 but has great sentimental value to Despondent and Despondent's family. Despondent, with the financial assistance of several family members, very much wishes to retain the property. What right, if any, does Despondent have to do so?

Now read § 506(d), which seemingly covers such situations.[5] It is the first of several provisions of the Bankruptcy Code that can be used to avoid a lien, either in whole or in part.

Subject to two minor exceptions, § 506(d) treats a lien as void to the extent that it secures a claim that is not an allowed secured claim. As we have already seen, § 506(a) treats an allowed claim as a secured claim only up to the value of the collateral. The implication of this is that § 506(d) invalidates a lien to the extent that a creditor is undersecured. Consider how this might work in the hypothetical illustration above.

> Despondent files a complaint to "strip down" Mortgagee's lien to the $39,000 value of the land, on the ground that under § 506(d) Mortgagee's lien is void to the extent it is not an allowed secured claim. Read literally, the provision allows Despondent and the court to do this. If Despondent can borrow enough money to redeem the land by paying off the remaining amount of the lien ($39,000), Despondent can not only keep the property and its sentimental value, but Despondent would also realize any subsequent increase in value of the land. Conversely, Mortgagee would lose that appreciation, something Mortgagee might have been able to realize under nonbankruptcy law, which would normally permit Despondent to free the property from the lien only by paying the full amount of the debt: $120,000.[6]

---

[5]   Because the property is real estate, it is not covered by § 722 and thus Despondent has no right to redeem it. Reaffirmation pursuant to § 524 would not seem to make much sense because the property is worth so much less than the debt. Nevertheless, if the valuation is correct, the mortgagee's economic interest in the property is limited to its $39,000 value and it would arguably be unfair to require payment of any more than that for the debtor to retain it. We will consider redemption and reaffirmation in chapter eight.

[6]   If Mortgagee had foreclosed on the real property, in those states that allow post sale redemption, Despondent would be able to redeem by paying the foreclosure sale price to the purchaser at the foreclosure sale.

Now consider this variation.

> Distressed owns a home worth $95,000 but subject to a first mortgage in favor of Bank and a second mortgage in favor of Finance Company. Distressed owes Bank $100,000 but is current on all payments. Distressed owes Finance Company $40,000 and is a few months in arrears. Distressed files for Chapter 7 bankruptcy protection and wishes to retain the home. Bank is willing, even in the absence of a reaffirmation agreement, to allow Distressed to remain in possession as long as Distressed makes the required monthly payments. Distressed is keen to do this, in part because Distressed has no source of credit to finance the acquisition of another home and in part because Distressed hopes to build up equity in the property by making the monthly payments. However, for Distressed to retain any equity resulting from postpetition payments to Bank (or from any appreciation in the value of the home), Distressed must avoid – "strip off" – the second mortgage. Otherwise, Finance Company stands to capture much of that equity. If read literally, § 506(d) allows Distressed to avoid the second mortgage completely because it does not secure an "allowed secured claim" at all.

Most courts adopted this literal interpretation of § 506(d). However, in *Dewsnup v. Timm*,[7] the Supreme Court rejected this reading of § 506(d) in a strip down case similar to the first illustration. Justice Blackmun, writing for the Court, noted that prior to enactment of the Bankruptcy Code, liens passed through bankruptcy unaffected. *Long v. Bullard*. Under this rule, debtors could not redeem property from a mortgagee unless they paid the debt in full. He then concluded that the new Code did not unambiguously repeal this rule and decided not to assume that Congress wished to grant debtors a broad new remedy to strip down liens. Blackmun therefore interpreted "allowed secured claim" in § 506(d) as not necessarily referencing the definition of that phrase in § 506(a). In his view, all § 506(d) does is avoid liens that secure disallowed claims; that is, claims the debtor does not legally owe. Thus, if an obligation is not truly owing, any lien securing the obligation is void. In essence, the majority read § 506(d) as though the word "secured" in the phrase "allowed secured claim" were deleted. Thus, after *Dewsnup*, a debtor's attempt to strip down a lien in a situation like that involving Despondent would fail. Future appreciation belongs to the secured creditor.

The Court's decision left most commentators astonished. The Court seized on a nonliteral interpretation of the Code that no lower court had adopted and which none of the litigants had even advocated. Justice Scalia was almost apoplectic in dissent. Although he readily conceded that allowing the secured creditor to retain the benefit of subsequent appreciation was quite defensible on policy grounds, the Court's almost

---

[7]   502 U.S. 410 (1992).

anti-textual statutory interpretation was both highly dubious and inconsistent with the Court's prior bankruptcy jurisprudence. On its face, § 506(d) voids a lien to the extent the claim it secures is not both an "allowed claim" and a "secured claim" under § 506(a). Scalia derided the premise of the majority: that somehow "allowed secured claim" in § 506(d) meant something different from the definition of that phrase in § 506(a), another subsection of the very same section! Such one-subsection-at-a-time interpretation was for him frightful, and cast doubt on the meaning of many provisions of the Code using the term.

Some lower courts, concerned about the policy ramifications of retaining completely under water liens, have refused to extend *Dewsnup* to strip off situations akin to that involving Distressed.[8] However, such situations seem on their face to be controlled by the Supreme Court's analysis and a greater number of courts, including two circuit courts, have concluded that liens securing wholly unsecured claims survive.[9] As we shall see, though, something similar to lien stripping may be available through a plan under Chapter 11 or 13, even for partially secured claims if the collateral is not the debtor's home.

One important impact of *Dewsnup* has little to do directly with lien stripping. Prior to the decision, secured claimants in Chapter 7 cases often had to choose between competing strategies. If, in an effort to speed their recovery, they moved for relief from the stay, arguing that the debtor had no equity in the property, they submitted evidence tending to minimize value of the collateral. This set the debtor up to strip down the lien, and effectively redeem the property for potentially far less than the debt. After *Dewsnup*, with lien stripping unavailable, there is no longer such a disincentive to seeking relief from the stay under § 362(d)(2).[10]

---

[8]   *E.g., In re Smith*, 247 B.R. 191 (W.D. Va. 2000), *aff'd*, 1 Fed. Appx. 178 (4th Cir. 2001), *cert. denied*, 532 U.S. 1052 (2001); *In re Yi*, 219 B.R. 394 (E.D. Va. 1998). Of course, if the collateral is consumer goods, then the debtor does not need § 506(d) to avoid the under water lien: the debtor could redeem the property from the lien using § 722 while paying nothing to the lien creditor. We will discuss redemption in chapter eight.

[9]   *See, e.g., In re Talbert*, 344 F.3d 555 (6th Cir. 2003); *Ryan v. Homecomings Financial Network*, 253 F.3d 778 (4th Cir. 2001); *In re Laskin*, 222 B.R. 872, 875-76 (9th Cir. BAP 1998) (also ruling that the debtor had no standing to raise the issue).

[10]   In Chapter 11 and 13 cases, however, the creditor still faces a dilemma. To obtain relief from the stay under § 362(d)(2), the creditor needs to show that debt exceeds the value of the collateral, and thus the creditor normally tries to prove that the collateral has a low value. If relief is nevertheless denied, perhaps because the property is necessary to a successful reorganization, that low valuation may be used to calculate the creditor's secured claim, thereby reducing the creditor's recovery under a plan or reorganization.

C. LIENS ON COLLATERAL ACQUIRED POSTPETITION

The postpetition effect of prepetition security interests is an important issue in business bankruptcies. Section 9-204(a) of the Uniform Commercial Code allows a security interest to attach to personal property acquired by the debtor after the security agreement is signed. In inventory and accounts financing, secured creditors commonly take advantage of this by acquiring a "floating lien" on all of the debtor's inventory and accounts, whether then owned or subsequently acquired. In commercial real estate financing, mortgagees typically take an interest in future rents and profits, as well as in the real estate itself.

The Bankruptcy Code is a little bit hostile to these arrangements. Section 552(a) invalidates prepetition security interests in property acquired postpetition. Because inventory and accounts constantly turn over and newly acquired property is not covered by the security interest, a secured creditor's floating lien could well lose its buoyancy, sinking to insignificance within weeks after the debtor files.

However, § 552(b) significantly limits the effect of § 552(a). Section 552(b)(1) allows secured claimants to retain their liens on postpetition *proceeds* of prepetition collateral. Because "proceeds" is a value-tracing concept while "after-acquired property" is not, the general policy underlying these two provisions seems to be that the creditor's position should not be enhanced by postpetition transactions, but it should not be wholly destroyed by them either. In applying these rules and the policy underlying them, the Fourth Circuit Court of Appeals suggested the following analytical approach:

> In order to determine the applicability of the exception in Section 552(b), we must undertake a [three]-part inquiry. First, is there a prepetition security agreement that by its terms extends to [the creditor's] prepetition inventory, accounts and proceeds? Second, did [the creditor] receive the proceeds of the prepetition inventory and accounts after the filing of the petition? Third, is [the creditor's] postpetition inventory second generation proceeds of prepetition inventory and accounts, and are [the creditor's] postpetition accounts proceeds of postpetition inventory?[11]

In analyzing these questions, the court cited, quoted, and relied on the definition of proceeds under old Article 9. That raises two questions. First, why should the term "proceeds" in § 552(b) carry the meaning ascribed to it in a state law? Second, assuming that the state-law definition is relevant, will the revised Article 9's expansion of the term "proceeds," *see* U.C.C. § 9-102(a)(64), alter the meaning of § 552(b) and expand the postpetition reach of security interests?

---

[11] *In re Bumper Sales, Inc*, 907 F.2d 1430, 1437-37 (4th Cir. 1990).

A related problem is whether postpetition rents are covered by a prepetition mortgage. Invariably, mortgagees of commercial real estate include an assignment of rents with their mortgage, and the postpetition treatment of these rents is often a critical aspect of any subsequent bankruptcy proceeding. Prior to 1994, postpetition rents were covered by a prepetition lien only to the extent provided for by the agreement and by applicable nonbankruptcy law.[12] This created much confusion and variation throughout the country, since real estate law is notably nonuniform and occasionally requires the creditor to take certain actions before the lien on rents arises. The 1994 amendments effectively removed the quoted language, and made the collateralization of postpetition rents more uniform. *See* § 552(b)(2).

There still remains the problem, however, of determining what receivables qualify as "rents." This issue frequently arose in connection with hotels. If the postpetition room charges constitute "rents," they are covered by a prepetition assignment; if not, if they are personal property, such as after-acquired "accounts," they are unencumbered. Courts were split on this issue. The weight of authority held that hotel and motel revenues are "accounts" (*i.e.*, personal property), rather than "rents" (*i.e.*, real property), and thus not encumbered by a prepetition lien.[13] There was, however, significant authority to the contrary, including two circuit court decisions.[14] The 1994 Amendments also addressed this issue by expressly making "fees, charges, accounts, or other payments for the use or occupancy of rooms and other public facilities in hotels, motels, or other lodging properties" subject to a prepetition lien. However, whether this includes hotel charges for food and drink remains open. Moreover, the larger issue remains: when something other than lodging yet related to real estate is involved, are the postpetition monies generated by the activity "rents," and therefore subject to a prepetition lien, or are they "accounts," and therefore free of any prepetition security interest? This issue can be very critical to a bankruptcy case. Consider the amounts charged by nursing homes, for example.[15]

Another related issue derives from the fact that, by its terms, § 552(a) applies only to consensual security interests and mortgages: "liens resulting from any security agreement." Nowhere does it or any comparable provision of the Bankruptcy Code deal with nonconsensual liens. Some state statutes governing attachment and execution

---

[12] *See Butner v. United States*, 440 U.S. 48 (1979).

[13] *See, e.g., In re Northview Corp.*, 130 B.R. 543 (9th Cir. BAP 1991) (applying California law).

[14] *E.g., Financial Sec. Ass., Inc. v. Tollman-Hundley Dalton, L.P.*, 74 F.3d 1120 (11th Cir. 1996) (treating the issue as one of federal law); *In re T-H New Orleans Ltd. Partnership*, 10 F.3d 1099 (5th Cir. 1993), *cert. denied,* 511 U.S. 1083 (1994) (applying Louisiana law).

[15] *See, e.g., In re Hillside Assocs., Ltd. Partnership*, 121 B.R. 23 (9th Cir. BAP 1990) (involving postpetition revenues generated by a nursing home).

allow a creditor to obtain a lien not only on existing property of the debtor, but also on property acquired by the debtor in the future. Garnishment statutes are a common example. While the Supreme Court has ruled that the fresh start policy of bankruptcy prevents a pre-bankruptcy assignment of wages from applying to post-bankruptcy wages,[16] it was never settled under the Bankruptcy Act whether that policy applied to the assignment of other types of future property. With respect to consensual liens, § 552(a) now decides that question against the secured creditor. The ability of nonconsensual liens to encumber postpetition property is an issue that remains open.[17]

Problem 6-1

A. Dragster Auto Mechanics, Inc. runs an automobile repair service. Three years ago, Dragster obtained an operating loan from First Finance and to secure that loan granted First Finance a security interest in all its "inventory and accounts now owned or hereafter acquired." First Finance properly perfected its security interest. Dragster's business has not done well and the corporation recently filed for bankruptcy protection under Chapter 11. After the filing, Dragster purchased $4,000 in new inventory, paying $3,000 in cash and promising to pay the balance in 45 days. After that, Dragster generated $2,000 in accounts receivable based on services rendered to customers after the bankruptcy filing. To what extent, if any, do the inventory and accounts acquired postpetition serve as collateral for Dragster's debt to First Finance? *See* § 522. *See also* §§ 363, 364.

B. Dillon owns and runs Rumble Fish Co., a small, incorporated business. Dillon guaranteed a loan from Lender to Rumble Fish, and secured that guaranty with a mortgage on Dillon's house. The guaranty agreement covers all existing and future indebtedness of Rumble Fish to Lender. After Dillon files for Chapter 7 bankruptcy protection, Lender makes an additional advance to Rumble Fish. Does Lender's claim against Dillon include the postpetition advance? Is the postpetition advance secured by Dillon's house? *See In re Stanton*, 303 F.3d 939 (9th Cir. 2002).

---

[16] *Local Loan Co. v. Hunt*, 292 U.S. 234 (1934).

[17] Yet another related issue involves future advances. In many lending arrangements, the debtor gives the creditor not merely an interest in after-acquired collateral and proceeds to secure existing debt, but also an interest in the collateral to secure any additional loans or credit that the lender may extend to the debtor in the future. These "future advances" clauses are not dealt with in § 552. Instead, the creditor's ability to secure obligations that the bankruptcy estate incurs subsequent to the filing of the petition with property of the estate is governed by § 364. That provision is covered *infra* in chapter twelve.

D. POSTPETITION INTEREST AND EXPENSES

Pursuant to § 502(b), the amount of a claim is determined as of the petition date. Claims for postpetition interest are normally disallowed. § 502(b)(2). Thus, creditors are generally not entitled to compensation for any delay in payment that results from the bankruptcy process. One rare exception occurs when the debtor is actually solvent and is able to pay all claims in full. In such instances, § 726(a)(5) provides that interest at the "legal rate" is payable from the date of the petition. "Legal rate" is not defined.

Another, far more common exception deals with secured claims. Section 506(b) allows an oversecured creditor – that is, a creditor whose interest in the collateral exceeds the amount of the debt owed – to recover from the collateral "interest on such claim, and any reasonable fees, costs, or charges provided for under the agreement under which such claim arose." There are three important points to note about this rule.

First, the introductory clause of the subsection limits the amount of interest the creditor may recover; interest is allowable only to the extent the creditor is oversecured. Thus, for example, a creditor with an allowed claim for $999 and a lien on property worth $1,000 is entitled to only $1 in interest.

Second, the Supreme Court ruled that the presence of the comma after "costs" in § 506(b) indicated that the phrase "provided for under the agreement" modified only the word "charges," not the word "interest."[18] As a result, interest is allowable on oversecured claims regardless of whether the lien was created by agreement or through some nonconsensual manner.[19] This represents a change from pre-Code law, which allowed postpetition interest only on claims secured by consensual liens, and demonstrates a type of strict textual analysis seemingly inconsistent with the Court's methodology in *Dewsnup* three years later.

Third, nothing in § 506(b) dictates what interest rate is to be used. In general, courts have used the contract rate of interest in cases involving consensual liens while resorting to the legal rate of interest with respect to judicial or statutory liens.[20] Query what is most appropriate.

---

[18]   *United States v. Ron Pair Enterprises*, 489 U.S. 235 (1989).

[19]   Charges, however, remain available only if authorized by agreement, and thus are available only to consensual lienors, not statutory lienors. *In re EnRe LP*, 457 F.3d 493 (5th Cir. 2006).

[20]   *See also In re Megafoods*, 163 F.3d 1063 (9th Cir. 1998) (requiring the legal rate of interest on statutory trust funds: funds collected by the debtor as sales taxes and deemed to be held in trust for the state).

Problem 6-2

Creditor has a mortgage on Duplex's apartment building. The mortgage debt is $1,000,000 and the value of the building is at least $1,300,000. The mortgage note calls for interest at the rate of 9% up until default and at 18% after default. The legal rate of interest is 12%, the prime lending rate is 5%, and the market rate for similar apartment mortgage loans is currently about 8%. The mortgage note provides that filing for bankruptcy protection is an event of default. What interest rate should apply postpetition to Creditor's claim? Why?

E.   AVOIDING LIENS

All the information about secured claims in this chapter assumes that the claimant's lien will not be avoided – that is, invalidated – in bankruptcy. However, several different Code provisions allow the trustee or debtor to avoid a creditor's lien.[21] These provisions serve a variety of different policies, yet each is important. If some provision of the Bankruptcy Code allows the debtor or the trustee to avoid the lien, then to the extent the lien is avoided the creditor is left with an unsecured claim. In this context, recall that secured claims are generally paid in full whereas unsecured claims rarely fare so well. In addition, avoiding a lien frees up more of the collateral's value for the estate, or, if the debtor can exempt that value, for the debtor. *See* § 522(g), (h), (i). Thus, lien avoidance is one of the most critical moves that the players may make in the game of bankruptcy. The stakes are often very high.

1.   *Strong-Arm Powers – § 544*

In chapter three we examined the power of the bankruptcy trustee under § 544(b) to avoid certain fraudulent prepetition transfers of the debtor. That power is derived from the nonbankruptcy rights – typically under state law – of an actual unsecured creditor to avoid the transfer. An additional power is granted to the trustee under § 544(a), commonly referred to as the strong-arm clause. This power is based on the power – again under nonbankruptcy law – of a creditor or purchaser to avoid certain liens and other transfers of an ownership interest in property.

---

[21]   In Chapter 11 cases, the debtor in possession has most of the rights and powers of the trustee, including the right to pursue lien avoidance actions. § 1107(a).

There are two principal parts to § 544(a). First, the trustee is granted, as of the date of the bankruptcy petition, the status of a creditor with a judicial lien on all of the debtor's property. § 544(a)(1). If, under nonbankruptcy law, that status gives the trustee priority over some other entity's interest in property of the debtor or property transferred by the debtor, then the trustee may use § 544(a)(1) to invalidate such entity's property rights.

The primary effect of § 544(a)(1) is to invalidate security interests that were unperfected when the bankruptcy petition was filed. Under § 9-317(a)(2) of the Uniform Commercial Code, a lien creditor has priority over a creditor with an unperfected security interest. By granting the bankruptcy trustee the status of a lien creditor, § 544(a)(1) allows the trustee to use U.C.C. § 9-317(a)(2) to invalidate any unperfected security interest in the debtor's property. Note, however, that this right is limited by § 546(b)(1)(A). If the creditor has a PMSI, and therefore has a 20-day grace period in which to perfect under U.C.C. § 9-317(e), the trustee cannot avoid the lien if the debtor files bankruptcy during that period. *See also* § 362(b)(3) (allowing the creditor to file a financing statement despite the automatic stay).

The second major part of § 544(a) is § 544(a)(3). This gives the trustee the status of a bona fide purchaser of all the debtor's real property. Combining this authority with state real property law, the trustee may invalidate unrecorded mortgages on and unrecorded deeds of real property of the debtor.[22]

One major point to note about § 544(a) is that any knowledge the trustee may have of an unperfected or unrecorded interest is irrelevant. Even if state law limits avoidance to those without knowledge of the unrecorded interest, for this purpose the trustee is conclusively presumed to lack that knowledge. § 544(a).[23] More than that, even if every creditor of the debtor had advance knowledge of the unrecorded lien, and thus could not avoid it under state law, the trustee can nevertheless still avoid it. This is in contrast to § 544(b) (discussed in chapter three), which permits the trustee to invoke state fraudulent transfer law. Under that provision, there must be an actual creditor who has the power to avoid the fraudulent transaction, into whose shoes the trustee may step.

One minor point to note about § 544(a)(3) is its potential interaction with § 541(d). Recall that § 541(d) keeps out of the estate the equitable rights to property in which the debtor has merely legal title. Thus, if state law creates a constructive trust in favor of

---

[22] There is occasionally overlap between § 544(a)(1) and (a)(3). In some states, both a judicial lienor and a bona fide purchaser have priority over an unrecorded mortgage. In others, a bona fide purchaser has priority over an unrecorded mortgage, but an unrecorded mortgage has priority over a judicial lien. In instances when both a judicial lienor and a purchaser would have priority, the trustee may use the authority under either paragraph to avoid the mortgage lien.

[23] Although the matter is in some dispute, apparently a debtor in possession in Chapter 11, exercising the powers of the trustee, *see* § 1107, is also conclusively deemed to be without knowledge. *See In re Kim*, 161 B.R. 831 (9th Cir. BAP 1993).

some creditors, those creditors may be able to recover the assets imbued with that trust and avoid loss in bankruptcy.[24] However, if § 544(a)(3) allows the trustee, as a bona fide purchaser of real estate, to take priority over the beneficiary of a constructive trust, then the trustee will be able to keep the property in the estate.[25]

Problem 6-3

On February 1, Diner gave a security interest in certain ovens used as equipment to Bank One for a loan. Bank One never filed a financing statement and thus its security interest is unperfected. On July 1, Diner gave a security interest in the same equipment to Bank Two in return for a loan. Bank Two perfected by filing a proper financing statement the day it advanced the funds. In December, Diner files for Chapter 7 bankruptcy protection. What happens to the two security interests and who among Bank One, Bank Two, and the trustee has priority? *See* §§ 544, 551. *See also* U.C.C. §§ 9-317(a), 9-322(a).

2.   Preferences Revisited – § 547

There are two main intersections of preference law and secured claims. The first involves whether a prepetition *payment* to a secured creditor is an avoidable preference. The second, and by far more important, is whether the *creation of the lien* itself – either voluntarily through grant of a security interest or involuntarily by creation of a judicial lien – is a preferential transfer of property rights.

(a) Prepetition Payments

Recall that an avoidable preference is a transfer that enables the creditor to receive more than such creditor would have received had the transfer not been made and the debtor's estate liquidated under Chapter 7. § 547(b)(5). If a creditor is fully secured – in other words, if the collateral is worth more than the amount of the debt it secures – then the creditor would receive full payment upon liquidation of the debtor's assets.[26] Accordingly, any prepetition payment to such a creditor could not have increased such

---

[24]   *See supra* pages 59-64.

[25]   *See Belisle v. Plunkett*, 877 F.2d 512 (7th Cir. 1989).

[26]   As we have seen, this payment is unlikely to occur in a Chapter 7 bankruptcy proceeding itself because the trustee rarely makes distributions on secured claims, *see* §§ 726, 363. It typically occurs outside bankruptcy when the creditor forecloses on the collateral.

creditor's recovery. In short, it could not be preferential as to that creditor. Looking at it from the trustee's perspective, the estate was not depleted by the transfer. Although the estate lost cash equal to the amount of the payment, it gained an equal amount in the equity in the collateral. Case law on this point is quite sparse, perhaps because the issue is so basic, but it all supports this analysis.[27]

If the creditor were undersecured, however, the result would be very different. For example, consider a creditor who is owed $1,000 and has a valid and unavoidable lien on property worth $800. If the debtor were to pay the entire debt within the preference period and while insolvent, the creditor would be preferred and the transfer would be avoidable (barring the availability of one of the preference defenses). In essence, the creditor would get the $1,000 payment instead of $800 on the secured claim and something less than $200 on the unsecured claim. In fact, if the debtor made only a partial payment to the secured creditor, that too would be preferential. Because the collateral would still remain, any payment necessarily reduces first the unsecured portion of the creditor's claim. If the debtor is truly insolvent and cannot pay creditors in full, the prepetition payment will be preferential and avoidable (again, barring the availability of a preference defense).

So, in sum, prepetition payments to undersecured creditors have preferential effect, and will be avoidable unless some preference defense exists. Prepetition payments to fully secured creditors have no preferential effect as to the secured creditor. The one exception to this is when the creditor's lien is itself avoidable, either as a preference or for some other reason. If the creditor's lien can be eliminated in bankruptcy, then any prepetition payment to such a creditor is essentially a payment to an unsecured creditor.

In some circumstances, however, payments to a fully secured creditor may be recovered because they have the effect of benefitting a different creditor. Consider the following problem.

Problem 6-4

Several years ago, Doubletime gave First National Bank a security interest in certain equipment to secure a loan. First National properly perfected that interest. A few months ago, in desperate need of cash, Doubletime borrowed money from Second Place Finance Company, granting Second Place a security interest in the same property. Second Place perfected its interest that same day. On May 1, Doubletime filed for bankruptcy protection. At that time, the

---

[27] *See In re Powerline Oil Co.*, 59 F.3d 969, 972 (9th Cir. 1995), *cert. denied*, 516 U.S. 1140 (1996) (dicta quoting 4 Collier on Bankruptcy ¶ 547.08, at 547-47 (Lawrence P. King ed., 15th ed. 1995)); *In re C-L Cartage Co.*, 899 F.2d 1490, 1493 (6th Cir. 1990); *Hashimoto v. Clark*, 264 B.R. 585, 608 (D. Ariz. 2001); *In re Teligent, Inc.*, 2006 WL 1030417 (Bankr. S.D.N.Y. 2006) (also noting that the preference plaintiff has the burden of proving that the secured party was undersecured).

debt to First National was $50,000, the debt to Second Place was $20,000 and the collateral was worth $65,000. Previously, in mid-February, Doubletime made a $5,000 payment to First National Bank. Is that payment avoidable as a preference? *See* 547(b)(1). If so, who is liable for it? *See* § 550.

(b) Creation of the Lien

Generally speaking, if a debtor pays an unsecured, nonpriority creditor within the preference period, that payment will be an avoidable preference. § 547(b). The same is true with respect to transfers of property other than cash: § 547(b) applies to transfers of any "interest of the debtor in property" and payments in kind deplete the estate just as much as payments in cash do.

Well, if the debtor transfers a limited property right, such as a lien, rather than complete ownership of a piece of property, the same principle applies. If value was transferred, then the creditor was preferred. Remember too, that an avoidable transfer need not be a voluntary one. *See* § 101(54) (defining "transfer"). If a creditor acquires a lien without the aid of the debtor, which is how most judicial liens are created, that too can be a preferential transfer.

Problem 6-5

Demobilized owns a car worth $8,000. Last week, Chiropractor, who had an outstanding $6,000 judgment against Demobilized, had the sheriff levy on the car. This gave Chiropractor a judicial lien on the car. This week, Demobilized filed for bankruptcy protection. May the trustee avoid Chiropractor's lien as a preference?

Before you jump to the conclusion that all security interests obtained in the preference period are avoidable, remember that an avoidable preference must be a transfer on account of an antecedent debt. § 547(b)(2). Consider the following problem.

Problem 6-6

On February 1, Diner gave a security interest in certain equipment to Bank One to secure a long overdue $6,000 debt. Bank One perfected its lien that day. On February 3, Diner gave a security interest in the same equipment to Bank Two in return for a $8,000 loan. Bank Two advanced the funds and perfected its security interest on that day. On March 1, Diner filed for Chapter 7 bankruptcy protection. What happens to the two security interests?

Assuming the collateral is worth $10,000, who among Bank One, Bank Two, and the trustee has priority and to what extent? *See* §§ 544, 551. *See also* U.C.C. §§ 9-317(a), 9-322(a).

Even if a lien is granted to secure an antecedent debt, any of several preference defenses may come to the aid of the secured party. Their collective reach protects the vast majority of most consensual liens from preference attack. Before examining those defenses, however, one more point must be made. Occasionally, what appears to be one transaction may involve two or more transfers of the debtor's property. When that is the case, it is important to analyze each transfer separately to determine whether it is an avoidable preference. Consider the following problem. In doing so, begin by identifying the different transfers. Then analyze the transfers in chronological order.

Problem 6-7

Digger is a gardener with a number of residential clients. While insolvent and less than three months before filing for Chapter 7 bankruptcy protection, Digger traded a back hoe for a riding mower. The back hoe was subject to a perfected security interest in favor of Seller, who neither knew of nor consented to the trade. At the time, the debt to Seller was $7,000 and the back hoe was worth $6,000 (as was the riding mower). Assume that under Article 9, Seller's security interest continues in the back hoe. Is there an avoidable preference here? *See* § 547(b)(5); U.C.C. §§ 2-312, 9-315(a)(2). In answering this, consider how Digger's other creditors might be affected.

(i) Contemporaneous Exchanges – § 547(c)(1)

One element of an avoidable preference is that the transfer be "for or on account of an antecedent debt." § 547(b)(2). Thus, if an insolvent buyer purchases goods and pays for them at the time of sale by transferring money or other property to the seller, there is no preference because the buyer's payment is contemporaneous with buyer's acquisition of the goods. Put another way, the buyer's assets change form but their overall value remains relatively stable, and thus the buyer's creditors are not injured.

However, suppose there is a short delay between the time the obligation is incurred and the time when property in payment of the obligation is transferred. Does the short delay make the debt antecedent? The Supreme Court considered this issue in *Dean v. Davis*.[28] On September 3, the debtor obtained a loan from Dean on the debtor's promise

---

[28]   242 U.S. 438 (1917).

to secure the loan by a mortgage on all of his property. The proceeds of the loan were used by the debtor to pay a debt owed to a bank. The mortgage was executed on September 10 and recorded the next day. Within a few days, a petition for involuntary bankruptcy was filed against the debtor. The trustee in bankruptcy brought an action under the old Bankruptcy Act to set aside the mortgage. The Supreme Court, in reversing the court of appeals' conclusion that the mortgage could be set aside as a preference, stated:

> Preference implies paying or securing a pre-existing debt of the person preferred. The mortgage was given to secure Dean for a substantially contemporaneous advance. The bank, not Dean, was preferred. The use of Dean's money to accomplish this purpose could not convert the transaction into a preferring of Dean, although he knew of the debtor's insolvency.[29]

Section 547(c)(1) codifies this holding of the Supreme Court. If the parties intend a contemporaneous exchange of a loan for a security interest or mortgage and the transfer of the lien is delayed for a short time but is nevertheless substantially contemporaneous, then the security interest or mortgage cannot be avoided. Now consider the following problem.

Problem 6-8

Finance Company made an unsecured demand loan to Discovered on the morning of April 1. Finance Company believed that Discovered was financially sound. Later that day Finance Company received a credit report indicating that Discovered was in financial difficulty and might be insolvent. Finance Company immediately talked to Discovered, who acknowledged the truth of the credit report. When Finance Company demanded immediate payment of the loan, Discovered offered instead to secure the loan by a mortgage on real property worth more than the amount of the loan. Finance Company agreed and the mortgage was executed on the evening of April 1 and recorded the next day. If Discovered was insolvent on April 1 and filed a petition in bankruptcy on June 1 can the mortgage be avoided as a preference? *See* § 547(b) & (c)(1).

A superficially similar but nevertheless distinct problem arises when the making of the loan and the creation of the security interest are contemporaneous, but there is a delay between the creation of the security interest – *i.e.*, attachment – and perfection of that security interest. There is no true preference in these cases because the transfer of

---

[29] *Id.* at 443.

the security interest to the creditor was not on account of an antecedent debt. *Cf.* § 547(b)(2). Rather, the problem of delayed perfection is the perceived evil of the secret lien. The classic case is that of a debtor in financial difficulty who wants to conceal from general creditors the true state of its financial condition. The debtor obtains an emergency loan from a creditor and grants that creditor a mortgage on real property or a security interest in personal property to secure the loan. The property involved might well be most of the debtor's previously unencumbered assets. If public notice of the transaction were given by recording the mortgage or filing a financing statement with respect to the security interest, the result might be that other creditors will be deterred from giving the debtor further unsecured credit because of the absence of unencumbered assets. To avoid this result the creditor might be induced not to record the mortgage or file the financing statement.

Essentially, the issue is fraud on creditors, not preference. Usually an unrecorded real property mortgage has priority over a creditor who subsequently levies on the property. The holder of an unperfected security interest in personal property takes a greater risk by not promptly perfecting, because an unperfected Article 9 security interest does not have priority over a subsequent judicial lien. However, as we have seen, both an unrecorded mortgage and an unperfected security interest are avoidable by a bankruptcy trustee. § 544(a). Nevertheless, in either case the creditor can protect its lien by promptly perfecting at the first sign that other creditors may levy on assets of the debtor or that a petition for bankruptcy relief is forthcoming. In the classic case, the creditor is an insider with access to information that provides some assurance that the creditor will have sufficient advance notice of facts that will allow the creditor to perfect in time.

It is understandable that there should be a policy against secret liens, and such a policy is expressed in the Bankruptcy Code. However, instead of dealing with the problem directly as a case of fraud on creditors, Congress discouraged the secret lien by a provision in the preference section. In other words, Congress dealt with the evil of secret liens by turning them into constructive preferences. This is accomplished through a conclusive presumption that the lien becomes effective at the time it is perfected, rather than at the time it is actually created. Certain grace periods are allowed for the creditor to perfect. If the creditor does not perfect within these periods, the lien is treated as having been given for an antecedent debt. The relevant provision is § 547(e)(2). Consider the following hypothetical.

> On July 1, Bank lends money to Debtor and receives in return a security interest in some of Debtor's assets. Some time later, Bank perfects its security interest. Unfortunately, a few months later, Debtor defaults and files for bankruptcy protection. Is the transfer of the security interest an avoidable preference?

Under § 547(e)(2), the transfer of a security interest will be deemed to have occurred when the interest attached, if perfection occurred within the following 30 days. Thus, for example, if Bank perfected on July 12, the transfer of the security interest is deemed to have occurred on July 1:

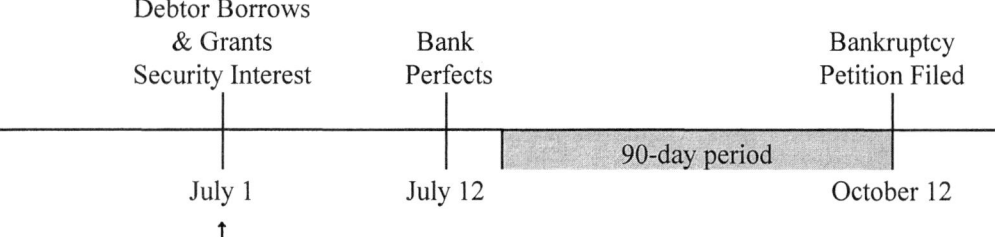

Because of this, the transfer of the security interest is simultaneous with the loan, and not on account of an antecedent debt. The transfer of the security interest therefore cannot be avoidable as a preference. *See* § 547(b)(2).

If, however, perfection occurred more than 30 days after the security interest attached, the transfer of the security interest will be deemed to have occurred when the security interest became perfected. § 547(e)(2). Thus, if the Bank in our hypothetical perfected on August 10, the security interest will be deemed to have been transferred on August 10:

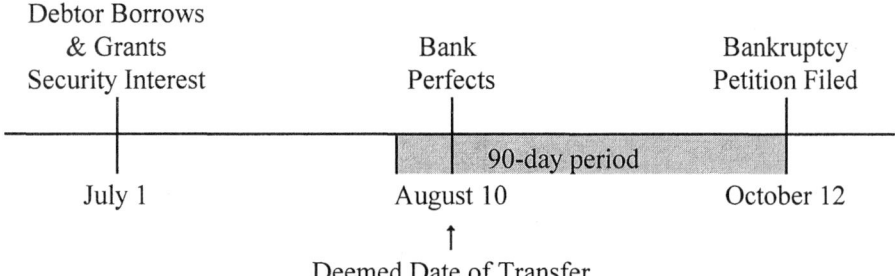

Two consequences flow from this. First, the transfer of the security interest is no longer simultaneous with the loan. Instead, it is substantially after the loan was made and thus on account of an antecedent debt. Second, the transfer of the security interest is more likely to fall within the 90-day preference period, and indeed on these facts now does. The transfer therefore appears to satisfy the prima facie case for avoidance under § 547(b) and can be saved only if it is still a contemporaneous exchange for new value.

In fact, § 547(c)(1) may not provide relief in this situation. Some courts believe that the grace period in § 547(e)(2) effectively places a limit on when grant of a security interest with delayed perfection can still be "contemporaneous" under § 547(c)(1).[30] As a result, while § 547(e)(2) may effectively eliminate the evils of the secret lien, it also ensnares some secured creditors who do not perfect within the 30-day time limit. Other courts were a bit more forgiving when the grace period in § 547(e)(2) was only 10 days.[31] It is unlikely, though, that many courts will treat a lien that, under current § 547(e)(2), is deemed to be transferred more than 30 days after the loan was made, as substantially contemporaneous with the loan.[32] But this does not render § 547(c)(1) meaningless. Consider the following problem.

Problem 6-9

Digger is a gardener with a number of residential clients. While insolvent and less than three months before filing for Chapter 7 bankruptcy protection, Digger sold a front loader for $8,000, its fair market value. Digger had purchased the front loader two years earlier from Supplier, who retained a perfected security interest in it to secure the unpaid portion of the purchase price. At the time Digger sold the front loader, Supplier had been pressuring Digger for payment of the $10,000 remaining due and threatening to repossess the machine. Digger figured that if he went into bankruptcy, the adequate protection payments he'd be required to make to retain possession of the front loader would cost more than the revenue the loader could generate. So he obtained Supplier's permission to sell the front loader free of Supplier's lien. Twelve days after the sale, Digger gave Supplier the $8,000 received from the buyer. Does this transaction involve an avoidable preference? *See* U.C.C. § 9-315(a)(2), (c), (d). In answering this question, be sure to identify each transfer and the date on which it is deemed to have occurred.

When § 547(c)(1) does not apply, there may be one hope for the lienholders who delayed recording their mortgage or perfecting their security interest. Consider the following problem.

---

[30] *See, e.g, In re Arnett*, 731 F.2d 358 (6th Cir. 1984) (so ruling when the § 547(e)(2) grace period was only 10 days).

[31] *See In re Dorholt, Inc.*, 224 F.3d 871 (8th Cir. 2000); *Pine Top Ins. v. Bank of American Nat'l Trust & Sav.*, 969 F.2d 321 (7th Cir. 1992); *In re Marino*, 193 B.R. 907 (9th Cir. BAP 1996), *aff'd without opinion*, 117 F.3d 1425 (9th Cir. 1997); *In re Stephens*, 242 B.R. 508 (D. Kan. 1999).

[32] *But cf. In re Kerst*, 347 B.R. 418 (Bankr. D. Colo. 2006) (treating a 47-day delay in perfection as substantially contemporaneous because the delay was largely attributable to a third party over whom neither the debtor nor the preference defendant had any control).

Problem 6-10

When interest rates started to fall, Dryden decided to refinance the $95,000 mortgage on Dryden's home. On July 1, Dryden closed on the refinancing transaction by executing a note and mortgage in favor of Refinance Company. On the same date Refinance Company disbursed the loan proceeds to Original Mortgagee. Because of a clerical error in Refinance Company's office, the new mortgage (and the release of the original mortgage) were not recorded until August 15. Dryden filed for Chapter 7 bankruptcy protection on October 20. May the trustee avoid Refinance Company's mortgage? *Compare In re Lazarus*, 478 F.3d 12 (1st Cir. 2007), *with In re Lee*, 339 B.R. 165 (E.D. Mich. 2006).

(ii) PMSI Protection – § 547(c)(3)

Constructive preferences also arise – probably even more frequently – when a lender takes a PMSI. This is because, for preferences purposes, the transfer of the lien cannot occur until the debtor acquires rights in the collateral, § 547(e)(3), and the debtor typically does not obtain such rights until after the loan is made. For these constructive preferences, § 547(c)(3) provides a bit more protection. It too has a 30-day time limit of perfection, but that limit – like the 20-day grace period in U.C.C. § 9-317(e) – begins not when the loan is made, but when the debtor receives possession of the property, which is usually some time later.

Problem 6-11

On April 1, Bank loaned $30,000 to Doctor by crediting that amount to Doctor's checking account. The loan agreement signed on that day provided that certain described equipment already owned by Doctor would secure the debt.

A. Doctor filed a Chapter 7 bankruptcy petition on June 1. When is the security interest deemed to have been transferred and is that transfer avoidable if:
1. Bank filed a financing statement covering the equipment on April 16? *See* § 547(b), (c)(1),(e)(2).
2. Bank filed a financing statement covering the equipment on May 5?
3. Bank never filed a financing statement.

B. How, if at all, would the analysis of Part A change if both parties intended that Doctor would use the loaned funds to buy some new equipment,

Doctor did so use the funds, and Doctor received the new equipment on April 10? *See* § 547(c)(1), (3), (e)(2), (3).

(iii) Improvement of Position Test – § 547(c)(5)

Some types of collateral – accounts receivable and inventory, in particular – normally turn over within a relatively short period of time. As the debtor operates its business, old accounts are collected and inventory is sold, while new accounts are generated and new inventory is acquired. Creditors who provide accounts or inventory financing do not want to restrict themselves merely to accounts and inventory on hand when the loan is made and the security agreement is signed. Such assets are likely not to be around by the time the debtor defaults. Instead, they typically want a "floating lien," one that extends to the new accounts and inventory as soon as the debtor acquires it. Article 9 of the Uniform Commercial Code expressly authorizes such floating liens by allowing a security interest to attach to after-acquired property. *See* U.C.C. § 9-204(a).

For debtors who seek bankruptcy protection, it is of course likely that some of the accounts and inventory on hand at the date of the petition will have been acquired within the preference period. Because a security interest in this new collateral is, by virtue of § 547(e)(3), deemed to have been transferred to the secured party when the debtor acquired it, that transfer might be an avoidable preference under § 547(b) if the debtor was insolvent at the time. Remember, there is a rebuttable presumption that debtor is insolvent during the 90 days preceding bankruptcy. § 547(f).

Section 547(c)(5) provides a limited exemption to such preference avoidance, in recognition of the fact that the secured creditor is not really preferred to the extent the new collateral replaces old collateral. A typical case to which § 547(c)(5) applies is as follows:

Scenario One

Secured Party is secured by all accounts receivable of Debtor, who at all relevant times is insolvent. The amount of the debt and the value of the collateral are as follows on the beginning of the preference period and on the day of the bankruptcy filing:

	90th Day Before Petition	Petition Day
Debt	$100,000	$100,000
Value of Collateral	$60,000	$60,000
Insufficiency	$40,000	$40,000

Despite the seeming constancy of these numbers, assume that, as is likely, some portion of the collateral – say $10,000 – on hand on the date of the petition, was acquired within the preference period. Let's stop for a moment. How can it be that the debtor acquired collateral worth $10,000 during the preference period but the overall value of the collateral did not change? The most likely explanation is that the debtor also sold collateral worth $10,000 during the period. The point is that you must begin the preference analysis by identifying the potentially avoidable transfers within the preference period (*e.g.,* the attachment of the creditor's security interest to newly acquired inventory), and those transfers need not be reflected in the chart depicted above. Let's now return to the analysis.

Although § 547(e)(3) would deem the security interest in that new collateral to have been acquired during the preference period and therefore potentially avoidable under § 547(b), § 547(c)(5) provides a preference defense. Because Secured Party's net position has not been improved by the additional collateral (the creditor was undersecured by $40,000 at both the start and the end of the preference period), the transfer of the security interest is not avoidable.

Under 547(c)(5), a secured creditor's position is deemed to be improved – thereby giving rise to an avoidable preference – not if its secured claim is increased, but only if its unsecured claim is reduced. Consider this variation:

Scenario Two

	90th Day Before Petition	Petition Day
Debt	$100,000	$110,000
Value of Collateral	$60,000	$70,000
Insufficiency	$40,000	$40,000

This time, although the total value of the collateral increased by only $10,000, assume that $20,000 of the collateral on hand on the date of the petition was acquired within the preference period. Assume that the increase in the debt is attributable to interest that has accrued on the secured obligation.

Under § 547(b) there is a potential $20,000 preference. Nevertheless, § 547(c)(5) protects all of it. Secured Party was $40,000 undersecured on the 90th day before the petition and was also $40,000 undersecured on the petition date. Secured Party's position has not really improved, and thus there is no avoidable preference.

Of course even with § 547(c)(5), creation of the security interest in some of the new collateral may be avoidable. Consider this version of the facts:

Scenario Three

	90th Day Before Petition	Petition Day
Debt	$100,000	$110,000
Value of Collateral	$60,000	$75,000
Insufficiency	$40,000	$35,000

Although the total value of the collateral increased by only $15,000, assume that $25,000 of the collateral on hand on the date of the petition was acquired within the preference period. As in Scenario Two, the increase in the debt is attributable to interest that has accrued on the secured obligation.

Under § 547(b) there is a potential $25,000 preference. This time § 547(c)(5) protects only part of it. Secured Party was $40,000 undersecured on the 90th day before the petition but is only $35,000 undersecured on the petition date. Secured Party's position has improved by $5,000 and thus the § 547(c)(5) defense is unavailable to protect that $5,000 in improvement.

Now let's throw in a wrinkle:

Scenario Four

	90th Day Before Petition	Petition Day
Debt	$100,000	$90,000
Value of Collateral	$60,000	$70,000
Insufficiency	$40,000	$20,000

Assume that $20,000 of the collateral was acquired in the preference period. The reduction in the debt was the result of pre-bankruptcy payment on the secured obligation.

Note, there are two potentially preferential transfers here: (1) the $10,000 prepetition payment; and (2) the security interest in the $20,000 of newly acquired collateral. Thus, the Secured Party's preference exposure is $30,000.

Whether the payment is in fact avoidable will probably depend on whether it was made in the ordinary course of business. *See* § 547(c)(2). However, the ordinary course of business defense has no applicability to the creation of the security interest in the new collateral. It applies only to payments.[33]

In contrast, § 547(c)(5) defense does not apply – at least not directly – to the payment. According to its language, it applies only to the creation of a security interest. Thus, the transfer of the security interest in the new collateral will be protected, if at all, by § 547(c)(5). Here, Secured Party went from being $40,000 undersecured to only $20,000 undersecured. Secured Party's position was therefore improved by $20,000. As a result, the transfer of a security interest in the $20,000 of new collateral is avoidable; § 547(c)(5) provides no help.

Problem 6-12

Does this result of Scenario Four make sense? In answering this question, consider what would have happened if there had been no prepetition $10,000 payment and the debt had remained $100,000. How much of the security interest in the new $20,000 of collateral would have been avoidable?

---

[33] *See, e.g., In re Four Winds Enterprises, Inc.*, 100 B.R. 24 (Bankr. S.D. Cal. 1989); *In re Silve*, 86 B.R. 230 (Bankr. D. Mont. 1988).

As confusing as § 547(c)(5) may seem, this rule is reasonably workable when applied to accounts receivable. To calculate the reduction of the deficiency (or, in other words, the improvement of position) it is necessary to value the collateral. Because accounts are simply claims against third parties, they are normally valued at face value, *i.e.*, the amount owed by the account debtors, perhaps reduced by some statistically determined amount that reflects the fact that some accounts will turn out to be uncollectible or will entail collection costs.[34]

The valuation problem created by § 547(c)(5) is far more complex with respect to inventory. If the unit value of inventory is constant and the number of units of inventory on hand at the date of bankruptcy is greater than the number of units on hand at the beginning of the preference period, § 547(c)(5) can properly be applied to make voidable as a preference the improvement in position represented by the increased number of units. However, in some cases the value of a secured party's collateral may increase during the preference period without the increase being preferential. To take a case not covered by § 547(c)(5), suppose Secured Party has a security interest in Airline's inventory of fuel and the price of oil – and hence the value of fuel – simply increased in during the preference period. No preference results from the improvement in Secured Party's position because the appreciation was not the result of any transfer from the debtor.

This analysis is consistent with the very notion of a security interest. Under the Uniform Commercial Code, security interests attach to property of the debtor, not to the value represented by such property. It is quite clear that if an undersecured secured party has a security interest in a unit of oil which doubles in value because of a change in world oil prices, the secured party is entitled to the benefit of the increase in value. The security interest is in the unit of oil, not in its value. As is the case generally with owners of property interests, the secured party takes the risk, and gets the benefit, of changes in value of the interest.

Sometimes, however, changes in value result both from appreciation and from additions to the collateral. Because § 547(c)(5) does not purport to deal with the former but certainly covers the latter, sorting through the details can be quite problematic. Moreover, an increase in value of inventory often is partly the result of an investment of labor or materials. The best example is a security interest in inventory consisting of unfinished goods. As those goods are transformed into finished goods – contributions of value made by the debtor – § 547(c)(5) may properly be read to mean that the secured party is the recipient of preferential transfers.

The case that follows considers the question of how the inventory of a retailer should be valued for the purposes of § 547(c)(5).

---

[34] *Cf.* Neil B. Cohen, *Value Judgments: Accounts Receivable Financing and Voidable Preferences Under the New Bankruptcy Code*, 66 MINN. L. REV. 639, 664 (1982) (suggesting a number of other possible definitions of value).

IN RE EBBLER FURNITURE AND APPLIANCES, INC.
804 F.2d 87 (7th Cir. 1986)

Flaum, Circuit Judge.

This suit involves an issue of first impression in this circuit. We are asked to define the word "value" as used in § 547(c)(5). We affirm the bankruptcy court and district court in their use of "cost" as the proper measurement in this case. However, we remand this case for further proceedings to determine the precise amount of the preference payment that the defendant received.

The present action is by the trustee in bankruptcy under § 547(b) and (c)(5), to recover preference payments received by the defendant. Ebbler Furniture and Appliance, Inc. ("Ebbler"), filed a voluntary petition for relief pursuant to the Chapter 7 liquidation provisions of the Bankruptcy Code.

The appellant, Alton Bank & Trust Co. ("the Bank"), was the inventory financier for Ebbler. * * *

The issue presented is the interpretation of "value" as used in § 547(c)(5) of the Bankruptcy Code. * * * Section 547(c)(5) prevents a secured creditor from improving its position at the expense of an unsecured creditor during the 90 days prior to filing the bankruptcy petition.

The first step in applying section 547(c)(5) is to determine the amount of the loan outstanding 90 days prior to filing and the "value" of the collateral on that day. The difference between these figures is then computed. Next, the same determinations are made as of the date of filing the petition. A comparison is made, and, if there is a reduction during the 90 day period of the amount by which the initially existing debt exceeded the security, then a preference for section 547(c)(5) purposes exists. The effect of section 547(c)(5) is to make the security interest voidable to the extent of the preference. Of course, if the creditor is fully secured 90 days before the filing of the petition, then that creditor will never be subject to a preference attack.

The language of section 547(c)(5), the "value of all security interest for such debt," was purposely left without a precise definition. Furthermore, it has been persuasively argued that the other Bankruptcy Code sections' definitions of "value" would not be useful for section 547(c)(5) purposes. Thus, the only legislative guidance is "that we are to determine value on case-by-case basis, taking into account the facts of each case and the competing interests in the case." *Matter of Lackow Bros., Inc.*, 752 F.2d 1529, 1532 (11th Cir. 1985).

The method used to value the collateral is crucial in determining whether or not the bank received a preference. The Bank urges that we adopt an "ongoing concern"[35] value standard, which, in this case, would be cost plus a 60% mark-up. * * *

Another view as to how value should be defined is proposed by Professor Cohen. He proposes an after-the-fact determination of value. In his article discussing accounts receivable, Cohen argues that the courts should look at the actual manner in which the collateral was liquidated, *i.e.*, cost or ongoing concern. Whatever method is used to dispose of the collateral, Cohen argues, should be used to value the collateral 90 days before the filing of the bankruptcy petition. Neil Cohen, *"Value" Judgments: Account Receivable Financing and Voidable Preferences Under the New Bankruptcy Code*, 66 Minn. L. Rev. 639, 664 (1982). At least one circuit has found Cohen's reasoning useful, though not necessarily adopting it as a rigid rule. *Matter of Missionary Baptist Foundation*, 796 F.2d 752, 761-62 (5th Cir. 1986).

In *Missionary Baptist Foundation*, the appellate court remanded to the district court for factual determinations as to whether or not the bank improved its position during the preference period. The court noted, however, that merely remanding for factual findings may not be sufficient in light of the ambiguous meaning of "value" in section 547(c)(5). The Fifth Circuit quoted with approval Cohen's admonition of an individualized approach in defining value and his hindsight solution of the problem. We follow the Fifth Circuit's lead and hold that under Section 547(c)(5) value should be defined on a case by case basis, with the factual determinations of the bankruptcy court controlling.

In the present case we affirm the bankruptcy court's use of cost as the method for valuing the collateral for 547(c)(5) purposes. * * *

Easterbrook, Circuit Judge, concurring.

This case involves the meaning of "value" under § 547(c)(5). I join the court's opinion, which concludes that the statute does not require bankruptcy judges to use one universal definition. The history of condemnation litigation shows that a single definition of "value" is not within judicial grasp. Still, we need not leave bankruptcy judges and litigants adrift. Security interests must be appraised with some frequency in bankruptcy litigation. The greater the uncertainty in the legal rule, the harder it is to settle pending cases. "Anything goes" is not a durable rule. The parties cannot know their entitlements until bankruptcy, district, and appellate courts have spoken. One

---

[35] The authors of Collier on Bankruptcy suggest that in a liquidation case under chapter 7, "it would seem that liquidation value should be used, although other standards of value may be appropriate under certain circumstances. In a case under chapter 9, 11, or 13, it would seem that a going concern value should be used although liquidation value may be appropriate in certain cases." We deem it inappropriate to bind this circuit to these distinctions at the present time. We note, however, that the Eleventh Circuit has cited this distinction, although commenting that it "is not set in cement." We believe that the definition of "value" should be individualized and variable enough so as to be tailored to each situation.

important function of appellate courts is to provide additional clarity, when that is reasonably possible. It is possible here. The bankruptcy judge did better than to avoid an abuse of discretion. He decided the case correctly.

"Value" is defined for a purpose, which sets limits on the admissible standards of appraisal even though it does not govern all cases. Section 547(c)(5) requires the court to find whether the secured creditor improved its position at the expense of other investors during the 90 days before the filing of the petition in bankruptcy. This calls for two appraisals, one on the day of filing and one 90 days earlier, using the same method each time, to see whether there was an improvement in position. The only standard that might plausibly be used in this case is wholesale cost of goods, because that is the only standard that could have been applied on both dates.

Wholesale cost is also the appropriate standard as a rule because wholesale and retail goods are different things. A furniture store, a supermarket, or the manufacturer of a product (the three situations are identical) uses raw materials purchased at wholesale to produce a new item. In the retailing business the difference between the wholesale price and the retail price is the "value added" of the business. It is the amount contributed by storing, inspecting, displaying, hawking, collecting for, delivering, and handling warranty claims on the goods. This difference covers the employees' wages, rent and utilities of the premises, interest on the cost of goods, bad debts, repairs, the value of entrepreneurial talent, and so on. The increment of price is attributable to this investment of time and other resources. The Bank does not have a security interest in these labors. It has an interest only in its merchandise and cash on hand.[36] The value of its interest depends on what the Bank could do, outside of bankruptcy, to realize on its security. What it could do is seize and sell the inventory. It would get at most the wholesale price – maybe less because the Bank would sell the goods "as is" and would not offer the wholesaler's usual services to its customer. The Bank does not operate its own furniture store, and if it did it would still incur all the costs of retailing the goods, costs that would have to be subtracted from the retail price to determine the "value" of the inventory on the day the Bank seized it.

To give the Bank more than the wholesale value is to induce a spate of asset-grabbing among creditors, which could make all worse off. If the Bank gets the whole increment of 'value (from wholesale to retail) during the last 90 days, other creditors may respond by watching the debtor closely and propelling it into bankruptcy when it has a lower inventory (and therefore less "markup" for the Bank to seize). The premature filing may reduce the value of the enterprise. There are other defensive measures available to creditors. The principal function of § 547(c)(5) is to reduce the

---

[36] The Bank's interest in the proceeds of sales is not the same as an interest in the whole retail price for unsold inventory. An ongoing financing arrangement provides for operating expenses, too, to come out of proceeds. The security interest on any given day covers only identified proceeds, an asset that is identifiable and significantly smaller than the wholesale or retail value of the entire inventory.

need of unsecured creditors to protect themselves against the last-minute moves of secured creditors. It would serve this function less well if goods subject to a security interest were appraised at their retail price.

Too, the Bank's security interest does not reach the "going concern" value of the debtor; it had security in the *goods*, not in the *firm*. To value the inventory in a way that reflects "going concern" value is to give the Bank something for which it did not contract. At all events, this wrinkle does not make a difference. If Ebbler had been sold as a going venture 90 days before the filing of the bankruptcy petition, the buyer of the business would have paid only wholesale price for Ebbler's inventory. If Ebbler had been at the peak of health, the buyer would have paid no more for inventory. A buyer would not have paid retail, because it would have had to invest the additional time and money necessary to obtain the retail price. So whether Ebbler is valued as a defunct business or as a going business sold to a hypothetical buyer on the critical date, wholesale is the right valuation, because it reflects the price that a willing buyer would pay after arms'-length negotiation. (The "going concern" value of Ebbler is reflected in its name, reputation, customer list, staff, and so on – things in which the Bank did not have a security interest.)

To put this differently, a willing buyer of a flourishing retail or manufacturing business will not pay more than the wholesale price for inventory of goods or parts on hand, because this buyer could purchase the same items on the market from the original sellers. Why pay Ebbler $500 for a sofa when you can get the same item for $200 from its manufacturer? Nothing would depend on whether Ebbler planned to stay in business. The court therefore properly does not allow the outcome of this case to turn on the fact that Ebbler chose a Chapter 7 liquidation rather than a Chapter 11 reorganization. Chapter titles are of little use in valuing assets under § 547(c)(5). A "liquidation" may be a sale of the business en bloc as an ongoing concern, and a "reorganization" may be a transition from one line of business to another.

The difference between the wholesale and retail prices of the inventory is the compensation that the other factors of production – the employees, landlords, utilities, *etc.* – obtain for their services. To appraise Ebbler's inventory at "retail" is to award to the Bank the entire value of the work done during the last 90 days by these other creditors of Ebbler. It is to allow the Bank to improve its position at their expense. Because a valuation at "retail" would produce exactly the consequence that § 547(c)(5) is designed to avert, the bankruptcy court wisely chose to appraise the goods at wholesale. The court leaves to another day the question whether retail price is ever an appropriate measure of value under § 547(c)(5). The observation that the bankruptcy court has leeway, however, does not imply that the court's discretion should be exercised without reference to the function of § 547(c)(5) and the limits of the security interest.

QUESTION

How, if at all, would the analysis of the court in *Ebbler Furniture* have been different if the Bank had held a perfected security interest in all of the debtor's assets, rather than merely its inventory?

(iv) Trilateral Preferences

Recall the discussion of the *DePrizio* case beginning on page 107. The initial legislative effort to overrule that case was not fully effective. At least one court, following the lead of a few commentators, noted that use of the term "recover" in § 550(c) limits the scope of that provision to payments, and that avoidance of a security interest under § 547 does not involve a recovery of property.[37] Thus, if a debt guaranteed by an insider is secured or, as in the case itself, a previously existing security interest is perfected, more than 90 days but less than one year before the bankruptcy filing, the security interest could be avoided.

The more recent 2005 Amendments added subsection (i) to § 547 to change this result. It completely insulates the noninsider from preference avoidance for any kind of transfer made more than 90 days before the petition was filed.

(v) Statutory Liens – § 547(c)(6)

Statutory liens, even those arising during the preference period, are immune to preference avoidance. § 547(c)(6). The rationale for this is probably related to the fact that the timing of their creation is not something readily subject to the control of either the debtor or the creditor. It may also have to do with the fact that statutory liens necessarily protect creditors whom the law wishes to favor. However, such liens are subject to their own special avoidance rules in § 545. *See infra* page 243.

3.   *Liens Impairing Exemptions – § 522(f)*

(a) Consensual Liens

Section 9-204(b)(1) is one of the few consumer protection rules incorporated into Article 9 of the Uniform Commercial Code. It prohibits a security interest from

---

[37] *E.g., In re Williams*, 234 B.R. 801 (Bankr. D. Ore. 1999).

attaching to after-acquired consumer goods unless the debtor acquires rights in the collateral within 10 days after the secured party gives value. The theory underlying it is that consumer debtors might not comprehend the significance of an after-acquired property clause in a written security agreement, and thus might well unintentionally encumber their property if the law allowed them to do so.

Nevertheless, creditors can still acquire a security interest in consumer goods. Typically this occurs when the creditor obtains a PMSI, by providing the funds the debtor uses to purchase the collateral. However, it can arise in other circumstances as well. Article 9 allows a creditor to take a security in whatever consumer goods the debtor already owns.

When the creditor perfects a nonPMSI through possession – a transaction commonly referred to as a pledge – the debtor likely understands the significance of parting with the goods: fail to pay and the goods will be sold. If the creditor perfects by filing, however, consumer debtors may not appreciate the significance of any security agreement they sign. This is particularly troublesome if the property involved is something the debtor could otherwise exempt. Such property – *e.g.*, clothes and household furnishings – is generally far more valuable to the debtor than to any creditor because the debtor's cost to replace it will likely exceed whatever amount a creditor could realize through a forced sale.

This is where § 522(f)(1) comes in. It allows a debtor in bankruptcy to avoid a nonpossessory, nonPMSI in household goods and furnishings, tools of trade, and professionally prescribed health aids to the extent that the lien impairs an exemption to which the debtor would otherwise be entitled. In essence, it provides a level of consumer protection that Article 9 fails to provide.

It is important to recognize, however, four limitations on the scope of this provision. First, it applies only if the security interest is not a PMSI. This limitation probably exists for two reasons: (1) even consumer debtors probably expect that if they buy goods on credit and don't pay, they'll lose the goods; and (2) without this limitation, consumers would find it extremely difficult to obtain credit for many needed purchases.

The Bankruptcy Code does not define or identify when a security interest is a PMSI. As a result, courts have generally looked to state law to determine whether a security interest qualifies as a PMSI.[38] Article 9 of the Uniform Commercial Code, as revised in 1998, provides that neither refinancing a PMSI nor providing additional collateral will undermine PMSI status. U.C.C. § 9-103(f). However, these rules are expressly made inapplicable to consumer transactions, *see* U.C.C. §§ 9-102(a)(26), 9-103(h), and thus pre-revision case law on these issues remains relevant.[39] Many courts treated

---

[38] *See, e.g., In re Billings*, 838 F.2d 405, 406 (10th Cir. 1988); *Pristas v. Landaus of Plymouth, Inc.*, 742 F.2d 797, 800 (3d Cir. 1984).

[39] In addition, even if Congress implicitly adopted the state-law meaning of a PMSI when it enacted

refinancing and cross-collateralization as things which destroyed PMSI status under old Article 9.[40] Accordingly, several courts have made similar rulings for the purposes of § 522(f) of the Bankruptcy Code.[41] Others have ruled to the contrary and treated refinancing as irrelevant.[42] Still others, dissatisfied with either position, have taken a case-by-case approach:

> The courts in this Circuit which have discussed this issue have not adopted the Transformation Rule or the dual status rule. The courts view a strict application of the Transformation Rule as working "unintended and inequitable results" including the result of discouraging creditors from refinancing consumer loans. The problem with the dual status rule is the difficulty of determining when any one item is paid off and released from the security agreement. Thus, the courts have taken a case by case approach which examines whether the refinancing agreement can be characterized as merely a renewal of the original obligation or as a novation. A renewal allows the purchase-money character of the security to survive. A novation, on the other hand, extinguishes the purchase-money character of the loan.
>
> The * * * test for delineating between a novation and a renewal is the "degree to which the original obligation of the debtor has changed and, to some extent, on any additional consideration which was conveyed by the debtor to the creditor." The greater degree of change in obligation or increase in obligation, the more likely a novation will be found. The Court believes this middle-of-the-road approach is the proper test.
>
> In applying the test * * * to the facts in the present case, this Court finds that the purchase-money character of the security interest * * * did not survive the refinancing. The entire character of the Debtor's obligation to the Creditor was changed by the loan agreement entered into on May 25, 2001. Not only was additional money loaned, but the repayment period was extended from one year to 31 months and the interest rate was increased from a "one year, same

---

the Bankruptcy Code in 1978, it is not clear that the meaning of the term does or should change when state law changes.

[40]   Refinancing occurs when a new debt is substituted for the old debt and the debtor is released on the old debt. Some courts refer to this as transformation of the debt from a PMSI debt to a non-PMSI debt. Cross collateralization occurs when the PMSI collateral also secures non-PMSI debt or when non-PMSI collateral secures PMSI debt.

[41]   *See, e.g., Dominion Bank of the Cumberlands v. Nuckolls*, 780 F.2d 408, 413 (4th Cir.1985); *In re Matthews*, 724 F.2d 798 (9th Cir. 1984) (per curiam).

[42]   *See, e.g., Billings*, 838 F.2d 405; *Pristas*, 742 F.2d 797; *First Nat'l Bank & Trust Co. v. Daniel*, 701 F.2d 141 (11th Cir. 1983).

as cash" arrangement to the rate of 21% per annum. Finally, the items of furniture which were originally security only for the $1,250 loan became collateral for both loans; and, on this basis, the Court finds that the refinancing agreement at bar must be characterized as a novation, rather than merely a renewal of the original obligation.[43]

The second limitation is that § 522(f)(1)(B) covers only that property which would otherwise be exempt. If the debtor lives in a jurisdiction that offers very limited exemptions to debtors, then § 522(f)(1)(B) will be of very limited help.

Third, it covers only specified – albeit in broad terms – types of property. Consider the following brief case.

IN RE MCGREEVY
955 F.2d 957 (4th Cir. 1992)

Luttig, Circuit Judge:

* * * Section 522(f) allows debtors to avoid liens on "household goods" that are "held primarily for the personal, family, or household use of the debtor or a dependent of the debtor." The issue presented in this case – an issue of first impression in this Circuit – is whether Mrs. McGreevy's shotgun and rifle are "household goods" within the meaning of [§ 522(f)(1)(B)].

Essentially two different definitions of "household goods" have achieved prominence in the bankruptcy courts since the adoption of the Bankruptcy Code in 1978. For the reasons explained below, we reject both of these definitions in favor of a definition that we are convinced is more faithful to congressional intent as evidenced in the language of section [522(f)(1)(B)].

The first definition used by the bankruptcy courts focuses upon the necessity of the goods to the debtor as he emerges from bankruptcy. Under this definition, only those goods that are found and used in or around the debtor's home *and* that are necessary to a debtor's fresh start after bankruptcy constitute "household goods. * * *

The "necessity" requirement is derived not from the language of the statute itself, but from a passage in the House Report to the Bankruptcy Reform Act of 1978 which emphasizes that the purpose of the Bankruptcy Code is to ensure debtors a fresh start after bankruptcy. The courts that have imposed a "necessity" requirement have extrapolated from this statement of general purpose the requirement that household goods must be necessary to a fresh start to be eligible for lien avoidance. The courts that have adopted this definition have uniformly held that firearms are not "household goods" within the meaning of section [522(f)(1)(B)].

---

[43]   *In re Snyder*, 2001 WL 34059294 (Bankr. C.D. Ill. 2001).

We reject this definition of "household goods" because it is without foundation in the statute. Section [522(f)(1)(B)] does not limit those household goods that are eligible for lien avoidance to only those goods that are necessary to a debtor's fresh start. It allows debtors to avoid liens on *all* exempt household goods that are held primarily for personal, family, or household use. Congress, in effect, decided that all such goods are important to a debtor's fresh start following discharge from bankruptcy, and it effected that decision by the inclusion – without limitation – of "household goods" in the list of personal property eligible for lien avoidance.

The second definition adopted in the bankruptcy courts is more defensible as a matter of statutory construction than the first definition, but it is still, we believe, inadequate. Under the second definition, "household goods" include *all* goods typically found and used in or around the home, whether or not they would be considered strictly necessary to a debtor's fresh start.[44] * * *

This second definition is more tenable than the necessity definition because it is grounded at least generally in the statutory text. Ultimately, however, it fails to capture fully the functional nexus between the good and the household that distinguishes a household good from a good that happens (even typically so) to be used in the house. We therefore reject this definition as well.

We adopt for this Circuit, instead, a definition of "household goods" that explicitly incorporates a requirement of a functional nexus between the good and the household. Such a requirement, we believe, is necessary for the term to have the ordinary, common-sense meaning that was intended by Congress. Any definition that does not include a functional requirement will inevitably suffer from either the underinclusiveness of the necessity definition, because some goods are used to support and facilitate daily life within the home that are not strictly necessary to day-to-day living, or the overinclusiveness of the proximity definition, because some goods are found and used within the home that are not used to support and facilitate home life. Indeed, the absence of such a requirement in the two generally accepted definitions is, we suspect, the cause of the inability of the courts to agree on either definition.

---

[44] Some courts have expanded this proximity definition to include "personal property that enables the debtor and his dependents to live in a usual convenient and comfortable manner or that has entertainment or recreational value . . . *even though it is used away from the residence or its curtilage." In re Bandy,* 62 B.R. 437, 439 (Bankr. E.D. Cal. 1986) (emphasis added) (televisions, VCR, computer, answering machine, video game, stereo system, golf clubs, exercise equipment, tools, and lawnmower are household goods). * * * These courts have not attempted to justify this definition under either the language or the structure of the statute, and we are unable to do so. A *sine qua non* of a "household" good must be use in or around the house. Any definition that does not incorporate *at least* this requirement is wholly without mooring in the statute. Congress provided lien avoidance for "household goods," not for all "goods."

We conclude that the requisite functional nexus exists where – and only where – the good is used to support and facilitate daily life within the house. It is the household good's use *for these purposes* that distinguishes it from a good that is merely located and used within the house. Pots and pans are household goods *because* they are used to support and facilitate daily household living; a model car collection, by contrast, is not a household good because it serves no such purpose.

We therefore hold that "household goods" under section [522(f)(1)(B)] are those items of personal property that are typically found in or around the home and used by the debtor or his dependents to support and facilitate day-to-day living within the home, including maintenance and upkeep of the home itself.

There are doubtless many goods found and used in the house for which a *per se* rule will be possible under the definition that we adopt above. For other goods, whether or not they constitute "household goods" will necessarily depend in whole or in part upon the cultural environment of the debtor or the geographic location of the debtor's household. We are not prepared to conclude at this time that firearms *per se* can never be household goods under our newly-adopted definition, and we need not go so far on the record before us. Even assuming that firearms can be household goods under certain circumstances, it is clear that Mrs. McGreevy's firearms are not household goods.

The McGreevys live in a townhouse that adjoins other townhouses in a complex of twenty-five to thirty townhouses. Mrs. McGreevy testified that her husband uses the rifle primarily to hunt deer in Maryland, West Virginia, and Pennsylvania, and occasionally uses both firearms for target practice at her uncle's house or in Mount Airy. Mrs. McGreevy noted only as an afterthought that the shotgun and rifle are also available for protection of their home and persons. It is evident from this testimony that the McGreevys' firearms are usually, if not exclusively, used away from the McGreevy household and its curtilage and that they are not used by the McGreevys to support or facilitate their day-to-day household living. Accordingly, they do not constitute "household goods" under [§ 522(f)(1)(B)], as we define that term today.

———

NOTES

1.   Enactment of § 522(f) led the FTC to promulgate a rule imposing similar restraints outside bankruptcy. The rule was adopted in part to respond to charges of abusive creditor tactics and in part to limit any special incentive to file bankruptcy. The FTC rule makes it an unfair credit practice for a creditor to take a nonpossessory, nonPMSI in certain listed household goods. *See* 16 C.F.R. §§ 444.1 & 444.2.

2.   In the 2005 Amendments to the Bankruptcy Code, Congress incorporated into § 522(f) a slightly modified version of the FTC definition of "household goods." *See* § 522(f)(4).

Problem 6-13

Several months before filing for bankruptcy, Disconnected granted Lender a nonpossessory, nonPMSI in the following items:

Item	Value
Diamond Ring	$500
DVD Player	$50
Laptop Computer	$200
High-Definition TV	$900
iPod	$100

The security agreement does not cover either of the other two televisions that Disconnected owns. On which of these items, if any, may Disconnected use § 522(f)(1)(B) to avoid the lien? *See* § 522(f)(4).

Problem 6-14

In November 2002, Dentist borrowed money from Centennial Bank, granting Centennial in exchange a security interest in Dentist's existing professional equipment (hydraulic chairs, x-ray machines, *etc.*). Centennial perfected by filing an appropriate financing statement. On August 1, 2004, after Dentist had defaulted on the loan, Centennial repossessed the equipment. One week later, Dentist filed for Chapter 7 bankruptcy protection. Dentist now moves to avoid Centennial's lien under § 522(f)(1)(B), as a nonpossessory lien on tools of trade, and for turnover of the equipment. Centennial agrees that the repossessed equipment constitutes tools of Dentist's trade, but nevertheless objects to Dentist's motion. Is the lien avoidable? Why or why not? What is the textual issue? *See In re Vann*, 177 B.R. 704 (D. Kan. 1995); *In re Kinnemore*, 181 B.R. 516 (Bankr. D. Idaho 1995).

The final limitation on the scope of § 522(f)(1)(B) is in § 522(f)(3), which places a dollar limit on the debtor's ability to avoid liens that impair an exemption in tools of trade. Congress deemed this necessary because some states provide an unlimited or very high exemption for tools of trade. However, the provision does not reach debtors each of those states. Its rather cumbersome and confusing language restricts its applicability to states that either (i) offer an unlimited exemption for tools of trade; or (ii) prohibit avoidance of consensual liens on otherwise exempt property.[45] Some states with high exemptions for tools of trade do neither.[46] As a result, § 522(f)(3) has a very limited scope.

(b) Judicial Liens

Whereas § 522(f)(1)(B) allows the debtor to avoid certain specified consensual liens on certain specified exempt property, § 522(f)(1)(A) allows the debtor to avoid judicial liens – other than those securing a domestic support obligation – on any exempt property.

Problem 6-15

Given that exempt property ordinarily cannot, by definition, be levied upon, why is § 522(f)(1)(A) necessary? Put another way, how can there ever be a judicial lien on exemptible property? *See* § 522(b).

The brevity of § 522(f)(1)(A) does not, alas, imply simplicity. Courts have had to wrestle with several interpretive problems posed by its language and two of these have generated decisions by the Supreme Court.

In *Farrey v. Sanderfoot,*[47] the Court was faced with a common situation. Husband and Wife divorced. Pursuant to the property settlement, Husband got the marital home but was obligated to pay Wife over a period of time for her share of the house's value. To secure this obligation, Wife got a lien on the property. While it is common for such a lien to be created consensually, as part of a settlement agreement, in *Farrey* there was no consensual lien; instead the divorce court granted Wife a lien on Husband's property in its decree. A few months later, Husband filed for bankruptcy, claimed the property as exempt, and moved to avoid Wife's judicial lien under the provision that is now designated as § 522(f)(1)(A).

The equities of the situation strongly favored Wife, and the Court came to her rescue. It ruled:

---

[45] For a very thorough and thoughtful analysis of the rather cumbersome and confusing language of § 522(f)(3), see *In re Duvall*, 218 B.R. 1008 (Bankr. W.D. Tex. 1998).

[46] *See In re Ehlen*, 207 B.R. 179 (W.D. Wis. 1997); *In re Zimmel*, 185 B.R. 786 (Bankr. D. Minn. 1995).

[47] 500 U.S. 291 (1991).

The statute does not say that the debtor may undo a lien on an interest in property. Rather, the statute expressly states that the debtor may avoid "the fixing" of a lien on the debtor's interest in property. The gerund "fixing" refers to a temporal event. That event – the fastening of liability – presupposes an object onto which the liability can fasten. . . . Therefore, unless the debtor had the property interest to which the lien attached at some point *before* the lien attached to that interest, he or she cannot avoid the fixing of the lien under the terms of [§ 522(f)(1)(A)].[48]

Husband countered that he had owned the residence with Wife before the judicial lien was created. However, looking to local property law, the Court concluded that the Husband's prior ownership of the property was terminated by the divorce decree. His current interest in the property came into being as a result of that decree, but did so at the same moment the judicial lien in Wife's favor of attached. Because he had not owned his current interest before the lien attached, he could not use § 522(f)(1) to avoid Wife's lien.

The Bankruptcy Reform Act of 1994 responded to the Supreme Court's decision in *Farrey* by amending § 522(f)(1) to make judicial liens for support obligations unavoidable. This amendment, though, does not apply to property settlement obligations, the type of obligation really at issue in *Farrey*. Moreover, the amendment does not address the Court's analysis of when a lien attaches to property, but leaves that issue to the vagaries of state property law. Accordingly, depending both on state law and on how a divorce decree or settlement is structured, a debtor may in rare instances be able to use § 522(f) to avoid a lien designed to enforce a divorce decree's division of property.[49]

As a result, *Farrey* continues to have some relevance outside the context of a marital estate. In some jurisdictions, a judicial lien can extend to after-acquired property, particularly real property. When that occurs, the lien and the debtor's interest arise simultaneously. Under *Farrey*'s analysis, such a lien cannot be avoided.[50]

Many of the remaining interpretive issues concerning § 522(f)(1)(A) arise from the phrase "to the extent such lien impairs an exemption." When does a lien impair an exemption? In some states, for example, exemptions are defined in reference to the

---

[48] *Id.* at 296.

[49] *But see In re Catli*, 999 F.2d 1405 (9th Cir. 1993) (under Washington's community property law, a division of property incident to divorce creates a new interest, and thus any lien created to enforce a payment obligation incident to divorce does not attach to a pre-existing interest).

[50] *See In re Scarpino*, 113 F.3d 338 (2d Cir. 1997); *In re Pederson*, 230 B.R. 158 (9th Cir. BAP 1999).

debtor's equity in the property. Thus, there can be no exemption to the extent that the property is encumbered. Do judicial liens in such states impair exemptions? If not, then states could effectively "opt out" of § 522(f)(1)(A) by the way they draft their exemption statutes. The Supreme Court rejected this on the same day it decided *Farrey*. Put simply, it ruled that to determine whether § 522(f) applies, "ask not whether the lien impairs an exemption to which the debtor is in fact entitled, but whether it impairs an exemption to which he *would have been* entitled but for the lien itself.[51]

Another recurring problem in determining whether a judicial lien impairs an exemption arises when there are other, consensual liens on the property. Consider the case of a debtor who has real property worth $58,000 that is subject to the following liens (listed in order of priority):

Lien	Amount
First Mortgage	$25,000
Judgment Lien	$14,000
Second Mortgage	$41,000
Total:	**$80,000**

Obviously, if none of the liens is avoided, no equity in the property remains for the debtor. Accordingly, the first mortgagee would extract $25,000 in value from the property, the judgment lienor would get $14,000, and the second mortgagee would get the remaining $19,000 (retaining an unsecured claim for the balance remaining due).

If, however, the property subject to these liens qualifies as a homestead (and is therefore otherwise exemptible up to some statutory limit, say $20,000), the question becomes whether the judgment lien impairs the debtor's exemption, and thus whether the judgment lien is avoidable under § 522(f)(1)(A). If the judgment lien is avoidable, a related question arises: does the freed-up value go to the debtor or to the second mortgagee? These were the issues presented in *In re Simonson*.[52]

The bankruptcy court concluded that the judgment lien was avoidable, but that the freed-up value went to the second mortgagee. Thus, the first mortgagee got $25,000 in value and the second mortgagee got the remaining $33,000 in value. Arguably, this provided a windfall to the second mortgagee, who, absent avoidance, would have received only $19,000. In other words, the second mortgagee was permitted to reap the only benefit of a provision of the Code designed to benefit debtors. More to the point, because a second mortgagee will normally take subject to a judgment lien only if the

---

[51] *Owen v. Owen*, 500 U.S. 305, 310-11 (1991).

[52] 758 F.2d 103 (3d Cir. 1985).

judgment lien is recorded before the second mortgage, the second mortgagee should expect to take the property subject to that judgment lien, and need not get the freed-up value to obtain the benefit of its bargain.

A divided Third Circuit reversed. The majority concluded that the judgment lien did not impair the debtor's exemption of "an interest of the debtor in property" because the second mortgage wiped out the debtor's equity and, therefore, destroyed the debtor's "interest." Accordingly, it left all of the liens in place. This result arguably created a windfall to the judgment lienor, whose lien is fortuitously protected from avoidance only because of the existence of a subsequent second mortgage. It is also arguably inconsistent with the Supreme Court's analysis in *Whiting Pools*, where there was an "interest[] of the debtor in property" within the meaning of § 541(a)(1), despite the debtor's lack of equity and even the lack of possession.

Judge Becker, in dissent, argued that the lien should be avoided and then preserved for the benefit of the debtor under § 522(i).[53] The following table illustrates the difference in approaches.

Bankruptcy Court		*Circuit Court*		*Judge Becker*	
Property Value	$58,000	Property Value	$58,000	Property Value	$58,000
First Mortgage	− $25,000	First Mortgage	− $25,000	First Mortgage	− $25,000
	$33,000		$33,000		$33,000
Second Mortgage ($41,000)	− $33,000	Judgment Lien	− $14,000	Debtor	− $14,000
	$0		$19,000		$19,000
		Second Mortgage ($41,000)	− $19,000	Second Mortgage ($41,000)	− $19,000
			$0		$0

The Bankruptcy Reform Act of 1994 adopted Judge Becker's position. It added § 522(f)(2) to the Code. Under the formulaic rule of that provision, the judgment lien described above is avoidable.[54] Although the Act did not indicate that such an avoided lien was to be preserved for the benefit of the debtor under § 522(i), such a result seems the best interpretation of the Code and in fact is what courts are doing.[55]

Another issue that continues to arise is the extent to which an avoidable judicial lien should be avoided. Consider the following case.

---

[53] This result is generally favored by most commentators. *See* National Bankruptcy Conference, Reforming the Bankruptcy Code – Final Report 110-12 (May 1, 1994).

[54] *See, e.g., In re Brinley*, 403 F.3d 415 (6th Cir. 2005); *In re Taras*, 131 Fed. Appx. 167 (11th Cir. 2005); *In re Kolich*, 328 F.3d 406 (8th Cir. 2003) (all ruling even liens junior to the judicial lien are considered in the formula).

[55] *See In re Hanger*, 196 F.3d 1292 (9th Cir. 1999).

IN RE SILVEIRA
141 F.3d 34 (1st Cir. 1998)

Stahl, Circuit Judge.

This bankruptcy appeal requires us to decide the extent to which a Chapter 7 debtor may, pursuant to § 522(f)(1) & (f)(2)(A), avoid the fixing of a judicial lien on the debtor's property, when the market value of the property exceeds the sum of (1) all consensual (non-judicial) liens on the property and (2) the amount of the debtor's exempt interest under § 522(d). We hold that, in such a situation, section 522(f)(1) permits the avoidance of the targeted judicial lien only in part, not in its entirety. Because the district court concluded otherwise, we vacate the judgment and remand for further proceedings.

I

The debtor and appellee in this action, Thomas J. Silveira, owns, as his primary residence, a property that has been stipulated for purposes of this appeal to have a fair market value of $157,000. The property is subject to a mortgage of $117,680. The appellant, East Cambridge Savings Bank ("the Bank"), holds a $209,500 judicial lien on the property.

On May 9, 1995, Silveira filed a voluntary petition under Chapter 7 of the Bankruptcy Code. He claimed an exemption of $15,000 in the property pursuant to § 522(d)(1). Silveira then filed a motion to avoid the Bank's $209,500 judicial lien pursuant to § 522(f)(1) and (f)(2)(A). The bankruptcy court ruled that those provisions permitted the debtor to avoid the Bank's lien in its entirety and thus granted Silveira's motion. The Bank appealed to the district court, arguing that on the facts of this case, § 522(f)(1) & (f)(2)(A) permitted only a partial avoidance of its judicial lien. The district court disagreed and entered an order affirming the bankruptcy court's determination. This appeal followed.

II

* * * In this case, it is undisputed that the sum of the targeted judicial lien ($209,500), all other liens ($117,680) and the amount of the debtor's exemption ($15,000) exceeds the (stipulated) value of the debtor's property ($157,000), by $185,180. Thus, the Bank's judicial lien clearly does "impair" an exemption of the debtor within the meaning of § 522(f)(2)(A). The question here concerns the extent of the debtor's power under § 522(f)(1) to alleviate this "impairment."

The district court concluded that once a debtor's power of avoidance is triggered by the fact of an impairment of whatever size, that power permits the debtor to avoid the judicial lien causing the impairment in its entirety. The court thus held that Silveira was entitled to avoid the entire amount of the Bank's $209,500 lien. The Bank now argues that the district court misapplied § 522(f)(1)(A), and that Silveira is in fact entitled to avoid only so much of the Bank's lien as necessary to prevent impairment of the debtor's exemption within the meaning of § 522(f)(2)(A). We agree.

As an initial matter, we find unpersuasive Silveira's argument that the "plain language" of the statute supports the district court's view. On the contrary, the language of the relevant provisions seems to us to support the Bank's position. Section 522(f)(1) permits a debtor to "avoid the fixing of a lien on an interest of the debtor in property *to the extent that* such lien impairs an exemption [of the debtor]." § 522(f)(1) (emphasis added). Section 522(f)(2)(A), similarly, provides that a judicial lien "impair[s] an exemption *to the extent that*" the targeted lien, in combination with other liens and the value of the debtor's exemption, exceeds the value of the debtor's property. § 522(f)(2)(A) (emphasis added). If Congress intended for avoidance of judicial liens to be an "all-or-nothing" matter, one might wonder why the provisions' drafters chose to use the connective phrase "to the extent that," in lieu of the word "if," which obviously would have been a simpler construction. The statutory directive that a debtor may avoid a judicial lien "to the extent that" the lien impairs an exemption favors – or is at least readily amenable to – reading the definition of "impairment" in § 522(f)(2)(A) not only as a *condition* of avoidability, but also as a *proportional measure* of the scope of the debtor's avoidance power.

But even if the statute's language does not settle the issue, the debtor's proposed interpretation is unacceptable in view of the statute's intended purposes. Consider the following two hypothetical scenarios:

> *Hypothetical A*: The debtor owns a primary residence with a market value of $100,000, subject to an outstanding mortgage balance of $55,000, a judicial lien of $30,000 (not securing a debt), and no other liens. The debtor is entitled, under § 522(d)(1), to claim an exemption of $15,000 with respect to the property.

> *Hypothetical B*: Same as Hypothetical A, except that the debtor's property is subject to a judicial lien of $30,001 instead of $30,000.

In Hypothetical A, we can see that the sum of the judicial lien ($30,000), other liens ($55,000) and the debtor's exemption ($15,000) does *not* exceed the value of the debtor's property ($100,000). Thus the judicial lien in Hypothetical A does *not* impair the debtor's exemption within the meaning of § 522(f)(2)(A), and the debtor is *not* entitled to avoid any portion of that lien under § 522(f)(1).

In Hypothetical B, however, the sum of the judicial lien ($30,001), other liens ($55,000) and the debtor's exemption ($15,000) *does* exceed the property's value (by $1), and so the targeted judicial lien is deemed under § 522(f)(2)(A) to impair the debtor's exemption. Under Silveira's proposed interpretation, the fact of this impairment requires that the debtor in Hypothetical B be permitted to avoid the $30,001 judicial lien *in its entirety*. Thus, as Silveira would have it, a $1 *increase* in the amount of the (unavoidable) judicial lien in Hypothetical A would result in the debtor's acquiring the power to avoid the lien in full.[56]

We find it difficult to conceive of any reason that would counsel in favor of interpreting § 522(f)(1)(A) & (f)(2)(A) to produce such a result. * * *

Here, the sum of the debtor's exemption ($15,000) and all consensual liens on his property ($117,680) is $24,320 *less* than the value of the property ($157,000); in other words, there is $24,320 of excess equity available. This means that if the Bank's judicial lien here had been for $24,320 or less, that lien would have been absolutely unavoidable under § 522(f)(1), because there would have been no "impairment" within the meaning of § 522(f)(2)(A).[57] The fact that the Bank's actual lien is for more than $24,320 surely provides no reason to place the Bank in a position worse than it would have been had its lien originally been limited to that amount. Fairness requires, therefore, that the Bank be permitted to pursue the fixing of its $209,500 judicial lien *up to* the amount of $24,320.

In more intuitive terms, it is obvious that the value of the debtor's property in this case is sufficient to cover the entire amount of the debtor's mortgage ($117,680) plus his claimed exemption ($15,000), with $24,320 of equity to spare. Nothing in § 522(f)(1) or § 522(f)(2) can be read to require that this excess equity be preserved either for the debtor or the bankruptcy estate, rather than being made available for the partial satisfaction of a judicial lien. And, as shown above, the fixing of a judicial lien in an amount equal to this excess equity would not create any impairment of the debtor's $15,000 exemption. It follows that no legitimate purpose underlying the statute would be served by permitting Silveira to avoid so much of the Bank's lien – $24,320 – as could be covered by the excess equity available in the property.

In summary, we apply § 522(f)(1)(A) and § 522(f)(2)(A) to the facts of this case as follows. First, pursuant to § 522(f)(2)(A), we determine that the sum of (i) the targeted judicial lien ($209,500), (ii) all other liens ($117,680), and (iii) the amount of the debtor's exemption ($15,000) – which sum equals $342,180 – exceeds the value that the debtor's property would have in an unencumbered state ($157,000), and exceeds that value by $185,180. Thus, the Bank's judicial lien impairs the debtor's exemption to the extent of $185,180. Because Silveira is entitled to avoid the Bank's lien to the extent of any impairment, Silveira is entitled to avoidance in the amount of $185,180. *See* § 522(f)(1)(A). The remainder of the Bank's judicial lien, in the amount of $24,320

---

[56] The debtor in Hypothetical A would also acquire full avoidance power (according to Silveira's approach) if the value of the debtor's property were reduced, or the amount of consensual liens were increased, by $1.

[57] That is, the sum of (i) the judicial lien ($24,320), (ii) other liens ($117,680), and (iii) the debtor's exemption ($15,000) would not have exceeded the value of the debtor's property ($157,000).

($209,500 minus $185,180), is not subject to avoidance by the debtor under § 522(f)(1)(A). * * *

QUESTION

The court concluded that the judicial lien should not be avoided in full in part because that would lead to absurd results. Assuming that is correct, was the court right in avoiding the lien to the extent of $185,180 or should it have avoided the lien only to the extent of $15,000 (the debtor's exemption limit)? Why does this matter?

When the debtor is not the sole owner of the property, computing the extent to which the lien impairs the exemption also requires ascertaining the value of the debtor's share of the property, and then deducting the amount of prior liens from that figure. *See* § 522(f)(2). This makes sense when the debtor is the sole obligor of the debt secured by the prior liens, but seems questionable when all the co-owners are jointly obligated on the prior lien debts. In such instances, it would seem to make more sense to deduct the lien amounts from the total value of the property, not merely the debtor's share. Consider the following illustration:

Debtor and Spouse own realty as tenants in common (each with a 50% share). The property is valued at $100,000 and is subject to a mortgage debt, on which both of them are liable, of $45,000. There is a judicial lien against the property for $4,000 (arising from some debt of the debtor) and the debtor is entitled to an exemption of $20,000. The different computations can be illustrated as follows:

Value of Property	$100,000	Value of Property	$100,000
Debtor's ½ Share	$50,000	Mortgage Lien	($45,000)
Mortgage Lien	($45,000)		$55,000
	$5,000	Debtor's ½ Share	$27,500
Exemption	($20,000)	Exemption	($20,000)
Net Equity	$0	Net Equity	$7,500

Under the approach on the left, which subtracts the entire senior lien amount from Debtor's share, the judicial lien impairs the exemption and may be avoided. However, doing so would effectively leave Debtor with property worth $27,500 (one-half of the couple's net equity), which is more than the exemption amount. Under the approach on the right, which subtracts the senior lien from the total value of the property before computing Debtor's proportionate share, the $4,000 judicial lien does not impair the exemption and cannot be avoided. Even so, Debtor is still able to enjoy the full value of the exemption.

Courts are divided. A few follow a literalist (left) approach, and deduct the lien amounts from the value of the debtor's share.[58] Most follow an approach (right) more in keeping with the purpose of the provision and deduct the amount of such liens from the full value of the property.[59]

When the property concerned is held in a tenancy by the entireties, the problem is even more difficult because the interests of the husband and wife may not readily be severable.[60]

One final issue concerning § 522(f)(1)(A) is whether the debtor can use it to avoid a lien on property that is not properly exemptible if no objection to the debtor's claimed exemption was filed. Recall that the Supreme Court has held that if no objection is timely filed, the exemption is valid even if there is no reasonable basis for claiming it.[61] Nevertheless, several courts have ruled, based on varying rationales, that the judicial lienor may defend the avoidance action by arguing that the property is not exemptible.[62]

---

[58] *E.g., In re Cozad,* 208 B.R. 495 (10th Cir. BAP 1997).

[59] *E.g., In re Miller,* 299 F.3d 183 (3d Cir. 2002); *In re Lehman,* 205 F.3d 1255 (11th Cir. 2000); *Nelson v. Scala,* 192 F.3d 32 (1st Cir. 1999); *In re Meyer,* 2007 WL 2200565 (9th Cir. BAP 2007); *In re Ware,* 274 B.R. 206 (Bankr. D.S.C. 2001) (reconsidering the issue in light of the 1st and 11th Circuit rulings).

[60] For an interesting discussion and resolution of this issue, see *In re Snyder,* 249 B.R. 40 (1st Cir. BAP 2000), *aff'd,* 2 Fed. Appx. 46 (1st Cir. 2001).

[61] *Taylor v. Freeland & Kronz,* 503 U.S. 638 (1992) (excerpted *supra* beginning on p. 136).

[62] *See, e.g., In re Schoonover,* 331 F.3d 575 (7th Cir. 2003) (the clock for lienholders begins running when the § 522(f) avoidance motion is served, not when the meeting of unsecured creditors is held); *In re Morgan,* 149 B.R. 147 (9th Cir. BAP 1993) (§ 522(f) empowers the debtor to avoid a lien impairing an exemption only if the debtor "would have been entitled" to the exemption at the time the petition is filed, but because the debtor becomes entitled to a baseless exemption under *Taylor* only later, upon the running of the objection period, avoidance is not permitted; also due process requires that the lien creditor receive notice that the encumbered property is claimed as exempt before the lienholder is barred from objecting).

(c) Claiming Exemptions After Using the Trustee's Avoiding Powers

We have just seen that § 522(f) authorizes the debtor to avoid certain liens that impair exemptions. In addition, the debtor may benefit from the trustee's avoiding powers. This can occur in either of two ways. First, if the trustee uses the strong-arm powers to avoid a lien or successfully brings a preference claim to recover property or avoid a lien, the debtor may be able to claim an exemption in the property concerned. *See* § 522(g). Second, if the trustee declines to bring such an action, the debtor may be able to use the trustee's powers to avoid a lien or recover property. *See* § 522(h).

Each of these provisions has its limitations. In particular, if the avoidable transfer was a voluntary one on the debtor's part, the debtor will not be able to claim an exemption in the otherwise recoverable property.[63]

Problem 6-16

Demobilized owns a car worth $8,000. State law affords debtors a $5,000 exemption for a motor vehicle. Last year, Demobilized granted Chiropractor a security interest in the car to secure Demobilized's obligation to pay for $6,000 of professional services from Chiropractor. Chiropractor never perfected the security interest. This week, Demobilized filed for bankruptcy protection.

A. May the trustee avoid Chiropractor's lien? *See* § 544(a).
B. If the trustee does, to what extent may Demobilized claim the car as exempt? *See* § 522(g); *In re Hicks*, 342 B.R. 596 (Bankr. W.D. Mo. 2006).
C. If the trustee does not, may Demobilized avoid the lien? *See* § 522(h).
D. Assume that Demobilized never granted Chiropractor a security interest but that two months ago Chiropractor obtained a $6,000 judgment against Demobilized and last week Chiropractor had the sheriff levy on the car. This gave Chiropractor a judicial lien on the car. How, if at all, would the analysis of each of the questions above change?

4. *Statutory Liens – § 545*

Section 545 governs the validity of statutory liens. "Statutory lien" is defined in § 101(53) as "a lien arising solely by force of a statute on specified circumstances or

---

[63] *See also* § 522(j), (k) (imposing additional limitations on the debtor's ability to benefit from the trustee's avoiding powers).

conditions." It is distinguished from a "security interest," which includes any type of consensual lien created by agreement, § 101(51), and from a "judicial lien," which is one obtained by a legal or equitable proceeding or process, § 101(36). It does not encompass, however, most common-law liens.[64]

Section 545(2) avoids any statutory lien (other than a tax lien) that would be ineffective against a bona fide purchaser of the property. This test is similar to the rule in § 544(a)(3) (applicable only to real estate) and is more stringent than the one in § 544(a)(1) (applicable to all property). In this sense, statutory liens are disfavored in bankruptcy relative to consensual and judicial liens.

One of the most important modern statutory liens is the mechanic's or materialman's lien, through which the unpaid suppliers of labor or material used in the improvement of real property are given a lien on the property improved to secure payment of their claims. Creation or enforcement of the lien often requires the filing of notice of lien in the appropriate public office. Normally, filing must be made within a specified period after the labor has been performed or the materials supplied. Failure to file such a notice will normally make the lien junior to the rights of a bona fide purchaser, and thus subject the lien to avoidance under § 545(2).[65] In this sense, failure to file has much the same effect as failing to perfect a security interest, which subjects the secured party to the trustee's strong-arm powers.

5.   Liens Securing Fines & Penalties – § 724(a)

In Chapter 7, fines, penalties, and awards for multiple or punitive damages are subordinated to other claims. § 726(a)(4). Congress decided that, as a matter of equity, creditors should not recover on these noncompensatory claims until other creditors had been compensated for their actual losses. In particular, it was concerned that penalty claims, especially for taxes, would swallow up too much of the estate, to the detriment of general, unsecured claimants.

To effectuate this policy, the subordination applies to both secured and unsecured claims. Query if this is necessary, however, given that § 724(a) authorizes the Chapter 7 trustee to avoid the lien. Thus, a lien supporting a claim for fines, penalties, multiple damages, or punitive damages will be avoided. The claimholder then shares in the estate assets only if there is enough to pay all nonpriority, unsecured claims in full.

---

[64]   Over the years, courts have created a variety of special liens to protect certain creditors.

[65]   Failure to file may also subject the lien to avoidance under § 544(a)(3).

6.   Limitations on Setoff – § 553(b)

As a general rule, bankruptcy does not enhance creditors' rights; it selectively recognizes some, delays enforcement of others, and eliminates many. One of the few exceptions to this is setoff. Setoff rights are not treated as a lien under nonbankruptcy law. Rather, they are simply a method by which two entities, each of whom owes a debt to the other, may settle up with each other on a net basis.[66] However, the Bankruptcy Code elevates the creditor with setoff rights to the status of a secured claimant. § 506(a). *See also* § 542(b) & 553(a). The effect of this is to virtually ensure that creditors with setoff rights will obtain the benefit of those rights in bankruptcy.

There are at least three important limitations on this generality, however. First, the Bankruptcy Code does not explain when setoff rights exist. For that, recourse must be made to state law, which is remarkably nonuniform and occasionally quite confusing on this subject.

Second, setoff rights are not recognized in bankruptcy if they are created in a preferential manner. This rule is codified in § 553(a)(2) & (3). Note, however, that the rule regarding setoff rights is different from the rules regarding preference transfers. For example, a security interest or judicial lien created within the 90 days preceding bankruptcy and that collateralizes a pre-existing debt meets the prima facie case of an avoidable preference. *See* § 547(b). In contrast, setoff rights created within the 90 days before bankruptcy are, by and large, invalidated only if the creditor's obligation to the debtor was created "for the purpose of obtaining a right of setoff against the debtor." § 553(a)(3)(C). In essence, avoidance of setoff rights under this rule requires a sort of intent to be preferred, a requirement that does not exist under § 547(b).[67]

Problem 6-17

Dutiful wanted to start a new business, but because of a poor credit history had great difficulty obtaining the needed financing until Dutiful went to Friends and Family Savings & Loan. Dutiful's cousin is a loan executive at the S&L and personally approved a $45,000 unsecured loan to Dutiful. For the next year, Dutiful was careful always to make the monthly payments to the S&L on time, even when other bills went unpaid for weeks or months. When

---

[66]   Because setoff rights do not qualify as a lien, the setoff claimant often loses setoff rights when a third payment has a lien on the claimant's obligation to pay. *See* Stephen L. Sepinuck, *The Problems with Setoff: A Proposed Legislative Solution*, 51 WM. & MARY L. REV. 51 (1988).

[67]   On the other hand, the § 547(c)(2) preference defense for transfers in the ordinary course severely limits the transfers that are avoidable. While it does not on its face impose a requirement of an intent to prefer or to be preferred, it may have a somewhat similar effect

it became clear that the business would fail, Dutiful wanted to do everything possible to make sure that the S&L got paid, so that Dutiful's cousin would not get in trouble. Dutiful knew that paying the S&L off in full or making any unusually large payment on the eve of bankruptcy would be an avoidable preference. So, Dutiful simply deposited all spare cash in a checking account at the S&L the day before filing for bankruptcy. Will this action have the preferential effect that Dutiful seeks? *See* § 553(a) & (b).

Third, § 553(b) places limits on the efficacy of setoff rights exercised prepetition. These limits are known as the "improvement in position test," and they are similar to the rule in § 547(c)(5). Unfortunately, the provision is notoriously difficult to understand and apply, probably because it is so poorly written. Read § 553(b) and then consider the following hypothetical.

On January 2, 90 days before Debtor's bankruptcy, Debtor owed Bank $10,000 on an unsecured demand note. On that date, Debtor's checking account at Bank had a $1,000 balance. On March 20, Debtor deposited a check for $15,000 in the checking account. The deposit was made in the ordinary course of business and with the expectation that the proceeds of the check would be available for withdrawal when the check was collected. The check was collected on March 25 and as a result Debtor's credit balance was $16,000. Checks of Debtor were paid by Bank after that date. On March 29, Bank learned that Debtor was in serious financial difficulty. Bank immediately demanded payment of the note. Debtor could not pay and, on March 30, Bank exercised its state-law setoff rights by debiting Debtor's checking account $10,300, the amount then due under the note. After the setoff, Debtor's account was reduced to $2,000. The following chart depicts these transactions.

Date	Debt	Deposit Balance
January 2	$10,000	$1,000
March 25	$10,300	$16,000
March 30	$10,300	$12,300
April 1	$0	$2,000

On April 2, Debtor filed in Chapter 7 bankruptcy. On March 29 and at all times thereafter Debtor was insolvent. Is the trustee in bankruptcy entitled, under § 553(b), to recover from Bank any part of the setoff?

Under § 553(b)(1), Bank's secured position must be calculated at two points: (1) at the date setoff is exercised; and (2) the earliest date, beginning 90 days before the petition, when there was an "insufficiency" in Bank's position, in this case January 2. The insufficiency is the extent to which Bank is unsecured under § 506(a).

On January 2, Bank was owed $10,000 and held $1,000 on deposit for Debtor. It thus had a secured claim for $1,000 and an unsecured claim – an "insufficiency" – for $9,000. By March 30th, the day it exercised setoff, Bank's claim had risen to $10,300 but was fully secured. Thus, there was no insufficiency on the date the setoff was made. Accordingly, from the beginning of the 90-day period to the date setoff was made, Bank's secured position improved by $9,000. As a result, § 553(b)(1) deprives Bank of this benefit; the trustee may recover this amount from Bank.

There are two things to note about this rule. First, § 553(b)(1) requires a comparison of the insufficiency on only two dates. It does not take into account any intermediate increases or decreases in the insufficiency. Second, if Bank had not effected setoff before bankruptcy, it would have been able to assert setoff rights in bankruptcy to the full extent of its claim. Section 553(a) recognizes the right of setoff "except as otherwise provided in this section." Section 553(b) is a limitation on § 553(a), but it applies only to a setoff made "on or within 90 days before the date of the filing of the petition." Thus, a postpetition setoff is not affected by § 553(b) (although it would likely be enjoined by the automatic stay, as we will see in the next chapter). In this sense, the rule of § 553(b) is distinguishable from the improvement of position test in § 547(c)(5), which applies even when the secured party refrains from enforcing its security interest prepetition.

The rule of § 553(b) has what some regard as a drafting glitch, leading to absurd results. Consider the following problem.

Problem 6-18

At all relevant times until Bank exercised its setoff rights, Distressed owed Bank $25,000 of an outstanding loan. The amounts that Distressed had on deposit with Bank were as follows:

	Account Balance	Debt to Bank	Insufficiency
90th day	$25,000	$25,000	$0
89th day	$8,000	$25,000	$17,000
88th – 16th day	various	various	various
15th day*	$26,000	$27,000	$1,000
14th day	$0	$1,000	$1,000

* (day of setoff)

On the 15th day before the bankruptcy petition, Bank set off the $24,000 in Distressed's account.

A.   How much, if anything, may the trustee recover from Bank?

B.   How, if at all, would the analysis of Part A change if on the 90th day before the petition the deposit account had a balance of $24,999?

Prior to July 2001, when revised Article 9 of the Uniform Commercial Code went into effect, it was possible to obtain a security interest in a deposit account but Article 9 did not apply to such a transaction.[68] As a result, there was no guidance on how to perfect such a security interest and few attempted to obtain one. Revised Article 9 governs security interests in deposit accounts and virtually all deposit account agreements expressly grant the depositary bank a security interest in the deposits to secure whatever obligations the depositor may owe or come to owe to the bank. Such security interests are automatically perfected. *See* U.C.C. §§ 9-104(a)(1), 9-314(a). As a result, whereas most depositary institutions had to rely on their common-law setoff rights when the Bankruptcy Code was adopted, most now supplement those rights with an Article 9 security interest.

Problem 6-19

The facts are the same as in Problem 6-18 but Bank has at all times had a perfected security interest in Distressed's deposit account. May the trustee recover anything from Bank?

---

[68]   A few states, including California, had a nonuniform version of Article 9 that governed such security interests. In all states, Article 9 applied to a security interest in a deposit account to the extent it contained proceeds of other collateral.

CHAPTER SEVEN
THE AUTOMATIC STAY AND OTHER DEBTOR PROTECTIONS

Several provisions of the Bankruptcy Code kick in immediately upon the filing of a bankruptcy petition to enjoin a wide variety of behavior by entities other than the debtor. These provisions include:

- § 362, which prohibits virtually all creditor collection activity against the debtor, against property of the debtor, or against property of the estate.

- § 525, which prohibits certain discrimination merely because the debtor has filed a bankruptcy petition or received a discharge.

- § 366, which prohibits utilities from withholding service (*e.g.*, electricity, gas, water, telephone) from a debtor merely because of the petition or the debtor's failure to pay a prepetition bill. Utilities are permitted, however, to require a reasonable deposit to cover future service.

- § 108, which tolls certain statutes of limitations, as well as time periods in both the rules of court procedure and certain private agreements.

Another injunction, imposed by § 524, prohibits acts to collect discharged debts. That provision will be discussed in chapter nine.

A.   THE AUTOMATIC STAY

Without doubt, the most important and far-reaching of these provisions is § 362, which creates what is known as the automatic stay. It is one of the most litigated aspects of the Bankruptcy Code. As its legislative history indicates:

> The automatic stay is one of the fundamental debtor protections provided by the bankruptcy laws. It gives the debtor a breathing spell from his creditors. It stops all collection efforts, all harassment, and all foreclosure actions. It permits the debtor to attempt a repayment or reorganization plan, or simply to be relieved of the financial pressures that drove him into bankruptcy. The automatic stay also provides creditor protection. Without it, certain creditors would be able to pursue their own remedies against the debtor's property. Those who acted first would obtain payment of the claims in preference to and to the detriment of other creditors. Bankruptcy is designed to provide an orderly liquidation procedure under which all creditors are

treated equally. A race of diligence by creditors for the debtor's assets prevents that.[1]

In short, the automatic stay is an almost necessary corollary to bankruptcy. It is doubtful that any effective, centralized and deliberate bankruptcy process could be created without an injunction against creditor collection activity.

1. Scope of the Stay

The stay is quite broad. Any postpetition act to collect a prepetition claim is enjoined, whether the act is directed against the debtor, property of the debtor, or property of the estate. *See* § 362(a)(1)-(7). In addition, all efforts to collect a postpetition claim that are directed against property of the estate are also stayed. § 362(a)(3) & (4). The combined effect of these rules is that almost all creditor activity must come to an immediate halt once the bankruptcy petition is filed. Still, some actions escape the stay's broad scope. Consider the following scenario:

> On March 1, Defunct Airlines filed a chapter 11 bankruptcy petition. Until that date, Defunct had maintained four arrival and departure slots (gates) at Airport. These slots had been allocated to it by the FAA two years before pursuant to the applicable federal regulations.[2] On the date of the petition, Defunct ceased operations and stopped using the slots. FAA regulations permit the holders of slots to sell or lease the slots to others, but provide that after a two-month grace period following bankruptcy "any slot not utilized 65 percent of the time over a two-month period shall be recalled by the FAA."[3] On July 15, the FAA notified Defunct that its four slots had been withdrawn for nonuse and that they would be reallocated to another carrier in ten days. Has the FAA violated the stay?

The answer is no. Because the FAA lacks discretion in this matter, recall of the slots is deemed to have occurred automatically, by operation of law. Thus, nothing the FAA did postpetition affected property of the estate.[4] Put another way, § 362(a) does not stay the automatic expiration of property rights, only actions and efforts to transfer property

---

[1]   H.R. Rep. No. 95-595, at 340.

[2]   14 C.F.R. §§ 93.211–93.227.

[3]   14 C.F.R. § 93.227(a).

[4]   *In re Gull Air, Inc.,* 890 F.2d 1255 (1st Cir. 1989).

rights.[5] Similarly, it does nothing to toll the expiration of rights of redemption,[6] or prevent a lease from expiring.

Problem 7-1

Which of the following actions, if taken by a creditor postpetition, would violate the automatic stay? For each action that does violate the stay, identify which paragraph or paragraphs of subsection (a) applies.

A.   Sending the debtor a bill for a prepetition debt.

B.   Sending the debtor a bill for a postpetition debt.

C.   Bringing suit against the debtor for a prepetition debt.

D.   Filing a motion to dismiss for failure to state a claim in a state-court action brought by the debtor prepetition. *See Martin-Trigona v. Champion Fed. Sav. & Loan Ass'n*, 892 F.2d 575 (7th Cir. 1989); *In re Merrick*, 175 B.R. 333 (9th Cir. BAP 1994).

E.   Recording a prepetition judgment against the debtor.

F.   Receiving wire transfers from debtor's employer pursuant to a prepetition order garnishing the debtor's wages. Does the answer depend on whether the creditor received notice of the bankruptcy? *See In re McCall-Pruitt*, 281 B.R. 910 (Bankr. E.D. Mich. 2002); *In re Roberts*, 175 B.R. 339 (9th Cir. BAP 1994).

G.   Refusing to sell the debtor goods or services unless the debtor pays a prepetition debt.

H.   Refusing to sell the debtor goods or services unless the debtor pays for them in advance.

I.   Demanding payment of a prepetition debt from a guarantor of debtor. *See Credit Alliance Corp. v. Williams*, 851 F.2d 119 (4th Cir. 1988).

J.   Bringing an action against debtor's liability insurer for a prepetition claim. *Compare In re Minoco Group of Companies, Ltd*, 799 F.2d 517 (9th Cir. 1986); *A.H. Robins Co. v. Piccinin*, 788 F.2d 994 (4th Cir. 1986), *with In re Edgeworth*, 993 F.2d 51 (5th Cir. 1993).

---

[5]   *See In re Yellow Cab Co-op. Ass'n*, 132 F.3d 591 (10th Cir. 1997) (taxicab medallions forfeited for nonuse); *United States v. Kansas Personal Communication Servs.*, 256 B.R. 807 (D. Kan. 2000) (FCC licenses forfeited for nonpayment was not an "act" in violation of the stay), *rev'd on other grounds*, 56 Fed. Appx. 910 (10th Cir. 2003).

[6]   *Johnson v. First Nat'l Bank of Montevideo*, 719 F.2d 270 (8th Cir. 1983), *cert. denied*, 465 U.S. 1012 (1984). *But see* § 108, discussed *infra* at the end of this chapter.

Problem 7-2

Dorothy owns a small office building in which she has equity. On March 1, Dorothy files a Chapter 7 petition. On April 1, Dorothy negligently operates her car, injuring Penny.

A. May Penny sue Dorothy in state court on April 20th? *See* § 362(a)(1).
B. If Penny is permitted to sue Dorothy and obtains a judgment against her, may Penny execute on Dorothy's office building? *See* §§ 362(a)(3), 541(a)(1). May Penny garnish Dorothy's postpetition wages? *Compare* § 362(a)(3) *with* § 362(a)(6).
C. Is there anything Dorothy could do to enhance the scope of the stay with respect to Penny's claim? *See* § 109(g); *In re Hopkins*, 261 B.R. 822 (Bankr. E.D. Pa. 2001); *In re Haney*, 241 B.R. 430 (Bankr. E.D. Ark. 1999).

In analyzing stay issues, it is important to remember that one of the main purposes of the stay is to preserve the status quo. With respect to actions against the debtor, this can provide a needed respite from the financial stress that precipitated the bankruptcy filing. With respect to actions against estate assets, this is even more important. It prevents dissipation of the estate in a manner inconsistent with the policies and rules of the bankruptcy process. Sometimes, however, these concerns can be in conflict. Consider the next problem. In doing so, begin by identifying the property that is at issue and who owns it. Then consider the subsequent problem, and how it differs from the first.

Problem 7-3

Depositor had $1,000 in a savings account at Local Bank when Depositor filed for Chapter 7 bankruptcy protection. Depositor claimed the entire savings account as exempt. One week after the filing, Depositor sought to withdraw funds to pay rent. Local Bank refused to honor the withdrawal order, causing Depositor's landlord to threaten eviction. Does Depositor have a cause of action against Local Bank for violation of the stay? Should Depositor have such a cause of action? *See* § 542(a), (b); Rule 4003(b). *See also In re Calvin*, 329 B.R. 589 (Bankr. S.D. Tex. 2005); *In re Jimenez*, 335 B.R. 450 (Bankr. D.N.M. 2005). If you were counsel to Local Bank, how would have advised it to respond to Depositor's withdrawal request?

Problem 7-4

Depositor borrowed $50,000 from Security Bank to help finance a new business venture. Unfortunately, the business venture has serious cash flow problems, and Depositor recently filed for bankruptcy protection while still owing Security Bank about $47,000. At the time of the bankruptcy filing, Depositor had $4,000 on deposit in a checking account at Security Bank. After the filing, Security Bank placed an administrative "freeze" on the checking account and refused to honor checks drawn on it. Has Security Bank violated the automatic stay? *See* §§ 362(a)(3), (4) & (7), 363(e), 542(b). *See also* §§ 506(a), 553(a); *Citizens Bank v. Strumpf*, 516 U.S. 16 (1995).

For many debtors, the automatic stay is one of the most desired features of bankruptcy. They file, in large measure, to stop a particular creditor from taking a particular action, such as foreclosing on the debtor's home. For such debtors, timing is critical. The debtor needs to file before that action is taken. If the debtor waits too long, such as until after the foreclosure sale is completed, the stay will provide no assistance.

In some cases, however, the debtor times the bankruptcy petition more with an eye on the past than to the future. For example, occasionally the debtor voluntarily pays a favored creditor and wants to ensure that the trustee will not be able to avoid the payment as a preferential transfer. In such a case, the debtor may wish to file only after the 90-day preference period has expired. Of course, this is one of the reasons that the preference period for insiders is one year. These are the persons the debtor is most likely to favor and it is far more difficult for a debtor who needs bankruptcy protection to delay filing for a year than for only 90 days.

Other timing considerations may apply. Consider the following problem.

Problem 7-5

Disabled was injured in a one-car automobile accident and incurred significant medical expenses that insurance would not cover. Eventually, Hospital obtained a judgment against Disabled and began garnishing her wages. Under the garnishment order, Disabled's employer pays $110 to Hospital every two weeks. Disabled comes to see you after this has gone on for two months. She very much wants to stop the garnishment because without that money she simply cannot pay her other living expenses. You conclude that in a bankruptcy liquidation, creditors would receive nothing, and in fact Disabled would have substantial, unused exemptions that she could use to protect additional property of any kind, including cash. Do you advise Disabled to file immediately? Why or why not? Consider §§ 522(g), (h) & 547(c)(8).

We saw in chapter one that the 2005 amendments to the Bankruptcy Code added a requirement that debtors seek credit counseling before petitioning for bankruptcy relief. *See* § 109(h). This requirement does not directly affect the scope of the stay, but by placing a hurdle in the debtor's path to bankruptcy protection, it obstructs debtors' ability to access the automatic stay. Consider the following problem.

Problem 7-6

This afternoon, Despondent came to you for help for the first time. Despondent shows you a judgment of foreclosure and a notice of foreclosure sale, dated nineteen days ago, indicating that the sheriff will be selling Despondent's home tomorrow at 9:00 a.m. You contact the local debt counseling agency and are advised that it cannot provide in-person counseling for three days and even internet counseling cannot be completed before 9:00 a.m. tomorrow. Can you help Despondent stop the sale? Put another way, will the filing stay the foreclosure even if the case is dismissed shortly thereafter? *See* § 109(h)(3). *See also In re Dixon*, 338 B.R. 383 (8th Cir. BAP 2006). *Compare In re Seaman*, 340 B.R. 698 (Bankr. E.D.N.Y. 2006).

Because the automatic stay is so wide-sweeping, virtually every revision to the Bankruptcy Code has added one or more exceptions to it. *See* § 362(b). For the most part, these exceptions fall into four general categories. One category includes the exceptions that are directed at specific creditors. Chief among these are: § 362(b)(2), which allows for collection of postpetition spousal and child support against non-estate property; § 362(b)(3), which authorizes the filing of a U.C.C. Article 9 continuation statement; and § 362(b)(10) and (22), which authorize a lessor of nonresidential property to obtain possession of the property if the lease expired before the bankruptcy petition or the lessor obtained a judgment for possession prepetition.[7] Note, however, that although the Code itself does not expressly so provide, it is generally understood that filing a proof of claim with the bankruptcy court does not violate the stay. If it did, the bankruptcy system obviously could not function.

Problem 7-7

Duke and Duchess have been married for fourteen years but are now separated. Duchess had filed for divorce and the case was still pending when

---

[7]   *See also* § 362(b)(23) (excepting from the stay an eviction action based on the debtor's endangerment of the property or use of controlled substances on the premises); (b)(19) (permitting postpetition deductions from the debtor's wages to repay a loan from an employer-sponsored, ERISA-qualified plan).

Duke filed for bankruptcy protection. What aspects of the case, if any, may Duchess pursue and the family court still deal with prior to the bankruptcy court granting relief from the stay? Specifically:

A. May the divorce decree itself be entered?
B. May the court enter an order dividing the marital estate?
C. May the court enter an order assigning custody of the children and visitation rights for the noncustodial parent?
D. May the court set the amount of spousal or child support?
E. May the court enjoin Duke from contacting Duchess?

Problem 7-8

Nine months ago, Duke and Duchess were divorced. The divorce decree ordered Duke to pay Duchess $2,000/month for three years but Duke has made no payments to Duchess and last week filed for Chapter 7 bankruptcy protection.

A. To collect the prepetition arrearages, may Duchess levy on Duke's car?
B. May Duchess garnish Duke's postpetition wages?
C. How, if at all, would the analysis to Parts A and B change if Duke had filed under Chapter 13? *See* § 1306.

A second category of exceptions to the stay are those designed to prevent the stay from undermining certain commercial markets or corrupting certain financial products. *See* § 362(b)(6), (7) & (11). *See also* § 362(b)(17), (27) (based on a similar concern).

A third category of actions excepted from the stay is designed to deal with debtors who file a bankruptcy petition after having a previous bankruptcy case dismissed or the stay lifted in the previous case. *See* § 362(b)(20), (21).

By far the most common – and unsurprising – exceptions are those in the fourth category, which deals with governmental actions. For example, criminal proceedings against the debtor are not stayed. § 362(b)(1). Were the law otherwise, bankruptcy would become the haven of every culprit seeking to avoid or delay punishment for criminal conduct. Read § 362(b) and then consider the following problem.

Problem 7-9

Deceptive is indicted for passing bad checks. Under applicable state law, conviction of the offense requires the criminal court to order the defendant to make restitution. Before the criminal trial begins, Deceptive files a bankruptcy petition.

A. May the state try Deceptive? Should the answer depend on what the prosecutor's motive is? *See In re Gruntz*, 202 F.3d 1074 (9th Cir. 2000).

B. If trial is held and results in conviction, may the court order restitution? May such a restitution order be enforced? *See Pennsylvania Dep't of Public Welfare v. Davenport*, 495 U.S. 552, 560-61 (1990).

C. What actions may a creditor take to press criminal charges? *Compare In re Shake*, 154 B.R. 270 (Bankr. D. Neb. 1993); *with In re Williamson-Blackmon*, 145 B.R. 18 (Bankr. N.D. Ohio 1992).

Of course, criminal proceedings represent only a small fraction of what states and the federal government do to enforce laws and regulations. Just as bankruptcy should not be a haven for the criminal, it should not be a sanctuary for those who would, for example, pollute the environment, practice medicine without a license, maintain unsafe working conditions, or issue unregistered securities. Not surprisingly, therefore, governmental agencies are generally permitted to continue exercising their police, regulatory, and taxing authority, as are accrediting bodies, licensing boards, and stock exchanges. *See* § 362(b)(4), (9), (12)–(16), (18), (25), (26), (28).

However, there are limits on the government's immunity from the stay. In particular, while § 362(b)(4) allows governmental units to enforce their police and regulatory powers and to obtain money judgments, they are not permitted to enforce money judgments. The idea behind this is fairly simple: the government is not subject to the stay when it acts as a *regulator*, but it is bound by the stay when it acts as a *creditor* or as an agent of private creditors. Unfortunately, this seemingly simple distinction is not always easy to apply. Consider the following case.

IN RE FIRST ALLIANCE MORTGAGE CO.
263 B.R. 99 (9th Cir. BAP 2001)

Marlar, Bankruptcy Judge.

INTRODUCTION

The bankruptcy court ruled that monetary claims asserted in a state court consumer protection action against the debtor were not exempt from the automatic stay, under the exception for an action to enforce a governmental unit's police or regulatory power. The Commonwealth of Massachusetts ("Commonwealth") appealed, and we reverse that portion of the order.[8]

---

[8]   The bankruptcy court ordered that the injunctive relief count of the Commonwealth's action was not subject to the automatic stay and could proceed. That portion of the order has not been appealed, and shall stand.

FACTS AND PROCEDURAL HISTORY

First Alliance Mortgage Co. ("FAMCO" or "debtor") is a financial services company and one of the affiliate debtors in jointly administered chapter 11 cases. FAMCO did business in several states, including Massachusetts.

Prepetition, the Commonwealth obtained a preliminary injunction against FAMCO, which prohibited it from engaging in the loan origination business. The preliminary injunction ensued from the Commonwealth's lawsuit, filed under the Massachusetts Consumer Protection Act, on October 30, 1998. The Commonwealth asserted claims for injunctive relief, civil penalties, attorneys' fees and costs, and restitution on behalf of 299 Massachusetts consumers who had borrowed money from FAMCO. Litigation was pending in that action when FAMCO filed for bankruptcy protection on March 23, 2000.

The Stay Relief Proceedings

On May 9, 2000, the Commonwealth filed a motion entitled "Commonwealth's Motion for Determination that the Automatic Stay Provision of the Bankruptcy Code Does Not Prevent the Commonwealth from Continuing its Superior Court Enforcement Action." It sought to continue to prosecute the state court action to a money judgment, but not to enforce such judgment. The Commonwealth alleged that the complaint was filed pursuant to the Massachusetts Consumer Protection Act, Mass. Gen. Laws ch. 93A § 4, which authorizes the Attorney General to commence an enforcement action against any person who is alleged to be engaging in unfair or deceptive acts or practices in violation of § 2(a) of the Act. The Commonwealth argued that the action was exempt from the automatic stay, under § 362(b)(4), which provides an exception to the automatic stay for "the commencement or continuation of an action or proceeding by a governmental unit . . . to enforce such governmental unit's . . . police and regulatory power." In the alternative, the Commonwealth sought relief from the automatic stay.

* * * The Commonwealth alleged in its motion that the debtor had been charging excessive points for mortgage loans, and had engaged in deceptive sales and training techniques designed to conceal and mislead borrowers regarding the true measure of points charged by FAMCO.

FAMCO filed its opposition, and the attached declaration of its executive vice president and CEO Jeffrey W. Smith. * * * In paragraph 10, Smith acknowledged the pending state court action, and stated: "I am informed and therefore believe that the Commonwealth . . . is seeking restitution and damages for 299 of its citizens that were among the over 35,000 borrowers on loans issued by Debtor nationwide." FAMCO also acknowledged, in its opposition, that the Commonwealth was seeking, in the state court action, the remedies of permanent injunction, restitution, civil penalties, and attorneys' fees and costs. Believing the injunctive relief to be moot because its operations had ceased, FAMCO also argued, in its brief, that the Commonwealth had "conced[ed] that the State Court Action was commenced 'to enjoin [the Debtor] from charging excessive points in its mortgage loans to Massachusetts borrowers . . . and from otherwise engaging in conduct that is unfair or deceptive.' " * * *

The Creditors' Committee joined in the opposition, and based its objection on the litigation costs to the estate, which could deplete the assets needed for the debtor's liquidation plan.

At the hearing, the bankruptcy court * * * discussed the merits of the stay exception as applied to the Commonwealth's claims. The court discussed the existence of about 35,000 potential claims against the debtor, all of which were similar to the 299 monetary claims asserted by the Commonwealth, and stated that all such claims should be liquidated in the bankruptcy case in order to treat similarly situated creditors fairly, and not deplete the liquidating estate.

The court then * * * accepted the undisputed facts, and determined that only the injunctive relief was exempt from the automatic stay. The court stated:

> * * * [I] believe that it is appropriate to let the Commonwealth proceed with respect to any injunctive relief, and to show to the people of its – of the Commonwealth, that it is attempting to exercise its police powers on their behalf and it has – it may proceed to enjoin.
>
> But other than that, this Court will not grant relief from stay, to allow the Commonwealth to proceed with respect to determining any damages, or any restitution, or any award, or any civil penalties amounts at this time.

* * *

ISSUE

The sole issue is whether the Commonwealth's consumer protection action for civil penalties, attorneys' fees, and restitution for borrowers is exempt from the automatic stay under § 362(b)(4).

* * *

DISCUSSION
A. Scope of § 362(b)(4)

The filing of a bankruptcy petition operates as a stay, applicable to all entities, of "the commencement or continuation . . . of a judicial, administrative, or other action or proceeding against the debtor." § 362(a)(1). The general policy behind the automatic stay is to grant complete and immediate, albeit temporary, relief to the debtor from creditors, and to prevent dissipation of the debtor's assets before orderly distribution to all creditors can be effected. A main purpose of the stay is to protect the priority of payments to creditors.

The Code provides certain exceptions to the automatic stay, which are read narrowly. Section 362(b)(4) provides an exception for certain governmental police and regulatory actions. Section 362(b)(4) provides that the filing of a petition does not stay

> the commencement or continuation of an action or proceeding by a governmental unit . . . to enforce such governmental unit's . . . police and regulatory power, including the enforcement of a judgment other than a money judgment, obtained in an action or proceeding by the governmental unit to enforce such governmental unit's . . . police or regulatory power.

This provision permits a governmental unit to "commence or continue any police or regulatory action, including one seeking a money judgment, but it may enforce only those judgments and orders that do not require payment or authorize the government to exercise control over property of the estate." 3 Collier on Bankruptcy, § 362.05[5][b] at 362-59 to 362-60 (15th ed. 2001).

The legislative history of this section indicates that when a debtor is sued by a governmental unit in order "to prevent or stop violation of fraud, environmental protection, *consumer protection,* safety, or similar police or regulatory laws, *or attempting to fix damages for violation* of such a law, the action or proceeding is not stayed under the automatic stay." H.R. Rep. No. 595, 95th Cong., 1st Sess. 343 (1977) (emphasis added). By allowing such actions to proceed, this exemption prevents the bankruptcy court from becoming a "haven for wrongdoers." *In re Berg,* 230 F.3d 1165, 1167 (9th Cir. 2000).

Not every police or regulatory action is automatically exempt, however. Enforcement of laws that affect health, welfare, morals, and safety will not be stayed, but regulatory laws that directly conflict with the control of the *res* or property by the bankruptcy court will be stayed. *See In re Universal Life Church, Inc.,* 128 F.3d 1294, 1297 (9th Cir. 1997). The Ninth Circuit applies two tests for determining whether a state's actions fall within the scope of § 362(b)(4): the "pecuniary purpose" test and the "public policy" test. *Id.*

Under the "pecuniary purpose" test, the court must determine "whether the government action relates primarily to the protection of the government's pecuniary interest in the debtor's property or to matters of public safety and welfare." *Id.* at 1297. The relevant inquiry is whether the action is being pursued "*solely* to advance a pecuniary interest of the governmental unit," in which case the stay will be imposed. *Id.* Such actions have been described as those that would "result in an economic advantage to the government or its citizens over third parties in relation to the debtor's estate." *In re Charter First Mortg., Inc.,* 42 B.R. 380, 382 (Bankr. D. Or. 1984).

* * *

Courts also apply the "public policy" test in order to "distinguish between government actions that effectuate public policy and those that adjudicate private rights." *Universal Life Church,* 128 F.3d at 1297. Under this test, the court considers whether the government is exercising its legislative, executive, or judicial functions. *In re Poule,* 91 B.R. 83, 86 (9th Cir. BAP 1988). "Where the agency's action concerns only the parties who are immediately affected the debtor is entitled to the same protection it would receive under the automatic stay if the proceeding were instead in a judicial forum." *Charter First,* 42 B.R. at 384.

In the instant case, the bankruptcy court allowed the Commonwealth's action for injunctive relief to proceed, but held that the claims for civil penalties, attorneys' fees and restitution were stayed, because those actions did not meet the "pecuniary purpose" or "public policy" tests.

B. Civil Penalties and Attorneys' Fees

The Commonwealth initiated a lawsuit against FAMCO under the provisions of its consumer protection act. The purpose of that law is "to improve the commercial relationship between consumers and business persons and to encourage more equitable behavior in the marketplace." *Poznik v. Mass. Medical Prof'l Ins. Ass'n,* 628 N.E.2d 1, 4 (Mass. 1994). It "proscribes unfair or deceptive acts or practices in conduct of trade or commerce." *Veranda Beach Club Ltd. P'ship v. Western Sur. Co.,* 936 F.2d 1364, 1385 (1st Cir. 1991). As a deterrence measure, it also "imposes liability on persons seeking to profit from unfair practices." *Id.;* Mass. Gen. Laws ch. 93A § 2.

From legislative history and case law, it is well-established that consumer protection is a valid exercise of the police and regulatory power for purposes of § 362(b)(4). Here, the Commonwealth sought to impose civil penalties against FAMCO for its alleged unfair and deceptive loan practices. This action falls squarely within its public policy of protecting consumers and deterring violators.

Where the debtor is being prosecuted for engaging in fraudulent conduct, the automatic stay should not allow the debtor to be shielded from the government's attempt to protect its citizens and uphold its laws related to the health and welfare of its citizens. The Ninth Circuit recognized in *Universal Life Church* that the "[d]etection of fraud ha[s] been sustained as a valid basis for invoking the exception even when there is an additional pecuniary interest at stake." 128 F.3d at 1298. It further opined that "[i]ndeed, most government actions which fall under this exemption have some pecuniary component, particularly those associated with fraud detection." *Id.* at 1299.

Even courts that would treat restitution as outside the scope of § 362(b)(4) treat civil penalties and attorneys' fees as being within the scope of the exception.

The bankruptcy court in the case at bar expressed concern about the potential for multiple prosecutions in the various states where FAMCO did business, and the financial effect of such litigation on the bankruptcy estate. However, to hold that a governmental action does not come within § 362(b)(4) for such reason would run counter to the fundamental policy behind the exception, which is to prevent the bankruptcy court from becoming a haven for wrongdoers. *Berg,* 230 F.3d at 1167. The bankruptcy court has other avenues to prevent general harm to the estate, *i.e.,* its powers under § 105(a) to "issue any order, process, or judgment that is necessary or appropriate to carry out the provisions of this title."

FAMCO also contends that these causes of action are unnecessary since it has already ceased its loan origination business. However, civil penalties may be assessed for violations of the statute. Mass. Gen. Laws ch. 93A § 4. The penalties imposed for consumer fraud meet both the pecuniary purpose test and the public policy test. * * *

Therefore, we hold that § 362(b)(4) exempts the Commonwealth's prosecution to judgment of its claims for civil penalties and attorneys' fees from the automatic stay.

C. Restitution Claims

The Commonwealth is also seeking to recover restitution, in the form of money damages, on behalf of 299 Massachusetts borrowers, who are also creditors of the estate. The Commonwealth contends that the restitution claims are not "solely pecuniary" because they further the state's consumer protection policies, and the Commonwealth will not seek to enforce the judgment outside of the bankruptcy case. The Commonwealth further contends that *it* is the plaintiff, not such private third parties; therefore, continuing with the claims liquidation process in state court would promote public policy. FAMCO contends, on the other hand, that the restitution action is solely pecuniary and for the benefit of private parties.

Under the "pecuniary purpose" test, the inquiry is whether the action "relates *primarily* to the protection of the government's pecuniary interest in the debtor's property, or to matters of public policy." *Berg,* 230 F.3d at 1167 (emphasis added). Traditionally, courts have looked at what effect the action will have on the bankruptcy estate, and the supremacy of federal laws. Here, the bankruptcy court determined that the 35,000 similar, unliquidated claims against the estate could be more equitably adjudicated in the bankruptcy claims process.

We believe that a trilogy of Ninth Circuit cases supports the Commonwealth's position and requires us to reverse the bankruptcy court's decision.

The power to determine a debtor's liability or to liquidate a damages claim may legitimately be part of an exempt police or regulatory action. The Ninth Circuit Court of Appeals has held:

> Indeed, most government actions which fall under this exemption have some pecuniary component.... This does not abrogate their police power function.
> Only if the action is pursued "*solely* to advance a pecuniary interest of the governmental unit" will the automatic stay bar it.

Universal Life Church, 128 F.3d at 1299.

In *Universal Life Church,* the Ninth Circuit Court of Appeals held that the IRS issuance of a letter revoking the debtor's tax exempt status was exempt from the stay, even though the IRS also required the Church to file tax returns, and which also estimated the outstanding tax to be more than $6 million. The appellate court rejected the debtor's position "that the IRS must have *no* pecuniary motive at all to fall within section 362(b)(4)," and held that the revocation letter was exempt from the stay because it served a "public policy purpose." 128 F.3d at 1298-99 (emphasis added).

In *Berg,* the Ninth Circuit Court of Appeals held that the purpose of pursuing litigation sanctions was to effectuate public policy, even though the monetary penalty would enure to the benefit of a private party. 230 F.3d at 1168. The court agreed with the reasoning that "although private parties may benefit financially from sanctions, the deterrent effect of monetary penalties can be essential for the government to protect its regulatory interests." *Id.*[9]

The third Ninth Circuit opinion in the trilogy convincing us that the Commonwealth's restitution claims are exempt from the automatic stay is *NLRB v. Continental Hagen Corp.*, 932 F.2d 828 (9th Cir. 1991). There, the National Labor Relations Board had filed an unfair labor practices complaint against the debtor, and sought damages consisting of back wages for unionized employees and truck drivers. The Court of Appeals made the important distinction that the NLRB was not seeking to enforce a judgment, but only to obtain a money judgment and liquidate its claim. Therefore, the back pay provision would not jeopardize nor interfere with the pending bankruptcy proceeding. *Id.* at 834-35. The action also passed the public policy test, the court held, because the NLRB was not providing a forum for private parties, but was acting in its own name in furtherance of the policies of the federal labor laws. *Id.* at 834.

* * *

We * * * find a similarity between the cases which exempt actions for back pay, and the present action for restitution to citizens of Massachusetts for the debtor's violation of the consumer protection laws, so long as the Commonwealth seeks only the entry, and not the enforcement, of the money judgment.

These cases provide authority for the Commonwealth's argument that its money claims, which are part of the totality of its consumer protection remedies, are for a public purpose, and not solely for the pecuniary gain to the Commonwealth or its individual citizens. Nor does the entry of a monetary judgment reduce the estate or interfere with the bankruptcy. Such a judgment only serves to liquidate the Commonwealth's claim against the estate. FAMCO will be entitled to all of its defenses to the Commonwealth's action in the Massachusetts state court action. Furthermore, these cases support the conclusion that the Commonwealth was not seeking to adjudicate private rights, but was primarily pursuing remedies for alleged violations of its consumer protection laws.

A few courts in the Ninth Circuit, including a BAP panel, have held that a restitution judgment would create an unfair advantage for those victims over other

---

[9]   We note that *Berg* involves sanctions rather than restitution, but the powerful policy considerations which the Ninth Circuit has articulated apply with equal force.

creditors of the estate by interfering with the bankruptcy court's exclusive jurisdiction to adjudicate claims in bankruptcy. Those cases are * * * distinguishable * * *.

In *Poule*, the BAP held that the State Registrar of Contractors' assessment of an order of corrections, which required the debtor to reimburse a customer, resulted from the adjudication of purely private rights and thus did not fall under the § 362(b)(4) exception. 91 B.R. at 87. The assessment of civil penalties, on the other hand, served the public policy of punishing the debtor for fraudulent conduct, and therefore that portion of the action was not stayed. *Id.* at 86.

In *In re Dunbar*, 235 B.R. 465 (9th Cir. BAP 1999), *aff'd*, 245 F.3d 1058 (9th Cir. 2001), * * * the California Contractors' State License Board had issued an order of correction, following an administrative hearing, which required the debtor to pay $27,000 in restitution for the debtor's violations of the Business and Professions Code. The debtor argued that the government action should be enjoined because it violated the automatic stay. The BAP remanded the matter with instructions that the bankruptcy court should determine if the action violated the automatic stay. The BAP examined § 362(b)(4) and held that, to the extent the state agency had instituted proceedings to seek restitution based on a determination of the debtor's personal liability, such action was not excepted from the automatic stay. *Id.* at 474-75.

Poule and *Dunbar* are distinguishable on their facts. First, they involved violations of legislation enacted to protect individual consumers, who are injured by the acts of building contractors on specific jobs. The remedy typically sought is the assessment of restitution and damages for repair of shoddy workmanship. Thus, the debtor's noncompliance with an order of correction could lead to license revocation proceedings against the debtor. In such instances, almost always initiated by private citizens acting in their individual interests, the restitution action is an action to enforce private rights rather than to protect public interests.

In contrast, in this case, the state attorney general commenced a consumer protection action on behalf of 299 persons who were victimized by the debtor's violation of laws enacted to protect consumers. Thus, viewed in its entirety, the Commonwealth's efforts are not intended "solely" to advance a pecuniary interest or primarily to adjudicate private rights. Rather, the focus of the Commonwealth's action is to enjoin illegal conduct and achieve penalties and restitution as a deterrent to future unlawful activity.

* * *

The Commonwealth argues that the trend in the law is to look at restitution as just one arrow in the entire consumer protection quiver. For example, in *In re Luskin's, Inc.*, 213 B.R. 107 (D. Md. 1997), the Maryland Attorney General's Consumer Protection Division prosecuted an action against the debtor for advertising tactics that were in violation of the Consumer Protection Act. The state sought to obtain restitution for consumers who had relied on the advertisements. The debtor argued that the state was pursuing a pecuniary interest in his property by attempting to adjudicate the private rights of consumers adversely affected by the advertisements. The district court reversed the stay that had been imposed by the bankruptcy court, and determined that the consumer protection action, which included injunctive relief and restitution, was "a legitimate use of . . . police power and/or regulatory power even though it seeks to reduce a monetary claim to judgment." The state, it found, was attempting to halt unfair trade practices by implementing the statutory purpose of its consumer protection law, *i.e.,* to protect the public interest. *Id.* at 110.

The facts in our case are similar to those in *Luskin's.* The Massachusetts Consumer Protection Act was designed to impose liability on persons seeking to profit from unfair or deceptive acts or practices. The restitution count is only one component of an action that is concerned with the overall protection of the public. Moreover, the restitution judgment would simply liquidate all or part of the Commonwealth's unsecured claim against the debtor. It would not give priority of the estate's assets to the Commonwealth or elevate its citizens' rights over the rights of other claimants. We reject the view that merely because the police or regulatory action will determine the debtor's liability for a potpourri of money damages – including damages inuring to the benefit of third parties – that such portion must be severed from the entire action, and stayed.

* * *

Therefore, we hold that the bankruptcy court erred by determining that the Commonwealth's restitution claims were not exempt from the automatic stay pursuant to § 362(b)(4).

NOTE

More recent cases have ruled that § 362(b)(4) also exempts from the stay a state court action to enforce federal antitrust laws,[10] and a civil forfeiture action against the debtor's property brought by the government because of the debtor's use of the property for illegal purposes.[11]

Problem 7-10

Which of the following actions may be taken postpetition without violating the automatic stay? For each permissible action, identify which paragraph or paragraphs of subsection (b) apply.

---

[10]   *Lockyer v. Mirant Corp.*, 398 F.3d 1098 (9th Cir. 2005).

[11]   *See In re Chapman*, 264 B.R. 565 (9th Cir. BAP 2001).

A. The county assesses a tax against debtor's real estate.
B. The state bar suspends the debtor from practicing law after investigating an ethics complaint filed against the debtor for the debtor's prepetition conduct. *See In re Wade*, 948 F.2d 1122 (9th Cir. 1991). *See also In re McMullen*, 386 F.3d 320 (1st Cir. 2004).
C. The Department of Motor Vehicles suspends debtor's driver's license for:
    1. Driving while intoxicated.
    2. Failing to pay a prepetition speeding ticket. *See In re Duke*, 167 B.R. 324 (Bankr. D.R.I. 1994); *In re North*, 128 B.R. 592 (Bankr. D. Vt. 1991).
D. The EEOC orders the debtor to:
    1. Rehire an employee it concludes the debtor illegally terminated.
    2. Pay the illegally terminated employee wages for the period the employee was out of work. *See NLRB v. Continental Hagen Corp.*, 932 F.2d 828 (9th Cir. 1991); *EEOC v. McLean Trucking Co.*, 834 F.2d 398 (4th Cir. 1987).
E. The EPA orders the debtor to:
    1. Stop polluting. *See In re Gandy*, 327 B.R. 796 (Bankr. S.D. Tex. 2005).
    2. Clean up a site on which debtor had dumped toxic chemicals. *Compare Penn Terra Ltd. v. Department of Environmental Resources*, 733 F.2d 267 (3d Cir. 1984), *with In re Kovacs*, 681 F.2d 454 (6th Cir. 1982), *vacated*, 459 U.S. 1167 (1983).

Problem 7-11

The Venn diagram below expands upon the diagram used in Problem 5-2 by adding the set of rights subject to the automatic stay. Determine where to place within the diagram each of the following:

A. A former spouse's unmatured right to support.
B. A lender's right to repayment of a term loan whose term has not yet expired.
C. A guarantor's contingent right to reimbursement from the debtor.
D. A criminal prosecution of the debtor for writing a bad check.
E. A homeowner association's right pursuant to the covenants in the chain of title to the debtor's real property to make the owner pay postpetition assessments.
F. A counter-party's right to setoff pursuant to a repurchase agreement entered into by the debtor.

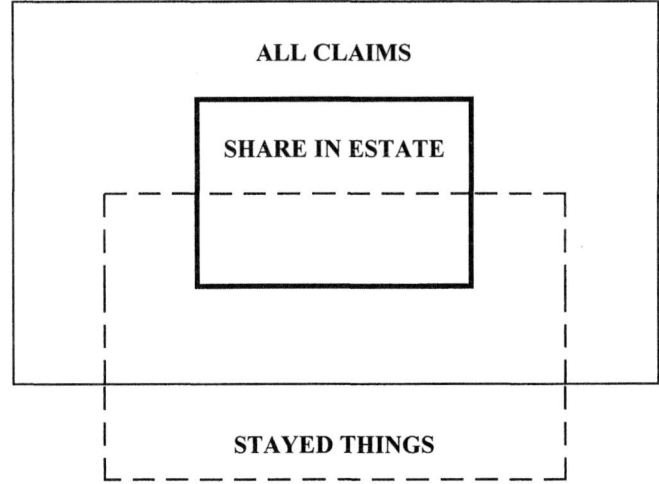

2.   Duration of and Relief from the Stay

The duration of the stay is governed by § 362(c). With regard to actions against property of the estate, the stay expires when the property ceases to be property of the estate.[12] For all other acts, the stay expires when the bankruptcy case is closed or dismissed or the debtor is either granted or denied a discharge, whichever occurs first.

Problem 7-12

Degree has an outstanding student loan debt to College. This debt first became due two years ago, upon Degree's graduation. After Degree filed for bankruptcy protection, College refused to release a copy of Degree's transcript even though Degree had tendered the appropriate $3.00 fee. Has College violated the stay? *See In re Merchant*, 958 F.2d 738 (6th Cir. 1992). Does it matter whether the debt to College is nondischargeable under § 523(a)(8)? Should it?

In some situations, the bankruptcy court may lift the stay before it would otherwise terminate to permit certain actions to occur. § 362(d). A party seeking such relief must file a motion therefor, *see* Rules 4001, 9014, and bankruptcy courts normally deal with those motions on a fairly expeditious basis. Indeed, unless the court rules otherwise, the

---

[12]   The stay might expire earlier – or not come into existence at all – if the debtor had one or more bankruptcy proceedings pending during the year preceding the petition in the current case. *See* § 362(c)(3), (4).

stay will normally terminate automatically 30 or 60 days after the motion is filed. § 362(e).

The main bases for granting relief from the stay are: (i) for cause, including lack of adequate protection of an interest in property; and (ii) with respect to particular property, when the debtor lacks equity in it and the property is not necessary for a successful reorganization. § 362(d)(1) and (2). Both of these grounds are primarily relevant only to creditors with secured claims. Let's consider the latter ground first.

Suppose the debtor owes a creditor $10,000 and the debt is secured by an automobile worth $8,000. Clearly, the debtor has no equity in the collateral; the car is not worth more than the debt it secures. If, in addition, the car is not necessary to a successful reorganization, then the creditor is entitled to relief from the stay. Once that relief is granted, the creditor may then pursue whatever rights the creditor has under nonbankruptcy law, most probably the right to repossess the car and foreclose its lien. Note, if the debtor is undergoing liquidation in Chapter 7, then by definition there will be no reorganization and the second prong of this test is satisfied. The only issue will be whether the collateral is worth more than the debt. If it is, then the estate (or the debtor, if the property is exempt) has equity and the stay will not be lifted under § 362(d)(2). In other words, if the property is worth something to the estate, relief from the stay will be denied to permit the trustee to try to extract value from the property for the benefit of claimants. If the property is worth something to the debtor, then relief from the stay will be denied so as to give the debtor time to find a way to preserve that value, before the creditor is permitted to use its nonbankruptcy rights to foreclose.

Now let's consider § 362(d)(1), which authorizes relief from the stay for cause, including lack of adequate protection of an interest in property. Lack of adequate protection most commonly exists when the secured creditor has little equity cushion and the collateral is depreciating or threatening to depreciate faster than the debtor is paying off the debt.

For example, suppose the debtor owes a creditor $10,000 secured by an automobile worth $10,500. If the debtor is continuing to use the car, the car will almost assuredly fall in value (it would be highly unusual for the car's value to rise with use). If the debtor has ceased making monthly payments on the car loan, the creditor is in jeopardy of not having its fully secured claim paid. In a situation such as this, the creditor is likely to move for relief from the stay. The court will then either grant such relief or issue an order requiring the debtor to make periodic – probably monthly – payments to the creditor to protect it from the likely diminution in value of the collateral. Which the court chooses to do will likely depend on whether the debtor is able and willing to make such adequate protection payments.

Problem 7-13

Other than future depreciation, what else would likely constitute a lack of adequate protection of an interest in property? Put another way, what are the other risks to the value of the creditor's interest in the estate property?

Although most of the § 362(d)(1) litigation focuses on lack of adequate protection, the provision is not so limited; it authorizes relief from the automatic stay whenever there is "cause." In rare situations, even unsecured creditors can get relief from the stay for cause. For example, suppose that a creditor were three weeks into a four-week trial against the debtor on a complex and hotly disputed antitrust claim when the debtor seeks bankruptcy protection. The bankruptcy court might well conclude that legal fees on both sides would be saved – and thus it would be in the best interest of the debtor and the creditors alike – if the trial were allowed to continue, rather than to start it anew in bankruptcy as part of the process of adjudicating claims.[13] In general, courts have identified three factors that should be considered in deciding whether to lift the stay for such reasons:

> (1) whether the issues in the pending litigation involve only state law, so the expertise of the bankruptcy court is unnecessary; (2) whether modifying the stay will promote judicial economy and whether there would be greater interference with the bankruptcy case if the stay were not lifted because matters would have to be litigated in bankruptcy court; and (3) whether the estate can be protected properly by a requirement that creditors seek enforcement of any judgment through the bankruptcy court.[14]

3.   *Violations of the Stay*

Most bankruptcy courts zealously enforce the stay. Violations are punishable as civil contempt and compensatory damages are readily available.[15] In this respect, it is

---

[13]   *See In re Holtkamp*, 669 F.2d 505 (7th Cir. 1982). *See also* H.R. Rep. No. 95-595, at 341 & 343 ("it will often be more appropriate to permit proceedings to continue in their place of origin, when no great prejudice to the bankruptcy estate would result, in order to leave the parties to their chosen forum and to relieve the bankruptcy court from many duties that may be handled elsewhere," and thus "a desire to permit an action to proceed to completion in another tribunal" may be cause for lifting the automatic stay).

[14]   *In re Robbins*, 964 F.2d 342, 345 (4th Cir. 1992).

[15]   *See In re Skinner*, 917 F.2d 444 (10th Cir. 1990) (relying on the grant of authority to bankruptcy courts in § 105).

important to note that, technically, no intent to violate is required. Indeed, the violator need not even be aware that a bankruptcy petition has been filed. However, an unknowing violation of the stay is unlikely to result in a finding of contempt.[16]

In 1984, Congress amended § 362 by adding subsection (h), which the 2005 amendments later re-designated as § 362(k)(1). That paragraph provides that an "individual" injured by a willful violation of the stay may recover actual damages, attorneys' fees, and in appropriate circumstances, punitive damages. In essence, this amendment gave debtors a private cause of action for willful violations of the stay, thus allowing them to avoid what may be a stricter standard under the civil contempt procedure.

The willfulness requirement does not mean that the creditor must intend to cause harm or even intend to violate the stay. It merely means that the creditor was informed of the stay and acted deliberately.[17] Thus, a creditor willfully violates the stay simply by not stopping its computer from sending bills to the debtor after the creditor has received notice of the bankruptcy filing.[18]

What constitutes "actual damages" for the purposes of § 362(k)(1) is a matter of some dispute. Certainly any type of economic injury qualifies. There is also a growing consensus that damages for emotional distress are available, although some courts disagree and some limit such damages to cases where they accompany a demonstrable financial loss.[19]

An award of punitive damages must normally be predicated on some maliciousness or bad faith. Even so, the availability of punitive damages remains a hotly litigated issue; Congress' use of the term "individual" in § 362(k)(1) has created a difficult – though interesting – problem of statutory construction. The Code does not define the

---

[16] *See In re Crysen/Montenay Energy Co.*, 902 F.2d 1098, 1104 (2d Cir. 1990) ("a party generally would not have sanctions imposed for its violation of an automatic stay as long as it had acted without maliciousness and had had a good faith argument and belief that its actions did not violate the stay").

[17] *Crysen*, 902 F.2d at 1104; *In re Bloom*, 875 F.2d 224, 227 (9th Cir. 1989).

[18] *See In re Rijos*, 263 B.R. 382, 392 (1st Cir. BAP 2001) (expressly rejecting "the computer did it" defense). *See also In re Vivian*, 150 B.R. 832 (Bankr. S.D. Fla. 1992) (reaching a similar conclusion with regard to a violation of the discharge injunction and, in a tongue-in-cheek opinion, fining the offending computer megabytes of memory).

[19] *Compare In re Dawson*, 390 F.3d 1139 (9th Cir. 2004); *Fleet Mortgage Group, Inc. v. Kaneb*, 196 F.3d 265 (1st Cir. 1999) (both ruling that damages for emotional distress are available), *with Aiello v. Providian Financial Corp.*, 239 F.3d 876 (7th Cir. 2001) (no recovery in bankruptcy for emotional distress unless there is also some financial loss, but tort action may exist for emotional distress if creditor engaged in oppressive debt collection tactics or creditor's behavior was extortionate). *See also In re Rivera Torres*, 432 F.3d 20 (1st Cir. 2005) (questioning whether damages for emotional distress are available under § 105 for willful violation of the § 524(a)(2) discharge injunction but in any event ruling that the federal government is immune from having to pay such damages).

term and courts have struggled with whether it encompasses corporate and partnership debtors. There is probably no good policy reason why punitive damages should be available only to human beings, however every other Code reference to "individuals" is clearly limited to human beings. *See* §§ 101(18)(A), 101(30), 101(41), 522(b)(1), 523(a), 727(a)(1), 1141(d)(2). Moreover, the 1984 amendments which added § 362(k)(1) to the Code dealt almost exclusively with consumer bankruptcies. Perhaps not surprisingly, courts have split on this issue. Several, including two circuit courts, have ruled that corporate and partnership debtors do qualify for punitive damages under § 362(k)(1).[20] Others, including five circuit courts, have followed a more textual approach and ruled to the contrary.[21]

Despite the ambiguity as to which debtors may benefit from § 362(k)(1), it is clear that some of those debtors who are so entitled relish the opportunity to pursue a claim for punitive damages for what is largely a minor stay violation. Because of this, courts have begun to express concern that some debtors and their counsel use § 362(k)(1) more as a sword than as a shield and that rewarding debtors too lavishly will create a cottage industry of precipitous § 362(k)(1) litigation.[22]

One of the other issues that arises periodically with respect to the stay is whether actions taken in violation of the stay are void or voidable. Consider the following case.

IN RE SCHWARTZ
954 F.2d 569 (9th Cir. 1992)

Wiggins, Circuit Judge:

Debtors Russell and Linda Schwartz appeal from a Bankruptcy Appellate Panel (BAP) decision that an IRS tax penalty assessed in violation of the Bankruptcy Code's automatic stay provision is voidable but not void. We reverse the judgment of the BAP.

---

[20]   *E.g., In re Atlantic Bus. & Community Corp.*, 901 F.2d 325 (3d Cir. 1990); *Budget Services Co. v. Better Homes of Va., Inc.*, 804 F.2d 289 (4th Cir. 1986).

[21]   *E.g., In re Spookyworld, Inc.*, 346 F.3d 1 (1st Cir. 2003); *In re Just Brakes Corporate Systems, Inc.*, 108 F.3d 881 (8th Cir. 1997); *In re Jove Engineering, Inc.*, 92 F.3d 1539 (11th Cir. 1996); *In re Goodman*, 991 F.2d 613 (9th Cir. 1993); *In re Chateaugay Corp.*, 920 F.2d 183 (2d Cir. 1990). *See also In re Pace*, 67 F.3d 187 (9th Cir. 1995) (the trustee, as the representative of the estate, is not an "individual" for the purpose of § 362(k)(1)). *Contra In re Garofalo's Finer Foods, Inc.*, 186 B.R. 414 (E.D. Ill. 1995).

[22]   *See, e.g., In re Roman*, 283 B.R. 1 (9th Cir. BAP 2002). *Cf. In re Baggs*, 283 B.R. 726 (Bankr. C.D. Ill. 2002) (awarding debtor $750 in punitive damages and attorneys' fees merely because creditor sent two bills after receiving notice of the bankruptcy filing).

BACKGROUND

The essential facts of this case are not in dispute. On February 25, 1983, the Schwartzes and their corporation, R.H. Schwartz Construction Specialties, Inc., filed a Chapter 11 bankruptcy petition. On October 8, 1984, the IRS, apparently unaware of the bankruptcy filing, assessed a 100% tax penalty, totaling $65,819.25, against Russell Schwartz pursuant to 26 U.S.C. § 6672 (1988). The Schwartzes did not challenge the tax assessment within the Chapter 11 bankruptcy and stipulated to their dismissal from the Chapter 11 bankruptcy on March 27, 1985.

In August 1987, the IRS filed a Federal Tax Lien with the King County Auditor pursuant to the penalty assessment. The IRS claimed that the penalty had increased to $86,296.60. On October 8, 1987, the Schwartzes filed a Chapter 13 bankruptcy petition. The IRS filed a Proof of Claim in the Chapter 13 bankruptcy on February 19, 1988, alleging that the Schwartzes owed the IRS $90,787.67 for the 1984 tax assessment.

The Schwartzes objected to the IRS claim. They argued that the tax assessment, which originally occurred during their prior Chapter 11 bankruptcy, violated the automatic stay provision of the Bankruptcy Code and was therefore void. The bankruptcy court agreed and ruled that the IRS tax assessment was void and without effect. The government appealed to the BAP, which rejected the Schwartzes' argument and reversed the judgment of the bankruptcy court. The BAP held that acts in violation of the automatic stay are voidable, not void. Because the tax assessment was not affirmatively challenged by the Schwartzes in the original Chapter 11 bankruptcy, the BAP held that the assessment was valid and enforceable in the subsequent Chapter 13 bankruptcy. This appeal followed.

DISCUSSION

The sole issue before us is whether creditor violations of the Bankruptcy Code's automatic stay provision are void or simply voidable. If violations of the automatic stay are void, the IRS tax assessment made against the Schwartzes in the Chapter 11 bankruptcy is without effect. If, however, such violations are merely voidable, the assessment is valid because the Schwartzes made no attempt to have the assessment voided in the Chapter 11 bankruptcy. The issue in this appeal is one of law; we review the BAP's conclusions of law de novo.

It is undisputed that the IRS tax assessment violated the Bankruptcy Code's automatic stay provision. § 362(a)(4)-(6). The Ninth Circuit has stated generally that violations of the automatic stay are "void." *See, e.g., In re Shamblin*, 890 F.2d 123, 125 (9th Cir. 1989) ("Judicial proceedings in violation of [the] automatic stay are void"); *In re Stringer*, 847 F.2d 549, 551 (9th Cir. 1988) ("Any proceedings in violation of the automatic stay in bankruptcy are void"). Although *Shamblin* and *Stringer* suggest that violations of the automatic stay are void and not merely voidable, the void/voidable distinction was not dispositive in those cases, and the Ninth Circuit has not directly addressed the precise issue presented in this appeal. * * *

In light of the automatic stay's purpose, the issue before us requires some analysis of the relevant policy considerations. Either the debtor must affirmatively challenge creditor violations of the stay, or the violations are void without the need for direct challenge. If violations of the stay are merely voidable, debtors must spend a considerable amount of time and money policing and litigating creditor actions. If violations are void, however, debtors are afforded better protection and can focus their attention on reorganization.

Given the important and fundamental purpose of the automatic stay and the broad debtor protections of the Bankruptcy Code, we find that Congress intended violations of the automatic stay to be void rather than voidable. Nothing in the Code or the legislative history suggests that Congress intended to burden a bankruptcy debtor with an obligation to fight off unlawful claims. The position championed by the IRS in this case would impose severe hardships on debtors trying to regain their financial footing.

The district court in *In re Garcia*, 109 B.R. 335 (N.D. Ill. 1989), explained that if violations of the automatic stay were merely voidable, creditors would be encouraged to violate the stay:

> [T]he fundamental importance of the automatic stay to the purposes sought to be accomplished by the Bankruptcy Code requires that acts in violation of the automatic stay be void, rather than voidable. Concluding that acts in violation of the automatic stay were merely voidable would have the effect of encouraging disrespect for the stay by increasing the possibility that violators of the automatic stay may profit from their disregard for the law, provided it goes undiscovered for a sufficient period of time. This may be an acceptable risk to some creditors when measured against a delayed pro rata distribution.

Id. at 340. Like the court in *Garcia*, we will not reward those who violate the automatic stay. The Bankruptcy Code does not burden the debtor with a duty to take additional steps to secure the benefit of the automatic stay. Those taking postpetition collection actions have the burden of obtaining relief from the automatic stay.

Our conclusion is supported by the great weight of authority. The majority of courts have long stated that violations of the automatic stay are void and of no effect. Indeed, many courts have specifically held that violations of the automatic stay are void and not merely voidable.

The courts which have found the automatic stay voidable rather than void have relied primarily on sections 362(d) and 549 of the Bankruptcy Code to support their conclusion. *See, e.g., Sikes v. Global Marine, Inc.*, 881 F.2d 176, 178-79 (5th Cir. 1989) (concluding that violations of the automatic stay are voidable); *In re Oliver*, 38 B.R. 245, 248 (Bankr. D. Minn. 1984). These courts have reasoned that (1) the court's power under section 362(d) to annul an automatic stay and (2) the trustee's duty under section 549 to bring an action to void an unauthorized transfer are inconsistent with violations of the stay being void and thus demonstrate that violations of the automatic stay are merely voidable. We find this reasoning erroneous.

Section 362(d)

Section 362(d), a subsection of the automatic stay provision, gives the bankruptcy court the power to grant creditors relief from the stay. It provides in part:

> On request of a party in interest and after notice and a hearing, the court shall grant relief from the stay provided under subsection (a) of this section, such as by terminating, annulling, modifying, or conditioning such stay.

Thus, section 362 gives the bankruptcy court wide latitude in crafting relief from the automatic stay, including the power to grant retroactive relief from the stay. Some courts have reasoned that the power to grant retroactive stay relief means that actions which violate section 362(a) cannot be absolutely void, for if they were, section 362(d) would be meaningless. *See, e.g., Sikes*, 881 F.2d at 178-79; *Oliver*, 38 B.R. at 248.

However, section 362(d) is not inconsistent with the conclusion that any action in violation of the automatic stay is void and of no effect. Section 362(d) outlines the bankruptcy court's authority to make exceptions to the general operation of the stay. If a creditor obtains retroactive relief under section 362(d), there is no violation of the automatic stay, and whether violations of the stay are void or voidable is not at issue.

The *Sikes* and *Oliver* courts read far too much into the meaning and operation of section 362(d). The power to grant relief, even retroactively, simply does not mean that violations of the stay must be merely voidable rather than void. As was explained by the court in *In re Garcia*, 109 B.R. at 339, "that Congress saw fit to include specific exceptions to the automatic stay does not require the conclusion that actions in violation of the automatic stay are merely voidable." It is entirely consistent to reason that, absent affirmative relief from the bankruptcy court, violations of the stay are void.

Statements from leading authorities on bankruptcy generally support this conclusion: "The use of the word 'annulling' [in § 362(d)] permits the [court's] order to operate retroactively, thus validating actions taken by a party at a time when he was unaware of the stay. *Such actions would otherwise be void.*" 2 Collier on Bankruptcy § 362.07 (emphasis added). With that understanding, section 362(d) gives the court the power to ratify retroactively any violation of the automatic stay which would otherwise be void. Simply put, there is nothing remarkable or inconsistent about the normal operation of the automatic stay being subject to a specific statutory exception such as that found in section 362(d). *See Sikes*, 881 F.2d at 180 (Johnson, J., dissenting) (noting that although violations of the automatic stay are void, "a bankruptcy court may validate an otherwise void filing in violation of the automatic stay").

Section 549

The more important potential conflict with interpreting the automatic stay as voiding violations is provided by section 549 of the Code. *See, e.g., Sikes*, 881 F.2d at 179 (court determining that § 549 is inconsistent with automatic stay voiding violations). Section 549 allows the bankruptcy trustee to avoid certain authorized transfers and all unauthorized transfers of estate property. Section 549 includes a statute of limitation which requires the trustee to commence an action to void a transfer either within two years of the transfer or before the close of the case, whichever is earlier. § 549(d). The Code's definitions dictate that section 549 can apply to a wide variety of transactions. "Transfer" is defined as "every mode, direct or indirect, absolute or conditional, voluntary or involuntary, of disposing of or parting with property or with an interest in property." § 101(50). Further, "property of the estate" includes all legal interests in property. § 541.

The supposed conflict between section 549 and section 362 can be explained by the following reasoning. First, the expansive definition of "transfer" means that sections 362 and 549, at times, cover the same transactions. Second, section 549 implies that some of these overlapping transactions will be valid unless affirmatively challenged by the trustee. Therefore, some argue that section 362 cannot be interpreted to void these overlapping transactions, for doing so would render section 549 moot. *See, e.g., Sikes*, 881 F.2d at 179.

On the surface, this conflict appears troublesome. However, a straightforward analysis of section 549 reveals that it is not intended to cover the same type of actions prohibited by the automatic stay nor rendered moot by section 362's voiding of all automatic stay violations. Section 549 applies to unauthorized transfers of estate property which are not otherwise prohibited by the Code. *Garcia*, 109 B.R. at 338-40; *In re R & L Cartage & Sons*, 118 B.R. 646, 650-51 (Bankr. N.D. Ind. 1990) (adopting *Garcia* analysis). In most circumstances, section 549 applies to transfers in which the debtor is a willing participant. *See Garcia*, 109 B.R. at 339. For example, in a transfer unrelated to any antecedent debt, the debtor may sell a portion of the estate's property to a third person. The trustee has the power to avoid such a transfer under section 549.

Section 362's automatic stay does not apply to sales or transfers of property initiated by the debtor. Thus, section 549 has a purpose in bankruptcy beyond the potential overlap with section 362. In other words, the automatic stay can void any violation and still leave section 549 with a valid and important role in bankruptcy. Section 549 exists as a protection for creditors against unauthorized debtor transfers of estate property. Although there are circumstances where section 362 overlaps section 549 and renders it unnecessary, this overlap falls far short of rendering section 549 meaningless.

Similarly, subsection 549(c)'s protection of good faith purchasers carves out an extremely specific and narrow exception to the automatic stay when section 362 overlaps subsection 549(c). There is no reason to infer from this narrow exception that violations of the automatic stay are not void. It is disingenuous to argue that the general rule must be invalid simply because there is a narrow exception to the rule. If violations of the automatic stay are not void because there is a narrow exception under subsection 549(c), then by the same reasoning the rest of section 549 would be invalid because subsection 549(c) creates an exception to the trustee's power to avoid postpetition transfers.

Indeed, subsection 549(c) sheds no light on the void/voidable distinction. Subsection 549(c) is an exception to section 362 regardless of whether violations of the automatic stay are void or merely voidable. Congress did not draft subsection 549(c) to demonstrate that violations of the automatic stay are merely voidable; Congress drafted subsection 549(c) to protect good faith purchasers where the sale would otherwise be subject to avoidance under section 549 or void under section 362. * * *

CONCLUSION

Because violations of the automatic stay are void, we reverse the decision of the BAP. The bankruptcy court's order granting the Schwartzes' objection to the IRS's penalty assessment is correct and should not be disturbed.

NOTE

A majority of circuit courts agree that actions in violation of the stay are void, not voidable. As one noted:

> Treating an action taken in contravention of the automatic stay as void places the burden of validating the action after the fact squarely on the shoulders of the offending creditor. In contrast, treating an action in contravention of the automatic stay as voidable places the burden of challenging the action on the offended debtor.[23]

Other courts disagree.[24] The Sixth Circuit would prefer to scrap the void/voidable distinction:

> We think that "invalid" is a more appropriate adjective to use when defining action taken against the debtor during the duration of the automatic stay. Like the word "void," "invalid" describes something that is without legal force or effect. However, something that is invalid is not incurable, in contrast to a void action which is incapable of being ratified.[25]

---

[23] *In re Soares*, 107 F.3d 969, 976 (1st Cir. 1997).

[24] *See, e.g., Bronson v. United States*, 46 F.3d 1573 (Fed. Cir. 1995); *Easley v. Pettibone Michigan Corp.*, 990 F.2d 905 (6th Cir. 1993); *Picco v. Global Marine Drilling Co.*, 900 F.2d 846, 850 (5th Cir. 1990).

[25] *Easley*, 990 F.2d at 909.

It would apparently agree with the Ninth Circuit's decision in *Schwartz* that the debtor should not have to incur the burden and expense of invalidating creditor actions that violate the stay. However, in appropriate circumstances, it would allow the bankruptcy court to ratify – and thereby give effect to – actions involving small, technical violations of the stay.

4. *Application of the Stay to Rejected Leases*

Review the discussion of executory contracts and unexpired leases in chapter five. Many debtors with rented property – either residential or commercial – default on their rental obligations prior to filing for bankruptcy protection. Others are current on all lease payments. In either situation, particularly when residential property is involved, the lease will have no value to the estate in a Chapter 7 case. Accordingly, the trustee will reject the lease. Unfortunately, "[t]he effect of rejection is one of the great mysteries of bankruptcy law."[26] There are several interrelated issues.

Technically, rejection constitutes a prepetition breach, § 365(g)(1), thus giving rise to a prepetition claim by the lessor against the estate.[27] Although the amount of the lessor's claim may be limited by § 502(b)(6), treating the lessor as having a prepetition claim makes sense if the debtor is already in default or plans to default. After all, the lease is a prepetition contract and the only way the lessor can share in estate assets to cover whatever losses arise is if the lessor has a prepetition claim. If, however, the debtor is current on all lease payments and plans to remain current, treating rejection as a breach is more problematic, at least if such treatment will precipitate an eviction. Indeed, because of this possibility, some courts have refused to treat the mere rejection of a residential lease as a breach for any purpose other than claim allowance.[28]

Related to all this is whether and how the stay applies to property subject to a rejected lease. Generally, at least with respect to personal property and residential realty, rejection gives rise to a prepetition breach but does not terminate the lease.[29]

---

[26] *In re Henderson*, 245 B.R. 449 (Bankr. S.D.N.Y. 2000).

[27] Accordingly, the claim will be generally dischargeable, even with respect to payments that were due postpetition. *Chateau Communities, Inc. v. Miller*, 252 B.R. 121 (E.D. Mich. 2000).

[28] *E.g., In re Knight*, 8 B.R. 925 (Bankr. D. Md. 1981).

[29] *See Henderson*, 245 B.R. at 453; *In re Beacon*, 212 B.R. 66, 69 (Bankr. E.D. Pa. 1997) ([l]ease rejection is not synonymous with lease termination," it is merely "a bankruptcy concept that determines whether the estate will administer the lease asset") (citing Jay L. Westbrook, *A Functional Analysis of Executory Contracts*, 74 MINN. L. REV. 227, 248 (1989)). *See also In re Lavigne*, 114 F.3d 379, 386-87 (2d Cir. 1997) (discussing the effect of rejection on executory contracts).

Instead, rejection effects an abandonment of the lease to the debtor.[30] A slightly different rule applies when non-residential real property is involved. If the trustee constructively rejects the lease by failing to assume it, the trustee must immediately surrender the property to the lessor. § 365(d)(4). In such a case, rejection is tantamount to termination.

Because rejection constitutes an abandonment of the estate's interest in both the lease and the leased property,[31] § 362(a)(3) will no longer stay eviction actions by the landlord. Nevertheless, other aspects of the stay may apply must be considered:

> The debtor and estate inevitably have personal property on the premises, and the termination of the lease does not affect those interests. Any act by the landlord that interferes with or exercises control over the estate's property violates the automatic stay. *See* § 362(a)(3). In addition, any attempt to collect a prepetition claim from property of the estate or property of the debtor violates the stay. *See* § 362(a)(2), (6).[32]

The upshot of this is clear: a landlord whose debtor has defaulted on lease payments – either prepetition or postpetition – must obtain relief from the stay to evict the debtor and obtain control of the premises unless some exception to the stay applies.[33] Such relief should be reasonably easy to get after a postpetition default in payment, but may be difficult to obtain if the only default is prepetition.

B.   ACTIONS AGAINST NONDEBTORS

Section 362(a) applies to actions and other proceedings against the debtor or the bankruptcy estate. It does not apply to actions against a third party. Although § 1301(a) extends the stay in Chapter 13 cases to individual co-obligors, the absence of such a provision in Chapters 7 and 11 suggests that Congress intended no protection for anyone other than the debtor in such cases.

However, § 105 gives bankruptcy courts authority to issue orders necessary to protect the bankruptcy process. May a court use § 105 to provide relief to someone other than the debtor? Not if the only purpose of such an order would be to protect the

---

[30]   *E.g., In re Couture*, 225 B.R. 58, 64 (D. Vt. 1998); *In re Beacon*, 212 B.R. at 68; 3 COLLIER ON BANKRUPTCY ¶ 365.09[3] at 365-84 (15th ed. rev. 2005).

[31]   *But cf.* § 554(d) (suggesting that abandonment may not result from rejection).

[32]   *In re Henderson*, 245 B.R. at 454 n.14.

[33]   *See* § 362(b)(10), (23).

third party.[34] However, courts have stayed actions against nondebtors in a number of Chapter 11 cases after concluding that successful reorganization of the debtor would be jeopardized by continued action against a third party. For example, some have enjoined actions against an insider/guarantor of the debtor's obligations because the guarantor's assets were needed to provide capital to the debtor in possession.[35] However, such decisions have been sharply criticized,[36] in part because they fail to explain why the creditor who bargained for the guaranty should be made to wait and perhaps never be paid merely so that the guarantor may make a risky investment in a bankrupt business. Accordingly some courts have expressly rejected this use of § 105.[37]

If the bankruptcy court does not intervene to enjoin a creditor's action against a nondebtor, then discovery relating to that action is, of course, not stayed. This is apparently true even with respect to discovery aimed at the debtor, so long as it relates to the claim against the nondebtor. *Cf.* § 362(a)(1) (staying "employment of process" against the debtor). In other words, the creditor is entitled to discovery against the debtor – and if necessary, to an order compelling the debtor to comply – despite the presence of the automatic stay and even if the information sought could eventually adversely affect the debtor.[38] However, prudence dictates that the party seeking discovery from the debtor first obtain relief from the stay.

C. PROHIBITIONS ON DISCRIMINATION

Insolvent debtors seeking a fresh start would have their hopes and plans seriously undermined if they could lose their jobs because of their financial difficulties. Yet outside of bankruptcy, there is little protection for debtors in this regard. One of the few laws that provides some is the Consumer Credit Protection Act, which prohibits employers from firing employees whose earnings have been subjected to garnishment for any *one* indebtedness. 15 U.S.C. § 1674(a). Yet the narrowness of this rule is staggering. First, it applies only to debt collection through garnishment; it does nothing to protect debtors who have been subjected to other types of collection efforts or who are simply insolvent. Second, it does not protect debtors whose earnings have been garnished twice, no matter how far apart the two garnishments were. Third, it does not

---

[34] *See, e.g., Lynch v. Johns-Manville Sales Corp.*, 710 F.2d 1194 (6th Cir. 1983).

[35] *E.g., In re Otero Mills, Inc.*, 25 B.R. 1018 (D.N.M. 1982).

[36] *See* Howard C. Buschman & Sean P. Madden, *The Power and Propriety of Bankruptcy Court Intervention in Actions Between Nondebtors*, 47 BUS. LAW. 913 (1992).

[37] *E.g., In re Supermercado Gamboa, Inc.*, 68 B.R. 230 (Bankr. D.P.R. 1986).

[38] *See In re Miller*, 262 B.R. 499 (9th Cir. BAP 2001).

prohibit a prospective employer from refusing to hire a job applicant merely because the applicant once had earnings garnished. Finally, although violations of this provision are punishable by fine or imprisonment, *see* 15 U.S.C. § 1674(b), they apparently do not give rise to a private cause of action.[39]

Debtors who file for bankruptcy protection fare somewhat better. The Bankruptcy Code prohibits public entities from denying licenses to, denying employment to, or terminating the employment of a bankruptcy debtor merely because the debtor is insolvent or has filed for bankruptcy protection. § 525(a). Even private employers are prohibited from discharging an employee who filed for bankruptcy merely because of the filing or the employee's insolvency. § 525(b).

These protections are not without their limits, though. Public agencies may, for example, refuse to renew the lease of a tenant in a public housing project whose lease was terminated prepetition for nonpayment of rent.[40] They apparently may also terminate the benefits – such as a low income housing subsidy – of debtors who violated regulations or contracts under which the benefits are provided.[41] They may also deny credit based solely on a person's recent bankruptcy discharge.[42] Private employers, while prohibited from firing employees because of their pending bankruptcy, may nevertheless refuse to hire someone who is or has been in bankruptcy. *Compare* § 525(a) *with* (b).[43] They may also fire an employee who *intends* to file for bankruptcy protection because § 525(b), by its very nature, offers no protection prior to the actual filing.[44]

The newest protection of this type for debtors is § 525(c), which was added as part of the 1994 amendments to the Code. It was intended to prevent banks from discriminating in the making of student loans against prospective borrowers who have a bankruptcy filing on their record.[45] The quality of legislative drafting being what it is,

---

[39] *See LeVick v. Scaggs Cos.*, 701 F.2d 777 (9th Cir. 1983); *Smith v. Cotton Bros. Baking Co.*, 609 F.2d 738 (5th Cir.), *cert. denied*, 449 U.S. 821 (1980).

[40] *See In re Robinson*, 169 B.R. 171 (N.D. Ill. 1994).

[41] *In re Smith*, 259 B.R. 901 (8th Cir. BAP 2001). *But cf. Stoltz v. Brattleboro Housing Authority*, 259 B.R. 255 (D. Vt. 2001) (public housing authority may not evict tenant for failing to pay discharged rent).

[42] *Toth v. Michigan State Housing Dev. Auth.* 136 F.3d 477 (6th Cir.), *cert. denied*, 524 U.S. 954 (1998).

[43] *See also Fiorani v. CACI*, 192 B.R. 401 (E.D. Va. 1996); *In re Stinson*, 285 B.R. 239 (Bankr. W.D. Va. 2002). *But see Leary v. Warnaco, Inc.*, 251 B.R. 656 (S.D.N.Y. 2000).

[44] *See In re Majewski*, 310 F.3d 653 (9th Cir. 2002).

[45] *But cf. In re Taylor*, 263 B.R. 139 (N.D. Ala. 2001) (provision does not prohibit prospective lender from *considering* a past bankruptcy, merely from making a past bankruptcy the sole basis of denying

however, the provision on its face does something entirely different and much more broad: instead of preventing discrimination against bankruptcy debtors when making federally guaranteed student loans (after all, why should the bank care about the borrower's bankruptcy filing if the loan is federally guaranteed?), it prohibits all banks that make student loans from discriminating against bankruptcy debtors when deciding to make any loan! The jury is still out on whether bankruptcy courts will restrict the provision to its intended meaning.

Another limit on discrimination is found in § 366, which applies to providers of utility services, such as gas, water, and electricity. If, postpetition, a utility provider threatened to cut off service unless the debtor or trustee paid off any debt remaining for prepetition services, that threat would violate the automatic stay. *See* § 362(a)(1). However, no part of the stay would prevent a utility provider from demanding payment in advance or an excessively large deposit to cover postpetition services. This is where § 366 comes in. Read it and then answer the following problem.

Problem 7-14

Displaced has filed a Chapter 7 bankruptcy petition. Among the debts to be discharged is a $420 bill for three months of electricity and natural gas. The supplier, Power Company, informs Displaced that service will be discontinued unless Displaced posts a $500 bond. Displaced does not have $500. What do you advise? *See* § 366. As a practical matter, can consumer debtors afford to litigate this issue? Can you identify any factors that might tend to keep utility companies' requests for consumer deposits within reason?

D.   TOLLING RULES

When a Chapter 7 bankruptcy petition is filed and the trustee assumes responsibility for all of the debtor's assets, or at least the nonexempt assets, the trustee may understandably need some time to ascertain where they are, determine how valuable they are, and decide what to do with them. This task can be particularly difficult and time consuming with respect to those rights consisting of claims by the debtor against some other entity. Yet such claims may be subject to strict time limits of one sort or another. For example, a statute of limitations may be about to expire or a deadline for filing a pleading may be only a day or two away. Creditors can face a similar problem. For example, claims against the debtor are generally subject to the stay even though they are not dischargeable. If the bankruptcy petition were filed a few days or weeks before

---

a loan; provision also does not create a private right of action for its violation).

the applicable statute of limitations were to expire, the creditor could find itself barred from bringing an action until after the limitations period had run out.

Section 108 deals with all of these problems by imposing various tolling periods that delay expiration of some legal and contractual time periods. Each of its three subsections tolls a different type of time period:

§ 108(a)	§ 108(b)	§ 108(c)
Tolls statutes of limitation for actions that could be brought by the debtor	Tolls time for trustee to file pleadings and do other similar things.	Tolls statutes of limitation for actions against the debtor.

Read § 108 and then attempt the following problems.

Problem 7-15

On June 1, Bank conducted a proper foreclosure sale of Dispossessed's home. Under state law, Dispossessed has six months to redeem the property from the foreclosure sale buyer by paying the foreclosure sale price (which is often significantly less than fair market value). On November 15th, two weeks before Dispossessed's statutory right of redemption would expire, Dispossessed filed for bankruptcy protection. Does the stay prevent the right of redemption from expiring? Does § 108(b) toll the period of redemption? *See In re Canney*, 284 F.3d 362 (2d Cir. 2002).

Problem 7-16

On June 1, Dealer purchased for $25,000 an option to buy a parcel of real property for $300,000 any time before December 1. On November 1, without having exercised the option, Dealer filed a Chapter 7 bankruptcy petition. Does the trustee have any right to exercise the option after December 1? *See* § 108(b). *See Good Hope Refineries v. Benavides*, 602 F.2d 998 (1st Cir. 1979); *In re Yates Dev., Inc.*, 256 F.3d 1285 (11th Cir. 2001); *In re Santa Fe Dev. & Mortgage Corp.*, 16 B.R. 165 (9th Cir. BAP 1981); *In re Durability, Inc.*, 273 B.R. 647 (Bankr. N.D. Okla. 2002), *rev'd on other grounds*, 166 Fed. Appx. 321 (10th Cir. 2006).

PART III

LIQUIDATION IN CHAPTER 7

CHAPTER EIGHT
THE LIQUIDATION PROCESS

A. DEALING WITH ESTATE ASSETS GENERALLY

For each asset included in the estate, only a limited number of interested parties are likely to seek control over the asset or assert the right to extract value from it. Chief among these is, of course, the trustee. The others may include: the debtor, if all or part of the asset is exempt; any creditor with a lien on the asset; and anyone else with an ownership interest in the asset.

Initially, of course, the debtor must assign a valuation to each asset listed in the schedules filed with or shortly after the petition. The trustee and others may choose to accept that valuation or to conduct an independent investigation or appraisal. For example, with respect to real estate the trustee may hire an appraiser, review any existing appraisals of the property that the debtor may have, or simply drive by the property and examine it. For intangible assets, such as a tort claim, the trustee may speak with the attorney already handling the case, if there is one, in an effort to discern the likelihood of success and the probable amount of any recovery.

Regardless how the trustee determines an asset's value, in most cases the trustee will decide fairly quickly whether the asset is worth anything to the estate. In other words, whether the estate's interest in the asset is worth more than: (i) any exemption amount to which the debtor is entitled in the asset; and (ii) the amount of all claims secured by unavoidable liens on the property. When valuing the estate's interest, the trustee will take into consideration whether anyone else has an ownership interest in the asset. Thus, the trustee's calculus might look something like this:

> Total Value of Asset
> – Portion of Value Allocable to Another Owner
> – Amount of Unavoidable Liens on the Asset
> – Amount of Exemption to Which Debtor is Entitled in Asset
> = Value of Estate's Interest

If the asset has minimal or no value to the estate, the trustee will abandon the asset and, indeed, can be compelled to do so by anyone who does have an interest in it. *See* § 554(a), (b).[1] To abandon an asset, the trustee files a motion to do so and sends a copy of it to the debtor, the U.S. Trustee, and to all creditors. *See* Rule 6007(a). If no one

---

[1] *See also* § 725 (requiring the trustee, before final distribution, to dispose of property in which an entity other than the debtor has an interest).

objects, the court will issue an order authorizing the abandonment. Such an order divests the estate of any ownership rights in the asset and, in most cases, revests the property in the debtor.[2] If a party in interest does object, the court will conduct a hearing to determine whether abandonment is in the best interests of the estate.

If, on the other hand, the trustee's computation suggests that the asset is worth more to the estate than the cost of administering it, the trustee will take control over the asset and, in all likelihood, sell it. Section 363 is the provision that authorizes the trustee to use, sell, and lease property of the estate. When selling assets, the trustee need not follow the procedures required of lien creditors under state law. In other words, there are no specified advertising requirements and the sale need not be conducted as an auction. The trustee often simply finds a willing buyer and negotiates a price. Exactly how the trustee does this typically depends on the type of asset involved and on how owners of such assets normally locate interested buyers. Regardless of the method used, however, the trustee must send at least 20 days in advance a notice explaining the proposed transaction to the U.S. Trustee and to the creditors committee. § 363(b).[3] If no one objects by the applicable deadline (usually five days before the sale),[4] the trustee will consummate the transaction. If someone does object, the court will conduct a hearing to determine whether to permit the trustee to sell the asset as proposed.

If the debtor's estate includes business assets, the court may authorize the trustee to operate the business for a limited period of time, if that is likely to be in the estate's best interest. § 721. In other words, the business may be worth more as a going concern, so the court may allow the trustee to continue the debtor's business operations pending a sale of the business. In such cases, the trustee may sell assets in the ordinary course of business even without notice and a hearing. § 363(c)(1). The trustee may also incur debt in the ordinary course of the business. § 364(a).

In some cases the estate may share ownership of an asset with another person. For example, the debtor may own a tract of land as tenants in common with siblings or as tenants by the entireties with a spouse. In such cases, the trustee has three options for dealing with the property. First, the trustee may seek to partition the property, using whatever rights a co-owner has under nonbankruptcy law to achieve such a division. In other words, the applicable real estate law may permit each tenant in common to bring an action to physically divide the property among the co-owners. This will not always be practical, however. For example, the divided portions might be too small under the

---

[2]   In some cases, the court may order abandonment directly to someone other than the debtor, usually someone who already has an ownership interest in the property.

[3]   *See* § 363(b); Rule 2002(g), (i), (k). Note, because orders authorizing the sale are normally automatically stayed for 10 days to facilitate a possible appeal, *see* Rule 6004(g), notification of the sale probably needs to be given at least 30 days in advance.

[4]   *See* Rule 6004(b).

governing zoning laws to permit development or the whole property may have a single use – such as a ski slope – that would make splitting it up undesirable for all concerned.

Second, the trustee may simply try to sell the estate's interest. However, this will often be difficult and unwise. Few people are likely to be interested in buying the estate's undivided interest, given that any buyer of that interest would have to share ownership with the nondebtor co-owner, someone the buyer probably does not know and who may not be particularly gracious about the prospect of sharing the property with a stranger. In short, even though the property as a whole may be worth a great deal, the presence of a co-owner may significantly undermine the market for the estate's undivided share.

Third, if the trustee is unlikely to realize the full value of the estate's interest using either of the prior two options, the trustee may sell the entire property. In other words, the trustee may sell the interests of both the estate and the co-owner, provided of course that a proportionate share of the sale proceeds are distributed to the co-owner. *See* § 363(f)(2), (5), (h).

As you may remember from chapter five, the estate may contain one or more executory contracts or unexpired leases that the debtor entered into prepetition. Because such contracts and leases still require performance by both sides, they represent both potential assets and potential liabilities of the estate. The trustee will therefore evaluate each contract and lease to determine if it is of net value to the estate. The trustee will likely assume those with such value and reject those without it. § 365(a). In connection with this choice, the trustee may decide to assume an executory contract or unexpired lease solely for the purpose of assigning it to another party (*i.e.*, selling it). § 363(f).

B. WHAT HAPPENS TO COLLATERAL

Almost everything written in the last few pages also applies to estate assets subject to one or more unavoidable liens. However, there are often competing interests at stake with respect to such property: (i) the trustee wants to extract whatever value the asset may have for the estate; (ii) the secured claimant certainly wants to preserve the asset's function as security and may want to promptly liquidate the collateral so as to realize upon its value; and (iii) the debtor may want to preserve the value of any exemption rights in the asset and, regardless of whether any portion of the asset's value is exempt, may want to retain possession and use of the asset. After all, the asset may be something the debtor needs – such as a house or motor vehicle – and the debtor may have little or no ability to obtain a replacement for it.

How these competing interests are treated in bankruptcy is a major aspect of many bankruptcy cases. It is also often a major factor in the debtor's decision about whether to file for bankruptcy protection at all and, if so, whether to do so under Chapter 7, 11,

12, or 13. We will explore the treatment of collateral under Chapters 13 and 11 in later chapters of this book. At present, we focus on what happens in Chapter 7 cases. In that context, the most significant factor in determining the fate of collateral is whether the collateral is worth more or less than the total of the claims it secures and any exemption amount to which the debtor is entitled. If it is worth more, then the collateral is of value to the estate and the trustee is the one with the incentive to maximize the price at which it will be sold. Accordingly the trustee will conduct the sale.

1.   Sale by the Trustee

In general, the trustee sells estate assets subject to the lien of any secured claimant. When this occurs, the buyer typically pays the secured claimant – often immediately but occasionally over time – to redeem the property from the lien. If the buyer fails to do this, the secured claimant may use whatever nonbankruptcy rights are available to enforce the lien.[5]

However, the trustee is also authorized to sell property free and clear of liens, *see* § 363(f), provided the trustee adequately protects the interest of the secured claimant, *see* § 363(e). As a practical matter, this means the holder of the secured claim is paid the amount of the claim from the proceeds of the sale. In some cases, the secured claimant wants the trustee to use this approach, perhaps to avoid the hassle of conducting the sale itself. Sometimes, though, it is for more significant reasons. For example, the collateral may be personal property for which there is no customary market and the creditor may be unsure how to comply with the requirement of conducting a commercially reasonable sale.[6] Alternatively, the collateral may be real estate, as in the following problem.

Problem 8-1

Security Bank has for several years provided financing for Developer, who recently filed for Chapter 7 bankruptcy relief. Security Bank holds a properly recorded mortgage on all of Developer's real estate, which is spread over eight different Midwestern states. For each parcel, Developer owes Security Bank more than the property is worth. Several of these states do not permit nonjudicial foreclosure, and as a result the foreclosure procedures are slow. Because time is money (at least with respect to interest that will accrue

---

[5]   Nothing in § 362(a) would stay the creditor's efforts to foreclose on property sold by the trustee to anyone other than the debtor.

[6]   *See* U.C.C. § 9-610(b).

but not be paid), Security Bank would like to avoid the whole nonbankruptcy foreclosure process by having the trustee sell the real estate under § 363(f). Is that permissible? Should it be? What if Developer is not in default on the mortgage loan? *See In re Feinstein Family Partnership*, 247 B.R. 502 (Bankr. M.D. Fla. 2000).

Section 506(c) permits the trustee to recover from the collateral the costs of preserving and disposing of it, to the extent this benefits the secured claimant. This rule is easy to state but less easy to apply, because there is some disagreement about what sort of "benefit" is necessary. On one hand, so the argument goes, if the trustee sells the creditor's collateral, the creditor is saved the expenses associated with conducting such a sale – appraisal fees, advertising costs, storage expenses, *etc.* – and thus can be called upon to reimburse the estate. Otherwise, so the argument continues, the secured claimant gets a windfall.[7] However, this argument makes sense only insofar as the costs are ones which the secured claimant would have actually incurred if it were conducting the sale outside bankruptcy. If the creditor is oversecured and such costs can be charged to the collateral under nonbankruptcy law, then arguably the creditor would never really incur those costs; the costs would always be charged to and come out of the collateral, still leaving enough value for the creditor to be paid in full. In short, if the creditor is oversecured, the trustee's expenses in caring for and selling the collateral should normally come out of the estate's equity in the collateral. If the creditor is undersecured, then the trustee should abandon the collateral, thereby leaving the costs of dealing with the collateral to the creditor. Thus, it is not clear when, if ever, § 506(c) may properly be used to charge the secured claimant with the costs of caring for or selling the collateral.

2.   *The Four Rs*

Whenever the collateral is worth less than the combined total of the debts it secures and any exemption amount to which the debtor is entitled, the trustee will probably abandon the property under § 554(a), and can even be forced to abandon it under § 554(b). If the debtor is a business entity or the collateral consists of business assets, the secured party will then probably seek relief from the stay and use its nonbankruptcy

---

[7]   *See IRS v. Boatman's First Nat'l Bank*, 5 F.3d 1157, 1159 (8th Cir. 1993). Note, only the trustee or debtor-in-possession may charge the collateral for their expenses; other creditors with administrative expense claims may not. *Hartford Underwriters Ins. Co. v. Union Planters Bank*, 530 U.S. 1 (2000).

rights to repossess and foreclose upon the collateral.[8] If the debtor is a consumer and the collateral consists of something the consumer needs – such as a house, car, or household goods – one of several things will likely occur: reaffirmation; redemption; repossession; or, perhaps, retention.

(a) Reaffirmation

In some cases, particularly when the debtor has built up a substantial amount of exempt equity in the collateral, the debtor may wish to reaffirm the debt. This allows the debtor to keep the collateral while making periodic payments to the secured creditor. In essence, the debt will not be discharged in the bankruptcy proceeding. *See* § 524(c). If the debtor defaults after bankruptcy, the secured creditor may exercise all of its nonbankruptcy remedies with regard to the collateral, including repossession and foreclosure. More significantly, the creditor may attempt to collect any deficiency from the debtor, since the debtor will remain obligated on the underlying obligation.

Reaffirmation is often the only feasible means for a Chapter 7 debtor to retain possession of desired collateral. Yet it has its drawbacks. First, the creditor will almost certainly require the debtor to reaffirm the entire obligation. For example, if a debt for $8,000 were secured by a lien on a car worth only $6,000, the debtor would likely have to promise to pay the entire $8,000 debt, perhaps with interest, costs, and the creditor's attorneys' fees added on. It is for this reason that reaffirmation is normally used only with respect to property in which the debtor has equity. Second, reaffirmation requires the consent of the creditor. Some lenders prefer to cut their losses and terminate relationships with bankrupt borrowers. Reaffirmation cannot be imposed on them. Third, reaffirmation agreements cannot impose an undue hardship on the debtor or the debtor's dependents. To ensure this, reaffirmation agreements are subject to a sort of certification process. They must be filed with the court and either: (i) accompanied by a representation of no undue hardship by the debtor's attorney; or (ii) approved by the court after a hearing on the matter. Read § 524(c). As a debtor's attorney, what would you think about when deciding whether to make the required representation to the court? Does making a representation of no undue hardship place your ethical obligation to the client in conflict with your ethical obligation to the court? Consider the following case that explores the meaning of the undue burden requirement.

---

[8]   Although abandonment by the trustee makes § 362(a)(3) and (4) inapplicable, § 362(a)(5) will continue to prevent the secured party from enforcing its lien. That is why the secured party must first obtain relief from the stay.

IN RE RIGGS
2006 WL 2990218 (Bankr. W.D. Mo. 2006)

Federman, Bankruptcy Judge.

Debtor Rebecca Ann Riggs owns a 1993 Ford Explorer which is subject to a lien held by Super Cars, Inc. The Debtor filed a Statement of Intention with her Petition, stating she intended to reaffirm the debt to Super Cars. She then signed and filed a Reaffirmation Agreement for a debt of $4,822.69 with an annual percentage rate of 18.9% and requests that I approve the Agreement. Her attorney did not sign Part C of such Agreement. For the reasons that follow, the request to approve the reaffirmation agreement is denied.

DISCUSSION
The Debtor's Requirements Regarding Property of the Estate
Securing Consumer Debts

* * * [U]nless the court fixes additional time, Chapter 7 debtors must, within the earlier of thirty days after the filing of the petition or on or before the meeting of creditors, file their statement of intention regarding property of the estate securing consumer debts, and must perform the intention with respect to such property within thirty days after the first date set for the meeting of creditors.

Prior to the enactment of the BAPCPA amendments, there was significant dispute among courts as to whether § 521(a)(2)(A) provided debtors with four options as to retention or surrender of such personal property, the fourth being that debtors could simply retain the property and keep making payments. That issue was effectively resolved, however, when Congress enacted § 326(h), § 521(a)(6), and § 521(d) as part of the BAPCPA amendments: Although the post-BAPCPA Code does not expressly prohibit the fourth "retain and pay" option, the Code now provides adverse consequences if the debtor does not perform one of the three specifically-enumerated options. Thus, the Code now effectively limits debtors' options with regard to personal property to (1) surrender; (2) retention coupled with redemption; or (3) retention coupled with reaffirmation of the debt. * * *

Requirements and Enforceability of Reaffirmation Agreements

When, as in this case, the debtor timely chooses the third option, to retain the property and reaffirm the debt, § 524(c) comes into play. * * *

In sum, with certain exceptions regarding the debtor's real estate not applicable here, in order for a signed reaffirmation agreement to be enforceable by the creditor, a number of conditions must be met. First, it must be signed, filed, and approved before the debtor's discharge is entered. Second, the agreement must contain the many disclosures described in § 524(k). Most of the current standard reaffirmation forms filed in this district contain the necessary disclosures. Third, the debtor must not have rescinded the agreement prior to discharge. And fourth, either (i) the debtor must have been represented by an attorney during the course of negotiating the reaffirmation agreement or (ii) the court, after notice and hearing, must approve the agreement as not imposing an undue hardship on, and being in the best interest of, the debtor.

This fourth requirement presents the most difficulty. Part C of the standard reaffirmation agreement allows the attorney to attest that the debtor was fully informed and advised of the consequences of reaffirming the debt, that the debtor voluntarily entered into the agreement, and that the agreement does not impose an undue hardship on the debtor or a dependent of the debtor. If the attorney does not sign Part C of the reaffirmation agreement, the Court has no way to know whether the debtor was "represented by an attorney during the course of negotiating the reaffirmation agreement." Therefore, in order to approve a reaffirmation agreement that is not signed by an attorney, the court must conduct a hearing and determine that the reaffirmation agreement does not impose an undue hardship and is in the debtor's best interest.

In determining whether the agreement imposes an undue hardship on the debtor, the court starts with § 524(m), which was added by BAPCPA. That section provides:

> (1) Until 60 days after an agreement of the kind specified in subsection (c) is filed with the court (or such additional period as the court, after notice and a hearing and for cause, orders before the expiration of such period), it shall be presumed that such agreement is an undue hardship on the debtor if the debtor's monthly income less the debtor's monthly expenses as shown on the debtor's completed and signed statement in support of such agreement required under subsection (k)(6)(A) is less than the scheduled payments on the reaffirmed debt. This presumption shall be reviewed by the court. The presumption may be rebutted in writing by the debtor if the statement includes an explanation that identifies additional sources of funds to make the payments as agreed upon under the terms of such agreement. If the presumption is not rebutted to the satisfaction of the court, the court may disapprove such agreement. No agreement shall be disapproved without notice and a hearing to the debtor and creditor, and such hearing shall be concluded before entry of the debtor's discharge.
>
> (2) This subsection does not apply to reaffirmation agreements where the creditor is a credit union.

The signed statement required under subsection (k)(6)(A) is found in Part D of the standard reaffirmation agreements filed in this district. According to Rule 4008, the amounts listed by the debtor in Part D should be the same as shown in the debtor's

Schedules I and J. If there is a difference between the Part D amounts and Schedules I and J, the debtor must explain why there is a difference.

Unless the creditor is a credit union, if Part D shows the debtor does not have enough income after expenses (including other debts to be reaffirmed) to make the payment on the submitted reaffirmation agreement, there is a presumption that reaffirming the debt will impose an undue hardship on the debtor. In order to rebut that presumption, the debtor must demonstrate, in writing, to the satisfaction of the court, how he or she will come up with the money each month to make the payment. Examples of this might be cutting costs in other categories of expenses or earning additional income through overtime or the like. If the court is not satisfied with the explanation, and there is a presumption that the payment imposes an undue hardship on the debtor, then the court cannot approve the agreement, regardless of whether the attorney signed off on it.

Assuming the § 524(m) presumption does not apply, the agreement is only enforceable if the attorney signs it, or if the Court approves it. In either situation, the issue is whether the agreement imposes an undue hardship and is in the best interests of the debtor. Thus, as to reaffirmation agreements (other than those involving a consumer debt secured by real property), the statute places attorneys in the uncomfortable position of deciding whether such reaffirmation imposes an undue hardship and whether it is in the client's best interests. Oftentimes, their clients desperately want to keep their cars, and to continue making regular payments. But in signing the reaffirmation agreement, attorneys expose their clients to a potential deficiency judgment, which would be avoided if the reaffirmation agreement were held not to be enforceable.

In determining whether to sign off on a reaffirmation agreement, attorneys should be aware of the types of agreements which I have concluded should be subject to the closest scrutiny. First, I look at whether Part D shows an ability to make payments presently. If it does show that the debtor has the ability to make the payments, then the question is: In the event that circumstances in the future leave the debtor unable to make the payments, how devastating will a deficiency judgment be? This is primarily a function of two factors, the interest rate and the amount being reaffirmed. Here, the debt to be reaffirmed carries an interest rate of 18.9%. As a consequence, it will take more than two years for the debtor to repay the loan on a 1993 model car. If the car stops running at any time during that period, and the reaffirmation is enforceable, the debtor will then be obligated to Super Cars for the unpaid balance, and will need to be paying on another car as well. And, she will not be able to obtain a Chapter 7 discharge of the debt due to Super Cars until eight years after this case was filed. For those reasons, I will not approve the Reaffirmation Agreement. As a rule of thumb, if a creditor on a personal property loan requires an interest rate over 10%, or if the amount to be reaffirmed is in excess of $20,000, attorneys should not be reluctant to leave it up to the Court to determine whether the agreement is in the debtor's best interests.

Pursuant to § 524(c), my declining to approve the Reaffirmation Agreement renders it unenforceable, even though the Debtor signed it. Thus, Super Cars cannot seek a deficiency against the Debtor if she defaults. And, since the Debtor has performed her duty under § 521(a)(2) in filing her statement of intention and signing and filing the reaffirmation agreement within the prescribed time limits, § 362(h) and § 521(c)(6) are not applicable. Once the discharge is entered, Super Cars may repossess the vehicle only if there is a payment or insurance default, or if its position has been significantly impaired. If Super Cars does later repossess the vehicle, any deficiency after sale will have been discharged in this bankruptcy case.

The request for approval of the reaffirmation agreement between debtor and Super Cars, Inc., is denied.

———————

Nothing in the Code explains how the stay operates with respect to negotiations over reaffirmation agreements. Nevertheless, just as courts have had no difficulty concluding that filing a proof of claim does not violate the stay, they have not hesitated to conclude that a creditor may solicit a reaffirmation agreement.[9] Indeed, for the most part they may, without violating the stay, play hardball during reaffirmation negotiations, such as by conditioning agreement to reaffirm a secured debt on reaffirmation of unrelated unsecured debts.[10]

(b) Redemption

The second option some debtors have is to redeem the property under § 722. To redeem, the debtor must pay the lienor the amount of the "allowed secured claim." As discussed at the beginning of chapter six, that amount is limited by the value of the collateral. Thus, using the example above of an $8,000 debt secured by a lien on a $6,000 car, the debtor could redeem the car by paying the secured creditor $6,000 in

———————

[9]   *E.g., In re Duke*, 79 F.3d 43 (7th Cir. 1996); *Morgan Guar. Trust Co. v. American Sav. & Loan*, 804 F.2d 1487 (9th Cir. 1986).

[10]   *See In re Jamo*, 283 F.3d 392 (1st Cir. 2002). *See also In re Briggs*, 143 B.R. 438 (Bankr. E.D. Mich. 1992) (concluding after lengthy analysis that creditor may even threaten to foreclose if debtor does not reaffirm; creditor's action in seeking reaffirmation violates the stay only if it: "(1) could reasonably be expected to have a significant impact on the debtor's determination as to whether to repay, and (2) is contrary to what a reasonable person would consider to be fair under the circumstances"). *But cf. In re Walker*, 194 B.R. 165 (Bankr. E.D. Tenn. 1996) (ruling that letter requesting reaffirmation and enclosing reaffirmation agreement violated the stay because the agreement did not fully comply with § 524(c)).

cash. The debtor need not pay the $2,000 balance; that is treated as an unsecured claim in the bankruptcy case, and will usually be discharged following whatever distributions the trustee makes.

Redemption is far from a panacea for debtors, however, because it suffers from three significant drawbacks. First, the debtor must come up with the necessary cash. Most courts do not permit the debtor to redeem in installments.[11] Of course, most bankrupt debtors do not have a ready supply of cash. To get it, they must normally either borrow it or convert some of their exempt property into a liquid form. Borrowing may be impossible, because bankruptcy debtors typically have great difficulty finding willing lenders, and liquidating exempt assets may be undesirable.

Second, the value of the property to be redeemed – and therefore the redemption price – is measured by the property's replacement value, without reduction for the costs of sale or marketing. *See* § 506(a)(2). This will normally mean the price a retail merchant would charge for such property, given its age and condition. § 506(a)(2).[12] As a result, the debtor is likely to have to pay more for the property than the debtor could turn around and sell it for.

Third, redemption is available in only limited circumstances. It applies only to individual debtors and covers only tangible personal property that is intended primarily for personal, family, or household purposes. It is unavailable to corporate debtors and cannot be used either for real property or for property used in a business. Moreover, the property must be either wholly exempt or have been abandoned by the trustee. For the most part, redemption is a paper right that is rarely exercised.

(c) Repossession

By far the most common thing that happens to the collateral is repossession. Secured claimants do not relish the idea of waiting a long time before getting paid, and thus are often eager to enforce their liens, using whatever nonbankruptcy rights they have. Most debtors in bankruptcy have already defaulted on their obligations and have

---

[11] *See, e.g., In re Bell*, 700 F.2d 1053 (6th Cir. 1983), cited approvingly for this point by *In re Taylor*, 3 F.3d 1512, 1515 (11th Cir. 1993); *In re Belanger*, 962 F.2d 345, 347 (4th Cir. 1992); *In re Edwards*, 901 F.2d 1383, 1386 (7th Cir. 1990).

[12] This measure applies whenever the property was "acquired for personal, family, or household purposes." Because redemption is limited to property "intended primarily for personal, family, or household use," § 722, this standard will typically apply to any proffered redemption. However, in unusual cases the property may not have been originally acquired for personal, family, or household purposes even though the debtor now intends to use it for such. In those cases, redemption is permissible but the Code does not necessarily measure value as the price a retail merchant would charge.

no ability or desire to try to cure those defaults. A note of caution for the creditor is in order, however. Even though secured claimants in a Chapter 7 case are not paid by the trustee, or indeed out of the bankruptcy estate at all, they are subject to the automatic stay. They may therefore take no action to collect the debts due to them. *See* § 362(a)(6).

The Code does not merely prohibit collection activity, however; it also expressly enjoins acts against the collateral. Specifically, it prohibits creditors from doing any act to create, perfect, or enforce a lien against property of the estate. § 362(a)(4). This gives the trustee time to determine if there is any basis for challenging the validity of a creditor's lien. It also bars such acts against property of the debtor to the extent that the lien secures a prepetition claim. § 362(a)(5). Because of this latter rule, the stay technically remains in effect even after the trustee has abandoned the property,[13] and protects the debtor who has exempt equity in the property. Finally, the Code prohibits creditors from doing any act to obtain possession of property of the estate. § 362(a)(3).

Collectively, and perhaps individually, these provisions prohibit secured creditors from either repossessing their collateral or conducting a foreclosure sale after a bankruptcy petition has been filed. Indeed, many bankruptcy petitions are filed to get precisely this benefit: to stop the repossession or sale of the debtor's property, particularly a home.

Application of the stay to secured claims has raised three recurring questions. First, does a creditor who repossessed collateral *before the bankruptcy petition was filed* violate the stay simply by refusing to return it postpetition upon the debtor's demand?[14] One circuit court has ruled that such a refusal does violate the stay.[15] Several other

---

[13]   Generally, abandoned property revests in the debtor upon leaving the estate. When that occurs, there is no doubt that the stay of § 362(a)(5) still applies. Occasionally, however, courts order the property abandoned directly to the secured creditor. The legislative history apparently supports this practice, stating that "[a]bandonment may be to any party with a possessory interest in the property abandoned." S. Rep. No. 989, 95th Cong., 2d Sess. 92 (1978), *reprinted in* 1978 U.S.C.C.A.N. 5787, 5878; H. Rep. No. 595, 95th Cong., 1st Sess. 377 (1977), *reprinted in* 1978 U.S.C.C.A.N. 5963, 6333. This practice may take the property outside the scope of the stay, obviating the need for the creditor to seek relief under § 362(d). *See* S. Rep. No. 989 at 52, *reprinted in* 1978 U.S.C.C.A.N. at 5838; H. Rep. No. 595 at 343, *reprinted in* 1978 U.S.C.C.A.N. at 6299 (both indicating that abandonment does not terminate the stay against property of the debtor "if the property leaves the estate and goes to the debtor").

[14]   There is no question that collateral remains property of the estate and must be returned in response to a turnover order under § 542. *See United States v. Whiting Pools, Inc.*, 462 U.S. 198 (1983) (excerpted on pages 50-54).

[15]   *See In re Knaus*, 889 F.2d 773 (8th Cir. 1989) (ignoring the necessity of adequate protection and the possible impact of § 363(e)).

courts have followed this decision.[16] About the same number have criticized it or otherwise ruled to the contrary.[17] The issue therefore remains unresolved and creditors in possession of collateral should be very cautious, particularly given the damages potentially available to an aggrieved debtor. *See* § 362(k)(1).

Second, does a creditor violate the stay by postponing, rather than cancelling, a foreclosure sale? The problem emanates from the language of § 362(a)(1), which prohibits the "continuation" of an action or proceeding that was or could have been commenced against the debtor prepetition. The Third Circuit analyzed the issue thus:

> "The primary purposes of the automatic stay provisions are to effectively stop all creditor collection efforts, stop all harassment of a debtor seeking relief, and *to maintain the status quo* between the debtor and [his] creditors, thereby affording the parties and the Court an opportunity to appropriately resolve competing economic interests in an orderly and effective way." *Zeoli v. RIHT Mortgage Corp.*, 148 B.R. 698, 700 (D.N.H. 1993) (emphasis added).
>   * * * [T]he filing of a bankruptcy petition prohibits the beginning ("commencement") of a judicial proceeding and the carrying forward ("continuation") of a proceeding that has already begun.
>   The "continuation" of a sheriff's sale, on the other hand, connotes the postponement of a proceeding, and effectuates the purposes of § 362(a)(1) by preserving the status quo until the bankruptcy process is completed or until the creditor obtains relief from the automatic stay. * * * [It therefore] comports with § 362(a)(1).[18]

Postponing a foreclosure sale – rather than cancelling it – can save the creditor more than time if the stay is lifted and the sale allowed to proceed. It can also save the

---

[16]   *E.g., In re Yates*, 332 B.R. 1 (10th Cir. BAP 2005); *In re Sharon*, 234 B.R. 676 (6th Cir. BAP 1999) (rejecting assertion that the creditor's right to adequate protection allows it to retain possession until such protection is provided); *In re Abrams*, 127 B.R. 239, 241 (9th Cir. BAP 1991).

[17]   *E.g., In re Kalter*, 292 F.3d 1350 (11th Cir. 2002) (secured party had right to possession of and title to repossessed automobile; debtor's mere right to redemption did not make car property of the estate under Florida law); *In re Lewis*, 137 F.3d 1280 (11th Cir. 1998) (same based on Alabama law). *See also* Thomas E. Plank, *The Creditor in Possession under the Bankruptcy Code: History, Text, and Policy*, 59 MD. L. REV. 253, 314 n.299 (2000) (referring to rulings that such conduct does violate the stay as "the most egregious examples of judicial misunderstanding of the stay and property of the estate"). *But see In re Moffett*, 356 F.3d 518 (4th Cir. 2004) (rejecting the Eleventh Circuit's analysis in *Lewis* and concluding that the debtor's redemption rights do make the collateral property of the estate).

[18]   *Taylor v. Slick*, 178 F.3d 698, 702 (3rd Cir. 1999).

creditor substantial money in advertising costs.[19] While these expenses normally come out of the foreclosure sale proceeds,[20] if the collateral is not worth enough to cover these expenses and pay the full amount of the debt, the creditor of an insolvent debtor is the one who ultimately bears these costs.

The third question arising from application of the stay to secured creditors is under what circumstances may the creditor obtain relief from the stay to foreclose on the collateral while the bankruptcy case is still pending? This is by far the most important question because it is very common for secured claimants to move for relief from the stay immediately after receiving notice of the debtor's bankruptcy filing.

A creditor's right to such relief is governed by § 362(d), which requires that the stay be lifted either (1) for cause, including the lack of adequate protection of the secured claimant's interest in the property; or (2) if the debtor has no equity in the property and the property is not necessary to a successful reorganization. In Chapter 7 cases, "cause" and lack of adequate protection are rarely an issue.[21] Instead, secured creditors in Chapter 7 liquidations typically seek relief under § 362(d)(2), because the property is by definition not needed for a successful reorganization. Relief for them therefore depends on whether the property is worth more than the debt. In many cases it is not, and the secured party obtains quick relief from the stay,[22] repossesses the property using its nonbankruptcy rights, and then forecloses its lien by selling the property under whatever nonbankruptcy rules are applicable.[23] Even if relief from the stay is not available, perhaps because the debtor has exempt equity in the property, as soon as the stay expires under § 362(c) the secured claimant may take whatever steps are allowed under nonbankruptcy law to enforce its lien.

---

[19]   *See In re Atlas Machine & Iron Works, Inc.*, 239 B.R. 322 (Bankr. E.D. Va. 1998) (ruling that creditor who spent more than $30,000 to advertise a foreclosure sale of equipment did not violate the stay by informing interested buyers that the sale was postponed).

[20]   *See, e.g.,* U.C.C. § 9-615(a)(1).

[21]   For that reason, these terms are discussed in Chapter Fourteen.

[22]   In general, the stay expires with respect to the property 30 days after the motion for relief is filed unless, before that period expires, the bankruptcy court orders otherwise. *See* § 362(e)(1).

[23]   There is one trap for the unwary here. Under Bankruptcy Rule 4001(a)(3), an order granting relief from the stay is itself stayed for ten days, unless the court orders otherwise. This is designed to give the debtor time to request a stay pending appeal of the order granting relief. If a creditor goes forward with collection activities within the ten-day period, the creditor risks contempt and sanctions for violating the stay. *See In re Banks*, 253 B.R. 25 (Bankr. E.D. Mich. 2000).

(d) Retention

There may be one other option for the debtor. Consider the case that follows. After that, we will explore how the 2005 Amendments to the Bankruptcy Code have dealt with this issue.

IN RE BOODROW
126 F.3d 43 (2d Cir. 1997)

Feinberg, Circuit Judge:

This case presents an issue of first impression in this circuit: whether a bankruptcy court may allow a debtor, who files for bankruptcy and is "current" on a car-purchase loan, to retain the collateral securing the loan and continue making monthly payments under the original loan agreement. * * *

FACTS AND PRIOR PROCEEDINGS

The material facts in this case are not in dispute. In May 1995, Boodrow filed for relief pursuant to Chapter 7. Prior to filing, Boodrow had borrowed $15,900 from Creditor Capital Communications Federal Credit Union (Capital) to purchase a 1992 Pontiac Grand Am. As of the petition date, Boodrow owed Capital $8,820, which sum was secured by a first priority lien on the vehicle. Capital agrees that the market value of the vehicle on that date was $9,650.

After filing his Chapter 7 petition, Boodrow filed a statement of intention pursuant to § 521(2), indicating that he intended to retain the vehicle and reaffirm his debt to Capital. However, Boodrow, who had been receiving workmen's compensation and disability payments for an injury, discovered sometime thereafter that he was permanently disabled and would not be able to return to full-time employment. For this reason, Boodrow says, he did not execute a reaffirmation agreement with Capital but rather retained the car, remained "current" on his monthly installment payments and maintained adequate insurance on the car. Apparently, as part of the loan contract with Capital, Boodrow had purchased disability insurance, which was the source of the monthly payments due under the loan. Indeed, it is undisputed that at all times up to the argument of this case before us, Boodrow has remained current on his payments and maintained adequate insurance for the vehicle.

In July 1995, Capital moved to lift the automatic stay and for other relief on the ground that Boodrow had not complied with § 521(2), and that this failure constituted cause under § 362(d)(1) for lifting the stay to enable Capital to recover the vehicle. Capital maintained that Boodrow was required under § 521(2) to either enter into a reaffirmation agreement, surrender the vehicle to Capital, or redeem it by immediately paying Capital the market value of the vehicle.

Bankruptcy Judge Littlefield conducted a hearing on Capital's motion in August 1995 and * * * in December, * * * denied Capital's motion for relief from the automatic stay. The court held that Capital had not demonstrated cause for lifting the stay because § 521(2) allowed a debtor in Boodrow's position to retain the collateral and continue making monthly payments. The court concluded that Capital had not demonstrated that it would suffer harm if the stay was not lifted.

Capital appealed to the district court, and Chief Judge McAvoy affirmed the bankruptcy court * * *. This appeal followed.

DISCUSSION
* * *

Capital argues primarily that it did show cause to lift the stay because Boodrow violated § 521(2) by not electing to reaffirm the debt or surrender or redeem the vehicle. In other words, Boodrow could not simply retain the vehicle and continue to make monthly payments. Courts in several circuits have taken the position that § 521(2) confines a debtor to the options specifically listed in that section. *E.g, In re Edwards*, 901 F.2d 1383, 1387 (7th Cir. 1990); *In re Taylor*, 3 F.3d 1512, 1517 (11th Cir. 1993); *In re Johnson*, 89 F.3d 249, 252 (5th Cir. 1996).

Boodrow responds that no cause existed to modify the stay because he complied with § 521(2) by indicating to Capital that he would retain the vehicle and continue making payments due under the loan agreement. Courts in other circuits have held that, consistent with § 521(2), a debtor who is current on a loan may follow this course of action. *E.g., In re Belanger*, 962 F.2d 345, 348-49 (4th Cir. 1992); *Lowry Federal Credit Union v. West*, 882 F.2d 1543, 1547 (10th Cir. 1989). Boodrow also argues that Capital alleged no affirmative harm justifying the lifting of the stay.

It is not clear to us that violation of § 521(2) would automatically require a bankruptcy court to lift the automatic stay. However, even assuming that such violation constitutes cause for lifting the stay, we find, for reasons discussed below, that Capital has not shown that Boodrow violated § 521(2).

Text of Section 521(2)

Section 521(2) was added to the Bankruptcy Code by the Bankruptcy Amendment and Federal Judgeship Act of 1984 and states in relevant part that

> the debtor shall file with the clerk a statement of his intention with respect to the retention or surrender of such property and, *if applicable*, specifying that such property is claimed as exempt, that the debtor intends to redeem such property, or that the debtor intends to reaffirm debts secured by such property.

§ 521(2)(A) (emphasis added). As Capital points out, surrender requires a debtor to return the collateral to the creditor. Redemption is governed by § 722. That section allows a debtor to retain the collateral by paying the creditor the value of the property.

Most courts require a debtor to pay the creditor in one "lump sum" payment rather than in installments, unless the creditor agrees otherwise. Alternatively, a debtor can reaffirm a debt by entering into a new loan agreement with the creditor, a legal obligation that survives the debtor's discharge from bankruptcy. *See* § 524(c). Capital observes, however, that in a reaffirmation agreement the parties can negotiate new terms to supplant those in the original loan agreement, and that the creditor's acceptance of the agreement must be voluntary.

It is clear that the "starting point in every case involving construction of a statute is the language itself. But the text is only the starting point," *Kelly v. Robinson*, 479 U.S. 36, 43 (1986), especially when the language is ambiguous. The Supreme Court has thus explained in interpreting other sections of the Bankruptcy Code that "we must not be guided by a single sentence or [part] of a sentence, but look to the provisions of the whole law, and to its object and policy." *Id.* With these principles in mind, we first turn to the text of § 521(2).

The bankruptcy and district courts in this case both held that the language of § 521(2)(A), quoted above, did not prevent the bankruptcy court from allowing Boodrow to retain the collateral and continue to perform under the loan agreement. (This course of action has been described as "reinstatement,"[24] a term we use at times hereafter in this opinion.) Both courts relied on *In re Belanger*, where the Fourth Circuit explained that

> [t]he fact that the statutory options are stated in the disjunctive shows that the words "if applicable" are unnecessary under a construction of the statute that makes the options exclusive. But if the phrase "if applicable" is given effect, it plays an important role. . . . [T]he debtor must specify a choice of the options if applicable. But if these options are not applicable, the debtor need not specify them.

962 F.2d at 348. The *Belanger* court noted that its reading of the statute complied with the "canon that courts should give effect, if possible, to every word in a statute." *Id.*

In support of this interpretation, Collier states that "[n]othing in section 521(2) requires the debtor to choose redemption, reaffirmation or surrender of the property to the exclusion of all other alternatives. Section 521(2) merely requires a statement of

---

[24] Professor Joann Henderson describes reinstatement as:

the debtor's right to retain the collateral by continuing regular payments under the security agreement and thereby completing the contract, albeit a somewhat different contract because any personal obligation has been discharged. To qualify for reinstatement, debtors cannot be in default, except for technical defaults such as bankruptcy clause defaults, and must pay the entire debt in accordance with the contract. This right is called reinstatement because it prevents foreclosure and reinstates the contract. Reinstatement allows debtors to continue with business as if bankruptcy had no effect on the secured creditor's position.

Joann Henderson, *The Gaglia-Lowry Brief: A Quantum Leap from Strip Down to Chapter 7*, 8 Bankr. Dev. J. 131, 137 (1991).

whether the debtor intends to choose any of those options, if applicable." Collier, ¶ 521.10, at 521-34 to 521-35. * * *

Capital counters that the plain language of § 521(2)(A) shows that Congress intended the options set forth to be the only ones available to a debtor. Capital relies on the reasoning of *In re Taylor*, where the [Eleventh] Circuit explained the meaning of the phrase "if applicable" as follows:

> [I]t is clear when the options of redemption and reaffirmation would not be applicable. This language does not apply to a debtor's surrender of the property; it therefore must apply to a debtor's retention of property. If a debtor retains secured property, then the options of redemption and reaffirmation are applicable and the debtor is required to redeem or reaffirm.

3 F.3d at 1516. Capital argues that § 521(2)(A) would be confusing without "if applicable" because it would require a debtor who decides to surrender the collateral to indicate an intention to reaffirm or redeem, two choices that do not logically apply if the debtor is giving back the collateral.

Both parties assert that their interpretation of § 521(2)(A) better comports with other subsections of § 521(2). Capital maintains that reinstatement cannot be reconciled with § 521(2)(B), which states in relevant part that "within forty-five days after the filing of a notice of intent . . . the debtor shall perform his intention with respect to such property." Admittedly, retaining the collateral and continuing to make scheduled payments is not action that typically can be performed within 45 days. Capital also insists that the options listed in § 521(2)(A) must be exclusive because nowhere else does the Code provide for additional options.

Boodrow argues, on the other hand, that his interpretation of § 521(2)(A) is reinforced by § 521(2)(C), which states that "nothing in subparagraphs (A) and (B) of this paragraph shall alter the debtor's or the trustee's rights with regard to such property under this title." The district court here agreed, relying on *In re Belanger*, where the Fourth Circuit noted that, before the enactment of § 521(2), one bankruptcy court had held that a debtor who was not in default on a loan was entitled to retain the collateral securing the loan as long as he remained current on the loan payments.

Although § 521(2)(A) clearly imposes a mandatory obligation on a debtor to state whether he intends to retain or surrender collateral, we find the section to be ambiguous as to whether Congress intended the options there listed to be exclusive, and we believe that the "plain" language arguably supports either of the interpretations described above. We thus turn to other sources for evidence of congressional intent as to the meaning of § 521(2).

Legislative History and Policy

The bankruptcy court in this case concluded that review of the legislative history of § 521(2) did "not assist resolution of this matter," noting that no Senate or House report became part of the record regarding § 521(2). Nevertheless, the district court found that the "limited legislative history points to the general conclusion that Section 521(2) is meant to be a notice provision." Judge Small, the bankruptcy judge in *In re Belanger*, came to the same conclusion based on detailed statements made at a congressional subcommittee hearing by "a coalition of bankers, credit unions, finance companies, oil companies and retailers." *In re Belanger*, 118 B.R. at 370. Those statements indicate that § 521(2)(A) was intended specifically to eliminate the problem that secured creditors could not determine what a debtor who had filed for bankruptcy was going to do with collateral securing a debt. Instead of the creditor having to spend time and money obtaining this information through judicial proceedings, § 521(2) placed on a debtor "the responsibility of giving creditors information . . . as to what they intend to do with the collateral." *Id.* at 370 n.5.

We agree that § 521(2) appears to serve primarily a notice function, not necessarily to restrict the substantive options available to a debtor who wishes to retain collateral securing a debt. With respect to Capital's argument that the time limit in § 521(2)(B) precludes such a conclusion, the district court here reasoned that "[o]bviously, under such a scheme it is appropriate to set a time limit for action upon such a statement, but that limit does not necessarily change the nature of the section" as one aimed at providing notice to creditors of a debtor's intentions. We note also that a bankruptcy court has discretion under § 521(2)(B) to give a debtor "additional time . . . for cause" beyond the 45-day deadline to perform a stated intention.

Moreover, we believe that the interpretation advocated by Boodrow and adopted by the courts below better comports with the policies behind the Bankruptcy Code. The bankruptcy court viewed Boodrow's interpretation of § 521(2) as "most consistent with balancing the 'fresh start' policy underlying the Code and the rights of the . . . secured creditor[s]." The policy embodied in the Code that a debtor discharged from bankruptcy should receive a "fresh start" has been emphasized time and again by the Supreme Court and this court.

Confining an individual Chapter 7 debtor to the choices of surrender, redemption or reaffirmation can severely interfere with providing the debtor a fresh start. As Judge Butzner explained in *In re Belanger*, a debtor is "unlikely to be able to redeem the collateral in a lump sum as required by § 722," and "reaffirmation requires the consent of the creditor in order to comply with § 524(c)." 962 F.2d at 348. Thus, if the options listed in § 521(2) were exclusive, a debtor's only real choices would be either to reaffirm the debt under whatever new terms the creditor requires or to surrender the property. Because reaffirmation involves negotiation between parties with unequal bargaining power and requires voluntary agreement by both debtor and creditor, it gives a creditor an effective veto on the "fresh start." Yet, surrender may deprive a debtor of much needed property, such as disabled debtor Boodrow's vehicle in this case.

Capital responds that a creditor faces the possibility of "substantial financial danger" and "very real loss" when a bankruptcy court allows a debtor to retain property without redeeming or reaffirming. Capital explains that because bankruptcy discharges a debtor from personal liability on outstanding loans, Capital's only remedy if Boodrow defaulted on the loan after discharge would be to commence legal action to recover the vehicle. Capital would not then be entitled to recover the difference, if any, between the outstanding balance on the loan and the value of the vehicle. Further, Capital argues that a debtor whose personal liability is discharged through bankruptcy has no incentive to maintain the collateral in good condition or to continue making payments if the value of the collateral drops below the amount outstanding on the loan. Finally, Capital contends that Boodrow's interpretation of § 521(2) would in effect negate reaffirmation because no debtor would reaffirm personal liability rather than simply continue to make payments on the loan and retain the collateral. Capital asserts, as the court stated in *In re Taylor*, that this additional option gives the debtor "not a 'fresh start' but a 'head start.' " 3 F.3d at 1516.

It is true that a debtor's discharge from bankruptcy eliminates personal liability on the loan, thereby theoretically limiting the amount a creditor could recover if the debtor defaults. However, we disagree with Capital's assumption that a creditor will necessarily or even probably suffer financial injury when a debtor who is current on a loan retains the collateral and continues to make the payments required under the loan agreement. As the court in *In re Crouch* observed, because a creditor can recover the collateral from a discharged debtor who defaults on a loan, the creditor's main concern should be that, upon default, the value of the collateral exceeds the amount outstanding on the loan. *In re Crouch*, 104 B.R. at 773. The bankruptcy court here characterized Capital's suggestion that Boodrow would not have any incentive to maintain the collateral as "uninformed with regard to the realities of the typical Chapter 7 case." Boodrow argues that "there is a great incentive for [him] to maintain current on the debt and to preserve the auto since he has no means to acquire another auto." Indeed, the bankruptcy court explained that

> a debtor's ability to obtain credit on the same (or comparable) terms as nondebtors, is generally impaired by filing bankruptcy. If a debtor fails to maintain or permits a waste of collateral, such as an automobile, he is therefore less able than a nondebtor to obtain financing required to replace the collateral. As a result, debtors are generally likely to have a greater incentive than nondebtors to stay current on payments and to maintain the value of the collateral.

In any event, other courts have noted that a debtor's failure, after discharge, to insure or maintain collateral typically permits a creditor to

> accelerate the indebtedness and repossess the collateral. In fact default clauses which permit the lender to declare a default in the event that the creditor deems its security interest insecure are specifically authorized by the Uniform

Commercial Code and may be exercised by a secured lender if it has a good
faith belief that the prospect for payment is impaired.
In re Belanger, 118 B.R. at 372. We thus disagree that a creditor invariably, or even
probably, will lose the benefit of its bargain under the original loan agreement when a
bankruptcy court permits reinstatement.

With regard to Capital's contention that Boodrow's interpretation of § 521(2) reads
reaffirmation out of the statute, amicus NACBA points out that sometimes a debtor has
an incentive to reaffirm a debt. The NACBA brief explains that a debtor may seek to
reaffirm in order to reestablish credit standing after a bankruptcy discharge or, if the
debtor was not current on the loan when the bankruptcy petition was filed, to obtain a
new agreement that would provide for the right to cure the arrearage and avoid default.
The brief also notes that sometimes a debtor may want to reaffirm in order to retain the
benefit of certain consumer protection provisions contained in the original loan
agreement. They thus challenge Capital's assumption that no debtor would choose
reaffirmation.

In any event, Capital's argument misapprehends the scope of the holding that we
review in this case. The district court explained that a bankruptcy court must exercise
its discretion in determining whether a debtor may retain collateral and keep making
payments by considering the debtor's "previous payment record, a comparison of the
value of the collateral and the amount of debt, and other relevant facts." Thus, a debtor
in default on a loan at the time of the bankruptcy petition or whose behavior indicates
that he will not be able to continue making scheduled payments might well suffer a
lifting of the stay. In fact, Judge Littlefield – the bankruptcy judge in this case – recently
granted summary judgment to a creditor because a debtor not current on his loan
obligation had not reaffirmed the loan or redeemed or surrendered the collateral. *In re
Bushey*, 204 B.R. 661, 663-64 (Bankr. N.D.N.Y. 1997).

After considering the text of § 521(2), its legislative history and the policies
informing the Bankruptcy Code, we hold that § 521(2) does not prevent a bankruptcy
court from allowing a debtor who is current on loan obligations to retain the collateral
and keep making payments under the original loan agreement.

Shadur, District Judge, dissenting:
[After making several textual points, Judge Shadur argued that an option to retain
would often be far more desirable than the other stated options. Redemption requires
that the debtor raise the funds needed to pay off, in one lump sum, the full amount of the
secured claim and reaffirmation requires that the debtor remain personally liable for
otherwise dischargeable debt. In contrast, with retention "the debtor effectively converts
his secured obligation from recourse to nonrecourse with no downside risk for failing
to maintain or insure the lender's collateral." *Taylor*, 3 F.3d at 1516. He suggested that
it would be bizarre indeed for the statute to expressly mention the less desirable choices
while leaving the most desirable one unstated. Judge Shadur concluded by noting that

Congress explicitly provided in Chapter 13 for a process by which a debtor may retain collateral over the objection of the secured party simply by keeping current on his or her payments. It would be inappropriate for courts to infer such a right in Chapter 7 given the omission of such an express right there.]

NOTES

1.   The *Boodrow* court stated that "if the options listed in § 521(2) were exclusive, a debtor's only real choices would be either to reaffirm the debt under whatever new terms the creditor requires or to surrender the property." That is not entirely accurate. As noted in Judge Shadur's dissent, if the debtor were eligible for and filed for relief under Chapter 13 (or were undergoing reorganization under Chapter 11), the debtor would be able to reinstate the contract – indeed, a debtor in default on the contract could cure the default and still reinstate – without the consent of the secured party. An interpretation of § 521 that gives debtors another incentive to file under Chapter 13, and thereby commit future income to the payment of creditors, may not be so bad.

2.   There are really two separate but related issues here: (1) whether § 521 authorizes a debtor who is not in default to retain the collateral without redeeming it or reaffirming the debt; and (2) if so, whether the debtor is in default.
     With regard to the first issue, the circuits are now divided as follows:

Retention Permitted	Retention Not Permitted
2nd, 3rd, 4th, 9th & 10th	1st, 5th, 7th & 11th

The Supreme Court has twice denied certiorari on the issue: in the cases from the Second and Ninth Circuits.
     With regard to the second issue, many security agreements include clauses that make filing for bankruptcy protection a default, and nothing in Article 9 invalidates such provisions. The Bankruptcy Code makes such "bankruptcy clauses" ineffective for some purposes. For example, a contract provision purporting to deprive the debtor of an interest in property in the event of insolvency or a bankruptcy filing is ineffective, and the property becomes part of the bankruptcy estate despite such a clause. § 541(c)(1). Similarly, a contract clause allowing an executory contract or unexpired lease of the debtor to be terminated for either of those reasons does not prevent the trustee from

assuming the contract for the benefit of the estate. § 365(e)(1). Nevertheless, until the 2005 amendments, nothing in the Code suggested that Congress intended to invalidate the common practice of including in a security agreement a provision that makes insolvency or filing for bankruptcy protection an event of default.

Nevertheless, a number of bankruptcy courts have shown hostility to default-on-bankruptcy clauses. Before enactment of § 521(2) in 1984, the two circuit courts that had ruled were divided on the issue. *In re Bell*,[25] ruled that a bankruptcy clause did create a default on a contract once the trustee had abandoned the collateral to the debtor. *Riggs Nat'l Bank v. Perry*,[26] held that a default-on-filing clause was unenforceable as contrary to the fresh start policy of the Code. Since enactment of § 521, courts have had little to say on this issue. The *Boodrow* court suggested in footnote 6 that such clauses are unenforceable; the First Circuit BAP suggested the opposite.[27]

The 2005 amendments to the Bankruptcy Code appear to have restricted, but not totally removed, the debtor's right to retain collateral without redeeming it or reaffirming the debt. Read § 521(a)(6).[28] It requires the debtor to reaffirm the debt or redeem the collateral – not merely to file a statement of intention, but to actually complete one of these tasks – within 45 days of the § 341 meeting.[29] If the debtor fails to do so, the stay will expire as to the collateral.[30] However, this new rule applies only

---

[25]   700 F.2d 1053 (6th Cir. 1983).

[26]   729 F.2d 982 (4th Cir. 1984).

[27]   *In re Burr*, 218 B.R. 267, 272 & n.5 (1st Cir. BAP), *rev'd on other grounds*, 160 F.3d 843 (1st Cir. 1998). *See also In re Sokolowski*, 227 B.R. 16 (Bankr. D. Conn. 1998) (canvassing the cases on the issue and concluding such clauses are unenforceable).

[28]   Note, § 521(2) has been re-designated as § 521(a)(2).

[29]   *Cf. In re Blakeley*, 363 B.R. 225 (Bankr. D. Utah 2007) (ruling that the debtor had complied with § 521(d) by simply *submitting* a reaffirmation agreement for court approval, and that court rejection of the agreement would not trigger relief from the stay or permit repossession of the collateral).

[30]   In contrast, if the debtor fails to file all the required schedules within 45 days of the petition, the entire case must be dismissed. *See* § 521(i). Courts have no discretion not to dismiss if the debtor fails to file the statement or a request for an extension before the 45-day period expires. *See, e.g., In re Ott*, 343 B.R. 264 (Bankr. D. Colo. 2006); *In re Fawson*, 338 B.R. 505 (Bankr. D. Utah 2006). *But cf. In re Parker*, 351 B.R. 790 (Bankr. N.D. Ga. 2006). If the debtor fails within 30 days of the petition to file a statement of intention with respect to collateral – all collateral, not merely personal property securing a purchase-money obligation – the stay will expire as to that collateral. *See* § 362(h); *In re Root*, 2006 WL 1050687 (Bankr. N.D. Iowa 2006); *In re Cracker*, 337 B.R. 549 (Bankr. M.D.N.C. 2006).

if the creditor has a purchase-money security interest ("PMSI") in personal property collateral. It therefore does not apply to realty collateral or to non-PMSI security interests in personalty.[31] It also applies only if the creditor has an *allowed* claim. Thus, if the creditor does not file a proof of claim – and in no-asset cases, no creditor does – the creditor will not have an allowed claim and arguably § 521(a)(6) cannot apply.[32] Perhaps more significantly, the new rule expressly relegates the secured creditor to whatever rights it may have under nonbankruptcy law. Section 521(d) then makes clear that default-on-bankruptcy clauses are not invalidated by the Bankruptcy Code. However, if the agreement lacks a default-on-bankruptcy clause or such clause is not enforceable under applicable nonbankruptcy law, and the debtor is not otherwise in default, retention may still be permitted.[33]

To the extent that § 521(a)(6) does not apply, such as when the collateral is real estate or the security interest does not secure the purchase price, and retention is permitted, either by the court or voluntarily by the secured creditor, the stay remains in effect. As always, creditors in such situations must be careful about what they do and do not do. A bankruptcy court summed up what is permissible:

> Debtors' Intentions
> * * * Where an individual debtor files a chapter 7 case and the schedules include a consumer debt secured by property of the debtor, § 521(2) gives the debtor 30 days to file "a statement of his intention with respect to the retention or surrender of such property . . . ." * * *
> Where a debtor files the statement of intention within the statutory period, there is no need for the secured creditor to contact the debtor to determine

---

Arguably, the 45-day period in § 521(a)(6) for the debtor to surrender, redeem, or reaffirm will always be trumped by the 30-day period in both § 521(a)(2)(B) and § 362(h), which commences on the date first set for the § 341 meeting, rather than the date of the actual meeting. *See In re Norton*, 247 B.R. 291, 300 n.10 (Bankr. E.D. Tenn. 2006).

[31] As to whether refinancing can undermine PMSI status, see *supra* chapter six notes 38-42 and accompanying text.

[32] *See In re Blakeley*, 363 B.R. 225 (Bankr. D. Utah 2007); *In re Anderson*, 384 B.R. 652 (Bankr. D. Del. 2006); *In re Donald*, 343 B.R. 524 (Bankr. E.D.N.C. 2006). *Contra In re Steinhaus*, 349 B.R. 694 (Bankr. D. Id. 2006); *In re Rowe*, 342 B.R. 341 (Bankr. D. Kan. 2006) (both ruling that the "allowed" requirement should be ignored in this context because it makes no sense).

[33] *See In re Rowe*, 342 B.R. 341 (Bankr. D. Kan. 2006) (ruling that a default-on-bankruptcy clause was unenforceable under the Kansas version of the Uniform Consumer Credit Code and that the 2005 revisions to § 521 merely relegated secured creditor to nonbankruptcy rights). *See also In re Riggs*, 2006 WL 2990218 (Bankr. W.D. Mo. 2006) (suggesting that a default-on-filing clause may not be enforceable in Missouri under Mo. Stat. § 408.552). *But cf. In re Anderson*, 384 B.R. 652 (Bankr. D. Del. 2006) (ruling that a default on bankruptcy clause is valid in Delaware).

what the debtor's intentions are with respect to the property. This is especially true where, as in this case, the statement is filed with the bankruptcy petition itself. The creditor can determine the debtor's intentions from the papers filed with the court, and has no need to contact the debtor whatsoever on this subject. In this manner the creditor can avoid a violation of the automatic stay.

* * *

5. Creditor Contacts Where Debtor Intends to Make Payments

A secured creditor should be encouraged to send out payment coupons, envelopes and periodic statements if a debtor has filed a statement that the debtor plans to keep property subject to secured debt and to make payments. Debtors frequently complain to the court that they want to make their payments, but their creditors do not cooperate by providing payment coupons. Secured creditors hesitate to provide such cooperation for fear of violating the automatic stay or the discharge injunction.

* * * [However, it is proper] for the secured creditor to send monthly statements to the debtor after the bankruptcy filing, and payment coupons or other means to facilitate the making of monthly postpetition payments by the debtor. If the promissory note has an adjustable interest rate (as it did in this case), the creditor may properly give notice of changes in the interest rate.

If the debtor defaults in making postpetition payments, the creditor may properly give notice thereof, and any other notices that are appropriate and customary in connection with lien enforcement action based on the postpetition default. Further, if there are arrearages in payments at the time of filing, the creditor may properly contact the debtor to arrange for the payment or refinancing of the arrearages. However, the creditor may not use a monthly statement to collect anything more than current payments. In contrast, such conduct would violate the automatic stay for any unsecured debts, or any secured debts as to which the debtor does not indicate in the Statement of Intention that the debtor intends to keep the property.

Proper communications in this context initiated by a creditor are limited to written communications. One benefit of a written communication is that it creates a record which permits the evaluation of whether the communication was proper, and did not stray into improper collection activities.

Throughout this process, the creditor may properly respond to any inquiries initiated by the debtor. Any communication that is initiated by the debtor is not a violation of the automatic stay or the discharge injunction, insofar as the creditor responds to the inquiry. If a debtor calls, the creditor is both entitled to take the call, and to call back if necessary to provide the information requested. However, the creditor should not use such a call as an occasion for collection activities.[34]

Problem 8-2

Driver filed for Chapter 7 bankruptcy protection in a state with a $2,500 motor vehicle exemption. Driver owns a car subject to a perfected security interest in favor of Lender and has made all the required monthly payments on time. For each of the situations below, determine: (i) what, if anything, Driver could do to keep the car; (ii) if redemption is available, what it would cost Driver to redeem the car; (iii) what Driver's best option is; and (iv) what Lender's best course of action is.

A.   Driver uses the car for family and household purposes.
1.   The car is worth $8,000, the secured debt is $10,000, and the secured obligation represents the remainder due on the purchase price of the car.
2.   The car is worth $8,000, the secured debt is $10,000, and the secured obligation consists of a loan for home repair.
3.   The car is worth $12,000, the secured debt is $10,000, and the secured obligation represents the remainder due on the purchase price of the car.
4.   The car is worth $12,000, the secured debt is $10,000, and the secured obligation consists of a loan for home repair.

B.   Driver uses the car primarily for business purposes.
1.   The car is worth $8,000, the secured debt is $10,000, and the secured obligation represents the remainder due on the purchase price of the car.
2.   The car is worth $8,000, the secured debt is $10,000, and the secured obligation consists of a loan for home repair.
3.   The car is worth $12,000, the secured debt is $10,000, and the secured obligation represents the remainder due on the purchase price of the car.

---

[34]   *In re Henry*, 266 B.R. 457, 471-73 (Bankr. C.D. Cal. 2001). *See also Arruda v. Sears, Roebuck & Co.*, 310 F.3d 13 (1st Cir. 2002) (creditor may seek and enter into "redemption agreement" without violating § 524); *In re Garske*, 287 B.R. 537 (9th Cir. BAP 2002) (secured creditor does not violate § 524 by contacting the debtor – telephonically or in writing – to ascertain the debtor's plans after missing payments as long as the creditor does not seek to collect the debt as a persona liability of the debtor); *In re Ramirez*, 280 B.R. 252 (C.D. Cal. 2002) (secured creditor does not violate § 524 by sending the debtor monthly statements listing the debtor's voluntary payments and describing the future payments that the debtor must make to avoid repossession).

4. The car is worth $12,000, the secured debt is $10,000, and the secured obligation consists of a loan for home repair.

C. CONVERTING TO ANOTHER CHAPTER

It is very common for a Chapter 11 or Chapter 13 case to be converted to a Chapter 7 proceeding. Typically this occurs when it becomes apparent that the reorganization effort will fail for some reason. Much less commonly, a Chapter 7 proceeding is converted to a case under Chapter 11 or Chapter 13. Indeed, a debtor in good faith apparently has the right to such a conversion if the case was not previously converted from one of those chapters to Chapter 7 and the debtor qualifies for relief under the chapter to which the case will be converted. *See* § 706(a), (d).

By far the most common situation in which the debtor seeks to convert a case from Chapter 7 to Chapter 11 or 13 is when the court has ruled that the Chapter 7 proceeding should be dismissed for cause under § 707, a subject that is discussed in chapter ten of this book. Typically, the court gives the debtor the option of dismissing the case or agreeing to a conversion, but the court need not always do so. A debtor who has acted in bad faith, such as by purposefully omitting or undervaluing assets on the bankruptcy schedules, has no right to convert to Chapter 13.[35]

A less common reason for converting arises when the case was commenced by an involuntary petition. For example, creditors filing an involuntary petition usually do so under Chapter 7. If the court enters the order for relief, the debtor may well exercise its right to convert the case to a reorganization, and thereby remain in control of the estate assets. In fact, the debtor may convert the case prior to entry of the order for relief, in which case all issues surrounding whether relief should be granted become moot.[36]

A debtor may also seek to convert after the bankruptcy court determines that a particular debt is nondischargeable, particularly if the debt would be dischargeable under another chapter.[37] The debtor may even seek to convert after receiving the discharge,[38] although that is fairly rare.[39]

---

[35] *Marrama v. Citizens Bank of Massachusetts*, 127 S. Ct. 1105 (2007).

[36] *See, e.g., In re J.B. Lovell Corp.*, 876 F.2d 96 (11th Cir. 1989); *In re Technical Fabricators, Inc.*, 65 B.R. 197 (S.D. Ala. 1986).

[37] This was more common prior to the 2005 amendments. Now, there are few debts that are nondischargeable in Chapter 7 but dischargeable in Chapter 13.

[38] *See, e.g., In re Young*, 237 F.3d 1168 (10th Cir. 2001).

[39] In such a case, eligibility for relief under Chapter 13 is apparently determined from the date of the petition, not the date of the conversion. *In re Stern*, 266 B.R. 322 (Bankr. D. Md. 2001). Thus, the

---

debtor cannot discharge debts in Chapter 7 so as to fall under the debt limitations for Chapter 13 eligibility, *see* § 109(e), and then convert the case.

CHAPTER NINE
PRIORITIES & DISTRIBUTION

In a Chapter 7 proceeding, the trustee is authorized – and can be compelled – to abandon any property that is burdensome or of inconsequential value to the estate. § 554(a), (b). With respect to other, valuable property, the trustee is required to "collect and reduce to judgment the property of the estate . . . and close such estate as expeditiously as is compatible with the best interests of the parties in interest." § 704(a)(1). Basically, this means that the trustee must liquidate the valuable property of the estate as quickly as possible. The court may, if it is in the best interest of the estate, authorize the trustee to operate the debtor's business for a limited time. *See* § 721. This may occur when the business is to be sold as a going concern or, more rarely, when the business is actually generating a profit. More commonly, however, the trustee plans to sell all of the property in the estate.

The main provision authorizing the trustee to liquidate the estate is § 363. It authorizes the trustee to use, sell, or lease most property in the ordinary course of business without court permission. § 363(c)(1). It authorizes the trustee to use, sell, or lease property outside the ordinary course of business – and to use, sell or lease cash collateral – only with court approval after notice and a hearing. § 363(b)(1), (c)(2). The trustee is even permitted to sell property in which some entity other than the estate has an interest, and on occasion can be given authority to sell such property free of the other party's interest. *See* § 363(f).

Just as under Article 9 of the Uniform Commercial Code, sales may be conducted by public auction or through private negotiation. Rule 6004(f)(1). Because private sales are generally thought to yield higher prices than public auctions, they are more common. To facilitate such sales, the trustee may, with court approval, hire an appraiser or broker. § 327(a).

Of course, liquidating the estate is only part of the trustee's job. The trustee is also required to distribute money to claimants "as promptly as practical." Rule 3009. No court approval is needed for the trustee to distribute estate assets to creditors, but if there is any dispute about how the assets should be divided, the trustee is likely to seek a court order resolving the issue. Moreover, the United States Trustee is charged with supervising both the trustee appointed in each case and the disbursements the trustee makes. On occasion, particularly when there are significant liquid assets on hand but recovery or liquidation of other assets is expected to take some time, the trustee may make preliminary distributions, followed by a final distribution at a later date. More commonly, the trustee makes either no distribution or only one distribution.

When distributing the estate to claimants, the trustee must follow the Code's priority and distribution scheme. That scheme is depicted in the chart on the next page.

DISTRIBUTION OF THE ESTATE UNDER § 726(a)

1a	Trustee expenses incurred in administering the estate to pay support obligations	**Administrative expenses**
1b	Spousal & child support claims	
2	Costs & expenses of preserving the estate	**Administrative expenses § 503(b)**
	Compensation to professionals: trustees, attorneys, accountants, *etc.* – § 330(a)	
	Reimbursement of certain creditor expenses	
	Compensation for certain creditor services	
3	Certain expenses arising from involuntary filings	**Priorities § 507(a)**
4	Certain employee wage claims (up to $10,950)	
5	Certain employee benefit claims (up to $10,950 per employee)	
6	Certain agricultural and aquicultural bailment claims (up to $5,400)	
7	Certain consumer deposits (up to $2,425)	
8	Certain tax claims	
9	Claims owed by depositary institutions to maintain capital levels	
10	Personal injury claims resulting from drunk driving	
11	Timely unsecured claims	
12	Untimely unsecured claims	
13	Prepetition claims for fines & penalties	
14	Interest on any of the claims listed above	
15	To debtor	

As you can see, this scheme is the product of several different Code provisions: §§ 330(a), 503(b), 507(a), and 726(a).[1] Pursuant to this scheme, bankruptcy claimants seeking a distribution from the vat comprising the bankruptcy estate present their little tin cup at the spigot on the right. In doing so, however, the claimants must first queue up in the order of their statutory priority, and then wait their turn.

Property of the Estate

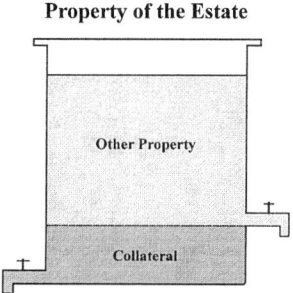

Claims within each ranking are to be paid in full before claims of a lower ranking are entitled to any payment at all. If there are insufficient assets to pay all the claims within a single ranking, those claims share on a pro rata basis. § 726(b).

Even a cursory reading of these provisions should reveal two things. First, no single bankruptcy estate is likely to have claims from every rung in the distribution ladder. This is in part because several of the priorities are highly specialized and, consequently, rather rare. *See* § 507(a)(3), (6), (9). It is also because some priorities apply only to individual debtors, *see* § 507(a)(1)(A), (1)(B), (10), while several others apply only to businesses, and indeed to different types of businesses, *see* § 507(a)(4), (5), (6), (7), (9).

Second, the entire distribution scheme has a glaring omission: secured claims. That is because the trustee in a Chapter 7 case does not pay secured claims. Instead, as we saw back in chapter six of these materials, the creditor will be paid in one of several alternative ways. If the estate has no interest in the collateral (either because the creditor is undersecured or all the equity is exempt), the creditor may obtain relief from the stay (or wait for the stay to expire) and use its nonbankruptcy rights to foreclose on the collateral. Alternatively, the trustee may abandon the collateral to the debtor, who may then choose to stave off foreclosure by voluntarily paying the secured creditor. Such payments may occur either during the bankruptcy process (through redemption) or after the bankruptcy process (pursuant to a reaffirmation agreement or the creditor's tacit willingness to allow the debtor to retain the collateral if current on payments). If the estate does have an interest in the collateral, § 725 directs the trustee to sell the property prior to completing the distribution process detailed in § 726. That sale will either be

---

[1]   It is helpful to review these sections in reverse order, since the bulk of the scheme is laid out in § 726(a). It in turn references § 507, which references § 503, which references § 330(a).

subject to the lien, in which case the secured creditor will seek payment from the buyer, or free of the lien, in which case the trustee will pay the creditor the amount of the secured claim. In either case, the trustee will put the remainder of the sale proceeds in the "vat" for distribution to creditors pursuant to the distribution priorities stated in § 726.

Third, although all of the various priorities are designed to benefit the creditor holding the priority claim, they do so for different reasons. For some, Congress has made the judgment that the creditor is likely to be particularly needy. In other words, that nonpayment by the estate may cause the creditor severe hardship and possibly even impel the creditor to seek bankruptcy protection. Congress enacted some of the other priority rules simply to protect the public fisc. Finally, at least one of the priorities is based on a process concern: without it the bankruptcy system itself might not be able to function. As you study these materials and the related statutory provisions, determine the underlying rationale for each priority rule discussed.

While the distribution scheme of § 726(a) applies only in Chapter 7 cases, the priorities listed in § 507(a) are also recognized in Chapter 11, 12, and 13 cases. Being accorded priority status is extremely important. In most Chapter 7 cases, little or nothing is paid to the nonpriority, unsecured claimants. While such creditors often fare a bit better in Chapter 11, 12, or 13 proceedings, they nevertheless remain at a distinct disadvantage.

A. PRIORITIES

1. Support Claims

Until recently, claims for spousal and child support were a fifth priority claim. The 2005 amendments to the Bankruptcy Code raised them to a first-tier priority, largely for political reasons. During the years that Congress wrestled with bankruptcy reform, many drafts of the legislation increased the types of debts that were nondischargeable. In particular, they frequently made a portion of the debts owed to credit card companies nondischargeable. Although support claims already enjoyed exception from the discharge, *see* § 523(a)(5), critics of the reform proposals claimed that support claimants – ex-spouses and minor children – would be hurt by the proposals because they would have to compete for the debtor's postpetition assets against more creditors. Beyond that, their new competitors would be entities with experience in and resources devoted to debt collection.

To counter this argument, supporters of the legislation decided to raise the priority of support claims in bankruptcy. Many regard this change as nothing more than a dismissive gesture. Nondischargeability and priority are two entirely different – and unrelated – points. When a claim is nondischargeable, the claimant remains free, after the stay expires or is lifted, to go after the debtor's nonexempt assets. Typically this means trying to get at the debtor's postpetition income. Priority, in contrast, deals with distributions of the bankruptcy estate. In short, priority is about what the claimant collects in the bankruptcy process, nondischargeability is about the claimant's ability to collect outside the bankruptcy process. Thus, the elevation in priority of support claims did nothing to address the point raised about increased competition outside of bankruptcy. Beyond that, the vast majority of individuals in Chapter 7 have no unencumbered, nonexempt assets, and thus the trustee makes no distribution. The level of a claim's priority is therefore often irrelevant.

Another point worth noting about the first-tier priority for support claims is their interaction with administrative expenses. One of the arguments against elevating support claims was that placing them ahead of administrative expenses would be unworkable. Trustees would still have the duty to administer the estate, *see* § 704, but might never be paid for the work involved if the estate were exhausted by paying the support claims. To deal with this, some of the trustee's expenses in "administer[ing] assets that would otherwise be available for the payment of [support] claims" come ahead of the support claims. *See* § 507(a)(1)(C) (referencing expenses incurred under § 503(b)(1)(A), (2) and (6)). Precisely how this will work is not yet clear.

The priority treatment of support claims is one of several provisions in the Bankruptcy Code designed to protect support obligations. We have already seen that such claims have immunity from both preference liability and the debtor's exemptions, partial immunity from the stay, and protection from certain lien avoidance actions. *See* §§ 522(f)(1)(A), 547(c)(7), 522(c)(1), 362(b)(2)(B). As we will see in upcoming chapters, they are also protected from the discharge. *See* §§ 523(a)(5), 1328(a)(2). Collectively, these provisions make support claims the most favored type of claim in the bankruptcy process. However, such favor is qualified by some rather bizarre language in § 101(14A)(B). That language defines a "domestic support obligation," a term used in § 507(a)(1) and directly or indirectly used in all of the other provisions favoring support, as one "in the nature of alimony, maintenance, or support . . . without regard to whether such debt is expressly so designated."

What does this language mean? Well consider a married couple in the process of getting divorced. They have the following assets:

Cash	$25,000
Home Equity	$75,000
Family Business	$300,000
Total:	$400,000

Although both spouses work, only one works in the family business. They agree – or the family court decides – to divide the marital assets equally. That means each should get $200,000 in assets (½ of $400,000). They also agree that the spouse who works in the family business should retain sole ownership of the business.[2] However, even if the other spouse gets the cash and the house, the total marital assets will not be divided equally. To remedy this, the parties agree – or the court orders – that the spouse who retains the business interest must pay the other spouse $100,000. Because he or she does not have the cash to do that up front, the arrangement further provides for payments of $2,025 per month for five years. This is the equivalent of $100,000 at approximately 8% interest.

This monthly payment – which in reality is part of the equitable distribution of marital assets – resembles support. In short, periodic payments to be made incident to divorce might be support or might be a division of property over time. There is really no easy way to tell the difference. Moreover, any label the court or the parties put on the payment obligation cannot really be determinative because there are a variety of factors and incentives that go into choosing that label.[3]

Section 507(a)(1), through its implicit incorporation of § 101(14A)(B), requires courts to analyze each payment obligation to determine if it really is support, in which case it is a priority claim, or if it is something else, in which case it is not a priority. Over the years, this issue has been heavily litigated, although more commonly in the context of a challenge to the dischargeability of the claim rather than to its priority.[4] When resolving such controversies, courts have been very protective of the creditor spouse and have engaged in some analytical gymnastics to interpret debts to a former spouse as support obligations, and therefore as nondischargeable. For example, in *Shaver v. Shaver*,[5] a bankruptcy court, district court, and circuit court all ruled that a

---

[2]   Note, in some instances this may be required. For example, if the business were a law firm, the lawyer would not be permitted under the Model Rule of Professional Conduct 5.4 to allow the former spouse to have an ownership interest in the firm.

[3]   Most notably, spousal support payments (not child support payments) are deductible to the payor and income to the recipient, whereas a division of property generates neither a deduction nor income. *See* I.R.C. § 71. If the spouses are likely to be in different tax brackets, there will be a tax incentive to label the payments either as support or as a property division, and that incentive may have no relationship to why the obligation was created.

[4]   *See* § 523(a)(5). In 1994, Congress added § 523(a)(15) to the Code to make property settlement claims incident to divorce also nondischargeable, albeit subject to a balancing of equities. In 2005, Congress removed that balancing limitation, making all support and property settlement obligations to a former spouse nondischargeable. As a result, future litigation seeking to distinguish a support obligation from a property settlement debt is unlikely to arise in the context of dischargeability determinations and will probably significantly abate.

[5]   736 F.2d 1314 (9th Cir. 1984).

$190,000 debt to a former spouse was for support – largely because the debt terminated on the creditor spouse's death and she had no other means of support – even though (i) the family court decree described it as in exchange for property rights; (ii) the amended decree described it as in exchange for marital and dower rights; and (iii) the state court had no authority to award alimony in the case. In another case, *In re Brody*,[6] the separation agreement provided for payment of: (i) $1 million over four years, in satisfaction of the wife's right to equitable distribution of the marital estate; and (ii) $3,250/month for support for 36 months, terminable on her death, remarriage, or cohabitation. The wife had even asserted in state court that the first obligation was a property settlement. Nevertheless, a bankruptcy court, district court, and circuit court all treated both obligations as support claims.

According to these and other courts, subjective intent and the substance of the obligation are the relevant inquiries, and neither state court treatment nor settlement labeling is to be regarded as conclusive.[7] One of the most critical factors is the duration of the payments. Specifically, if payments are to continue even after the creditor spouse dies or remarries, they are unlikely to qualify as support.[8] On the other hand, if the amount or duration of payments is subject to change if the creditor spouse's circumstances change, then the payment is likely to be support, because a property settlement would not normally be affected by a change in circumstances.[9]

B. Administrative Expenses

After support claims, administrative expenses have the highest priority. *See* § 507(a)(2). These include the costs of preserving and liquidating the estate.

---

[6]   3 F.3d 35 (2d Cir. 1993). *See also In re Werthen*, 329 F.3d 269 (1st Cir. 2003) ($833,000 state court property division award treated as additional support because alimony award was inadequate to meet the needs of the creditor spouse and children).

[7]   Some courts have ruled that the debtor's tax treatment of the payment obligations may collaterally estop *the debtor* from asserting the obligation is dischargeable. *See In re Robb*, 23 F.3d 895, 898-99 (4th Cir. 1994) (debtor who deducted payments to former spouse collaterally estopped from claiming they are dischargeable support obligation to former spouse's daughter rather than nondischargeable spousal support); *In re Davidson*, 947 F.2d 1294, 1297 (5th Cir. 1991). Other courts have disagreed. *E.g., In re Kritt*, 190 B.R. 382, 388-89 (9th Cir. BAP 1995); *In re Sampson*, 997 F.2d 717, 724-25 (10th Cir. 1993).

[8]   *Compare* I.R.C. § 71(b)(1)(D). Note, however, that the converse is not necessarily true: even if the payments are to cease on the creditor spouse's death, they may still be a property settlement rather than a support obligation.

[9]   *See Shaver,* 736 F.2d at 1316. *See also In re Davidson*, 133 B.R. 795 (N.D. Tex. 1990) (listing other factors), *rev'd on other grounds*, 947 F.2d 1294 (5th Cir. 1991).

§ 503(b)(1). This means that the costs of insuring estate assets, preparing them for sale, and the like are all a top priority. In reorganization cases, which may last many months or even years, the administrative expenses are frequently quite substantial and eat up the entire estate. This is because the administrative expenses will include virtually all the costs of running the debtor's business – including employees' wages, postpetition taxes, utilities, supplies, and even tort damages arising out of the normal operation of the business[10] – and the business may well be earning less money than it takes to run. Read § 503(b). Notice that in order to be paid, administrative expenses must be approved by the court after notice and a hearing.

As broad as the administrative expenses priority is, it is not limitless, as the following case demonstrates.

PENNSYLVANIA DEPARTMENT OF ENVIRONMENTAL RESOURCES V. TRI-STATE CLINICAL LABORATORIES, INC.
178 F.3d 685 (3d Cir. 1999)

McKee, Circuit Judge.

We are asked to decide if a criminal fine is entitled to priority as an administrative expense under Chapter 7 of the Bankruptcy Code. The fine was imposed upon a debtor in possession for postpetition conduct that violated Pennsylvania's Solid Waste Management Act. Pennsylvania's Department of Environmental Resources ("DER") filed a proof of claim in which it asserted that it was entitled to have the fine paid as an administrative expense under § 503(b) of the Bankruptcy Code. The bankruptcy court disagreed, and sustained the trustee's objection to the proof of claim. The district court affirmed. We hold that a postpetition criminal fine is not an administrative expense under Chapter 7, and therefore we affirm.

I. Factual Background and Procedural History

On August 14, 1990, Tri-State Clinical Laboratories, Inc. filed a voluntary petition under Chapter 11 of the United States Bankruptcy Code. A few months later, on October 4, 1990, two municipal workers were sprayed with blood while emptying a dumpster located behind Tri-State's place of business. The blood came from test tubes that Tri-State had illegally placed in the dumpster. The test tubes would have been collected and deposited in a municipal landfill had they not been discovered.

On January 21, 1992, the Office of Attorney General filed a criminal complaint charging Tri-State with violations of Pennsylvania's Solid Waste Management Act for illegally disposing of infectious waste. Count I of the complaint charged Tri-State with unlawfully storing municipal waste on or about July 18, 1990 (before Tri-State had filed

---

[10]   *See, e.g, In re Eagle-Picher Industries, Inc.*, 447 F.3d 461 (6th Cir. 2006) (damages for patent infringement arising from postpetition sales were an administrative expense).

its Chapter 11 petition). Count II charged Tri- State with unlawfully disposing of infectious waste in the dumpster on or about October 4, 1990 (after Tri-State had filed its Chapter 11 petition).

On September 10, 1992, Joseph P. Nigro was appointed Chapter 11 Trustee. Shortly thereafter, on October 6, 1992, the case was converted to Chapter 7, and Mr. Nigro was appointed the Chapter 7 Trustee.

On July 28, 1994, while the Chapter 7 proceedings were still pending, the Court of Common Pleas of Westmoreland County convicted Tri-State on Counts I and II of the complaint and imposed a fine of $10,000 for the violation charged in Count I, and a fine of $20,000 for the violation charged in Count II. It is undisputed that these fines were punitive in nature, and unrelated to actual costs or expenses incurred by the DER.

On August 19, 1994, the DER filed a proof of claim asserting a $10,000 subordinated unsecured claim under § 726(a)(4); and a $20,000 claim for administrative expenses pursuant to §§ 503(b), 507(a)(1), and 726(a)(1). The trustee objected to treating the $20,000 fine as an administrative expense. However, there was no objection to allowing the $10,000 claim for pre-petition conduct under § 726(a)(4), and that fine is not an issue in this appeal.

The bankruptcy court concluded that administrative expenses must be claimed by filing a "request for payment," and not by filing a "proof of claim." Accordingly, the bankruptcy court held that "[its previous] order granting the DER leave to file its proof of claim beyond the bar date is, in effect, a nullity." In the alternative, the court held that the $20,000 fine for postpetition criminal conduct is not an administrative expense under § 503(b). Instead, the court allowed the DER to pursue the fine as an unsecured claim.

The district court subsequently affirmed the bankruptcy court's determination that the $20,000 fine was not an administrative expense. Thus, it was not necessary for the district court to decide if it agreed with the bankruptcy court's conclusion that an administrative expense must be asserted in a request for payment, rather than a proof of claim. This appeal followed.

II. Discussion
A

The DER contends that the $20,000 fine imposed upon the debtor in possession for conduct that occurred after it filed the petition must be given priority status as an administrative expense under § 503(b)(1)(A) of the Bankruptcy Code. The DER bases its argument upon the nonexclusive nature of the list of expenses in § 503(b), and the fact that other courts have held that tort damages, postpetition civil penalties, and civil environmental fines are administrative expenses. The DER insists that there is no rational basis to distinguish those civil penalties from these criminal fines. According to the DER, both must be treated as an "actual necessary expense of preserving the estate" under § 503(b). The DER seeks to bolster this argument with policy considerations. It insists that if criminal fines are not given priority, "Chapter 11 debtors in possession [will be encouraged] to disregard criminal statutes and other valid laws that might impede a debtor in possession's effort to turn a profit," because such a debtor can violate the law "secure in the knowledge that no economic punishment would follow." The DER warns that this would "create[ ] an incentive for any marginal corporate business to attempt to free itself from regulatory restraints by seeking the safe haven of Chapter 11 protection."

The trustee's rejoinder relies heavily upon our decision in *Commonwealth of Pennsylvania Dept. of Environmental Resources v. Conroy*, 24 F.3d 568 (3d Cir. 1994). The trustee argues that we drew a distinction in *Conroy* between compensatory assessments which may enjoy priority status as actual administrative expenses, and noncompensatory assessments which do not reimburse creditors for actual expenses. The trustee argues that because Congress expressly refers to non-compensatory criminal fines and penalties elsewhere in the Code, it would have expressly included such fines under § 503(b) if it intended to treat them as administrative expenses. The trustee also adds its own policy "spin" to rebut the policy considerations that the DER urges upon us. The trustee argues that non-compensatory criminal fines survive bankruptcy, and can be assessed against the corporation or corporate officers individually. Thus, those who are responsible for the operation of the business have no incentive to cut costs by violating the law as the DER suggests.

B

The starting point of any statutory analysis is the language of the statute. Thus, we begin at the beginning by examining the text of the statute. In doing so, "we must not be guided by a single sentence or member of a sentence, but look to the provisions of the whole law, and to its object and policy." *Kelly v. Robinson*, 479 U.S. 36, 43 (1986).

Section 503(b)(1)(A) of the Bankruptcy Code provides:

(b) [T]here shall be allowed, administrative expenses, ... including –

(1)(A) the actual, necessary costs and expenses of preserving the estate, including wages, salaries, or commissions for services rendered after the commencement of the case.

Thus, for a claim to be given priority as an administrative expense under this provision of the Code, it must be (1) a "cost" or "expense" that is (2) "actual" and "necessary" to (3) "preserving the estate."

We construe the words of a statute according to their ordinary meaning, unless the context suggests otherwise. In *Reading Co. v. Brown*, the Supreme Court concluded that "the words 'preserving the estate' include the larger objective, common to arrangements, of operating the debtor's business with a view to rehabilitating it." 391 U.S. 471, 476-77 (1968). The dictionary defines "necessary" as "absolutely required" or "needed to bring about a certain effect or result." Webster's II New Riverside University Dictionary 787

(1994). However, the Supreme Court has held that the concept of "necessary costs" under the Code is somewhat broader than would be suggested by the dictionary definition. Thus, " 'usual and necessary costs' should include costs ordinarily incident to operation of a business, and not be limited to costs without which rehabilitation would be impossible." *Reading*, 391 U.S. at 483.

To determine Congress' intent in enacting § 503(b)(1)(A), we also must consider the other provisions of § 503. *See Neal v. Clark*, 95 U.S. 704, 708-09 (1877) ("a word is known by the company it keeps"). Section 503(b) specifically lists several expenditures that are included within the meaning of "administrative expenses." These include certain taxes and fines or penalties that relate to those taxes, § 503(b)(1)(B) & (C); compensation for services rendered by trustees and indenture trustees, § 503(b)(2) & § 503(b)(5); the actual, necessary expenses incurred by certain creditors pressing their claims, § 503(b)(3); reasonable compensation for the professional services of attorneys and accountants who provide particular services, § 503(b)(4); and other specified fees and mileage, § 503(b)(6). These specified administrative expenses all describe compensation for services that are necessarily incident to the operation of a business, *see, e.g.*, § 503(b)(2), (4) & (5), or reimbursement for actual expenses incurred, *see, e.g.*, § 503(b)(3) & (6).[11] Moreover, paragraph (1)(A) designates "wages, salaries, or commissions *for services rendered* after the commencement of the case" as "actual, necessary costs and expenses of preserving the estate." See § 503(1)(A) (emphasis added). Thus, the language of § 503(b), read as a whole, suggests a quid pro quo pursuant to which the estate accrues a debt in exchange for some consideration necessary to the operation or rehabilitation of the estate. Priority, therefore, is afforded such expenses to compensate the providers of necessary goods, services or labor.

Such a construction is supported by the purposes of the Bankruptcy Code. Chapter 11 is intended to "rehabilitat[e] the debtor and avoid[ ] forfeiture by creditors." *Pioneer Investment Services v. Brunswick Associates Ltd. Partnership*, 507 U.S. 380, 389 (1993). The drafters of the Code recognized that to achieve that purpose, the debtor has to

---

[11] Although taxes incurred by the estate, as well as fines and penalties relating to those taxes, are expressly included in § 503's definition of administrative expense, taxes are treated uniquely throughout the Bankruptcy Code, and the policies underlying the treatment of taxes do not apply to other debts and expenses. Thus, the inclusion of taxes and tax penalties in this section is not particularly helpful to our analysis. Indeed, to the extent that the express reference to tax penalties in § 503 implies anything, it implies that Congress did not intend to include noncompensatory criminal fines and penalties within the category of "administrative expenses." Pursuant to well-established canons of construction, the fact that Congress expressly included tax fines and penalties in § 503 implies that had Congress intended to include other types of fines and penalties within the class of administrative expenses, it would have done so expressly. *See Bates v. United States*, 522 U.S. 23 (1997) (" '[W]here Congress includes particular language in one section of a statute but omits it in another section of the same Act, it is generally presumed that Congress acts intentionally and purposefully in the disparate inclusion or exclusion.' ") (quoting *Russello v. United States*, 464 U.S. 16, 23 (1983)).

continue to operate between the filing of the petition and the adjudication of bankruptcy. This can result in additional expenses that are necessary to the continued operation of the business or to successfully winding it down. Congress recognized this need to provide an incentive to creditors who otherwise would not continue to provide services to a failing business. Accordingly, "the actual, necessary costs and expenses of preserving the estate" are given priority under the Code. *See* H.R. Rep. No. 95-595, at 186-87 (1977) ("Those who must wind up the affairs of a debtor's estate must be assured of payment, or else they will not participate in the liquidation or distribution of the estate"). Absent the priority established under § 503, a debtor in possession could not keep its employees, nor obtain services necessary to its operation as it attempts to reorganize, or wind-down pending ultimate liquidation. We believe the relevance of this consideration extends to interpreting Congress' intent in according priority to certain claims under Chapter 7.

The Supreme Court's holding in *Reading* illustrates these principles. In *Reading*, I.J. Knight Realty Corporation filed a petition for an arrangement under Chapter 11 of the Bankruptcy Act which was then in effect.[12] The district court appointed a receiver, and authorized him to continue to conduct the debtor's business of leasing an industrial building. Thereafter the building was totally destroyed by a fire which spread to the surrounding property. In a resulting tort action, one of the adjacent property owners recovered a judgment against the receiver in an effort to obtain compensation for the damage the fire inflicted upon its property as a result of the receiver's negligence. Because the debtor in possession was in bankruptcy, an issue arose as to the priority that the judgment should be accorded against the bankrupt estate. The Supreme Court held that the tort judgment was entitled to priority as an administrative expense under § 64a(1) of the Bankruptcy Act, even though the expense was not technically a cost of preserving the estate.

The Court's holding was motivated by the considerations of fairness and practicality which underlie the purposes of the bankruptcy laws. The Court believed that those who continue to transact business with the debtor during the Chapter 11 case, and who suffer financially as a result, are entitled to priority over other creditors who have not affirmatively assumed such risk. The Court reasoned that fairness dictates that those injured by the operation of a bankrupt business by a receiver acting within the scope of his authority be compensated for the injury. The Court concluded that it simply is not fair to deny innocent victims compensation for injuries they would not have incurred had the law not allowed the debtor to continue operating its business. * * *

The Court also considered the practical consequences of not allowing the tort claimant to recover ahead of other creditors.

More directly in point is the possibility of insurance. An arrangement may provide for suitable coverage, and the Court below recognized that the cost of insurance

---

[12]   The prior Bankruptcy Act is analogous to the current version.

against tort claims arising during an arrangement is an administrative expense payable in full under § 64a(1) . . . . It is . . . obvious that proper insurance premiums must be given priority, else insurance could not be obtained; and if a receiver or debtor in possession is to be encouraged to obtain insurance in adequate amounts, the claims against which insurance is obtained should be potentially payable in full.
Id. at 483.

* * *

Here, allowing the DER's claim to be treated as an administrative expense will allow that claim to be paid to the exclusion of, and out of the resources otherwise available for, claims of other creditors. The practical result would be that fines for committing crimes would be paid by innocent third persons – the creditors – rather than TriState – the criminal. That is as unfair as it is impractical. The payment of the criminal fine would not compensate for any damages resulting from Tri-State's conduct. It would merely cause Tri-State to satisfy its obligations to the state out of the pockets of Tri-State's creditors.

The DER argues that the cost of complying with the criminal laws is a necessary cost of doing business (no less than taxes, wages, or fees), and therefore any criminal penalties in the form of fines resulting from violating the law must be treated as an administrative expense. Thus, the DER would have us hold that a violation of a criminal law intended to protect public safety is necessary or ordinarily incident to operating a business, and therefore, is incurred as an expense of "preserving the estate." However, the DER fails to recognize that, even if the costs associated with operating a business in accordance with the law are necessary to preserving the estate, it does not follow that criminal fines and the conduct they attempt to punish are ordinarily incident to operating a business. We refuse to adopt an analysis of administrative expenses that is based upon the assumption that legitimate businesses engage in a "cost-benefit" analysis to determine if they will comply with criminal laws that protect the very public that the owners and operators of those legitimate businesses are part of. It is neither reasonable nor necessary for a commercial enterprise to violate criminal laws and endanger the public to preserve the estate or to conduct legitimate business operations, and we refuse the DER's invitation to hold otherwise. Rather, we believe Congress intended only for those "actual necessary costs and expenses" that arise in the context of, or compensate for, legitimate business activity, or the losses resulting therefrom, to be treated as expenses of preserving the estate, and accorded priority as an administrative expense.

Although both parties to this appeal rely upon our holding in *Conroy* to support their arguments, we view *Conroy* as supporting the distinction we draw between claims for compensatory expenses and those for criminal fines. In *Conroy*, the DER filed a claim for reimbursement for costs incurred in cleaning up hazardous chemicals at a site the Chapter 11 debtors had attempted to abandon. In holding that those costs were administrative expenses entitled to priority we said:

> [I]f the DER had not itself undertaken to clean up the [site,] the Conroys could not have escaped their obligation to do so by abandoning the hazardous property in question. Furthermore, if Frank Conroy had arranged for cleanup of the facility after he had filed a Chapter 11 petition, the costs of this cleanup would have constituted administrative expenses under § 503(b)(1)(A), since they are a portion of "the actual, necessary costs and expenses of preserving the estate."

24 F.3d at 569. We also held that reimbursement for that portion of the administrative and legal costs incurred in arranging for cleanup which the DER had "sufficiently substantiated" as reasonable compensation also qualified as an administrative expense. *Id.* at 570-71. By cleaning up the site, the DER provided a service to the debtor – a service that the debtor itself would have had to perform during the course of normal operations – and therefore, the DER was entitled to compensation for that service.

The situation here is quite different. Tri-State was not required to endanger the health and welfare of residents of the community by illegally disposing of test tubes containing blood, and the sanction that was imposed as punishment for doing so has nothing to do with compensation or proper business operations. Rather the purpose of this criminal fine is deterrence, retribution, and punishment.

C

Our conclusion is also consistent with the legislative history relating to the classification of non-compensatory criminal fines and penalties. [a lengthy discussion of legislative history followed – ed.] * * *

We conclude that the policy considerations evidenced by the aforementioned legislative history, as well as the text of the Code and the cases interpreting it, support our view that non-compensatory criminal fines imposed on a Chapter 7 debtor or trustee should not be deemed administrative expenses. This interpretation also is consistent with Congress' limitation on the dischargeability of criminal fines and penalties. Under Chapter 7, that portion of a fine that is compensatory is discharged. § 523(a)(7). We do not believe that Congress intended for us to ignore the non-compensatory character of a criminal fine in deciding if it is an administrative expense under § 503, while explicitly requiring that consideration under § 523(a)(7). Rather, for the reasons previously stated, we conclude that § 503's restriction to "expenses of preserving the estate" limits such expenses to those that constitute compensation for expenditures necessary to the operation of the debtor-in-possession's business. As we noted above, we will not stretch our policy analysis to include within this category the payment of the criminal fines for Tri-State's conduct here.

We recognize, of course, that Tri-State may not have the funds to pay this fine after the estate is liquidated. However, that is often a possibility when criminal fines are imposed, and we see nothing in the statutes that Tri-State has violated, nor anything endemic to the process of bankruptcy, that would justify us in removing the Commonwealth's hand from the empty pockets of the criminal, and placing it in the pockets of creditors merely because those pockets are deeper. Tri-State was sentenced while in bankruptcy for an act that occurred after it filed its bankruptcy petition. The sentencing judge clearly knew that Tri-State's ability to pay any fine was suspect at best. Yet, the sanction here was on the corporate entity, not upon the responsible individuals. It should not now come as any great surprise that the bankrupt debtor lacks the resources to pay this criminal fine and meet its obligations to creditors. Tri-State's precarious financial condition does not, however, allow us to stretch the concept of administrative expense to remedy the DER's predicament.

D

Finally, we realize, of course, that there is a certain tension between our analysis here, and the analysis in *Alabama Surface Mining Commission v. N.P. Mining Co.*, 963 F.2d 1449 (11th Cir. 1992). There, the court held that civil fines imposed solely as punishment for violation of environmental regulations were entitled to priority as an administrative expense under Chapter 11. The holding was based upon the requirement in § 969(b) that the trustee or debtor in possession manage and operate the property in compliance with state law. The court of appeals reasoned that

> [i]f postpetition costs "ordinarily incident to operation of a business" that do not confer a benefit on the estate [the tort claims in Reading] can indeed qualify as "actual, necessary" expenses of preserving the estate, then a strong case can be made that when a licensed business operates in the regulated atmosphere of strip mining in Alabama, incurring regulatory penalties is a cost ordinarily incident to operation of a business and should be accorded administrative-expense priority.

Id. at 1454-5.

However, we do not think that rationale applies here, even if it is appropriate for a civil fine on a business in a heavily regulated industry. As noted above, doing so would require us to infer that disposing of infectious human waste in a manner that not only endangers members of the general public, but also constitutes criminal activity, is part of the ordinary and necessary operations of a business. Moreover, the court in *N.P. Mining* stressed that the violation before it did not involve safety. *See* 963 F.2d at 1458. We are not convinced the court's holding would be the same if it were faced with the kind of reckless conduct in which Tri-State engaged. Finally, the court in *N.P. Mining* did not consider the extensive legislative history regarding prepetition penalties to be as relevant as we do in determining whether punitive criminal fines should be given preferential treatment. Accordingly, we are not persuaded by *N.P. Mining*, the cases upon which it relies, or the cases that have relied upon *N.P. Mining*.

III. Conclusion

In sum, based on the plain language of the Bankruptcy Code, its purpose and legislative history, and the principles of fairness upon which the Code is grounded, we hold that punitive criminal fines arising from postpetition behavior are not administrative expenses under § 503(b), and therefore, are not accorded priority status pursuant to § 507(a)(1). Therefore, the orders of the Bankruptcy Court and the District Court will be affirmed in accordance with this decision.

––––––––––––––

Even in Chapter 7 cases, the administrative expenses can be significant. This is often because the cost of paying many of the people involved in the bankruptcy case will be borne by the estate.

(a) The Trustee's Compensation

In Chapter 7 cases, the trustee receives $45 for each case filed. § 330(b). This amount comes out of the filing fee. In addition, the trustee is entitled to reasonable compensation for services but such compensation is capped at a percentage of the distributions to the claimants. *See* §§ 326(a), 330(a).[13] Because this compensation is fairly minimal, trustees usually look for other ways to enhance their income. Because a majority of trustees are lawyers, most also seek employment as professionals under § 327 in those cases in which employing a professional is necessary and appropriate. This typically occurs when there will be litigation to recover a preference or fraudulent transfer. In essence, the trustees hire themselves as lawyers (subject to court approval), *see* § 327(d), and compensation for such professional services is not capped by a percentage of the distributions in the case. § 330(a). In the few districts that do not routinely permit a trustee to serve as his or her own lawyer, the trustees typically hire each other or their law firms, again subject to court approval. § 327(a).

––––––––––––––

[13]   Technically, § 326(a) fixes a maximum fee. However, in many districts the trustee is permitted to take the maximum without having to provide any specific justification for it. For some reason, the additional $45 fee is not thought to be extra compensation that would take the trustee beyond the maximum permitted by § 326(a).

(b) Compensation for Employed Professionals

Generally speaking, the debtor's attorney in a Chapter 7 case is not compensated out of the estate. This is because the debtor's interests are typically adverse to those of the creditors, for whose benefit the estate is administered.[14] Accordingly, most debtor's attorneys get their fees up front before the bankruptcy petition is filed. Failure to do this will subject the unpaid fee obligation to the debtor's discharge.

Even though the debtor's attorney is seldom paid out of estate assets, and may well be paid through a prepetition retainer, the Bankruptcy Court has the authority and the duty to review the reasonableness of those fees and to order that any unreasonable amount either not be collected or be disgorged if already paid. *See* § 329(b). To permit the court to perform this review, the debtor's attorney must disclose all payments and fee arrangements. *See* § 329(a); Rule 2016(b). Many courts do not hesitate to reduce the fee charged by the debtor's attorney.[15] The following case illustrates the procedural and substantive hurdles that the debtor's counsel faces in obtaining payment for bankruptcy legal services. It also involves a rather unusual solution to the problem.

IN RE LEITNER
221 B.R. 502 (Bankr. D. Nev. 1998)

Minahan, Jr., Bankruptcy Judge.

A myriad of issues are raised in this Chapter 7 case because, before filing this bankruptcy case, debtors' counsel obtained a promissory note and mortgage from debtors to assure payment for bankruptcy related legal services. I conclude that these extraordinary pre-bankruptcy transactions with counsel are legal and appropriate, provided that the multiple requirements of the Bankruptcy Code and Rules are met.

At the time the debtors sought legal advice from attorney Mr. Bert Blackwell, they agreed to pay Mr. Blackwell $1,100.00, and the bankruptcy filing fee in installments of $100.00 per month. He agreed to represent them in a Chapter 7 bankruptcy case and to advance the $175.00 filing fee. The debtors granted Mr. Blackwell a mortgage in their residence to secure the $1,275.00 debt. The mortgage was duly recorded prior to filing

---

[14] The debtor's attorneys' fees generally do not qualify for administrative expense treatment under § 503(b)(1) because they are typically not incurred to "preserve the estate." In addition, they do not qualify under § 503(b)(2), which references compensation authorized under § 330(a), because § 330(a) in turn references professionals employed under § 327 and the debtor's attorney is not normally hired under § 327. This latter point was actually the subject of some confusion because of a poorly drafted 1994 amendment to § 330(a), but the Supreme Court has now made it clear that the debtor's attorney does not qualify for payment from the estate except in the rare instance when the attorney is hired under § 327. *Lamie v. U.S. Trustee*, 540 U.S. 526 (2004).

[15] *See, e.g., In re Day*, 213 B.R. 145 (C.D. Ill. 1997).

this bankruptcy case. Debtors' residence is valued at $11,800.00, and is encumbered only by Mr. Blackwell's mortgage. The debtors claim the remaining equity in the real estate as an exempt homestead under § 40-101 of the Nebraska Revised Statutes.

The debtors filed a reaffirmation agreement with the Clerk of the Bankruptcy Court seeking leave of the court to affirm their $1,275.00 obligation to Mr. Blackwell. The United States Trustee objected to approval of the reaffirmation agreement, asserting that the monthly installment payments of $100.00 may impose an undue hardship on the debtors. When the debtors sought leave to withdraw the reaffirmation agreement, I scheduled a hearing to examine the debtors' transactions with Mr. Blackwell.

The fee agreement between Mr. Blackwell and debtors represents a good faith attempt to deal with a difficult problem faced by bankruptcy practitioners whose clients cannot afford to pay Chapter 7 legal expenses in advance. However, the fee agreement and mortgage present a number of legal issues which I will address with the objective of providing counsel guidelines for structuring agreements with clients for the payment of Chapter 7 legal expenses on a deferred basis.

Bankruptcy practitioners are faced with a difficult situation when a financially troubled debtor wants to file a Chapter 7 bankruptcy case and cannot afford to pay attorney fees in advance. Prudent counsel will not agree to pay the bankruptcy filing fees and to file the bankruptcy case without a retainer because the debtor's obligations to pay for pre-bankruptcy legal services will be discharged in the bankruptcy case. One alternative is for counsel to suggest that the client file a Chapter 13 bankruptcy case so that the attorney fees can be paid on a deferred basis as an allowed administrative expense. However, the selection of the appropriate bankruptcy chapter should not be influenced by the need to pay attorney fees. Chapter 13 is most appropriate for debtors who want to retain non-exempt assets and make payments to creditors. If a debtor has few non-exempt assets and no debts excepted from discharge under § 523, Chapter 7 may be the most appropriate chapter for the insolvent debtor who has no desire or ability to make payments to creditors.

What course of action should bankruptcy counsel recommend to a debtor who has no ability to pay for legal services in advance, but whose circumstances strongly suggest that Chapter 7 liquidation is the most suitable bankruptcy alternative? Mr. Blackwell addressed this problem by obtaining a promissory note and mortgage and filing a Chapter 7 case. His clients are thus in the appropriate bankruptcy Chapter, but the transaction between counsel and his clients raises several specific issues:

> 1. Is debtors' counsel disqualified from representing the bankruptcy debtors because counsel is a prepetition creditor, holding a lien in property of the bankruptcy estate?

> 2. Are the debtors or counsel required to disclose the prepetition mortgage transaction and fee agreement to the court and to creditors?

3. Must the debtors' counsel file a fee application in the Chapter 7 case seeking allowance of his fees and approval of the fee agreement and mortgage?

4. Absent reaffirmation, will the Chapter 7 discharge order extinguish the debtors' personal obligation to pay for the legal services?

5. If a reaffirmation agreement is not approved, does the lien securing the obligation to pay attorney fees pass through the bankruptcy case unimpaired, thus permitting counsel to enforce the mortgage after the bankruptcy discharge is entered and the bankruptcy case is closed?

1. *Disqualification of Counsel*

The Eighth Circuit Court of Appeals has held that an attorney who is a prepetition creditor holding a mortgage on the debtor's real estate for prepetition and postpetition services related to a bankruptcy case, is not a "disinterested person," and thus does not qualify for employment under § 327(a) in a Chapter 11 bankruptcy case. *See In re Pierce*, 809 F.2d 1356 (8th Cir.1987). However, the "disinterested" requirements of §§ 327 and 328 do not apply to an attorney representing the debtor in a Chapter 7 case. The "disinterested" requirements of §§ 327 and 328 of the Bankruptcy Code apply to professionals who provide services to or for the benefit of the bankruptcy estate such as counsel for the standing trustee. These professionals must be retained with court approval and are generally compensated from property of the bankruptcy estate. Debtor's counsel does not represent the bankruptcy estate in a Chapter 7 case, except by special order of the court. Mr. Blackwell is not disqualified from representing the Chapter 7 debtors simply because he is a secured creditor of the debtors respecting unpaid fees for bankruptcy related legal services.

Attorney and clients are almost always in a debtor-creditor relationship respecting the provision of legal services. The fact that a client is indebted to counsel for undisputed charges for services rendered within the scope of the current representation does not provide an ethical or statutory basis for disqualification of counsel.

2. *Disclosure of Fee Arrangement and Mortgage*

Counsel's § 329 and Rule 2016 Statement must disclose the fee agreement. The debtors' bankruptcy schedules and statement of financial affairs must disclose the mortgage securing the fee agreement.

Section 329, in relevant part, requires that:

(a) Any attorney representing a debtor in a case under this title, or in connection with such a case, whether or not such attorney applies for compensation under this title, shall file with the court a statement of the compensation paid or agreed to be paid, if such payment or agreement was made after one year before the date of the filing of the petition, for services

rendered or to be rendered in contemplation of or in connection with the case
by such attorney, and the source of such compensation.

Bankruptcy Rule 2016 further elaborates the disclosure requirements. However, Bankruptcy Rule 2016(b) and § 329(a) make no explicit requirement that liens be disclosed.

The existence of the encumbrance to secure the obligation to pay is an integral part of the fee agreement and it is highly relevant to the bankruptcy proceedings. Certainly, each and every term and provision of a fee agreement need not be disclosed, but in the context of a bankruptcy case, the existence of an encumbrance to secure payment of attorney fees is arguably an essential term of the bargain. I construe Rule 2016(b) to require disclosure of any lien that secures payment of counsel's fees. The Rule explicitly requires disclosure of "the source of such compensation." I hold that a mortgage securing a fee agreement is a potential "source of compensation" which must be disclosed in the Rule 2016(b) statement.

It is clear that the debtor must also disclose the mortgage. A bankruptcy debtor is required to list the name and address of all entities holding claims secured by property of the debtor as of the date of filing of the petition. *See* Schedule D, Creditors Holding Secured Claims. The bankruptcy schedules in this case list Mr. Blackwell as a secured creditor holding a mortgage on the debtors' real estate to secure a $1,275.00 debt. The statement of financial affairs also requires disclosure of the mortgage. The debtor must list all payments made or property transferred by or on behalf of the debtor to any person for consultation concerning debt consolidation, relief under the Bankruptcy Code, or preparation of a petition in bankruptcy within one year immediately preceding the commencement of the case. *See* Question Number 9, Statement of Financial Affairs.

In summary, an agreement between debtor and counsel for the payment of bankruptcy legal fees secured by a mortgage on debtors' property, must be disclosed (i) by counsel in the § 329 and Rule 2016(b) statement, and (ii) by debtor in the bankruptcy schedules and statement of financial affairs.

3. *Fee Application Requirement*

Bankruptcy Rule 2016(a) requires any entity seeking compensation or reimbursement of expenses from the bankruptcy estate to file a fee application. A Chapter 7 debtor's counsel is not a professional retained to represent the bankruptcy estate, and debtor's counsel is not paid from the property of the estate. Debtors' counsel, Mr. Blackwell, does not seek compensation from the bankruptcy estate and he is not required to file a fee application.

However, the court may examine the fee agreement. Under Bankruptcy Rule 2017, the court has broad authority to determine whether the payment of money or transfer of property to an attorney for services is excessive. Bankruptcy Rule 2017 provides a procedural mechanism for the court to examine the reasonableness of a prepetition fee agreement. In appropriate circumstances the fees could be reduced, and the mortgage limited or avoided.

4. *Discharge of Debtors' Personal Liability*

The Chapter 7 debtor's personal obligation to pay for prepetition legal services will be discharged by the Chapter 7 discharge order, unless the debtor reaffirms the debt under § 524 of the Bankruptcy Code. A reaffirmation agreement between debtor and counsel will not be enforceable unless it is filed with the court. Counsel, as a party to the fee agreement, may not represent the debtor in regard to the reaffirmation agreement. Since the debtors are not represented by counsel in connection with the reaffirmation agreement, and there is no counsel to file the affidavit or declaration required by § 524(c)(3), the reaffirmation agreement is not enforceable unless approved by the court after a hearing attended by the debtors.

If the obligation to pay attorney fees is discharged, § 524(a)(2) enjoins counsel from any attempt to collect the debt as a personal obligation of the debtor.

5. *Mortgage Passes Through Bankruptcy*

Even though the Chapter 7 debtors' personal obligation to pay prepetition attorney fees will be discharged absent a valid reaffirmation of the debt, the mortgage will pass through the bankruptcy proceeding unimpaired. On the facts of this case, there is no suggestion that the mortgage is avoidable as a preference or fraudulent conveyance. None of the trustee's avoiding powers seem applicable. Section 522(f), which can be used to avoid certain non-purchase money security interests, is not applicable to security interests in real property, such as Mr. Blackwell's mortgage. However, § 522(f) could be used to avoid liens in the types of exempt personal property listed in that subsection of the Bankruptcy Code. In effect, § 522(f) will limit the ability of counsel to structure secured deferred financing.

Under § 506(a), Mr. Blackwell's prepetition claim is an allowed secured claim to the extent of equity in collateral. On the facts of this case the mortgage is fully secured. Thus, even if counsel fails to file a proof of claim, the mortgage will not be avoided under § 506(d). The discharge order entered in this case will discharge debtors' personal obligation, but the mortgage will survive and may be enforced. After the discharge order is entered in this case, the debtors will no longer be personally liable to Mr. Blackwell, however, Mr. Blackwell will be free to enforce the mortgage.

Finally, it should be noted that to the extent services are provided by the Chapter 7 debtor's attorney postpetition, many of the above issues become moot. In that instance, although the fee agreement must still be disclosed, the attorney is a postpetition creditor, the postpetition debt for attorney fees is not dischargeable, and a reaffirmation agreement is not necessary as to postpetition services.

Conclusion

Counsel is not disqualified from representing the Chapter 7 debtors by virtue of his holding a secured claim for undisputed prepetition legal services. The prepetition agreement between debtors and counsel concerning the payment of legal fees in installments and the granting of the mortgage must be disclosed (i) by counsel in the § 329 and Bankruptcy Rule 2016(b) statement, and (ii) by debtors in the bankruptcy schedules and statement of financial affairs. Counsel is not required to file a fee application or obtain bankruptcy court approval of the fee agreement, but the court may examine the fee agreement under Rule 2017. Unless the debtors' reaffirm their obligation to pay counsel, the prepetition debt will be discharged by the Chapter 7 discharge order. Counsel may enforce his prepetition mortgage against the debtors' property under applicable non-bankruptcy law after the automatic stay of § 362 terminates.

Mr. Blackwell may continue to represent the debtors in this case. The motion to withdraw the reaffirmation agreement is sustained.

Problem 9-1

Was the Leitners' arrangement with their attorney, Mr. Blackwell, designed solely to ensure payment of his legal services or did it also serve some additional objective? If so, what was that objective?

In those situations where the efforts of the debtor's attorney really do benefit the estate, compensation from the estate will be possible. This is quite rare in Chapter 7 cases but common in Chapter 11, where the debtor is functioning as debtor-in-possession, retains control over the estate, and has many of the trustee's powers. *See* § 1107(a).

The trustee's attorney and accountant are normally paid out of the estate, as are the professionals hired by a debtor-in-possession or a creditors' committee. However, there are several protections built into the process to make sure that estate assets are not wasted in the process of employing and paying these professionals. First, the court must approve the employment in advance. Second, except for those hired by a creditors' committee, the professional to be hired must be "disinterested." *See* §§ 327(a), 330(a), 1107. *Cf.* § 1103(a), (b).

Because anyone who holds a prepetition claim cannot be disinterested, § 101(14)(A), an attorney or accountant whose bill for prepetition services remains even partly unpaid cannot be employed postpetition by the trustee or debtor-in-possession, at least not unless the professional waives the right to payment for such services.[16] As may be evident, these are often the professionals who are most familiar with the debtor's legal or financial affairs, and who therefore are often the persons best suited to provide postpetition services. Nevertheless, as one court noted, when Congress enacted § 327(a) it "made a conscious choice that efficiency would be sacrificed for the appearance of propriety."[17] Moreover, paying the professional in full shortly before bankruptcy will likely not solve the problem. Because such a payment may well constitute an avoidable preference, the professional would have an interest adverse to the estate, and thus still not qualify as disinterested.[18]

There are four noteworthy exceptions to this main rule, but all are rather narrow. First, if the prepetition claim arose out of services to be provided in connection to the bankruptcy case – for example, if the claim arises because the debtor promises to pay an attorney for bankruptcy services but provides no retainer – then the professional may still be employed.[19] This of course in no way helps a trustee or debtor employ attorneys or accountants who acquired insight into the debtor's situation by providing prepetition services for which they remain unpaid.

Second, § 327(b) permits the trustee to retain salaried professionals. However, only the largest businesses maintain attorneys or accountants on salary. The trustee for most debtors and most debtors-in-possession will be unable to use this provision.

Third, § 1107(b) indicates that a professional is not disqualified for employment merely because the debtor had employed the professional prepetition. However, by its terms this provision applies only in Chapter 11 cases and only to debtors-in-possession, not to trustees.[20] More importantly, the provision does not circumvent the requirement that employed professionals be disinterested or alter the fact that a holder of an unpaid claim is not disinterested. As a result, most courts treat this provision merely as a

---

[16] *See, e.g., In re Fulgham Enterprises, Inc.*, 181 B.R. 139 (Bankr. N.D. Ala. 1995); *In re Hub Business Forms, Inc.*, 146 B.R. 315 (Bankr. D. Mass. 1992).

[17] *In re Siliconix, Inc.*, 135 B.R. 378, 380 (Bankr. N.D. Cal. 1991).

[18] *See In re Pillowtex, Inc.*, 304 F.3d 246 (3d Cir. 2002) (so ruling even though no determination had been made that the payment was preferential and the professional agreed to return the funds and waive any revived claim for payment if the payment was determined to be a preference); *In re Triple Star Welding, Inc.*, 324 B.R. 778 (9th Cir. BAP 2005) (agreeing with *Pillowtex* but suggesting that the conflict would be removed if the professional returned the payment). *But cf. In re Enron*, 2003 WL 223455 (S.D.N.Y. 2003) (if the professional agrees to waive the right to litigate the preference issue and be bound by an examiner's determination, the conflict is removed and the professional is disinterested).

[19] *In re Martin*, 817 F.2d 175 (1st Cir. 1987).

[20] *Hub Business Forms*, 146 B.R. at 318 n.2.

statement that working in a professional capacity for both the debtor and the debtor-in-possession is not inherently a conflict of interest.

Finally, § 327(e) permits employment of an attorney *for a special purpose,* even though the attorney is not disinterested, provided the attorney does not hold an interest adverse to the debtor on the matter that is the subject of the employment. Thus, an attorney of the debtor who is owed money for prepetition services may continue to represent the trustee or debtor-in-possession on a specific matter. For example, an attorney may continue to litigate a claim by or against the debtor or to negotiate a particular contract. The exception does not, however, contemplate more general representation. Moreover, it does not extend to other professionals, such as accountants.[21] Thus, if the debtor owes money for prepetition services to a particular accounting firm, then neither the trustee nor the debtor-in-possession may employ that firm even though it may have great familiarity with the debtor's books and records.

The remaining – and perhaps most significant – method for ensuring that estate assets are not wasted through the employment of professionals is through substantial judicial oversight of the fees awarded. Such oversight can occur in either of two ways.

First, the bankruptcy court may determine and approve the terms of the professional's compensation in the appointment order. If the court does this, such as by setting an hourly rate or a contingent fee, the court may later reduce that compensation only if "the terms and conditions prove to have been improvident in light of developments not capable of being anticipated at the time" they were fixed. § 328(a).[22]

Second, and more commonly, the court evaluates the reasonableness of the fee by examining the services with the benefit of hindsight. In doing so, the court is expressly charged with considering the nature and value of the services, and the amount and reasonableness of the time spent. § 330(a)(3). Beyond this, courts routinely examine other factors, such as "the novelty and difficulty of the task, the requisite skill level, whether the case precluded other employment, the contingent nature of the fee, time limitations, the amount of money involved and results obtained, and the experience, reputation, and ability of the [professional]."[23] As a result, courts may – and frequently do – refuse to compensate the professional fully for the work performed, and instead approve a fee request only in part. The following case is an example of this.

---

[21]   *See, e.g., In re South Shore Golf Club Holding Co.,* 182 B.R. 94 (Bankr. W.D.N.Y. 1995).

[22]   *See also In re Texas Securities, Inc.,* 218 F.3d 443, 445-46 (5th Cir. 2005).

As to the formalities necessary to show such advance approval of the compensation terms, *compare In re Circle K Corp.,* 279 F.3d 669 (9th Cir. 2002), and *Zolfo, Cooper & Co. v. Sunbeam-Oster Co., Inc.,* 50 F.3d 253, 261 (3d Cir. 1995), *with In re Airspect Air, Inc.,* 385 F.3d 915, 921-22 (6th Cir. 2004).

[23]   *In re Commercial Financial Services, Inc.,* 427 F.3d 804, 811 (10th Cir. 2005).

IN RE GIC GOVERNMENT SECURITIES, INC.
122 B.R. 148 (Bankr. M.D. Fla. 1990)

Paskay, Chief Judge.

This is a Chapter 7 stockbroker liquidation case and the matter under consideration is the Application for Fees filed by Addison, Ketchey & Horan, P.A. (Addison, Ketchey). Addison, Ketchey was authorized by this Court to serve as special counsel for George Hadley, the Trustee in this Chapter 7 liquidation case after the Trustee filed an Application for Authorization To Employ Addison, Ketchey in order to pursue claims in excess of $6 million from E.F. Hutton & Co., Inc., and other major security brokerage houses. Addison, Ketchey seeks fees of $336,414.80 for services rendered to the Trustee for the period from May 7, 1987 through June 21, 1990, claiming to have spent 3,483.4 hours in conjunction with the services rendered to the Trustee.

At the initial hearing on the Application to employ Addison, Ketchey, this Court expressed its reluctance to authorize the employment for the purpose of filing a suit on behalf of the Trustee to recover damages from E.F. Hutton & Co., Inc., in light of the Supreme Court decision *in Caplin v. Marine Midland Grace Trust Co.,* 406 U.S. 416 (1972). In *Caplin*, the Supreme Court held that a reorganization trustee had no standing to assert against a third party, the trustee for debenture holders, claims on behalf of holders of the debtor's debentures. *Caplin* was decided under the Act of 1898; however, *Caplin* has been held still the law by several circuits.

Notwithstanding this Court's reluctance to authorize the employment of Addison, Ketchey in light of *Caplin* and its progeny, the "victims committee" urged that the Application for Employment should be approved because of the potential recovery of $6 million. This Court did ultimately approve the Application for employment of Addison, Ketchey, and the law firm filed suit on behalf of the Trustee in the Circuit Court, which was removed to the district court based on diversity jurisdiction.

In the District Court, the Trustee's Motion for Summary Judgment on the issue of standing was granted initially in part, and E.F. Hutton's Motion for Summary Judgment on the same issue was denied. However, because the standing issue concerned a question of law involving a substantial ground for difference of opinion, the District Court certified the standing issue for an immediate interlocutory appeal. On appeal, the Eleventh Circuit Court of Appeals determined that the Trustee lacked standing to bring an action on behalf of creditors of the debtor. The Circuit Court remanded the case back to the District Court with instructions to dismiss the case for lack of standing. The Circuit Court in its decision relied heavily on the Supreme Court's decision in *Caplin, supra,* a case which was of concern to this Court initially when it considered the Application To Employ Addison, Ketchey as special counsel.

Pursuant to the mandate issued by the Eleventh Circuit Court of Appeals, the District Court entered a Final Judgment on September 6, 1990, in favor of E.F. Hutton, and against the Trustee.

In reviewing the Fee Application under consideration, it should be noted at the outset that this Court has no quarrel with the number of hours spent by the law firm, nor does the Court find the blended hourly rate of $96 per hour to be excessive. Thus, based on the lodestar principle, this Court ordinarily would not have any difficulty to conclude that the fees sought by Addison, Ketchey are more than reasonable. However, in evaluating fee applications, this Court must also consider the factors identified in *Johnson v. Georgia Highway Express, Inc.,* 488 F.2d 714 (5th Cir. 1974), which were made applicable to bankruptcy proceedings in *In re First Colonial Corp. of America,* 544 F.2d 1291 (5th Cir. 1977), *cert. denied,* 431 U.S. 904 (1977). One of the factors in *Johnson* considers the amount involved and the ultimate results obtained.[24]

---

[24]   The *Johnson* court listed the following factors, 488 F.2d at 717-19:

(1) *The time and labor required.* Although hours claimed or spent on a case should not be the sole basis for determining a fee, they are a necessary ingredient to be considered. The trial judge should weigh the hours claimed against his own knowledge, experience, and expertise of the time required to complete similar activities. If more than one attorney is involved, the possibility of duplication of effort along with the proper utilization of time should be scrutinized. The time of two or three lawyers in a courtroom or conference when one would do, may obviously be discounted. It is appropriate to distinguish between legal work, in the strict sense, and investigation, clerical work, compilation of facts and statistics and other work which can often be accomplished by non-lawyers but which a lawyer may do because he has no other help available. Such non-legal work may command a lesser rate. Its dollar value is not enhanced just because a lawyer does it.

(2) *The novelty and difficulty of the questions.* Cases of first impression generally require more time and effort on the attorney's part. Although this greater expenditure of time in research and preparation is an investment by counsel in obtaining knowledge which can be used in similar later cases, he should not be penalized for undertaking a case which may "make new law." Instead, he should be appropriately compensated for accepting the challenge.

(3) *The skill requisite to perform the legal service properly.* The trial judge should closely observe the attorney's work product, his preparation, and general ability before the court.

(4) *The preclusion of other employment by the attorney due to acceptance of the case.*

(5) *The customary fee.* It is open knowledge that various types of legal work command differing scales of compensation. At no time, however, should the fee for strictly legal work fall below the $20 per hour prescribed by the criminal justice act, 18 U.S.C. § 3006A(d)(1), and awarded to appointed counsel for criminal defendants. As long as minimum fee schedules are in existence and are customarily followed by the lawyers in a given community, they should be taken into consideration.

(6) *Whether the fee is fixed or contingent.* The fee quoted to the client or the percentage of the recovery agreed to is helpful in demonstrating the attorney's fee expectations when he accepted the case. But, such arrangements should not determine the court's decision. The criterion for the court is not what the parties agreed but what is reasonable. In no event, however, should the litigant be awarded a fee greater than he is contractually bound to pay, if indeed the attorneys have contracted as to amount.

Thus, if this Court considers only the results obtained, this Court might be inclined to disapprove the Fee Application in toto. It is clear that the efforts of the law firm, notwithstanding the fact that the quality of the services rendered might have been adequate or even superior, produced no benefit at all for the Debtor's estate. However, this Court is mindful of the fact that the law firm was not employed to serve as special counsel for the Trustee on a contingency fee basis. Thus, it would be patently unfair to disapprove the Fee Application in toto. Notwithstanding, this Court must be mindful of the fact that considering the Supreme Court's decision in *Caplin*, it was likely that the undertaking by the law firm involved substantial risk, and it was also more than likely that the Trustee would have no standing to sue E.F. Hutton.

Thus, while it would be patently unfair to the law firm to disapprove in toto the Application for Allowance, it is equally clear that it is appropriate to reduce the amount of fees. In *Hensley v. Eckerhart,* 461 U.S. 424 (1983), the Supreme Court held that "the extent of a plaintiff's success is a crucial factor in determining the proper amount of an award of attorney's fees under 42 U.S.C. § 1988." In sum, this Court is satisfied that it is appropriate to consider the lack of success of the law firm when determining the appropriate fee award. Accordingly, this Court is constrained to conclude that some reduction of the amount sought is appropriate under the circumstances, and the award shall not be more than $285,000.

Accordingly, it is ordered, adjudged and decreed that the First Application for Reimbursement of Fees by Addison, Ketchey & Horan, P.A., be, and the same is hereby,

---

(7) *Time limitations imposed by the client or the circumstances.* Priority work that delays the lawyer's other legal work is entitled to some premium. This factor is particularly important when a new counsel is called in to prosecute the appeal or handle other matters at a late stage in the proceedings.

(8) *The amount involved and the results obtained.*

(9) *The experience, reputation, and ability of the attorneys.* Most fee scales reflect an experience differential with the more experienced attorneys receiving larger compensation. An attorney specializing in civil rights cases may enjoy a higher rate for his expertise than others, providing his ability corresponds with his experience. Longevity per se, however, should not dictate the higher fee. If a young attorney demonstrates the skill and ability, he should not be penalized for only recently being admitted to the bar.

(10) *The "undesirability" of the case.* Civil rights attorneys face hardships in their communities because of their desire to help the civil rights litigant. Oftentimes his decision to help eradicate discrimination is not pleasantly received by the community or his contemporaries. This can have an economic impact on his practice which can be considered by the court.

(11) *The nature and length of the professional relationship with the client.* A lawyer in private practice may vary his fee for similar work in the light of the professional relationship of the client with his office. The court may appropriately consider this factor in determining the amount that would be reasonable.

(12) *Awards in similar cases.*

approved in part and disapproved in part, and the law firm of Addison, Ketchey & Horan, P.A., is awarded fees in the amount of $285,000.

Problem 9-2

Which of the following can qualify as administrative expenses in a Chapter 7 case?

A. Fees of the trustee's attorney incurred in challenging the discharge. *See* §§ 704(a), 503(b)(2), 330(a), 327(a).
B. Fees of the trustee's attorney incurred in seeking to avoid a preferential transfer.
C. Fees of the debtor's attorney incurred in defending the debtor against a challenge to the discharge. *See Lamie v. U.S. Trustee*, 540 U.S. 526 (2004).
D. Fees of a creditor's attorney incurred in challenging the discharge.

(c) Allocation Problems

While virtually all allowable claims arise prepetition, administrative expenses are expenses that necessarily arise postpetition. Occasionally, determining whether a bill for payment represents a prepetition claim (with little or no priority) or a postpetition administrative expense (with a high priority) is difficult. The issue is most likely to arise in a Chapter 11 case in which the debtor is seeking to maintain and reorganize an ongoing business. It occasionally comes up in Chapter 7 cases, though, particularly if the trustee is temporarily operating the debtor's business in the hope of selling it as a going concern. *See* § 721. We therefore consider the issue here.

IN RE JARTRAN, INC.
732 F.2d 584 (7th Cir. 1984)

Cudahy, Circuit Judge.

Appellants Reuben H. Donnelley Corporation ("Donnelley") and Sandra C. Tinsley, Inc. ("Tinsley") filed a claim for administrative priority against appellee Jartran, Inc.'s ("Jartran") estate. The bankruptcy judge denied the claim and, on appeal, the district court affirmed. [F]or the reasons set forth below, we affirm.

I

The facts are undisputed and can be stated briefly. Jartran is in the business of leasing trucks to consumers nationwide. Pursuant to an agreement dated September 11, 1979 (the "Agreement"), Tinsley, an advertising agency, placed Jartran's orders for classified advertisements in telephone directories (the "Yellow Pages") with Donnelley. Donnelley, in turn, arranged with the Yellow Pages' publishers nationwide for Jartran's ads to appear. Under the Agreement, Tinsley and Jartran were liable to Donnelley for the cost of the advertising. Donnelley was liable to the publishers of the various directories. Although the parties were irrevocably committed to pay for the advertising several months before the ads were to appear,[25] the Agreement provided that Tinsley and Jartran would be billed for the ads only after they were published.

On December 31, 1981, Jartran filed for reorganization under Chapter 11 of the Bankruptcy Code. At that time, the closing date had passed for many directories which had not yet been published. Appellants claim that the amount owing for ads placed in such directories, $1,311,695.50, should be treated as an administrative expense.[26] As is apparent from our discussion of the law relating to the allowance of administrative expenses, the key fact is that the irrevocable commitment by Jartran, Donnelley and Tinsley to place the ads was made before the filing of the petition in bankruptcy.

II

Section 503(b) of the Bankruptcy Code provides as follows:

(b) After notice and a hearing, there shall be allowed, administrative expenses . . . including--

(1)(A) The actual, necessary costs and expenses of preserving the estate, including wages, salaries or commissions for services rendered after the commencement of the case[.]

It is well settled that expenses incurred by the debtor-in-possession in attempting to rehabilitate the business during reorganization are within the ambit of § 503. Appellants claim that, because the ads involved in the case were not published until after the "commencement of the case" and presumably aid Jartran in its efforts to rejuvenate its business, the cost of those ads should be treated as an administrative expense. As an administrative expense, the fees for the ads would be afforded priority ahead of certain pre-petition creditors.

---

[25] The date upon which ads were irrevocably placed is referred to in the Agreement and by the parties as the "closing date." On that date, up to six months prior to actual publication, ads could no longer be withdrawn from the directory. Each directory had its own closing date, but Donnelley uniformly billed the advertisers after publication. The Agreement provided that cancellations were effective only with respect to directories for which the closing date had not passed.

[26] Appellants agree that billing for ads published before the petition for reorganization was filed should be treated as non-priority, prepetition debts. The parties also agree that expenses for ads for which the closing date occurred after the petition was filed are entitled to § 503 priority.

The policies underlying the provisions of § 503 (and its predecessor, § 64(a)(1) of the Bankruptcy Act) are not hard to discern. If a reorganization is to succeed, creditors asked to extend credit after the petition is filed must be given priority so they will be moved to furnish the necessary credit to enable the bankrupt to function. *See In re Mammoth Mart, Inc.*, 536 F.2d 950, 954 (1st Cir. 1976). Thus, "[w]hen third parties are *induced* to supply goods or services to the debtor-in-possession . . . the purposes of [§ 503] plainly require that their claims be afforded priority." *Id.* (emphasis added). Without a provision like § 503, efforts to reorganize would be hampered by the necessity of advance payment for all goods and services supplied to the estate since presumably no creditor would willingly assume the status of a non-priority creditor to a debtor undergoing reorganization.

This involves no injustice to the pre-petition creditors because it is for their benefit that reorganization is attempted. If reorganization successfully rehabilitates the debtor, presumably the pre-petition creditors will be better off than in a liquidation. * * *

Recognizing the need for careful criteria in granting priority, the court in *Mammoth Mart* established a two part test for determining whether a debt should be afforded administrative priority. Under these criteria a claim will be afforded priority under § 503 if the debt both (1) "arise[s] from a transaction with the debtor-in-possession" and (2) is "beneficial to the debtor-in-possession in the operation of the business." 536 F.2d at 954. This test is, of course, essentially an effort to determine whether the underlying statutory purpose will be furthered by granting priority to the claim in question, and we will apply it in that spirit.

There is no question that the appearance of ads in Yellow Page directories throughout the country is beneficial to Jartran, as a debtor-in-possession, in the operation of its business. After filing the petition in bankruptcy, Jartran continued to place new ads in directories throughout the nation, thus evidencing the importance of Yellow Pages advertising to the success of the Jartran business. Therefore, the only serious question on appeal is whether the district court incorrectly concluded that the claim did not arise from a transaction with the debtor-in-possession.

Stated this simply, we believe that the district court's conclusion was correct: the agreement among the parties was entered into, and the ads were placed without possibility of revocation, before the petition was filed. Appellants urge, however, that the *publication date* rather than the closing date is the key date for § 503 purposes. They argue forcefully that, because the ads were *published* after the petition in bankruptcy was filed, appellants "supplied [consideration] to the debtor-in-possession in the operation of the business." *Mammoth Mart*, 536 F.2d at 954. Appellants support this argument by pointing out that appellants provided additional services after the closing date, and, presumably, after the petition was filed, including "review of advertising copy for correctness, size of advertisement, placement by page and category, accuracy of telephone listings and addresses, review of art work, and response to numerous queries from publishers concerning the advertisements." Appellants' brief at 7. It was also necessary for Donnelley and Tinsley (presumably after the filing of the petition) to examine the final, published ads to ascertain their correctness. Then, and only then, would Jartran be billed for the advertisements.

We recognize that the services performed by appellants after the closing date, and after the filing of the petition, were significant and of value to Jartran. However, appellants do not allege that Jartran, after the filing of the petition, requested that appellants continue work on ads for which the closing date had passed. Nor is it claimed that Jartran had a duty to take affirmative steps to prevent Donnelley from engaging in postpetition performance. Thus, it was the pre-petition Jartran and not Jartran as debtor-in-possession that *induced* appellants to perform these services. To serve the policy of the priority, inducement of the creditor's performance by the *debtor-in-possession* is crucial to a claim for administrative priority in the context of the furnishing of goods or services to the debtor. Because the closing date occurred before the debtor-in-possession came into existence (through the filing of the Chapter 11 petition), the bankruptcy court in the case before us held that the debtor-in-possession did not induce appellants' performance.

As noted, the reason that *inducement* of the creditor's performance by the debtor-in-possession is crucial to a claim for administrative priority is rooted in the policies that gave rise to the creation of the priority. Thus, administrative priority is granted to postpetition expenses so that third parties will be moved to provide the goods and services necessary for a successful reorganization. In the case before us, no inducement by the debtor-in-possession was required because the liability for the costs of the ads was irrevocably incurred before the petition was filed. This construction of the requirements for the administrative priority provides as full an opportunity as can be furnished for rehabilitation of the debtor. And this approach simply carries out the teaching of the Supreme Court, "that fairness requires that any claims incident to the debtor-in-possession's operation of the business be paid before those for whose benefit the continued operation of the business was allowed." *Mammoth Mart*, 536 F.2d at 954 (citing *Reading Co. v. Brown*, 391 U.S. 471, 478 (1968) (first priority for tort claims based upon negligence attributable to debtor-in-possession)). It is clear, however, that appellants' claim here arises out of commitments made before the debtor-in-possession came into existence. * * *

Problem 9-3

The *Jartran* case is complicated a bit by the fact that several parties were involved. If the debtor had contracted directly with the publisher of the Yellow Pages, would the result be any different? If not, is there anything the publisher could do to better protect itself? *See* § 365.

Problem 9-4

Office Station provides and delivers office supplies to large businesses in several major metropolitan areas. One of its regular customers is Daylight Software, which places orders every other week. On March 15, Daylight faxed a purchase order for some $8,000 in office supplies to Office Station. On March 17, Daylight filed for Chapter 7 bankruptcy protection and the following day the court authorized the trustee to operate Daylight's business. On March 20, Office Station delivered the supplies and the trustee accepted them. Is Office Station's bill entitled to administrative expense treatment? *See* § 503(b); *In re Russell Cave Co.*, 249 B.R. 145 (Bankr. E.D. Ky. 2000). If not, what could Office Station do to better protect itself? *See* § 546.

3.   *Wage & Benefit Claims*

For fairly obvious reasons, the Bankruptcy Code assigns priority status to the claims of the debtor's employees for up to $10,950 in pay and benefits earned during the 180 days immediately preceding the petition. § 507(a)(4), (5). Query, though, whether the rule is fully adequate to protect the debtor's employees. Consider the following problem.

Problem 9-5

Diabolical Corp. engaged in unfair and discriminatory labor practices, resulting in the February 1 discharge of Emma, a senior management employee. Emma sued and, on October 31, received a reinstatement order and an award of back pay for the nine months she was out of work. Diabolical filed a bankruptcy petition the next day. How much, if any, of the back pay award qualifies for priority treatment under § 507(a)(4)? In answering this, think about the policies that may underlie § 507(a)(4).

The priority rule of § 507(a)(4) presents few problems with respect to wages, salary, or commissions.[27] With respect to vacation pay or sick leave pay, however, significant allocation problems can exist. Consider a situation in which the debtor's employees' right to vacation pay vests on a particular date each year, say on August 1. Is the

---

[27]   In contrast, circuit courts were split on whether § 507(a)(5)'s priority for contributions to an employee benefit plan extends to an employer's obligation to pay worker's compensation insurance premiums, until the Supreme Court ruled that it does not. *See Howard Delivery Serv., Inc. v. Zurich American Ins. Co.,* 126 S. Ct. 2105 (2006).

vacation pay "earned" within the meaning of § 507(a)(4) on the date of vesting, or ratably over the year? The answer to this can be significant. If it is all "earned" on August 1, the debtor may be able to time its petition so that none of its employee's vacation pay will be earned within 180 days before the petition and thus none of it will be accorded priority status.

In *In re Northwest Engineering Co.*,[28] Judge Easterbrook faced this issue and ruled that benefits such as vacation pay should be deemed to be "earned" ratably over the year, regardless of when vesting occurs. Vesting is still a necessary condition to having a valid claim – not merely to having priority, but to having a claim allowable under § 502 – but as long as the employees' right to the benefits have vested, they will be deemed to have been earned on a *per diem* basis over the year.

4. Taxes

One of the most common priority claims is for unpaid taxes. Not all unpaid taxes are granted priority status, however. For the most part, only recent taxes are accorded priority. Read § 507(a)(8). Now consider the following problem.

Problem 9-6

Down & Out Corp., which has a fiscal and taxable year beginning on July 1, filed a bankruptcy reorganization petition on June 30, 2006. Since that time, Down & Out has operated and continues to operate its business as debtor-in-possession.

A. What is the priority of Down & Out's federal income tax obligations for the taxable year ending June 30, 2005?

B. What priority are Down & Out's federal income tax obligations for the taxable year ending on June 30, 2007?

C. What is the priority of the interest on such obligations? *See* § 726(a)(5); *In re Weinstein*, 272 F.3d 39 (1st Cir. 2000).

The time limitations on the tax debts that qualify for priority under § 507(a)(8) are intended to impel the IRS to collect quickly. If the IRS allows a debtor's tax liability to languish, the resulting claim will not be a priority. In connection with this, however, it is important to note that the taxpayer may have been the debtor in a previous bankruptcy case. If so, even though the debtor's unpaid tax liability was not discharged,[29] the

---

[28] 863 F.2d 1313 (7th Cir. 1988).

[29] *See* § 523(a)(1).

automatic stay in that earlier case may have greatly reduced the time available to the IRS to assess and collect the taxes due. Although § 108(c) and the Internal Revenue Code toll some periods, the time for priority treatment is not one of them.[30] In other words, serial bankruptcy filings may significantly delay IRS collection efforts, while the clock on priority status is ticking away.

Circuits were divided on whether a prior bankruptcy suspended the clock on priority status.[31] The Supreme Court unanimously ruled that the clock was indeed tolled during the pendency of a prior bankruptcy petition,[32] and the 2005 amendments to the Bankruptcy Code confirmed and expanded this result by adding the last clause of § 507(a)(8). It provides that the clock is suspended for however much time a prior automatic stay enjoined the IRS from collecting, plus 90 days.

The discussion so far of the priority accorded to tax claims applies only to unsecured tax claims. Secured tax claims are subject to a variety of special rules. *See, e.g.,* § 724(b).

Problem 9-7

    A.   How, if at all, does the answer to Problem 9-6, Part A change if, prior to the bankruptcy petition, the IRS filed a notice of tax lien against the debtor?

    B.   Down & Out's estate includes a piece of real property worth $10,000 subject to three encumbrances in following order of priority: (i) a $2,000 first mortgage; (ii) a tax lien securing a debt of $4,000; and (iii) a $3,000 second mortgage. None of the liens is avoidable under either § 544 or § 547. There are $2,500 in administrative expense claims for which there are no other assets of the estate to pay those claims. If the property is sold free and clear of all liens, how should the proceeds be disbursed?

---

[30] *See* I.R.C. § 6503(h).

[31] At least six circuit courts treated tolling of the priority period as automatic during the pendency of a prior bankruptcy stay. *See In re Young,* 233 F.3d 56 (1st Cir. 2000); *In re Waugh,* 109 F.3d 489 (8th Cir. 1997); *In re Taylor,* 81 F.3d 20 (3d Cir. 1996); *In re West,* 5 F.3d 423 (9th Cir. 1993); *In re Richards,* 994 F.2d 763 (10th Cir. 1993); *In re Montoya,* 965 F.2d 554 (7th Cir. 1992). Three others permit tolling after the equities are considered on a case-by-case basis. *See In re Palmer,* 219 F.3d 580 (6th Cir. 2000); *In re Morgan,* 182 F.3d 775 (11th Cir. 1999); *In re Quenzer,* 19 F.3d 163 (5th Cir. 1993).

[32] *Young v. United States,* 535 U.S. 43 (2002).

5.   Other Priorities

Two other priorities worthy of note are contained in § 507(a)(7) and (10).   The former protects consumers who have paid a deposit in connection with the purchase or lease of goods or the purchase of services, if the seller or service provider seeks bankruptcy protection and never performs.   The latter is a new rule that gives priority status to personal injury claims against the debtor for driving while intoxicated.

Problem 9-8

What is the policy underlying § 507(a)(10)?   In answering this, consider who the claimant may be.   How should a Chapter 7 debtor who owes such a claim feel about this priority?   *See* § 523(a)(9).

Problem 9-9

Duchovney filed a Chapter 7 bankruptcy petition on February 12, 2007. The trustee amassed and sold Duchovney's nonexempt assets for $29,000, obtained and collected a $6,000 preference judgment, and thus has $35,000 for distribution.   The claims filed in the bankruptcy case are for the following obligations:
1. $21,000 in federal income taxes: $13,000 for 2002; $5,000 for 2003; and $3,000 for 2006.
2. $500 for postpetition gas and electricity service at Duchovney's home.
3. $2,000 to Duchovney's lawyer for work performed in preparing the bankruptcy filing.
4. $15,000 to Duchovney's former wife pursuant to their divorce decree.
5. $10,000 in other general unsecured claims.
In addition, the bankruptcy trustee sought permission to pay the following expenses out of the estate:
6. $5,000 to the trustee for administering the assets of the estate.
7. $2,000 to the trustee for legal services in bringing the preference action.
8. $250 for insurance on the nonexempt assets prior to their sale.
9. $500 for the costs associated with selling (including advertising) the nonexempt assets.
Determine how much each creditor will receive from the bankruptcy estate. If there is a priority that is uncertain, determine which parties have the greatest incentive to litigate the issue.

B.   DEALING WITH JOINTLY HELD & COMMUNITY PROPERTY

The way the Bankruptcy Code deals with jointly held property – including property held in common and property held by the entireties – is not particularly complicated. First and foremost, the debtor's undivided interest is initially included in the bankruptcy estate. *See* § 541(a)(1).[33] Second, the debtor may exempt his or her interest *to the extent* that it would be exempt from process under applicable non-bankruptcy law. § 522(b)(2)(A). If the debtor is using state exemptions, this *may* depend on whether there are creditors with claims against both the debtor and the debtor's spouse.[34] However, in some states even such joint creditors may not be able to attach entireties property, and thus the debtor should be able to exempt it.[35]

If some portion of jointly held property remains in the estate, the trustee is empowered to administer it for the benefit of the estate. This means that the trustee will either sever the debtor's interest from that of the nondebtor spouse and liquidate only the debtor's interest, or the trustee will sell the entire property and give the nondebtor spouse one-half the proceeds. *See* § 363(f), (h), (j). Of course, if the two spouses have filed jointly, the trustee would not have to release any of the sale proceeds.

The way the Bankruptcy Code deals with community property, on the other hand, is unfortunately – but necessarily – complicated. Consider the following scenario, which was something that could have occurred under the old Bankruptcy Act:

> Debtor, who is married and resides in a community property state, files for bankruptcy protection and receives a discharge. Subsequently, Debtor acquires property. Applicable law treats such property as community property. A prepetition creditor of Debtor, whose claim *against Debtor* was discharged, then relies on its rights against Debtor's spouse to go after such property. The end result: the discharge is effectively circumvented.

To avoid such an outcome, several issues needed to be resolved. They included: (1) what property is initially included in the estate? (2) what property may then be exempted? (3) what property may the trustee administer (to the extent this somehow differs from the resolution of the two previous issues)? (4) should community and jointly held property be distributed differently from other property? (5) should community and

---

[33] *See also In re Garner*, 952 F.2d 232 (8th Cir. 1991).

[34] *See In re Williams*, 104 F.3d 688 (4th Cir. 1997) (indicating that exemption applies only to creditors of the debtor, not to joint creditors). *See also In re Bunker*, 312 F.3d 145 (4th Cir. 2002) (noting the same for the Virginia exemption for property held by the entireties and ruling that, because there were no joint creditors, such property was wholly exempt even though the spouses filed a joint petition).

[35] *See In re Hunter*, 970 F.2d 299 (7th Cir. 1992).

joint claims be treated differently from other claims? and (6) how will the discharge operate on community and jointly held claims? As if this were not enough, the resolution of several of these issues might be affected by whether the spouses file jointly or serially, or whether only one of the spouses files.

The Bankruptcy Code takes three main steps to deal with these issues. First, the property interests of both the debtor and the debtor's spouse in community property are, for the most part, included in the estate. *See* § 541(a)(2). Second, community property is segregated from the rest of the estate and used solely to pay community creditors. It does this through special distribution rules that are similar to a marshaling of assets. *See* § 726(c). Third, the discharge bars community creditors with unpaid prepetition claims from going after community property acquired after the petition. Such creditors may proceed in the future only against the separate property of the non-bankruptcy spouse. *See* § 524(a)(3), (b).[36] The cumulative effect of these rules is to give the debtor a meaningful discharge.

The special distribution rules for community claims are themselves a bit complicated. They involve the creation of four "sub-estates," each of which is available only for specified classes of claims and each of which must be distributed in the proper order. One court explained the rules as follows:

> Sub-estates are created in Section 726(c), consisting only of section 541(a)(2) property (*i.e.*, community property subject to community claims). Community claims – even community claims that would otherwise fit within the rubric of section 507 as priority claims – must look solely to the sub-estates (and distribution scheme) set up by section 726(c). § 726(c)(2). There are four sub-estates set up under section 726(c)(2), but community claims assertable against the non-debtor are restricted to recoveries out of the first and last sub-estates only. The last estate, being residual, might well be empty because the other sub-estates may (and usually will) be exhausted by satisfying other claims.
>
> The first sub-estate pays all community claims – including community claims assertable against the non-debtor spouse. The sub-estate consists only of Section 541(a)(2) property excluding property that is solely liable for debts of the debtor. § 726(c)(2)(A). The second sub-estate pays only community claims assertable against the debtor, to the extent not already satisfied out of the first sub-estate. The second sub-estate contains the section 541(a)(2) property that was excluded from the first sub-estate, *i.e.*, section 541(a)(2) property that is solely liable for debts of the debtor. § 726(c)(2)(B). If the community claim is assertable against the non-debtor, it does not get to participate in this second tranche of property. The third sub-estate pays

---

[36] *See also In re Dyson*, 277 B.R. 84 (Bankr. M.D. La. 2002).

community claims assertable against only the debtor (and not the nondebtor spouse), to the extent not already paid from the first two sub-estates. This third sub-estate consists solely of non-community property. § 726(c)(2)(C). Finally, the residual sub-estate permits community claims assertable against the nondebtor spouse to re-enter the distribution, permitting recovery out of the general assets of the estate, if there are any left. Thus, only after exhausting community property in the estate may community claimholders then look to all remaining property of the estate. Community claimholders whose claims are assertable against the nonfiling spouse must, after sharing with everyone else from the first sub-estate, then wait patiently on the sidelines while everyone else's claims are paid from the other two sub-estates, hoping that, at the end of the day, there will be something left. Usually there is not. And the community claimholders whose claims are assertable against the nonfiling spouse are relegated to this position even if they would be classified as priority under section 507![37]

The distribution scheme is also depicted in the following chart:

	Sub-estate	Claims Distributed To
1	Community Property (other than property liable solely for the debts of the debtor)	All community claims
2	Community Property (only that liable solely for the debts of the debtor)	Community claims against the debtor
3	All other property	All claims against the debtor (using normal priority rules)
4	Remaining Property (*i.e.*, sub-estate # 2)	Community claims

---

[37]   *In re Whitus*, 240 B.R. 705, 709-10 (Bankr. W.D. Tex. 1999) [hyphens added for clarity – eds.].

CHAPTER TEN
DISCHARGE AND DISMISSAL

———————

In Chapter 7 cases, the debtor makes all nonexempt assets available for distribution to creditors. In exchange, the debtor is generally entitled to a discharge of personal liability on prepetition debts, to the extent they are unpaid in the bankruptcy process. Of course, in a large percentage of consumer bankruptcy cases there are no nonexempt assets for distribution to claimants. Even in these cases, § 727(a) provides the general rule that the court shall grant the debtor a discharge.

The scope of the discharge is quite broad. For the most part, it covers all prepetition debts, as well as some obligations treated as prepetition under § 502.[1] § 727(b). It even covers obligations for which the creditor has not filed a proof of claim. This is because a contrary rule would essentially allow creditors to opt in or out of the bankruptcy case, and that option would undermine the whole bankruptcy process.

As should not be surprising, because bankruptcy is an equitable proceeding, there are numerous exceptions to both the availability and the scope of the discharge. Some debtors are denied a discharge entirely. Read § 727(a). Others, even though granted a discharge, remain obligated on some specified debts; put another way, some prepetition debts are nondischargeable. Read §§ 727(b), 523(a).

A. DENIAL OF DISCHARGE

The grounds for denying a discharge are laid out in § 727(a). One of the most important is found in § 727(a)(8). That provision denies a discharge if the debtor has previously received a Chapter 7 or Chapter 11 discharge in a case commenced less than eight years before the petition date in the current case. A similar rule often denies a discharge to a debtor who received a discharge in a Chapter 12 or Chapter 13 case commenced less than six years before the current case. *See* § 727(a)(9). However, if in that earlier Chapter 12 or Chapter 13 case the creditors were paid in full or the debtor used his or her best efforts and paid the creditors 70% of their claims, this limitation on a new discharge does not apply.

The principal rationales for this rule are: (1) that it prevents the habitual or professional bankrupt, a person who makes it his or her business to run up debt and then take advantage of the Bankruptcy Code; and (2) a slightly more subtle notion that,

———————

[1] For example, as we have already seen, if a creditor repays a preference to the bankruptcy trustee, the debt is revived and treated as prepetition. § 502(h). That claim is then subject to the discharge.

regardless of any specific fraudulent intent, seeking a frequent discharge is itself a form of misconduct.

These policies are also evident in Chapter 13, which also contains limitations on the availability of multiple discharges.[2] We will study those limitations in chapter eleven. For now, though, the following chart contains a brief comparison of the different limitations.

		Current Case	
		Chapter 7 § 727(a)(8), (9)	**Chapter 13** § 1328(f)
Prior Discharge	**Chapter 7**	No new discharge if prior case was commenced within 8 years of new case	No new discharge if prior case was commenced within 4 years of new case[3]
	Chapter 11		
	Chapter 12	No new discharge if prior case was commenced within 6 years of new case	
	Chapter 13		No new discharge if prior case was commenced within 2 years of new case[3]

Perhaps the next most significant basis for denying a discharge is in § 727(a)(1). That provision limits a Chapter 7 discharge to individual debtors. The reason for this is that other entities, such as corporations and partnerships, do not need a discharge following their liquidation. A human debtor needs a discharge to protect future earnings from prepetition creditors.[4] A liquidated corporation or partnership is little more than a paper entity. The only reason it would need a discharge is if it somehow retained or received some assets, which it should not be doing in a liquidation proceeding if the bankruptcy process works as intended. Such entities can get a discharge in Chapter 11, but they need none in Chapter 7.

The remaining grounds for denying a discharge all involve the debtor's misconduct:

---

[2]   There are no similar restrictions on a discharge in Chapter 11 or Chapter 12.

[3]   The phrasing of § 1328(f), which was added in 2005, is ambiguous as to whether the petition in the prior case must have been filed or the prior discharge must have been granted within the applicable time period.

[4]   Recall that an individual debtor's postpetition earnings from personal services are not part of the bankruptcy estate in a Chapter 7 proceeding. § 541(a)(6).

1. making a fraudulent transfer or destroying property   § 727(a)(2)
2. failing to maintain adequate financial records   § 727(a)(3)
3. lying to the bankruptcy court   § 727(a)(4)
4. failing to explain any loss of assets   § 727(a)(5)
5. disobeying an order of the bankruptcy court   § 727(a)(6)

Although few discharges are denied under these provisions,[5] when a creditor objects to the discharge, it is not uncommon for the creditor to raise several or all of these grounds simultaneously. For example, consider a debtor who, prior to bankruptcy, gave the objecting creditor a signed financial statement listing the debtor's assets. The creditor, before making a loan or otherwise extending credit, verified the existence and value of those assets. Then, in the bankruptcy case, some or all of those assets are not included in the debtor's schedules. This discrepancy may be the result of a fraudulent transfer, § 727(a)(2), or due to the fact that the debtor has concealed assets from the court, § 727(a)(4). Even if neither of these is true, the debtor will need to come forward with some explanation for the discrepancy or face a loss of the discharge under either § 727(a)(3) or (a)(5).

We have already seen that a fraudulent transfer may occur in the context of converting nonexempt assets into exempt assets. Of course, fraudulent transfers are not so limited. They may involve moving assets to places or jurisdictions where creditors cannot readily locate or access them. Alternatively, they may involve putting assets into the name of someone else to hide the identity of the true owner.

Making a false statement to the bankruptcy court can occur during a hearing on a contested matter or at the § 341 meeting. More commonly, it occurs on the debtor's schedules of assets and liabilities, which are filed with or shortly after the petition. Courts are fairly lenient about mistakes on the schedules because it is difficult for anyone to make an exhaustive and fully accurate list of all his or her assets, liabilities, and recent transfers. Moreover, the discharge is to be denied only for false statements made "knowing and fraudulently." § 727(a)(4). Nevertheless, courts will protect the integrity of the process and even a failure to disclose exempt assets can be the basis for denying the discharge.[6] Consider the following cases.

---

[5]   One reason for this is that debtors who anticipate a problem often file under Chapter 11 or 13, where these grounds for denying a discharge do not apply. *Cf.* §§ 1141 & 1328. *But cf.* §§ 1129(a)(3), 1328(a)(3) (both requiring that to be confirmed a plan or reorganization must be proposed in good faith).

[6]   *See In re Murray*, 249 B.R. 223 (E.D.N.Y. 2000) (noting that all exempt assets begin in the estate and can become exempt only through a legal process that includes disclosure, which permits the trustee and creditors to test the exemption claim).

IN RE MITCHELL
102 F. Appx. 860 (5th Cir. 2004)

Per Curiam:

The bankruptcy court awarded Appellants James Richard Mitchell and Jackie Anice Mitchell a discharge of their Chapter 7 bankruptcy over the objection of their creditor, Appellee Cadle Company. The district court reversed the bankruptcy court on appeal, because it found that the Mitchells made several false oaths in their bankruptcy petition. We conclude that the Mitchells' bankruptcy petition demonstrates a reckless indifference to the truth sufficient to constitute a false oath. Agreeing with the district court, we affirm its reversal of the bankruptcy court.

* * *

A debtor may be denied discharge if he "knowingly and fraudulently, in or in connection with the case . . . [makes] a false oath or account." § 727(a)(4)(A). The party objecting to discharge must prove by a preponderance of the evidence that (1) the statement was made under oath, (2) the statement was false, (3) the debtor knew the statement was false, (4) the debtor made the statement with fraudulent intent, and (5) the statement related materially to the bankruptcy case.[7]

The Mitchells made the following errors and omissions in their bankruptcy filings: (1) they provided only half a month's income in response to a question that demanded a full month's income; (2) they initially listed a life insurance policy as having no cash value and a face value of $15,000, though it actually had a cash value of approximately $3,500 and a face value of $100,000; (3) they omitted multiple payments made to creditors within 90 days of bankruptcy; (4) in their initial filing, they did not list a counterclaim against Cadle as an asset even though they listed Cadle's claim against them as a liability; (5) they failed to list Mr. Mitchell's substantial vintage-car refurbishing tools in their initial schedules, and their final amended schedules did not include all of the tools and undervalued the remainder; and (6) they omitted a set of Wedgewood china. In their amended petition they corrected items (2) and (4).

The bankruptcy court held that the Mitchells did not have fraudulent intent because their mistakes were honestly made, minor in importance, and relatively few in number. We disagree. Fraudulent intent may be proved by showing either actual intent to deceive or a reckless indifference for the truth. *In re Sholdra,* 249 F.3d at 382. We conclude that the Mitchells demonstrated a reckless disregard for the truth, as evidenced by their repeated insistence that their errors were due to carelessness, not bad intent. In *In re Beaubouef,* we discussed the impact of honest mistakes:

---

[7] The statements were made under oath, because they were included in the Mitchells' sworn bankruptcy petition. *See* Rule 1008. Omissions and incorrect valuations qualify as false statements. The complaining party need not prove that the debtor consciously chose to omit or misstate information, only that the debtor knew the truth when the omission or misstatement was made.

> The bankruptcy court correctly noted that a discharge cannot be denied when items are omitted from the schedules by honest mistake. However, the bankruptcy court found that the existence of more than one falsehood, together with [the debtor's] failure to take advantage of the opportunity to clear up all inconsistencies and omissions when he filed his amended schedules, constituted reckless indifference to the truth and, therefore, the requisite intent to deceive. These findings are . . . not clearly erroneous.

966 F.2d at 178. The Mitchells had numerous errors and omissions in their original schedules; they did not amend their schedules to correct several of those errors and omissions; and their only excuse was that they filled out the forms in great haste and did not bother going over forms prepared by their attorney to make sure they were accurate. That is the essence of a reckless disregard for the truth.

We do not agree with the bankruptcy court's holding that the availability of correct information elsewhere in the bankruptcy petition "cured" the Mitchells' undervaluation of their monthly income and the omission of their counterclaim. Debtors have a duty to answer each question truthfully, so a false answer to one question cannot be cured by providing true information in response to another question.

The Mitchells made numerous material false statements in their original and amended bankruptcy petitions. Their careless approach to the completion of their schedules demonstrates a reckless indifference to the truth, and their errors amounted to false oaths. We therefore affirm the district court's reversal of the bankruptcy court's judgment awarding a discharge, and we remand to the district court for further remand to the bankruptcy court with instructions that it enter an order denying discharge.

IN RE BALDRIDGE
256 B.R. 284 (Bankr. E.D. Ark. 2000)

Scott, Bankruptcy Judge.

This cause came before the Court upon the trial of the adversary proceeding objecting to the debtor's discharge pursuant to sections 727(a)(2), (a)(4)(A). Trial was held on September 7, 2000, after which the parties submitted written post trial argument whereupon the matter was under submission.

I. FACTUAL BACKGROUND
Baldridge's Inheritance

Danny Baldridge's father died sometime in the early 1990's and his step mother died several years after that. When the estate was finally settled, it was discovered that Danny Baldridge had somehow obtained more than his fair share of the estate.

Accordingly, he was compelled to execute promissory notes to each of his four sisters in the amount of $18,452. When he did not pay on the notes, his sisters instituted a civil action in state court, sometime in 1999. These notes, listed on the schedules, constitute eighty percent of Baldridge's total debt.

Acquisition of Real Property

In September 1998, Baldridge's uncle was undergoing treatment for cancer and thought he was dying. In an effort to help his nephew, he decided to deed some rental property he owned to Baldridge. The uncle established the price of $30,000 for the property, which he believed had a value of $157,000, and executed and delivered a deed in favor of Baldridge who had prepared the deed for his uncle. Baldridge, unable to obtain any credit on his own, obtained the funds through his wife, with his mother-in-law providing the collateral for a loan. The next day, Baldridge approached his uncle with a substitute deed, this one granting the property solely to Kimberly Baldridge, Baldridge's wife. The uncle signed the substitute deed because Baldridge requested it. He had little interest in assisting Kimberly because, "I didn't hardly know Kimberly." As a condition of selling the property, the uncle also requested that Baldridge begin making payments to his sisters on the money he owed them. Baldridge made a couple of $100 payments, then ceased when his wife mortgaged the property and thereby incurred a new monthly household debt. The property was mortgaged in order to pay off Baldridge's substantial federal tax debt. The real property is not listed on the schedules although the debtor lists a $1,548 monthly mortgage payment as a household debt. The debtor also claims to own no real property, but he lists real estate taxes as an expense on his schedules.

Kimberly's Business

Kimberly Baldridge operates a medical care business known as DanAnne, Inc. which employs both Baldridge and Kimberly. Although Baldridge works a substantial number of hours at the business and, in the past, was paid for those hours, he now collects only $50 per week for his employment. This was done, he testified, because he had tax problems. That is, he did not want to pay taxes on the income he earned from his wife's business and therefore took a smaller sum as wages than in the past. Although he is entitled to between $400 and $600 per week for the work he performs, he reports only $50 in income from this work.

Instead of wages, the Baldridges arranged for substitute remuneration to be given to Baldridge. For example, debtor transferred the vehicle titled in his name to his wife's corporation which then purchased a new truck for his use. The business makes all of the loan and insurance payments on the vehicle which Baldridge uses for personal, rather than business, use. In fact, when his wife is required to travel for her business, she uses a car titled in her name and charges the corporation for the mileage.

Neither the sale of debtor's vehicle nor any ownership interest in any vehicle is listed on the schedules. In addition, although the debtor admits that the use of the truck constitutes income, that use is not reported on his federal tax returns.

Bank Accounts

Prior to filing his chapter 7 case, the debtor was either an owner of several bank accounts or authorized to sign on the accounts. Most, but not all, of the accounts were closed prior to the filing of the chapter 13 case because his accountant advised him that the IRS would soon levy on the accounts to collect on his federal tax obligations. Specifically, the debtor admitted to having at least three accounts, two with the Bank of the Ozarks and one at Metropolitan Bank. The accounts were either closed within the year prior to the filing of this case or soon thereafter. Maintenance of his own accounts are unnecessary because Baldridge has full access to his wife's bank accounts. He signs checks on his spouse's accounts as well as on her corporate account. These accounts are not listed on the petition.

II. CONCLUSIONS

A. False Oath: Section 727(a)(4)

Section 727(a)(4) provides the penalty for a debtor who fails to truthfully list all assets and fully answer the questions in the petition under oath. This section ensures that debtors will accurately report their interests in property in order that adequate information is available to anyone interested in the debtor's financial affairs. This serves the policy of permitting parties in interest to rely upon the information in the schedules without examination or investigation. In light of this requirement, the debtor has a "paramount duty" to ensure that the answers are made truthfully and completely. *In re Craig*, 252 B.R. 822, 828-29 (Bankr. S.D. Fla. 2000).

In order to demonstrate discharge should be denied under this paragraph, a plaintiff must prove by a preponderance of the evidence that:

(1) the debtor made a statement under oath;
(2) the statement was false;
(3) the statement related materially to the bankruptcy case;
(4) the debtor knew the statement was false; and
(5) the debtor made the statement with fraudulent intent.

False statements as well as omissions from the schedules may qualify as false oaths if they are made knowingly and with fraudulent intent. Of course, the omissions must relate to a material matter and may be material even if they do not cause financial prejudice. An omission is material if it relates to the discovery of assets. The materiality of an omission is not lessened by the fact that an omitted asset is exempt or otherwise unavailable for distribution to the creditors. * * *

1. *Failure to List Bank Accounts on the Schedules.* There is no dispute that the debtor failed to list at least three bank accounts on his schedules. Indeed, he freely admits to the existence of those accounts, merely shrugging that he forgot about them. Since one of the accounts at Bank of the Ozarks appears to have been utilized by both he and his wife for many personal and family expenses, this statement is not credible. The queries on the form schedules would have twice prompted Baldridge to recall that he owned or had access to several accounts. Moreover, the fact that he and his wife went through so many financial machinations, including closing accounts by removing his name, to avoid payment of his federal taxes, makes his statement that he didn't think of the accounts a clear falsehood.

Rather than contesting the omissions, Baldridge asserts that since there was little or no value in the accounts at the time they were closed, the omissions were not sufficiently material to permit denial of discharge. This argument ignores the purpose of the statute and improperly diminishes his obligations under the Bankruptcy Code. The value of property which is not disclosed on the petition, particularly as it relates to bank accounts, may have little relevance to the concept of materiality. Few, if any, assets are more material to a consumer debtor's financial affairs than a bank account, for it is from that kind of asset that the creditors can discern not only an overall picture of the debtor's financial affairs, but also the details of the debtor's finances. Accordingly, the omission of any and all bank accounts to which the debtor had access constituted a false statement that related materially to the case.

2. *Failure to Disclose Transfer of Real Property.* In September 1998, less than one year prior to the filing of the chapter 13 petition, Baldridge acquired title to real property. Since he did not disclose either the acquisition or the subsequent transfer to his wife, he made a false oath within the meaning of section 727(a)(4).

Under Arkansas law, a deed, signed and delivered passes title to the grantee. Delivery, a substantive and specific act, occurs if the grantor intends to deliver title and the grantee evidences an intent to accept the deed. Delivery occurs even if the deed is later returned to the grantor for some other act or alteration to be made.

The uncontroverted testimony of Baldridge, as well as that of his uncle, indicates the uncle's intent to deliver the deed to Baldridge. Baldridge's uncle thought he was dying, and he desired to help his nephew. Accordingly, he directed that a deed be prepared, signed it, and handed it over to Baldridge. Baldridge accepted the deed. Indeed, as his wife testified, "Danny desperately wanted to purchase the property." At that moment, title passed to Baldridge, whether or not Baldridge delivered the agreed consideration, and despite the fact that the deed was returned the next day, unrecorded. Thus, under Arkansas law, in September 1999, Baldridge acquired title to real property with a value of well over $100,000. The next day, he caused the property to be transferred to his wife. Both of these transactions occurred within one year of the filing of the chapter 13 petition. Thus, when he stated on his petition that he had made no transfers of property, that statement, made under oath, was false.

3. Failure to Disclose Transfer of Vehicle. In or around December 1998, within one year of the filing of the chapter 13 petition, Baldridge transferred his interest in his 1990 Chevrolet S-10 to his wife's corporation. The corporation then purchased a 1999 Sierra for Baldridge to use as his personal vehicle. Neither the transfer nor the interest in the vehicle is disclosed on the schedules filed in the case. The failure to disclose the transfer of this vehicle on his schedules is an omission constituting a knowingly false statement which is materially related to his bankruptcy case.

4. Fraudulent Intent. Not only did the debtor know his statements and omissions were false, as discussed above, he made the false statements with the requisite fraudulent intent. It is well settled that fraudulent intent may be inferred from circumstantial evidence or from a course of conduct. Moreover, statements made with reckless indifference to the truth are regarded as intentionally false. Baldridge and his wife freely admit to various financial schemes, including fraud on his federal income tax returns and transferring virtually all of his assets to his wife or his wife's corporation to ensure that his creditors not reach his assets.

Second, although specific questions on the bankruptcy schedule forms prompted disclosure of his bank accounts and other assets, he claims to have forgotten each and every bank account he held or had access to within a year. While a debtor may plausibly forget one of many accounts which may have been closed in the year prior to a bankruptcy filing, Baldridge's claim that he forgot that he held any accounts is so clearly false that the Court can infer a fraudulent intent.

In addition to the absurdity of forgetting all bank accounts, there are simply too many omissions of material matters for the Court to accept the Baldridge's assertion that they were "inadvertent." Not only does Baldridge fail to disclose his true income, he fails to disclose each and every asset or transfer of asset of any value. Finally, the debtor's demeanor at trial, including the palpable rancor in his voice when discussing his sisters and their attempts to obtain their inheritance, are indicative of the debtor's motives behind secreting his property from the reach of all his creditors, not merely the IRS. While it is true that the immediate threat of seizure of property by the IRS may have been an impetus for some of the transactions, he clearly intended that no creditors, including his sisters, should be able to reach his assets. Therefore, with fraudulent intent, he omitted information that would have revealed his assets and financial transactions.

B. Transfer of Property: Section 727(a)(2)

The Court also finds that the plaintiff sustained her burden with regard to section 727(a)(2)(A). In order to meet this burden, a plaintiff must show by a preponderance of the evidence that:

(1) a transfer or concealment of property occurred;

(2) the property was property of the debtor;

(3) the transfer occurred within one year of the filing of the petition; and

(4) the debtor had, at the time of the transfer, intent to hinder, delay or defraud a creditor.

In addition to the transfers themselves, omitting information from the schedules may be construed as a concealment occurring both before and after the filing of the case for purposes of this section. Moreover, maintaining bank accounts in someone else's name may also constitute a concealment.

The Court has already determined that transfers of property of the debtor occurred within one year before the filing of the petition. The debtor transferred his interest in real property and a vehicle to his wife and his wife's corporation prior to the filing of the bankruptcy case.

Section 727(a)(2) also requires the Court to find an intent to deceive and this element involves a two-part inquiry. First, the debtor's actual intent must be found as a matter of fact from the evidence presented. The second prong of the inquiry involves a determination, as a matter of law, as to whether the demonstrated intent constitutes the intent proscribed by the statute. The question is whether the intent is sufficiently abusive to merit denial of discharge. * * *

In addition to the facts discussed above, in determining whether fraudulent intent existed, the Court has also considered the demeanor and testimony of the debtor which indicated to the Court a lack of truthfulness. While the Court believes the debtor's admissions that he made the transfers with the intent to remove them from the reach of his creditors, the Court further infers from all of the facts and circumstances that he had the requisite fraudulent intent in so doing. The Court does not believe the minimal explanations of neglect, lack of knowledge and mere inadvertence. There are simply too many omissions and transfers of assets to accept these explanations. The failure to come forward with credible explanations for the transactions, the lack of candor with the Court, the transfers to his wife, combined with the fact that the debtor continues to live off the income secreted or derived from the property he transferred to his wife, lead inescapably to the conclusion that Baldridge's transfers were fraudulently intended to shield assets from his creditors, including his sisters. Accordingly, it is hereby ordered that judgment will be entered in favor of the plaintiff and the debtor will be denied his discharge pursuant to § 727(a)(2), (a)(4).

Cases involving inadequate records are fairly rare. When they do arise, they occasionally involve documents stored in boxes that have mysteriously vanished.[8] More often, they involve the debtor's failure to create records at all. Almost always, this arises in the context of a business. Debtors who had no business and whose income is derived from their personal services rarely lose a discharge under § 727(a)(3).

When a debtor has failed to maintain adequate records, the issue becomes whether that failure is justified. Courts have been somewhat lenient in this regard.[9] The applicable standard was articulated in *Meridian Bank v. Alton*:

> The Bankruptcy Code does not specify what constitutes justification for maintaining inadequate records; instead it requires the trier of fact to make a determination based on all the circumstances of the case. The issue of justification depends largely on what a normal, reasonable person would do under similar circumstances. The inquiry should include the education, experience, and sophistication of the debtor; the volume of the debtor's business; the complexity of the debtor's business; the amount of credit extended to debtor in his business; and any other circumstances that should be considered in the interest of justice.[10]

Of course, even in this setting judicial tolerance has its limits. One debtor who produced no records of the two businesses he owned and operated, not even the checkbook registers he admittedly possessed, was denied a discharge on summary judgment.[11]

Problem 10-1

Darlene was divorced from Harry six months ago. The marital property consisted principally of a $10,000 car. The court awarded the car to Darlene

---

[8] *See, e.g., In re Cromer*, 214 B.R. 86 (Bankr. E.D.N.Y. 1997); *In re Harron*, 31 B.R. 466 (Bankr. D. Conn. 1983).

[9] *See, e.g., In re Cox*, 41 F.3d 1294 (9th Cir. 1994) (debtor's failure to maintain business records justified because debtor's spouse handled all business affairs); *In re Sendecky*, 283 B.R. 760, 764 (8th Cir. BAP 2002) (debtor who operated concrete business and who had produced income tax returns, deposit account statements, and some credit reports was justified in not maintaining more detailed records because he was poorly educated, had no sophistication, had little business experience, and still lived with his parents).

[10] 958 F.2d 1226, 1231 (3d Cir. 1992).

[11] *In re Strbac*, 235 B.R. 880 (6th Cir. BAP 1999). *See also Union Planters Bank v. Connors*, 283 F.3d 896 (7th Cir. 2002) (denying discharge because of the failure to maintain – and also for discarding – records concerning four business ventures).

but ordered her to make a $5,000 equalization payment to Harry and gave Harry a lien on the car to secure that payment.

Three weeks ago, after Darlene consulted with a bankruptcy attorney and decided to file, but before actually filing, the "check engine" light came on Darlene's car while she was driving. She ignored it and a short time later the engine seized up. The engine is now worthless and the car has lost much of its value. If Harry files a complaint to deny Darlene a discharge under § 727(a)(2), how should the court rule?

Problem 10-2

Desperate has been in serious financial condition for several months. Two weeks ago, he sought the advice of a friend who works as a financial consultant. On that friend's advice, Desperate conveyed his only significant asset, a vacation home, to his daughter as a gift. Desperate has now come to you for assistance in obtaining bankruptcy relief.

A. If Desperate files a Chapter 7 bankruptcy petition, will Desperate have difficulty obtaining a discharge? *See* § 727(a)(2).

B. How, if at all, would the answer to Part A change if, before filing the bankruptcy petition, Desperate gets his daughter to transfer the vacation home back? *Compare In re Davis*, 911 F.2d 560 (11th Cir. 1990), *with In re Adeeb*, 787 F.2d 1339 (9th Cir. 1986). *See also In re Bajgar*, 104 F.3d 495 (1st Cir. 1997).

Problem 10-3

For the last four years Derek has been employed as a waiter at an upscale restaurant. Much of his income is in the form of tips. He has maintained no written records of his tip income. He and his co-workers have all declared exactly the same amount in tip income – three times their base salary – on their federal income tax returns. At the § 341 meeting, Derek acknowledged that he probably earned more tip income than he declared for tax purposes. Should the court deny Derek's discharge under § 727(a)(3)? Why or why not?

Problem 10-4

For the last several years, Darius earned a good living as a stockbroker. Nevertheless, he has run up rather large debts on his credit cards and recently lost his job when the brokerage decided to downsize. In reviewing his schedules and financial records, particularly the debtor's periodic cash withdrawals from his checking account, the Chapter 7 trustee cannot determine what happened to about $40,000 in income over the two years preceding Darius' bankruptcy petition. How should the court rule on a § 727(a)(5) complaint if Darius testifies that he used about $24,000 of the money to buy cocaine and lost the remainder gambling at casinos in Atlantic City? Does it matter if the court believes the testimony? What questions should the attorney for the plaintiff ask Darius at the hearing?

B.   NONDISCHARGEABLE CLAIMS

For numerous public policy reasons, Congress has chosen to make a growing variety of claims nondischargeable. That is, even if the debtor is granted a discharge, claims of these types will survive the bankruptcy process.

That said, it is important to remember one thing: even if a claim is nondischargeable, the claimant is still entitled to share in distributions from the bankruptcy estate. Nothing in § 726 excludes nondischargeable claims from the distribution scheme or subordinates them to dischargeable claims. If this seems counterintuitive, remember that some debtors may have no real prospect of earning money after bankruptcy. Thus, the bankruptcy process may well be the only place where the holder of a nondischargeable claim has any hope of receiving payment. Since the congressional decision to classify a claim as nondischargeable is based on the favored status of the claim, and is intended to enhance the prospect of repayment, such claims should not be and are not excluded from the distribution scheme.

Returning to our visual metaphor, unsecured bankruptcy claimants queue up – in order of their priority – for a distribution from the right-hand spigot of the estate vat. For those few who are paid in full, there is nothing left for them to do or to be concerned about. Most, however, are likely to receive little or nothing from the estate. If the debtor receives a discharge, most of those unpaid claimants are ineligible to go after assets in the debtor's vat. However, the unpaid claimants with nondischargeable claims are permitted to drain nonexempt assets from the debtor's vat. There will be no orderly, bankruptcy process for syphoning off such assets; the trustee will not be involved and bankruptcy priorities will be meaningless. Instead, the claimants with nondischargeable claims will be relegated to their nonbankruptcy creditor rights, which benefits them largely on a first-come, first-served basis.

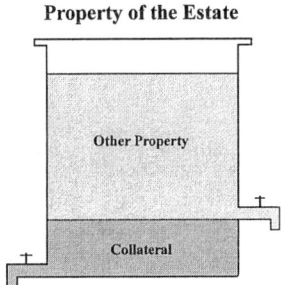
Property of the Estate

Other Property

Collateral

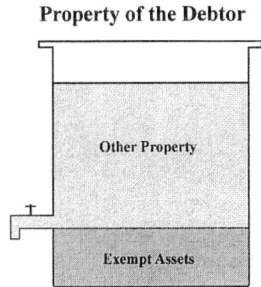
Property of the Debtor

Other Property

Exempt Assets

1.   *Unscheduled Debts*

From the creditor's perspective, the *quid pro quo* for having the debtor's obligation discharged is being able to participate in the bankruptcy proceeding and being entitled to share in any distributions from the estate. If the debtor fails to list a creditor on the debtor's schedule of debts, the court will not notify the creditor of the bankruptcy filing. If the creditor does not otherwise learn of the bankruptcy, the creditor is denied the right to participate. When this occurs, the creditor's claim is generally excepted from the discharge. § 523(a)(3).[12]

There is an exception to this exception in "no asset" cases, however. In such instances, the failure to list a claim on the schedule of debts is largely immaterial, because there would have been no distribution to the creditor anyway. As long as the creditor is still able to challenge the dischargeability of the debt on other grounds, the failure to list the claim caused no injury and should not render the claim nondischargeable.

While this makes perfect sense from a policy standpoint, courts have struggled with the text of the Code to reach this result. The particular controversy has centered on whether the debtor needs to reopen the case and amend the schedules in order to discharge the creditor's claim. The prevailing view is that such action is unnecessary.

> [Section] 523(a)(3)(A) excepts a debt from discharge if the debt was not scheduled in time for a timely filing of the proof of claim, *but not if,* despite the debt's not having been scheduled, the creditor nevertheless received notice of the bankruptcy in time to file a timely proof of claim. Put another way, the debt is discharged so long as it is scheduled in time for the creditor to file a proof of claim or the creditor finds out about the bankruptcy case in time to do

---

[12]   In short, the *creditor's* failure to file a proof of claim prevents the creditor from sharing in estate assets but does not affect the discharge. In contrast, the *debtor's* failure to schedule a debt to a creditor potentially prevents the creditor from sharing in the estate and makes the creditor's claim nondischargeable.

so. Scheduling the debt enables the bankruptcy court to provide the creditor with notice. Where the creditor, through some other means, finds out about the bankruptcy in time to assert his right to a portion of the proceeds of the estate, there is no reason to except an otherwise dischargeable debt from the effect of the discharge. But where the creditor is not aware of the bankruptcy, he cannot assert his right. Without the exception in § 523(a)(3)(A), the debtor could simply deny his uninformed creditors the opportunity to recover from the bankruptcy estate by omitting their debts from the schedule.

In a Chapter 7 no-asset case, however, the creditors cannot recover from the estate because there is nothing to recover. For this reason, there is no deadline for filing a timely proof of claim in a no-asset case. Technically speaking, therefore, no matter when the creditor learns of the bankruptcy, he is able to file a timely claim. Because § 523(a)(3)(A) excepts the unscheduled debt from discharge "unless such creditor had notice or actual knowledge of the case in time for such timely filing," the moment the creditor receives notice or knowledge of the bankruptcy case, § 523(a)(3)(A) ceases to provide the basis for an exception from discharge. Consequently, the debt is at that point discharged.[13]

The result might be different if the unlisted creditor contests the dischargeability of the debt owed or the availability of the discharge generally.[14]

Problem 10-5

Dependable is contemplating filing for Chapter 7 bankruptcy relief and has brought you a list of creditors, debts, and assets. The list of debts includes $700 remaining due to Employer on a loan made some time ago to enable Dependable to buy needed medication. Dependable does not want Employer to know of the bankruptcy and intends to pay back the debt in full as soon as possible. Thus, Dependable does not want to list the debt to Employer on the schedules. What do you advise? In answering this, consider what might happen if the schedules filed with the bankruptcy court omit the debt to Employer.

---

[13]   *In re Madaj*, 149 F.3d 467, 469-70 (6th Cir. 1998).

[14]   *See, e.g., Madaj*, 149 F.3d at 471 n.4 (dealing only with dischargeability, not the discharge).

2.   *Certain Priority Claims*

Review the list of claims treated as priorities in § 507(a). Some of these claims – not all, merely some – are also nondischargeable. It may be surprising that priority status and nondischargeability do not go fully hand-in-hand. If you think about it though, this makes perfect sense.   Priority status is about favored treatment in bankruptcy; specifically, priority claims are the first unsecured claims to be paid out of the bankruptcy estate (after allocating the value of any collateral to the payment of secured claims and removing exemptible property).   Nondischargeability provides a favored treatment outside of bankruptcy, out of whatever nonexempt assets the debtor is later able to acquire.   In general, claims are accorded priority status because of the perceived need of the creditor. In contrast, claims are generally made nondischargeable to prevent the debtor from escaping responsibility for them.   There is some overlap between these two concerns, but not much. Thus, for example, administrative expenses and employee wages are a top priority. However, they are dischargeable. Conversely, certain tort claims are, as we will see, nondischargeable, even though they are not entitled to any priority.

Two types of claims, though, get both priority treatment and nondischargeability: taxes and support obligations. Yet even with respect to these, the symmetry between the scope of the priority rule and the scope of the nondischargeability rule is not perfect.

(a) Taxes

In chapter nine we saw the priority accorded to tax claims. Recall that generally there is a three-year lookback regarding income taxes: taxes accruing in the three years prior to the bankruptcy filing are generally nondischargeable. *See* § 523(a)(1)(A). However, the nondischargeability of tax debts is a bit broader in several ways. First, it also covers taxes for which the debtor never filed a return or filed a fraudulent return. § 523(a)(1)(B), (C). Second, it covers debts incurred to pay the taxes. *See* § 523(a)(14), (14A). Thus, if a debtor obtains a loan or a cash advance on a credit card and uses the money to pay nondischargeable taxes, the resulting debt to the creditor is also nondischargeable.   There is no similar rule for debts incurred to pay other nondischargeable claims.

Problem 10-6

Taxpayer earned $29,000 last year, but changed jobs twice in the process. Because Taxpayer had three different employers, the total amount withheld from her pay for federal income taxes was not sufficient. In April, when

Taxpayer prepared her income tax return, she calculated that she owed $2,000 in back taxes, and another $500 in interest. To avoid further penalties, Taxpayer got a $2,500 cash advance through her Visa card and used the money to pay her taxes. This raised the outstanding balance on her Visa card to $4,000. During the early part of May, Taxpayer charged an additional $1,000 on her Visa card. At the end of the month, just before filing a bankruptcy petition, she made a $500 payment to the Visa card bank. What portion, if any, of her Visa bill is nondischargeable?

In general, creditors with nondischargeable claims cannot go after the debtor's exempt assets. In other words, the exemptions apply not only during the bankruptcy process, but after it as well. *See* § 522(c). There are, however, a few exceptions, most notably, for nondischargeable tax debts and nondischargeable support claims. *See* § 522(c)(1). Thus, creditors with these claims may seek recompense from three different spigots in the illustrations below: the right-hand spigot from the estate (queuing up in order of priority) and both spigots on the debtor's vat of assets.

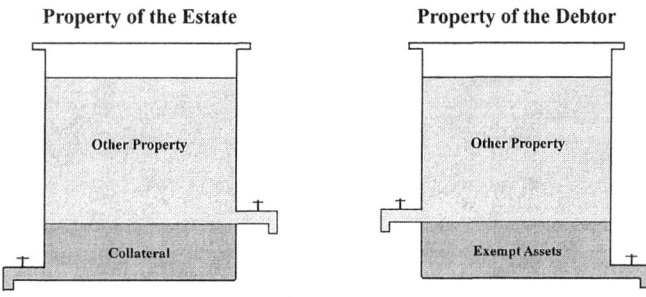

Problem 10-7

Explain the interaction and relationship of §§ 507(a)(8), 522(c), 523(a)(1), 523(a)(7), 724(a), and 726(a)(4) with respect to a claim for a tax penalty secured by a lien on the debtor's assets. In doing so, it may be useful to complete the right-hand column of the following table:

Attribute	Circle Correct Treatment		
Lien	survives		avoided
Priority	priority	normal	subordinated
Dischargeability	nondischargeable		dischargeable
Immune from Exemptions	yes		no

(b) Claims for Support

Section 523(a)(5) makes claims for domestic support obligations nondischargeable.[15] Review § 101(14A) and the discussion in chapter nine regarding how to distinguish spousal support from a property settlement obligation. Fortunately, for nondischargeability purposes, this distinction no longer matters in Chapter 7 cases. That is because while § 523(a)(5) is limited to support, § 523(a)(15) also makes nondischargeable property settlement obligations incident to divorce.

Congress added § 523(a)(15) to the list of nondischargeable claims in 1994, in part due to the realization that a spouse may agree to accept less alimony in exchange for a greater share of the marital estate or for a promise by the other spouse to assume responsibility for a larger share of the marital debts. Thus, it was thought unfair to make so much ride on the distinction. As originally enacted, the nondischargeability rule in § 523(a)(15) was subject to two exceptions: one dealing with the debtor's ability to pay and another requiring a balancing of the benefit to the creditor against the detriment to the debtor. In 2005, Congress removed these limitations. Thus, for the purposes of nondischargeability in Chapter 7, there is no need to distinguish true support from a property settlement obligation. Both are fully nondischargeable. Only the former, however, receives the other favored treatments the Code bestows: priority status, partial immunity from the stay, immunity from exemptions, immunity from preference liability, and protection from certain lien avoidance actions. *See* §§ 362(b)(2)(B), 522(c)(1), 547(c)(7), 522(f)(1)(A). Moreover, only true support obligations are nondischargeable in Chapter 13. *See* § 1328(a)(2).

3. *Misconduct Claims*

(a) Willful & Malicious Injuries

Section 523(a)(6) makes nondischargeable debts for injury to persons or property resulting from the "willful and malicious" conduct of the debtor. This means that the bully who batters a neighbor or the arsonist who burns down a building cannot escape civil liability for those acts in Chapter 7.[16] Perhaps more to the point, an insolvent

---

[15] You may remember from chapter five that § 502(b)(5) disallows claims for unmatured support. Thus only matured claims for support (*i.e.,* due or past due support obligations) get to share in distributions from the estate. However, under § 523(a)(5) all support claims – whether allowable or not – are nondischargeable.

[16] *See In re Thirtyacre*, 36 F.3d 697 (7th Cir. 1994) (debtor's liability for assault and battery was a nondischargeable debt).

person who plans to file for bankruptcy in a few days would not be able to do such acts with the intention of evading liability for them.

Of course, not all tortious acts involve the same degree of moral culpability that battery and arson do. The Code distinguishes those that give rise to dischargeable claims from those that create nondischargeable ones through use of the terms "willful" and "malicious." Those terms are somewhat vague, however, and the amount of litigation on this issue is extensive.

One of the first issues to arise in interpreting the "willful and malicious" standard was whether it requires an act done with intent to harm or merely an intentional act that results in injury.[17] The Supreme Court purported to answer that question in *Kawaauhau v. Geiger* – a medical malpractice case based on negligence – by stating that willfulness requires an intent to injure.[18] In other words, it is the injury – not the act– that must be willful. In reaching this conclusion, the Court relied upon Restatement (Second) of Torts § 8A comment a. Because that section also provides that intent to injure exists if the actor "believes that the consequences are substantially certain to result from [his act]," most lower courts have ruled that the willfulness requirement of § 523(a)(6) is satisfied if either the debtor desires the injurious consequences or believes that such consequences are substantially certain to result from the debtor's actions.[19] Note, this is not an objective test. It is not sufficient that the debtor should have known of the likely injurious consequences. Nor, at least in theory, is it sufficient to show that the injurious consequences were substantially certain to occur. The debtor must have subjectively believed that the debtor's volitional act was substantially certain to produce the injury. That said, subjective intent is typically inferred from objective evidence, so that a volitional act that is almost certain to cause harm will often be sufficient to satisfy the willfulness requirement.[20]

Maliciousness has also been the source of some controversy, but the consensus seems to be that it does not require a showing of biblical malice: personal hatred, ill-

---

[17] Compare *In re Cecchini*, 780 F.2d 1440 (9th Cir. 1986) (no intent to injure required), *with In re Compos*, 768 F.2d 1155 (10th Cir. 1985) (intent to injure required).

A similar issue arises under § 362(k)(1). For that purpose, most courts conclude that a willful violation of the stay does not require knowledge that the act will violate the stay, but merely knowledge of the petition and an intention to commit the act which does violate the stay. *E.g., In re Goodman*, 991 F.2d 613, 618 (9th Cir. 1993).

[18] 523 U.S. 57, 61 (1998).

[19] See *In re Jercich*, 238 F.3d 1202 (9th Cir.), *cert. denied*, 533 U.S. 930 (2001); *In re Markowitz*, 190 F.3d 455, 464 (6th Cir. 1999); *In re Jones*, 300 B.R. 133 (1st Cir. BAP 2003).

[20] See, e.g., *In re Langley*, 235 B.R. 651 (10th Cir. BAP 1999).

will or spite. Instead, an act is malicious if it is "wrongful and without just cause or excuse."[21]

The upshot of all this is that a great deal of conduct is treated as nondischargeable under § 523(a)(6):

- Willful and deliberate copyright infringement,[22] or trademark infringement.[23]

- Unauthorized reception and descrambling of cable TV service.[24]

- Illegally recording a conversation.[25]

- Deliberate breach of a covenant not to compete,[26] intentional interference with a business relationship,[27] or misappropriation of trade secrets,[28] but not necessarily every intentional breach of contract.[29]

---

[21]   *E.g., Ball v. A.O. Smith Corp.*, 451 F.3d 66, 69 (2d Cir. 2006).

[22]   *E,g., In re Pineau*, 149 B.R. 239 (D. Me. 1993).

[23]   *In re Whitner*, 179 B.R. 699 (Bankr. E.D. Okla. 1995) (giving collateral estoppel effect to state court judgment).

[24]   *In re Feiner*, 254 B.R. 266 (Bankr. D. Kan. 2000).

[25]   *Mazurczyk v. O'Neil*, 268 B.R. 1 (Bankr. D. Mass. 2001).

[26]   *See In re Sarff*, 242 B.R. 620 (6th Cir. BAP 2000) (also involving misappropriation of trade secrets and intentional interference with business relations); *In re Butler*, 297 B.R. 741 (Bankr. C.D. Ill. 2003).

[27]   *Piccicuto v. Dwyer*, 39 F.3d 37 (1st Cir. 1994).

[28]   *In re McCoy*, 189 B.R. 129 (Bankr. N.D. Ohio 1995).

[29]   *See In re Williams*, 337 F.3d 504 (5th Cir. 2003) (employer's intentional violation of collective bargaining agreement by hiring nonunion workers did not give rise to a nondischargeable claim because employer was motivated by a desire to compete with other business, not to injure union); *In re Jercich*, 238 F.3d 1202 (9th Cir.), *cert. denied,* 533 U.S. 930 (2001) (intentional breach of contract will give rise to nondischargeable claim only if accompanied by tortious conduct, although it is not necessary that the conduct be actionable if no contract existed; thus breach of duty to pay an employee his wages was nondischargeable).

- Sexual harassment,[30] sexual relations with a patient,[31] or transmission of a sexual disease.[32]

- Malicious prosecution,[33] filing a baseless lawsuit,[34] or otherwise engaging in vexatious litigation.[35]

- Even "slovenly living habits" that result in damage to a leased residence.[36]

In contrast, the failure to purchase insurance, even if required by law, does not generate a willful and malicious injury.[37]

One of the most commonly litigated disputes under § 523(a)(6) involves a debtor in a secured transaction who has converted the collateral by selling it and spending the proceeds. This kind of conversion is sometimes referred to as a "sale out of trust." Consider the following problem.

Problem 10-8

At the time Defoe borrowed $2,000 from Creditor, Defoe granted Creditor a security interest in some items of personal property. The security

---

[30]   *E.g., In re Jones*, 300 B.R. 133 (1st Cir. BAP 2003).

[31]   *In re Fors*, 259 B.R. 131 (8th Cir. BAP 2001) (debt of chiropractor for harm caused by sexual relations with employee/patient was nondischargeable). *But see In re Strybel*, 105 B.R. 22 (9th Cir. BAP 1989) (holding dischargeable debt of doctor who had housed woman when she feared violence from her husband and had terminated professional relationship before sexual relationship began).

[32]   *E.g., In re Moffitt*, 252 B.R. 916 (6th Cir. BAP 2000) (debt to ex-wife for intentional infliction of emotional distress, arising from transmission to her of sexually transmitted disease contracted through extra-marital affairs, was nondischargeable).

[33]   *In re Abbo*, 168 F.3d 930 (6th Cir. 1999).

[34]   *In re Amaranto*, 252 B.R. 595 (Bankr. D. Conn. 2000). *See also Ball v. A.O. Smith Corp.*, 451 F.3d 66 (2d Cir. 2006) (attorney's debt to opposing party for Rule 11 sanctions was nondischargeable).

[35]   *In re Keaty*, 397 F.3d 264 (5th Cir. 2005).

[36]   *In re Hatton*, 204 B.R. 470 (Bankr. E.D. Va. 1996). *See also In re Sintobin*, 253 B.R. 826 (Bankr. N.D. Ohio 2000) (debt for damage to rented property by the debtors' undisciplined children and the children's friends nondischargeable).

[37]   *See In re Walker*, 48 F.3d 1161 (7th Cir. 1995) (employer's failure to acquire worker's compensation insurance); *In re Shahrokhi*, 266 B.R. 702 (8th Cir. BAP 2001) (failure of taxi owner to purchase auto insurance). However, failure to purchase medical insurance for employees with funds withheld from their paychecks for that purpose does produce a willful and malicious injury, since that is effectively a defalcation. *In re Wright*, 209 B.R. 276 (E.D.N.Y. 1997).

agreement expressly prohibited Defoe from selling the collateral without Bank's prior written permission. Nevertheless, Defoe sold the collateral to a friend for $400 to finance a trip to the nearest casino, where Defoe promptly lost all the sale proceeds. At the time of sale, the collateral was worth $1,200.

A. Is some or all of Defoe's debt to Bank nondischargeable under § 523(a)(6)? Should it be? What additional facts would be relevant to these questions? *See, e.g., In re Whiters*, 337 B.R. 326 (Bankr. N.D. Ind. 2006).

B. If the Bankruptcy Court determines that Defoe acted willfully and maliciously in selling the collateral, how much of Defoe's debt to Creditor will be nondischargeable: all of it, $1200, or $400? *See In re Modicue*, 926 F.2d 452 (5th Cir. 1991); *In re Coltrane*, 273 B.R. 478 (Bankr. D.S.C. 2001).

C. Does it matter if Creditor failed to perfect the security interest, with the result that it would have been avoidable in bankruptcy? *See In re Collins*, 946 F.2d 815 (11th Cir. 1991); *In re Little*, 335 B.R. 376 (Bankr. N.D. Ohio 2005); *In re Thompson*, 316 B.R. 326 (Bankr. W.D. Mo. 2004).

Two additional points about § 523(a)(6) are worth noting. First, it does not distinguish between compensatory and punitive damages; both are nondischargeable.[38] Even attorneys fees incurred prepetition in an effort to recover for such injuries may be nondischargeable.[39] Second, claims for injuries or damage attributable to drunk driving, which are typically predicated on negligence, do not meet the "willful and malicious" standard for nondischargeability under § 523(a)(6). Because of that, in 1994 Congress added § 523(a)(9) to the Code. However, this rule makes nondischargeable only claims for personal injury; it does not cover debts for property damage.[40]

(b) Fraudulently Incurred Obligations

Debts incurred through fraud or under false pretenses, like those for willful and malicious injury, are nondischargeable. Read § 523(a)(2). The underlying principle is much the same. Debtors who engage in tortious – sometimes even criminal – conduct

---

[38] *In re Britton*, 950 F.2d 602, 605-06 (9th Cir. 1991); *In re Miera*, 926 F.2d 741, 745 (8th Cir. 1991).

[39] *See In re Feiner*, 254 B.R. 266 (Bankr. D. Kan. 2000); *In re Beale*, 253 B.R. 644 (Bankr. D. Md. 2000).

[40] *In re Brisson*, 186 B.R. 205 (Bankr. E.D. Va. 1995); *In re Williams*, 175 B.R. 17 (Bankr. M.D. Tenn. 1994).

should not be able to evade civil liability for their conduct through bankruptcy. There may, of course, be some overlap between paragraphs (2) and (6) of § 523(a) – in other words, some fraudulent conduct may cause a willful and malicious injury. Nevertheless, the two provisions have largely different scopes. Paragraph (a)(2) covers bad conduct that occurs in the creation of the debt – procurement of the debt through fraud or false pretenses – whereas paragraph (a)(6) deals with bad conduct that produces an injury for which the debtor is liable.[41]

The first two subparagraphs of § 523(a)(2) cover different types of misrepresentations. Subparagraph (B) deals with written misrepresentations about the "financial condition" of the debtor or an insider of the debtor. In addition, the creditor must prove: (i) the misrepresentations were materially false; (ii) the debtor intended to deceive; and (iii) the creditor reasonably relied on the facts misrepresented. Typically, all this occurs in connection with a loan application. The debtor submits a financial statement with major errors or omissions and the creditor later seeks to have the debt deemed nondischargeable when the debtor defaults and files for bankruptcy protection. The major hurdle for the creditor is often the reasonable reliance requirement. If the creditor neglected to take fairly simple steps to verify the debtor's statements or took but failed to perfect a security interest, the claim will be dischargeable.[42]

Subparagraph (A), in contrast, deals with misrepresentations – whether written or oral – about something other than the financial condition of the debtor or an insider. Most commonly this concerns the intent – or lack of intent – to repay the debt. The creditor asserts that the debtor expressly or implicitly misrepresented that the debtor intended to repay the debt.

One significant interpretative problem concerning subparagraph (A) arose from the fact that, whereas subparagraph (B) expressly requires reasonable reliance by the creditor, subparagraph (A) makes no mention of reliance. Most courts nevertheless imputed a reliance requirement into the provision in order to satisfy the element of causation inherent in the phrase "obtained by," and most required that such reliance be objectively reasonable.[43] However, in *Field v. Mans*,[44] the Supreme Court concluded

[41] *But cf. McClellan v. Cantrell*, 217 F.3d 890 (7th Cir. 2000) (applying § 523(a)(2) to a woman who knowingly participated in a fraudulent transfer by receiving property from her brother in an effort to shield it from one of her brother's creditors).

[42] *See, e.g., In re Cribbs*, 2006 WL 1875366 (10th Cir. 2006) (bank did not really rely on the promissory note that the debtor claimed in his financial statement to own and even, if it had, such reliance would not have been reasonable because the bank never asked to see it); *In re Flaherty*, 335 B.R. 481 (Bankr. D. Mass. 2005) (bank unreasonably failed to investigate the ownership of the offered collateral – it did not request bills of sale or other documentation).

[43] *See, e.g., In re Mullet*, 817 F.2d 677 (10th Cir. 1987) (bank failed to act reasonably in making a $86,000 loan to a 23-year-old man who claimed to have $134,000 in a Swiss bank because the bank made no effort to confirm this, other than noting that he spoke with a Swiss accent, and failed to

that justifiable reliance, not reasonable reliance, was needed. This standard, drawn from the common law, is apparently an easier standard for the creditor to meet. It not only takes into account the creditor's experience and sophistication,[45] but requires no investigation into the facts. All the creditor need do is examine the information and material provided to it.

Even before the Court's decision in *Field v. Mans*, credit card issuers made extensive use of § 523(a)(2) in efforts to have the debts due them declared nondischargeable. Since the decision, they have used the provision even more. They argue, often successfully, that every time the cardholder uses a credit card to purchase goods or services or to obtain a cash advance, the cardholder impliedly represents to the issuer the ability and intent to pay. If facts show that the cardholder did not intend to pay, the debt will be nondischargeable. Consider the following case.

IN RE HASHEMI
104 F.3d 1122 (9th Cir. 1997)

Kozinski, Circuit Judge.

Appellant didn't leave home without his American Express cards. In fact, he and his family traveled to Europe in style, and charged it all. On his return, appellant owed American Express more than $60,000, the bulk of which represented charges made during the six-week trip. He promptly filed for bankruptcy, and American Express petitioned to have his debt declared nondischargeable under § 523(a)(2)(A), which precludes discharge of debts obtained through "actual fraud." The bankruptcy court denied appellant's request for a jury trial, ruled the debt nondischargeable and ordered appellant to pay American Express $69,793.67 plus interest. The district court affirmed the bankruptcy court's judgment and Dr. Hashemi appeals again. We must decide whether * * * American Express adduced sufficient proof of "actual fraud." * * *

[A]ppellant claims the bankruptcy court erred in finding that he defrauded American Express. Section 523(a)(2)(A) precludes discharge of any debt obtained by

---

inquire about discrepancies between the borrower's unaudited financial statement and his credit report). *See also In re Britton*, 950 F.2d 602, 604 (9th Cir. 1991). *Contra In re Ophaug*, 827 F.2d 340, 343 (8th Cir. 1987) (requiring reliance but not reasonableness).

[44] 516 U.S. 59 (1995).

[45] Financial sophistication is routinely considered even under a reasonableness standard. Thus, a creditor not engaged in the business of extending credit is held to a lower duty of care. *See In re Hodges*, 116 B.R. 558, 561 (Bankr. N.D. Ohio 1990) (quoting *In re Phillips*, 804 F.2d 930, 933 (6th Cir. 1986)). Indeed, reasonable reliance can still exist even though the lender neglected to perfect its security interest. *In re Collins*, 946 F.2d 815 (11th Cir. 1991).

"false pretenses, a false representation, or actual fraud." In order to establish a debt's nondischargeability under this section, the creditor must show:

(1) the debtor made . . . representations;

(2) that at the time he knew they were false;

(3) that he made them with the intention and purpose of deceiving the creditor;

(4) that the creditor relied on such representations; [and]

(5) that the creditor sustained the alleged loss and damage as the proximate result of the misrepresentations having been made.

In re Britton, 950 F.2d 602, 604 (9th Cir. 1991). These requirements mirror the elements of common law fraud, and the creditor is required to prove each by a preponderance of the evidence. Appellant contends that American Express failed to establish his intent to defraud, that he made no false representations to American Express, and that if any such representations were made, American Express did not justifiably rely on them.

a. Fraudulent Intent. "[A] court may infer the existence of the debtor's intent not to pay if the facts and circumstances of a particular case present a picture of deceptive conduct by the debtor." *In re Eashai*, 87 F.3d 1082, 1087 (9th Cir. 1996). In *In re Dougherty*, 84 B.R. 653 (9th Cir. BAP 1988), our Bankruptcy Appellate Panel enumerated twelve factors relevant to determining a debtor's intent.[46] These factors are nonexclusive; none is dispositive, nor must a debtor's conduct satisfy a minimum number in order to prove fraudulent intent. So long as, on balance, the evidence supports a finding of fraudulent intent, the creditor has satisfied this element. We adopted *Dougherty*'s twelve-factor test as the law of the circuit in *Eashai*.

Applying the test set out in *Dougherty* and *Eashai*, as did the bankruptcy court, there is ample evidence to support the finding that appellant intended to defraud American Express. Appellant made nearly 170 charges totaling more than $60,000 during a six-week trip with his family to France. These charges exceeded appellant's annual income and, even before the trip, appellant already owed more than $300,000 in unsecured credit card debt. Appellant did have one major asset when he made the charges – a one-half ownership interest in an eight-unit condominium project. He claims the purpose of his trip was to borrow money from his mother-in-law to support this real estate venture. This does not explain why appellant stayed in France for six

---

[46] The factors are: (1) the length of time between the charges and the bankruptcy filing; (2) whether or not an attorney had been consulted concerning the filing of bankruptcy before the charges were made; (3) the number of charges made; (4) the amount of the charges; (5) the financial condition of the debtor at the time the charges were made; (6) whether the charges were above the credit limit of the account; (7) whether the debtor made multiple charges on the same day; (8) whether or not the debtor was employed; (9) the debtor's prospects for employment; (10) the financial sophistication of the debtor; (11) whether there was a sudden change in the debtor's buying habits; and (12) whether the purchases made were luxuries or necessities.

weeks, took his wife and two children with him, took a side-trip to the French Riviera, purchased cosmetics, expensive meals and other luxury items, and ultimately charged almost as much on his credit cards as he claims he planned to borrow. Moreover, while appellant was away, the holder of the second mortgage on his condominium project initiated foreclosure proceedings. This should have alerted appellant that he would not be able to repay his debt by selling his interest in the property. Given these facts, the bankruptcy court could reasonably infer that appellant tried to have a last hurrah at American Express's expense.

b. False Representations. Appellant also complains that he never made any fraudulent misrepresentations to American Express because American Express extended him an unlimited line of credit. We rejected the identical argument in *In re Anastas*, 94 F.3d 1280 (9th Cir. 1996). Each time a "card holder uses his credit card, he makes a representation that he intends to repay the debt. . . . When the card holder uses the card without an intent to repay, he has made a fraudulent representation to the card issuer." *Id.* at 1285. Because the bankruptcy court found that appellant had no intention of repaying his debt, each time he used his cards he made a fraudulent representation to American Express.

c. Justifiable Reliance. "[T]he credit card issuer justifiably relies on a representation of intent to repay as long as the account is not in default and any initial investigations into a credit report do not raise red flags that would make reliance unjustifiable." *Id.* at 1286. At the time appellant began his spending spree, his account was not in default. In fact, he owed American Express only $227. Moreover, appellant himself testified that he had repaid American Express balances of up to $60,000 "numerous times" before. American Express therefore had no reason to question the good faith of appellant's promise to repay. Because American Express provided ample evidence of each element of common law fraud, the bankruptcy court was fully justified in declaring appellant's debt nondischargeable.

———————

Although this decision has proven to be persuasive with some courts,[47] not all courts agree that a cardholder impliedly represents the ability and intent to repay by using a credit card or charge card. Some have followed an "assumption of the risk" theory, by which credit card issuers are deemed to have assumed the risk that the cardholder will use the card until it is revoked. Under this theory, fraud arises only when the cardholder has made charges after receiving notice that the card has been revoked.[48] While

———————

[47] *See, e.g., In re Mercer*, 246 F.3d 391 (5th Cir. 2001) (en banc; reversing a panel ruling that rejected the implied representation theory with respect to pre-approved credit cards).

[48] *First Nat'l Bank v. Roddenberry*, 701 F.2d 927 (11th Cir. 1983). *See also In re Kukuk*, 225 B.R.

§ 523(a)(2)(C), which was added to the Code in 1984, may protect credit card issuers in such jurisdictions from the most egregious examples of credit card abuse, issuers governed by the assumption of the risk rule will generally find the obligations due them to be dischargeable.

Even if a court employs the implied representation theory, the credit card issuer may still encounter a problem proving justifiable reliance. For example, *In re Ellingsworth*,[49] involved debtors who for years had depended on their credit cards to make ends meet. Based on their credit score, a bank then offered one of them another, pre-approved card with a $4,000 limit. The debtors verified by telephone their income and employment, but the bank sought no information about the value of their assets, the amount of their accumulated liabilities, or their monthly expenses. A full credit report would have listed their obligations in detail and implied their insolvency.

The debtors did not use the card for almost a year. Then, after one of them was demoted at work and they had exhausted their other sources of credit, they used the card until they reached the credit limit. The bulk of such use was to obtain cash advances. Then, without making a single payment on the card, they filed for bankruptcy. Because their monthly expenses left them with only about one half of what they needed to make even the minimum payments on their $70,000 in aggregate credit card debt, the court concluded that the debtors must have known that they could not repay the $4,000 debt on the new card and thus misrepresented their intent to repay. However, the court also concluded that if the debtors had applied to a bank for a $4,000 loan, and had revealed their true financial position on their credit application, the bank could not have justifiably relied on their promise to repay. It then questioned why credit cards should be treated differently and ruled that the bank's reliance was not reasonable.[50]

The *Ellingsworth* decision has been criticized for focusing the justifiable reliance inquiry too much on ability to pay, rather than on intent to pay.[51] One might also

---

778 (10th Cir. BAP 1998) (debtor makes representation of intent, but not ability, to repay).

[49]   212 B.R. 326 (W.D. Mo. 1997).

[50]   *See also In re Rembert*, 141 F.3d 277, 283-84 (6th Cir. 1998) (Krupansky, J., concurring) (suggesting that justifiable reliance transcends the time when the card is issued and requires thereafter routine or periodic investigations of the cardholder's credit worthiness).

The *Ellingsworth* court nevertheless ruled that the cash advances obtained within the 60 days preceding bankruptcy, and which are presumed nondischargeable under § 523(a)(2)(C), were not dischargeable. In short, the creditor did not have to demonstrate justifiable reliance for these charges to be nondischargeable. 212 B.R. at 330, 340.

[51]   *In re Herrig*, 217 B.R. 891, 900 (Bankr. N.D. Okla. 1998). *See also In re Mercer*, 246 F.3d at 411-25 (credit card issuer *actually* relies on cardholder's representation of intent to pay merely by extending credit; such reliance is *justifiable* if the account is not in default and no red flags were raised when the card was issued).

question the court's analogy to a request for a loan in which a financial statement is presented. After all, the debtors had provided no such statement and the Supreme Court's decision in *Field v. Mans* strongly suggests that justifiable reliance differs from reasonable reliance in that there is no duty to investigate. Still, the decision reveals the deep disagreement about whether consumers or credit card issuers are more at fault for the abuses of consumer credit.

The National Bankruptcy Review Commission described the law governing dischargeability of credit card debt as confusing, problematic and "fraught with doctrinal difficulty."[52] With increasing frequency, credit card issuers are challenging the dischargeability of the debts due them, even in the absence of actual fraud. Impoverished debtors often lack the resources to litigate the issue. The result is a large group of inconsistent decisions and a great deal of what the Commission regarded as unnecessary litigation. It proposed a bright-line rule designed to achieve rough justice. Under this proposal, credit card debts not covered by § 523(a)(2)(B) or (a)(14) would be dischargeable unless they exceeded the credit limit or were incurred within the 30 days preceding the bankruptcy filing. Section 523(a)(2)(A) would no longer be available for routine credit card use. The Commission acknowledged that some honest debtors would suffer under this rule, and that other debtors could abuse it, but noted that no solution could be wholly satisfactory, either in theory or in practice. It believed that by limiting the rule to 30 days, it would generally cover only those charges made in contemplation of bankruptcy. It suggested that the rule would walk a fine line: it would neither disrupt credit practices nor safeguard creditors from improvident lending decisions that the lenders themselves could avoid making.[53]

Congress did not adopt this recommendation, but it did tinker with § 523(a)(2)(C). It provides a presumption for the purposes of subparagraph (A) – not subparagraph (B) – that a credit card debt totaling more than $500 for the purchase of luxury goods within the 90 days preceding bankruptcy was obtained under false pretenses, as are cash advances in the 70 days before the petition totaling more than $750.

Problem 10-9

In the two months preceding Davidson's bankruptcy petition, Davidson obtained $500 in cash advances on a Visa card and $600 on a MasterCard. Davidson, who was unemployed at the time, used the money to buy food and to pay rent. Davidson hoped to land a new job, but so far has yet to obtain one. Are the debts for the cash advances dischargeable?

---

[52] National Bankruptcy Review Commission, *Bankruptcy: The Next Twenty Years* 181 (October 20, 1997).

[53] *Id.* at 195.

As noted above, those circuit courts with a ruling on the issue have all agreed that punitive damages resulting from a willful and malicious injury are covered by § 523(a)(6) and are nondischargeable. In contrast, the language of § 523(a)(2)(A), by making nondischargeable "any debt for money, property, services . . . obtained by false pretenses," arguably does not encompasses punitive damages.[54] Nevertheless, the Supreme Court has ruled that a treble damages award is wholly nondischargeable under § 523(a)(2).[55]

It will be interesting to see how broadly the Court's decision is interpreted. For example, it may implicitly overrule a disputed line of authority ruling that the finance charges on a § 523(a)(2) debt are not obtained by false pretenses, misrepresentation, or fraud, but merely represent the creditor's profit (contractual expectancy), which is not what the provision is designed to protect.[56] Note, this specific issue – while not normally momentous – serves as an important reminder that an obligation which appears to be a single debt may in fact be several debts, not all of which are entitled to the same treatment. The Court's decision may also have undermined another line of cases ruling that § 523(a)(2) applies only when the debtor benefits from the fraud. At least one court has so ruled.[57]

One interesting question concerning § 523(a)(2) is what happens if the fraudulently incurred obligation is replaced in a settlement agreement. Consider the following scenario:

> Borrower gives Lender false and misleading financial statements upon which Lender reasonably relies in deciding to make a loan. After discovering the fraud, Lender and Borrower enter into a settlement agreement. As part of the settlement, the parties tear up the old promissory note and Borrower signs a new one which, among other things, increases the interest rate on the loan.

---

[54] *See In re Levy*, 951 F.2d 196, 199 (9th Cir. 1991), *cert. denied*, 504 U.S. 985 (1992). *Contra In re St. Laurent*, 991 F.2d 672 (11th Cir. 1993).

[55] *Cohen v. de la Cruz*, 523 U.S. 213 (1998).

[56] *See, e.g., In re Smith*, 207 B.R. 403 (Bankr. W.D.N.Y. 1997) (merchant's service charges for bad check dischargeable); *In re Owen*, 181 B.R. 288 (Bankr. D.W. Va. 1995) (interest on debt incurred through fraud was dischargeable; it was not covered by § 523(a)(2)); *In re Bonnifield*, 154 B.R. 743 (Bankr. N.D. Cal. 1993) (interest on § 523(a)(2) claim is dischargeable). *But see In re Gosney*, 205 B.R. 418 (9th Cir. BAP 1996) (both prepetition interest and attorneys' fees generated in prepetition attempts to collect a nondischargeable debt are nondischargeable); *In re Dawson*, 163 B.R. 421 (Bankr. D.R.I. 1994) (interest nondischargeable); *In re Keller*, 125 B.R. 716 (Bankr. N.D.N.Y. 1989) (postpetition interest nondischargeable).

[57] *See In re Denbleyker*, 251 B.R. 891 (Bankr. D. Colo. 2000) (debtor's personal liability arising from loan to corporate entity following debtor's misrepresentation that corporate subcontractors were paid off was nondischargeable).

Before making the payments under the settlement agreement, Borrower files for bankruptcy protection. Does execution of the settlement agreement affect the dischargeability of the debt? Put another way, if the original indebtedness would have been nondischargeable under § 523(a)(2), (4) or (6), is the current debt under the settlement agreement also nondischargeable?

Until recently, courts were divided on this issue.[58] Then the Supreme Court ruled in *Warner v. Archer*,[59] that even if a settlement agreement released all the tort claims and left the creditor with only a contractual obligation, that obligation could still be nondischargeable:

> We agree with the Court of Appeals . . . that "[t]he settlement agreement and promissory note here, coupled with the broad language of the release, completely addressed and released each and every underlying state law claim." That agreement left only one relevant debt: a debt for money promised in the settlement agreement itself. To recognize that fact, however, does not end our inquiry. We must decide whether that same debt can *also* amount to a debt for *money obtained by fraud*, within the terms of the nondischargeability statute. Given this Court's precedent, we believe that it can.[60]

However, while agreeing that a novation does not necessarily change the character of the debt, the Court remanded for lower court consideration the debtor's argument that the particular settlement agreement not only worked a novation but also included an implicit promise not to challenge the dischargeability of the debt for fraud.

Problem 10-10

When buying a small business two years ago, Despicable gave Bank false and misleading financial statements upon which Bank reasonably relied. The parties are preparing now to enter into a settlement agreement, which will significantly increase the interest rate on the loan. You represent Bank and are

---

[58]   *Compare In re Warner*, 283 F.3d 230 (4th Cir. 2002); *In re Fischer*, 116 F.3d 388 (9th Cir.), *amended by* 127 F.3d 819 (9th Cir. 1997); *In re West*, 22 F.3d 775 (7th Cir. 1994) (all ruling that the settlement made the debt dischargeable); *with United States v. Spicer*, 57 F.3d 1152 (D.C. Cir. 1995); *Greenberg v. Schools*, 711 F.2d 152 (11th Cir. 1983); *In re Francis*, 226 B.R. 385 (6th Cir. BAP 1998) (all ruling that the settlement agreement has no impact on dischargeability).

[59]   538 U.S. 314 (2003).

[60]   *Id.* at 318-19.

preparing to draft the agreement. You are comforted by the Supreme Court's recent decision in *Warner v. Archer* but you are unsure how broadly lower courts may read that decision. How would you draft the settlement agreement to avoid jeopardizing the nondischargeability of Despicable's obligation?

(c) Embezzlement, Larceny & Fraud in Connection with a Fiduciary Duty

Section 523(a)(4) also makes nondischargeable debts derived from fraud in a fiduciary capacity, embezzlement, and larceny. There is much less litigation under § 523(a)(4) than under § 523(a)(2), in part because courts have been somewhat reluctant to imply fiduciary obligations in normal commercial transactions.[61] There is, however, one recent case that may be a harbinger for increased use of § 523(a)(4). In that case, *In re Ellison*,[62] the debtors owned and managed a corporation that operated a travel agency. The business failed to remit money it had collected from customers to the clearing house established by several airlines for the tickets purchased on those carriers. The debtors were personally liable for this debt under a guaranty agreement. While such liability would not normally give rise to a § 523(a)(4) debt, the court ruled that the confluence of the following four facts resulted in the debtors' obligation to the clearinghouse falling under § 523(a)(4) as a debt for defalcation in a fiduciary capacity:

(1) the guarantees;
(2) the fact that corporation's debt resulted from its breach of a fiduciary duty to the clearinghouse (pursuant to a written trust agreement);
(3) the fact that such debt was brought about by the debtors' personal conduct; and
(4) the fact that the debtors, as officers and directors of the corporation, breached a fiduciary duty to the corporation.

In a sense, this can be viewed as something like the mathematical concept of transition (if A=B and B=C, then A=C): if A breaches a fiduciary duty to B, causing B to breach a fiduciary duty to C, then A has breached a fiduciary duty to C. It will be interesting to see if the case is interpreted that broadly.

---

[61] *See In re Marchiando*, 13 F.3d 1111 (7th Cir.), *cert. denied*, 512 U.S. 1205 (1994) (debtor who owned a convenience store and who failed to remit to state amounts collected from customers through sales of lottery tickets did not incur a fiduciary liability despite state statute imposing a trust on the receipts); *In re Whiters*, 337 B.R. 326 (Bankr. N.D. Ind. 2006) (granting a security interest does not create a fiduciary relationship within the meaning of § 523(a)(4)).

[62] 296 F.3d 266 (4th Cir. 2002).

4. *Educational Loans*

Section 523(a)(8), as originally enacted, made educational loan debts to a governmental unit or nonprofit institution of higher learning nondischargeable if it became due less than five years before the petition was filed. Since then, in a series of amendments, Congress has expanded the nondischargeability by lengthening and then removing the time restriction and expanding the types of entities to whom the debt may be owed. The one major limitation on the scope of the rule is that the debt not impose an "undue hardship" on the debtor and the debtor's dependents. The phrase "undue hardship" is not defined but is explored in the following case.

IN RE GERHARDT
348 F.3d 89 (5th Cir. 2003)

Jones, Circuit Judge:

Over a period of years, Jonathon Gerhardt obtained over $77,000 in government-insured student loans to finance his education at the University of Southern California, the Eastman School of Music, the University of Rochester, and the New England Conservatory of Music. Gerhardt is a professional cellist. He subsequently defaulted on each loan owed to the United States Government.

In 1999, Gerhardt filed for Chapter 7 bankruptcy and thereafter filed an adversary proceeding seeking discharge of his student loans pursuant to § 523(a)(8). The bankruptcy court discharged Gerhardt's student loans as causing undue hardship. On appeal, the district court reversed, holding that it would not be an undue hardship for Gerhardt to repay his student loans. Finding no error, we affirm the district court's judgment.

I. STANDARD OF REVIEW
 * * * Generally, a bankruptcy court's findings of fact are reviewed for clear error and conclusions of law are reviewed de novo.

Whether courts review the "undue hardship" determination de novo is a matter of first impression in this circuit. A number of our sister circuits have confronted this precise issue, determining that the dischargeability decision is a question of law subject to de novo review. Similarly, this court has held that determining dischargeability of a debt arising from a willful and malicious injury under § 523(a)(6) is a question of law subject to de novo review. The decision to discharge Gerhardt's debts represents a conclusion regarding the legal effect of the bankruptcy court's factual findings as to his circumstances. Thus, the district court correctly applied de novo review to the bankruptcy court's dischargeability holding, and this court applies the same standard on appeal.

II. UNDUE HARDSHIP TEST

This circuit has not explicitly articulated the appropriate test with which to evaluate the undue hardship determination. The Second Circuit in *Brunner* crafted the most widely-adopted test. *See In re Cox,* 338 F.3d 1238, 1241 (11th Cir. 2003); *In re Ekenasi,* 325 F.3d 541, 546 (4th Cir. 2003); *Rifino,* 245 F.3d at 1087-88; *Brightful,* 267 F.3d at 327-28; *Roberson,* 999 F.2d at 1135-36. To justify discharging the debtor's student loans, the *Brunner* test requires a three-part showing:

> (1) that the debtor cannot maintain, based on current income and expenses, a "minimal" standard of living for [himself] and [his] dependents if forced to repay the loans; (2) that additional circumstances exist indicating that this state of affairs is likely to persist for a significant portion of the repayment period of the student loans; and (3) that the debtor has made good faith efforts to repay the loans. *Brunner,* 831 F.2d at 396.

Because the Second Circuit presented a workable approach to evaluating the "undue hardship" determination, this court expressly adopts the *Brunner* test for purposes of evaluating a Section 523(a)(8) decision.

A. Minimal Standard of Living

Under the first prong of the *Brunner* test, the bankruptcy court determined that Gerhardt could not maintain a minimal standard of living if forced to repay his student loans. Evidence was produced at trial that Gerhardt earned $1,680.47 per month as the principal cellist for the Louisiana Philharmonic Orchestra ("LPO"), including a small amount of supplemental income earned as a cello teacher for Tulane University. His monthly expenses, which included a health club membership and internet access, averaged $1,829.39. The bankruptcy court's factual findings are not clearly erroneous. Consequently, we agree with the bankruptcy court's conclusion of law, which we review de novo, that flows from these factual findings. Given that Gerhardt's monthly expenses exceed his monthly income, he has no ability at the present time to maintain a minimal standard of living if forced to repay his loans.

B. Persisting State of Affairs

The second prong of the *Brunner* test asks if "additional circumstances exist indicating that this state of affairs is likely to persist [for a significant period of time]." *Brunner,* 831 F.2d at 396. "Additional circumstances" encompass "circumstances that impacted on the debtor's future earning potential but which [were] either not present when the debtor [ ] applied for the loans or [have] since been exacerbated." *In re Roach,* 288 B.R. 437, 445 (Bankr. E.D. La. 2003). This second aspect of the test is meant to be "a demanding requirement." *Brightful,* 267 F.3d at 328. Thus, proving that the debtor is "currently in financial straits" is not enough. *Id.* Instead, the debtor must specifically prove "a total incapacity . . . in the future to pay [his] debts for reasons not within [his] control."[63] *In re Faish,* 72 F.3d 298, 307 (3d Cir. 1995) (quoting *In re Rappaport,* 16 B.R. 615, 617 (Bankr. D.N.J. 1981)).

Under the second prong of the test, the district court correctly concluded that Gerhardt has not established persistent undue hardship entitling him to discharge his student loans. Gerhardt holds a masters degree in music from the New England Conservatory of Music. He is about 43 years old, healthy, well-educated, and has no dependents, yet has repaid only $755 of his over $77,000 debt. During the LPO's off-seasons, Gerhardt has collected unemployment, but he has somehow managed to attend the Colorado Music Festival. Although trial testimony tended to show that Gerhardt would likely not obtain a position at a higher-paying orchestra, he could obtain additional steady employment in a number of different arenas. For instance, he could attempt to teach full-time, obtain night-school teaching jobs, or even work as a music store clerk. Thus, no reasons out of Gerhardt's control exist that perpetuate his inability to repay his student loans.

In addition, nothing in the Bankruptcy Code suggests that a debtor may choose to work only in the field in which he was trained, obtain a low-paying job, and then claim that it would be an undue hardship to repay his student loans. Under the facts presented by Gerhardt, it is difficult to imagine a professional orchestra musician who would not qualify for an undue hardship discharge. Accordingly, Gerhardt "has failed to demonstrate the type of exceptional circumstances that are necessary in order to meet [his] burden under the second prong" of *Brunner. Brightful,* 267 F.3d at 330. Finding no error, the judgment of the district court is affirmed.

NOTES

1. Although most courts apply the *Brunner* test,[64] a "totality of the circumstances test" has been adopted by the Eighth Circuit,[65] and by some

---

[63] Some examples of "additional circumstances" include "psychiatric problems, lack of usable job skills, and severely limited education." *Roach,* 288 B.R. at 445.

[64] As noted in *Gerhardt*, the *Brunner* test has been adopted by the Second, Third, Fourth, Fifth, Seventh, Ninth, and Eleventh Circuits. More recently, it has also been adopted by the Sixth and Tenth Circuits. *See In re Olyer*, 397 F.3d 382 (6th Cir. 2005); *Educational Credit Mgmt. Corp. v. Polleys*, 356 F.3d 1302, 1309 (10th Cir. 2004).

[65] *In re Long,* 322 F.3d 549, 553 (8th Cir. 2003).

courts in the First Circuit.[66] Unlike the *Brunner* test, the totality of the circumstances test considers whether the debtor has made, but does not require the debtor to have made, a good faith effort to repay the educational loans.

For certain health education assistance loans, a completely different standard and statute apply.[67]

2. The *Brunner* test can be difficult to satisfy. This was perhaps best illustrated in *In re Elpel*,[68] a case involving two Gonzaga Law School graduates. The bankruptcy court ruled that the couple's combined $194,000 educational loan indebtedness was a hardship, but not an undue one, even though neither was able to find permanent work as an attorney. Both passed the Washington State bar exam, but after efforts to obtain permanent employment in Washington proved unsuccessful, they moved to Arizona and began work for a title company. Because their combined monthly take-home pay was $3,615 and their monthly living expenses were $2,175, the court concluded they could make monthly payments of $1,413 on their educational loans without incurring an undue burden. The court noted that the debtors had "not yet obtained a middle class lifestyle" and acknowledged the emotional burdens this debt created, but it nevertheless declined to discharge any of their student loan debt.[69]

Another good example of the difficulty of satisfying the *Brunner* test is *In re Olyer*.[70] The debtor in the case was a 48-year-old married pastor with three children. Before founding his church, the debtor earned a master's degree, worked as a salesman and audio engineer, and once owned his own business. More recently, his family's annual income for the preceding two years was less than $10,000, well below poverty level for a family of five. The church congregation provided the family with an apartment and a monthly salary

---

[66]   *See In re Kelly*, 312 B.R. 200 (1st Cir. BAP 2004).

[67]   *See* 42 U.S.C. § 292f(g); *In re Rice*, 78 F.3d 1144 (6th Cir. 1996); *In re Johnson*, 787 F.2d 1179 (7th Cir. 1986).

[68]   No. 97-04740-WIR (Bankr. W.D. Wash. Sept. 1, 1998).

[69]   *See also In re Furneri*, 266 B.R. 447 (Bankr. D. Alaska 2001) (finding no undue hardship for two law school graduates with $230,000 in education loan debt because they chose nonlegal employment that did not maximize the use of their skills or their income). For a thoughtful and interesting decision going the other way, see *In re Speer*, 272 B.R. 186 (Bankr. W.D. Tex. 2001) (involving a technical school "supposedly" providing instruction in aircraft mechanics and repair that in reality "failed to educate the [debtor] properly, if at all").

[70]   397 F.3d 382 (6th Cir. 2005).

based on contributions that averaged about $1,200. The family had no health insurance and the debtor repeatedly experienced detached retinas as a result of a persistent medical condition. His only debts were $40,000 worth of student loans. Although the bankruptcy court and Bankruptcy Appellate Panel both held that the debtor qualified for a hardship discharge of his student loans, the Sixth Circuit concluded that the debtor failed to satisfy the second prong of the *Brunner* test and reversed. It ruled that the debtor's "choice to work as a pastor of a small start-up church cannot excuse his failure to supplement his income so that he can meet knowingly and voluntarily incurred financial obligations. By education and experience he qualifies for higher-paying work and is obliged to seek work that would allow debt repayment before he can claim undue hardship."[71]

3.   In *In re Roberson*,[72] the Seventh Circuit affirmed the bankruptcy court's conclusion that the debtor's educational loans were nondischargeable but nevertheless also affirmed its decision to allow the debtor a two-year deferment before he had to start paying the debt. Although there is no clear authority for this, several courts have done it.

A few courts have also held that even if the debtor fails to demonstrate undue hardship, a discharge of a portion of the student loan debt may be in order under the court's § 105 powers, so that the debtor will be able to pay.[73] The bulk of authority is to the contrary, however. Absent a finding of undue hardship, there can be no discharge of student loans at all, although if undue hardship is present, courts may use their § 105 powers to discharge only the portion of the student loan debt posing the hardship.[74] Most courts using this last approach refuse to bifurcate any single loan into dischargeable and nondischargeable portions but will apply the undue hardship analysis to each loan separately, and discharge some but not others.

Prior to the 2005 amendments, which slightly reordered the text of § 523(a)(8), divided the text in subparagraphs, and added what is now subparagraph (B), there were

---

[71]   *Id.* at 386.

[72]   999 F.2d 1132 (7th Cir. 1993).

[73]   *See, e.g., In re Hornsby*, 144 F.3d 433 (6th Cir. 1998).

[74]   *See, e.g., In re Aldrete*, 412 F.3d 1200, 1207 (10th Cir. 2005); *In re Miller*, 377 F.3d 616, 621-23 (6th Cir. 2004) (interpreting *Hornsby* as requiring undue hardship for whatever portion is discharged); *In re Cox*, 338 F.3d 1238, 1243 (11th Cir. 2003), *cert. denied*, 541 U.S. 991 (2004); *In re Saxman*, 325 F.3d 1168, 1174-75 (9th Cir. 2003).

at least three significant interpretive problems regarding the scope of the nondischargeability rule for educational debts.

The first is whether the provision applies when the debtor is not the student, but is a relative or friend who borrowed money or guaranteed a debt to help finance the student's education. Most of the courts dealing with the issue have ruled that the provision applies anyway, and that the obligation is generally nondischargeable.[75] A few courts disagree.[76]

The second question concerns whether the provision applies to former students who, after graduation, consolidate their student loans in order to alter the repayment schedule or get the benefit of a general decline in interest rates. The Higher Education Act of 1965 authorizes such consolidations. Technically, however, the consolidated loan proceeds are not used to pay educational expenses. Nevertheless, courts have had little difficulty concluding that such consolidated loans from a governmental or nonprofit institution are to be treated under § 523(a)(8) in the same manner as the obligations they replaced.[77] Borrowing from a bank, relative, or friend to repay student loans may, however, produce a different result.[78]

The third question is whether credit received in kind can result in a nondischargeable debt. Such credit is fairly common; it arises when the school allows the student to attend without prepaying tuition (*i.e.,* provides instruction for which the student promises to pay later) or provides room, board, or books on credit. Section 523(a)(8) covered – and subparagraph (A) still covers – only three types of indebtedness:

1. "an educational benefit overpayment" made or insured by a governmental unit or made or funded by a nonprofit institution;
2. a "loan" made or insured by a governmental unit or made or funded by a nonprofit institution; and
3. "an obligation to repay funds received as an educational benefit, scholarship, or stipend."

---

[75] *See, e.g., Pelkowski v. Ohio Student Loan Comm'n,* 990 F.2d 737 (3d Cir. 1993).

[76] *See, e.g., In re Pryor,* 234 B.R. 716 (Bankr. W.D. Tenn. 1999); *In re Kirkish,* 144 B.R. 367 (Bankr. W.D. Mich. 1992).

[77] *See, e.g., Sheer v. Educational Credit Mgmt. Corp.,* 245 B.R. 236 (D. Md. 1999); *In re Flint,* 238 B.R. 676 (E.D. Mich. 1999). *Cf. Hiatt v. Indiana State Student Assistance Commission,* 36 F.3d 21 (7th Cir. 1994) (consolidated loan is a new obligation for the purpose of determining when the 7-year clock on student loan debt dischargeability starts to run).

[78] *See, e.g., In re Nies,* 334 B.R. 495 (Bankr. D. Mass. 2005) (loan made by hospital pursuant to its physician recruitment program to enable the debtor to repay student loans was not a consolidated loan and served no educational purpose).

The first is fairly narrow in scope. An educational benefit is something that occurs under a program, such as the GI Bill, which provides funds to veterans who certify they are attending school. An overpayment of an educational benefit occurs when a person receives such funds for a period when that person is not in school. This type of situation is not common. The latter two types of indebtedness are broader, but it remains unclear whether credit in kind qualifies as either a "loan" or "funds received." A fair number of courts have ruled that such extensions of credit are not loans.[79]

The addition of subparagraph (B) was no doubt intended to expand the scope of the nondischargeability provision and to include virtually all credit associated with schooling, regardless of whether it was in the form of a loan and regardless of whether it was made, insured, or guaranteed by a governmental unit or nonprofit organization. In particular, it makes clear that refinanced educational debt is nondischargeable, apparently even if refinanced by a relative, bank, or credit card issuer.

Now that we've covered most of debts that are nondischargeable, try your hand at the following two problems. Each in its way requires that you integrate material from this chapter with that from almost all the earlier chapters in this book.

Problem 10-11

The Venn diagram below expands upon the diagram used in Problem 7-11 by adding the claims subject to the discharge. Review your response to Problem 7-11 and determine where within the revised diagram to place each of the specific rights listed in that problem. For each vacant portion of the diagram, identify at least one right that falls within it. Alternatively, if you prefer to use the matrix beneath the Venn diagram, identify an example of a right that fits within each blank cell.

---

[79] *See, e.g., In re Mehta*, 310 F.3d 308 (3d Cir. 2002) (attending classes is neither an educational benefit overpayment nor a loan, at least if not evidenced by a promissory note, and is not part of a funded program); *In re Renshaw*, 222 F.3d 84 (2d Cir. 2000) (providing tuition, room, and board on credit is not a loan and is not part of a funded "program," but rejecting notion that money need actually change hands).

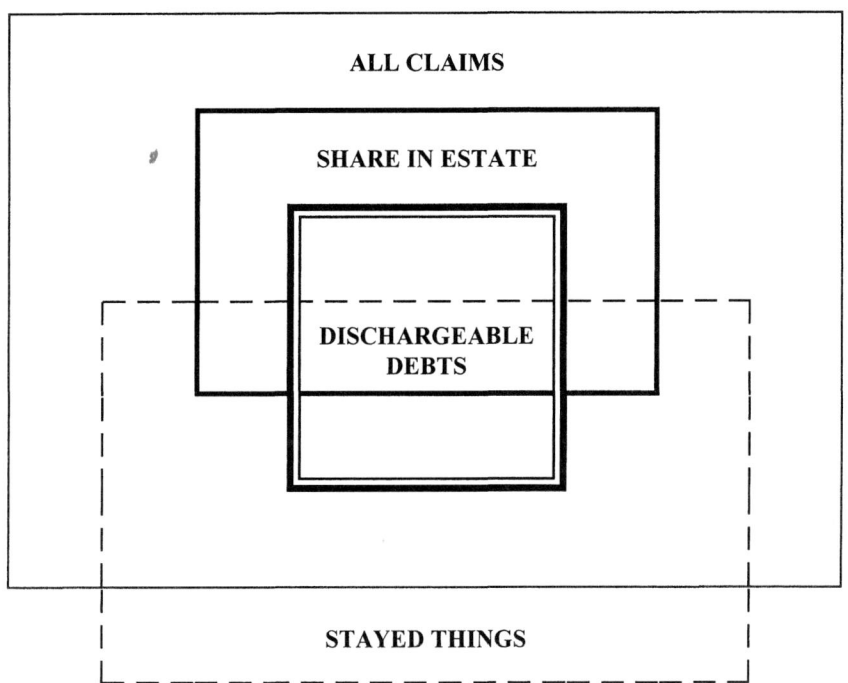

	Dischargeable		Nondischargeable	
	Stayed	Not Stayed	Stayed	Not Stayed
Allowed Claims				
Disallowed Claims				
Non-Claims				

Problem 10-12

Destitute, who has consulted with a local attorney about filing for bankruptcy, has the following assets and liabilities:

Assets	Value
Car (subject to lien)	$10,000
Exempt assets (clothes & household goods)	$5,000
Nonexempt Assets (cash & mutual fund account)	$5,000
Total:	$20,000

Liabilities	Amount
Educational Loans	$20,000
Spousal Support	$20,000
Credit Cards	$10,000
Car Loan (secured)	$10,000
Total:	$60,000

Although employed, Destitute sees no end in sight to debt and is contemplating filing for Chapter 7 bankruptcy relief. Assume that Destitute has not yet defaulted on any payment obligations, and largely for that reason still has $20,000 of unused credit on various major credit cards. What pre-bankruptcy transactions might Destitute engage in to enhance assets or reduce liabilities post-bankruptcy? Which of these transactions will have the desired effect? Consider §§ 507(a), 522(c), (g), 523(a), 547(b), (c), and 727(a).

5. Litigating Nondischargeability Issues

There are four points to note about how disputes concerning the dischargeability of a specific claim are resolved. First, most nondischargeable claims are automatically excluded from the discharge; the discharge order will simply exclude debts covered under most of the paragraphs of § 523(a) without expressly identifying them. As a result, disputes about whether a specific claim is or is not dischargeable need not be resolved by the bankruptcy court. Certainly, either party may ask the bankruptcy court for a declaratory order on the issue.[80] Rule 4007(a). Indeed, they may do so at any time during the bankruptcy case and may even petition the court to reopen the case if the issue arises after the case has been closed. Rule 4007(b). However, they also may litigate the issue in a nonbankruptcy forum. Typically this occurs when the creditor pursues the debtor to recover payment after the stay is lifted or expires and the debtor defends on the basis of the discharge. Thus, any state or federal court can resolve disputes about the scope and meaning of many of the nondischargeability provisions. That option is risky for the creditor, however. If the creditor is wrong about the nondischargeability of the debt, any effort to collect it post-discharge will violate the discharge injunction of § 524 and subject the creditor to damages (*i.e.*, the debtor's attorneys' fees).[81]

Claims covered by § 523(a)(2), (4), (6), and (15) are treated differently. They will be discharged unless the creditor specifically asks the bankruptcy court to declare them nondischargeable. § 523(c)(1). In other words, the bankruptcy court has exclusive jurisdiction to determine the dischargeability of a claim under these provisions. When the court sends creditors notice of the bankruptcy filing and of the first meeting of creditors, it will also fix a deadline for filing an objection to the discharge under § 727 and for filing complaints to determine the dischargeability of a debt under § 523(c). *See* Rule 2002(f). Normally this deadline is 60 days after the § 341 meeting. *See* Rule 4007(c).

Second, many claims allegedly covered by § 523(a)(2), (4), or (6) – all of which involve debtor misconduct – are based on a pre-bankruptcy judgment. When that is the case, the creditor will often try to collaterally estop the debtor from challenging the nondischargeability complaint. In other words, if the debtor had previously been held liable for fraud, theft, or the like, the creditor will seek to prevent the debtor from relitigating in the nondischargeability dispute the facts that formed the basis for that conclusion.

Before giving preclusive effect to a pre-bankruptcy judgment, bankruptcy courts are cautious to make sure that all the elements inherent in the § 523(a)(2), (4), or (6) exception were actually adjudicated. If the elements truly were adjudicated, however,

---

[80]   And the creditor may have incentive to do so, because litigating this issue in bankruptcy court may be less expensive than litigating it elsewhere.

[81]   *See In re Torres*, 117 B.R. 379 (Bankr. N.D. Ill. 1990) (noting that compensatory and remedial damages are appropriate for violating the discharge injunction, even if done in a good faith belief that the debt was nondischargeable). *See also In re Batla*, 12 B.R. 397, 400 (Bankr. N.D. Ga. 1981) (a creditor who is uncertain about whether its claim has survived the bankruptcy discharge and who chooses not to seek a declaratory order from the bankruptcy court "takes a calculated risk under threat of contempt" by attempting to collect the debt).

and if they were decided under the same or greater burden of proof,[82] collateral estoppel will apply.[83]   In this respect, a state court default judgment apparently can qualify as adjudication on the merits, and thus be accorded preclusive effect, if that is how the state would regard it.[84]   Similarly, a consent judgment can also be the basis for collateral estoppel.[85]

Third, the losing party in nondischargeability litigation may be liable for attorneys' fees. The debtor gets them if the court determines that the creditor's position was not "substantially justified" and the award would not otherwise be unjust. § 523(d). The creditor may be entitled to them by contract, statute, or other rule of law.[86] As one court put it:

> (1) If allegations are tried and adjudicated [in bankruptcy court], for the first time, in a § 523 action, attorneys fees must be awarded if a statute, a contract, or a black letter principle of law . . . so commands. And such fees *might* be awarded if a statute, contract, or black letter principle of law permits, but does not require, such an award.
>
> (2) If the underlying claim was tried and adjudicated before bankruptcy and was found to warrant an award of fees because of statute, contract, or black letter principle of law, then the debtor must ask herself whether what she is going to ask the bankruptcy court to decide (by defending the action) is the same thing that was decided before, albeit under § 523 rather than under non-bankruptcy law. She defends at her own peril because if the court concludes that there is no distinction, she will not be permitted to have foisted on her opponents the cost of demonstrating a second time in a second forum what the substance and nature of the claim and injury actually were.[87]

---

[82]   Ever since the Supreme Court's decision in *Grogan v. Garner*, 498 U.S. 279 (1991), that a "preponderance of the evidence" standard applies for all discharge exceptions under § 523(a), this is rarely an issue.

[83]   *See, e.g., In re Davis*, 3 F.3d 113 (5th Cir. 1993).

[84]   *See, e.g., In re Caton*, 157 F.3d 1026 (5th Cir. 1998), *cert. denied*, 526 U.S. 1068 (1999); *In re Nourbakhsh*, 67 F.3d 798 (9th Cir. 1995); *In re Bush*, 62 F.3d 1319 (11th Cir. 1995). *But cf. Spilman v. Harley*, 656 F.2d 224 (6th Cir. 1981).

[85]   *See Klingman v. Levinson*, 831 F.2d 1292 (7th Cir. 1987).

[86]   *Travelers Cas. & Sur. Co. v. Pacific Gas & Elec. Co.*, 127 S. Ct. 1199 (2007). *See also In re Busch*, 2007 WL 1584650 (10th Cir. BAP 2007).

[87]   *In re Behn*, 245 B.R. 444, 448 (Bankr. W.D.N.Y. 2000) (said in reference to litigation under § 523(a)(2), (4), or (6); it is unclear whether its analysis applies to litigation under some other provision of § 523(a)). *See also In re Hung Tan Pham*, 250 B.R. 93 (9th Cir. BAP 2000) (such an award should be made whenever the successful plaintiff would be entitled to it under nonbankruptcy

That said, much may depend on the wording of the agreement. Consider the following brief case excerpt and problem.

> If there is an attorney's fees provision in an agreement between the parties, we look to the language of the agreement to determine whether an award of attorney's fees is warranted in a tort action.
>
> * * * Here, the Agreement allowed attorney's fees to the prevailing party in "any action at law or in equity" if it was "to enforce or to interpret" the terms of the Agreement. * * * [T]he Complaint involved a § 523(a)(2)(A) action for fraud. Redwood's theory was that Debtor misrepresented that he was the sole buyer of the Theater when in fact he intended to transfer an interest to Mr. Knopf. Redwood did not allege any breach of the Agreement or seek to enforce any rights under the Agreement. Redwood also did not allege that the Agreement included any term requiring the identification of any prospective assignee of an interest in the Theater. To the contrary, the Agreement specifically permitted an assignment of Debtor's rights in the Theater. Therefore, in finding no fraud by Debtor, the bankruptcy court was not enforcing or interpreting the terms of the Agreement. Accordingly, * * * Debtor was not entitled to attorney's fees under the Agreement even though he was the prevailing party.[88]

Problem 10-13

You are drafting a form loan agreement for Bank to use in all its consumer loans. How should you phrase the attorneys' fees provision to best protect Bank's rights?

The fourth point about litigating nondischargeability is a tactical one. Should a creditor who has the choice of bringing a complaint under § 523(a) or § 727(a) bring both or only one? How should courts deal with such situations? Consider the following problem.

Problem 10-14

Desperate has been in serious financial condition for several months. During this time, Desperate as been "kiting credit": borrowing from new lenders to pay off existing creditors in order to forestall collection efforts. In

---

law).

[88] *In re Davison*, 289 B.R. 716, 724-25 (9th Cir. BAP 2003).

one such transaction, Desperate borrowed $25,000 from Savings & Loan after providing the loan officer with a personal financial statement that overstated assets and understated liabilities. More recently, as it became apparent that the whole scheme would come crashing down, Desperate conveyed a valuable painting that had been in the family for generations to Daughter as a gift. A few days later, Desperate filed for bankruptcy relief.

A   If Savings & Loan has an option, would it be better off challenging the discharge under § 727, the dischargeability of its claim under § 523(a), or both?

B.   If Savings & Loan and Desperate work out a deal under which Savings & Loan will dismiss its § 727 action and, in exchange, Desperate will consent to a judgment that the debt is nondischargeable, how should the court rule? *See In re de Armond*, 240 B.R. 51 (Bankr. C.D. Cal. 1999). *See also* Rule 7041.

C.   DISMISSAL FOR CAUSE

As an alternative or in addition to challenging the discharge or the dischargeability of a debt owed to it, a creditor may seek to have the entire bankruptcy case dismissed for cause. Section 707(a) lists three, nonexclusive examples of cause: (1) unreasonable delay by the debtor that is prejudicial to creditors; (2) nonpayment of the filing fee; and (3) failure to timely file a statement about what the debtor plans to do with property constituting collateral for a debt. Note, these specific examples and the provision generally, apply to all types of debtors, individuals and corporations, and without regard to how their debts arose.

A far more significant basis for dismissal exists in § 707(b), which applies only to individual debtors whose debts are primarily consumer debts.[89] It is an unusually long and cumbersome provision, and understanding it requires some background.

Congress added § 707(b) to the Code in 1984 to counter perceived abuses by debtors. At the time, it authorized the court to dismiss a case if granting relief would be a "substantial abuse" of the Chapter. No one was permitted to file a motion for dismissal under this rule; the issue had to be raised by the court on its own. In 1988,

---

[89] "Consumer debt" is a term defined in § 101(8). It includes the purchase-money mortgage debt on an individual's principal residence. *See, e.g., In re Price*, 280 B.R. 499 (9th Cir. BAP 2002). However, the term excludes not only debts incurred for business reasons, but also unpaid personal income taxes. *See, e.g., In re Wisher*, 222 B.R. 634 (Bankr. D. Colo. 1998); *In re Brashers*, 216 B.R. 59 (Bankr. N.D. Okla. 1998). *See also In re Westberry*, 215 F.3d 589 (6th Cir. 2000) (tax debts are not consumer debts for purpose of determining scope of the co-debtor stay in Chapter 13).

Congress loosened this restriction a bit by allowing the U.S. Trustee to suggest that a case be dismissed.

Because "substantial abuse" was undefined, courts struggled to supply it with meaning. Most adopted a "totality of the circumstances" approach.[90] As one circuit court described it:

> In determining whether to apply § 707(b) to an individual debtor, . . . a court should ascertain from the totality of the circumstances whether he is merely seeking an advantage over his creditors, or is "honest," in the sense that his relationship with his creditors has been marked by essentially honorable and undeceptive dealings, and whether he is "needy" in the sense that his financial predicament warrants the discharge of his debts in exchange for liquidation of his assets. Substantial abuse can be predicated upon either lack of honesty or want of need. . . .
>
> Among the factors to be considered in deciding whether a debtor is needy is his ability to repay his debts out of future earnings. That factor alone may be sufficient to warrant dismissal. For example, a court would not be justified in concluding that a debtor is needy and worthy of discharge, where his disposable income permits liquidation of his consumer debts with relative ease. Other factors relevant to need include whether the debtor enjoys a stable source of future income, whether he is eligible for adjustments of his debts through Chapter 13 of the Bankruptcy Code, whether there are state remedies with the potential to ease his financial predicament, the degree of relief obtainable through private negotiations, and whether his expenses can be reduced significantly without depriving him of adequate food, clothing, shelter and other necessities.[91]

There was some disagreement about whether ability to pay creditors out of future disposable income could, by itself, constitute a sufficient basis for finding substantial abuse,[92] but most said that it could be and all treated ability to pay creditors as the most important factor. Such ability to pay need not mean that the creditors would or could be paid in full; any meaningful distribution to creditors was apparently enough to prompt

---

[90] *See, e.g., In re Stewart*, 175 F.3d 796 (10th Cir. 1999); *In re Lamanna*, 153 F.3d 1 (1st Cir. 1998); *In re Green*, 934 F.2d 568 (4th Cir. 1991); *In re Krohn*, 886 F.2d 123 (6th Cir. 1989); *In re Walton*, 866 F.2d 981 (8th Cir. 1989); *In re Kelly*, 841 F.2d 908 (9th Cir. 1988).

[91] *Krohn*, 886 F.2d at 126-27.

[92] *Compare Green*, 934 F.2d at 572 (stating that ability to pay is insufficient, without more, for "substantial abuse" finding), *with Lamanna*, 153 F.3d at 5; *Krohn*, 886 F.2d at 126; *Walton*, 866 F.2d at 985; *In re Kelly*, 841 F.2d at 914-15 (all indicating that it could).

courts to dismiss a Chapter 7 petition.[93] In connection with this, bankruptcy courts were apparently free to consider post-petition events, such as whether the debtor has obtained new or more lucrative employment.[94]

In adjudicating these issue, several courts measured substantiality by focusing more on the amount – rather than the percentage – of repayment, because otherwise the grocery clerk who could pay 70% of a low debt load with only $300/month would be forced out of Chapter 7 while a surgeon who could repay 10% of a $1.6 million debt might not.[95] They were also not hesitant to scrutinize the debtor's financial situation in some detail and find substantial abuse if the debtor failed to minimize expenses,[96] unreasonably failed to earn income,[97] or possessed but failed to liquidate extensive exempt property.[98]

Other factors were also relevant to whether the debtor was substantially abusing the bankruptcy system so as to warrant dismissal of the case. For example, a debtor who misrepresented his or her financial condition,[99] "kited" credit prior to the filing,[100] or used nonexempt assets to acquire luxuries shortly before filing for Chapter 7 bankruptcy protection,[101] would be substantially abusing the bankruptcy process.

Despite all this, Congress believed that debtors were still abusing the bankruptcy process and in 2005 it significantly altered § 707(b). Read it. In doing so, note that its paragraphs are not logically arranged. Paragraph (1) contains the revised general rule

---

[93]   *See, e.g., In re Smith*, 269 B.R. 686 (Bankr. W.D. Mo. 2001) (ability to pay 27% made Chapter 7 filing a substantial abuse); *In re Scobee*, 269 B.R. 678 (Bankr. W.D. Mo. 2001) (ability to pay 26% made Chapter 7 filing a substantial abuse).

[94]   *See In re Cortez*, 457 F.3d 448 (5th Cir. 2006).

[95]   *E.g., In re Aiello*, 284 B.R. 756, 761 (Bankr. E.D.N.Y. 2002); *In re Falke*, 284 B.R. 133, 139-40 (Bankr. D. Or. 2002).

[96]   *See, e.g., In re Kornfield*, 164 F.3d 778 (2d Cir. 1999) ($53,640/year in education expenses for four children); *In re Burger*, 280 B.R. 444 (Bankr. S.D. Ind. 2002) (debtors allocated $1,147/month for vacation, recreation, internet access, and children's parochial schooling).

[97]   *See In re Stewart*, 175 F.3d 796, 809-10 (10th Cir. 1999) (debtor chose to forego more than $50,000 in annual earning capacity by entering a fellowship program); *In re Kelly*, 217 B.R. 273 (Bankr. D. Neb. 1997) (debtor chose to work part time while completing graduate school).

[98]   *E.g., In re Kornfield,* 164 F.3d 778 (2d Cir. 1999).

[99]   *See, e.g., In re Bryant*, 47 B.R. 21 (Bankr. W.D.N.C. 1984).

[100]   *See In re Wilson*, 125 B.R. 742, 745-46 (W.D. Mich. 1990) (debtor made minimal payments on credit cards with advances from other credit cards).

[101]   *See, e.g., In re Lenartz*, 263 B.R. 331 (Bankr. D. Idaho 2001) (debtors spent a $12,000 tax refund to acquire unnecessary, exempt goods within the month prior to bankruptcy).

and paragraph (3) expounds on it. Paragraph (2) contains the new means test, with paragraph (7) providing an income-based limitation on the means test. Paragraph (6) contains a similar income-based limitation on who may raise the issue of abuse based on something other than the means test. Paragraphs (4) and (5) contain rules about who can be made to pay for the cost of litigating a § 707(b) motion. While nothing can simplify the subsection, it is probably best to tackle its paragraphs in the order in which they were just mentioned.

There are four changes to note with respect to the general rule. First, the word "substantial" has been removed. Now the case is to be dismissed if granting relief would be an "abuse." It is not clear what effect this change will have. Second, the provision used to have a "presumption in favor of granting the relief requested by the debtor." That language too has been removed. Third, the restriction on who may raise the issue has been largely removed, although if the debtor's income falls below a certain threshold then only the judge or U.S. Trustee may raise it. *See* § 707(b)(6). Fourth, courts are instructed to consider the totality of the circumstances and whether the debtor filed the petition in good faith. § 707(b)(3). This latter point resolves a split among the circuits.[102]

Most of the remaining changes to § 707(b) deal with the new means test for Chapter 7 relief for individuals whose obligations are primarily consumer debts and whose income exceeds the state median. This means test creates a presumption of abuse if the debtor's projected postpetition monthly income, reduced by certain specified expenses, exceeds a specified level. The presumption is difficult to rebut. *See* § 707(b)(2)(B).

The basic structure of the means test is laid out in § 707(b)(2)(A)(i). It provides a rather complicated mathematical formula which is intended to ascertain whether the debtor will have more than a minimum amount of disposable income over the next five years. More specifically – and ramp up your tolerance for complexity here – the formula asks if :

$$(CMI - ME - (1/60 \times SO - 1/60 \times SP) \times 60) \geq \text{lesser of (greater of 25\% UC or \$6000) or \$10,000}$$

For this purpose:

CMI equals the debtor's Current Monthly Income, a term defined in § 101(10A) to mean, roughly, the debtor's average gross monthly income for the last six months.

---

[102] *Compare In re Padilla*, 222 F.3d 1184 (9th Cir. 2000) (good faith is not relevant to substantial abuse) *with In re Tamecki*, 229 F.3d 205 (3d Cir. 2000); *In re Zick*, 931 F.2d 1124 (6th Cir. 1991) (both ruling that good faith is relevant).

ME equals the debtor's Monthly Expenses pursuant to certain IRS National and Local Standards. The National Standards are intended to cover such things as food, clothing, housing supplies, and miscellaneous expenses. They vary with income and family size, ranging from a low of $367/month to a high of $1,564/month for cases filed after February 13, 2006. The Local Standards are intended to cover more variable costs, such as utility services and rent, and transportation. Monthly Expenses also include Other Necessary Expenses, a term which, judging by the official form debtors are to use in computing the means test, includes income taxes, social security taxes, mandatory retirement fund contributions, life insurance expenses, and health care costs (beyond the cost of insurance premiums). In addition to all this, the debtor's Monthly Expenses include:

(1) Reasonable expenses for health insurance;
(2) Expenses to protect against family violence;
(3) Up to 5% more for food and clothing;
(4) Costs of caring for elderly, infirm or disabled household or family member;
(5) The administrative expenses that would arise in a Chapter 13 case (if the debtor would be eligible);
(6) Actual expenses, up to $1,500/minor child to attend school; and
(7) Actual home energy costs, in excess of the IRS allowance, if reasonable;

SO equals the total payments due on the debtor's Secured Obligations for the next 60 months.

SP equals the total Support Payments the debtor is obligated to make for the next 60 months.

UC equals the amount of the Unsecured Claims against the debtor.

Okay, now that you have all that, try the following problem, using the charts in the appendix.

Problem 10-15

Dennis and Deirdre were married six years ago, shortly after they completed college. They currently live in Spokane, Washington, where Dennis is employed as an architect. Deirdre was employed as a claims specialist with an insurance company until the birth of their daughter Evangeline three years ago. Since then, she has elected to stay home and care for the baby, in part because Evangeline has had a series of minor but recurring illnesses. With the loss of Deirdre's income, the couple has had a difficult time making ends meet.

They left school with a combined $80,000 in student loan debt, which they elected to pay over 15 years at $630 per month. They pay monthly rent of $1,250 for a two-bedroom apartment. They each have a car. Dennis purchased his car three years ago. It is currently worth about $8,000 and he pays $340/month on what was originally a four-year, $15,000 loan. Two years ago Deirdre entered into a four-year lease of a new car. The lease calls for $225 in monthly payments.

Dennis earns $6,000 per month. From that, the following deductions are taken:

Income Taxes	$520
Social Security	$430
401k Plan Contribution	$300
Health Insurance	$200
	$1,450

With their rent, car payments, student loans, medical co-pays, not to mention food, clothing, utilities, gasoline, insurance, and other living expenses, they find themselves falling further behind each month. To cover their expenses they have done what so many do: taken cash advances on their various credit cards. As a result, they have built up a substantial credit card debt and can no longer make even the minimum monthly payments. They currently owe the following:

Student Loans	$65,000
Car Loan	$3,800
Credit Cards	$16,200
	$85,000

A. Are Dennis and Deirdre eligible for Chapter 7 bankruptcy relief? *See* Selected Means Test Data, which is one of the appendices to this book.

B. How, if at all, would the result be different if Dennis earned $5,000 per month, from which the deductions listed below were taken? *See* § 707(b)(7).

Income Taxes	$375
Social Security	$360
401k Plan Contribution	$250
Health Insurance	$200
	$1,185

C. How, if at all, would the result be different if Dennis earned $4,900 per month, from which the deductions listed below were taken? *See* § 707(b)(7).

Income Taxes	$365
Social Security	$350
401k Plan Contribution	$245
Health Insurance	$200
	$1,160

D. How, if at all, would the results in Part A be different if the debtors indicated on their Statement of Intention that they planned to surrender Deirdre's car to the lessor? What if they had in fact surrendered the car prior to the trustee's motion to dismiss the case? *See In re Singletary*, 354 B.R. 455 (Bankr. S.D. Tex. 2006).

E. In reviewing the formula in § 707(b)(2), what might debtors do to satisfy the means test? In other words, what, if any, prepetition transactions could debtors enter into to make it more likely they will satisfy the means test?

D. EFFECT OF THE DISCHARGE

Once a debt is discharged, the creditor is permanently enjoined from trying to collect it. § 524(a)(2). A creditor who, with knowledge of this injunction, willfully violates it, will be in civil contempt and sanctioned accordingly.[103] However, most courts have held that there is no private right of action for violations. In other words, the debtor has no claim for damages arising from violations of the discharge injunction.[104]

Despite the injunction on creditor efforts to collect a discharged debt, nothing stops the debtor from voluntarily paying such an obligation. *See* § 524(f). This raises some interesting problems. For example, what if a creditor refuses to do further business with the debtor unless the discharged debt is paid? Does the communication of such a policy

---

[103] *See, e.g., In re Waswick*, 212 B.R. 350 (Bankr. D.N.D. 1997).

[104] *See, e.g., Walls v. Wells Fargo Bank*, 276 F.3d 502 (9th Cir. 2002); *Cox v. Zale Delaware, Inc.*, 239 F.3d 910 (7th Cir. 2001); *Pertuso v. Ford Motor Credit Co.*, 233 F.3d 417 (6th Cir. 2000) (all ruling that no private cause of action exists for violations of the discharge injunction). *But cf. Bessette v. AVCO Financial Services, Inc.*, 230 F.3d 439 (1st Cir. 2000), *cert. denied*, 532 U.S. 1048 (2001) (agreeing that there is no private right of action but noting that the bankruptcy court may use § 105 to enforce the discharge injunction by awarding damages for its violation).

constitute an effort to collect the debt and thus violate § 524(a)(2)? Consider the following case.

IN RE VOGT
257 B.R. 65 (Bankr. D. Colo. 2000)

Matheson, Bankruptcy Judge.

The Plaintiffs filed this adversary proceedings alleging that the Defendant extracted payment of a debt that had been discharged in the Plaintiffs' earlier bankruptcy proceeding by promising to withdraw or amend a credit report that showed the debt to still be owing. * * *

As is often the case in consumer bankruptcy proceedings, matters that appear on their face to be simple and straightforward turn out to be inordinately complex. Such is the case with the instant proceeding.

* * *

As to the * * * allegations that the acts of the Defendant violated the injunctive provisions of section 524(a)(2) of the Code, the initial question is whether any remedy is available for a violation of those provisions. None is explicitly provided for by the statute.

* * * This factor might not be particularly troublesome, but for the fact that the parallel stay provision of section 362 does contain an explicit remedy for a violation of the 362(a) stay. But, that remedy is limited to cases involving an "individual" debtor who is injured by a willful violation of the stay. [§ 362(k)(1).] Because of this limiting factor, some courts have held that there is no remedy available for a corporate debtor that has suffered injury because of a stay violation. *In re Chateaugay Corp.*, 920 F.2d 183 (2d Cir. 1990). If that case, and others like it, are correct, then it is difficult to extrapolate a remedy for a violation of the statutory stay under section 524.

Notwithstanding the limiting language of section [362(k)(1)], other courts have fashioned an implied remedy under section 105 of the Code. *In re Skinner,* 917 F.2d 444 (10th Cir. 1990); *In re Atlantic Business & Community Corp.,* 901 F.2d 325 (3d Cir. 1990). This Court believes that this is clearly the better view and that the same reasoning applies when section 524(a) has been violated. The Court adopts the reasoning of the court in *Molloy v. Primus Automotive Financial Services,* 247 B.R. 804, 816-20 (C.D. Cal. 2000), finding that section 524 carries with it an "implied private right of action." The question, then, is whether the Plaintiffs have established a claim that may give rise to a remedy.

The allegations of the complaint, supplemented by counsel's representations at the hearing, show that at the time the Plaintiffs filed bankruptcy they had a debt outstanding to Dallas Leasing, aka Illinois Capitol Group ("Dallas"). Dallas was timely scheduled as a creditor and given notice of the bankruptcy proceeding. At some point, believed to be after the filing of the bankruptcy, Dallas assigned its claim to the Defendant.

In the spring of 1999, some five years after filing bankruptcy, the Plaintiffs applied for a home mortgage loan. They were then informed that the Defendant still asserted that the Dallas debt was due and owing and that the same had been assigned to the Defendant for collection. The existence of this outstanding debt disqualified the Plaintiffs from receiving the loan they sought.

The Plaintiffs contacted the Defendant "in an effort to clarify the error" and to explain that the debt had been discharged in the earlier bankruptcy. At that point the Defendant agreed to correct "the erroneous information" only if the Plaintiffs paid the debt in the amount of $2,582. The Plaintiffs paid this amount because they feared they would lose their home loan if they did not do so.

The Plaintiffs ultimately got a home loan. However, they allege "on information and belief" that the Defendant had failed to modify the "negative" credit information even after having been paid the $2,582. The result was that Plaintiffs incurred additional closing costs and fees and had to pay a higher interest rate to obtain their loan.

The Court must initially observe that the Plaintiffs' complaint evidences some misconceptions about the effect of an order of discharge. Section 727 of the Code specifies that a discharge "discharges the debtor from all debts that arose before the date of the order for relief under this chapter, and any liability on a claim that is determined under section 502." Section 524(a), then, specifies the effect on the creditors of the discharge. In particular, section 524(a)(2) provides that a discharge:

> Operates as an injunction against the commencement or continuation of an action, the employment of process, or an act, to collect, recover or offset any such debt as a personal liability of the debtor.

It is apparent from the complaint in this case that the Plaintiffs believe that the effect of the order of discharge is to wipe away the debt. But that clearly is not the case. For example, pursuant to section 524(a)(3), it is clear that a creditor that holds security for the discharged debt can still foreclose on the collateral to collect that debt. And, the debtor's discharge does not affect the ability of a creditor to seek repayment of the debt from a third party surety or guarantor. § 524(e). Thus, the discharge does not wipe away the debt. It only serves to eliminate the debtor's personal responsibility to pay the debt.

The distinction is important, because the initial suggestion here is that the Defendant was somehow in error, or, perhaps, in violation of some provision of the Bankruptcy Code, when it continued to report that, in its records, the Dallas debt was still due and owing, notwithstanding the order of discharge in the Plaintiffs' bankruptcy case. But the Court cannot fault the Defendant for taking this position. At least, it cannot be said that the Defendant's position in this regard, standing alone, was in any way "an act" to effect collection of the debt. Nor can the Defendant be faulted, under section 524, for refusing to correct this report. If there is a violation of section 524(a)(2), that violation must be found in the alleged position taken by the Defendant that the information would be corrected only if the Plaintiffs paid the debt.

There are many cases that consider what constitutes "an act" to force collection of a debt. The efforts of the courts to parse this phrase require the wisdom of Solomon to interpret, or at least the interpretive skill of a Florida ballot counter. It is largely a matter of the court knowing it when it smells it. Some examples may be instructive.

In *In re Olson,* 38 B.R. 515 (Bankr. N.D. Iowa 1984), a doctor's office sent a letter to a debtor. It advised the debtor that, in view of the bankruptcy, the doctor could provide no further medical services unless "you wish to pay your account voluntarily." The doctor was found to have violated section 524(a)(2).

Olson leaves many questions. For example, what would have been the result had the doctor merely written and said "no more medical services will be provided," in response to which the debtor, sorely in need of the doctor's services, then went to the doctor and tendered payment? Clearly, no violation of section 524 would have occurred. Would the result change if, after receiving the letter, the debtor called the doctor to inquire what might be done to enable the debtor to continue to be treated, and the doctor responded, "pay your bill"? In reality, the doctor's actions are equally coercive in each instance. It is hard to see the logic of the court's position.

In *In re Esposito,* 119 B.R. 305 (Bankr. M.D. Fla. 1990), the creditor, much like the doctor in *Olson,* advised the debtor that their previous business relationship could be continued postdischarge, and the creditor would ship new merchandise to the debtor, provided the debtor paid $8,000 on the discharged debt. The debtor paid the money but, despite repeated promises and misrepresentations, no merchandise was ever delivered. The court there found that the action of the creditor was "nothing more than a subterfuge and an underhanded act to collect" and violated section 524.

Esposito poses the same kinds of questions as did *Olson.* The *Esposito* court may well be correct that the creditor engaged in an underhanded subterfuge, and should perhaps be held liable for breach of an agreement to send new merchandise (which gave the court the necessary aroma to discern a violation of section 524). But, what would have been the result had the creditor performed his promise and shipped new merchandise?

In *Van Meter v. American State Bank,* 89 B.R. 32 (W.D. Ark. 1988), a bank required a customer to pay an earlier loan that had been discharged in bankruptcy before the bank would extend new credit to the debtors. The court there found that the loan repayment was not "voluntary" and that the creditor's action violated 524(a)(2).

It is interesting that none of the cases consider the provisions of section 525 of the Code. That section deals with discriminatory acts by a governmental unit. It specifies that a governmental unit may not discriminate against a debtor who has not paid a dischargeable debt by refusing to renew a franchise, charter or permit, or by conditioning such a renewal on payment. Thus, pursuant to 525(a), the government could not, for example, condition the grant of a new agricultural loan on a debtor's repayment of a discharged debt. Similarly, section 525 prohibits a student loan lender from denying new credit to a debtor, or conditioning the extension of new credit on the repayment of a discharged debt.

The provisions of section 525 become meaningless if the courts in the cases discussed above are correct. If section 524(a)(2) bars a lender from conditioning the making of a new student loan on the repayment of a discharged loan, as the court concludes in *Van Meter,* then it adds nothing for Congress to add section 525 to the Code. *See, Brown v. Pennsylvania State Employees Credit Union,* 851 F.2d 81 (3d Cir. 1988) (recogniz[ing] that the Code must be read to give effect to both 524 and 525, and [ruling] that it was not a violation of 524 for a credit union to send a letter to a debtor saying, in effect, "if you pay your debt we will extend continued services").

In all of these cases the courts have split hairs into microscopic fragments. Clearly, section 524(a)(2) is implicated if the creditor, after the debtor's discharge, writes a letter to the debtor saying: "Your discharge be damned – pay your debt!" This is exactly the kind of hectoring, dunning demand that Congress intended to stop. But what of the following:

1. A creditor writes saying: "I won't provide future services unless you pay."
2. The creditor writes saying: "I would be pleased to do business with you in the future, but only if you pay what is owed."
3. The debtor says: "If I pay you my past debt, will you reinstate my credit line?"
4. The debtor says: "I very much want to do business with you again. Is there anything I can do to reinstate our business relationship?" And the lender replies: "Yes. Pay your account in full."

It is difficult to conclude that, in all of these cases, the creditor has crossed over the line.

In the instant case it is the Debtors who approached the creditor. The creditor was under no obligation under the Bankruptcy Code to change the way it reported the status of the loan. False reporting, if not done to extract payment of the debt, is simply not an act proscribed by the Code. There is absolutely no showing in this case that the Defendant had manufactured a false report in order to extract payment. To the contrary, here, nearly five years had elapsed since the order of discharge had entered and the Defendant had apparently never made an effort to contact the Plaintiffs or to otherwise seek to collect the discharged debt. Under these circumstances, the Court does not consider the demand of the creditor for payment, as a condition to changing its credit report, as "an act" to extract payment.

It appears that the real complaint here is less that the creditor demanded payment, and more with the allegation that the Defendant, having received payment, failed to perform. But that allegation is made "on information and belief." No evidence has been proffered to the Court to show whether the Defendant failed to perform, or whether the credit reporting agencies failed to correct their credit reports.

This case must be contrasted with *Esposito*. There the creditor told the debtor that new merchandise was available and would be released upon payment of the discharged debt. It is not clear from the decision whether the initial contact was made by the debtor or the creditor. After the debtor made the payment he was repeatedly told that merchandise was on its way, and relied on those representations in expending money to start a new business. It is small wonder that the court took exception to the creditor's actions.

This case is simply not the same as any of those discussed. The facts here may present a claim by the Plaintiffs for breach of contract, or perhaps even for fraud, if evidence can be generated to show that the Defendant did indeed take the money and failed to perform. Those are not claims over which this Court has jurisdiction. * * * And, as to the 524 claim set forth in the Second Claim for Relief, the Court concludes that a claim has not been established. Accordingly, the case is dismissed, without prejudice.

Problem 10-16

Dayton recently received a Chapter 7 discharge. One of the obligations discharged was a $5,000 debt to Neighbor, who lives across the street. Neighbor has long believed that credit is a sacred responsibility and that bankruptcy discharges are sought only by the immoral and irreligious. Upon learning of the discharge, Neighbor posts the following sign with large block letters on his front yard: "Beware all who come this way. Dayton is a Deadbeat who has discharged his debts and ripped off his rightful creditors." Has Neighbor violated the discharge injunction? *See In re Andrus*, 189 B.R. 413 (N.D. Ill. 1998). Does he have a defense under the First Amendment? *See In re National Service Corp.*, 742 F.2d 859 (5th Cir. 1984); *In re Crudup*, 287 B.R. 358 (Bankr. E.D.N.C. 2002); *In re Stoneking*, 222 B.R. 650 (Bankr. M.D. Fla. 1998).

Problem 10-17

Before filing for bankruptcy protection, Davis defaulted in paying rent to Landlord on a residential apartment. The trustee, as is typical, did not assume the lease. Thus, the lease was deemed rejected, and the default gave rise to a prepetition claim. No distributions were made to any creditors and Davis never paid the rental arrearages. After the bankruptcy court entered an order granting Davis a discharge, Landlord brought a state-court action to evict Davis. Does that proceeding violate the discharge injunction? Does it matter whether Landlord is also attempting to collect the back rent? *See, e.g., In re Stephens,* 53 Fed. Appx. 392 (8th Cir. 2002); *In re Dabrowski,* 257 B.R. 394 (Bankr. S.D.N.Y. 2001).

E.   TAX IMPLICATIONS OF THE DISCHARGE

In general, a discharge of indebtedness creates taxable income to the debtor. I.R.C. § 61(a)(12). Although this may not intuitively seem correct, it really does makes sense. Consider a borrower who borrows $100 from a friend. This transaction does not have tax consequences. While the borrower now has $100 in cash that the borrower did not have before, the borrower also has an obligation to repay an equal amount. Taking the loan and the obligation to repay it together, there's been no change to the net worth of the borrower (or to the lender). If the lender forgives the debt, however, the borrower's net worth will change. In essence, the borrower would have received cash and have no duty to repay it. That change is treated as gross income.

If this general rule were applied in bankruptcy cases, the debtor who is struggling to overcome crippling financial problems would potentially be burdened with a large tax liability by virtue of the bankruptcy discharge. To avoid this, the Internal Revenue Code excludes from gross income any discharge of indebtedness that occurs in a case under Title 11. I.R.C. § 108(a)(1)(A). It also excludes from gross income a discharge of indebtedness that occurs outside of bankruptcy when the debtor/taxpayer is insolvent. I.R.C. § 108(a)(1)(B).

This exclusion is not an unqualified boon for bankruptcy debtors, however. To the extent discharge of indebtedness income is excluded from gross income under this rule, the debtor's "tax attributes" are reduced. I.R.C. § 108(b). This means that if the debtor has a net operating loss, that loss – which can be used to offset future income for tax purposes – will be reduced. If the debtor has no net operating loss, the debtor's basis in property can be reduced, creating a larger taxable gain if it is ever sold. *See* I.R.C. § 108(b)(2).

F.   BANKRUPTCY CRIMES

A variety of conduct that might lead to a denial of discharge under § 727 is also criminal. For example, a debtor who conceals assets or knowingly files false schedules can be fined and imprisoned for up to five years. 18 U.S.C. § 152.[105] A creditor who files a fraudulent claim or a trustee who embezzles from the estate is also guilty of a crime and is subject to the same penalty. 18 U.S.C. §§ 152 & 153.

In 1994, Congress created a new bankruptcy crime entitled "bankruptcy fraud." It covers any person who, as part of a scheme to defraud, files a bankruptcy petition or files a document in a bankruptcy proceeding. 18 U.S.C. § 157. This crime too is punishable by up to five years in prison.

The definition of bankruptcy fraud is extremely broad. It appears to cover the "credit card spree" case, in which a debtor enjoys a luxurious vacation, made possible by charging as much as possible on credit cards, with the intention of filing bankruptcy upon returning home. It remains to be seen whether this provision will be interpreted so expansively and invoked as frequently as this type of abuse occurs. At present, bankruptcy lawyers should advise clients to be very cautious, particularly during that period between the time they decide to file for bankruptcy and the time they actually do.

---

[105] An attorney who knowingly assists in such activity can similarly be punished. _See United States v. Webster_, 125 F.3d 1024 (7th Cir. 1997). _See also_ STEPHANIE WICKOUSKI, BANKRUPTCY CRIMES (2000).

PART IV

REORGANIZATION

CHAPTER ELEVEN
INDIVIDUAL DEBT ADJUSTMENT IN CHAPTER 13

A. IN GENERAL

In Chapter 7 liquidations, the debtor's assets and liabilities are essentially frozen as of the moment of the bankruptcy filing. The case then generally proceeds as follows. The debtor's assets – to the extent not exempt – go into the bankruptcy estate. The debtor keeps the exempt assets while the trustee liquidates the estate's assets and distributes the proceeds to prepetition creditors. The debtor is then relieved of the duty to pay most prepetition debts and all the debtor's subsequent earnings are free from the reach of prepetition creditors. Property subject to a valid security interest is either relinquished to the creditor or a mutually acceptable payment schedule is worked out.

There are several drawbacks to this procedure. The most notable from the debtor's standpoint is that, if the debtor has equity in a home in excess of the exemption amount, the debtor will likely lose the home. The main problem from the creditors' standpoint is that many of them receive little or no payment of their claims, even from debtors with the potential to earn substantial income.

Chapter 13 is intended to address these drawbacks. It focuses largely on future income rather than on accumulated assets. In essence, the debtor agrees to turn over a portion of future income to pay prepetition claims. In exchange, the debtor will keep most assets, regardless of whether their value exceeds any exemption amount to which the debtor is entitled. In short, the debtor keeps assets and pays creditors out of future income. Payments are actually made periodically to a trustee, who applies them first to administrative expenses and then distributes the remainder to creditors pursuant to a court-approved plan. When the debtor has fully complied with the plan – that is, when the debtor has made all required payments – the debtor's prepetition obligations are discharged to the extent they remain unpaid.

Thus, many debtors facing bankruptcy must make a fundamental choice: to give up nonexempt assets and seek an immediate discharge under Chapter 7 or to try paying creditors over time under Chapter 13. Several rules and incentives in the Bankruptcy Code have great impact on this choice. Among them are:

Rules & Incentives Against Chapter 13

1. Only individual debtors (*i.e.*, human beings) with a regular source of income and fairly modest levels of debt are eligible for Chapter 13. § 109(e).

2. The Chapter 13 plan must pay creditors at least what they would get in Chapter 7, § 1325(a)(4), and must always do so within five years and often within three, § 1322(d).

3. The plan must provide for full payment of all priority claims, unless the holder agrees to something less. § 1322(a)(2). This can be particularly problematic (*i.e.* make it impossible to draft a confirmable plan) if the debtor owes a large amount for priority taxes, support arrearages, or for a personal injury resulting from drunk driving.

4. If all creditors are not to be paid in full, the debtor must for at least three years, and possibly for as long as five, turn over all "disposable income" (*i.e.*, income over reasonable and necessary living expenses) to the trustee for payment to creditors. § 1325(b).

5. The administrative expenses generated by a Chapter 13 case – comprised largely of the trustee's fees – must be paid first, *see* § 1322(a)(2), and can substantially increase the cost of completing a Chapter 13 plan.

Rules & Incentives Against Chapter 7

1. Debtors with high income may fail the means test, thus causing any Chapter 7 petition to be dismissed as an abuse of the bankruptcy process. § 707(b).

2. Debtors who received a bankruptcy discharge in the last several years and thus are ineligible for a Chapter 7 discharge, § 727(a)(9), may be able to get a new discharge in Chapter 13. § 1328(f).

3. Debtors receive a sightly broader discharge in Chapter 13 than in Chapter 7 (in other words, some debts that are nondischargeable in Chapter 7 can be discharged in Chapter 13). § 1328(a).

4. Because civil fines are dischargeable, a Chapter 13 debtor whose driver's license has been suspended *solely* for failure to pay traffic tickets is entitled to have the license restored. § 525(a).

5. Debtors in Chapter 13 can cure defaults on secured obligations, "de-accelerate" debts, and strip down some secured claims (except home mortgages and purchase-money loans). § 1322(b)(2), (b)(5) & (c).

The trouble with Chapter 13 is that it does not address the sources of the debtor's financial problems. Put another way, both Chapters 7 and 13 treat the debtor's accumulated debt *as* the problem. This works fairly well in Chapter 7 because it freezes everything as of the petition date and does not try to deal directly with the future. Chapter 13, on the other hand, is a lengthy process which seeks to "rehabilitate" the debtor by putting the debtor on a tight budget that provides for regular payment to creditors.[1] However, Chapter 13 does little to deal with or even identify whatever created the debtor's financial distress. A new requirement, added in 2005, makes a Chapter 13 discharge conditional on the debtor's completion of a course on personal financial management. § 1328(g).[2] This may help debtors whose problems are in fact attributable to poor financial management but is unlikely to assist those whose circumstances arose from a job loss, divorce, medical condition, or other event beyond their control. Moreover, by providing for all disposable income to be paid to creditors for the next several years, Chapter 13 presumes that the causes of the debtor's financial distress will not continue or recur. As a result, most Chapter 13 debtors fail to make all the scheduled payments and never get a discharge. Indeed, a recent study of all Chapter 13 cases closed within a six-month period in one federal district indicated that in only 32.4% did the debtor complete the plan and receive a discharge.[3] Consider the following brief excerpt from the report of the National Bankruptcy Review Commission.

> While the concept of a repayment plan is valuable . . . [t]he high non-completion rate of Chapter 13 plans is cause for substantial concern. For more than a decade, two-thirds of all Chapter 13 plans have failed before the debtor completes payments, and sometimes before unsecured creditors have received anything at all. While some of the debtors convert to Chapter 7 when plan payments become infeasible, about half of all debtors who initially file for Chapter 13 are dismissed with no resolution of their financial problems and no discharge.
>
> Noncompletion may have a number of causes. Some commentators suggest that debtors frequently encounter repeated financial difficulties or face

---

[1]   Note, however, that because of differing priorities and other reasons, the plan may provide for paying some creditors before others.

[2]   This is to be distinguished from and is apparently more significant than the credit counseling that is an eligibility requirement for bankruptcy relief. *See* § 109(h).

[3]   *See* Ed Flynn, *A Small New Window on Outcomes in Chapter 13*, 19 AM. BANKR. INST. J. 22 (March 2000) (summarizing Scott F. Norberg, *Consumer Bankruptcy's New Clothes: An Empirical Study of Discharge and Debt Collection in Chapter 13*, 7 ABI L. REV. 415 (1999)). In 49.3%, the case was dismissed after confirmation of a plan; the remaining 18.3% were dismissed before a plan was confirmed.

Interestingly, there was no statistically significant relationship between completion of the plan and debtor income, percentage payback, or plan duration. However, debtors with higher secured debt were more likely to complete their plan, as were debtors who had filed an earlier Chapter 13 petition.

new crises, such as the loss of a job or a health emergency. Bankruptcy does not insulate against subsequent disaster. The same kinds of spotty employment or medical problems that caused debtors' initial financial problems may reemerge, or new problems might appear. Subsequent difficulties, coupled with the higher "catch-up" payments on secured debt, can foil well-intentioned repayment efforts. Others suggest that debtors propose unrealistic plans that are doomed from the inception, sometimes due in part to inadequate advice. In an effort to meet the requirements of the Bankruptcy Code in the treatment of certain creditors or to meet the informal payment requirements of some judges or trustees, debtors may commit to payment plans that would consume or exceed every dollar of discretionary income, and make optimistic assumptions about their income, expected over-time pay, and so on, but do not allow for even minimal unforeseen expenses. Some simply cannot sustain such payments over time. Another theory holds that some debtors file for Chapter 13 never intending to complete their payments; they may cure a default on a secured debt on a home or a car, then leave bankruptcy when their secured debt payments are current. A related, but more troubling theory suggests that some number of Chapter 13 debtors have filed only to get an automatic stay to stop a foreclosure or eviction. When they are unable to bring the underlying obligation current, they dismiss with an intent to buy another automatic stay by filing again.

Whatever the causes for the high rate of noncompletion, several consequences are troubling. First, the many dismissals serve as a reminder that under the current system, choosing Chapter 13 over Chapter 7 does not guarantee meaningful repayment to unsecured creditors. For example, in the many jurisdictions that permit the deferral of unsecured debt payment until the end of the plan, unsecured creditors may receive a negligible collective payout. For debtors who file only to avoid foreclosure or eviction, payouts range from nominal to non-existent.

In addition, for the debtors who filed for legitimate purposes but who are too poor or too disaster-prone to complete their plans, filing and dismissing add to their financial burdens. When noncompletion leads to dismissal rather than discharge, as it so often does, debtors exit the system having paid a substantial filing fee and attorneys' fees but have not discharged any debt. Because interest continues to accrue and compound on nondischarged debt, the debtor may have an even higher debt load after making a determined – but ultimately unsuccessful – effort to pay off debts.[4]

---

[4]   National Bankruptcy Review Commission, *Bankruptcy: The Next Twenty Years* 233-35 (October 20, 1997).

1. Eligibility

The requirements for eligibility are set forth in § 109(e). The first limitation is that the debtor must be an "individual with regular income." This means that the debtor must be a human being. Partnerships and corporations are not eligible and must seek relief under either Chapter 7 or 11. It also means that the debtor must have income that is "sufficiently stable and regular to enable such individual to make payments under a plan under chapter 13." § 101(30). The source of the income is not material. Debtors who make a wage, earn a salary, or are self-employed are eligible. Even unemployed or retired individuals are eligible so long as they receive regular income, which might be from investments, social security, private pensions, or even a welfare program. Spouses of debtors with regular income are eligible for Chapter 13 even though they have no income.

The second major limitation is that the debtor must have unsecured debts of less than $336,900 and secured debts of less than $1,010,650.[5] Debts counting toward these limits must be noncontingent and liquidated, but they may be disputed.[6] The amounts were chosen to make Chapter 13 available to most consumer debtors and many small business debtors, while leaving Chapter 11 to those cases involving greater debt.[7] The value of the debtor's assets, in contrast, is never relevant.

Problem 11-1

For each of the following claims, determine how, if at all, it affects the debtor's eligibility for Chapter 13 relief under § 109(e).

A. Devalued's family residence secures a $600,000 debt to Bank. Because a recent hurricane has severely damaged much of the local community, real estate values have plunged and the residence is now worth only $250,000. *See In re Scovis*, 249 F.3d 975 (9th Cir. 2001); *In re Balbus*, 933 F.2d 246 (4th Cir. 1991); *Miller v. United States*, 907 F.2d 80 (8th Cir. 1990).

---

[5]   These amounts are adjusted every three years. § 104. To the extent a lien is obviously avoidable, the claim associated with it is apparently to be regarded as an unsecured claim for eligibility purposes. *In re Scovis*, 249 F.3d 975 (9th Cir. 2001); *In re Hanson*, 282 B.R. 240 (Bankr. D. Colo. 2002).

[6]   *In re Claypool*, 142 B.R. 753 (Bankr. E.D. Va. 1990).

[7]   Note that in community property states, community obligations for which the debtor is not individually liable but which may be enforced against community property are to be counted toward the debt limits. *See In re Monroe*, 282 B.R. 219 (Bankr. D. Ariz. 2002).

B.   Dolly owes Lender $100,000. The debt is secured by some real property worth $100,000, which Dolly transferred by quitclaim deed to her daughter on the eve of bankruptcy. *See In re Valenti*, 310 B.R. 138 (9th Cir. BAP 2004).

C.   Dell has leased a new Mercedes for four years from Car Dealer. Dell is current on the lease payments. Postpetition monthly payments will total $30,000. *See In re Smith*, 325 B.R. 498 (Bankr. D.N.H. 2005).

D.   Dean owes $100,000 secured by property worth $120,000. Dean has a one-half interest in the collateral. *See In re Lower*, 311 B.R. 888 (Bankr. D. Colo. 2004).

E.   Dubois pledged some corporate stock worth $200,000 as security for a loan to Child. Dubois has no personal liability on the loan. *See In re Glance*, 487 F.3d 317 (6th Cir. 2007).

F.   Darren owes $40,000 to Bank for student loans. Darren has $15,000 on deposit at Bank in a checking account. *See* § 506(a).

G.   Delilah hit Pedestrian with her car. Pedestrian has a pending lawsuit against Delilah for $10,000 in medical expenses incurred and $200,000 in pain and suffering. Delilah denies liability and claims the amount sought for pain and suffering is grossly excessive. The case is in the discovery phase. *Cf. In re Mazzeo*, 131 F.3d 295 (2d Cir. 1997); *In re Verdunn*, 89 F.3d 799 (11th Cir. 1996); *In re Knight*, 55 F.3d 231 (7th Cir. 1995).

2.   The Mechanics of Chapter 13

As is true for proceedings under other Chapters, a Chapter 13 debtor must file with the bankruptcy petition or shortly thereafter a variety of schedules giving information about the debtor's employment, income, expenses, debts, and property, as well as estimates of future monthly income and expenses. Rule 1007(c). The debtor must file a plan with the petition or within 15 days thereafter unless an extension is granted. Rule 3015(b). Some districts use a standardized, model plan which the debtor or the debtor's attorney simply fills in. The model Chapter 13 plan for the Eastern District of Washington is in the Appendix at the end of this book.

The debtor must begin making payments to the trustee within 30 days after the plan is filed, even if the plan is not yet confirmed. § 1326(a)(1). Any payment received by the trustee before confirmation is to be held by the trustee until the plan is either confirmed or not confirmed. If the plan is not confirmed, the trustee gives the money back to the debtor; if the plan is confirmed, the trustee will distribute the money pursuant to the plan. § 1326(a)(2).

The Chapter 13 trustee does not have the same duties as a Chapter 7 trustee. A Chapter 13 trustee does not, for example, collect, preserve, or sell property of the estate. § 1302(b)(1). Nonetheless, the Chapter 13 trustee does have important functions, including objecting to improper creditor claims and, when appropriate, objecting to the debtor's discharge. § 1302(b)(1). The trustee's main duties, though, relate to the plan. The trustee is expected to recommend approval or disapproval of the plan, § 1302(b)(2)(B), ensure that the debtor commences making payments within 30 days, § 1302(b)(5), and make payments to creditors under the plan. § 1326(c). If the debtor falls behind in making payments, it is the trustee who monitors the debtor's performance, urges compliance, and if necessary moves to dismiss the case. If the debtor fails to commence payments on time, the court "may" convert the case to Chapter 7 or dismiss it. § 1307(c)(4). Courts have been known to dismiss a case merely because the debtor is late on the first payment.[8]

Within 20 to 50 days after the petition, the U.S. Trustee must call a meeting of creditors pursuant to § 341(a). Rule 2003(a). Proofs of claim are to be filed within 90 days after the first date set for the meeting of creditors. Rule 3002(c). The notice of the confirmation hearing must include either the plan or a summary of it so that creditors can determine whether they wish to object to it at the confirmation hearing. Rule 3015(d). Although the U.S. Trustee or a designee presides at the meeting of creditors, Rule 2003(b), and the court ultimately decides whether to confirm the debtor's plan, the true gatekeeper in the Chapter 13 confirmation process is usually the trustee. The trustee's staff examines the debtor's plan before the creditors' meeting and the trustee uses that meeting to raise with the debtor's counsel any deficiencies in the plan. Further information may be sought from the debtor who must be present at the meeting. § 343. If these problems can be worked out at the meeting, the trustee may place the debtor's case on what amounts to a consent calendar and, unless there are valid creditor objections, confirmation will follow. In some districts confirmation may occur immediately after the creditors' meeting. Unsecured creditors have no right to vote on the plan; the court's decision on confirmation is based solely on whether the plan complies with the Code's requirements. Money may be paid to the trustee directly by the debtor or, pursuant to court order, by the debtor's employer or other source of income. § 1325(c). After confirmation the trustee will disburse the money to creditors under the plan. When, and if, all payments under the plan have been completed, the debtor is discharged. § 1328(a).

---

[8]   *In re McDonald*, 118 F.3d 568 (7th Cir. 1997).

3.   *The Stay*

In all types of bankruptcy proceedings, the debtor's creditors are enjoined from making any effort to collect a prepetition claim from the debtor. *See* § 362(a)(6). While nothing in the language of § 362 purports to alter the scope of the stay in Chapter 13 cases, other provisions of the Code impact the reach of the stay in Chapter 13. Consider the following problem.

Problem 11-2

Dominick, who filed for Chapter 13 relief three weeks ago, owes several thousand dollars in past due, prepetition child support to his ex-wife, Carlotta. He is also failing to pay postpetition support. May Carlotta use the state's support enforcement mechanisms – including garnishment and contempt – to enforce either or both of these obligations? *See* §§ 362(b)(2)(B), 541(a)(6), 1306(a)(2). *See also In re Steenstra*, 280 B.R. 560 (Bankr. D. Mass. 2002).

4.   *The Co-Debtor Stay*

As a general rule, the automatic stay does not protect co-debtors: people other than the debtor who are also liable on one or more of the debtor's obligations. Thus, in most bankruptcy cases, creditors are free to pursue co-debtors while the debtor's bankruptcy case is pending. Such co-debtors are often friends or family members, many of whom may not have fully appreciated the consequences of co-signing or guaranteeing the debtor's obligation. Creditors often use the threat of collecting against co-debtors to coerce debtors into paying or reaffirming the debt. In short, after a debtor defaults and files bankruptcy, the creditor in effect says "pay me or grandma pays." Faced with this pressure, the debtor may capitulate.

To prevent such tactics, and perhaps to entice debtors into Chapter 13, Congress included the co-debtor stay in Chapter 13. § 1301(a). It prevents creditors from attempting to collect a consumer debt from an individual co-debtor during the pendency of the bankruptcy case. Because Chapter 13 plans typically call for payments over several years, the co-debtor gets substantial protection from this rule. More importantly, the Chapter 13 bankruptcy debtor, now relieved of the pressure to protect co-debtors, can deal with the creditor on the same basis as other creditors, and obtain a more complete fresh start.

The co-debtor stay is not absolute. Congress included several significant limitations. First, it covers only individual (*i.e.*, human being) co-debtors. Second, it applies only to consumer debts. These are defined as debts incurred for personal, family, or household purposes. § 101(8). It thus covers the home mortgage loan, but apparently not tax liability.[9] Third, relief from the stay is available if the co-debtor actually received the consideration giving rise to the debt (*i.e.*, if the bankruptcy debtor is really the co-debtor, rather than the other way around). § 1301(c)(1). Fourth, relief from the stay is available to the extent the plan does not provide for full payment to the creditor. § 1301(c)(2). Thus, if the debtor owes $100 and the plan proposes to pay $70, the creditor can get relief to collect the remaining $30, plus any interest, fees, and other charges to which the creditor is otherwise entitled.[10] Similarly, if the plan does not provide for paying postpetition interest, the creditor may get relief from the stay to recover that from the co-debtor.[11] Finally, if the creditor's interests would be "irreparably harmed," such as if the co-debtor's financial situation were deteriorating or the co-debtor was about to flee the jurisdiction, the stay may be lifted. § 1301(c)(3).

B. THE PLAN

1. General Requirements

Three main provisions govern the contents of Chapter 13 plans. The first, § 1322(a), identifies a few, very general requirements. The most notable of these is that priority claimants must be paid in full. The second, § 1322(b), identifies a few additional things a plan *may* do. These too are phrased very generally and, with some exception, permit the debtor to do most anything. For example, the debtor may pay all or any part of a claim. § 1322(b)(6) & (8). To do this, the plan may classify claims into different groups, provided it does not "discriminate unfairly" among classes of claims and provided it treats all claims within a class alike. § 1322(a)(3) & (b)(1). The plan may also modify most secured claims and cure defaults, § 1322(b)(2), (3) & (5).

The third main provision governing plans is § 1325, which provides the rules on confirmation. Although some of its requirements are also fairly general – even vague – others provide a lot more detail. Of particular note are the rules in § 1325(a)(3)–(6) & (b). They require that the plan be proposed in good faith, that each claimant receive the liquidation value of its claim, that secured and priority claimants be paid in full (or agree to some other treatment), and that nonpriority unsecured creditors either be paid in full or that the debtor allocate all disposable income for the "applicable commitment period"

---

[9] *See, e.g., In re Westberry*, 215 F.3d 589 (6th Cir. 2000).

[10] *See* H.R. Rep. 595, 95th Cong., 1st Sess. 122 (1977).

[11] *Southeastern Bank v. Brown*, 266 B.R. 900 (S.D. Ga. 2001).

to the payment of creditors. The applicable commitment period depends on income but is usually either three or five years. § 1325(b)(4).

The materials that follow explore each of these requirements in some detail. In order to see the whole picture, however, it is useful to keep all of them in mind as each is studied individually. Toward this end, the chart on the following page should help compare some of Chapter 13's requirements to the distribution scheme of Chapter 7 (it also depicts the rules applicable in Chapter 11).

Although this chart is relatively simple, it is worth thinking about the implications of the rules it depicts. For example, because a Chapter 13 plan must pay priority claims in full (unless, as is unlikely, the creditor agrees to accept less), the debtor must have sufficient income to pay spousal and child support arrearages and accrued tax liability in order to consummate a Chapter 13 plan and receive a Chapter 13 discharge. The chief benefit to Chapter 13 with respect to such claims is that the claims may be paid over a three- or five-year period, and they may be paid without interest.[12] Thus, for example, a debtor who owed $10,000 in priority income taxes would have to pay that amount over the multi-year life of the plan, even though the present value of such payments would be substantially less than $10,000.[13]

---

[12] Although this is certainly true for taxes and technically true for support, because support claims are nondischargeable in Chapter 13 (whereas tax debts are dischargeable), postpetition interest on support claims, if not paid under the plan, will remain and will not be discharged. *In re Pitt*, 240 B.R. 908 (Bankr. N.D. Cal. 1999). *See also In re Pardee*, 218 B.R. 916 (9th Cir. BAP 1998), *aff'd on other grounds*, 193 F.3d 1083 (9th Cir. 1999).

Of course, even when interest is not required, the plan must pay creditors, in present value terms, what they would get in a Chapter 7 liquidation. § 1325(a)(4). Thus, if – but only if – there would be enough to pay these priority claims in full in a liquidation, then interest is effectively required in Chapter 13.

[13] If paid in equal monthly installments of $27.78, the present value of all payments would be slightly less than $875, using a 9% discount rate. If the payment were made in one lump sum at the end of the three-year plan, the present value would be less than $765, again using a 9% discount rate.

TREATMENT OF CLAIMS AGAINST THE ESTATE

	Distribution in Chapter 7	Chapter 11	Chapter 13
1a	Trustee expenses in administering the estate to pay support claims	*See* 3–7 below	Unless creditor agrees otherwise, must be paid in full (without interest), over life of plan § 1322(a)(2)
1b	Spousal & child support claims		
2	Costs & expenses of preserving the estate	Unless creditor agrees otherwise, must be paid in full on the effective date of the plan § 1129(a)(9)(A)	
	Compensation to professionals: attorneys, accountants, *etc*		
	Reimbursement of certain creditor expenses		
	Compensation for certain creditor services		
3	Certain expenses arising from involuntary filings	Must be paid in full on the effective date of the plan, unless creditor agrees otherwise or class agrees to be paid in full (with interest), over life of plan § 1129(a)(9)(B)	n/a
4	Certain employee wage claims (up to $10,950)		Unlikely to exist; if it does, unless creditor agrees otherwise, must be paid in full (without interest), over life of plan § 1322(a)(2)
5	Certain employee benefit claims (up to $10,950 per employee)		
6	Certain agricultural and aquicultural bailment claims (up to $5,400)		
7	Certain consumer deposits (up to $2,425)		
8	Certain tax claims	Must be paid in full within five years	*See* 1–2 above
9	Claims owed by depositary institutions to maintain capital levels	Classified by and treated under plan, subject to rules on confirmation	n/a
10	Personal injury claims resulting from drunk driving		*See* 1–2 above
11	Timely unsecured claims		Classified by and treated under plan, subject to rules on confirmation
12	Untimely unsecured claims		
13	Prepetition claims for fines & penalties		
14	Interest on the claims listed above	Plan may provide for on nonpriorities	Paid on nondischargeable debts if claims are fully paid
15	To debtor	To the extent the plan provides	Except as otherwise provided

2. *Disposable Income*

In exchange for allowing debtors to keep their property and discharge their debts, Chapter 13 contemplates that a plan will be worked out that will result in some payment to creditors. But as originally enacted, Chapter 13 required merely that unsecured claimants receive as much in Chapter 13 as they would have received in a Chapter 7 liquidation, taking into account the fact that payment in Chapter 13 is on a deferred basis. Since many debtors, even those with good incomes, have no nonexempt assets, this requirement was literally met by a plan that called for paying nothing to unsecured creditors, even though the debtor could afford to pay more. Judicial tolerance for such zero-payment plans was low, and some courts rejected them as not being proposed in good faith under § 1325(a)(3). On the whole, though, judicial reaction was uneven and unpredictable.

Discontent from the creditor community led Congress to add § 1325(b)(1)(B), which requires that the plan either pay creditors in full or allocate all of the debtor's "projected disposable income" to the plan for the applicable commitment period. "Disposable income" is defined primarily to mean income which is not reasonably necessary to be expended for the maintenance or support of the debtor or a dependent of the debtor. § 1325(b)(2)(A).

This requirement has proven very difficult to apply. On the income side, it requires courts to prognosticate about what the debtor's income will be. Predicting the overall state of the economy for a three- or five-year period is notoriously difficult; predicting the specific financial circumstances of an individual debtor is virtually impossible. As a result, courts tend to deal with income projections in a rough-and-ready manner, relying on the power to modify plans when conditions change. § 1329. One court admitted that "[p]rojected disposable income typically is calculated by multiplying a debtor's monthly income at the time of confirmation by 36 months."[14] This is not a very sophisticated solution, but given their case load, courts can do little else.

Courts have also had to deal with several other thorny issues about the income side of this requirement. For example, several have ruled that income which is exempt under law is nevertheless still included in the calculation of disposable income, in part because the plan is voluntary and the income is therefore still not involuntarily attached or levied upon.[15] Numerous others have ruled that the income of a nondebtor spouse must be

---

[14]   *In re Solomon*, 67 F.3d 1128, 1132 (4th Cir. 1995).

[15]   *See In re Taylor*, 212 F.3d 395, 397 (8th Cir. 2000) (income from ERISA-qualified pension); *In re Koch*, 109 F.3d 1285, 1289 (8th Cir. 1997) (worker's compensation benefits); *In re Freeman*, 86 F.3d 478 (6th Cir. 1996) (tax refund); *In re Hagel*, 184 B.R. 793 (9th Cir. BAP 1995) (social security disability benefits); *In re Schnabel*, 153 B.R. 809, 817-18 (Bankr. N.D. Ill. 1993) (social security and pension income). *But see In re Hunton*, 253 B.R. 580 (Bankr. N.D. Ga. 2000). *Cf. In re Solomon*, 67 F.3d 1128 (4th Cir. 1995) (retired debtor who could withdraw funds from IRA without penalty but

added in, or at least considered, because it reduces the amount of the debtor's income that is "reasonably necessary" for the maintenance and support of the debtor's household.[16] Perhaps most significant, the requirement that all projected disposable income be allocated to the plan may obligate the debtor to get a job.[17]

On the expense side, the requirement is even more difficult to apply. If the debtor's income exceeds the median for a household of the same size, reasonable expenses are to be computed using the formula in the means test. § 1325(b)(3). If the debtor's income does not exceed the state median, the court must determine whether each of the debtor's listed expenses – for telephone, cable television, schooling, as well as for food, clothing, shelter, and transportation – is necessary. This is a thankless and somewhat distasteful job for bankruptcy judges. Some judges have responded by not scrutinizing all expenses, and instead focusing on luxury items and obvious indulgences. Others conduct a more full inquiry to determine which expenses are unnecessary for a reasonable (*i.e.,* Spartan) lifestyle.[18] Not surprisingly, the different standards, compounded by different judicial notions of what is reasonable, have led to very inconsistent results, particularly with respect to such items as clothing,[19] recreation,[20]

---

who planned not to, need not include funds in computation since they are not a source of regular income).

Note, though, that incoming child support does not count as income for this purpose. § 1325(b)(2).

[16] *See, e.g., In re Falke*, 284 B.R. 133, 138 (Bankr. D. Or. 2002) (citing other cases); *In re McNichols*, 249 B.R. 160, 169 (Bankr. N.D. Ill. 2000) (citing other cases).

Similarly, at least one court has ruled that a debtor's undivided half-interest in the income of a nondebtor spouse in a community property jurisdiction – specifically, Washington – is estate property. *In re Hull*, 251 B.R. 726 (9th Cir. BAP 2000). Arguably this implies that the nondebtor spouse's half interest in the debtor's income removes such half of that income from the estate, but the court did not discuss that implication.

[17] *In re Jobe*, 197 B.R. 823 (Bankr. W.D. Tex. 1996) (the debtor, an able-bodied man in his early 50s with a pension from the U.S. Army, must find work to meet the "best interests" test; failure to do so, combined with a few misrepresentations, constitutes bad faith).

[18] *See In re McGovern*, 278 B.R. 888 (Bankr. S.D. Fla. 2002), *vacated on other grounds*, 297 B.R. 650 (S.D. Fla. 2003).

[19] *Compare In re McGovern*, 278 B.R. at 901 (allowing $175/month for a single, professional debtor but cutting the laundry budget from $162/month to $120/month); *In re Williams*, 201 B.R. 579 (Bankr. M.D. Fla. 1996) (budget of $100/month for one adult and $50/month for laundry was not excessive); with *In re Gillead*, 171 B.R. 886 (Bankr. E.D. Cal. 1994) (concluding that $200/month for clothes for two adults was excessive, as was $100/month for laundry). *See also In re Webb*, 262 B.R. 685, 692-93 (Bankr. E.D. Tex. 2001) (indicating that $200/month for dry cleaning was unreasonable).

[20] *Compare In re Lampman*, 2006 WL 167832 (Bank. N.D. Iowa 2006) (rejecting as excessive $225/month for recreation and $80/month for satellite television for joint debtors with two young children and suggesting $100/month for recreation and $45 for television would be acceptable); *In re*

and education expenses.[21] Courts have even disagreed about pension contributions withheld from the debtor's paycheck.   While most courts agree the voluntary contributions and loan repayments are not expenses that reduce disposable income,[22] there is no consensus on how to deal with mandatory contributions over which the

---

McGovern, 278 B.R. at 900 (cutting $150/month for recreation down to $100/month for single debtor); *In re Riegodedios*, 146 B.R. 691 (Bankr. E.D. Va. 1992) (allowing $60/month for recreation), *with In re Gillead*, 171 B.R. 886 ($86/month for entertainment and $75/month for health club dues were both unwarranted discretionary expenses); *In re Wood*, 92 B.R. 264 (Bankr. S.D. Ohio 1988) (half of $100 monthly recreation expense for two adults and one teenager is excessive). *See also In re Kelly*, 841 F.2d 908, 915 n.9 (9th Cir. 1988) (suggesting, in the context of § 707(b), that $500/month for entertainment was excessive); *In re Nissly*, 266 B.R. 717, 721 (Bankr. N.D. Iowa 2001) ($370/month for recreation, children's activities, internet access, cable tv, and family gifts is excessive); *In re Webb*, 262 B.R. at 692-93 (suggesting that $300/month for recreation, cable, and children's allowances is unreasonable).

[21]   *Compare In re Webb*, 262 B.R. 685 ($550/month for private schooling of 12-year-old son with ADHD was reasonable); *In re Summer*, 255 B.R. 555 (Bankr. S.D. Ohio 2000) ($925/month for son's final year of private schooling was reasonable, but $410/month to pay off loans incurred to finance education of daughter who was now an employed adult was not); *In re Burgos*, 248 B.R. 446 (Bankr. M.D. Fla. 2000) ($590/month to send two daughters to private religious school was reasonably necessary); *In re Nicola*, 244 B.R. 795 (Bankr. N.D. Ill. 2000) ($260/month for daughter's Catholic schooling was reasonably necessary); *In re Riegodedios*, 146 B.R. 691 (permitting debtors to pay $614/month for daughter's final year of college); *In re Navarro*, 83 B.R. 348 (Bankr. E.D. Pa. 1988) (permitting expense of $100/month for son's parochial schooling), *with In re Watson*, 309 B.R. 652 (1st Cir. BAP 2004) ($735/month for Catholic school for two minor children was not reasonably necessary); *Univest-Coppell Village, Ltd. v. Nelson*, 204 B.R. 497 (E.D. Tex. 1996) ($395/month for daughter's tuition at private high school was not reasonably necessary); *In re Stout,* 336 B.R. 138 (Bankr. N.D. Iowa 2006) ($700/month for home schooling 12-year-old daughter not reasonably necessary); *In re Rathburn*, 309 B.R. 901 (Bankr. N.D. Tex. 2004) ($900/month for private school tuition is excessive); *In re Ehret*, 238 B.R. 85 (Bankr. D.N.J. 1999) ($2,000/month for son's special education in private school was not reasonably necessary); *In re MacDonald*, 222 B.R. 69 (Bankr. E.D. Pa. 1998) ($175/month to send debtor's child to parochial school in another state was not reasonably necessary); *In re Jones*, 55 B.R. 462 (Bankr. D. Minn. 1985) ($500/month for 18-year-old child's college tuition and a similar amount for a younger child's private schooling are both excessive). *See also In re Attanasio*, 218 B.R. 180, 231 & n.77 (Bankr. N.D. Ala. 1998) (collecting cases on the issue); *In re Davis*, 269 B.R. 747 (Bankr. S.D. Ohio 2001) (plan allocating $350/month for ten months for a daughter's college education was in good faith; no objection made under the disposable income requirement).

[22]   *See In re Anes,* 195 F.3d 177 (3d Cir. 1999); *In re Harshbarger*, 66 F.3d 775 (6th Cir. 1995) (both dealing with repayment of a loan from the debtor's retirement fund). *But cf. Hebbring v. U.S. Trustee*, 463 F.3d 902 (9th Cir. 2006) (voluntary contributions to be reviewed on a case-by-case basis to determine whether they are reasonably necessary; 8% contribution was necessary for 33-year old with $49,000 per year in income).

debtor has no control.[23] The one circuit court with a decision on point ruled that no bright line rule is appropriate and that bankruptcy judges should exercise their discretion after reviewing all the evidence properly before them.[24]

Some courts do not seem to be particularly bothered by the general lack of consistency about what constitutes disposable income. Consider the following excerpt:

> Since § 1325(b)(2)(A) speaks in terms of expenditures that are "reasonably necessary," it is safe to assume that the judicial distinction between disposable and nondisposable income must be made by an objective, reasonable-person standard. The more difficult question concerns how one defines this standard.
>
> There are expenditures that a chapter 13 debtor might make which all reasonable people would agree are excessive – such as for a yacht or personal jet. At the other end of the spectrum, there are expenditures nobody could reasonably challenge – such as for food and shelter. The problem lies in the vast gray area between these extremes – *i.e.*, those expenditures with respect to which reasonable people could disagree on the question of whether they are appropriate under the circumstances.
>
> One approach a court could take in deciding this question would be to hold a particular expenditure to be "reasonably necessary" if it concludes that reasonable persons could disagree as to whether the expenditure is reasonably necessary. Because this in effect means that an expenditure would be allowed even if only a small minority of reasonable people would view the expenditure as appropriate, it is too lenient.
>
> Conversely, a court might hold an expenditure to be excessive if *any* reasonable person could view it as such. This standard swings too far in the opposite direction, making it virtually impossible for the debtor to justify other than the most vital of expenditures.
>
> A third approach would follow the simple majority. If the court concludes that most (reasonable) people would view the expenditure as excessive, then the expenditure will be so treated. There is much to recommend this approach: it is more moderate than either of the other two approaches mentioned and, because it yields to the perceived consensus, it could promote consistency and uniformity among the courts regarding this issue.

---

[23] *Compare In re Awuku*, 248 B.R. 21 (Bankr. E.D.N.Y. 2000); *In re Davis*, 241 B.R. 704 (Bankr. D. Mont. 1999) (both ruling that such payments do or at least can reduce disposable income), *with In re Nation*, 236 B.R. 150 (Bankr. S.D.N.Y. 1999).

[24] *In re Taylor*, 243 F.3d 124 (2d Cir. 2001).

In most cases, however, this approach is unworkable because there is little or no evidence upon which the judge can rely in determining whether "most people" would regard a particular expenditure as reasonable. And while it is always appropriate to refer to whatever case law is on point, the infinite variety of factual contexts in which these cases are decided, as amply demonstrated by a review of the reported decisions in this field, along with what is likely to be a relatively small number of pertinent decisions, do not make this source a particularly reliable means for eliciting a consensus.

Given these limitations, the decision of whether a particular expense is reasonable is and ought to be based on the judge's own opinion, for the judge is, in § 1325(b)(2) decision-making, the hypothetical reasonable person.[25]

Picking up on this, several courts have adopted a sort of amalgam approach for dealing with the issue of what expenses are reasonably necessary. Consider the following excerpt:

Whether income is "reasonably necessary" for the debtors' maintenance and support is open to interpretation. The Code requires a meaningful and realistic budget, accompanied by the devotion of most of the debtor's surplus income to repay creditors. Chapter 13 debtors are not required to adopt a totally spartan existence; neither are they permitted to continue an extravagant lifestyle at the expense of creditors. Courts apply § 1325(b) to allow debtors to maintain a reasonable lifestyle while simultaneously insuring they make a serious effort to pay creditors by eliminating unnecessary and unreasonable expenses. This section contemplates some sacrifices or alteration in prepetition consumption levels by Chapter 13 debtors, while allowing them to sustain basic needs not related to their former lifestyles.

Some expenditures are clearly essential, or nondiscretionary, such as reasonable amounts budgeted for food, clothing and shelter. The Code, however, recognizes that debtors "cannot live by bread alone." *In re Gonzales*, 157 B.R. 604, 608 (Bankr. E.D. Mich. 1993). Chapter 13 debtors are allowed some latitude regarding discretionary spending for items such as recreation, clubs, entertainment, newspapers, charitable contributions and other expenses in their budget. Excessive amounts allocated to nondiscretionary expenses also constitute discretionary spending. The Court has the duty to examine the entire budget in Chapter 13 cases to determine whether all listed expenses are reasonable and necessary under § 1325(b).

No matter where the "fat" is hidden, such discretionary expenditures typically have more to do with enhancing one's quality

---

[25]   *In re Gonzales*, 157 B.R. 604, 607-08 (Bankr. E.D. Mich. 1993).

of life, acquiring spiritual fulfillment, or just simply relaxing and enjoying oneself, than with subsistence. Since no two people have the same tastes, interests or philosophical dispositions, these discretionary costs can run the gamut from making charitable donations to buying a ticket for a tractor-pull event.[ ] By lumping all discretionary expenses together, whether they derive from categories more commonly thought of in subsistence terms or from categories commonly thought of as clearly discretionary in nature, the bankruptcy specific expenditures, that is to say, micromanage the details of a debtor's life. * * *

The proper methodology is to aggregate all expenses projected by the debtor which are somewhat more discretionary in nature, and any excessive amounts in the relatively nondiscretionary line items such as food, utilities, housing, and health expenses, to quantify a sum which, for lack of a better term, will be called "discretionary spending." *Id.* at 609. * * *

Discretionary expenses identified by courts include charitable contributions, gifts, recreation, private school tuition, payments for boats, campers and other luxuries, health club and country club dues, and newspapers and magazines. Courts also scrutinize cable TV services, veterinary expenses, cell phones, unspecified home repairs, and deductions for voluntary retirement funds.[26]

While this approach of aggregating all the expenses and looking for the collective fat may seem reasonable, it can allow the court to essentially obscure what it truly finds objectionable. Indeed, in the excerpted case, the court went on to identify the monthly expenses for school activities, recreation, gifts, food, home maintenance, and medical expenses – totaling $1,350 – as all involving some discretionary spending. It then calculated the discretionary amount as $550-$650 per month, but gave no indication where the excess came from. Query how debtors and their counsel are to devise Chapter 13 plans without more guidance.

The National Bankruptcy Review Commission viewed the "reasonably necessary" test as so indeterminant that it recommended dropping it altogether:

[I]t is all too clear that after thirteen years' experience with the disposable income requirement, courts seem no closer to sharing a collective view of what constitutes "reasonably necessary expenses" than they were at the inception. Some courts believe that private schools are necessary, while others do not. Orthodontia, piano lessons, college tuition, home repairs, dry cleaning,

---

[26] *In re Gleason*, 267 B.R. 630, 633-34 (Bankr. N.D. Iowa 2001).

newspapers, tithing, utility payments, and food allocations are just a few of the expenses that are scrutinized in this context. Personal views of what is and what is not necessary for the family inescapably factor into the equation. The amount that debtors must pay to their unsecured creditors will differ from courtroom to courtroom not because of different circumstances, but because of divergent views on the expenses perceived to be reasonably necessary. Because the inquiry is so fact-specific and non-legal, published opinions have little precedential value. Any party can threaten to litigate, knowing that there is some case law to support any position. The confusion over standards increases the leverage of any party with the resources and the stamina to fight about disposable income.[27]

Congress responded in 2005 by adding § 1325(b)(3), which requires Chapter 13 debtors whose income exceeds the state median to compute their disposable income pursuant to the standards used in the means test of § 707(b)(2). While this provides greater certainty for some debtors, it does nothing to deal with the debtors whose income is below the state median. Moreover, for high-income debtors, the means test computations occasionally generate a figure for disposable income:

> that is dramatically at odds with the reality of the debtor's ability to pay. Often this occurs because the starting point for the calculation – current monthly income – does not represent "current" income at all but rather the average monthly income received in the six months preceding the filing of the chapter 13 petition. A debtor who was unemployed for a substantial portion of that period but who now has a well-paying job, for example, will show little or nothing in the way of disposable income under the means test while the schedules I and J will show substantial surplus income with which to make plan payments. The reverse can also occur: a debtor who has recently lost a high-paying job or who received unusual payments in the six-month period leading up to the chapter 13 filing may show disposable income that is far beyond his or her actual ability to pay. Distortions can also occur with respect to the allowed deduction from current monthly income. For example, the means test envisions a hypothetical chapter 13 scenario in which secured debts are paid in full, while the debtor's actual plan may propose to surrender the collateral or (if permitted) to bifurcate an under-secured claim into secured and unsecured components.[28]

---

[27] National Bankruptcy Review Commission, *Bankruptcy: The Next Twenty Years* 263-65 (October 20, 1997).

[28] *In re Mitchell*, 2007 WL 1075195 (Bankr. E.D. Va. 2007).

Courts noting these distortions have responded in different ways. Some have regarded the distortions as a congressional mandate and taken no corrective action. Others have found some flexibility in the Code. They note that, technically, § 1325(b)(3) applies to the term "disposable income," as defined in § 1325(b)(2). However, § 1325(b)(1) requires that the debtor either pay claimants in full or allocate all "*projected* disposable income" to the plan. From this they conclude that debtors whose income or expenses have recently changed – or are about to change – may be permitted or required to take such changes into account in calculating their projected disposable income.[29]

One class of expenses that gets some special treatment are charitable contributions. The Religious Liberty and Charitable Donation Protection Act of 1998 changed the definition of disposable income in § 1325(b)(2)(A) by adding charitable contributions – up to 15% of the debtor's gross income for the year in which the contributions are made – to the amounts considered reasonably necessary for the debtor's support. There is no requirement that the debtor have a prior practice of making charitable contributions, as would normally be true for debtors who tithe. Apparently, therefore, at least some Chapter 13 debtors may make annual gifts – under the 15% ceiling – to a qualified charity at the expense of creditors.[30]

Problem 11-3

You represent Dauphin, the manager of several upscale coffee shops. Dauphin's annual income is slightly over $90,000. Dauphin lives as if it were even higher. Dauphin, who is single and has no dependents, has a $600,000 home subject to a $500,000 mortgage. The monthly mortgage payment is $3,675. Dauphin also owns a $45,000 Mercedes subject to a $40,000 security interest. Dauphin's monthly car payments are $975.

---

[29] *See In re Kibbe*, 361 B.R. 302 (1st Cir. BAP 2007) (projected disposable income should not be calculated solely from debtor's income for the prior six months, but should take into account fact that debtor recently accepted a higher paying job); *In re Jass*, 340 B.R. 411 (Bankr. D. Utah 2006) (debtors' projected disposable income should take into account recent need for increased medical expenses, if the debtors substantiate them). *But see In re Kolb*, 336 B.R. 802 (Bankr. S.D. Ohio 2007) (requiring a simple, mechanical calculation); *In re Tuss*, 360 B.R. 684 (Bankr. D. Mont. 2007) (same).

[30] *In re Cavanagh*, 250 B.R. 107 (9th Cir. BAP 2000) (so ruling with regard to measuring disposable income, but noting that the debtor's reason for commencing or increasing donations in the plan may be relevant to good faith); *In re Kirschner*, 259 B.R. 416 (Bankr. M.D. Fla. 2001) (same, but also imposing monitoring conditions to ensure contributions are made); *In re Watson*, 309 B.R. 652, 662 n.3 (1st Cir. BAP 2004) (agreeing in dicta with *Cavanagh*). *But see In re Davis*, 272 B.R. 5 (Bankr. D. Wyo. 2001) (requiring that such contributions be reasonable and denying confirmation of plan that included a tithe substantially above debtors' pre-bankruptcy practices); *In re Buxton*, 228 B.R. 606 (Bankr. W.D. La. 1999) (refusing to permit "unreasonable" donations even if under the statutory limit).

A. If Dauphin seeks Chapter 13 relief, to what extent will the mortgage and car payments affect Dauphin's disposable income? *See* § 1325(b)(2), (3).

B. How, if at all, would the analysis to Part A change if Dauphin's plan provided for Dauphin to surrender the Mercedes to the secured party? *Compare In re Love*, 350 B.R. 611 (Bankr. M.D. Ala. 2006), *with In re Oliver*, 2006 WL 2086691 (Bankr. D. Or. 2006).

C. If Dauphin has made monthly $100 donations to National Public Radio for the last four years, may Dauphin's Chapter 13 plan continue such payments, thereby reducing the distribution to claimants? *See* § 1325(b)(2), (3).

3.   Treatment of Secured Claims

(a) In General

The main rules applicable to secured claims are in § 1322(b)(2), (5) and § 1325(a)(5). Read those provisions. To understand their collective meaning, we start with § 1322(b)(2). It permits a Chapter 13 plan to modify secured claims other than those secured by a principal residence. If you think about it, this is a staggering grant of authority. It means, among other things, that the debtor may use a Chapter 13 plan to cure a default, modify the payment terms, and alter the interest rate, all while retaining the collateral. There are three principal limitations on this power. First, as in proceedings under other bankruptcy chapters, the debtor must adequately protect the creditor's interest in the collateral. § 361. This means, among other things, that if the debtor is going to retain the collateral, the debtor must protect the secured claimant from depreciation of the collateral, typically by making periodic payments on the secured obligation at a rate at least equal to the depreciation. Second, pursuant to a provision enacted in 2005, any periodic payments must be made on a monthly basis and must not vary in amount. *See* § 1325(a)(5)(B)(iii).

Problem 11-4

In reviewing the remaining discussion of how secured claims are treated in Chapter 13, consider how the new requirement that periodic payments be both monthly and equal might affect the debtor's plan. What was this requirement probably intended to prevent and why? What else may it also prevent and how important might the loss of that flexibility be to the debtor?

The final major limitation on the debtor's authority to modify secured claims is that the debtor must pay secured claimants, in present value terms, the amount of their "secured claim," unless the claimant agrees to some other treatment or the debtor surrenders the collateral. § 1325(a)(5)(B)(ii).[31] Thus, we need to know how to compute two things: (i) the amount of the secured claim; and (ii) the claim's present value.

The amount of a secured claim is something we discussed at the beginning of chapter six. According to § 506(a), the creditor's "secured claim" is limited by the value of the collateral. Thus, a creditor owed $10,000 who has the only lien on property worth $8,000 has a secured claim for $8,000 and an unsecured claim for $2,000. Determining value is often a difficult task. When a dispute arises, each of the parties involved may submit the opinion of one or more expert witnesses, and those opinions may well differ widely. Compounding that is the problem of ascertaining what the proper valuation standard is.[32] Should value be based on what the creditor could get if the debtor surrendered the collateral: liquidation value? Or should it be based on the benefit to the debtor from retaining the collateral: replacement value?

In *Associates Commercial Corp. v. Rash*,[33] the Supreme Court ruled that the latter standard applied. At the time, § 506(a) mandated simply that value "be determined in light of the . . . proposed disposition or use" of the collateral. The Court concluded that the "disposition or use" of the collateral turns on the alternative the debtor chooses: surrender or retention. If the plan provides for the debtor to retain the collateral, the valuation must be based on such "disposition or use." Applying a foreclosure-value standard when the retention option is invoked attributes no significance to that decision. A replacement-value standard, on the other hand, distinguishes retention from surrender.

Of course, merely settling on a replacement-value standard does not solve all valuation questions. The Court recognized this in a notorious footnote:

> Our recognition that the replacement-value standard, not the foreclosure-value standard, governs in cram down cases leaves to bankruptcy courts, as triers of fact, identification of the best way of ascertaining replacement value on the basis of the evidence presented. Whether replacement value is the equivalent of retail value, wholesale value, or some

---

[31] Some courts do not permit the debtor to use both § 1325(a)(5)(B) and (C) with respect to the same loan, such as by surrendering some of the collateral and paying off the secured claim on the remainder. *See In re Williams*, 168 F.3d 845 (5th Cir. 1999). Other courts permit the debtor to do this. *See, e.g., United States v. White*, 340 B.R. 761 (E.D.N.C. 2006); *In re McCommons*, 288 B.R. 594 (Bankr. M.D. Ga. 2002).

[32] This problem was already discussed with respect to determining insolvency for preference purposes (chapter three, part G.1.(a)(iv)), the process of claiming exemptions (chapter four, part D.2.), and the improvement of position test in § 547(c)(5) (chapter six, part F.3.(b)(iii)).

[33] 520 U.S. 953 (1997).

other value will depend on the type of debtor and the nature of the property. We note, however, that replacement value, in this context, should not include certain items. For example, where the proper measure of the replacement value of a vehicle is its retail value, an adjustment to that value may be necessary: A creditor should not receive portions of the retail price, if any, that reflect the value of items the debtor does not receive when he retains his vehicle, items such as warranties, inventory storage, and reconditioning. Nor should the creditor gain from modifications to the property – *e.g.*, the addition of accessories to a vehicle – to which a creditor's lien would not extend under state law.[34]

Perhaps in response to this, Congress amended § 506(a) in 2005 to add more clarity, at least in some cases. Read § 506(a)(2).

Regardless of what the applicable standard is, it is clear that the parties and the bankruptcy courts cannot undertake a costly, fact-intensive litigation in every case.[35] Prior to *Rash*, some courts commonly started with the average of the NADA retail and wholesale amounts, and then made adjustments if special circumstances dictated.[36] Although *Rash* appears to reject such an approach, some post-*Rash* opinions have held that it is not really inconsistent with *Rash*, provided the parties are permitted to show reasons for increasing or decreasing that amount.[37]

Section 1325(a)(5)(B) requires that a secured creditor retain its lien and receive property with a present value – *i.e.*, as of the date of confirmation – equal to the allowed amount of its secured claim. What does this present value requirement mean? Let's return to our example of a creditor with a $10,000 claim secured by property valued at $8,000, and who thus has an $8,000 secured claim. The plan could provide for payment of the full $8,000 on the date of confirmation. That is unlikely, however. More commonly, it would provide for monthly payments until the secured claim is paid off. If the plan provided for 20 monthly payments of $400, the total amount paid would be $8,000. However, even though that stream of 20 monthly payments of $400 *totals* $8,000, it is not *worth* $8,000. Think about it, would you rather have $8,000 now or that stream of 20 payments? If you had the cash up front, you could use it or invest it (*e.g.*, earn interest on it). In short, the present value of that stream of 20 payments is less than

[34]   *Id.* at 965 n.6.

[35]   *See In re Younger*, 216 B.R. 649 (Bankr. W.D. Okla. 1998), in which the court noted that it heard nearly 3,000 Chapter 13 cases in 1997, many of which required vehicle valuations.

[36]   *E.g., In re Valenti*, 105 F.3d 55 (2d Cir. 1997).

[37]   *E.g., In re De Anda-Ramirez*, 359 B.R. 794 (10th Cir. BAP 2007); *In re Getz*, 242 B.R. 916 (6th Cir. BAP 2000).

the sum of the payments. Determining how much less depends largely on what prevailing interest rates are; valuing the stream of payments requires that we discount each payment by the interest that could have been earned if the payment had been made immediately.

The Code offers no specific guidance on the interest rate to be used in discounting future payments to arrive at the present value of a secured claim. Some courts favored the contract rate, in part because it was easy to determine. However, in *Till v. SCS Credit Corp.*,[38] the Supreme Court ruled that bankruptcy courts should use a "formula approach," which begins by looking to the national prime rate – what commercial banks charge creditworthy commercial borrowers to compensate for the opportunity costs of the loan, the risk of inflation, and the relatively slight risk of default – and then, because bankrupt debtors pose a greater risk of nonpayment than solvent commercial borrowers, adjust the prime rate upward accordingly. The appropriate size of that risk adjustment "depends on such factors as the circumstances of the estate, the nature of the security, and the duration and feasibility of the reorganization plan."[39]

So, where does this leave us? Consider the following scenario:

> Eighteen months ago, Debtor purchased a $4,000 high-definition television from Creditor. Debtor paid nothing down but agreed to pay $140 each month for three years. This payment stream amortizes the debt at 15% interest. Creditor retained a security interest in the television. Debtor stopped making payments after twelve months and, because the agreement imposes interest at a higher rate upon default, currently owes $3,200. The television is now worth $1,500.

> Creditor has a secured claim of $1,500 and an unsecured claim of $1,700. Debtor may retain the television and modify the claims as long as the plan calls for Creditor to retain its lien on the secured claim and payments with a present value of $1,500 (plus whatever distribution is appropriate on Creditor's unsecured claim). If we were to compute present value using the pre-default contract rate of interest, monthly payments would be approximately $50 if the plan called for payment over three years. If payment were to be made over a shorter period, payments would be higher; if payments were to be made over a longer period, they would be lower. Because the contract rate of interest is so much higher than prevailing market interest rates, the court might permit the debtor to compute present value using a lower interest rate, thereby reducing the amount of the required monthly payment.

---

[38]   541 U.S. 465 (2004).

[39]   *Id.* at 479.

As you can see, this gives the debtor a great deal of flexibility in dealing with secured creditors. In essence, the right to modify permits the debtor to bifurcate a secure creditors' claim into its secured and unsecured components and to treat the two claims very differently. Because the creditor need retain its lien only with respect to its secured claim, *see* § 1325(a)(5)(B)(i)(I), these rules essentially permit a Chapter 13 debtor to strip down a lien, something the Supreme Court ruled that the debtor cannot do in Chapter 7.[40] As a result, if the property appreciates postpetition, the debtor will reap that benefit.[41]

Problem 11-5

Two years ago, Dwyer purchased furniture on credit and gave the seller a security interest in the furniture to secure the $5,400 purchase price. The sales agreement called for payment of $150/month for three years – in essence, a 0% interest rate. When Dwyer filed for Chapter 13 bankruptcy protection, Dwyer was current on all payments. The furniture is now worth $1,800, the amount Dwyer still owes. If Dwyer proposes a plan that calls for payment at the contract rate until the debt is paid off, and the seller objects, may the bankruptcy court confirm the plan? *See, e.g., In re Soards*, 344 B.R. 829 (Bankr. W.D. Ky. 2006); *In re Scruggs*, 342 B.R. 571 (Bankr. E.D. Ark. 2006); *In re Pryor*, 341 B.R. 648 (Bankr. C.D. Ill. 2006).

Of course, even though the debtor has the right to strip down a lien does not mean the debtor will choose to exercise that right. On occasion, the debtor will simply not have a need for the collateral or enough income to pay for it. In such cases, the debtor may propose a plan that provides for surrender of the collateral to the secured party. This can present a bit of a procedural problem for the creditor if it is undersecured. Rule 3002 imposes a deadline for filing a proof of claim. If the debtor proposes to surrender colateral to the secured creditor, who will then foreclose its lien, the resulting deficiency may not be known until after the proof of claim filing deadline. What should the potentially undersecured creditor do? One court recently answered this question:

> An undersecured creditor should file, within the bar date for unsecured claims, a proof of claim. The claim may be filed as fully secured or, alternatively, the amount of the unsecured component may be estimated or may simply be shown as undetermined. When the collateral is subsequently liquidated and the deficiency determined, the creditor may file an amended claim for the then-

---

[40] *See Dewsnup v. Timm*, 502 U.S. 410 (1992) (discussed in chapter six, part C.).

[41] *See Massachusetts Housing Finance Agency v. Evora*, 255 B.R. 336 (D. Mass. 2000).

quantified unsecured amount. The amended claim relates back to the timely filed claim and will not be objectionable on the basis of timeliness. Even creditors who believe themselves to be safely oversecured may file a cautionary claim for a potential deficiency, thus protecting themselves against that eventuality. If it turns out that no deficiency is realized, the cautionary claim may be withdrawn.[42]

(b) Limitations on Modification

There are three limitations on modification of secured claims in Chapter 13. First, § 1322(b)(2) does not permit the debtor to modify a claim secured solely by the debtor's principal residence. The debtor is not powerless over such mortgage debts; in particular, the debtor may cure a prepetition default. *See* § 1322(b)(5). Thus, a debtor in default on a home mortgage loan may propose a plan providing for payment of the amount of the arrearages over the three- to five-year life of the plan while paying the current installments as they come due under the mortgage.[43] If the debtor has the resources to carry out such a plan, the mortgage is reinstated and the loss of the home that might have occurred in Chapter 7 is avoided. What the debtor may not do is modify the home mortgage debt. Thus, the debtor cannot alter the interest rate or payment period on such debts.[44]

Although some debtors argued that this anti-modification rule applies only to the secured portion of an undersecured claim, thus still permitting bifurcation of a claim into its secured and unsecured components and modification of the unsecured portion, The Supreme Court rejected that argument in *Nobelman v. American Sav. Bank*.[45] As a result, claims secured solely by the debtor's home cannot be modified at all, although most courts permit modification if the claim is wholly unsecured, as in the case of a second mortgage when the debt to the first mortgagee exceeds the value of the property.[46]

---

[42]   *In re Brooks*, 2007 WL 1810491 at *5 (Bankr. C.D. Ill. 2007).

[43]   *See* §1322(b)(5) (suggesting that installments may then continue after the plan is completed), § 1328(a)(1) (indicating that the discharge does not extent to long-term obligations treated under § 1322(b)(5)).

[44]   For examples of other things that would constitute an impermissible modification, see *In re Collins*, 2007 WL 2116416 (Bankr. E.D. Tenn. 2007).

[45]   508 U.S. 324 (1993).

[46]   *See, e.g., In re Zimmer*, 313 F.3d 1220 (9th Cir. 2002); *In re Lane*, 280 F.3d 663 (6th Cir. 2002); *In re Pond*, 252 F.3d 122 (2d Cir. 2001); *In re Tanner*, 217 F.3d 1357 (11th Cir. 2000); *In re Bartee*,

It is important to note that the limitation on modifying home mortgage claims does not apply if collateral in addition to the debtor's home secures the debt. Thus, for example, if the debt is secured by a multi-unit dwelling and the debtor resides in only one unit, the debtor may modify the mortgage loan.[47] Prior to the 2005 amendments, other boilerplate clauses in the mortgage often triggered a similar result. For example, several courts held that the debtor could modify a home mortgage loan because the mortgage included appliances, machinery, furniture and equipment on premises."[48] Others ruled that a home mortgage loan would be modifiable if the loan agreement required the mortgagor to buy life or disability insurance, the proceeds of which would be used to pay the balance of the loan if the mortgagor dies or is disabled.[49] Similarly, mortgage loans often include in the debtor's monthly mortgage payment one-twelfth of the amount necessary to pay the real estate taxes and casualty insurance on the property. Such sums are typically held in escrow until used by the mortgagee to pay the taxes and insurance. If the mortgage goes further and gives the mortgagee a lien on the escrowed sums, some courts ruled that the mortgage no longer fell under the anti-modification rule.[50] The 2005 amendments broadened the scope of the anti-modification rule by adding a definition of "debtor's principal residence" and a related definition of "incidental property." *See* § 101(13A), (27B). Now, the use of such escrows, and possibly the use of such insurance policies, will not make a mortgage loan modifiable in Chapter 13.[51]

---

212 F.3d 277 (5th Cir. 2000); *In re McDonald*, 205 F.3d 606 (3d Cir.), *cert. denied*, 531 U.S. 822 (2000); *In re Griffey*, 335 B.R. 166 (10th Cir. BAP 2005); *In re Mann*, 249 B.R. 831 (1st Cir. BAP 2000). *But cf. In re Dickerson*, 222 F.3d 924 (11th Cir. 2000), *cert. denied*, 532 U.S. 972 (2001) (treating *Tanner* as binding but expressing disagreement with it).

[47]   *See In re Scarborough,* 461 F.3d 406 (3d Cir. 2006); *Lomas Mortgage Inc. v. Louis,* 82 F.3d 1 (1st Cir. 1996).

[48]   *See In re Johns*, 37 F.3d 1021 (3d Cir. 1994); *Wilson v. Commonwealth Mortgage Corp.*, 895 F.2d 123 (3d Cir. 1990). *But see In re Mendez,* 255 B.R. 143 (Bankr. D.N.J. 2000) (because fixtures are realty, not personalty under N.J. law, mortgage on residence and fixtures could not be modified); *In re Lee,* 215 B.R. 22 (9th Cir. BAP 1997) (a lien on appliances and other fixtures in the home does not take the mortgage out of § 1322(b)(2) because these items are "inextricably bound to the real property itself").

[49]   *See, e.g., In re Washington*, 967 F.2d 173 (5th Cir. 1992) (viewing the trend of authority as holding that such clauses do not allow modification of the claim).

[50]   *See In re Hughes,* 333 B.R. 360 (Bankr. M.D.N.C. 2005); *In re Donadio,* 269 B.R. 336 (Bankr. M.D. Pa. 2001). *But see In re Ferandos,* 402 F.3d 147 (3d Cir. 2005) (ruling that the debtor lacked rights in the escrowed funds and thus no security interest attached to them).

[51]   *See also In re Lunger,* 2007 WL 1970807 (Bankr. M.D. Pa. 2007).

Despite the general prohibition on modifying home mortgage claims, if final payment on the debt falls due during the life of the plan, bifurcation of the claim into its secured and unsecured portions is permitted under § 1322(c)(2).[52] What if final payment became due before the petition? Consider the following problem.

Problem 11-6

Dirigible gave Creditor a note for $100,000 providing for 36 monthly interest payments and a final "balloon" payment of the $100,000 principal on the third anniversary of the note. The note was secured by a mortgage on Dirigible's residence. Dirigible made all the interest payments on time but failed to pay the principal. Dirigible then filed a petition in Chapter 13. Dirigible's plan proposed to pay the $100,000 principal in sixty monthly installments with interest.

A. Should confirmation be denied on the ground that the plan is a modification of the rights of Creditor under § 1322(b)(2)? *See* § 1322(c)(2). *See also In re Watson*, 190 B.R. 32 (Bankr. E.D. Pa. 1995); *In re Jones*, 188 B.R. 281 (Bankr. D. Or. 1995); *In re Chang*, 185 B.R. 50 (Bankr. N.D. Ill. 1995).

B. How, if at all, would the analysis change if Dirigible's mortgage had required equal monthly payments over 30 years but Dirigible defaulted and the mortgagee accelerated the debt and obtained a foreclosure judgment for the full, accelerated amount prepetition? *See, e.g., In re Rowe*, 239 B.R. 44 (Bankr. D.N.J. 1999). *See also* § 1322(c)(1).

The second limitation on modification emanates from the language of § 1325(a)(5)(B)(ii), which requires the present value of property "distributed under the plan" to equal or exceed the amount of the secured claim. Several authorities suggest that this means that all payments on the secured claim must be made during the life of the plan.[53] If the debtor is so restricted, in other words, if amounts distributed *under the plan* means only amounts paid *during the plan*, then the debtor's ability to strip down secured claims in Chapter 13 through modification is effectively limited to fairly small claims. More significantly, such an interpretation of § 1325(a)(5) would seem to

---

[52] *See In re Paschen*, 296 F.3d 1203 (11th Cir. 2003); *In re Eubanks*, 219 B.R. 468 (6th Cir. BAP 1998). *But see In re Witt*, 113 F.3d 508 (4th Cir. 1997).

[53] *See, e.g., In re Barnes*, 32 F.3d 405 (9th Cir. 1994) (accepting the litigants' assumption that this provision meant that payment of the secured claim had to be completed during the life of the plan); *In re Nenonen*, 232 B.R. 803 (M.D. Fla. 1998). *Cf.* § 1222(b)(9) (expressly authorizing payments on secured claims to extend beyond the length of the plan).

conflict the with the debtor's right under § 1322(b)(5) to cure a home mortgage default and then continue to make the contractually required monthly payments on the mortgage loan.[54] The case law on this issue is surprisingly sparse but it seems highly doubtful that Congress expected debtors to pay off their home mortgages in 3-5 years. Indeed, the ability to keep one's home is one of the main enticements of Chapter 13.

The final limitation on modification was added by the 2005 amendments. It is the final – so-called "hanging" – paragraph of § 1325(a), which is difficult to cite because it is not incorporated into a numbered paragraph. Read it and then consider the following problem. For each portion of the problem, identify the textual issue.

Problem 11-7

Fifteen months before filing a Chapter 13 petition, Detroit purchased a new car on credit from Car Dealer, who retained and perfected a security interest in the car to secure the purchase price. Detroit uses the car to travel to and from work, for personal errands, and to shuttle family members. On the petition date, the car was worth $23,000 and the amount remaining due on the secured loan was $29,000.

A. How much is the secured claim: $29,000? $23,000? $0? *Compare In re Carver*, 338 B.R. 521 (Bankr. S.D. Ga. 2006), *with In re Brown*, 339 B.R. 818 (Bankr. S.D. Ga. 2006). *See also* 8 COLLIER ON BANKRUPTCY ¶ 1325.06[1][a] (15th ed. rev'd 2006).

B. How, if at all, would the answer change if Detroit purchased the car for Spouse and Spouse is the only one who drives it? *See In re Jackson*, 338 B.R. 923 (Bankr. M.D. Ga. 2006).

C. How, if at all, would the analysis change if Detroit acquired the loan nine months before filing for bankruptcy protection and the collateral was a car Detroit already owned? *See In re Quevedo*, 345 B.R. 238 (Bankr. S.D. Cal. 2006).

D. If Detroit's plan bifurcates Car Dealer's claim into a $23,000 secured claim and a $6,000 unsecured claim, can the plan be confirmed if Car Dealer consents? What if Car Dealer merely fails to object? *See* 1325(a)(5); *In re Montoya*, 341 B.R. 41 (Bankr. D. Utah 2006).

Perhaps the greatest controversy generated by the text of the hanging paragraph is what happens if the debtor surrenders the collateral. Consider the following opinion.

---

[54] *See In re Gordon*, 217 B.R. 973 (Bankr. M.D. Ga. 1997) (rejecting, for these reasons, the argument that all payments on secured claims must be made during the life of the plan).

IN RE WRIGHT
2007 WL 1892502 (7th Cir. 2007)

EASTERBROOK, Chief Judge.

Bankruptcy judges across the nation have divided over the effect of the unnumbered hanging paragraph that the Bankruptcy Abuse Prevention and Consumer Protection Act of 2005 added to § 1325(a) of the Bankruptcy Code. Section 1325 * * * specifies the circumstances under which a consumer's plan of repayment can be confirmed. The hanging paragraph says that, for the purpose of a Chapter 13 plan, § 506 of the Code does not apply to certain secured loans.

Section 506(a) divides loans into secured and unsecured portions; the unsecured portion is the amount by which the debt exceeds the current value of the collateral. In a Chapter 13 bankruptcy, consumers may retain the collateral (despite contractual provisions entitling creditors to repossess) by making monthly payments that the judge deems equal to the market value of the asset, with a rate of interest that the judge will set (rather than the contractual rate). *See Associates Commercial Corp. v. Rash,* 520 U.S. 953 (1997); *Till v. SCS Credit Corp.,* 541 U.S. 465 (2004). This procedure is known as a "cramdown" – the court crams down the creditor's throat the substitution of money for the collateral, a situation that creditors usually oppose because the court may underestimate the collateral's market value and the appropriate interest rate, and the debtor may fail to make all promised payments, so that the payment stream falls short of the collateral's full value. (The effect is asymmetric: if a judge overestimates the collateral's value or the interest rate, the debtor will surrender the asset and the creditor will realize no more than the market price. When the judge errs in the debtor's favor, however, the debtor keeps the asset and pays at the reduced rate. Creditors systematically lose from this asymmetry – and in the long run solvent borrowers must pay extra to make up for creditors' anticipated loss in bankruptcy.)

The question we must decide is what happens when, as a result of the hanging paragraph, § 506 vanishes from the picture. The majority view among bankruptcy judges is that, with § 506(a) gone, creditors cannot divide their loans into secured and unsecured components. Because § 1325(a)(5)(C) allows a debtor to surrender the collateral to the lender, it follows (on this view) that surrender fully satisfies the borrower's obligations. If this is so, then many secured loans have been rendered nonrecourse, no matter what the contract provides. The minority view is that Article 9 of the Uniform Commercial Code plus the law of contracts entitle the creditor to an unsecured deficiency judgment after surrender of the collateral, unless the contract itself provides that the loan is without recourse against the borrower. That unsecured balance must be treated the same as other unsecured debts under the Chapter 13 plan.

Craig Wright and LaChone P. Giles-Wright, debtors in this proceeding, owe more on their purchase-money automobile loan than the car is worth. Because the purchase occurred within 910 days of the bankruptcy's commencement, the hanging paragraph in § 1325(a)(5) applies. * * *

Debtors proposed a plan that would surrender the car to the creditor and pay nothing on account of the difference between the loan's balance and the collateral's market value. After taking the minority position on the effect of bypassing § 506, the bankruptcy judge declined to approve the Chapter 13 plan, because debtors did not propose to pay any portion of the shortfall.

* * *

Like the bankruptcy court, we think that, by knocking out § 506, the hanging paragraph leaves the parties to their contractual entitlements. True enough, § 506(a) divides claims into secured and unsecured components. * * * Yet it is a mistake to assume, as the majority of bankruptcy courts have done, that § 506 is the *only* source of authority for a deficiency judgment when the collateral is insufficient. The Supreme Court held in *Butner v. United States,* 440 U.S. 48 (1979), that state law determines rights and obligations when the Code does not supply a federal rule.

The contract between the Wrights and their lender is explicit: If the debt is not paid, the collateral may be seized and sold. Creditor "must account to Buyer for any surplus. Buyer shall be liable for any deficiency." In other words, the contract creates an ordinary secured loan with recourse against the borrower. Just in case there were doubt, the contract provides that the parties enjoy all of their rights under the Uniform Commercial Code. Section 9-615(d)(2) of the UCC, enacted in Illinois * * *, provides that the obligor must satisfy any deficiency if the collateral's value is insufficient to cover the amount due.

If the Wrights had surrendered their car the day before filing for bankruptcy, the creditor would have been entitled to treat any shortfall in the collateral's value as an unsecured debt. It is hard to see why the result should be different if the debtors surrender the collateral the day after filing for bankruptcy when, given the hanging paragraph, no operative section of the Bankruptcy Code contains any contrary rule. Section 306(b) of the 2005 Act, which enacted the hanging paragraph, is captioned "Restoring the Foundation for Secured Credit". This implies replacing a contract-defeating provision such as § 506 (which allows judges rather than the market to value the collateral and set an interest rate, and may prevent creditors from repossessing) with the agreement freely negotiated between debtor and creditor. Debtors do not offer any argument that "the Foundation for Secured Credit" could be "restored" by making all purchase-money secured loans non-recourse; they do not argue that non-recourse lending is common in consumer transactions, and it is hard to imagine that Congress took such an indirect means of making non-recourse lending *compulsory.*

Appearing as *amicus curiae,* the National Association of Consumer Bankruptcy Attorneys makes the bold argument that loans covered by the hanging paragraph cannot be treated as secured in any respect. Only § 506 provides for an "allowed secured claim," *amicus* insists, so the entire debt must be unsecured. This also would imply that a lender is not entitled to any post-petition interest. *Amicus* recognizes that § 502 rather than § 506 determines whether a claim should be "allowed" but insists that only § 506 permits an "allowed" claim to be a "secured" one.

This line of argument makes the same basic mistake as the debtors' position: it supposes that contracts and state law are irrelevant unless specifically implemented by the Bankruptcy Code. *Butner* holds that the presumption runs the other way: rights under state law count in bankruptcy unless the Code says otherwise. Creditors don't need § 506 to create, allow, or recognize security interests, which rest on contracts (and the UCC) rather than federal law. Section 502 tells bankruptcy courts to allow claims that stem from contractual debts; nothing in § 502 disfavors or curtails secured claims. Limitations, if any, depend on § 506, which the hanging paragraph makes inapplicable to purchase-money interests in personal motor vehicles granted during the 910 days preceding bankruptcy (and in other assets during the year before bankruptcy).

Both the debtors and the *amicus curiae* observe that many decisions, of which *United States v. Ron Pair Enterprises, Inc.,* 489 U.S. 235 (1989), is a good example, state that § 506 governs the treatment of secured claims in bankruptcy. No one doubts this, but the question at hand is what happens when § 506 does not apply. The fallback under *Butner* is the parties' contract (to the extent the deal is enforceable under state law), rather than non-recourse secured debt (the Wrights' position) or no security interest (the *amicus curiae's* position). And there is no debate about how the parties' contract works: the secured lender is entitled to an (unsecured) deficiency judgment for the difference between the value of the collateral and the balance on the loan.

By surrendering the car, debtors gave their creditor the full market value of the collateral. Any shortfall must be treated as an unsecured debt. It need not be paid in full, any more than the Wrights' other unsecured debts, but it can't be written off *in toto* while other unsecured creditors are paid some fraction of their entitlements.

Affirmed

Problem 11-8

Crafty Motors has been offering for sale one of its car models for $17,715 and extending customers 100% financing at a 4% annual interest rate. Under such a deal, customers pay $400/month for 48 months. To increase sales, Crafty is considering advertising a lower interest rate (but raising the price) or advertising a lower price (but raising the interest rate). It is trying to choose between a 0% deal based on a $19,200 price and an 8% deal based on a $16,385 price. Both would require payments of $400 for 48 months. Which option would be better for Crafty if the debtor goes into Chapter 13 and wants to keep the car? Which option would be better if the debtor filed for Chapter 7 relief and wants to keep the car? *See In re Taranto*, 365 B.R. 85 (6th Cir. BAP 2007).

(c) Payments "Outside the Plan"

One of the main drawbacks to Chapter 13 is its expense. The trustee receives a percentage – as much as 10% – of all disbursements to creditors made under the plan. With respect to unsecured creditors, unless the plan provides for payment to them in full, the trustee's fees effectively reduce the amount the creditors receive. With respect to secured claims, the burden of the trustees' fees falls initially on the debtor. If the debtor wants to retain the collateral, the debtor must pay the secured claim in full. § 1325(a)(5)(B). The trustee's fees therefore cannot reduce the secured creditor's take. In other words, to keep the collateral, the debtor will have to pay an additional percentage just for the privilege of having the trustee make the payments to the creditor. However, the debtor is usually already devoting all disposable income to the plan and has no more to contribute. The trustee's take thus comes out of that finite fund of disposable income, and as a result reduces the percentage recovery of the unsecured claimants. It is therefore the unsecured claimants who pay to have trustee make disbursements to secured claimants.[55]

It is easy to appreciate why the trustee should act as the disbursing agent generally. If the debtor were allowed to pay creditors directly, the trustee would not learn whether payments were being made unless creditors complained; the situation could become chaotic and difficult to administer. With respect to secured claims, however, this rationale is less powerful. In many instances, particularly in the case of a residential mortgage, the debtor will owe the same payments after confirmation as before. Moreover, these payments may well continue long after the plan is completed because debtors are not discharged from long-term debts. § 1328(a)(1). Thus, it makes some sense for the debtor to pay these claims directly.

The clear implications from § 1326(c) are that the court may approve a plan allowing the debtor to act as disbursing agent and that the trustee is not entitled to a commission on payments made directly by the debtor. *See* 28 U.S.C. § 586(e)(2). The savings generated by direct payments to creditors can be substantial, and can make the difference between a confirmable plan and a nonconfirmable one.[56]

---

[55] *See In re Chandler*, 210 B.R. 898, 904 (Bankr. D.N.H. 1997).

[56] *See, e.g., In re Slaughter*, 188 B.R. 29 (Bankr. D.N.D. 1995) (savings of $1,700 annually, without which the plan would be infeasible).

Nevertheless, courts have not reached total agreement about when it is appropriate to permit the debtor to pay claims directly. Most treat a residential mortgage debt as one the debtor may pay directly.[57] Debtors are sometimes allowed to be disbursing agents on other secured claim cases as well.[58] The willingness of courts to allow this practice – which if taken to an extreme could leave the trustee system seriously underfunded – apparently varies significantly from district to district and often depends on whether the plan modifies the obligation or on whether the debtor is in default.[59]

4. *Treatment of Unsecured Claims*

Assuming the plan allocates all the debtor's disposable income to the plan for the applicable commitment period, the debtor has almost unfettered discretion with respect to the treatment of unsecured claims. Almost. The debtor may alter the contractual payment schedule, pay only a small portion of the claim, and treat the claim differently from other unsecured claims, and yet still discharge the unpaid portion upon completion of the plan. There are, however, three important limitations on this freedom.

First, each priority claim – with the exception of support claims assigned to a governmental unit for a purpose other than collection – must be paid in full unless the claimant agrees to accept something less. § 1322(a)(2), (4). Second, unsecured creditors must receive at least the liquidation value of their claims. *See* § 1325(a)(4).

Problem 11-9

Diver received a college degree two years ago and accepted a job as an oceanographer trainee for $21,000 per year. Thrilled with being out of school and earning income, Diver went a little wild with consumer consumption. Diver has settled down now. Indeed, Diver recently married and has two stepchildren to support. Unfortunately, Diver is unable to pay off the large

---

[57] *See, e.g., In re Aberegg*, 961 F.2d 1307 (7th Cir. 1992). *See also In re Clay*, 339 B.R. 784 (Bankr. D. Utah 2006) (ruling that nothing in the 2005 amendments to the Bankruptcy Code requires a change in the practice of permitting the debtor to act as the disbursing agent on the home mortgage loan). *But see In re Perez*, 339 B.R. 385 (Bankr. S.D. Tex. 2006) (upholding a local rule that requires the trustee to disburse home mortgage payments unless the debtor applies for and merits an exception to that rule, and listing 21 factors to consider in determining whether to grant such an exception).

[58] *E.g., In re Bradley*, 705 F.2d 1409 (5th Cir. 1983) (auto loan).

[59] *Compare Haden v. Pelofsky*, 212 F.3d 466 (8th Cir. 2000) (debtor in Chapter 12 – which has provisions identical to Chapter 13 – may directly pay secured creditors with impaired claims); *with In re Fulkrod*, 973 F.2d 801 (9th Cir. 1992) (Chapter 12 debtor must make payments on modified claims through the trustee).

credit card bills generated in those wilder days and those bills are continuing to accrue interest. As a result, Diver has decided to file under Chapter 13. After reviewing Diver's assets, you determine that there would be $3,600 in nonexempt assets in a Chapter 7 case. Diver proposes a three-year plan calling for payments of $100/month, which is a fair estimate of Diver's disposable income. Assuming the Chapter 13 trustee's commission will be 10% of amounts disbursed under the plan, is such a plan confirmable? What else might you need to know? *See* § 326(a); *In re Dixon*, 140 B.R. 945 (Bankr. W.D.N.Y. 1992). What is the least amount that Diver could contribute to a three-year plan that would satisfy § 1325(a)(4)?

Third, disparate treatment of different unsecured claims – which is expressly authorized, *see* § 1322(b)(1) – is circumscribed in three ways:

(1)   the debtor may group claims into different "classes" but all the claims within a single class must be substantially similar, *see* § 1122(a);

(2)   all claims within a single class must be treated alike, § 1322(a)(3); and

(3)   the plan must not unfairly discriminate among the different classes of claims, § 1322(b)(1).

In Chapter 11 cases, creditors vote on a debtor's reorganization plan by class, and thus classification may play an important role in the debtor's strategy for gaining acceptance of the plan. In Chapter 13, debtors do not need creditors to approve the plan; the court will confirm the plan if it meets the requirements of § 1325. Thus the sole reason for a Chapter 13 debtor to separate nonpriority, unsecured claims into different classes is to prefer one class over another in the percentage or timing of payment.

The Code's prohibition on "unfair discrimination" – a term left undefined – implies that the debtor may discriminate to some extent. In other words, by prohibiting only "unfair" discrimination, the Code permits discrimination that is fair. On the other hand, the prohibition presumably has some relevance beyond the other statutory requirements for confirmation of a Chapter 13 plan. Thus, presumably it means more than merely ensuring that claimants receive the liquidation value of their claims, *see* § 1325(a)(4), or that debtors not paying creditors in full allocate all disposable income to the plan for the applicable commitment period, *see* § 1325(b).

There are innumerable bankruptcy court cases on the meaning of "discriminate unfairly," and they differ widely in their interpretation of the term. Some general themes are discernable, however.

Discrimination is permissible if it is necessary to have a successful plan that benefits all creditors. For example, a debtor who has a subsidized low-income lease which is in default may need to pay the arrearages in full in order to cure the default and assume the lease. Otherwise, the debtor will lose the subsidized housing, thus increasing monthly expenses. A plan which discriminates in order to cure the default on such a lease – even to the extent of paying 100% of the lease arrearages and only 10% of other unsecured claims – is not unfair.[60]

When the proposed discrimination serves some other purpose, it is more questionable. Several of the early cases on unfair discrimination involved claims on which there was a co-debtor, typically a family member or friend of the debtor. Often, the debtor would propose to separately classify such claims and pay the holder of the claims a greater percentage than that allocated to holders of other unsecured claims. For example, in *Barnes v. Whelan*,[61] the debtor's plan called for 100% payment on a co-signed debt and only 1% on the other unsecured claims. The court concluded that although there was a rational basis for this proposal, the 99% differential was unfair. Other courts disagreed, and Congress responded by adding the "however" clause to § 1322(b)(1). Unfortunately, this clause speaks only to different treatment, not to "unfair discrimination," leaving the precise meaning of the clause unclear. Most courts have interpreted the amendment as permitting disparate treatment in favor of co-debtor claims, but still subject to the unfair discrimination standard, and thus decline to confirm a plan that discriminates excessively.[62] A few other courts regard favored treatment of co-debtor claims as wholly exempt from unfair discrimination analysis,[63] although even they would presumably prohibit a debtor from discriminating among different co-debtor claims.[64]

In recent years, the bulk of the litigation on unfair discrimination has involved plans that prefer the holders of nondischargeable claims over other claimants. Although Chapter 13 offers debtors a slightly expanded discharge, several debts remain nondischargeable even after successful completion of a Chapter 13 plan. These include student loans, debts arising from drunk driving accidents, and restitution or fines stemming from criminal convictions. *See* § 1328(a).[65] Chapter 13 becomes very enticing to debtors if they can hold on to their homes and automobiles, use their

---

[60]   *In re Davis*, 209 B.R. 893 (Bankr. N.D. Ill. 1997).

[61]   689 F.2d 193 (D.C. Cir. 1982).

[62]   *See, e.g., In re Ramirez*, 204 F.3d 595 (5th Cir. 2000) (interpreting some rather contradictory statements in *In re Chacon*, 202 F.3d 725 (5th Cir. 1999)).

[63]   *See, e.g., In re Monroe*, 281 B.R. 398 (Bankr. N.D. Ga. 2002).

[64]   *See In re Janssen*, 220 B.R. 639, 643 (Bankr. N.D. Iowa 1998); *In re Young*, 102 B.R. 1022, 1023 (Bankr. W.D. Mo. 1989).

[65]   Support obligations are also nondischargeable, *see* § 1328(a)(2), but in 1994 they were also made priority claims. *See* § 507(a)(1). They therefore now *must* be classified separately – recall that only similar claims may be classified together, § 1322(b)(1) – and they must be paid in full. *See* § 1322(a)(2).

disposable income to pay off only their nondischargeable debts, pay their other unsecured creditors with little or nothing, and walk away with a fresh start. The issue arises frequently with respect to student loans. Consider the following hypothetical and the brief discussion which follows.

> Donald and Debra financed part of their college education through student loans. They live in an apartment; their possessions, including an automobile, are entirely exempt under state law. They owe $50,000 in student loans and, because of their excessive use of credit cards in the early years of their marriage, $25,000 to a variety of other creditors. They are behind on some of their payments and are being pressed by their creditors. They have consulted a financial counselor and have decided to turn over a new leaf and clear up their financial problems so that in the future they can consider buying a house and having a family. They do not wish to have a Chapter 7 discharge on their credit record because they believe it would inhibit their ability to obtain a home loan later on. They file under Chapter 13 and propose a five-year plan that classifies their student loan debts separately from their other unsecured obligations. The portion of their annual income that qualifies as "disposable" is $13,000. The plan calls for $12,000 per year to be devoted to paying their student loans and $1,000 per year to be paid on the debts owed to their "other creditors." By the end of the plan, Debtors will have paid off all of their student loans – including postpetition interest – but only 20% of the debts owing to their other creditors. Should the court deny confirmation on the grounds that the plan unfairly discriminates against the other creditors under § 1322(b)(1)?

Minority View: In order to be fair under § 1322(b)(1), the classification must rationally further a legitimate interest of the debtor and not be inconsistent with a policy explicit or implicit in the Code. This approach is appropriate because the right to preferentially classify is one of the incentives placed in Chapter 13 by Congress to induce debtors to choose Chapter 13 over Chapter 7, under which nonpriority creditors must be paid pro rata. If Donald and Debra were to exercise their right to convert to Chapter 7, the other creditors would get nothing and the debtors would have their postpetition income to pay off their nondischargeable student loans. With respect to student loan claims, even though they are not accorded priority status, Congress has favored them with nondischargeability to help ensure that they are paid. Favored treatment in a Chapter 13 plan does not frustrate that policy, it furthers it.[66]

---

[66]   For cases permitting favored treatment of education debt, *see, e.g., In re Sullivan*, 195 B.R. 649 (Bankr. W.D. Tex. 1996); *In re Gregg*, 179 B.R. 828 (Bankr. S.D. Tex. 1995) (but not permitting discrimination among different student loan creditors); *In re Tucker*, 159 B.R. 325 (Bankr. D. Mont.

Majority View: Section 1322(b)(1)'s reference to unfair discrimination means unfair *to the creditors*; it is a creditor protection device. While § 1322(b) implicitly allows debtors to discriminate in a reasonable manner in classifying claims, the discrimination in the hypothetical unfairly imposes on the other creditors the burden of paying the debtors' student loans. In 1990, when Congress made student loans nondischargeable in Chapter 13, it could have provided a special classification for student loans, as it did in 1984 for co-signed consumer debts, *see* § 1322(b)(1), or it could have made payment of student loans a priority in Chapter 13. It did neither. Hence, there is no reason to believe that Congress intended to favor student loans in Chapter 13 by, in effect, subordinating the claims of other creditors.[67]

Possible Alternatives: One possible alternative, if the applicable commitment period is only three years, is to lengthen the plan and discriminate only after the third year. If, under § 1325(b), debtors must allocate all disposable income to the plan for three years, general unsecured creditors simply have no right to expect income for a longer period of time. Any amount the debtors pay after this three-year period represents a voluntary effort. Even if general unsecured creditors do not benefit from this extra effort, arguably nothing has truly been taken away from them. Thus, while the debtors may not discriminate during the applicable commitment period, they may allocate payments after that time solely to the nondischargeable claims.[68]

Another approach taken or suggested by an increasing number of courts is to permit the debtor to deal with nondischargeable debt under § 1322(b)(5).[69] This provision allows the debtor to cure a default and remain current on a debt for which the contractual payments would continue beyond the duration of the plan. During the life of the plan these payment may be funneled through the trustee or, particularly if there has been no prepetition default, the debtor may be permitted to make them directly, thereby avoiding the trustee's fees on these disbursements.

1993). *See also* Stephen L. Sepinuck, *Rethinking Unfair Discrimination in Chapter13*, 74 AM. BANKR. L.J. 341 (2000).

[67]   *E.g., In re Groves*, 39 F.3d 212 (8th Cir. 1994).

[68]   *See, e.g., In re Simmons*, 288 B.R. 737 (Bankr. N.D. Tex. 2003); *In re Thibodeau*, 248 B.R. 699, 706 (Bankr. D. Mass. 2000).

[69]   *See, e.g., In re Groves*, 39 F.3d at 215 (quoting and expressing agreement with the bankruptcy court's statements on this issue).

5. Good Faith

(a) Minimal Payment Plans

One of the principal benefits to the debtor of Chapter 13 is the ability to save nonexempt assets that would go to creditors in Chapter 7. The price the debtor pays for this benefit, at least since the 1984 amendments, is that the debtor must pay into the plan all of the debtor's projected disposable income for three years. § 1325(b)(1)(B).

What if the debtor has no disposable income? Consider the following hypothetical.

> Debtor owns a house and an automobile that are subject to security interests that secure debts greater than the value of the collateral. Debtor is in default on these debts and, even under Chapter 7, would probably have to surrender the assets to the secured creditors. Debtor also has a large amount of unsecured debt, but unsecured creditors will receive nothing in Chapter 7 because Debtor has no unencumbered, nonexempt property. Debtor files for Chapter 13 bankruptcy protection and proposes to devote all projected disposable income for three years to the plan. However, all of this income will be paid to satisfy the claims of home mortgagee and auto lender. Thus, the effect of the plan is to save Debtor's house and automobiles but nothing is paid to other creditors with unsecured claims. Is this a proper use of Chapter 13?

In the early years of the Code, courts had difficulty with "zero payment" or nominal payment plans like this one. Some courts construed the "good faith" requirement of § 1325(a)(3) as barring zero payment plans. Most simply treated the debtor's proposed level of debt repayment as one of the most of important factors – in a long list of factors – for courts to consider in evaluating good faith.[70]

By enacting § 1325(b)(1)(B) – which requires that the debtor use all disposable income to pay creditors – Congress addressed the issue, but only obliquely. It did not specifically bar zero payment plans and, of course, some debtors with *regular* income have no *disposable* income. Indeed, the legislative history strongly suggests that Congress did not wish to limit Chapter 13 to those debtors willing and able to pay a certain percentage of their debts. Thus, plans calling for no or only minimal payments to unsecured creditors do not present a significant good faith problem. As the Tenth Circuit observed:

> The policy of allowing a fresh start does not license debtors to lightly rid themselves of the burden of their indebtedness without an honest attempt at repayment. Yet neither does that policy compel debtors, in Dickensian

---

[70]   *See, e.g., In re Estus*, 695 F.2d 311 (8th Cir. 1982) (identifying eleven criteria for courts to use).

fashion, to labor for the rest of their lives under the crushing weight of gigantic debt; under our law the world is not to be made a debtor's prison by a lifelong sentence of penury.[71]

When minimal payment is combined with heinous prefiling conduct, however, the situation is very different. Until recently, Chapter 13 offered debtors a substantially enhanced discharge. Certain obligations – including those for willful and malicious injuries – which could not be discharged in Chapter 7, were dischargeable in Chapter 13. The rationale for giving a broader discharge in Chapter 13 was premised on the assumption that the Chapter 13 debtor was actually paying creditors, whereas the typical consumer in Chapter 7 paid little or nothing to unsecured claimants.[72] If a substantial portion of the debtor's obligations were for claims that would be nondischargeable in Chapter 7 and the debtor proposed to pay those claims little or nothing in Chapter 13, courts generally balked.

For example, the Eighth Circuit upheld a bankruptcy court determination of bad faith based on three principal facts: (1) the plan was filed only eleven days before a civil suit claiming damages resulting from the debtor's sexual abuse of a minor was set to go to trial, thereby preventing the plaintiff from having her case heard; (2) the debtor filed not because of debts that came due in the ordinary course, but in anticipation of the likely damage award resulting from the civil suit; and (3) the initial plan offered only a meager payment plan, which the debtor increased only in response to the plaintiff's objection.[73]

The Sixth Circuit summed the matter up this way:

> The bankruptcy court made much of the point that an attempt to discharge a debt under Chapter 13 which is not dischargeable under Chapter 7 is not conclusive evidence that the Chapter 13 plan was not made in good faith. We agree. It is not conclusively bad faith for a debtor to seek to discharge a debt incurred through his own criminal or tortious conduct, but that factor may be considered. Although we consider as a factor what [the debtor] did to incur the judgment, it is what he has done since the judgment to avoid paying it that is

---

[71]   *In re Young*, 237 F.3d 1168, 1178 (10th Cir. 2001).

[72]   This premise is implicit in the scope of Chapter 13's more limited hardship discharge. A Chapter 13 debtor who, due to circumstances for which the debtor should not justly be held accountable, is unable to complete a plan, can nevertheless receive a discharge if the unsecured creditors have received as much as they would have received in a Chapter 7 liquidation, and modification of the plan to accommodate the debtor's new circumstances is not practicable. § 1328(b). However, such a hardship discharge does not rid the debtor of those debts that would have been nondischargeable in Chapter 7. § 1328(c).

[73]   *Noreen v. Slattengren*, 974 F.2d 75, 77 (8th Cir. 1992).

most important. Our decision rests on much more than the fact that this debt is not dischargeable under Chapter 7; it rests on [the debtor's] unrelenting efforts to reduce the assets available to his creditors, to make only minimal payments and over the shortest possible time, and to make even those only when threatened with garnishment. The plan before us was not tendered in good faith, but was one more effort to avoid paying the judgment creditors.[74]

The 2005 Amendments have significantly cut back on the scope of the discharge in Chapter 13, bringing it much closer to that available in Chapter 7. *See* § 1328(a).

Problem 11-10

Last year, Dastardly, then 19 years old, was indicted for raping a 16-year-old girl. Although the criminal case was dismissed, the girl's parents have brought a civil action against Dastardly on her behalf seeking $400,000 in compensatory damages and $1 million in punitive damages. Discovery has been completed and trial is scheduled to commence next week.

A. Is Dastardly eligible for Chapter 13 relief today? *See* § 109(e).

B. If Dastardly files for Chapter 13 relief today, the court confirms Dastardly's plan, and Dastardly completes the plan, will Dastardly's liability for damages arising from the rape be discharged? *See* § 1328(a), (h).

---

[74] *In re Caldwell*, 895 F.2d 1123, 1127-28 (6th Cir. 1990). *See also In re Scotten*, 281 B.R. 147 (Bankr. D. Mass. 2002) (refusing to confirm the plan of a statutory rapist who had made no payments on a civil judgment to the rape victim and whose plan provided for only a 10% distribution); *In re White*, 255 B.R. 737 (Bankr. W.D. Mo. 2000) (refusing to confirm plan of debtor who had liability of more than $300,000 for malicious prosecution because she had never made any payments on that judgment, failed to obtain employment, filed another vexatious suit against the judgment creditor, and filed her Chapter 13 petition just before a foreclosure sale, after the judgment creditor had already incurred substantial costs associated with the sale). *But cf. In re Smith*, 286 F.3d 461, 468 (7th Cir. 2002) (confirming a 5-year plan that paid a defrauded creditor less than 10% of her claim; "[a]lthough the nature of the underlying debt, not dischargeable in Chapter 7, weighs against a finding of good faith, this factor alone cannot defeat confirmation").

On the other hand, if debtors have made substantial payments on their tort liabilities before filing for Chapter 13 relief and propose to make significant payments under the plan, they may pass over the hurdle of good faith even if the main reason for seeking such relief is to discharge debts that would be nondischargeable in Chapter 7. *See, e.g., In re Francis*, 273 B.R. 87 (6th Cir. BAP 2002), *aff'd*, 69 Fed. Appx. 766 (6th Cir. 2003) (confirming a plan that paid only 2-3% on general claims because it allocated all disposable income to the plan for five years, the debtor had already paid $43,000 of a $229,000 debt for fraud, the debtor had waited several years after the state court judgment before filing, and the debtor's relatives were adding $15,000 to the pot).

C. How, if at all, would the analysis of each of the questions above change if Dastardly waits to file until after the trial and judgment is entered against him for $400,000?

D. If Dastardly files for Chapter 13 relief today and proposes a plan that pays unsecured claimants 5% of their claims over five years, should the plan be confirmed? *See* § 1325(a)(3).

Problem 11-11

Shortly after a state court entered a $25,000 judgment against Destructive for willful and malicious damage to private property, Destructive filed for bankruptcy protection under Chapter 13. To ensure that the bankruptcy court will regard the plan as filed in good faith, Destructive proposes to separately classify the tort claim and pay it at a higher rate than other general, unsecured claims. Is such a plan confirmable? *See In re Johnson*, 69 B.R. 726 (Bankr. W.D.N.Y. 1987).

(b) Repeated Filings

Section 727(a)(8) prevents a discharge in a Chapter 7 case if the debtor received a discharge in a previous case commenced less than eight years before. This rule reflects a policy against recidivism in bankruptcy. Congress apparently believes that one fresh start is okay, but a debtor who needs frequent fresh starts is abusing the bankruptcy process.

Until recently, there was no bar against successive discharges in Chapter 13. The reason for this was to encourage the use of Chapter 13. Because Chapter 13 was seen as a way for debtors to pay their debts, rather than escape them, it followed that debtors should be able to use Chapter 13 as often as they wished.

In reality, of course, Chapter 13 debtors do not normally pay their creditors in full and often pay them only a small fraction of their claims. Beyond that, debtors besieged by creditors sometimes file under Chapter 13 solely to obtain the protection of the automatic stay, with no intent to actually complete a repayment plan. Thus the debtor may simply be buying time until creditors are able to have the case dismissed, perhaps with the intent of filing again and again, thereby delaying creditors almost indefinitely.

In 1984, Congress added § 109(g) to address this problem. It prohibits refiling for 180 days after a dismissal resulting from the debtor's willful failure to obey a court order or failure to prosecute the case, or after voluntary dismissal following a creditor's motion for relief from the automatic stay. As with any effort to create a general rule to deal with highly individualized circumstances, this one is probably both underinclusive and overinclusive. For example, because of the different nature of Chapter 13, creditors of a Chapter 13 debtor do not regularly move for relief from the stay. Thus, a debtor may choose to file under Chapter 13 to stave off foreclosure or eviction, then voluntarily dismiss, only to file again when the mortgagee or landlord brings another action. Section 109(g) does not prohibit such behavior. On the other hand, debtors sometimes miss deadlines, such as those for the § 341 examination or for the filing of schedules or statements, because they lack adequate legal advice and are not aware of the deadlines. If the court dismisses for such errors, § 109(g) may delay the debtor from receiving much needed bankruptcy relief.

Another type of repeated filing involves what is euphemistically known as a "Chapter 20": a Chapter 13 petition filed shortly after receiving a Chapter 7 discharge. Congress probably envisioned Chapters 7 and 13 as offering alternative forms of relief for debtors. If a debtor is willing to turn over nonexempt property to a trustee for distribution to creditors, the debtor can receive a Chapter 7 discharge without using future income to pay creditors. Three drawbacks to this are that the debtor may be left with certain nondischargeable debts, must deal with secured creditors without much help from the bankruptcy court, and will not be able to get another discharge for six years. On the other hand, if a debtor is willing to use all disposable income for three years to pay creditors under Chapter 13, the debtor may retain possession of exempt and encumbered property and may strip down liens, other than home mortgages and some purchase-money security interests.

Some debtors have sought the best of both bankruptcy worlds by first getting rid of ordinary debts in Chapter 7 and then filing in Chapter 13 to deal with nondischargeable debts and security interests. This effectively allows them to target their postpetition disposable income toward payment of the debts that they cannot or do not wish to discharge. In essence, a Chapter 20 plan, if permitted, would allow the debtor to discriminate among creditors in a way that § 1322(b)(1) would not permit if the debtor had filed under Chapter 13 initially. Not surprisingly, courts have reacted with some hostility toward such Chapter 20 plans. Some courts even treated them as bad faith *per se* but the Supreme Court rejected that view largely because of the absence of a statutory bar to successive filings or discharges in Chapter 13.[75]

Indeed, there apparently are some justifications for filing under Chapter 13 shortly after receiving a Chapter 7 discharge, such as if the debtor has too much debt to be eligible for Chapter 13 relief or insufficient income to fund a feasible plan without first discharging some debt.[76] Nevertheless, Chapter 20 plans remained highly disfavored

---

[75]   *Johnson v. Home State Bank*, 501 U.S. 78, 87 (1991).

[76]   *See In re Cushman*, 217 B.R. 470, 476 n.10 (Bankr. E.D. Va. 1998).

and a major factor to consider in determining whether the debtor is acting in good faith.[77]

The 2005 amendments, by adding § 1328(f), have made Chapter 20 plans virtually impossible. Read that provision and then tackle the following problem.

Problem 11-12

Delaney filed a Chapter 7 bankruptcy petition on May 1, 2002, and received a discharge in that case on November 1, 2002. If Delaney files for Chapter 13 bankruptcy protection on August 1, 2006, and completes the plan on September 15, 2009, will Delaney be entitled to a discharge? *See* § 1328(f).

6. Avoidance Powers

In Chapter 7, the trustee uses a variety of powers to avoid certain prepetition and postpetition transfers. *See* §§ 544, 545, 547, 548, 549 & 553. These powers are a necessary aspect of the trustee's principal function of collecting and liquidating the property of the estate. § 704(a)(1). The Chapter 13 trustee, however, acts primarily as a disbursing agent and may choose not to exercise those powers. Indeed, the method of compensating trustees gives the Chapter 7 trustee an incentive to maximize the size of the bankruptcy estate through the use of avoiding powers, whereas a Chapter 13 trustee may not have such an incentive.

What if, however, the trustee or the debtor wishes to avoid a transfer? For example, suppose a creditor levied on substantial assets shortly before the bankruptcy petition were filed. In a Chapter 7 case, that preferential transfer, once avoided, might significantly enhance the recovery of general creditors. However, if the debtor files under Chapter 13, which requires that creditors receive at least what they would get in Chapter 7 – a calculation that necessarily factors in the impact of the trustee's avoiding powers – but is unable to avoid the preferential transfer, the debtor may not be able to fund a confirmable plan.

Chapter 5 of the Bankruptcy Code, which includes the avoiding powers, is expressly made applicable in Chapter 13 cases. § 103(a). However, in enumerating the powers of the Chapter 13 trustee, § 1302(b) makes no reference to the avoiding powers. Moreover, while a Chapter 11 debtor in possession is expressly granted the avoiding

---

[77] *See, e.g., In re Covino*, 245 B.R. 162 (Bankr. D. Idaho 2000). *But cf. In re Keach*, 243 B.R. 851 (1st Cir. BAP 2000) (concluding that judicial decision about "good faith" had gone far afield from what the drafters of the Code had intended, that many of the factors employed in the case law had been preempted by contrary judgments explicitly made by Congress, and that the inquiry into good faith was properly restricted to the debtor's postfiling conduct).

powers of a trustee, § 1107(a), there is no such grant of authority to a Chapter 13 debtor. Is there any way, then, to avoid preferences, fraudulent transfers, and the like in a Chapter 13 case? Several courts have ruled that there is not.[78]

A similar question arises with respect to the debtor's avoidance powers. Recall that the debtor has the power under § 522(f) to avoid certain liens that impair exemptions and the power under § 522(h) to avoid certain transfers of exempt property that the trustee chooses not to avoid. Given that exempt property does not serve the same function in Chapter 13 as it does in Chapter 7 – because a Chapter 13 debtor normally retains all property, exempt and nonexempt, while paying creditors out of future income – do such powers apply in Chapter 13? Should they?[79]

C.   THE EFFECT OF CONFIRMATION

Confirmation of the plan is *not* the culmination of a Chapter 13 case. In particular, it does not terminate the stay or qualify the debtor for a discharge. The discharge is not granted until the debtor finishes making all payments under the plan, § 1328(a), or becomes entitled to a hardship discharge, § 1328(b). The stay remains generally in effect until the case is closed, dismissed, or the debtor is either granted or denied a discharge. § 362(c)(2). Because the discharge does not come until all payments are made, the stay generally remains until that time as well.

What confirmation does do is vest all property of the estate in the debtor. § 1327(b).[80] More importantly, confirmation binds the debtor and all creditors to the plan. § 1327(a). The plan therefore becomes the blueprint for the parties' future relations. It is binding even on those creditors who are not provided for under it. In short, the plan is given *res judicata* effect.[81]

---

[78]   *See, e.g., In re Knapper,* 407 F.3d 573 (3d Cir. 2005) (Chapter 13 debtor could not invoke trustee's strong-arm powers); *In re Stangel,* 219 F.3d 498 (5th Cir. 2000) (debtor lacked standing to bring § 545 action); *In re Hanson,* 332 B.R. 8 (10th Cir. BAP 2005). *Contra In re Cohen,* 305 B.R. 886 (9th Cir. BAP 2004) (debtor has standing to use trustee's § 544 strong-arm powers); *Thacker v. United Companies Lending Corp.,* 256 B.R. 724 (W.D. Ky. 2000) (same).

[79]   *See, e.g., In re Hamilton,* 125 F.3d 292 (5th Cir. 1997); *In re Hall,* 752 F.2d 582 (11th Cir. 1985). *See also In re Maddox,* 15 F.3d 1347 (5th Cir. 1994) (Chapter 13 trustee may use § 522(f) to avoid transfers); *In re Stroud,* 219 B.R. 388 (Bankr. M.D.N.C. 1997) (debtor may use § 522(f) only after completing the Chapter 13 plan and becoming entitled to a discharge).

[80]   This means that § 362(a)(3) & (4) no longer apply to such property. *See* § 362(c).

[81]   *See, e.g., In re Layo,* 460 F.3d 289 (2d Cir. 2006) (confirmed plan which treats claimant as secured is res judicata and prevents subsequent lien avoidance action).

This effect engenders two recurring issues. First, what happens if the confirmed plan contains an improper or unauthorized provision? In general, a confirmed plan cannot be collaterally attacked. Thus, if a timely objection was not made and if the time for appealing the confirmation order has expired, the plan will normally be binding despite any impropriety in it. Despite that, the debtor cannot use the plan to circumvent other provisions of the Code. For example, the debtor cannot use the plan to reduce the amount of a claim if the debtor did not object to the claim under § 502(a).[82] Similarly, a plan that is confirmed despite its failure to provide for payment of priority claims, in violation of § 1322(a)(2), is null and void and therefore can be attacked after confirmation.[83] Similarly, and despite some disagreement, a debtor cannot engage in discharge by ambush: put language in the plan discharging an otherwise nondischargeable debt, have the plan confirmed without following the procedures for litigating nondischargeability issues (which are supposed to be resolved through adversary proceedings rather than the confirmation process), and then give preclusive effect to the plan.[84]

---

[82]   *See In re Linkous*, 990 F.2d 160 (4th Cir. 1993) (contrary holding would deny creditor due process).

[83]   *See In re Escobedo*, 28 F.3d 34 (7th Cir. 1994). *Cf. In re Szostek*, 886 F.2d 1405 (3d Cir. 1989) (confirmed plan's failure to pay present value of a secured claim, in violation of § 1325(a)(5)(B), could not later be attacked by the secured claimant who failed to object at the confirmation hearing because the present value requirement is not mandatory).

[84]   *See In re Hanson*, 397 F.3d 482 (7th Cir. 2005) (it would violate due process to discharge student loan debts in a plan without following the rules for an adversary proceeding); *In re Poland*, 382 F.3d 1185 (10th Cir. 2004) (refusing to treat plan as discharging student loan obligations and expressing view that earlier decision to the contrary in *In re Andersen*, 179 F.3d 1253 (10th Cir. 1999), was wrong); *In re Banks*, 299 F.3d 296 (4th Cir. 2002) (plan purporting to discharge postpetition interest on student loans was ineffective because it denied due process); *In re Repp*, 307 B.R. 144 (9th Cir. BAP 2004) (due process would be violated by discharging student loan debts in a plan without the notice required by an adversary proceeding); Kevin C. Driscoll, Jr., Note, *Eradicating the "Discharge by Declaration" for Student Loan Debt in Chapter 13*, 2000 U. Ill. L. Rev. 1311 (arguing against discharge by ambush). *But cf. In re Davis*, 188 Fed. Appx. 671 (10th Cir. 2006) (debtor may through language in confirmed plan avoid allegedly unperfected lien).

  Of course, if *before confirmation* the court notices the debtor's effort to make student loans dischargeable by putting a statement to that effect in the proposed plan, the court should and will deny confirmation even if no creditor objects. *E.g., In re Webber*, 251 B.R. 554 (Bankr. D. Ariz. 2000); *In re Mammel*, 221 B.R. 238 (Bankr. N.D. Iowa 1998). Moreover, an attorney's effort to circumvent proper procedures in this way is sanctionable conduct. *In re Patton*, 261 B.R. 44, 48 (E.D. Wash. 2001); *In re Lemons*, 285 B.R. 327 (Bankr. W.D. Okla. 2002); *In re Hensley*, 249 B.R. 318 (Bankr. W.D. Okla. 2000). *But cf. In re Wright*, 279 B.R. 886 (D. Kan. 2002) (agreeing with bankruptcy court that sanctions for such conduct should be imposed on a case-by-case basis, rather than through a per se rule).

Second, what happens if the debtor fails to perform under the plan? When that occurs, the debtor will not receive a discharge, the case will be converted to Chapter 7 or dismissed, and the claims of creditors will be restored to their original amount, less any payments actually received under the Chapter 13 plan. It will also usually be grounds for getting relief from the stay.

IN RE CARONA
254 B.R. 364 (Bankr. S.D. Tex. 2000)

Steen, Bankruptcy Judge.

Sterling Bank ("Sterling") seeks relief from the automatic stay to execute on its security interests in certain trucks and trailers because Richard Carona ("Debtor") has failed to make payments to the chapter 13 trustee in this case as required by the Debtor's confirmed chapter 13 plan. For reasons set forth below, relief from the stay is granted by separate order issued this date.

FACTS

The facts are undisputed.

August 27, 1999   Debtor filed this case under chapter 13 of the Bankruptcy Code.

March 23, 2000   Debtor's Chapter 13 plan was confirmed.

July 19, 2000   Sterling filed its motion for relief from the automatic stay, alleging principally that the Debtor had failed to make payments to the chapter 13 trustee as required by the Debtor's plan.

The Debtor's chapter 13 plan does not include any provision that would alter the post-confirmation vesting provisions of § 1327(b) of the Bankruptcy Code. There was no proceeding to avoid Sterling's security interests and the plan did not provide for vesting the trucks and trailers in the Debtor free and clear of Sterling's security interests. At the time of the hearing on Sterling's motion for relief from the stay, the Debtor was $8,700 delinquent in payments to the chapter 13 trustee.

Although Debtor's counsel was present at the hearing on Sterling's motion for relief from the stay and although counsel argued enthusiastically for the Court to deny the motion, the Debtor did not appear at the hearing and the Debtor presented no evidence at that hearing to refute Sterling's evidence that the Debtor was $8,700 delinquent in plan payments. The Debtor has not filed a motion to modify the plan to cure the payment defaults.

CONTENTIONS OF THE PARTIES

Sterling contends that the Debtor's default is sufficient "cause" to justify relief from the automatic stay to allow Sterling to execute on its security interests, and to sell the collateral. The Debtor contends (i) that the confirmation of its chapter 13 plan revests the trucks and trailers in the Debtor, (ii) that the trucks and trailers are, therefore, no longer property of the estate, (iii) that the bankruptcy automatic stay no longer applies since the property is no longer property of the estate, (iv) that confirmation of the chapter 13 plan, in effect, rewrites the contract between the Debtor and Sterling and (v) therefore Sterling's appropriate remedy is to seek dismissal of the case and the concomitant revocation of the effects of the confirmation order.

Neither party has briefed the issues or cited authority for its contentions.

CONCLUSIONS OF LAW

Analysis of the Debtor's argument requires an interpretation of the definition of property of the estate and an interpretation of the reach and termination of the automatic stay in bankruptcy. It is helpful to view these concepts in broad generalities, first, and then to look at the finer points of the Debtor's arguments.

1. GENERAL CONCEPTS AS APPLICABLE TO THIS CASE

At the moment that a bankruptcy petition is filed, Bankruptcy Code § 541 creates an estate consisting of all property interests owned by the Debtor. Also at the beginning of the case, Bankruptcy Code § 362(a) creates an automatic stay that prohibits creditor action to collect pre-petition debt. For purposes of this discussion, it is important to note that the stay prohibits: (i) collection of pre-petition claims against the debtor, (ii) acts to foreclose on property of the estate, and (iii) acts to enforce pre-petition liens against property of the debtor. The automatic stay terminates (as to property of the estate) when the property ceases to be property of the estate. Otherwise, (as applicable to the current facts) the automatic stay terminates when the case is dismissed or the debtor is discharged.

Confirmation of a chapter 13 plan: (i) binds the debtor and each creditor to its terms; and (ii) vests property of the estate in the debtor (unless the plan provides otherwise), subject to liens and security interests (unless those liens and security interests are voided by appropriate proceedings).

2. DOES THE AUTOMATIC STAY APPLY, POST-CONFIRMATION, TO STERLING?

The Debtor correctly argues that, as of the date that the chapter 13 plan was confirmed, the trucks and trailers ceased to be property of the estate and became property of the debtor. Therefore, the stay effected by Bankruptcy Code § 362(a)(2), (3), and (4) was terminated. However, Bankruptcy Code § 362(a)(5) provides that:

[Filing a bankruptcy] petition operates as a stay . . . of any act to create, perfect, or enforce against property of the debtor any lien to the extent that such lien secures a claim that arose before the commencement of the case.

There is no question that the trucks and trailers are now property of the debtor and there is no question that Sterling's security interests were liens to secure a pre-petition claim. The stay effected [by] § 362(a)(5) remains in effect. Therefore, the Debtor is incorrect in arguing that Sterling's motion should be denied as moot.

3.   DOES A POSTPETITION DEFAULT IN PAYMENTS TO THE CHAPTER 13 TRUSTEE CONSTITUTE SUFFICIENT "CAUSE" TO GRANT RELIEF FROM THE AUTOMATIC STAY?

The Debtor argues that the confirmation order, in effect, rewrote the contract between the Debtor and Sterling and that Sterling is bound by that order. Therefore, the Debtor argues, relief from the stay is inappropriate until the case is dismissed or until the confirmation order is revoked. The Court disagrees.

The Debtor's argument ignores the fact that the Debtor is *also* bound by the confirmation order. The Debtor is obligated by the plan and by the confirmation order to make payments to the Trustee. Even assuming the Debtor's conceptual approach, (*i.e.* that the confirmation order creates a new contract between the Debtor and Sterling), there does not appear to be any reason why (and the Debtor has pointed out no reason why) a postpetition default by the Debtor does not justify the same results that would occur outside of bankruptcy, that is, foreclosure on a lien or security interest. That foreclosure may first require permission of the bankruptcy court (*i.e.* relief from the automatic stay of § 362(a)(5)), but the Debtor has pointed out no reason why the Debtor's default is not "cause" sufficient to justify the court to grant that relief.

The jurisprudence and the principal treatise on chapter 13 support the view that a postpetition default is sufficient cause to grant relief from the stay to allow foreclosure by a secured creditor. Judge Ellington, in *In re Lee*, 167 B.R. 417, 426-27 (Bankr. S.D. Miss. 1992), *aff'd*, 22 F.3d 1094 (5th Cir. 1994) expresses the rule as follows, and cites no fewer than 5 cases in support of the proposition:

Since a creditor's rights are redefined by the terms of the confirmed plan, where a debtor materially defaults under the terms of his confirmed plan the creditor may be entitled to relief from the automatic stay under Bankruptcy Code § 362.

In the leading treatise on chapter 13, Judge Lundin indicates that a post-confirmation default is sufficient cause to grant relief from the stay unless the Debtor timely modifies the plan to cure the default. The Court of Appeals for the Fifth Circuit has clearly held that the chapter 13 plan can be modified to cure post-confirmation defaults. *Matter of Mendoza*, 111 F.3d 1264 (5th Cir. 1997). Therefore, if a debtor wants to avoid the possibility that the Court will grant relief from the stay on account of the debtor's postpetition defaults under the plan, the debtor should assure timely plan modification to cure the default.

CONCLUSION

In summary, the Court concludes that the automatic stay of § 362(a)(5) survives plan confirmation with respect to pre-petition claims. The Court further concludes that a material default in payments to the chapter 13 trustee constitutes sufficient cause to grant relief from the stay when the Debtor has taken no steps to cure the deficiency promptly or to modify the plan to cure the default. Therefore, an order will be issued this date granting Sterling relief from the automatic stay.

In researching the law for this opinion, the Court examined and considered a number of cases that deal with the intricacies of the interplay between §§ 362, 1306, and 1327. Because this case involves a *pre*-petition claim secured by property of the debtor and a postpetition default under a confirmed plan, the Court does not need to consider whether a stay exists with respect to postpetition claims and with respect to execution of those claims against property of the debtor. Nor does the Court need to consider the extent to which property/earnings of the debtor post-confirmation constitute property of the estate. Nor does the Court need to consider the applicable consequences, if any, of a plan provision that abrogates § 1327(b) to allow property to remain in the estate rather than being vested in the debtor post-confirmation. Each of these distinctions might be significant in different circumstances and for different purposes. Although the Court finds the decision in *In re Fisher*, 203 B.R. 958 (N.D. Ill. 1997) to be persuasive, and although the Court finds Judge Lundin's discussion of that case in his chapter 13 treatise to be especially illuminating, any further discussion of those issues in this decision would be dicta.

NOTE

The last paragraph of the *Carona* decision identifies a number of things the court did not need to address. To understand what the court was getting at, consider this. While any effort to collect a prepetition debt remains stayed, *see* § 362(a)(6), efforts to collect a postpetition debt directed at nonexempt property now vested in the debtor would not be stayed. Yet while that rule is fairly clear, what remains unclear is how it applies to the debtor's future income. Is the portion of the income allocated to the plan immune from reach of creditors? What about the remaining portion, the debtor's nondisposable income, which is by definition to be used to pay the debtor's necessary living expenses? The following case addresses this issue.

1. *Paying Postpetition Obligations*

IN RE LEAVELL
190 B.R. 536 (Bankr. E.D Va. 1995)

St. John, Bankruptcy Judge.

This case is before the court on the motion of the debtor, Alfreda Epps Leavell, for a finding of contempt and imposition of sanctions against Littmans, Inc., ("Littmans") and its counsel, W. Wayne Tiffany ("Tiffany"). After reviewing the evidence and arguments of counsel, we make the following determinations.

FINDINGS OF FACT

The debtor filed the instant Chapter 13 case on December 8, 1994. Six days later, she purchased a ring and a video cassette recorder from Littmans. The debtor did not disclose her bankruptcy status when she purchased these items. After the debtor failed to pay for these items, Littmans, through Tiffany, obtained a judgment against her on July 19, 1995 and began to garnish her postpetition earnings. Upon learning of the garnishment, counsel for the debtor notified Tiffany of the pending Chapter 13 case but her request to dismiss the garnishment was refused. Thereafter, the debtor filed this motion for contempt and sanctions, requesting damages, attorney fees, and sanctions on the grounds that the garnishment action violated the automatic stay.[85]

We note that the debtor's confirmed Chapter 13 plan required $75.00 per month for 36 months. According to her schedules, the debtor earns $1,550.00 per month. Under the terms of the plan, all property of the estate re-vested in the debtor upon confirmation. The Court entered an order confirming the Chapter 13 plan on February 6, 1995. Littmans did not file a proof of claim for the postpetition debts and the plan failed to provide for said debts.

ANALYSIS

The automatic stay operates to prohibit certain collection efforts upon the filing of the bankruptcy petition. It bars collection actions against the (1) debtor which actions could have been brought pre-petition; (2) property of the debtor in an effort to collect pre-petition debts; and (3) property of the estate regardless of whether the debt arose before or after the filing of the bankruptcy petition. In the case at bar, we are concerned only with the third prohibition since the debt was incurred postpetition. * * *

The case at bar poses two issues for the Court to consider. The threshold issue is whether there can be any property of the estate upon which the automatic stay can

---

[85]   The debtor did not argue that the lawsuit and judgment obtained by Littmans violated the stay. Therefore, we do not address this issue.

operate upon confirmation of a Chapter 13 plan. If the answer is negative, then Littmans and Tiffany did not violate the automatic stay since there was nothing upon which the stay can protect. If the answer is affirmative, then we must determine whether all postpetition earnings become property of the estate and thus protected by the automatic stay.

Littmans and Tiffany argued that property of the estate in the instant case ceased to exist upon the confirmation of the plan. Since the plan did not provide otherwise, they argue, the order of confirmation vested all property of the estate in the debtor. They conclude that they did not violate the stay because there was no property of the estate remaining upon which the stay can operate.

We first note that courts have disagreed on whether property of the estate exists after the Chapter 13 plan is confirmed. There are several lines of cases as to how to reconcile seemingly conflicting provisions of §§ 1306(a) and 1327(b). One line of cases has held that upon confirmation of the plan, property that is necessary to implement the Chapter 13 plan remains property of the estate upon which the stay operates to protect. In contrast, another line of cases has held that two things occur upon confirmation of the plan: (1) property of the estate is vested in the debtor unless provided for otherwise in the plan; and (2) there is no longer any property of the estate remaining upon which the stay can operate. In another line of reasoning, [one court has] held that although confirmation of the plan vests property of the estate with the debtor, the debtor's ownership interest in such property is limited to the extent that it is required to implement the plan. In other words, the debtor gets ownership and possessory rights to the property but the debtor is not free for all purposes to do with it as he pleases.

After reviewing the * * * cases and the reasoning therein, the Court agrees with the first line of cases. Upon confirmation of the plan, the estate continues to exist. There are several reasons for this conclusion. First, there must be some property of the estate remaining after confirmation for the Chapter 13 Trustee to administer and upon which the Trustee makes a final report. If there never is any property of the estate after confirmation, then what is there for the Trustee to collect from the debtor and then disburse to and for the benefit of the creditors under the confirmed plan? If they do not receive and disburse property of the estate, why are they needed?

Second, to determine that § 1327(b) mean[s] that there is no property of the estate after confirmation would render § 1306(a) superfluous. This is necessarily so because Congress intended to protect earnings and property that are acquired by the debtor postpetition and necessary to implement the plan. Without § 1306(a), any property that the debtor acquires post-confirmation can be seized without regards to the Chapter 13 process. Congress did not say in § 1306(a) that earnings and properties acquired postpetition are property of the estate until the Chapter 13 plan is confirmed. Rather, it said that such property and earnings are property of the estate until the case is closed, dismissed, or converted.

Third, our decision would also give § 1306(b) full effect. Section 1306(b) provides:
Except as provided in a confirmed plan or order confirming a plan, the debtor shall remain in possession of all property of the estate.
This section does not apply until confirmation. If at the time after confirmation there is no property of the estate, then there is no reason to grant the debtor possession.

Finally, the clear language of § 1306 demonstrates that confirmation of the plan is not relevant to determining whether property is or is not property of the estate. The relevant events in this determination are commencement of the case and either dismissal, closing or conversion of the case. If Congress had intended for confirmation to so drastically affect the expansive definition of property of the estate in § 1306, it knew how to draft such a provision.

We next address the effect of confirmation on the debtor's postpetition earnings. The debtor argues that all postpetition earnings are property of the estate under § 1306(a) and thus protected by the automatic stay from collection actions by post-confirmation creditors. Specifically, the debtor argues that not only postpetition earnings are property of the estate, but also that they remain so until the cases is closed, dismissed or converted to a case under Chapter 7, 11, or 12.

The debtor also argues that policy considerations favored a judgment in her favor. She argues that allowing Littmans to garnish the portion of the earnings over $75.00 would result in great prejudice to her. Such a garnishment threatens her ability to complete her plan payments because it reduces the debtor's already limited resources. The garnishment may force the debtor to use the money allocated to pay the plan and thus frustrate her ability to complete the Chapter 13 plan and thus destroy her ability to receive a discharge. Furthermore, if the plan cannot be consummated, the unsecured creditors would also be prejudiced since they would not receive any payments. We decline to adopt these arguments.

Addressing the debtor's legal argument, we conclude that earnings acquired post-confirmation and necessary to implement the Chapter 13 plan remains property of the estate after the plan is confirmed unless the plan states otherwise. Only that portion that is necessary to make the plan payments becomes property of the estate and protected by the automatic stay. The balance of such post-confirmation earnings belongs to the debtor as her individual property and is not insulated from postpetition claims nor protected by the automatic stay. Applying these conclusions of law to the facts of the instant case, only $75.00 of the debtor's monthly earnings is protected by the automatic stay. This meant that Littmans could garnish up to $1,475.00 per month from the debtor's net monthly income of $1,550.00. Littmans garnished $417.59. Accordingly, Littmans (and Tiffany) did not violate the automatic stay automatic stay when it garnished the debtor's income to satisfy the postpetition debts.

We note that [some] courts have reached even stronger conclusions. These courts held that pursuant to § 1327(b) all property of the estate vests in the debtor upon confirmation of the plan, without regard to whether or not such property is necessary to implement the plan. We disagree because this interpretation would allow the creditor to levy against all of the debtor's property, including that property in the hands of the Chapter 13 Trustee. The holding of these courts would require debtors to specifically delay re-vesting in the plan or to vest property of the estate in an entity other than the debtor. We do not believe that this was Congress' intent. Section 1327(b) is an efficient adaption of Bankruptcy Act Section 70(I). It implements a major theme of Chapter 13 by preserving to the debtor possession of all property, except as otherwise required to effectuate the confirmed plan.

Turning to the debtor's policy arguments, we find them equally unpersuasive. The primary concern proffered by the debtor is that the Court should protect the debtor from herself. She chose to purchase the ring and video cassette recorder when she possibly could not afford to pay for them. She was in bankruptcy and, according to her schedules, could barely pay her living expenses and make her plan payments. The prejudice the debtor raises was her own doing and the Court will not allow her to use the bankruptcy process as a sword against the unwary creditor who extended credit to her without knowledge of her bankruptcy.

Addressing the debtor's argument concerning the unsecured creditors, the Court finds that argument unpersuasive. Unsecured creditors have an interest in the debtor being able to perform under the plan to completion and without postpetition creditors being able to deprive the debtor of its ability to do so by seizing property or wages. If the case is dismissed, the unsecured creditors can pursue their claims through non-bankruptcy forums to obtain the benefit of their bargain. We do recognize that the unsecured creditors would receive 0% of their claims, according to the debtor's schedules, should the case be converted. However, the Code provides many provisions that favor postpetition creditors over pre-petition creditors. Therefore, we cannot conclude that the prejudice to the unsecured creditors is so severe to warrant another outcome.

Furthermore, we find the prejudice to Littmans more equitably compelling. First, it would have no remedy to enforce its claim until case is closed, dismissed or converted. Second, Littmans could not share in the distribution of this plan. It would not qualify to file a postpetition claim under § 1305(a) and § 1305(c) because the items purchased by the debtor were not necessary for the debtor's performance under the plan. Third, Littmans does not have standing to modify the plan to include his claims under § 1329. Since it cannot file a proof of claim as contemplated in § 1305 and thus get an allowed claim, it necessarily does not have standing to modify the plan.

As a final note, our decision is limited to postpetition earnings as contemplated by § 1306(a)(2). We do not deal with property acquired postpetition as set forth in § 1306(a)(1). Postpetition earnings dedicated to the Chapter 13 Trustee are easily discernible for purposes of determining whether such funds are necessary to implement the plan. Property other than earnings are not so readily discernible and must be determined on a case-by-case basis. Therefore, we expressly limit this opinion to the post-confirmations earnings.

NOTE

Some other courts have rejected this approach and held that all of the debtor's postpetition earnings are estate property and therefore are protected by the stay.[86] As one of them explained:

> The chapter 13 plan payment is not the only payment necessary for the successful completion of a chapter 13 plan. Frequently, the confirmed plan requires the debtor make payments directly to a secured creditor, in this case the mortgage company, and in other cases, the car finance company. If the direct payments are not timely made, the secured creditor will seek relief from the automatic stay in order to repossess the vehicle or sell the home at foreclosure. If relief is granted, the chapter 13 case typically converts to a chapter 7 proceeding or is dismissed, both to the prejudice of the unsecured creditors provided for in the chapter 13 plan. Saving the family home or the family car is a key incentive to selecting chapter 13 over chapter 7 – a selection frequently more beneficial to unsecured creditors than chapter 7. Not only is the plan payment to the chapter 13 trustee necessary for the success of the plan, but the direct payments to the secured creditors are also necessary.
>
> * * * In addition to these plan payments, the debtor must also be able to pay his living expenses. Confirmation requires that the debtor devote his entire net disposable income to the chapter 13 plan. § 1325(b). Confirmation also requires the court to find that the plan be feasible. § 1325(a)(6). Successful plans require strict adherence to the debtor's budget. A garnishment necessarily reduces the income available to the debtor to make his plan payment to the trustee, the direct payments to his secured creditors, and the payment of his current living expenses. Since the debtor's entire net disposable income must be devoted to the chapter 13 plan, there is

---

[86] *See, e.g., In re Fisher*, 203 B.R. 958 (N.D. Ill 1997); *In re Reynard*, 250 B.R. 241 (Bankr. E.D. Va. 2000); *In re Holden*, 236 B.R. 156 (Bankr. D. Vt. 1999), *aff'd*, 258 B.R. 323 (D. Vt. 2000); *In re Rangel*, 233 B.R. 191 (Bankr. D. Mass. 1999).

nothing left over for a creditor to seize that does not affect a debtor's ability to successfully complete the chapter 13 plan. All post-confirmation earnings – not just the amount of the plan payment-are necessary for the success of a chapter 13 plan and must be property of the post-confirmation chapter 13 estate. They are protected by the automatic stay.[87]

2. *Modifying a Confirmed Plan*

During the multi-year duration of the plan, many things may affect the debtor's finances. On the negative side, the debtor may experience a job loss, an illness with associated medical expenses and loss of income, a divorce, an uninsured casualty to property, or simply unanticipated expenses, such as for necessary repairs to a home or car. On the positive side, the debtor may receive a raise, find a better paying job, get married to a person with substantial assets or high income, or even win the lottery. Accordingly, § 1329 allows for post-confirmation modification of a plan. Unfortunately, that authorization includes no guidance on when a court may or must modify the plan. In other words, it provides no standard for determining whether or when modification is appropriate, although it does require that a modified plan satisfy all requirements normally applicable to plan confirmation. This raises a difficult question: given the *res judicata* effect of confirmation, what has to change before a court must or should entertain motions to modify? Given the lack of guidance in the Code, it is not surprising that courts have come to differing conclusions on this question. Some require that the proponent of modification show that there has been an unanticipated, substantial change in the debtor's financial circumstances.[88] Others have found no such requirement in § 1329 and declined to imply one.[89] This latter approach appears to be the prevalent view.[90]

Probably the most common reason debtors seek to modify a confirmed plan is a reduction in income. If the court believes that the modification is proposed in good faith and the debtor will be able to make the payments under the modified plan, it is likely to

---

[87]   *Reynard,* 250 B.R. at 248-49.

[88]   *See, e.g., In re Arnold,* 869 F.2d 240 (4th Cir. 1989).

[89]   *See, e.g., In re Witkowski,* 16 F.3d 739 (7th Cir. 1994).

[90]   *See Barbosa v. Solomon,* 235 F.3d 31 (1st Cir. 2000) (agreeing with *Witkowski* and leaving the decision on modification to the discretion of the bankruptcy judge, subject to review on an abuse-of-discretion standard); *In re Brown,* 219 B.R. 191 (6th Cir. BAP 1998); *In re Powers,* 202 B.R. 618 (9th Cir. BAP 1996).

approve the modification.[91] Apparently, debtors may even use § 1329 to modify their plans in order to cure post-confirmation defaults on their home mortgage loans.[92]

Another reason debtors sometimes seek modification is if property serving as collateral suddenly depreciates and the debtor no longer views it as worthwhile to continue making the payments called for under the plan in order to retain the property. For example, in *In re Coffman*,[93] the debtors owed $6,775 on a car valued at $5,450. Their plan stripped the lien down, treating the creditor as secured to the extent of $5,450 and unsecured as to the remainder, and required the debtors were to make monthly payments of $121.30 on the secured claim. Fifteen months into the plan, the car began to malfunction and repair efforts proved unsuccessful. The debtors then decided to surrender the car to the creditor and sought modification to avoid making the remaining $121.30 payments. The court refused to permit the modification, noting that debtors receive the benefit of any appreciation in property collateralizing a secured claim and thus it was only fair that they bear the risk of any depreciation.[94] It then regarded the debtor's request as a motion to reconsider a claim under § 502(j), for which the requisite "cause" was lacking.[95]

Occasionally, a creditor or the trustee seeks a modification. For example, in *In re Arnold*,[96] the debtor's income increased from a projected $80,000 at the inception of the plan to $200,000 two years later. The Fourth Circuit affirmed the bankruptcy court's decision to increase the monthly payments from $800 to $1500 and to extend the term of the plan to five years. A similar issue arises when assets that were part of the estate, but which confirmation revested in the debtor, appreciate postpetition. Consider the following problem.

---

[91] *Cf. In re Vasquez*, 261 B.R. 654 (Bankr. N.D. Tex. 2001) (it is bad faith to propose modifying a plan to stop all future payments if a hardship discharge is available).

[92] *See In re Mendoza*, 111 F.3d 1264 (5th Cir. 1997); *In re Hoggle*, 12 F.3d 1008 (11th Cir. 1994).

[93] 271 B.R. 492 (Bankr. N.D. Tex. 2002).

[94] *Id.* at 496.

[95] *See also In re Jackson*, 280 B.R. 703 (Bankr. S.D. Ala. 2001) (denying debtors' request to modify a plan by surrendering their car to the secured creditor and reclassifying the creditor's claim as unsecured; the debtors had put 10,000 miles on the car but paid the creditor only $12.31 on its claim). *But cf. In re Hernandez*, 282 B.R. 200 (Bankr. S.D. Tex. 2002) (permitting the debtors to modify a confirmed plan to surrender a car to the secured party because proposal was not abusive and debtors needed the money previously for debt service on the car to pay the home mortgage).

[96] 869 F.2d 240 (4th Cir. 1989).

Problem 11-13

Delighted's confirmed Chapter 13 plan called for Delighted to make direct payments on a home mortgage loan and payments of $1,200/month to the trustee for distribution to unsecured claimants. If those payments are made, and after deducting the trustee's fees, the resulting distributions will be sufficient to pay creditors approximately 24% of their claims. Eighteen months after confirmation, and after real estate values had appreciated substantially, Delighted sold the home for $137,000 more than the value listed in Delighted's schedules. Even after using some of the sales proceeds to pay off the mortgage loan, the remainder, if allocated to the plan, would be sufficient to pay off all creditors in full. What should the court do? *Compare In re Murphy*, 474 F.3d 143 (4th Cir. 2007)*, and Barbosa v. Soloman*, 235 F.3d 31 (1st Cir. 2000), *with In re Burgie*, 239 B.R. 406 (9th Cir. BAP 1999).

Even when modification is available, debtors should be careful about requesting it. As one commentator noted:

> Should you let a sleeping dog lie? Chapter 13 plans, once confirmed, can be modified. However, modification triggers a re-examination of the debtor's affairs, including his or her income and assets. Absent a modification of a chapter 13 plan, usually only the debtors are aware of their financial status and prospects; they have, in effect, an information monopoly. Modifying a plan requires disclosing financial information by debtors and the break-up of that monopoly.[97]

One recent case puts an interesting twist on this issue. In *Petro v. Mishler*,[98] the trustee was concerned that the debtors, because of their ages and work potential, might earn extra income not factored into their plan's payment schedules. At his request, the bankruptcy court required the debtors to provide the trustee with sworn statements of their income and check stubs every six months as a condition to approving the plan. The Seventh Circuit reversed, concluding that this effectively and impermissibly added a confirmation requirement to § 1325(a). It did, however, note that the debtors had to submit their income tax returns to the trustee, who could then use these as a basis for seeking to modify the plan under § 1329.

---

[97]   Joseph R. Prochaska, *Breaking the "Information Monopoly": The Perils to a Debtor of Modifying a Chapter 13 Plan*, 19 AM. BANKR. INST. J. 18 (March 2000).

[98]   276 F.3d 375 (7th Cir. 2002).

Problem 11-14

Shortly before filing a petition under Chapter 13, Disabled, a construction worker, developed a hernia that, unless repaired, would prevent Disabled from continuing his current employment. Disabled consulted Surgeon, who was informed about the bankruptcy petition. Disabled's health insurance will not cover all of the cost of the operation. Surgeon has never encountered a Chapter 13 patient before and calls you for legal advice concerning how the bankruptcy affects Surgeon's ability to obtain payment. Surgeon's normal practice is to send a bill for professional services after the services are performed. How would you advise Surgeon? *See* §§ 1305(a)(2), (c) & 1328(a), (d).

D. CONVERSION TO CHAPTER 7

If the plan proposed by the debtor fails to satisfy the criteria for confirmation, the bankruptcy court will typically give the debtor the opportunity to revise the plan so that it can be confirmed. If the debtor cannot devise a confirmable plan, the court may dismiss the case or convert it to Chapter 7. § 1307(c). Moreover, the debtor has a nonwaivable right to convert the case to one under Chapter 7 at any time. § 1307(a). Courts disagree about whether the means test applies upon conversion from Chapter 13 to Chapter 7.[99]

If conversion occurs before confirmation, there will typically be assets on hand – in particular, postpetition disposable income – that were part of the Chapter 13 estate but which would not have been part of a Chapter 7 estate if the case had been originally filed as a liquidation. *See* § 1326(a) (requiring the debtor to begin making payments within 30 days after a plan is filed but requiring the trustee to retain such payments until confirmation or denial of confirmation). Prior to 1994, it was very unclear what happened to these assets in the Chapter 7 proceeding. Circuit courts were split on whether the money remained in the estate for the benefit of creditors or was returned to the debtor.[100] In fact, the First Circuit described the issue as "excruciatingly close,"[101] and Judge Posner acknowledged that the arguments on both sides were "equally good

---

[99]   *Compare In re Perfetto*, 361 B.R. 27 (Bankr. D.R.I. 2007) (test does not apply after conversion), *with In re Fox*, 2007 WL 1576140 (Bankr. D.N.J. 2007) (test does apply).

[100]   *Compare In re Calder*, 973 F.2d 862 (10th Cir. 1992); *In re Lybrook*, 951 F.2d 136 (7th Cir. 1991) (both holding that such income remained in the estate) *with In re Young*, 66 F.3d 376 (1st Cir. 1995); *In re Bobroff*, 766 F.2d 797 (3d Cir. 1985) (both holding that it does not).

[101]   *Young,* 66 F.3d at 378.

alternative[s]."[102] Perhaps this was because of the strong policy supporting each side: failing to retain the income in the estate leaves open the possibility of "strategic conversions"; on the other hand, including it may discourage Chapter 13 filings.

The 1994 amendments to the Code resolved the issue by providing expressly that assets earned postpetition in a Chapter 13 case, and which remain on hand, are not part of the estate if the debtor converts to a Chapter 7 liquidation. *See* § 348(f).[103] The money is returned to the debtor.

Problem 11-15

Delinquent is employed, is paid weekly, and earns $30,000/year. Delinquent has $26,000 in reasonable annual living expenses, including income taxes and including payments on Delinquent's secured obligations (*see* the home and car loans described below). Delinquent has the following assets and liabilities.

Assets		Liabilities		Monthly Payment
$100,000	House	$93,000	Home Mortgage	$750
$4,500	Car	$6,000	Car Loan	$250
$3,900	Furnishings	$6,000	Battery Judgment	
$100	Cash	$60,000	Student Loans	
$3,500	Household Goods	$3,000	Credit Cards & Utilities	
$112,000		$165,000		

Delinquent is current in the car loan payments but two months behind on the home mortgage payments. Delinquent incurred the car loan two years ago. That loan calls for 48 equal monthly installments. The home mortgage secures a 20-year note that Delinquent signed four years ago. Interest is accruing on the student loans at an annual rate of 9% and on the battery judgment at a rate

---

[102] *Lybrook*, 951 F.2d at 137.

[103] *See also In re Stamm*, 222 F.3d 216 (5th Cir. 2000). *Cf. In re Pruneskip*, 343 B.R. 714 (Bankr. M.D. Fla. 2006) (equity in home built up postpetition during Chapter 13 proceeding was not in the estate upon conversion to Chapter 7).

There is an exception if the debtor converts the case in bad faith. *See* § 348(f)(2). In such instances, all property in the estate as of the date of the conversion remains property of the estate.

of 12% per annum. Would Delinquent be better off filing for bankruptcy protection under Chapter 7 or Chapter 13? Why?

CHAPTER TWELVE
THE CHAPTER 11 PROCESS

SECTION A.   STARTING A CHAPTER 11 CASE

1.   *Theory of Chapter 11*

Chapter 11 proceedings are somewhat similar to those under Chapter 13. In each, the debtor's future income is used to pay some portion of prepetition claims. In Chapter 13 proceedings, the future income is generated through the debtor's earnings. Hence, Chapter 13 proceedings are limited to debtors with regular income. § 109(e). In Chapter 11 cases, the future income is generated primarily by using the assets of a business, such as inventory, equipment, or account receivables. In Chapter 13, the future income used to pay prepetition claims is based on a budget that takes into account the debtor's anticipated living expenses. In Chapter 11, the future cash flow available to pay prepetition claims is calculated after taking into account the expenses necessary to generate that cash flow. In both types of cases, the debtor may also engage in a partial liquidation – that is, sell some assets – as part of the reorganization. In addition, both types of proceedings are based on the premise that a debtor's "going concern value" likely exceeds the debtor's liquidation value. In other words, a debtor who continues to generate income through gainful employment or operation of a business is worth more than a debtor who ceases all business activity.

While there are similarities, there are also some notable differences. Chapter 13 is restricted to individual debtors, whereas Chapter 11 is geared toward business debtors. That said, the proceedings are not wholly mutually exclusive. A sole proprietor of a business may use Chapter 13 to reorganize the business as long as the debtor is an individual with regular income and meets the debt thresholds.[1] Alternatively, an individual debtor may file a Chapter 11 petition even if the debtor does not have a business. Indeed, an individual whose debts exceed the limits of eligibility for Chapter 13 and whose income would presumptively make filing under Chapter 7 an abuse of the bankruptcy process, *see* § 707(b), may have no recourse other than to file under Chapter 11. Another difference between the two processes is that in a Chapter 13 case, the creditors may object to a reorganization plan as part of the confirmation process but they do not vote on the plan. § 1325. Chapter 11, on the other hand, is a largely consensual process. The creditors, once grouped into classes, vote on the proposed plan. The court will confirm the plan only if all classes of creditors accept the plan, § 1129(a)(8), or the

---

[1]   *See* Robert M. Lawless & Elizabeth Warren, *The Myth of the Disappearing Business Bankruptcy*, 93 CAL. L. REV. 743 (2005).

plan meets the exacting requirements necessary to confirm it over the objection of one or more classes. § 1129(b). This process leads to much more negotiation in advance of the confirmation hearing than is typical in a Chapter 13 case. There are other important differences between the confirmation requirements for each type of case. In Chapter 13, the court may confirm a plan over the objection of an unsecured creditor only if the plan satisfies the disposable income test, which requires that all future disposable income for the applicable commitment period be used to pay prepetition claims. § 1325(b). In Chapter 11, confirmation over the objection of an impaired class of creditors requires compliance with the absolute priority rule. § 1129(b). This means that no class of creditors may receive anything of value unless the plan provides for full payment to all objecting classes with a higher priority. It also means that debtor's interest holders (*e.g.*, stockholders) cannot retain any interest in the debtor unless all objecting classes of claims are paid in full.[2]

The bottom line is that many of the rules you will explore in this chapter of the book will be somewhat familiar to – but not precisely the same as – what we covered in the preceding chapter. The same is true for the policies underling the two types of reorganizations. Both are based on the fundamental belief in a second chance. A typical consumer debtor may have gotten in over his or her head because of job loss, medical crisis, divorce, excessive consumption or poor financial management. Chapter 11 cases typically involve a business debtor that has encountered difficulty because of business-related problems. Perhaps the market for the debtor's product or services was not as robust as predicted. Perhaps the debtor was the victim of bad management decisions or failed to implement an otherwise viable business plan. Perhaps the debtor encountered an excessive amount of liability due to some malfunction or defect in its product. Perhaps the debtor experienced problems not of its own doing, such as a general economic down turn or economic dislocation due to war, embargo, shortage of raw materials, or other causation not in its control. Chapter 11, like Chapter 13, is about permitting the debtor to deal with the causes of its financial difficulties and regroup for another try. In Chapter 13 this is thought good for society because it prevents individuals from becoming wards of the state and gives them a financial incentive to remain a productive member of the economy. In Chapter 11, this second chance may also benefit society given that businesses employ workers and presumably produce some product or service that is valued in the market.[3]

---

[2]   *See* Douglas G. Baird & Donald S. Bernstein, *Absolute Priority, Valuation Uncertainty, and the Reorganization Bargain*, 115 YALE L.J. 1930 (2006).

[3]   That being said, confirming a Chapter 11 plan is a difficult and expensive process. By some estimates, less than a third of filed Chapter 11 cases result in a confirmed plan. A. Mechele Dickerson, *A Behavioral Approach to Analyzing Corporate Failures*, 38 WAKE FOREST L. REV. 1, 33 & n.118 (2003).

However, there is a counter-policy at work in Chapter 11 that may not apply in Chapter 13. Chapter 13 debtors – who are, after all, individuals – necessarily survive the bankruptcy process.[4] Whether given or denied bankruptcy relief, the individual will continue to exist, and thus bankruptcy policy must be cognizant of that enduring fact. Businesses, on the other hand, need not survive. While it may be desirable that they do, their survival is not preordained. Nor is it clear that their survival is necessarily a good thing. Perhaps businesses that encounter financial distress should not be rehabilitated but liquidated, and the capital investment in the business put to a better use. In all likelihood, the better result will vary; some businesses should be liquidated and others reorganized. If that is true, the law must now confront a critical question: who should decide? Should the current managers and owners be in charge of this process or should the creditors of the business have control? What should be the role of the bankruptcy court in deciding these questions? These issues form the background for much of the debate regarding the viability of the Chapter 11 process itself.[5] As you study the Chapter 11 process, keep these questions in mind and ask yourself how they form the basis for the various rules we will encounter.

When considering these questions, also bear in mind that, by all accounts, successful reorganization in Chapter 11 may be rare. Many Chapter 11 cases produce no confirmed plan and are converted to Chapter 7 liquidations. In many others, the plan that is confirmed is essentially a liquidating plan: one that provides an orderly break up and sale of the estate assets rather than the continued operation of the debtor's business. In many of those that do yield a confirmed plan of reorganization, the debtor defaults on the plan, which may then lead to a new bankruptcy proceeding, often under Chapter 7. Few Chapter 11 cases produce a confirmed plan of true reorganization that the debtor performs and from which the debtor emerges as a viable business. Perhaps this should not be surprising, given that bankruptcy deals with the symptoms of the debtor's problems – excessive debt – rather than the root causes (*e.g.,* economic recession, poor management, fierce competition, and labor disputes).

---

[4]   A Chapter 13 debtor might, of course, die before completing the payment plan, but such an event would in all probability be unrelated to the bankruptcy proceeding itself.

[5]   *See, e.g.,* Douglas G. Baird & Edward R. Morrison, *Serial Entrepreneurs and Small Business Bankruptcies,* 105 COLUM. L. REV. 2310 (2005); Irit Haviv-Segal, *Bankruptcy Law and Inefficient Entitlements,* 2 BERKELEY BUS. L.J. 355 (2005); Lynn M. Lopucki, *A Team Production Theory of Bankruptcy,* 57 VAND. L. REV. 741 (2004); Jay Lawrence Westbrook, *The Control of Wealth,* 82 TEX. L. REV. 795 (2004); Douglas G. Baird & Robert K. Rasmussen, *The End of Bankruptcy,* 55 STAN. L. REV. 751 (2002); Douglas G. Baird & Robert K. Rasmussen, *Control Rights, Priority Rights, and the Conceptual Foundations of Corporate Reorganizations,* 87 VA. L. REV. 921 (2001); Elizabeth Warren, *Bankruptcy Policymaking in an Imperfect World,* 92 MICH. L. REV. 336 (1993).

2.   *Filing the Chapter 11 Case*

Section 109(d) provides that an entity eligible to seek relief under Chapter 7 – other than stockbrokers or commodity brokers – may file a Chapter 11 petition.[6] Individuals who file under Chapter 11 are subject to the same credit counseling provisions examined in chapter two of these materials. § 109(h). Repeat filers are subject to the dismissal provisions in § 109(g), discussed in chapter eleven of this book.

A Chapter 11 case may be commenced as either a voluntary case or an involuntary case. § 303.[7] However, few involuntary petitions are filed under Chapter 11 because most petitioning creditors prefer the Chapter 7 process under the oversight of a trustee.

Filing the Chapter 11 petition creates the bankruptcy estate. The estate includes all rights of the debtor in property as of the commencement of the case as well as all proceeds, profits or other products produced from property of the estate. § 541.[8] Given that a fundamental assumption underlying reorganization is that the debtor will use postpetition income to pay prepetition claims, it makes sense that all assets generated from the use of estate property likewise become property of the estate. Thus, in a typical Chapter 11 case, a debtor will use its equipment, inventory , accounts receivable, and other assets to produce income to be used in the reorganization process. That future income is then also property of the estate.

In a Chapter 11 case, the debtor remains in possession of property of the estate and operates the business unless there is cause for the court to appoint a trustee to take over. §§ 1101(1), 1107. The circumstances that justify appointment of a trustee will be discussed later in this chapter. For the moment, consider the implications of the debtor in possession concept. When a business debtor files a Chapter 11 petition, the same management team that was in charge of the business before the petition is generally still in charge of the business after the petition. Filing the petition does not magically make that team any better at its job of running a successful and profitable business. The petition gives the existing management no additional wisdom, skills, or ability to make accurate economic predictions. On the other hand, consider the alternative. To have a chance at a successful reorganization, the business must continue to operate and often cannot afford the significant amount of time it may take for a new management team to get up to speed on what needs to be done. Thus, while the existing management may

---

[6]   Uninsured state banks and certain financial clearing organizations are also permitted to file a Chapter 11 proceeding, even though they may not be eligible to file a Chapter 7 proceeding. *Compare* § 109(d) *with* § 109(b).

[7]   The rules relating to involuntary petitions were covered briefly in chapter two of this book.

[8]   If an individual files the Chapter 11 proceeding, earnings from the individual's postpetition services, as well as all property the individual acquires after commencement of the case, are included in the bankruptcy estate. § 1115. This rule virtually identical to the rule in Chapter 13. *See* § 1306.

not be the best team to run the business in the long run, there may be no other viable options for the short run.

In part because of this, Chapter 11 requires – particularly at the beginning of the process but continuing throughout the case – that the debtor in possession provide information about the operation of the business to the creditors, the court, and the U.S. Trustee's office. This allows those entities to monitor what the debtor in possession is doing. For example, within 15 days of when the debtor files a Chapter 11 petition,[9] the debtor must also file: schedules of assets, liabilities, executory contracts, and claimed exemptions if the debtor is an individual (Official Form 6); a statement of financial affairs (Official Form 7); and a list of the 20 largest unsecured creditors (Official Form 4). Rule 1007. Those forms provide creditors with their first look at the debtor's financial situation. sometime between the 20th and 40th day after the order for relief, the U.S. trustee will hold the first meeting of creditors. That meeting will enable creditors to ask the debtor questions concerning its assets, liabilities, and plans for the reorganization. § 341; Rule 2003. Unlike in Chapter 7, where few creditors are likely to attend the § 341 meeting, in Chapter 11 cases creditors often use that meeting to obtain the information they need to determine what actions to take to protect their interests.

3. *Immediate Considerations*

With or shortly after the petition, each of four provisions of the Bankruptcy Code may quickly come into play. First, as in Chapter 7 and 13 cases, filing the petition invokes the automatic stay. § 362. Thus, creditors with prepetition claims cannot seek to collect on those claims, absent relief from the stay. Similarly, creditors with liens on property of the estate cannot enforce those liens without first obtaining relief from the stay. Second, if the debtor is to continue to operate its business, it needs to be able to continue to sell its products, buy inventory and supplies, and collect its receivables. Section 363 gives the debtor in possession such authority, subject to various restrictions. The most stringent restrictions involve the use of cash collateral. Third, to finance its operations, the debtor may need continued access to credit. Such credit may be the intra-day credit extended by a bank when it allows a depositor to access newly deposited funds before they have cleared, the relatively short-term credit of suppliers who deliver without prepayment, or long-term capital financing. Section 364 gives the debtor in possession authority to incur such credit, again subject to a variety of limitations. Finally, the debtor in possession may need to decide quickly whether to assume or reject

---

[9] Of course the debtor must also pay the filing fee ($1,000) and other fees as specified in 28 U.S.C. § 1930. In a Chapter 11 case, there is also a quarterly fee to the U.S. Trustee's office depending upon the amount of disbursements in that quarter.

some of its unexpired leases or executory contracts. *See* § 365. The need for haste in this regard is sometimes attributable to the fact postpetition rent on an unexpired lease may qualify as an administrative expense, a prospect that could significantly burden the estate and make reorganization much more difficult.

Debtors who have planned well for bankruptcy know how they wish to deal with these issues when they file their petition. To the extent they need court approval under one or more of these provisions for any or all of what they want to do, the debtor's counsel usually prepares motions and proposed orders for the bankruptcy court to hear on an expedited basis. Such requests typically cover the debtor's proposed use of cash collateral to pay current operating expenses but may also deal with other matters, such as the sale of assets or incurring credit. Although local practice varies, these requests are often made and the orders entered on an *ex parte* basis. That is, the court reviews these requests on an emergency basis without the opportunity to conduct a full evidentiary hearing and without notice to all the creditors who may have an interest in what is being proposed. *Cf.* Rules 9013, 4001(b)(2), (c)(2). As a result, they are often referred to as "first day orders." When that occurs, the orders are typically limited to a few days or weeks, during which time the debtor may file and serve on creditors a motion for more long-term authority. Nevertheless, in some cases, the decisions made on these early requests can dramatically affect all future reorganization efforts. Consider the following case, which concerns the efforts of a debtor in possession to stay in operation.

IN RE KMART CORPORATION
359 F.3d 866 (7th Cir.), *cert. denied*, 543 U.S. 986 (2004)

Easterbrook, Circuit Judge.

On the first day of its bankruptcy, Kmart sought permission to pay immediately, and in full, the pre-petition claims of all "critical vendors." (Technically there are 38 debtors: Kmart Corporation plus 37 of its affiliates and subsidiaries. We call them all Kmart.) The theory behind the request is that some suppliers may be unwilling to do business with a customer that is behind in payment, and, if it cannot obtain the merchandise that its own customers have come to expect, a firm such as Kmart may be unable to carry on, injuring all of its creditors. Full payment to critical vendors thus could in principle make even the disfavored creditors better off: they may not be paid in full, but they will receive a greater portion of their claims than they would if the critical vendors cut off supplies and the business shut down. Putting the proposition in this way implies, however, that the debtor must *prove,* and not just allege, two things: that, but for immediate full payment, vendors *would* cease dealing; and that the business will gain enough from continued transactions with the favored vendors to provide some residual benefit to the remaining, disfavored creditors, or at least leave them no worse off.

Bankruptcy Judge Sonderby entered a critical-vendors order just as Kmart proposed it, without notifying any disfavored creditors, without receiving any pertinent evidence (the record contains only some sketchy representations by counsel plus unhelpful testimony by Kmart's CEO, who could not speak for the vendors), and without making any finding of fact that the disfavored creditors would gain or come out even. The bankruptcy court's order declared that the relief Kmart requested-open-ended permission to pay any debt to any vendor it deemed "critical" in the exercise of unilateral discretion, provided that the vendor agreed to furnish goods on "customary trade terms" for the next two years-was "in the best interests of the Debtors, their estates and their creditors". The order did not explain why, nor did it contain any legal analysis, though it did cite § 105(a). * * *

Kmart used its authority to pay in full the pre-petition debts to 2,330 suppliers, which collectively received about $300 million. This came from the $2 billion in new credit (debtor-in-possession or DIP financing) that the bankruptcy judge authorized, granting the lenders super-priority in post-petition assets and revenues. Another 2,000 or so vendors were not deemed "critical" and were not paid. They and 43,000 additional unsecured creditors eventually received about 10¢ on the dollar, mostly in stock of the reorganized Kmart. Capital Factors, Inc., appealed the critical-vendors order immediately after its entry on January 25, 2002. A little more than 14 months later, after all of the critical vendors had been paid and as Kmart's plan of reorganization was on the verge of approval, District Judge Grady reversed the order authorizing payment. He concluded that neither § 105(a) nor a "doctrine of necessity" supports the orders.

Appellants insist that, by the time Judge Grady acted, it was too late. Money had changed hands and, we are told, cannot be refunded. But why not? Reversing preferential transfers is an ordinary feature of bankruptcy practice, often continuing under a confirmed plan of reorganization. If the orders in question are invalid, then the critical vendors have received preferences that Kmart is entitled to recoup for the benefit of all creditors. Confirmation of a plan does not stop the administration of the estate, except to the extent that the plan itself so provides. * * *

Now it is true that we have recognized the existence of a longstanding doctrine * * * that detrimental reliance comparable to the extension of new credit against a promise of security, or the purchase of assets in a foreclosure sale, may make it appropriate for judges to exercise such equitable discretion as they possess in order to protect those reliance interests. Thus once action has been taken to distribute assets under a confirmed plan of reorganization, it would take some extraordinary event to turn back the clock. These appeals, however, do not question any distribution under Kmart's plan; to the contrary, the plan (which was confirmed after the district court's decision) provides that adversary proceedings will be filed to recover the preferences that the critical vendors have received. No one filed an appeal, which means that it is appellants in this court that now wage a collateral attack on the plan of reorganization.

Appellants say that we should recognize their reliance interests: after the order, they continued selling goods and services to Kmart (doing this was a condition of payment for pre-petition debts). Continued business relations may or may not be a form of reliance (that depends on whether the vendors otherwise would have stopped selling), but they are not *detrimental* reliance. The vendors have been paid in full for post-petition goods and services. If Kmart had become administratively insolvent, and unable to compensate the vendors for post-petition transactions, then it might make sense to permit vendors to retain payments under the critical-vendors order, at least to the extent of the post-petition deficiency. Because Kmart emerged as an operating business, however, no such question arises. The vendors have not established that any reliance interest – let alone any language in the Code – blocks future attempts to recover preferential transfers on account of pre-petition debts.

* * * Section 105(a) allows a bankruptcy court to "issue any order, process, or judgment that is necessary or appropriate to carry out the provisions of" the Code. This does not create discretion to set aside the Code's rules about priority and distribution; the power conferred by § 105(a) is one to implement rather than override. Every circuit that has considered the question has held that this statute does not allow a bankruptcy judge to authorize full payment of any unsecured debt, unless all unsecured creditors in the class are paid in full. We agree with this view of § 105. "The fact that a [bankruptcy] proceeding is equitable does not give the judge a free-floating discretion to redistribute rights in accordance with his personal views of justice and fairness, however enlightened those views may be." *In re Chicago, Milwaukee, St. Paul & Pacific R.R.*, 791 F.2d 524, 528 (7th Cir.1986).

* * * So does the Code contain any grant of authority for debtors to prefer some vendors over others? Many sections require equal treatment or specify the details of priority when assets are insufficient to satisfy all claims. *E.g.*, §§ 507, 1122(a), 1123(a)(4). Appellants rely on §§ 363(b), 364(b), and 503 as sources of authority for unequal treatment. Section 364(b) reads: "The court, after notice and a hearing, may authorize the trustee to obtain unsecured credit or to incur unsecured debt other than under subsection (a) of this section, allowable under section 503(b)(1) of this title as an administrative expense." This authorizes the debtor to obtain credit (as Kmart did) but has nothing to say about how the money will be disbursed or about priorities among creditors. * * * Section 503, which deals with administrative expenses, is likewise irrelevant. Pre-filing debts are not administrative expenses; they are the antithesis of administrative expenses. Filing a petition for bankruptcy effectively creates two firms: the debts of the pre-filing entity may be written down so that the post-filing entity may reorganize and continue in business if it has a positive cash flow. Treating pre-filing

debts as "administrative" claims against the post-filing entity would impair the ability of bankruptcy law to prevent old debts from sinking a viable firm.

That leaves § 363(b)(1): "The trustee [or debtor in possession], after notice and a hearing, may use, sell, or lease, other than in the ordinary course of business, property of the estate." This is more promising, for satisfaction of a pre-petition debt in order to keep "critical" supplies flowing is a use of property other than in the ordinary course of administering an estate in bankruptcy. Capital Factors insists that § 363(b)(1) should be limited to the commencement of capital projects, such as building a new plant, rather than payment of old debts – as paying vendors would be "in the ordinary course" but for the intervening bankruptcy petition. To read § 363(b)(1) broadly, Capital Factors observes, would be to allow a judge to rearrange priorities among creditors (which is what a critical-vendors order effectively does), even though the Supreme Court has cautioned against such a step. *See United States v. Reorganized CF & I Fabricators of Utah, Inc.,* 518 U.S. 213 (1996). Yet what [this decision] principally [said] is that priorities do not change unless a statute supports that step; and if § 363(b)(1) is such a statute, then there is no insuperable problem. If the language is too open-ended, that is a problem for the legislature. Nonetheless, it is prudent to read, and use, § 363(b)(1) to do the least damage possible to priorities established by contract and by other parts of the Bankruptcy Code. We need not decide whether § 363(b)(1) could support payment of some pre-petition debts, because *this* order was unsound no matter how one reads § 363(b)(1).

The foundation of a critical-vendors order is the belief that vendors not paid for prior deliveries will refuse to make new ones. Without merchandise to sell, a retailer such as Kmart will fold. If paying the critical vendors would enable a successful reorganization and make even the disfavored creditors better off, then all creditors favor payment whether or not they are designated as "critical." This suggests a use of § 363(b)(1) similar to the theory underlying a plan crammed down the throats of an impaired class of creditors: if the impaired class does at least as well as it would have under a Chapter 7 liquidation, then it has no legitimate objection and cannot block the reorganization. For the premise to hold true, however, it is necessary to show not only that the disfavored creditors *will* be as well off with reorganization as with liquidation-a demonstration never attempted in this proceeding-but also that the supposedly critical vendors would have ceased deliveries if old debts were left unpaid while the litigation continued. If vendors will deliver against a promise of current payment, then a reorganization can be achieved, and all unsecured creditors will obtain its benefit, without preferring any of the unsecured creditors.

Some supposedly critical vendors will continue to do business with the debtor because they must. They may, for example, have long term contracts, and the automatic stay prevents these vendors from walking away as long as the debtor pays for new deliveries. *See* § 362. Fleming Companies, which received the largest critical-vendors payment because it sold Kmart between $70 million and $100 million of groceries and related goods weekly, was one of these. No matter how much Fleming would have liked to dump Kmart, it had no right to do so. It was unnecessary to compensate Fleming for continuing to make deliveries that it was legally required to make. Nor was Fleming likely to walk away even if it had a legal right to do so. Each new delivery produced a profit; as long as Kmart continued to pay for new product, why would any vendor drop the account? That would be a self-inflicted wound. To abjure new profits because of old debts would be to commit the sunk-cost fallacy; well-managed businesses are unlikely to do this. Firms that disdain current profits because of old losses are unlikely to stay in business. They might as well burn money or drop it into the ocean. Again Fleming illustrates the point. When Kmart stopped buying its products after the contract expired, Fleming collapsed (Kmart had accounted for more than 50% of its business) and filed its own bankruptcy petition. Fleming was hardly likely to have quit selling of its own volition, only to expire the sooner.

Doubtless many suppliers fear the prospect of throwing good money after bad. It therefore may be vital to assure them that a debtor will pay for new deliveries on a current basis. Providing that assurance need not, however, entail payment for pre-petition transactions. Kmart could have paid cash or its equivalent. (Kmart's CEO told the bankruptcy judge that COD arrangements were not part of Kmart's business plan, as if a litigant's druthers could override the rights of third parties.) Cash on the barrelhead was not the most convenient way, however. Kmart secured a $2 billion line of credit when it entered bankruptcy. Some of that credit could have been used to assure vendors that payment would be forthcoming for all post-petition transactions. The easiest way to do that would have been to put some of the $2 billion behind a standby letter of credit on which the bankruptcy judge could authorize unpaid vendors to draw. That would not have changed the terms on which Kmart and any of its vendors did business; it just would have demonstrated the certainty of payment. If lenders are unwilling to issue such a letter of credit (or if they insist on a letter's short duration), that would be a compelling market signal that reorganization is a poor prospect and that the debtor should be liquidated post haste.

Yet the bankruptcy court did not explore the possibility of using a letter of credit to assure vendors of payment. The court did not find that any firm would have ceased doing business with Kmart if not paid for pre-petition deliveries, and the scant record would not have supported such a finding had one been made. The court did not find that discrimination among unsecured creditors was the only way to facilitate a reorganization. It did not find that the disfavored creditors were at least as well off as they would have been had the critical-vendors order not been entered. * * * Even if [§ 363(b)(1)] allows critical-vendors orders in principle, preferential payments to a class of creditors are proper only if the record shows the prospect of benefit to the other creditors. This record does not, so the critical-vendors order cannot stand.

———————————

QUESTION

The request for a critical-vendors order is premised on the belief that each critical vendor will refuse to do business with the debtor in possession unless the debtor's prepetition debt to the vendor is or will be paid. If the debtor has evidence that this is how critical vendors are acting, must the debtor capitulate to that pressure, or is there some other way to respond?

NOTES

1.   For a case approving payment of critical vendors, see *In re Tropical Sportswear Int'l, Inc.*, 320 B.R. 15 (Bankr. M.D. Fla. 2005).

2.   A motion to pay prepetition wage claims of critical employees may fare better than a request to pay critical vendors because employee wage claims are entitled, at least in part, to priority. *See In re CEI Roofing, Inc.*, 315 B.R. 50 (Bankr. N.D. Tex. 2004); § 507(a)(4), (5).

3.   The 2005 amendments to the Bankruptcy Code added some protection to vendors, whether "critical" or not. Those that sold goods to the debtor in the ordinary course of business may reclaim them if the goods were delivered within 45 days before the petition,[10] § 546(c)(1), and failing that, are entitled to administrative expense treatment for the sales price if the goods were delivered within 20 days before the petition, § 503(b)(9).

The *Kmart* case sets up a basic operational issue at the beginning of every Chapter 11 case in which the debtor plans to reorganize rather than liquidate. Who must the debtor pay to stay in operation and where does the debtor get the funds to pay those critical performers? Although these matter may, by necessity, be dealt with in haste in connection with the "first day orders," they are often given very substantial attention as the case progresses. Again, decisions made in connection with them can significantly affect the prospect for successful reorganization. Accordingly, in the next section, we consider the relevant Bankruptcy Code requirements in some detail.

---

[10]   The reclamation right is rarely helpful to vendors because the goods sold typically become part of the debtor's inventory and are encumbered by a security interest in favor of one or more of the debtor's creditors. Reclamation rights are subordinate to the rights of an unavoidable lien. *See* U.C.C. § 2-702(3). *See, e.g., In re Advance Marketing Systems*, 360 B.R. 421 (Bankr. D. Del. 2007).

SECTION B. MANAGING A CHAPTER 11 CASE

1. *Using Assets of the Estate to Generate Income*

(a) Section 364: Obtaining Credit

Few bankruptcy debtors are flush with cash. Most are insolvent and the few who are not are usually suffering from significant cash flow problems. Beyond that, in either the normal course of their businesses or on the path to bankruptcy, debtors will likely have collateralized almost all of their assets, including the liquid kind. Thus, as they enter bankruptcy, debtors are likely to have little unencumbered cash.

Obviously, the debtor in possession must obtain funds to pay current expenses – *e.g.,* employees, utilities, taxes – if its business is to survive. However, the debtor in possession cannot use cash collateral without either the consent of the secured party or a court order. § 363(c). Each of those will almost assuredly require some form of adequate protection of the creditor's interest. Without much in the way of unencumbered assets to offer in exchange for the use of cash collateral, the debtor in possession will need some source of financing (often referred to DIP financing) if it hopes to reorganize during the course of bankruptcy. Section 364 provides rules on how debtors in possession may obtain DIP financing and what they may provide in exchange for it. Read § 364.

As you can see, § 364 establishes a sort of hierarchy of preferred financing. It does so by placing more and higher hurdles in the path of financing the more unusual it is or the more the debtor in possession must provide in return. Its rules can be summarized as follows:

1. The debtor in possession may incur unsecured debt/credit in the ordinary course of business without court approval. § 364(a).

2. The debtor in possession may incur unsecured debt/credit outside the ordinary course of business only with court approval after notice and an opportunity for a hearing. § 364(b).

3. The debtor in possession may incur unsecured debt/credit with the highest administrative priority or junior secured debt/credit only with court approval after notice and an opportunity for a hearing and only if the types of financing discussed above are unavailable. § 364(c).

4. The debtor in possession may incur secured debt/credit with priority over existing liens only with court approval after notice and an opportunity for a hearing, only if the types of financing discussed above are unavailable, and only if the existing lienholder's interest is adequately protected. § 364(d).

Prior to filing the petition, the debtor will often have negotiated with its existing lenders for additional financing. If the existing lenders are unwilling to provide more financing (the court cannot order a lender to loan more money to the debtor), the debtor will usually try to obtain a new lender. Whoever the DIP financer is, whether an existing lender or a new lender, it will generally insist that the new debt be fully secured and superior in priority to all other debt obligations of the estate. Lenders willing to provide postpetition financing are typically in a very strong negotiating position.

If you were representing a lender approached to provide DIP financing, what conditions would you insist on? If you were representing existing creditors of the debtor, what provisions would you object to? If you objected to the financing proposed and the bankruptcy court approved the financing, what are your options for obtaining a reversal of the court's decision? Consider the following case.

IN RE SAYBROOK MANUFACTURING CO.
963 F.2d 1490 (11th Cir. 1992)

Cox, Circuit Judge:

Seymour and Jeffrey Shapiro, unsecured creditors, objected to the bankruptcy court's authorization for the Chapter 11 debtors to "cross-collateralize" their pre-petition debt with unencumbered property from the bankruptcy estate. The bankruptcy court overruled the objection * * *. We conclude that * * * cross-collateralization is not authorized under the Bankruptcy Code. Accordingly, we reverse and remand.

I. Facts and Procedural History

Saybrook Manufacturing Co., Inc., and related companies (the "debtors"), initiated proceedings seeking relief under Chapter 11 of the Bankruptcy Code on December 22, 1988. On December 23, 1988, the debtors filed a motion for the use of cash collateral and for authorization to incur secured debt. The bankruptcy court entered an emergency financing order that same day. At the time the bankruptcy petition was filed, the debtors owed Manufacturers Hanover approximately $34 million. The value of the collateral for this debt, however, was less than $10 million. Pursuant to the order, Manufacturers Hanover agreed to lend the debtors an additional $3 million to facilitate their reorganization. In exchange, Manufacturers Hanover received a security interest in all of the debtors' property – both property owned prior to filing the bankruptcy petition and that which was acquired subsequently. This security interest not only protected the $3 million of post-petition credit but also secured Manufacturers Hanover's $34 million pre-petition debt.

This arrangement enhanced Manufacturers Hanover's position vis-a-vis other unsecured creditors, such as the Shapiros, in the event of liquidation. Because Manufacturers Hanover's pre-petition debt was undersecured by approximately $24 million, it originally would have shared in a pro rata distribution of the debtors' unencumbered assets along with the other unsecured creditors. Under the financing order, however, Manufacturers Hanover's pre-petition debt became fully secured by all of the debtors' assets. If the bankruptcy estate were liquidated, Manufacturers Hanover's entire debt – $34 million pre-petition and $3 million post-petition – would have to be paid in full before any funds could be distributed to the remaining unsecured creditors.

Securing pre-petition debt with pre- and post-petition collateral as part of a post-petition financing arrangement is known as cross-collateralization. The Second Circuit aptly defined cross-collateralization as follows:

> [I]n return for making new loans to a debtor in possession under Chapter XI, a financing institution obtains a security interest on all assets of the debtor, both those existing at the date of the order and those created in the course of the Chapter XI proceeding, not only for the new loans, the propriety of which is not contested, but [also] for existing indebtedness to it.

In re Texlon Corp., 596 F.2d 1092, 1094 (2d Cir. 1979).

Because the Second Circuit was the first appellate court to describe this practice in *In re Texlon,* it is sometimes referred to as *Texlon*-type cross-collateralization. Another form of cross-collateralization involves securing post-petition debt with pre-petition collateral. This form of non-*Texlon*-type cross-collateralization is not at issue in this appeal. The Shapiros challenge only the cross-collateralization of the lenders' pre-petition debt, not the propriety of collateralizing the post-petition debt. . . .

The Shapiros filed a number of objections to the bankruptcy court's order on January 13, 1989. After a hearing, the bankruptcy court overruled the objections. * * * The Shapiros then appealed to this court.

* * *

B. Cross-Collateralization and Section 364

Cross-collateralization is an extremely controversial form of Chapter 11 financing. Nevertheless, the practice has been approved by several bankruptcy courts. Even the courts that have allowed cross-collateralization, however, were generally reluctant to do so.

In *In re Vanguard,* 31 B.R. 364 (Bankr. E.D.N.Y. 1983), for example, the bankruptcy court noted that cross-collateralization is "a disfavored means of financing" that should only be used as a last resort. *Id.* at 366. In order to obtain a financing order including cross-collateralization, the court required the debtor to demonstrate (1) that its business operations would fail absent the proposed financing, (2) that it is unable to obtain alternative financing on acceptable terms, (3) that the proposed lender will not accept less preferential terms, and (4) that the proposed financing is in the general creditor body's best interest. *Id.* This four-part test has since been adopted by other bankruptcy courts which permit cross-collateralization.

The issue of whether the Bankruptcy Code authorizes cross-collateralization is a question of first impression in this court. Indeed, it is essentially a question of first impression before any court of appeals. Neither the lenders' brief nor our own research has produced a single appellate decision which either authorizes or prohibits the practice.

* * * We conclude that cross-collateralization is inconsistent with bankruptcy law for two reasons. First, cross-collateralization is not authorized as a method of post-petition financing under section 364. Second, cross-collateralization is beyond the scope of the bankruptcy court's inherent equitable power because it is directly contrary to the fundamental priority scheme of the Bankruptcy Code. *See generally* Charles J. Tabb, *A Critical Reappraisal of Cross-Collateralization in Bankruptcy,* 60 S. Cal. L. Rev. 109 (1986).

Section 364 authorizes Chapter 11 debtors to obtain secured credit and incur secured debt as part of their reorganization. * * * By their express terms, sections 364(c) & (d) apply only to future – *i.e.*, post-petition – extensions of credit. They do not authorize the granting of liens to secure pre-petition loans. * * *

Given that cross-collateralization is not authorized by section 364, we now turn to the lenders' argument that bankruptcy courts may permit the practice under their general equitable power. Bankruptcy courts are indeed courts of equity, *see* § 105(a), and they have the power to adjust claims to avoid injustice or unfairness. This equitable power, however, is not unlimited.

> [T]he bankruptcy court has the ability to deviate from the rules of priority and distribution set forth in the Code in the interest of justice and equity. The Court cannot use this flexibility, however, merely to establish a ranking of priorities within priorities. Furthermore, absent the existence of some type of inequitable conduct on the part of the claimant, which results in injury to the creditors of the bankrupt or an unfair advantage to the claimant, the court cannot subordinate a claim to claims within the same class.

In re FCX, Inc., 60 B.R. 405, 409 (E.D.N.C.1986).

Section 507 of the Bankruptcy Code fixes the priority order of claims and expenses against the bankruptcy estate. Creditors within a given class are to be treated equally, and bankruptcy courts may not create their own rules of superpriority within a single class. Cross-collateralization, however, does exactly that. As a result of this practice, post-petition lenders' unsecured pre-petition claims are given priority over all other unsecured pre-petition claims. The Ninth Circuit recognized that "[t]here is no . . . applicable provision in the Bankruptcy Code authorizing the debtor to pay certain pre-petition unsecured claims in full while others remain unpaid. To do so would impermissibly violate the priority scheme of the Bankruptcy Code." *In re Sun Runner Marine, Inc.,* 945 F.2d 1089, 1094 (9th Cir. 1991).

The Second Circuit has noted that, if cross-collateralization were initiated by the bankrupt while insolvent and shortly before filing a petition, the arrangement "would have constituted a voidable preference." *In re Texlon,* 596 F.2d at 1097. The fundamental nature of this practice is not changed by the fact that it is sanctioned by the bankruptcy court. We disagree with the district court's conclusion that, while cross-collateralization may violate some policies of bankruptcy law, it is consistent with the general purpose of Chapter 11 to help businesses reorganize and become profitable. Rehabilitation is certainly the primary purpose of Chapter 11. This end, however, does not justify the use of any means. Cross-collateralization is directly inconsistent with the priority scheme of the Bankruptcy Code. Accordingly, the practice may not be approved by the bankruptcy court under its equitable authority.

Conclusion

Cross-collateralization is not authorized by section 364. Section 364(e), therefore, is not applicable and this appeal is not moot. Because *Texlon* -type cross-collateralization is not explicitly authorized by the Bankruptcy Code and is contrary to the basic priority structure of the Code, we hold that it is an impermissible means of obtaining post-petition financing. The judgment of the district court is reversed and the case is remanded for proceedings not inconsistent with this opinion.

QUESTION

Should other courts follow the *Saybrook* prohibition on cross collateralization? *Cf. In re Cooper Commons, LLC*, 430 F.3d 1215 (9th Cir. 2005) (discussing scope of financing orders under § 364(e)). See also the discussion of various DIP financing provisions in George W. Kuney, *Hijacking Chapter 11*, 21 EMORY BANKR. DEV. J. 19 (2004).

(b) Section 363

The estate of a typical Chapter 11 debtor includes inventory, equipment, deposit accounts, and account receivables. It also usually contains one or more interests in real estate, either in fee or as lessee, and a multitude of contracts on which performance is owed to the debtor. It may also include chattel paper, promissory notes, investment securities, and various types of intellectual property. In all likelihood, all or substantially all of these assets are encumbered by one or more liens. To determine whether and under what conditions the debtor in possession may use these assets to generate income, one must first look to § 363 and Bankruptcy Rule 4001. In general, these provisions are designed to strike a balance: allowing a business to continue its operations without excessive creditor interference or unnecessary court involvement while protecting creditors from dissipation of the estate's assets.

Section 363 contains a variety of rules concerning the ability of the debtor in possession to use property of the estate during the case.[11] These rules are separated into three different conceptual blocks, based on the type of asset and the kind of proposed use:

(i) assets that will be used, sold or leased in the ordinary course of business –
    § 363(c)(1);

(ii) cash collateral – § 363(c)(2); and

(iii) assets that will be used, sold or leased not in the ordinary course of business – § 363(b)(1).

Starting with first and the easiest category, the debtor in possession may use, sell or lease assets in the ordinary course of business without notice and hearing to creditors. § 363(c)(1). For example, if the debtor has a manufacturing business, the debtor in possession may use raw materials to manufacture its product and may sell its inventory, as long as it does so in the ordinary course of its business. What is ordinary course of business? We have seen that phrase in the § 547(c)(2) preference defense. Here, though, it has a slightly different and probably broader meaning. As the Second Circuit Court of Appeals stated:

> The term "ordinary course of business" generally has been accepted to embrace the reasonable expectations of interested parties of the nature of transactions that the debtor would likely enter in the course of its normal, daily business. Although never specifically articulated by this Court, two tests have emerged to determine whether a transaction is "ordinary." These tests are (1) the "creditor's expectation test" also known as the "vertical test," and (2) the "industry-wide test" also called the "horizontal test." * * *
>
> Under the vertical test, the court views the disputed transaction from the vantage point of a hypothetical creditor and inquires whether the transaction subjects a creditor to economic risks of a nature different from those he accepted when he decided to enter into a contract with the debtor.
>
> The horizontal test involves an industry-wide perspective in which the debtor's business is compared to other like businesses. In this comparison, the

---

[11] Note, § 363 is phrased as a grant of authority to the trustee. However, it also operates as a grant of authority to the debtor in possession because the debtor in possession is entitled to exercise the trustee's powers. § 1107(a).

test is whether the postpetition transaction is of a type that other similar businesses would engage in as ordinary business.[12]

Apparently, a proposed use of estate assets must satisfy both the vertical and horizontal tests to qualify as in the ordinary course of business.[13]

Of course, many of the estate's assets will be encumbered and the lienholder may not be happy about the debtor's proposed use of the assets. For example, a creditor with a security interest in the debtor's inventory will likely be very concerned if the debtor plans to sell the inventory postpetition. After all, buyers in the ordinary course will likely take free of the creditor's lien,[14] and, as we have seen, the creditor's interest in after-acquired inventory will likely be cut off by § 552(a) (assuming that any inventory acquired postpetition cannot be traced as proceeds of inventory or other collateral on hand as of the petition date). Thus, postpetition sale of the inventory may result in the rapid depletion of the creditor's collateral, particularly if the proceeds of that sale are used to pay employees, utilities, or other current expenses of the business. For this reason, a creditor with a security interest in assets that the debtor in possession wants to sell in the ordinary course often immediately moves for adequate protection of the value of its secured claim. *See* § 363(e). In fact, this is often part of the constellation of first day orders mentioned above. The creditor will move that the court adequately protect its secured claim in existing inventory, for example, by requesting a replacement lien in new inventory that the debtor in possession purchases subsequent to the petition.

The second category of assets covered by § 363 is "cash collateral," a term defined in § 363(a). To use cash collateral, the debtor in possession must first obtain either the approval of the court or the consent of any creditor with a lien on the cash collateral. § 363(c). This is true even if the proposed use would be in the ordinary course of the debtor's business. Why is cash collateral treated more restrictively than other types of assets in which a creditor may have an interest? Because cash – or at least a security interest in cash – can be ephemeral. When assets such as inventory are sold in the ordinary course of business, they generate proceeds. Any creditor with a security interest in the inventory will automatically have a security interest in all the identifiable proceeds.[15] While cash collateral too can generate proceeds – such as if used to buy other assets – it often does not. When cash is used to pay operating expenses –

---

[12]   *In re Lavigne*, 114 F.3d 379, 384-85 (2d Cir. 1997).

[13]   *See In re Roth America, Inc.*, 975 F.2d 949, 952-54 (3d Cir. 1992).

     Note, though, that there may be some redundancy in the two tests because a "reasonable hypothetical creditor would not expect a debtor to incur debt inconsistent with the actions of similar businesses." *See In re Husting Land Dev., Inc.*, 255 B.R. 772 (Bankr. D. Utah 2000).

[14]   *See* U.C.C. § 9-320(a).

[15]   *See* § 552(b); U.C.C. § 9-315(a)(2).

employees, taxes, or utilities – the value of the creditor's collateral simply dissipates. Because secured creditors are entitled to adequate protection of their secured claim, § 363(e), the Code requires creditor or court consent to the use of cash collateral. Predictably, therefore, an order regarding the debtor's use of cash collateral, and providing adequate protection of the creditors's lien, is one of the first day orders that enable the debtor in possession to operate the business.

The final category covered by § 363 is the use, sell or lease property of the estate outside the ordinary course of business. Any such action requires court approval after notice to creditors and the opportunity for a hearing. § 363(b)(1). Courts generally apply some version of the business judgment rule to these decisions: if there is a good business reason for allowing the proposed action, the court will approve the use, sale or lease of property of the estate.[16]

Problem 12-1

Dash Manufacturing, Inc. is in the business of manufacturing plastic component parts for, Hybrid Motor Corp., a major automobile manufacturer. When Hybrid needs components for a particular automobile, Hybrid and Dash engineers work on a design for the part, and Dash produces a mold for the plastic part. Once the engineers are satisfied that the part is correctly designed, Dash then manufactures the part from the specially designed molds.

Dash is financed by Intercontinental Bank. Intercontinental has a perfected security interest in Dash's equipment, inventory, and accounts. The current amount outstanding on that loan is $500,000. Intercontinental estimates that the total value of its collateral is $400,000 ($200,000 in equipment, $50,000 in inventory, and $150,000 in accounts). The bulk of those accounts ($120,000) are owed by Hybrid and more than half of Hybrid's obligation is more than 90 days past due. Hybrid's cars have not been selling well and there have been rumors in the popular press that Hybrid may file for bankruptcy. Intercontinental is considering accelerating the loan and foreclosing on its collateral pursuant to U.C.C. Article 9 because Dash has missed the last two months' payment of interest on the loan.

Yesterday, Dash informed Intercontinental that it would be filing a Chapter 11 petition by the end of the week. Dash told the loan officer that, after the filing, Dash will sell some trucks it no longer needs and will seek contracts to supply parts to another automobile manufacturer, Hotrod Cars, Inc. Dash also told the loan officer that Hybrid will be paying half the amount it owes to Dash so that Dash can fund its payroll at the end of the week. Dash

---

[16]   *E.g., In re Iridium Operating LLC*, 478 F.3d 452, 466 (2d Cir. 2007).

has asked Intercontinental to enter into a stipulated agreement allowing Dash to use proceeds from the trucks and the Hybrid payment to pay employees their regular salaries and wages the week following the petition and to pay the monthly rent coming due on Dash's manufacturing facility. Dash has also asked Intercontinental to provide postpetition financing in the form of a $100,000 line of credit.

A.   You represent Intercontinental. How do you advise it to respond to Dash's proposal? Should Intercontinental object to the sale of the trucks? If Intercontinental is willing to provide the line of credit provided it does not end up in a worse position, what terms should it insist on including in the stipulation regarding such financing?

B.   You represent Plastic Co., which sells Dash the ingredients Dash uses to make plastic auto parts. Dash owes Plastic Co. approximately $40,000 for past deliveries and Plastic Co. is scheduled to delivery $20,000 worth of product to Dash next week. Plastic Co. has received notice of Dash's Chapter 11 filing and a copy of a stipulated agreement between Intercontinental and Dash. The agreement provides that Intercontinental has a security interest in all inventory, equipment, accounts and proceeds of that collateral the debtor has an interest in at the time of the petition or acquires an interest in after the filing of the petition to secure any and all obligations owed to Intercontinental, whether those obligations were incurred pre-or postpetition. Should Plastic Products object to the stipulation? Should Plastic Products make the scheduled delivery?

Several issues arise in connection with § 363 sales outside the ordinary course of business. First, what happens if the assets to be sold are encumbered by one or more non-avoidable liens? Read § 363(e), (f), (k). Unless the order specifies otherwise, assets are sold subject to existing liens. Of course, most buyers want the assets they purchase to be unencumbered, so the court may order the assets to be sold free and clear of liens. In such cases, the lienholder is entitled to adequate protection, which typically is provided by granting the lienholder a lien on the sale proceeds or a replacement lien on some other assets of the estate. In the event that two or more lienholders are disputing who has priority, the court may either resolve that issue when authorizing the sale or simply order that they will retain their relative priorities – whatever they may be – in the sale proceeds, and then resolve the priority issue at a later date.

A second, less common, issue is whether asset sales under § 363 can make the buyer liable for claims against the debtor upon principles of successor liability. Successor liability is a common-law doctrine aimed at preventing an entity from forming a new business entity, transferring substantially all of its assets to the new entity, and then leaving its creditors without recourse to those assets. The doctrine applies whenever: (i) the sale is a de facto consolidation or merger; (ii) the purchaser is a mere continuation of the seller; or (iii) the transfer of assets is for the fraudulent purpose of escaping liability. In analyzing whether a transaction is a de facto merger and whether the buyer is mere continuation of the seller, courts look at such factors as whether the entities conduct the same business, whether the new entity operates from the same location as the old, whether the new entity has substantially the same employees, and whether the entity is controlled or managed by the same persons. Because the prospect of successor liability is likely to reduce the price buyers are willing to pay for the debtor's assets, it is a doctrine somewhat at odds with bankruptcy policy generally, which seeks to maximize the value of the estate for the benefit of the debtor's creditors. Accordingly, application of successor liability following § 363 sales is controversial, and courts sometimes expressly order the buyer to take free of such liability.[17]

A third issue is whether the debtor in possession may sell or lease substantially all of the assets of the estate prior to confirmation of a plan of reorganization. The debtor in possession may have important reasons for proposing such action. For example, it may have already negotiated a sale with a buyer who is unwilling to wait for months while a plan is negotiated and confirmed. On the other hand, a sale of substantially all of the estate assets will likely restrict the options available for reorganization and often lead to a liquidating plan. Moreover, to that extent that the sale order provides what will happen to the sale proceeds, it may effectively alter the priorities established by the Code and deprive creditors of both substantive and procedural rights inherent in the plan confirmation process. Even something more innocuous than a sale of most assets – such as a compromise of major prepetition litigation (which is a "use" of assets) – may significantly impact the confirmation process. How should courts respond to such motions? Consider the following case.

IN RE TORCH OFFSHORE, INC.
327 B.R. 254 (E.D. La. 2005)

Lemmon, District Judge.

A. Background.

On January 7, 2005, Torch Offshore, Inc., the owner and operator of an 11-vessel fleet in the Gulf of Mexico, filed a petition for bankruptcy protection under Chapter 11. Since entering bankruptcy protection Torch has repeatedly expressed its intention to sell off all or most of its assets due to its declining prospects for successfully reorganizing its business. On April 6, 2005, Torch filed a motion seeking bankruptcy court approval of the sale of the majority of its assets under § 363(b) to Cal Dive International, Inc. for

---

[17] *See In re Trans World Airlines, Inc.*, 322 F.3d 283 (3d Cir. 2003). *See also* Michael H. Reed, *Successor Liability and Bankruptcy Sales Revisited–A New Paradigm*, 61 BUS. LAW. 179 (2005).

$92 million. At a hearing on Torch's motion on April 27, 2005, Torch modified its proposal to reflect that (1) three vessels * * * that were subject to a lien in favor of General Electric Capital Corporation ("GECC") would be sold to GECC for $18.36 million, or to the highest bidder; and (2) six vessels * * * would be sold to Cal Dive for $80 million, or to the highest bidder. One other vessel, * * * estimated to bring in $2 million, would be auctioned separately. The effect of these sales would be to divest Torch of all of its operating assets.

On May 4, 2005, the bankruptcy court approved the sales procedures, and the auctions took place on June 2, 2005. An $18.36 million offer by GECC was the highest bid on the vessels subject to its lien. An $80.45 million offer by Cal Dive was the highest bid on the six vessels covered by its original proposal, and a $2.55 million offer by Cal Dive was the highest bid on the [remaining vessel]. Epic Divers was the highest bidder, at $2.8 million, on certain other equipment. The total amount of the proposed sale is $85.8 million.

On June 8, 2005, the bankruptcy court conducted a hearing on whether to approve the sales. The Official Committee of Unsecured Creditors (the "Committee") objected to the sales, arguing that they constituted a *sub rosa* plan of reorganization and violated the standards announced in *In re Braniff Airways, Inc.,* 700 F.2d 935 (5th Cir.1983) and *In re Continental Air Lines, Inc.,* 780 F.2d 1223 (5th Cir.1986). The bankruptcy court specifically instructed counsel for the Committee that under the theory of *Continental,* he had to "show specifically what protection is being denied to you by these sales under Section 363," and asked counsel several times to identify "what rights, what benefits are the unsecured creditors being deprived of by this sale rather than a sale through-rather than the benefits that would accrue to them under a plan of reorganization?" Although counsel for the Committee indicated that it wished the opportunity to file a reorganization plan, the court perceived that the unsecured creditors would receive no payments either under the sales or through a reorganization plan, and termed the Committee's objections to the asset sales to be "not specific enough to satisfy me or to satisfy the test from *Continental Air Lines.*"

At the end of the hearing, the court orally approved the sales, and entered written orders of approval on June 15, 2005. The court rejected the Committee's argument that the sales violated the standards of *Continental* and *Braniff* * * *.

The Committee appeals the ruling of the bankruptcy court approving the sales, arguing that there is no business justification for the sales and that they constitute a *sub rosa* reorganization plan in violation of *Braniff.* * * *

B. Analysis.

* * *

2. The proposed asset sales.

[Section] 363(b) provides that "[t]he trustee, after notice and a hearing, may use, sell, or lease, other than in the ordinary course of business, property of the estate." In *In re Continental Air Lines, Inc.,* 780 F.2d 1223 (5th Cir.1986), the debtor sought to enter into leases for new aircraft under § 363 after filing bankruptcy. Certain institutional creditors objected. The court held that when a proposed use, sale, or lease of assets is outside the ordinary course of business, the first step is for the debtor in possession to demonstrate that there are "business justifications" for the proposed transaction, necessitating an analysis of the factors enunciated in *In re Lionel Corp.,* 722 F.2d 1063 (2d Cir.1983):

> the proportionate value of the asset to the estate as a whole, the amount of elapsed time since the filing, the likelihood that a plan of reorganization will be proposed and confirmed in the near future, the effect of the proposed disposition on future plans of reorganization, the proceeds to be obtained from the disposition vis-a-vis any appraisals of the property, which of the alternatives of use, sale or lease the proposal envisions and, most importantly perhaps, whether the asset is increasing or decreasing in value. This list is not intended to be exclusive, but merely to provide guidance to the bankruptcy judge.

Continental, 780 F.2d at 1226. Additionally, lower courts facing a proposal to use, sell, or lease assets outside the ordinary course of business must determine "whether the proposed transactions otherwise violate or are incompatible with the provisions of Chapter 11," including the requirement that the sales not be a *sub rosa* plan of reorganization prohibited by *In re Braniff Airways, Inc.,* 700 F.2d 935 (5th Cir.1983).

(a) Are there business justifications for the proposed sales?

Consideration of the *Lionel* factors clearly reveals that there are business justifications for the asset sales. The fact that the sales encompass virtually all of the assets of the estate is not determinative, but one consideration in determining whether there is a business justification for the proposed sales. The auctions occurred approximately six months after the filing of the bankruptcy petition, and during these six months the debtor explored whether it could reorganize its business or had to liquidate its operating assets. No plan of reorganization has been proposed, and there is no indication that a sale of the debtor's assets pursuant to any such plan would result in a greater value to the estate than the proceeds realized by the auctions. The Committee points out that the assets were recently appraised at $228 million, but this is not an indication of market value because no firm was willing to offer this amount at the well advertised twelve-hour-long auctions, during which the debtor received almost 100 bids.

Most importantly, the undisputed evidence before the bankruptcy court indicated that maintaining the vessels was costing the debtor an exorbitant amount of money, and the condition of the vessels was deteriorating over time. The court affirms the bankruptcy court's finding that there are sound business justifications for the asset sales.

(b) Do the asset sales exceed the scope of § 363(b)?

The Fifth Circuit examined the scope of § 363(b) in *In re Braniff Airways, Inc.,* 700 F.2d 935 (5th Cir.1983). The *Braniff* debtor entered into an agreement to dispose of all of its assets to an entity known as PSA in exchange for travel scrip. Numerous creditor objections were filed. The court held that the PSA Agreement was invalid because the transaction was "much more than the 'use, sale or lease' of Braniff's property authorized by § 363(b):"

> Three examples will illustrate our rationale. The PSA Agreement provided that Braniff would pay $2.5 million to PSA in exchange for $7.5 million in scrip entitling the holder to travel on PSA. It further required that the scrip be used only in a future Braniff reorganization and that it be issued only to former Braniff employees or shareholders or, in a limited amount, to unsecured creditors. *This provision not only changed the composition of Braniff's assets, the contemplated result under § 363(b), it also had the practical effect of dictating some of the terms of a future reorganization plan.* The reorganization plan would have to allocate the scrip according to the terms of the PSA agreement or forfeit a valuable asset. *The debtor and the Bankruptcy Court should not be able to short circuit the requirements of Chapter 11 for confirmation of a reorganization plan by establishing the terms of the plan sub rosa in connection with a sale of assets.*
>
> Second, under the agreement between Braniff and its creditor, the secured creditors were required to vote a portion of their deficiency claim in favor of any future reorganization plan approved by a majority of the unsecured creditors' committee. Again, such an action is not comprised by the term "use, sell, or lease," and it thwarts the Code's carefully crafted scheme for creditor enfranchisement where plans of reorganization are concerned.
>
> Third, the PSA transaction also provided for the release of claims by all parties against Braniff, its secured creditors and its officers and directors. On its face, this requirement is not a "use, sale or lease" and is not authorized by § 363(b).

Id. at 940 (emphasis added). The court therefore determined that the PSA Agreement was not authorized under § 363(b) * * *. *Braniff* requires review of agreements that do more than constitute the simple "use, sale or lease" of assets to ensure that they do not exceed § 363(b) and constitute *sub rosa* plans of reorganization. *See Matter of The Babcock & Wilcox Co.,* 250 F.3d 955, 960 (5th Cir.2001) ("*Braniff* stands merely for the proposition that the provisions of § 363 permitting a trustee to use, sell, or lease the assets do not allow a debtor to gut the bankruptcy estate before reorganization or to change the fundamental nature of the estate's assets in such a way that limits a future reorganization plan."); *see also* 3 *Collier on Bankruptcy* ¶ 363.02[4], at 363-20 (Lawrence P. King ed., 15th ed. 1996) ("Attempts to determine plan issues in connection with the sale [under § 363(b)] will be improper and should result in a denial of the relief requested.")

In re Cajun Electric Power Cooperative, Inc., 119 F.3d 349 (5th Cir.1997) illustrates the limits of *Braniff.* The *Cajun Electric* debtor entered into a settlement regarding its obligations connected with the River Bend nuclear reactor (paying some monies, giving up some claims, and being released from future obligations pertaining to the plant). The court approved the settlement, rejecting the arguments of the creditors of the debtor that it was prohibited by *Braniff:*

> The instant settlement is not a *sub rosa* reorganization of the type disapproved in *Braniff.* It does not dispose of all claims against Cajun, nor does it restrict creditors' rights to vote as they deem fit on a proposed reorganization plan. Finally, the settlement does not dispose of virtually all of Cajun's assets, leaving "little prospect or occasion for future reorganization."[18] Instead it disposes of one particular "asset," River Bend, which is not so much the crown jewel of Cajun's estate but its white elephant. The removal of River Bend from the estate will facilitate Cajun's reorganization, and will do so without denigrating the rights of the unsecured trade creditors.

> Undeniably, the settlement removes $107 million in cash and transmission lines worth $20 million from the debtor's estate; it also precludes Cajun from pursuing litigation-an uncertain prospect at best-against Gulf States and RUS. However, Cajun retains as much as $1.1 billion in non-River Bend assets. In sum, the settlement does not "alter creditors' rights, dispose of assets, and release claims to the extent proposed in the wide-ranging transaction disapproved in" *Braniff.* The cases are entirely distinguishable, and the settlement at issue does not effect a *sub rosa* plan.

---

[18]   The fact that the sale disposes of essentially all of the assets of the estate does not necessarily disqualify the sale as a *sub rosa* plan. Several courts have approved the sale of all of an estate's assets under certain circumstances. *See In re Cummins Utility, L.P.,* 279 B.R. 195, 198 (Bankr. N.D. Tex. 2002) (approving the sale of all of the debtor's assets because all parties supported it, and the court "was persuaded by the parties that he Debtor's business was rapidly deteriorating"); *In re Condere Corp.,* 228 B.R. 615, 627 (Bankr. S.D. Miss. 1998) (approving sale of all debtor's assets because debtor would otherwise run completely out of money in two to four weeks, and "the proposed sale in the instant case is a simple exchange of assets for cash. It is unlike the far reaching terms of the sale the Fifth Circuit objected to in *Braniff* "). The current sales are only exchanges of assets for cash. They do not contain any provisions dictating the terms of any future reorganization plan, preordaining the way creditors will vote on such a plan, or attempting to vary the priorities of Torch's creditors.

Id. at 355 (citations omitted).

Because "each hearing on a § 363(b) transaction cannot become a mini-hearing on plan confirmation," the *Continental* court held:

> that when an objector to a proposed transaction under § 363(b) claims that it is being denied certain protection because approval is sought pursuant to § 363(b) instead of as part of a reorganization plan, the objector must specify exactly what protection is being denied. If the court concludes that there has in actuality been such a denial, it may then consider fashioning appropriate protective measures modeled on those which would attend a reorganization plan.

Continental, 780 F.2d at 1228.

The Committee does not demonstrate how any specific protection will be lost because the vessel sales will take place pursuant to § 363(b) rather than as part of a reorganization plan, and its complaints are simply a list of virtually every procedural protection afforded by Chapter 11, without a specific explanation of how these protections are being denied.

The Committee presented general arguments that the assets sales will cause them to lose the ability to receive a disclosure statement, will result in the failure of administrative and tax claims to be paid, will divest them of plan voting rights, and will deprive them of the ability to file a competing reorganization plan. The Committee fails to provide any specific reason why a disclosure statement would be valuable, other than a cryptic reference to "denied discovery," which denial was not appealed. Additionally, although the Committee argues that the "plan process" would require that administrative, priority, and tax claims would have to be paid in full, it fails to explain why this process would be different from what will occur pursuant to the asset sales. The entire argument that the Committee's proposal for its plan of reorganization may afford protections not available in the § 363(b) sales depends on the validity of the assertion that the [vessels] "could then be operated at a profit." This bare assertion has no factual basis in the record.

* * * Accordingly, the bankruptcy court's orders approving the sales are affirmed.
* * *

(b) Section 365: Executory Contracts and Unexpired Leases

In chapter five of this book, we briefly examined § 365, which governs the bankruptcy treatment of the debtor's executory contracts and unexpired leases. A Chapter 11 debtor in possession must carefully examine its executory contracts and unexpired leases to determine whether to assume, assign, or reject them. In making that decision the inquiry is – or at least should be – what is best for the estate; which action will generate the greatest revenue or impose the least cost. Although certain unexpired leases will be automatically rejected if not assumed within a specified time period, *see* § 365(d)(4), for most executory contracts and unexpired leases the debtor in possession need not make a decision until confirmation. *See* § 365(d)(1); Rule 6006. Indeed, if the debtor in possession intends to assume an executory contract or unexpired lease, the debtor will often include a provision to that effect in the reorganization plan itself. *See* § 1123(b)(2). This allows the debtor in possession to avoid binding itself before it knows whether the plan will be confirmed. If the debtor in possession chooses to assume or, more commonly, to reject before confirmation, it must file a motion to that effect. The court then reviews debtor's decision somewhat deferentially; the court normally defers to the debtor's business judgment unless there is evidence that the debtor is exercising its judgment for illegitimate reasons.[19]

Generally, a debtor in possession will take some time – often many months – to decide whether to assume or reject each executory contract and unexpired lease. The uncertainty during this period can be very frustrating for the counter-party, who will likely have several significant concerns: (i) how much time will the court give the debtor in possession to make a decision; (ii) must the debtor in possession perform its obligations during the period before assumption or rejection; (iii) must the counter-party perform its obligations before the debtor in possession assumes or rejects the unexpired lease or executory contract; and (iv) how, if at all, does rejection affect any interests in property that the counter-party has already transferred to the debtor.

With respect to the first issue, read § 365(d)(2) and (d)(4). Subsection (d)(2) allows a party to ask the court to set a deadline for assumption or rejection. Obviously, in setting such deadlines, courts must balance a variety of competing considerations. These include: (i) the potential harm to each party and the likelihood of such harm; (ii) the possible benefit to the estate; (iii) the debtor's ability to satisfy its postpetition obligations; (iv) the contract's importance to debtor's business and to a successful reorganization; and (v) whether debtor has had a sufficient time to appraise its financial situation and potential value of its assets in formulating plan.[20]

As to the second issue, whether the debtor in possession must perform its postpetition obligations under the contract or lease before assumption or rejection, § 365 provides no comprehensive answer. For unexpired leases of nonresidential real property, § 365(d)(3) requires that the debtor in possession timely perform all postpetition obligations. For unexpired leases of personal property used for business purposes, § 365(d)(5) requires that the debtor in possession timely perform all obligations arising more than 60 days after the petition. Both of these provisions clearly

---

[19]   *See In re Pomona Valley Medical Group, Inc.*, 476 F.3d 665, 670 (9th Cir. 2007).

[20]   *See In re Adelphia Communications Corp.*, 291 B.R. 283, 292-93 (Bankr. S.D.N.Y. 2003).

apply when the debtor is the lessee, but it is less clear whether they also apply when the debtor is the lessor. The Ninth Circuit has ruled they do not.[21] Do you agree? Compare the language of § 365(d)(3) to the language of (d)(4).

Even when the provisions do apply, there is occasionally some dispute as to which contractual obligations "aris[e]" after the petition and before rejection. For example, if the debtor in possession rejects a lease and vacates the property in the middle of a month, must it nevertheless pay the entire monthly rental that became due at the beginning of the month?[22] If the lease requires the debtor to pay the real estate taxes, what happens if the taxes accrue prepetition but, pursuant to the lease, the lessor does not bill the debtor for them until after the petition?[23] This latter question should be reminiscent of the issues discussed in chapters three and five concerning which assets and liabilities of the debtor are allocable to the prepetition period and which to the postpetition period.

Aside from § 365(d)(3) and (d)(5), nothing in § 365 specifies whether the debtor in possession must perform postpetition obligations. Because those provisions apply only to leases, nothing in the section covers executory contracts at all. The only marginally helpful provision is § 363(e), which permits a counter-party to seek adequate protection of its interests.

As to the third issue, whether the counter-party must perform prior to assumption or rejection, the Code says very little. Presumably if the counter-party suspends performance, it risks being in breach and liable for any resulting damages. It may, however, be able to treat the debtor's bankruptcy as grounds for demanding adequate assurance of future performance.[24] In other words, it may be able to seek adequate protection. *See* § 363(e). It may also be able to get the court to force the debtor to make a prompt decision on whether to assume or reject. Failing either of those, it may be able to claim administrative expense priority for the value of its postpetition performance accepted by the debtor. Review the *Jartran* case from chapter nine.

Of course, if the debtor assumes the executory contract or unexpired lease, the estate becomes bound and must perform all the debtor's obligations under the contract or lease, including curing any defaults. § 365(b). If the assumed contract or lease is not assigned to a third party, then any obligation the debtor in possession fails to perform

---

[21]   *See In re BCE West, L.P.*, 319 F.3d 1166 (9th Cir. 2003) (dealing with § 365(d)(3)).

[22]   *Compare HA-LO Indus., Inc. v. CenterPoint Properties Trust*, 342 F.3d 794 (7th Cir. 2003); *In re Koenig Sporting Goods, Inc.*, 203 F.3d 986 (6th Cir. 2000), *with In re Ames Dept. Stores*, 306 B.R. 43 (Bankr. S.D.N.Y. 2004).

[23]   *Compare In re Montgomery Ward Holding Corp.*, 268 F.3d 205 (3d Cir. 2001), *with In re Handy Andy Home Improvement Ctrs.*, 144 F.3d 1125 (7th Cir. 1998).

[24]   *See* U.C.C. § 2-609; Restatement of Contracts (Second) § 251 (1981).

will qualify as an administrative expense. § 503. Thus for anyone seeking to maximize the assets of the estate, the decision to assume an executory contract or unexpired lease is not a riskless proposition.

The last issue concerns the effect of a rejection of an executory contract or unexpired lease.[25] We already know that the counter party will have a claim against the estate for breach of contract and that claim will be treated as a prepetition obligation. § 365(g). We also know that, to the extent any executory (*i.e.*, unperformed) obligations remain on either side of the transaction, those executory obligations need not be performed. But what about obligations already performed? That is, suppose the debtor in possession has already received property pursuant to a rejected contract. Must the debtor in possession return the property to the counter party? Alternatively, assume the debtor has transferred property to the counter party. Does rejection of the contract nullify the transfer such that the assets are automatically revert to the estate?[26]

The answers to these questions are complicated by the fact that § 365 contains numerous rules relevant to these question, and many of the rules apply to only a narrow class of contracts or property. Beyond that, the rules are probably more attributable to lobbying by special interest groups than to fidelity to a consistent or coherent policy. Read § 365(h), (i), (n). Then consider the following case.

THOMPKINS V. LIL' JOE RECORDS, INC.
476 F.3d 1294 (11th Cir. 2007)

Tjoflat, Circuit Judge:

This appeal requires us to consider what happens when a debtor-in-possession in a Chapter 11 bankruptcy case, who negotiated the purchase of copyrights prior to the bankruptcy proceeding, later uses the bankruptcy code to reject those contracts that transferred ownership of the copyrights to the debtor. Our resolution of that question determines the outcome of much of this suit by a rap artist who created the works giving rise to the copyrights in question. The artist sold copyrights in his works to a music recording company in exchange for a recording contract that entitled the artist to future royalties. The recording company later went bankrupt, becoming the

---

[25] Collective bargaining agreements, a special type of executory contract, are dealt with specifically in §1113. To assume or reject a collective bargaining agreement, the Chapter 11 debtor must comply with this section. The debtor may use Chapter 11 as a mechanism to force renegotiation of collective bargaining agreements. *See, e.g., In re Northwest Airlines, Corp.*, 483 F.3d 160 (2d Cir. 2007). The intersections between bankruptcy law and labor law are complex and beyond the scope of an introductory course on bankruptcy, for which this book is designed.

[26] *Cf. Precision Indus., Inc. v. Qualitech Steel SBQ, LLC*, 327 F.3d 537 (7th Cir. 2003) (§ 363(f) sale of property the debtor had previously leased cut off the lessee's rights even though § 365(h)(1)(A) provides that rejection does not affect the lessee's rights).

debtor-in-possession. In confirming the debtor's reorganization plan, the bankruptcy court ordered that all of the debtor's contracts with the artist be rejected under the bankruptcy code and the copyrights sold to a rival recording company and its owner, two of the defendants in the instant case.

Years later, the artist sued the defendants, alleging that they did not actually gain ownership of the copyrights through the bankruptcy, or if they did, they now owe him royalties. Based on that premise, the artist asserts numerous claims sounding in federal and state law. The district court granted summary judgment in favor of the defendants on all claims, and for the reasons set forth below, we affirm.

I.
* * *
A.

[In May 1989, Luther Campbell ("Campbell"),a member of 2 Live Crew, signed Jeffrey J. Thompkins ("Thompkins") to an Exclusive Recording Agreement (the "1989 Agreement" or "Agreement") with a Campbell's recording company, Luke Records, Inc. ("Luke Records").

The Agreement covered a contract period of five years. Under its terms, Thompkins was required to record albums under the group name "Poison Clan" and deliver master recordings ("masters") for production and release by Luke Records. Luke Records was given "exclusive, unlimited and perpetual rights throughout the world" to the copyrights in the sound recordings and a license to exploit the musical compositions. In exchange, Luke Records agreed to pay Thompkins royalties according to specified rates.] The Agreement obligated Luke Records generally to "commercially release each LP [album] recorded and delivered" by Thompkins under certain conditions. * * *

From 1989 through 1994 (the year in which the 1989 Agreement expired by its terms), Thompkins recorded three albums as Poison Clan: *2 Low Life Muthas, Poisonous Mentality,* and *Rufftown Behavior.* Luke Records distributed each of these.

B.

On March 28, 1995, Luke Records became the subject of an involuntary Chapter 7 bankruptcy petition filed by its creditors in the U.S. Bankruptcy Court for the Southern District of Florida. That June, Campbell individually filed a voluntary Chapter 11 bankruptcy petition, and Luke Records moved to convert its Chapter 7 case into one under Chapter 11. The bankruptcy court granted Luke Records' motion on June 14, 1995 and jointly administered the Luke Records and Campbell bankruptcies. (footnote omitted)

* * *[The bankruptcy cases continued throughout the following months, and on March 22, 1996, the bankruptcy court confirmed a plan or reorganization. The confirmation order expressly provided that "all executory contracts and unexpired leases of the Debtors are hereby rejected." Following confirmation, the bankruptcy court issued orders in both bankruptcy cases setting bar dates for claims arising from rejected executory contracts. Parties to the rejected contracts were allowed thirty days to file "any claims arising as a result of such rejection," and claims not timely filed were to be "deemed waived and will not be entitled to distribution under the confirmed Joint Plan." Thompkins did not file any proof of claim for rejection damages. As a final step in the reorganization process, the parties executed an assignment to Lil' Joe Records, Inc. of all of Luke Records' and Campbell's copyrights.]

C.

Nearly six years later, on March 5, 2002, Thompkins filed the instant suit against Lil' Joe Records, Inc., Lil' Joe Wein Music, Inc., and Weinberger (hereinafter collectively, "Lil' Joe") in the U.S. District Court for the Northern District of Georgia seeking damages, declaratory relief, and permanent injunctive relief for alleged violations of the Copyright Act. * * * On December 7, 2004, the district court * * * granted Lil' Joe's motion for summary judgment on the ground that the earlier bankruptcy Confirmation Order precluded Thompkins's claims, and denied Thompkins's motion for summary judgment. The district court entered final judgment for Lil' Joe on December 16, 2004. Thompkins now appeals, challenging the district court's order granting Lil' Joe's motion for summary judgment.

II
* * *

Thompkins first asserts a claim of infringement under the Copyright Act, alleging that Lil' Joe has illegally exploited copyrights owned by Thompkins in dozens of songs that he authored and performed on recordings [pursuant to the 1989 agreement ("the Poison Clan Songs"). * * *

With regard to the Poison Clan Songs, Thompkins argues that any copyrights he transferred to Luke Records under the 1989 Agreement reverted to his ownership when Luke Records rejected the Poison Clan contracts as executory under the bankruptcy Joint Plan. Thompkins further argues that, upon reversion of the copyrights, those assets ceased to constitute part of the bankruptcy estate and thus were not transferred to Lil' Joe under the Joint Plan, notwithstanding the language of the Plan and the various supporting documents and bankruptcy orders suggesting that the copyrights were meant to be transferred. Accordingly, Thompkins argues, Lil' Joe infringed his copyrights when it exploited them after the plan confirmation. Lil' Joe disputes Thompkins's interpretation of the effect of the Joint Plan confirmation, arguing instead that Luke Records' ownership of the copyrights was unaffected by its rejection of any contracts. Thus, Lil' Joe contends, those copyrights were transferred to Lil' Joe among other Luke Records assets disposed of by the terms of the Joint Plan.

The terms of the 1989 Agreement clearly transferred ownership of the disputed copyrights to Luke Records in the course of its business relationship with Thompkins, well before the bankruptcy. The parties now dispute the effect on copyright ownership caused by Luke Records' rejection of the 1989 Agreement in the bankruptcy as an executory contract pursuant to § 365.[27] Because post-bankruptcy ownership of the copyrights determines Thompkins's ability to assert copyright claims on the Poison Clan Songs in this suit, we must decide whether Luke Records' rejection of the 1989 Agreement had any effect on Luke Records' – or, more precisely, its bankruptcy estate's – continued ownership of those copyrights in the bankruptcy.

We hold that the rejection of the 1989 Agreement did not cause ownership of the Poison Clan Song copyrights to revert to Thompkins; thus, the copyrights properly passed into Luke Records' bankruptcy estate and from there were legally assigned to Lil' Joe. In essence, Thompkins asks this court to deem an executory contract rejection under § 365 to be the functional equivalent of a rescission, rendering void the contract and requiring that the parties be put back in the positions they occupied before the

---

[27] Under § 365(a), "the trustee, subject to the court's approval, may assume or reject any executory contract . . . of the debtor." This provision has spawned much litigation over the proper definition of an "executory contract," and courts have struggled to formulate a coherent approach to the issue. The parties in this case have likewise grappled with the definition of the contracts at issue between Thompkins and Luke Records. On appeal, the parties agree that the contracts were "executory" for the purposes of § 365 and that Luke Records rejected them. But this rare point of agreement between the parties is unique to the appeal in this case; in the district court, Thompkins maintained exactly the opposite position, asserting that the contracts were improperly treated as executory by the bankruptcy court.

Fortunately, we need not descend into the morass and attempt to define "executory" in this case. The parties do not contest that issue on appeal, and even if they were so inclined, we might otherwise be precluded from reconsidering the "executoriness" of the contracts. That issue was already decided by various bankruptcy court orders deeming the relevant contracts to be executory and confirming their rejection. In addition to the Confirmation Order generally deeming any unassumed contracts to be rejected, the order setting the bar date for rejection claims in the Luke Records bankruptcy specifically designated the "exclusive recording contracts" with Poison Clan as rejected executory contracts.

Although we do not find it necessary to reexamine whether the 1989 Agreement was properly treated as "executory," we note that the bankruptcy court's approval of the rejection of the 1989 Agreement would be consistent with the "functional approach" to "executoriness" that we have tacitly approved in our precedent. That is, "[e]ven though there may be material obligations outstanding on the part of only one of the parties to the contract, it may nevertheless be deemed executory . . . if its assumption [ ][or] rejection would ultimately benefit the estate and its creditors." *In re Gen. Dev. Corp.,* 177 B.R. 1000, 1012 (S.D.Fla.1995), *aff'd,* 84 F.3d 1364, 1365, 1374 (11th Cir.1996). The bankruptcy court presumably determined that rejection of the 1989 Agreement would benefit the Luke Records estate by maximizing the value of the copyrights. The enhanced value of the copyrights in turn increased the value of the estate and the amount available to be paid to all of Luke Records' creditors-including Thompkins, had he properly filed a claim in the bankruptcy.

contract was formed. (footnote omitted) This is not the purpose of § 365, nor does Thompkins cite any authority to show otherwise.

In support of his argument, Thompkins relies on the proposition that a debtor cannot accept only the benefits of an executory contract while eschewing the burdens. He also correctly observes that § 365 of the bankruptcy code ordinarily deems rejection of an executory contract to be "a breach of such contract . . . immediately before the date of the filing of the [bankruptcy] petition." § 365(g). Thompkins apparently concludes that because Luke Records' rejection of the 1989 Agreement constituted a pre-petition breach of that contract, that event somehow reverses any transfer of asset ownership previously carried out by the rejected contract. In other words, Luke Records' rejection of the "burdens" of the 1989 Agreement prevents Luke Records from keeping the "benefits," which, in Thompkins's view, are the copyrights Luke Records received.

It is true that a debtor must either assume an executory contract in its entirety or completely reject it, but Thompkins misunderstands the implications of rejection under § 365. Thompkins's argument basically calls for an interpretation of rejection as an outright dissolution of the contract. But rejection "does not embody the contract-vaporizing properties so commonly ascribed to it. . . . Rejection merely frees the estate from the obligation to perform; it does not make the contract disappear." *In re Drexel Burnham Lambert Group, Inc.,* 138 B.R. 687, 703 (Bankr. S.D.N.Y. 1992). More specifically, "[r]ejection has absolutely no effect upon the contract's continued existence; the contract is not cancelled, repudiated, rescinded, or in any other fashion terminated." *Id.* at 703.

The *Drexel Burnham Lambert Group* case, cited by Thompkins himself, presents a useful illustration of what a § 365 rejection does and does not affect. The corporate debtor, in an attempt to avoid its prospective obligations to compensate its former general counsel under the terms of an employment agreement, sought to reject the agreement as executory under § 365. Among the compensation provided for in the agreement were various monetary payments, plus three stock portfolios purchased by the former general counsel from the debtor upon execution of the agreement and held in escrow for future disbursement. The debtor claimed that by rejecting the employment contract-the means by which the stock portfolios were purchased and escrowed by the general counsel-the debtor "pull[ed] the plug" on the general counsel's rights to the escrowed portfolios. *Id.* at 695.

The bankruptcy court granted the debtor's motion to reject the contract, resulting in a prepetition breach under the terms of § 365(g) and converting the monetary balance owed to the general counsel into "a general unsecured claim that can be paid in 'tiny Bankruptcy Dollars.' " *Id.* at 711. As to the stock portfolios, however, the court "repudiate[d] Debtor's contention that rejection vaporizes or otherwise avoids [the general counsel's] interest in the escrowed funds." *Id.* The terms of the agreement gave the general counsel "both legal title and the equitable interest" in the escrowed stock, and the only right the debtor company retained in the stock upon execution of the agreement was a contingent interest subject to a condition subsequent, which ultimately never materialized. *Id.* at 710. When the condition subsequent became moot, the general counsel "became entitled to immediate possession" of the stocks, and that possession was unaffected by the rejection of the contract. *Id.*

Like the debtor in *Drexel Burnham Lambert Group,* Thompkins argues that Luke Records "pulled the plug" on its own claim of ownership over the copyrights when it rejected the contract; thus, he contends, the copyrights could not have been assigned to Lil' Joe out of Luke Records' estate. But like the bankruptcy court in *Drexel Burnham Lambert Group,* other courts have observed that rejection differently affects the unperformed portions of an executory agreement and those provisions of the agreement that, by their nature, are fully executed. The rejection of a pre-petition executory contract pursuant to which the debtor acquired property does not obligate the debtor to return the property.

There is no debate that Thompkins's transfer of his copyrights to Luke Records under the 1989 Agreement was an executed sale of property. The terms of the Agreement leave Thompkins not even so much as a contingent interest in the copyrights. Nor did Thompkins negotiate any specific requirements for the sale or promotion of his records; Luke Records needed only to "commercially release" each record, which it undisputedly did, and all matters of business judgment in such efforts were reserved to Luke Records and binding on Thompkins. To the extent the 1989 Agreement was "executory," in the sense of not being fully executed, it was only insofar as Luke Records was required to pay Thompkins royalties based on any future sales of his records. The transfer of the copyrights was fully executed, however, and Luke Records held full legal and equitable title under the terms of the Agreement.

Thus, when the bankruptcy court approved the rejection of the Agreement, it freed Luke Records from the obligation, or "burden," to pay royalties under the contractual terms and gave Thompkins a pre-petition claim for damages resulting from the breach. It also would have released Thompkins from any outstanding obligation to perform under the Agreement – *i.e.*, to convey any as-yet unrealized "benefit" to Luke Records. But the bankruptcy court's Confirmation Order did not effectively rescind the 1989 Agreement and reverse the executed transfer of the Poison Clan Song copyrights to Luke Records. The rejection had no effect on Luke Records' ownership of the copyrights, and they passed from the estate to Lil' Joe under the terms of the Joint Plan and Confirmation Order (and the later documents executing the agreed upon and confirmed terms of the reorganization). Accordingly, Thompkins cannot support a claim of copyright infringement against Lil' Joe as to the Poison Clan Songs, and we affirm the grant of summary judgment on that claim in favor of Lil' Joe. * * *

Problem 12-2

Darling Home Services, Inc. provides repair services to homeowners. It has leased office space in a strip mall. Monthly lease payments are $1,000. The lease is in the second year of a four-year term. Darling also leases a high-speed copier and three computers from Computing Supply, Inc. This lease is for 12 months and was executed two months ago. It obligates Darling to pay $300 per month and obligates Computer Supply to provide up to 10 hours of network support services each month for no additional charge (if Computing Supply provides more than 10 hours of such services in a month, it is entitled to be paid $50 per hour for any portion of an hour spent above the 10 hours in the month for network support services). Darling also recently entered into a contract with a condominium association to provide home repair services to the homeowners in the association for $35 per hour up to 50 hours per month. Darling filed a Chapter 11 petition last week.

A. What are Darling's options and obligations regarding each of the three contracts while it is in the process of formulating its reorganization plan?

B. What would you advise the landlord, Computing Supply, or the condominium association to do in terms of each of their relationships with Darling?

(d) Lien and Transfer Avoidance

In chapters two and six of this book, we explored the bankruptcy code provisions on recovering prepetition payments as avoidable preferences. In chapter six we also covered the various provisions that empower the trustee to avoid liens, including: § 544 (the strong arm power), § 545 (statutory liens); and § 547 (preferences). Added to them is § 549, which allows the trustee to avoid any postpetition transfer of estate property that is not authorized by the code or approved by the court. In Chapter 11 cases, all of these avoidance powers may be exercised by the debtor in possession. § 1107.

The power of the debtor in possession to avoid these types of transfers influences the bankruptcy process. It can affect the terms of a plan reorganization, the plan confirmation process and, more preliminarily, the negotiations over the debtor's authorization to continue operations and use estate property. To illustrate this dynamic, consider the following situation.

First Bank has been providing operating financing for DEF, Inc., a debtor that has filed a Chapter 11 bankruptcy. First Bank has a properly perfected security interest in DEF's inventory and accounts but is undersecured. That is, the value of the inventory and accounts on the day the bankruptcy was filed was less than the amount owed to First Bank. Prior to the bankruptcy filing, First Bank received several payments on its debt that are preferential given the undersecured nature of its claim (and that are not protected from avoidance under § 547(c)). DEF has filed a cash collateral motion to use the proceeds of inventory sales and account collections to pay employees. First Bank has objected to the debtor's motion and has requested adequate protection of its security interest in the inventory and accounts. If the debtor filed a preference action and won, First Bank would have to return the preference payments. This would have the effect of increasing the amount of First Bank's unsecured claim in the debtor's bankruptcy but also increasing the amount of cash in the bankruptcy estate. In the negotiations between First Bank and the debtor, the debtor and First Bank might agree that the debtor will not pursue its preference action against First Bank in return for First Bank dropping its objection to the debtor's use of cash collateral and agreeing to a lesser standard of adequate protection for the use of that cash collateral. Similarly, if there is some issue regarding whether First Bank's security interest is perfected, the debtor will use that fact in negotiating with First Bank regarding use of cash collateral. Obviously, if the security interest is in fact unperfected, First Bank's security interest in the proceeds of the collateral does not have to be adequately protected.

These simple examples illustrate that the transfer avoidance issues play out differently in a Chapter 11 proceeding. They form the backdrop of considerations that the creditor and debtor take into account in negotiating how that creditor will be treated during the process of the case and ultimately the plan proposal.

Problem 12-3

Revisit the facts of Problem 12-1. What clauses, if any, does the discussion of lien and transfer avoidance suggest that Intercontinental Bank should seek to include in the postpetition financing stipulation and order?

(e) Employment of Professionals in Chapter 11

In previous chapters, most notably chapter nine, we discussed the employment of professionals in a bankruptcy case, including the treatment of the fees of such professionals as administrative expenses. While creditors often complain about the cost of the Chapter 11 process, and in particular about the amount of professional fees, there is little empirical data that demonstrates those costs are excessive.[28] Moreover, there are several protections in the system to prevent excessive fees. First, the bankruptcy court must approve the attorney that the debtor in possession wishes to hire and that attorney must be disinterested. § 327. Second, that attorney must disclose all compensation received from the debtor in the year prior to the petition date. § 329. Finally, to be paid from the estate, the attorney must submit fee applications and those applications must be approved by the court. §§ 330, 328. Section 330 sets forth the criteria that the bankruptcy court takes into account in determining the amount of the reasonable compensation for the attorney for the debtor in possession. These provisions also apply to other professional persons employed by the debtor in possession, including accountants, appraisers, and consultants. Review the discussion in chapter nine on compensation for employed professionals.

2. Creditors' Involvement in the Chapter 11 Case

(a) Individual Creditors

Creditors in Chapter 11 cases may need to file a proof of claim. § 501. Bankruptcy Rule 3003 provides that if the creditor's claim is not included in the debtor's schedules or is scheduled as "disputed, contingent, or unliquidated," the creditor must file a proof of claim to be dealt with in the plan. Thus it is important for a creditor in a Chapter 11 case to consult the schedules to determine how its claim is treated. Even if the creditor agrees with the designation of the claim on the schedules, the creditor may still file a proof of claim. The debtor in possession will examine the proofs of claim and object to those it thinks should be disallowed. *See* § 502; Rule 3007.

Aside from filing a proof of claim, an unsecured creditor may have little involvement in the proceeding. If the creditor's claim is small or the distribution on the claim is likely to be minimal, it may not be worth the creditor's time to be involved. Unsecured creditors with substantial claims, however, may deem it prudent to carefully review and potentially object to any of a variety of actions that might reduce their recovery. The actions they are likely to be particularly concerned with include: the terms of any proposed DIP financing; the terms of a proposed sale of assets outside the ordinary course of business (*i.e.,* whether the estate is to get full or fair value); the decision to assume or reject executory contracts and unexpired leases; and requests to pay administrative expenses, in particular the salaries of the debtor's highly paid

---

[28] *See, e.g.*, Stephen J. Lubben, *Choosing Corporate Bankruptcy Counsel*, 14 AM. BANKR. INST. L. REV. 391 (2006); Stephen P. Ferris & Robert M. Lawless, *The Expenses of Financial Distress: The Direct Costs of Chapter 11*, 61 U. PITT. L. REV. 629 (2000).

executives and the fees of the debtor's counsel. In addition, creditors with large unsecured claims may actively participate in negotiating the plan of reorganization.

Secured creditors are more likely to be actively involved in the case. While unsecured claimants are typically concerned with the estate as a whole, secured claimants are concerned with protecting their interest in the collateral. Anything that might jeopardize that interest is a cause for concern. Thus, they carefully consider and may object to efforts by the debtor to sell or lease their collateral, whether inside or outside the ordinary course of business. They take great interest in the terms of any DIP financing, and in particular whether that financing might impair their priority. And, of course, they defend lien avoidance actions.

In addition to all this, secured claimants often demand adequate protection of their liens or seek relief from the automatic stay under § 362(d). Review the material in chapter seven on relief from the stay. This is a particularly fertile area for litigation in Chapter 11 because it often takes many months before a plan is confirmed (if indeed one ever is confirmed). During that time, the collateral may be depreciating in value. In addition, while oversecured creditors are entitled to postpetition interest on their claims (up to the value of their interest in the collateral), § 506(b), undersecured creditors do not accrue interest on either the secured or unsecured portion of their claims.[29] Accordingly, undersecured creditors often evaluate whether the debtor will be able to confirm a feasible reorganization plan within a reasonable time. If it appears that the debtor will not be able to do so, the creditor is likely to move for relief from the stay under § 362(d)(2), which as you may recall has two elements: that the debtor lacks equity in property and the property not necessary to an effective reorganization. The creditor has the burden of proof to show the debtor's lack of equity in the property but the debtor has the burden to show the property is necessary for an effective reorganization. § 362(g). This burden of the debtor can be difficult to satisfy. As the Supreme Court stated:

> What this requires is not merely a showing that if there is conceivably to be an effective reorganization, this property will be needed for it; but that the property is essential for an effective reorganization *that is in prospect.* This means, as many lower courts, including the en banc court in this case, have properly said, that there must be "a reasonable possibility of a successful reorganization within a reasonable time." (citation omitted) The cases are numerous in which § 362(d)(2) relief has been provided within less than a year from the filing of the bankruptcy petition. And while the bankruptcy courts demand less detailed showings during the four months in which the debtor is given the exclusive right to put together a plan, see § 1121(b), (c)(2), even

---

[29]   *See United Sav. Ass'n of Texas v. Timbers of Inwood Forest Assocs., Ltd.*, 484 U.S. 365 (1988).

within that period lack of any realistic prospect of effective reorganization will require § 362(d)(2) relief.[30]

Obviously, as part of any motion for relief from the automatic stay under § 362(d) or for adequate protection under § 363(e), a creditor will have to prove the validity of its secured claim. If the debtor in possession has a possible ground for avoiding the creditor's lien or for recovering a preferential payment to that creditor, the creditor may hesitate to make such motions. In fact, such a creditor may seek to provide the DIP financing, and as part of the financing package have the debtor in possession (and successors in interest, such as a trustee), to waive all such claims as against that creditor.

The bottom line of such interaction is that not only must creditors in a Chapter 11 proceeding scrutinize the activities of the debtor in possession, they must also be vigilant regarding the actions of other creditors, who may be seeking to improve their relative position through their dealings with the debtor in possession.

(b) The Creditors Committee

Another way in which unsecured creditors monitor what is happening in the debtor's Chapter 11 case is through the unsecured creditors committee. The U.S. Trustee's office appoints an unsecured creditors' committee that consists of the creditors willing to serve who have the seven largest claims of similar types. § 1102(a), (b). Additional committees of creditors may be appointed to represent other types of claimants. § 1102(a). The purpose of the committee is to provide information to other creditors with similar types of claims, to provide comments to the debtor from those creditors, to investigate the debtor's financial condition, to consult with the debtor in possession regarding the case administration, and participate in the formulation of a confirmable plan. §§ 1102(b)(3); 1103(c). In large cases involving thousands of creditors, where it is often impractical to send notice of every minor matter to every creditor, the court may order that some notices be sent only to the unsecured creditors committee. Rule 2002(i). The committee may employ attorneys and other professional to perform services for the committee. § 1103(a). The committee often uses these professionals to participate in actions that can significantly affect the estate, such as major preference litigation and objections to sizeable claims.[31] The professionals employed by the committee generally receive compensation from the estate pursuant to §§ 328 and 330, and qualify for administrative expense priority to the extent not paid

---

[30]   *Id.* at 375-76.

[31]   Recall from chapter four that claims owed to the debtor's interest holders are sometimes recharacterized as equity. *See supra* p. 192

during the case. § 503(b)(2). As with other professional persons paid from estate assets, the bankruptcy court must scrutinize such fee requests for reasonableness.[32]

(c) Appointment of a Trustee or Examiner

If creditors are dissatisfied with how the debtor in possession is managing the business or administering the estate, they have two additional tools at their disposal. First, they may seek to replace the debtor in possession with a trustee, who will administer the estate. Second, they may request appointment of an examiner to investigate the debtor's conduct. Read §§ 1104, 1106. Both of these are regarded as rather extreme measures. After all, the debtor in possession's existing management often has an ownership interest in the debtor, and hence a financial incentive to successfully reorganize. In addition, the existing management usually has substantial familiarity with the debtor's business; it often has expertise in the production of the debtor's products, a relationship with the debtor's suppliers and customers, and awareness of the strengths and limitations of the debtor's personnel. Shunting this experience aside in favor of a court-appointed guardian of the estate will often cause a major disruption of the business while that guardian tries to learn the ropes.

On the other hand, the existing management may be the source of many of the debtor's financial problems. It may be incompetent. It may be receiving compensation far beyond the worth of the services it is providing. It may even be looting the estate. If the creditors can prove this, if they can prove that the debtor in possession is not moving toward proposing a plan of reorganization, is not dealing fairly with one or more creditors or classes of creditors, or is engaged in fraud or excessive mismanagement, the court may appoint a trustee or examiner.[33] Even acrimony between the debtor in possession and its creditors may be sufficient cause to appoint a trustee or examiner.[34] However, there is a presumption against granting such relief and the creditors will have to prove their point by clear and convincing evidence.[35]

---

[32] For a discussion of some of the issues that may arise in utilizing creditors committees, see Kurt F. Gwynne, *Intra-committee Conflicts, Multiple Creditors' Committees, Altering Committee Membership and Other Alternatives for Ensuring Adequate Representation under Section 1102 of the Bankruptcy Code*, 14 AM. BANKR. INST. L. REV. 109 (2006); Daniel J. Bussel, *Creditors' Committees as Estate Representatives in Bankruptcy Litigation*, 10 STAN. J. L. BUS. & FIN. 28 (2004).

[33] *See, e.g.*, Clifford J. White, III & Walter W. Theus, Jr., *Chapter 11 Trustees and Examiners After BAPCPA*, 80 AM. BANKR. L.J. 289 (2006).

[34] *See In re Marvel Entm't Corp.*, 140 F.3d 463 (3d Cir. 1998).

[35] *See In re G-I Holdings, Inc.*, 385 F.3d 313 (3d Cir. 2004).

(d) Dismissal or Conversion of the Chapter 11 Case

A creditor, a creditors' committee, or the U.S. Trustee may also move to dismiss the Chapter 11 case or, provided the debtor is eligible to be in Chapter 7, to convert the case to a liquidation proceeding.[36] Read § 1112. In addition to the reasons listed in that section for dismissal or conversion of the Chapter 11 case, some courts grant such motions if the court finds the case has not been filed in good faith.[37] The usual reason for obtaining such a dismissal or conversion is the inability to formulate a confirmable plan of reorganization.[38]

In the event the case is converted to a Chapter 7 case, administrative expenses incurred in the Chapter 11 case are subordinated to the administrative expenses incurred in the Chapter 7 case. § 726(b).

QUESTION

How does the ever-present possibility that the case may be converted to Chapter 7, coupled with that subordination of pre-conversion administrative expenses to post-conversion administrative expenses pursuant to § 726(b), affect the terms of DIP financing?

3.   Role of the U.S. Trustee

The U.S. Trustee's office monitors all Chapter 11 cases. 28 U.S.C. § 586. It is particularly concerned with preventing fraud and abuse, reviewing professional fees for reasonableness, appointing and monitoring creditors' committees, ensuring that the estate is administered promptly and efficiently, and reviewing disclosure statements and financial reports.[39] In a Chapter 11 case, the debtor in possession must provide periodic financial reports to the court and the U.S. Trustee. *See* §§ 704(a)(8), 1107, 1106(a)(1); Rule 2015. These periodic reports of the financial activities of the debtor in possession provide valuable information regarding the estate's income and disbursements during

---

[36]   The debtor may also seek to convert the case to Chapter 7 pursuant to § 1112(a).

[37]   *See, e.g., In re Integrated Telecom Express, Inc.*, 384 F.3d 108 (3d Cir. 2004).

[38]   *See, e.g., In re Wiersma*, 2007 WL 1073782 (9th Cir. 2007); *In re Hedquist*, 450 F.3d 801 (8th Cir. 2006).

[39]   See the U.S. Trustee's website at http://www.usdoj.gov/ust/eo/ust_org/about_ustp.htm.

the case.[40] Failure to file the required reports may result in dismissal or conversion of the Chapter 11 case pursuant to § 1112.[41]

Problem 12-4

Revisit the facts of Problems 12-1 and 12-3. Dash has been in bankruptcy for six months and has not yet proposed a plan of reorganization. During that time, Dash has generated approximately $60,000 in income each month. Monthly operating expenses have averaged $58,000. Its inventory and accounts (all of which were acquired postpetition) are now worth only about $60,000, in part because Dash has been much more successful in collecting its accounts. Intercontinental Bank estimates that the current value of Dash's equipment is about $150,000 due to depreciation. Intercontinental had provided a postpetition line of credit up to $75,000 secured by all assets of Dash, and Dash has drawn $70,000 on that line of credit. Dash has spent quite a bit on marketing pitches in an effort to get new business, but has been largely unsuccessful. Almost $35,000 in cash has been paid to Dash's lawyers pursuant to court approval. Hybrid is still Dash's major customer and Hybrid just filed a Chapter 11 bankruptcy petition. You represent Intercontinental. What actions do you recommend that Intercontinental take now?

SECTION C. CONFIRMING A CHAPTER 11 PLAN

1. Overview of Confirmation Process

While the debtor in possession is operating the business, it is also negotiating with creditors for purposes of proposing a plan of reorganization. The debtor in possession prepares two basic documents, a disclosure statement and a reorganization plan. The disclosure statement is designed to give information to all creditors regarding the financial condition of the debtor and its plans for the future operation of its business. The reorganization plan details how existing claims against the estate will be paid. After circulating the disclosure statement and reorganization plan, the creditors and equity holders entitled to vote on the plan will cast their ballots. After that, the bankruptcy court will hold a confirmation hearing. If all classes of creditors and equity holders have accepted the plan, and the plan complies with the statutory requirements, *see* § 1129(a), the court will confirm the reorganization plan. If any class of creditors or equity holders

---

[40]   For an example of the monthly reporting forms, see http://www.usdoj.gov/ust/r18/k_mor1.pdf.

[41]   *See, e.g., In re All Denominational New Church*, 268 B.R. 536 (8th Cir. BAP 2001).

entitled to vote on the plan does not accept the plan, then the debtor may ask the court to confirm the plan anyway in a process known as a "cramdown." A reorganization plan confirmed through a cramdown must meet additional statutory requirements, *see* § 1129(b). A confirmed reorganization plan then governs the relationship between the debtor and the creditors as to all claims that arose before confirmation. § 1141. In other words, the debtor remains obligated on prepetition claims only to the extent so provided in the plan.

As discussed more fully below, other parties in interest may seek to file their own plans of reorganization. Those other parties in interest, particularly creditors, often seek to file a liquidating plan of reorganization as they generally have less information and expertise in running the debtor's business. The U.S. Trustee is not authorized to file a plan of reorganization. § 307.

The process of formulating a plan simultaneously involves negotiating for positive votes on the plan. As we study the requirements for plan confirmation and the process of plan confirmation, consider how the debtor's need to get positive votes may influence how certain types of creditors are treated. Also consider which types of creditors are likely to have the most negotiating leverage and are thus likely to be able to obtain (extort?) the best treatment in the reorganization plan.

2.   *Exclusive Period for Filing a Plan*

To facilitate an orderly reorganization process and give the debtor a reasonable chance to solve its financial problems, § 1121(b) gives the debtor in possession the exclusive right to file a plan for the first 120 days after the order of relief. Other parties in interest (such as creditors) may not file a plan until after this period expires.[42] The court may extend or reduce the 120-day period for cause, but may not extend it beyond 18 months after the date of the order for relief. § 1121(d). The debtor's exclusivity period also will end even if the debtor has filed a plan of reorganization if that plan is not been accepted by the creditors within 180 days after the order for relief. § 1121(c)(3). The bankruptcy court can also extend the 180-day time period but not beyond 20 months after the date of the order for relief. § 1121(d). How does the exclusivity period impact the negotiations between the debtor in possession and the creditors over the plan's contents? What should a bankruptcy court consider when deciding whether to extend or reduce these time periods? Consider the following case.

---

[42]   This exclusivity also ends immediately if a trustee is appointed; once a trustee is appointed, the trustee or any party in interest may file a reorganization plan. § 1121(c)(1).

IN RE HOFFINGER INDUSTRIES, INC.
292 B.R. 639 (8th Cir. BAP 2003)

Kressel, Chief Judge.

Leesa Bunch and Brad Rinehart appeal from the order of the bankruptcy court which extended the debtor's plan exclusivity periods through May 1, 2003 and October 1, 2003. Because we believe the bankruptcy court did not abuse its discretion, we affirm.

BACKGROUND

Appellee, Hoffinger Industries, Inc., is a manufacturer of above ground swimming pools, vinyl liners, filters and pool accessories. The debtor's principal manufacturing facility is located in West Helena, Arkansas. Hoffinger filed a voluntary petition seeking relief under Chapter 11 on September 13, 2001. Hoffinger filed its petition after entry of a judgment against it on August 23, 2001 in the Superior Court of the State of California in favor of Leesa Bunch in the amount of $12,526,890.70 plus costs.

On December 7, 2001, Hoffinger filed its first Motion for Extension of Debtor's Exclusivity Periods to File a Plan of Reorganization and to Obtain Acceptances Thereof, requesting a 90 day extension of the 120 day and 180 day exclusivity periods. The motion was granted on March 6, 2002. On April 18, 2002, Hoffinger filed its Motion for Second Extension of Debtor's Exclusivity Periods to File Plan of Reorganization and to Obtain Acceptances Thereof requesting an additional 120 day extension of the exclusivity periods. The second motion was granted on May 29, 2002.

On August 8, 2002, Hoffinger filed its Motion for Third Extension of Debtor's Exclusivity Periods to File Plan of Reorganization and to Obtain Acceptances Thereof. In its motion, Hoffinger set forth a number of matters that would need to be resolved prior to formulation of a plan of reorganization including completion of the Unsecured Creditor Committee investigation of various transactions between Hoffinger and related parties. Furthermore, because of the substantial size and complexity of its bankruptcy, its appeal of the Bunch judgment and issues related to developing a plan of reorganization, Hoffinger requested that the debtor's exclusivity periods to file its plan of reorganization and to obtain acceptances be extended until 60 and 120 days after final adjudication or resolution of the Bunch Judgment, or alternatively, that each period be extended for an additional 120 days or other period of time as the bankruptcy court might deem cause to exist.

Bunch and Rinehart filed objections to Hoffinger's third Motion for Extension. The Unsecured Creditors Committee and the U.S. Trustee also objected to an unlimited extension of the exclusivity periods. After an evidentiary hearing on the motion the bankruptcy court extended the plan exclusivity period until May 1, 2003 and the confirmation period until October 1, 2003. Bunch and Rinehart filed a timely appeal.

* * * We review the bankruptcy court's decision to extend the debtor's exclusivity periods for abuse of discretion. An abuse of discretion may only be found if the lower court's judgment was based upon clearly erroneous factual findings or erroneous legal conclusions. * * *

THE MERITS

[Section] 1121 establishes the time lines for filing plans of reorganization. Section 1121(a) permits the debtor to file a plan of reorganization at any time. However, § 1121(b) gives the debtor in possession the exclusive right to file a plan during the 120 day period after the date of the order of relief under Chapter 11. If the debtor in possession files a plan during this 120 day period, § 1121(c)(3) grants the debtor in possession 180 days from the date of the order of relief to solicit acceptances of the plan.

While the exclusivity periods in § 1121(b) and (c) may be sufficient for most debtors to file a plan, there are some situations where longer exclusivity periods are appropriate. Section 1121(d) states:

> On request of a party in interest made within the respective periods specified in subsections (b) and (c) of this section and after notice and a hearing, the court may for cause reduce or increase the 120 day period or the 180 day period referred to in this section.

The factors that must be established to constitute "cause" to reduce or increase the exclusivity periods are not described within § 1121(d), yet the legislative history of this section reveals what may establish cause.

First, the legislative history reveals the intent to facilitate the rehabilitation of debtors in Chapter 11, and therefore the party requesting an extension of the exclusivity period has the burden of establishing good cause. The legislative history also reveals that Congress intended that the granting of an extension would be based "on a showing of some promise of probable success [for reorganization]." *Matter of Newark Airport/Hotel, Ltd.,* 156 B.R. at 451 (quoting S. Rep. No. 95-989). Furthermore, "[a]n extension should not be employed as a tactical measure to put pressure on parties in interest to yield to a plan they consider unsatisfactory." *Id.*

In deciding whether or not to extend or shorten the exclusivity periods, courts have relied on such factors as: (1) the large size of the debtor and the consequent difficulty in formulating a plan of reorganization for a huge debtor with a complex financial structure; (2) the need of the creditors' committee to negotiate with the debtor and the ability to prepare adequate information; (3) the existence of good faith progress towards reorganization; (4) the existence of an unresolved contingency; (5) the fact that the debtor is paying bills as they become due; (6) the length of previous extensions of exclusivity; (7) breakdowns in plan negotiations, such that the continuation of the debtor's exclusivity period would result in the debtor having an unfair bargaining position over creditors; (8) the debtor's failure to resolve fundamental reorganization matters essential to its survival; (9) the gross mismanagement of the debtor.

As always, we emphasize that these are only factors, not all of which are relevant in every case. Nor is it simply a question of adding up the number of factors which weigh for and against an extension. It is within the discretion of the bankruptcy court to decide which factors are relevant and give the appropriate weight to each. As long as the bankruptcy court does not abuse its discretion, its decision will be affirmed.

In this case, evidence in the record reveals that the debtor met its burden of establishing good cause, and that the bankruptcy court did not abuse its discretion in granting extensions under § 1121(d). Hoffinger's president, Wayne Hollowell, Jr., testified that early reports regarding the fiscal year ending July 31, 2003 were encouraging, and that the company's sales were at an all time high from 1999. Moreover, Hollowell testified that the debtor, in an effort to further the reorganization process, has hired expert appraisers approved by the court to appraise equipment as well as real estate, has hired insurance experts to study the adequacy of their products liability insurance which is an ongoing process. He also testified that Hoffinger is paying its post petition expenses as they become due and adequate cash and lines of credit are in place to pay administrative claims in the future. Thus, it was not clearly erroneous for the bankruptcy court to conclude that reorganization is feasible for Hoffinger.

Finally, based on testimony from Hollowell, the court reasonably concluded that this is a complex case. The debtor has annual gross sales of approximately $36 million dollars, it has unresolved issues regarding completion of the Unsecured Creditor's Committee investigation of various transactions between the debtor and related parties, it is in the process of securing financing, finishing audits and appraisals. The Bunch appeal was but one of the issues the court considered as being a contributing factor to the complexity of the debtor's case. Thus it was not an abuse of the court's discretion to give the debtor an extension of its exclusivity period.

The appellants also complain that the length of the period granted to the debtor to obtain confirmation of its plan for five months, from May 1 to October 2, 2003, is too long. Rule 2002(a) requires twenty five days notice of the time fixed for filing objections and the hearing to consider approval of the disclosure statement and confirmation of the plan. If the objection deadline is five days before the hearing, then notice would have to be mailed at least thirty days before the hearing. Allowing a week from the filing of the disclosure statement to prepare notices and copies and mail them, thirty seven days would elapse from filing a plan and disclosure statement until a hearing on the adequacy of the disclosure statement.

The time periods from the time a disclosure statement is approved and a hearing on confirmation of the plan are similar. Thus, under ideal conditions, it would take seventy four days to get from plan filing to confirmation. We think the bankruptcy court's allowance of another eighty days to allow for contingencies like attorneys' and clients' schedules, the clerk's workload, and the court's calendar, not to mention time for the parties to negotiate and the court to make its decisions, is not an abuse of discretion.

---

3.   *Preparing a Disclosure Statement*

Section 1125 details the requirements of the disclosure statement. A disclosure statement must be distributed to all holders of claims or interests before or at the time that solicitations for acceptances of the plan of reorganization are made. The disclosure statement must also be approved by the bankruptcy court prior to such circulation. § 1125(b). The bankruptcy court holds a hearing on whether the disclosure statement satisfies the requirements of the Code and parties in interest are given a chance to object to it. Rule 3017. If the bankruptcy court approves the disclosure statement, the court will establish a time line for the confirmation process and a deadline by which the votes on the plan must be cast. Rule 3017. A party circulating an approved disclosure statement in good faith is insulated from liability under other law for the content of the disclosure statement, most notably the liability under securities laws. § 1125(e).

The key substantive requirement for a disclosure statement is that it provide "adequate information" so that the recipients are able to reach an informed decision on how to vote on the plan. Read § 1125(a). What is "adequate information"? One court has adopted the following list of 19 factors to consider:

1. The circumstances that gave rise to the filing of the bankruptcy petition;
2. A complete description of the available assets and their value;
3. The anticipated future of the debtor;
4. The source of the information provided in the disclosure statement;
5. A disclaimer, which typically indicates that no statements or information concerning the debtor or its assets or securities are authorized, other than those set forth in the disclosure statement;
6. The condition and performance of the debtor while in Chapter 11;
7. Information regarding claims against the estate;
8. A liquidation analysis setting forth the estimated return that creditors would receive under Chapter 7;
9. The accounting and valuation methods used to produce the financial information in the disclosure statement;
10. Information regarding the future management of the debtor, including the amount of compensation to be paid to any insiders, directors, and/or officers of the debtor;
11. A summary of the plan of reorganization;

12. An estimate of all administrative expenses, including attorneys' fees and accountants' fees;

13. The collectability of any accounts receivable;

14. Any financial information, valuations or *pro forma* projections that would be relevant to creditors' determinations of whether to accept or reject the plan;

15. Information relevant to the risks being taken by the creditors and interest holders;

16. The actual or projected value that can be obtained from avoidable transfers;

17. The existence, likelihood and possible success of non-bankruptcy litigation;

18. The tax consequences of the plan; and

19. The relationship of the debtor with affiliates.[43]

The court then cautioned

that the list is but a yardstick against which the adequacy of disclosure may be measured; the precise information required will be governed by the facts and circumstances presented in each case. * * *

Generally, a disclosure statement must contain all pertinent information bearing on the success or failure of the proposals in the plan of reorganization. A disclosure statement should likewise contain all material information relating to the risks posed to creditors and equity interest holders under the proposed plan of reorganization. The disclosure statement, on the other hand, should not be burdened with "overly technical and extremely numerous additions," where such information would serve only to diminish the understanding of a typical creditor or interest holder.[44]

4. *Confirmation Requirements*

As noted above, confirmation requires either the consent of all classes or, failing that, compliance with the requirements for cramdown. The court holds a confirmation hearing at which the votes are counted and any objections to the plan are considered. § 1128. If both the consensual and cramdown processes fail, the debtor in possession

---

[43] *In re Cardinal Congregate I*, 121 B.R. 760, 765 (Bankr. S.D. Ohio 1990).

[44] *Id.* at 765-66 (citations omitted).

will not have a confirmed plan of reorganization. Inability to confirm a plan is grounds for dismissal or conversion of the Chapter 11 case. § 1112.

(a) Consensual Confirmation

(i) Claim Classification

A reorganization plan must classify claims and interests to facilitate the voting process prescribed in § 1126. *See* § 1129(a)(1), 1123(a)(1). A reorganization plan cannot be confirmed through a consensual process unless all classes of impaired claims or interests accept the plan. § 1129(a)(8). Creditors and equity holders vote on a plan of reorganization individually, but creditors' claims and equity holders' interests are grouped into classes of claims and interests for purposes of determining acceptance of the plan. § 1122.

All of the claims or interests within a class must be "substantial similar" to each other. Thus claims are not classified with interests. Secured claims are not classified with unsecured claims. Priority claims are not classified with nonpriority claims. Beyond that, whether substantially similar claims must be classified together, is a matter of some controversy.[45] Because voting is by class, the debtor may try to classify claims in such a way as to get the class to vote positively on the plan. Claims or interests that are not impaired are deemed to have accepted the plan. § 1126(f). At least one class of impaired claims must accept the plan, without counting votes of any insider, if there is at least one impaired class. § 1129(a)(10).

A claim or interest is impaired unless the creditor' or holder's rights are not altered by the plan, or the plan reinstates the claim or interest to its original terms with compensation for the damages caused by the debtor's default. § 1124. The plan must expressly designate which classes of claims and interests, if any, are not impaired. §§ 1129(a)(1), 1123(a)(2). The plan must also specify the treatment of all impaired class of claims or interests. §§ 1129(a)(1), 1123(a)(3). Unless a class member agrees to less favorable treatment as to its claim or interest, each claim or interest must be treated the same as others within its class. §§ 1129(a)(1), 1123(a)(4).

---

[45] *See, e.g.*, Bruce A, Markell, *A New Perspective on Unfair Discrimination in Chapter 11*, 72 AM. BANKR. L.J. 227 (1998); G. Eric Brunstad, Jr. & Mike Sigal, *Competitive Choice Theory and the Unresolved Doctrines of Classification and Unfair Discrimination in Business Reorganizations under the Bankruptcy Code*, 55 BUS. LAW. 1 (1999); Scott F. Norberg, *Classification of Claims under Chapter 11 of the Bankruptcy Code: The Fallacy of Interest Based Classification*, 69 AM. BANKR. L.J. 119 (1995); Linda J. Rusch, *Gerrymandering the Classification Issue in Chapter Eleven Reorganizations*, 63 U. COLO. L. REV. 163 (1992).

A class of impaired claims accepts the plan only if, of those voting, the positive votes are at least two-thirds in dollar amount of the claims in that class and more than one half in number of the claims in the class. § 1126(c). To illustrate, assume that a class of claims consists of ten claimants with a total dollar amount of claims of $60,000. If all ten claimants vote, at least six must vote yes, and the amount of claims voting yes must be at least $40,000. If only nine claimants vote and the total amount of those nine claims is $55,000, then number of claims voting yes must be at least five and the total dollar amount of those claims voting yes must be $36,667 (two-thirds of $55,000). If any one claimant in this hypothetical class (ten claimants with $60,000 in total claims) has a claim for more than $20,000, it can control the voting in that class by voting no (regardless of how many other creditors in that class vote yes) because that will prevent two-thirds in amount of the claims in that class from accepting the plan.[46]

A class of impaired interests is deemed to accept if at least two thirds in amount of interests voting in that class accept the plan. The voting requirement for impaired interests does not include the one half in number requirement applicable to impaired claims. § 1126(d).

If a vote is not made in good faith, or if the vote is not solicited in good faith, a party may request the court to "designate" the vote. § 1126(e). The effect of such designation is that the vote is not counted in the numerical thresholds for acceptance by the class of claims or interests.

(ii) Feasibility

To confirm the plan, the court must find that the plan is feasible. This means that the plan must provide adequate means for the debtor to implement it. §§ 1129(a)(1), 1123(a)(5). It also means that confirmation is not likely to be followed by liquidation or further reorganization, unless those actions are contemplated by the plan itself. § 1129(a)(11). In short, if the plan provides for the debtor's business to continue, it must provide for whatever financing the business needs and not leave the business overburdened with debt. The plan must also identify principals who will be involved in running the debtor after confirmation. §§ 1129(a)(1), (5), 1123(a)(6), (7). This provision allows the creditors and interest holders to determine whether the persons so identified are capable of running the debtor after confirmation of the plan. In assessing feasibility, the information in the disclosure statement will often be critical. The disclosure statement should contain fairly detailed information about the past and projected business operations of the debtor.

---

[46] It cannot, however, dictate the outcome by voting yes. Even if a single claimant had 99% of the amount of the claims in a class, its vote alone does not satisfy the requirement that more than a majority of the claimants in the class vote yes.

If the reorganization plan is for an individual debtor, the debtor's future income sufficient to consummate the plan must be devoted to the plan. § 1123(a)(8).

(iii) Compliance with Bankruptcy Code and Other Law

The proponent of the plan must also comply with the applicable provisions of the Bankruptcy Code. § 1129(a)(2). If the debtor is the proponent, this means that the debtor must have operated the business postpetition in accordance with all the Code requirements, including circulating the requisite financial reports, and complied with all court orders. The proponent of the plan must also propose the plan in good faith and not by any means forbidden by law. § 1129(a)(3). This term is generally interpreted to mean that there exists "a reasonable likelihood that the plan will achieve a result consistent with the objectives and purposes of the Bankruptcy Code."[47] All transfers of property for which the plan provides must comply with applicable law outside the Bankruptcy Code. § 1129(a)(16). If the debtor is subject to rate regulation, the debtor must obtain approval of the regulatory body for any proposed rate changes. § 1129(a)(6).

(iv) Required Payments of Claims and Expenses

Payments made pursuant to the plan to a person who rendered services to the debtor in possession or who has paid expenses chargeable to the estate must be approved by the court as reasonable. § 1129(a)(4). This requirement operates in addition to the payments to professional persons approved pursuant to § 330 and § 328. In addition, all required bankruptcy related fees must be paid no later than the effective date of the plan. § 1129(a)(12).

Payment to priority claimants depends upon the type of priority claim involved. Administrative expenses must be paid in full in cash equal to the allowed amount of the claim no later than the effective date of the plan, unless the administrative expense claimant has agreed to a different treatment. § 1129(a)(9)(A).

Each holder of most other priority claims must receive – if its class has accepted the plan – deferred cash payments that have a present value as of the effective date of at least the allowed amount of the claim. § 1129(a)(9)(B)(i). In other words, such priority claimants must be paid in full over time, but with post-confirmation interest. If such claimant's class has rejected the plan, the claimant must be paid in full in cash on the effective date of the plan. § 1129(a)(9)(B)(ii). Of course, any individual claimant may agree to less favorable treatment.

---

[47] *In re Madison Hotel Assocs.*, 749 F.2d 410, 425 (7th Cir. 1984).

Unsecured priority tax claims are entitled to cash payments in regular installments with a present value at least equal to the amount of the claim. The distributions on such claims must be made within five years of the order for relief and on at least as favorable of terms as the most favored non priority unsecured claimants. § 1129(a)(9)(C). The tax claimant may agree to less favorable treatment. Secured tax claims that would qualify for § 507(a)(8) priority but for their secured status are entitled to the same treatment. § 1129(a)(9)(D).

Claimants with impaired nonpriority claims who have not accepted the plan are entitled to receive the present value of the liquidation value of their claim. § 1129(a)(7). This rules is know as the "best interests of creditors test" but could probably be described more accurately as the "liquidation value test." To apply this rule, the court must estimate the liquidation value of the estate – as of the date of confirmation – and what each creditor would get under a hypothetical distribution pursuant to § 726. That in effect means that a secured claim gets the value of its collateral. As we have repeatedly encountered, valuation issues are a critical part of bankruptcy. Because this is a hypothetical distribution, a dissenting secured creditor will try to prove that the value of its collateral is higher than the value that the debtor in possession has allocated to that creditor. Similarly, dissenting unsecured creditors will try to demonstrate that the debtor in possession has not allocated enough value to paying its unsecured claims based upon this hypothetical liquidation based distribution.

A creditor whose claim is partially secured (so that the creditor has both a secured claim and an unsecured claim) has a choice to elect to treat its entire claim as a secured claim, in effect waiving its unsecured claim, and receive the present value of its collateral value in a payment stream that equals the dollar amount of its entire claim. §§ 1129(a)(7)(B), 1111(b)(2). Thus if the creditor has a $10,000 total claim, secured by $4,000 in collateral value (in essence a $4,000 secured claim and a $6,000 unsecured claim), a creditor making the § 1111(b)(2) election must receive a total stream of payment totaling $10,000 with a present value of at least $4,000. Few creditors make this election. Those that do usually anticipate that the collateral will appreciate post-confirmation and that the debtor will nevertheless default. If so, the creditor will then have a lien for the full, appreciated value of the collateral.

In addition, holders of unsecured claims who have objected to confirmation of an individual debtor's Chapter 11 plan must either receive full payment of the amount of the claim or the debtor's entire disposable income for five years (or for the plan period if longer) must be devoted to payments under the plan. § 1129(a)(15). This provision is comparable to the provision found in § 1325(b).

Finally, retiree benefits are given special protection by virtue of § 1114. *See* § 1129(a)(13).

(b) Cramdown

If not all classes of impaired claims and interests vote yes on the plan, the debtor in possession (or other plan proponent) may attempt to obtain confirmation through the cramdown process of § 1129(b). Cramdown requires compliance with all rules discussed for consensual confirmation, except for the requirement that all impaired classes must accept the plan. It also requires compliance with three other rules designed to protect creditors. Note, however, that cramdown protections apply only if one or more impaired *classes* of creditors vote against the plan; they do not apply if *individual creditors* vote against the plan but are outvoted by the other members of their class.

The first additional requirement for cramdown is that at least one class of impaired claims (if there are any such classes) must accept the plan. § 1129(a)(10), (b). The second cramdown requirement is that the plan must not discriminate unfairly. This is similar to the requirement in § 1322(b)(1), explored in chapter eleven. In general, it does not prohibit all disparate treatment of classes but does require that:

> (i) there is a reasonable basis for discriminating, (ii) the debtor cannot consummate the plan without discrimination, (iii) the discrimination is proposed in good faith, and (iv) the degree of discrimination is in direct proportion to its rationale."[48]

Third, the plan must be fair and equitable as to all dissenting classes of claims and interests. § 1129(b). "Fair and equitable" is defined differently for secured claims, unsecured claims, and interests. For secured claims, there are three alternative methods for satisfying the fair and equitable test: (i) allow the secured claimant to retain its lien (to the extent of the amount of the secured claim) and provide for cash payments with a present value of the secured claim; (ii) sell the collateral and give the secured claimant the proceeds of the sale; or (iii) provide the secured claimant with the "indubitable equivalent" of the claim. This typically means providing some appropriate alternative collateral. However, as the Ninth Circuit Court of Appeals has indicated, the substitute "must both compensate for present value and insure the safety of the principal. To the extent a debtor seeks to alter the collateral securing a creditor's loan, providing the 'indubitable equivalent' requires that the substitute collateral not increase the creditor's risk exposure."[49]

As to unsecured claims classes, the fair and equitable requirement means that either the dissenting class of unsecured claimants will receive property with a present value equal to the full amount of their claims or all classes of claims and interests that are

---

[48] *Mercury Capital Corp. v. Milford Connecticut Assocs., L.P.*, 354 B.R. 1, 10 (D. Conn. 2006).

[49] *In re Wiersma*, 2007 WL 1073782 (9th Cir. 2007) (citations and internal quotations omitted).

junior in priority to the dissenting class will not "receive or retain" any property under the plan "on account of such junior claim or interest." § 1129(b)(2)(B). This is known as the "absolute priority rule." The rule for dissenting classes of interests is similar. *See* § 1129(b)(2)(C).

The rules on confirmation generally – and the absolute priority rule, in particular – have a significant impact on the negotiations over the content of the reorganization plan. The absolute priority rule implies that, unless all classes of creditors accept the plan, the equity holders will not be permitted to retain any interest in the reorganized debtor. The only hope those owners have of recovering anything on their investment is if the debtor in possession – whose representatives are really bargaining on behalf of the debtor's equitable owners – can get the creditors to accept the plan. The creditors, however, cannot force the debtor in possession to pay them anything. Thus the dynamic often ends up something like this:

> The debtor in possession offers creditors plan payments equal to some (small) percentage of their claims. The creditors insist on more, and threaten to vote against the plan unless the debtor in possession agrees. This would invoke the absolute priority rule and leave the owners with nothing. The debtor in possession responds by threatening to convert the case to Chapter 7, in which case the business will be liquidated for presumably less than its value as a going concern. This may deprive creditors of their best source of recovery. It is as if the parties were seated around a pot of money and none of them has the ability to grab it. All they can do is thwart each other's attempts. Superimposed on this is the frequent reality that the debtor in possession is losing money. Often its operating costs – when combined with the administrative expenses (*e.g.*, legal fees) of the bankruptcy proceeding – exceed its incoming revenue. It is like a bunch of hungry people bargaining over a dish of ice cream . . . in a very hot room.

One wrinkle in all this the fact that often the debtor needs an infusion of capital to have a feasible reorganization. The debtor's equitable owners are the logical source for that new capital because they were the ones who initially had faith in the debtor's business and are the ones most likely to want an ownership interest in the reorganized debtor once the plan is confirmed. In recognition of this, and to facilitate reorganizations, many courts have allowed one or more of the existing owners to contribute new capital and then retain some or all of the ownership of the reorganized debtor, even though some dissenting classes of creditors are not paid in full. The existence and operation of this "new value exception" to the absolute priority rule is hotly debated. The first time the Supreme Court dealt with the issue, it ruled that even if the "new value" exception exists, contribution of labor and expertise by the prior owner (so called "sweat equity") is not sufficient "new value."[50] Now consider the Supreme Court's slightly more recent discussion of the new value exception.

BANK OF AMERICA NATIONAL TRUST AND SAVINGS ASSOCIATION V. 203 NORTH LASALLE STREET PARTNERSHIP
526 U.S. 434 (1999)

Justice Souter delivered the opinion of the Court.

The issue in this Chapter 11 reorganization case is whether a debtor's prebankruptcy equity holders may, over the objection of a senior class of impaired creditors, contribute new capital and receive ownership interests in the reorganized entity, when that opportunity is given exclusively to the old equity holders under a plan adopted without consideration of alternatives. We hold that old equity holders are disqualified from participating in such a "new value" transaction by the terms of § 1129(b)(2)(B)(ii), which in such circumstances bars a junior interest holder's receipt of any property on account of his prior interest.

I

Petitioner, Bank of America National Trust and Savings Association (Bank), is the major creditor of respondent, 203 North LaSalle Street Partnership (Debtor or Partnership), an Illinois real estate limited partnership. The Bank lent the Debtor some $93 million, secured by a nonrecourse first mortgage on the Debtor's principal asset, 15 floors of an office building in downtown Chicago. In January 1995, the Debtor defaulted, and the Bank began foreclosure in a state court.

In March, the Debtor responded with a voluntary petition for relief under Chapter 11 of the Bankruptcy Code, which automatically stayed the foreclosure proceedings. The Debtor's principal objective was to ensure that its partners retained title to the property so as to avoid roughly $20 million in personal tax liabilities, which would fall due if the Bank foreclosed. The Debtor proceeded to propose a reorganization plan during the 120-day period when it alone had the right to do so, *see* § 1121(b). The Bankruptcy Court rejected the Bank's motion to terminate the period of exclusivity to make way for a plan of its own to liquidate the property, and instead extended the exclusivity period for cause shown, under § 1121(d).

The value of the mortgaged property was less than the balance due the Bank * * *. Under the plan, the Debtor separately classified the Bank's secured claim, its unsecured deficiency claim, and unsecured trade debt owed to other creditors. *See* § 1122(a). The Bankruptcy Court found that the Debtor's available assets were prepetition rents in a cash account of $3.1 million and the 15 floors of rental property worth $54.5 million.

---

[50] *Norwest Bank Worthington v. Ahlers*, 485 U.S. 197 (1988).

The secured claim was valued at the latter figure, leaving the Bank with an unsecured deficiency of $38.5 million.

So far as we need be concerned here, the Debtor's plan had these further features:

(1) The Bank's $54.5 million secured claim would be paid in full between 7 and 10 years after the original 1995 repayment date.

(2) The Bank's $38.5 million unsecured deficiency claim would be discharged for an estimated 16% of its present value.

(3) The remaining unsecured claims of $90,000, held by the outside trade creditors, would be paid in full, without interest, on the effective date of the plan.

(4) Certain former partners of the Debtor would contribute $6.125 million in new capital over the course of five years (the contribution being worth some $4.1 million in present value), in exchange for the Partnership's entire ownership of the reorganized debtor.

The last condition was an exclusive eligibility provision: the old equity holders were the only ones who could contribute new capital.[51]

The Bank objected and, being the sole member of an impaired class of creditors, thereby blocked confirmation of the plan on a consensual basis. *See* § 1129(a)(8). The Debtor, however, took the alternate route to confirmation of a reorganization plan, forthrightly known as the judicial "cramdown" process for imposing a plan on a dissenting class. § 1129(b).

There are two conditions for a cramdown. First, all requirements of § 1129(a) must be met (save for the plan's acceptance by each impaired class of claims or interests, see § 1129(a)(8)). Critical among them are the conditions that the plan be accepted by at least one class of impaired creditors, *see* § 1129(a)(10), and satisfy the "best-interest-of-creditors" test, *see* § 1129(a)(7). Here, the class of trade creditors with impaired unsecured claims voted for the plan, and there was no issue of best interest. Second, the objection of an impaired creditor class may be overridden only if "the plan does not discriminate unfairly, and is fair and equitable, with respect to each class of claims or interests that is impaired under, and has not accepted, the plan." § 1129(b)(1). As to a dissenting class of impaired unsecured creditors, such a plan may be found to be "fair and equitable" only if the allowed value of the claim is to be paid in full, § 1129(b)(2)(B)(i), or, in the alternative, if "the holder of any claim or interest that is junior to the claims of such [impaired unsecured] class will not receive or retain under the plan on account of such junior claim or interest any property," § 1129(b)(2)(B)(ii). That latter condition is the core of what is known as the "absolute priority rule."

The absolute priority rule was the basis for the Bank's position that the plan could not be confirmed as a cramdown. As the Bank read the rule, the plan was open to

---

[51] The plan eliminated the interests of noncontributing partners. More than 60% of the Partnership interests would change hands on confirmation of the plan. The new Partnership, however, would consist solely of former partners, a feature critical to the preservation of the Partnership's tax shelter.

objection simply because certain old equity holders in the Debtor Partnership would receive property even though the Bank's unsecured deficiency claim would not be paid in full. The Bankruptcy Court approved the plan nonetheless, and accordingly denied the Bank's pending motion to convert the case to Chapter 7 liquidation, or to dismiss the case. The District Court affirmed, as did the Court of Appeals.

The majority of the Seventh Circuit's divided panel found ambiguity in the language of the statutory absolute priority rule, and looked beyond the text to interpret the phrase "on account of" as permitting recognition of a "new value corollary" to the rule. According to the panel, the corollary, as stated by this Court in *Case v. Los Angeles Lumber Products Co.,* 308 U.S. 106 (1939), provides that the objection of an impaired senior class does not bar junior claim holders from receiving or retaining property interests in the debtor after reorganization, if they contribute new capital in money or money's worth, reasonably equivalent to the property's value, and necessary for successful reorganization of the restructured enterprise. The panel majority held that

"when an old equity holder retains an equity interest in the reorganized debtor by meeting the requirements of the new value corollary, he is not receiving or retaining that interest 'on account of' his prior equitable ownership of the debtor. Rather, he is allowed to participate in the reorganized entity 'on account of' a new, substantial, necessary and fair infusion of capital."

In the dissent's contrary view, there is nothing ambiguous about the text: the "plain language of the absolute priority rule . . . does not include a new value exception." (opinion of Kanne, J.). Since "[t]he Plan in this case gives [the Debtor's] partners the exclusive right to retain their ownership interest in the indebted property *because of* their status as . . . prior interest holder[s]," *id.,* the dissent would have reversed confirmation of the plan.

We granted certiorari to resolve a Circuit split on the issue. * * * We do not decide whether the statute includes a new value corollary or exception, but hold that on any reading respondent's proposed plan fails to satisfy the statute, and accordingly reverse.

II

The terms "absolute priority rule" and "new value corollary" (or "exception") are creatures of law antedating the current Bankruptcy Code, and to understand both those terms and the related but inexact language of the Code some history is helpful. The Bankruptcy Act preceding the Code contained no such provision as subsection (b)(2)(B)(ii), its subject having been addressed by two interpretive rules. The first was a specific gloss on the requirement of § 77B (and its successor, Chapter X) of the old Act, that any reorganization plan be "fair and equitable." The reason for such a limitation was the danger inherent in any reorganization plan proposed by a debtor, then and now, that the plan will simply turn out to be too good a deal for the debtor's owners. *See* H.R. Doc. No. 93-137, pt. I, p. 255 (1973) (discussing concern with "the ability of a few insiders, whether representatives of management or major creditors, to use the reorganization process to gain an unfair advantage"; "[I]t was believed that creditors, because of management's position of dominance, were not able to bargain effectively without a clear standard of fairness and judicial control"). Hence the pre-Code judicial response known as the absolute priority rule, that fairness and equity required that "the creditors . . . be paid before the stockholders could retain [equity interests] for any purpose whatever." *Northern Pacific R. Co. v. Boyd,* 228 U.S. 482, 508 (1913).

The second interpretive rule addressed the first. Its classic formulation occurred in *Case v. Los Angeles Lumber Products Co.,* in which the Court spoke through Justice Douglas in this dictum:

> "It is, of course, clear that there are circumstances under which stockholders may participate in a plan of reorganization of an insolvent debtor. . . . Where th[e] necessity [for new capital] exists and the old stockholders make a fresh contribution and receive in return a participation reasonably equivalent to their contribution, no objection can be made. . . .

> [W]e believe that to accord 'the creditor his full right of priority against the corporate assets' where the debtor is insolvent, the stockholder's participation must be based on a contribution in money or in money's worth, reasonably equivalent in view of all the circumstances to the participation of the stockholder." 308 U.S. at 121-122.

Although counsel for one of the parties here has described the *Case* observation as "black-letter' principle," it never rose above the technical level of dictum in any opinion of this Court, which last addressed it in *Norwest Bank Worthington v. Ahlers*, 485 U.S. 197 (1988), holding that a contribution of "labor, experience, and expertise" by a junior interest holder was not in the "money's worth" that the *Case* observation required. Nor, prior to the enactment of the current Bankruptcy Code, did any court rely on the *Case* dictum to approve a plan that gave old equity a property right after reorganization. Hence the controversy over how weighty the *Case* dictum had become, as reflected in the alternative labels for the new value notion: some writers and courts (including this one, see *Ahlers*, 385 U.S. at 203-04, n.3) have spoken of it as an exception to the absolute priority rule, while others have characterized it as a simple corollary to the rule..

Enactment of the Bankruptcy Code in place of the prior Act might have resolved the status of new value by a provision bearing its name or at least unmistakably couched in its terms, but the Congress chose not to avail itself of that opportunity. In 1973, Congress had considered proposals by the Bankruptcy Commission that included a recommendation to make the absolute priority rule more supple by allowing nonmonetary new value contributions. Although Congress took no action on any of the ensuing bills containing language that would have enacted such an expanded new value concept, each of them was reintroduced in the next congressional session. *See* H.R. 31,

94th Cong., 1st Sess., §§ 7-303(4),[52] 7-310(d)(2)(B) (1975).[53] After extensive hearings, a substantially revised House bill emerged, but without any provision for nonmonetary new value contributions. After a lengthy markup session, the House produced H.R. 8200, 95th Cong., 1st Sess. (1977), which would eventually become the law. It had no explicit new value language, expansive or otherwise, but did codify the absolute priority rule in nearly its present form. *See* § 1129(b)(2)(B)(iv) ("[T]he holders of claims or interests of any class of claims or interests, as the case may be, that is junior to such class will not receive or retain under the plan on account of such junior claims or interests any property").

For the purpose of plumbing the meaning of subsection (b)(2)(B)(ii) in search of a possible statutory new value exception, the lesson of this drafting history is equivocal. Although hornbook law has it that "Congress does not intend *sub silentio* to enact statutory language that it has earlier discarded," *INS v. Cardoza-Fonseca,* 480 U.S. 421, 442-43 (1987), the phrase "on account of" is not *silentium,* and the language passed by in this instance had never been in the bill finally enacted, but only in predecessors that died on the vine. None of these contained an explicit codification of the absolute priority rule, and even in these earlier bills the language in question stated an expansive new value concept, not the rule as limited in the *Case* dictum.

The equivocal note of this drafting history is amplified by another feature of the legislative advance toward the current law. Any argument from drafting history has to account for the fact that the Code does not codify any authoritative pre-Code version of the absolute priority rule. Compare § 1129(b)(2)(B)(ii) ("[T]he holder of any claim or interest that is junior to the claims of such [impaired unsecured] class will not receive or retain under the plan on account of such junior claim or interest any property") with *Boyd,* 228 U.S. at 508 ("[T]he creditors were entitled to be paid before the stockholders could retain [a right of property] for any purpose whatever"), and *Case,* 308 U.S. at 116 ("[C]reditors are entitled to priority over stockholders against all the property of an insolvent corporation").

---

[52] Section 7-303(4) read: "[W]hen the equity security holders retain an interest under the plan, the individual debtor, certain partners or equity security holders will make a contribution which is important to the operation of the reorganized debtor or the successor under the plan, for participation by the individual debtor, such partners, or such holders under the plan on a basis which reasonably approximates the value, if any, of their interests, and the additional estimated value of such contribution."

[53] Section 7-310(d)(2)(B) read: "Subject to the provisions of section 7-303(3) and (4) and the court's making any findings required thereby, there is a reasonable basis for the valuation on which the plan is based and the plan is fair and equitable in that there is a reasonable probability that the securities issued and other consideration distributed under the plan will fully compensate the respective classes of creditors and equity security holders of the debtor for their respective interests in the debtor or his property."

The upshot is that this history does nothing to disparage the possibility apparent in the statutory text, that the absolute priority rule now on the books as subsection (b)(2)(B)(ii) may carry a new value corollary. Although there is no literal reference to "new value" in the phrase "on account of such junior claim," the phrase could arguably carry such an implication in modifying the prohibition against receipt by junior claimants of any interest under a plan while a senior class of unconsenting creditors goes less than fully paid.

III

Three basic interpretations have been suggested for the "on account of " modifier. The first reading is proposed by the Partnership, that "on account of " harks back to accounting practice and means something like "in exchange for," or "in satisfaction of." On this view, a plan would not violate the absolute priority rule unless the old equity holders received or retained property in exchange for the prior interest, without any significant new contribution; if substantial money passed from them as part of the deal, the prohibition of subsection (b)(2)(B)(ii) would not stand in the way, and whatever issues of fairness and equity there might otherwise be would not implicate the "on account of " modifier.

This position is beset with troubles, the first one being textual. Subsection (b)(2)(B)(ii) forbids not only receipt of property on account of the prior interest but its retention as well. A common instance of the latter would be a debtor's retention of an interest in the insolvent business reorganized under the plan. Yet it would be exceedingly odd to speak of "retain[ing]" property in exchange for the same property interest, and the eccentricity of such a reading is underscored by the fact that elsewhere in the Code the drafters chose to use the very phrase "in exchange for," § 1123(a)(5)(J) (a plan shall provide adequate means for implementation, including "issuance of securities of the debtor . . . for cash, for property, for existing securities, or in exchange for claims or interests"). It is unlikely that the drafters of legislation so long and minutely contemplated as the 1978 Bankruptcy Code would have used two distinctly different forms of words for the same purpose. . . .

The second difficulty is practical: the unlikelihood that Congress meant to impose a condition as manipulable as subsection (b)(2)(B)(ii) would be if "on account of " meant to prohibit merely an exchange unaccompanied by a substantial infusion of new funds but permit one whenever substantial funds changed hands. "Substantial" or "significant" or "considerable" or like characterizations of a monetary contribution would measure it by the Lord Chancellor's foot, and an absolute priority rule so variable would not be much of an absolute. Of course it is true (as already noted) that, even if old equity holders could displace the rule by adding some significant amount of cash to the deal, it would not follow that their plan would be entitled to adoption; a contested plan would still need to satisfy the overriding condition of fairness and equity. But that general fairness and equity criterion would apply in any event, and one comes back to the question why Congress would have bothered to add a separate priority rule without a sharper edge.

Since the "in exchange for " reading merits rejection, the way is open to recognize the more common understanding of "on account of " to mean "because of." This is certainly the usage meant for the phrase at other places in the statute, *see* § 1111(b)(1)(A) (treating certain claims as if the holder of the claim "had recourse against the debtor on account of such claim"); § 522(d)(10)(E) (permitting debtors to exempt payments under certain benefit plans and contracts "on account of illness, disability, death, age, or length of service"); § 547(b)(2) (authorizing trustee to avoid a transfer of an interest of the debtor in property "for or on account of an antecedent debt owed by the debtor"); § 547(c)(4)(B) (barring trustee from avoiding a transfer when a creditor gives new value to the debtor "on account of which new value the debtor did not make an otherwise unavoidable transfer to . . . such creditor"). So, under the commonsense rule that a given phrase is meant to carry a given concept in a single statute, the better reading of subsection (b)(2)(B)(ii) recognizes that a causal relationship between holding the prior claim or interest and receiving or retaining property is what activates the absolute priority rule.

The degree of causation is the final bone of contention. We understand the Government, as *amicus curiae,* to take the starchy position not only that any degree of causation between earlier interests and retained property will activate the bar to a plan providing for later property, but also that whenever the holders of equity in the Debtor end up with some property there will be some causation; when old equity, and not someone on the street, gets property the reason is *res ipsa loquitur.* An old equity holder simply cannot take property under a plan if creditors are not paid in full.

There are, however, reasons counting against such a reading. If, as is likely, the drafters were treating junior claimants or interest holders as a class at this point,[54] then the simple way to have prohibited the old interest holders from receiving anything over objection would have been to omit the "on account of " phrase entirely from subsection (b)(2)(B)(ii). On this assumption, reading the provision as a blanket prohibition would leave "on account of " as a redundancy, contrary to the interpretive obligation to try to give meaning to all the statutory language. One would also have to ask why Congress would have desired to exclude prior equity categorically from the class of potential

---

[54]   It is possible, on the contrary, to argue on the basis of the immediate text that the prohibition against receipt of an interest "on account of " a prior unsecured claim or interest was meant to indicate only that there is no *per se* bar to such receipt by a creditor holding both a senior secured claim and a junior unsecured one, when the senior secured claim accounts for the subsequent interest. This reading would of course eliminate the phrase "on account of " as an express source of a new value exception, but would leave open the possibility of interpreting the absolute priority rule itself as stopping short of prohibiting a new value transaction.

owners following a cramdown. Although we have some doubt about the Court of Appeals's assumption that prior equity is often the only source of significant capital for reorganizations, old equity may well be in the best position to make a go of the reorganized enterprise and so may be the party most likely to work out an equity-for-value reorganization.

A less absolute statutory prohibition would follow from reading the "on account of" language as intended to reconcile the two recognized policies underlying Chapter 11, of preserving going concerns and maximizing property available to satisfy creditors. Causation between the old equity's holdings and subsequent property substantial enough to disqualify a plan would presumably occur on this view of things whenever old equity's later property would come at a price that failed to provide the greatest possible addition to the bankruptcy estate, and it would always come at a price too low when the equity holders obtained or preserved an ownership interest for less than someone else would have paid.[55] A truly full value transaction, on the other hand, would pose no threat to the bankruptcy estate not posed by any reorganization, provided of course that the contribution be in cash or be realizable money's worth, just as *Ahlers* required for application of *Case*'s new value rule.

IV

Which of these positions is ultimately entitled to prevail is not to be decided here, however, for even on the latter view the Bank's objection would require rejection of the plan at issue in this case. It is doomed, we can say without necessarily exhausting its flaws, by its provision for vesting equity in the reorganized business in the Debtor's partners without extending an opportunity to anyone else either to compete for that equity or to propose a competing reorganization plan. Although the Debtor's exclusive opportunity to propose a plan under § 1121(b) is not itself "property" within the meaning of subsection (b)(2)(B)(ii), the respondent partnership in this case has taken advantage of this opportunity by proposing a plan under which the benefit of equity ownership may be obtained by no one but old equity partners. Upon the court's approval of that plan, the partners were in the same position that they would have enjoyed had they exercised an exclusive option under the plan to buy the equity in the reorganized entity, or contracted to purchase it from a seller who had first agreed to deal with no one else. It is quite true that the escrow of the partners' proposed investment eliminated any formal

---

[55] Even when old equity would pay its top dollar and that figure was as high as anyone else would pay, the price might still be too low unless the old equity holders paid more than anyone else would pay, on the theory that the "necessity" required to justify old equity's participation in a new value plan is a necessity for the participation of old equity as such. On this interpretation, disproof of a bargain would not satisfy old equity's burden; it would need to show that no one else would pay as much. No such issue is before us, and we emphasize that our holding here does not suggest an exhaustive list of the requirements of a proposed new value plan.

need to set out an express option or exclusive dealing provision in the plan itself, since the court's approval that created the opportunity and the partners' action to obtain its advantage were simultaneous. But before the Debtor's plan was accepted no one else could propose an alternative one, and after its acceptance no one else could obtain equity in the reorganized entity. At the moment of the plan's approval the Debtor's partners necessarily enjoyed an exclusive opportunity that was in no economic sense distinguishable from the advantage of the exclusively entitled offeror or option holder. This opportunity should, first of all, be treated as an item of property in its own right. While it may be argued that the opportunity has no market value, being significant only to old equity holders owing to their potential tax liability, such an argument avails the Debtor nothing, for several reasons. It is to avoid just such arguments that the law is settled that any otherwise cognizable property interest must be treated as sufficiently valuable to be recognized under the Bankruptcy Code. Even aside from that rule, the assumption that no one but the Debtor's partners might pay for such an opportunity would obviously support no inference that it is valueless, let alone that it should not be treated as property. And, finally, the source in the tax law of the opportunity's value to the partners implies in no way that it lacks value to others. It might, indeed, be valuable to another precisely as a way to keep the Debtor from implementing a plan that would avoid a Chapter 7 liquidation.

Given that the opportunity is property of some value, the question arises why old equity alone should obtain it, not to mention at no cost whatever. The closest thing to an answer favorable to the Debtor is that the old equity partners would be given the opportunity in the expectation that in taking advantage of it they would add the stated purchase price to the estate. But this just begs the question why the opportunity should be exclusive to the old equity holders. If the price to be paid for the equity interest is the best obtainable, old equity does not need the protection of exclusiveness (unless to trump an equal offer from someone else); if it is not the best, there is no apparent reason for giving old equity a bargain. There is no reason, that is, unless the very purpose of the whole transaction is, at least in part, to do old equity a favor. And that, of course, is to say that old equity would obtain its opportunity, and the resulting benefit, because of old equity's prior interest within the meaning of subsection (b)(2)(B)(ii). Hence it is that the exclusiveness of the opportunity, with its protection against the market's scrutiny of the purchase price by means of competing bids or even competing plan proposals, renders the partners' right a property interest extended "on account of " the old equity position and therefore subject to an unpaid senior creditor class's objection.

It is no answer to this to say that the exclusive opportunity should be treated merely as a detail of the broader transaction that would follow its exercise, and that in this wider perspective no favoritism may be inferred, since the old equity partners would pay something, whereas no one else would pay anything. If this argument were to carry the day, of course, old equity could obtain a new property interest for a dime without being seen to receive anything on account of its old position. But even if we assume that old equity's plan would not be confirmed without satisfying the judge that the purchase price was top dollar, there is a further reason here not to treat property consisting of an exclusive opportunity as subsumed within the total transaction proposed. On the interpretation assumed here, it would, of course, be a fatal flaw if old equity acquired or retained the property interest without paying full value. It would thus be necessary for old equity to demonstrate its payment of top dollar, but this it could not satisfactorily do when it would receive or retain its property under a plan giving it exclusive rights and in the absence of a competing plan of any sort. (footnote omitted) Under a plan granting an exclusive right, making no provision for competing bids or competing plans, any determination that the price was top dollar would necessarily be made by a judge in bankruptcy court, whereas the best way to determine value is exposure to a market. This is a point of some significance, since it was, after all, one of the Code's innovations to narrow the occasions for courts to make valuation judgments, as shown by its preference for the supramajoritarian class creditor voting scheme in § 1126(c). In the interest of statutory coherence, a like disfavor for decisions untested by competitive choice ought to extend to valuations in administering subsection (b)(2)(B)(ii) when some form of market valuation may be available to test the adequacy of an old equity holder's proposed contribution.

Whether a market test would require an opportunity to offer competing plans or would be satisfied by a right to bid for the same interest sought by old equity is a question we do not decide here. It is enough to say, assuming a new value corollary, that plans providing junior interest holders with exclusive opportunities free from competition and without benefit of market valuation fall within the prohibition of § 1129(b)(2)(B)(ii).

The judgment of the Court of Appeals, accordingly, is reversed, and the case is remanded for further proceedings consistent with this opinion.

In the 2005 amendments to the Bankruptcy Code, Congress did enact an exception to the absolute priority rule. If the Chapter 11 debtor is an individual, the debtor may retain property of the estate that is included in the estate pursuant to § 1115. While this includes postpetition earnings, the confirmed plan must still satisfy a new provision – § 1129(a)(15) – which incorporates the disposable income concept from Chapter 13 cases. Section 1115 is not limited to postpetition earnings, however, and would also include other property acquired by the individual post petition. Thus arguably the 2005 amendments opened a rather large hole in the absolute priority rule in the Chapter 11 case of an individual debtor. Does this amendment have a negative effect on the availability of the "new value exception" in a non-individual debtor's Chapter 11 case?

Problem 12-5

Joyce Duong operated a grocery store as a sole proprietor, Joyce's Foods. State Bank had a properly perfected security interest in the inventory to secure an operating loan. The security agreement provided for all proceeds of inventory to be applied to payment of the loan. State Bank then advanced monthly operating expenses as that money was required in the business. Monthly operating expenses were approximately $100,000 per month. Monthly proceeds of the inventory and accounts varied from $80,000 to $120,000 per month. Joyce's Foods has been in operation for over 5 years.

Last year, SuperFoods, built a supermarket within one mile of Joyce's Foods. That supermarket opened six months ago. On the day the supermarket opened, Joyce's Foods inventory had a value of $100,000 if sold in the ordinary course of business. Since the supermarket opened, monthly proceeds of inventory dropped to $70,000 to $90,000 per month. During the six months, the amount of the outstanding loan balance grew from $100,000 to $250,000.

On July 1, Duong, d/b/a Joyce's Foods, filed a bankruptcy petition under Chapter 11 of the Bankruptcy Code. At the time of the filing, the loan had a principal balance of $250,000 and the inventory had a liquidation value of $50,000 and a value of $100,000 if sold in the ordinary course of business. At the time of the filing, Duong owed $5,000 to the IRS for personal income taxes from the prior year. The IRS has assessed the taxes but has not filed a notice of tax lien for those taxes. Also at the time of filing, Duong was in the second year of a five-year contract with Fresh Foods Supply in which Fresh Foods promised to supply specified groceries to Joyce for resale in the store with a minimum monthly purchase obligation of $10,000. At the time of filing Duong owed Fresh Foods $50,000 for past deliveries.

During the first two months of Duong's Chapter 11 case, the inventory was sold and the money from the sale of inventory was used to buy new inventory and pay most of the ongoing business operating expenses. State Bank obtained a cash collateral order that granted it a security interest in the new inventory as a replacement lien for the loss of its lien in the prepetition inventory. State Bank has not advanced any additional funds during the pendency of this bankruptcy case. After the petition was filed, Duong did not purchase any groceries from Fresh Foods.

On the day that Duong filed her plan and disclosure statement for court approval, the inventory had a value of $80,000 if sold in the ordinary course of business. The entire $80,000 value was composed of inventory purchased after the commencement of the case. The plan provided as follows:

Class 1: $50,000 in expenses used to run the business during the bankruptcy case by incurring unsecured credit and attorney's fees will be paid over the course of one year with 5% interest ($4,280 per month)

Class 2: State Bank's secured claim of $50,000 will be paid with 6% interest over the course of 2 years ($2,216 per month).

Class 3: State Bank's unsecured claim of $200,000 will be paid $20,000 without interest over the course of 1 year ($1,667 per month).

Class 4: Fresh Foods unsecured claim of $50,000 will be paid $25,000 without interest over the course of 5 years ($417 per month).

Class 5: Internal Revenue Service claim of $5,000 for unpaid income taxes will be paid in full without interest over the course of 1 year ($417 per month).

The plan also provided that all executory contracts that were not assumed were rejected. The plan provided that operating expenses were reduced to $70,000 per month and income had remained steady and was expected to remain steady at $80,000 per month. Duong will continue to own and operate the grocery store. The plan states that the liquidation value of the business is $60,000.

A. Your client is State Bank. Identify and explain all the arguments State Bank might raise to keep this plan from being confirmed. Evaluate the merits and likelihood of success of each argument. How would you advise State Bank to vote on the plan and why?

B. Your client is Joyce Duong. Determine whether the plan can be confirmed in a cramdown. If not, restructure the plan so that a cramdown would be possible.

5. Effect of Confirmation

A confirmed reorganization plan binds all claimants and interest holders to its terms. § 1141(a). It also revests all estate property in the debtor. § 1141(b). Unless the debtor is an individual, a confirmed plan also discharges all pre-confirmation debts, except to the extent it provides otherwise. § 1141(d). However, this discharge does not apply to certain liquidating plans. *See* § 1141(d)(3). If the debtor is an individual, the debtor, the discharge does not cover debts made nondischargeable by § 523(a) and, as in Chapter 13, receives no discharge at all unless the debtor makes all payments required by the plan. § 1141(d)(2), (5)(A). However, the court may under certain circumstances grant an individual debtor a sort of hardship discharge prior to completion of payments. § 1141(d)(5)(B) and (C).

After confirmation, the debtor must carry out the plan and is subject to the court orders that help implement of the plan. §§ 1142, 1143. Within 180 days after confirmation, a party in interest may request revocation of the confirmation if the confirmation was procured by fraud. § 1144.

6. *Modification of Confirmed Plans*

After confirmation but before substantial completion of the plan, the non-individual reorganized debtor or plan proponent may seek to modify the confirmed plan. Any modification must be such that the plan, as modified, still complies with the requirements for confirmation. § 1127(b). If the debtor was an individual, § 1127(e) allows modification even if the plan has been substantially consummated and the debtor, any holder of an unsecured claim, a trustee, or the U.S. Trustee may make the request for modification. The modification of an individual's reorganization plan may not need to meet the requirements of § 1129 as the new subsection (e) does not so state, in contrast to the explicit statements in subsection (b).

SECTION D. SPECIAL CASES

Congress enacted the Bankruptcy Code in 1978. On many occasions since then, as a result of changing economic circumstances and lobbying by specific industries, Congress has amended the Code to deal with evolving practices or concerns. While many of these concerns have been in the consumer context, Chapter 11 has not been immune from this periodic amendment process. The following three situations are examples of what has resulted. As you think about these situations and what you have learned about Chapter 11 so far, is there a need for further refinement of the Chapter 11 process?

1. *Pre-packaged Chapter 11 Plans*

Given the time and expense in putting together a reorganization plan, some debtors file for Chapter 11 relief with the disclosure statement, plan of reorganization, and creditors' acceptances, all ready to go. These debtors file the case and want to go immediately to confirmation. This phenomena is known as a "pre-packaged plan."[56] Section 1121 allows a debtor to file a plan at the same time as the petition for relief. Section 1125(g) allows pre-filing solicitations of votes on a plan as long as that solicitation complies with non bankruptcy law. Section 1126(b) allows prepetition votes on the plan. *See also* Rule 3018(b).

---

[56] *See* 4 WILLIAM L. NORTON, JR., NORTON BANKRUPTCY LAW & PRACTICE ch. 86 (2d ed. 2007).

2. Single Asset Real Estate Cases

Many of the cases raising difficult issues in Chapter 11 reorganizations have been so called "single asset" cases. The typical "single asset" case is a partnership or corporate debtor that owns an apartment building, hotel, or some other piece of income-generating real property.[57] Typically, the real property generates a cash flow that is not adequate to pay back both the mortgagee who helped finance the debtor's acquisition or remodeling of the property and the trade creditors who provide services and supplies to the property. The real property is also often worth less than the amount of the debt which the property secures. The debtor files bankruptcy to stop the inevitable foreclosure process and to strip the value of the mortgage down to the value of the property. With a stripped down mortgage, the property might have a neutral or positive cash flow (sufficient to pay the mortgage payments and trade creditors necessary to run the property). The current owners of the debtor also need to remain in ownership positions in order to avoid adverse tax consequences, as in the *LaSalle* case. The mortgage holder generally prefers to foreclose its interest rather than to be forced into a continuing relationship with the debtor. The mortgage lender also generally asserts the real property is worth much more than the value the debtor proposes to pay the mortgage holder.

This single asset case was common in the early 1990's, a time of extreme devaluation of real estate properties. Thus in 1994, Congress added several Bankruptcy Code provisions to deal with the issues that frequently arise in such cases. Most of the amendments were designed to protect the mortgage lender. For example, the holder of a secured claim in a single asset case is now able to get relief from the automatic stay if the debtor has not filed a confirmable reorganization plan within 90 days after the order for relief or the debtor has not been paying the secured claimant at least interest on the secured claim. § 362(d)(3). The secured party is also protected against multiple bankruptcy filings. § 362(d)(4).

3. Small Business Cases

Because of the expense and time believed to be involved in Chapter 11 reorganizations, in 2005 Congress enacted several provisions designed to make the process more feasible for small business debtors. A small business debtor is defined in § 101(51D), (51C). That definition excludes real estate single asset debtors and is subject to a debt cap (adjustable periodically under § 104). A small business debtor has additional reporting requirements, § 308, and may be prevented in some circumstances

---

[57] *See* § 101(51B) (defining a "single asset real estate" case).

from having the automatic stay apply, § 362(n). In a Chapter 11 small business case, the U.S. Trustee may decide to not appoint a creditors' committee. § 1102(a)(3). A small business debtor also has additional duties under § 1116. The small business debtor has a longer period of exclusivity for filing a plan of reorganization, § 1121(e), and may not have to file a disclosure statement if the reorganization plan contains adequate information, § 1125(f). The court may also speed up the plan confirmation process by conditionally approving a disclosure statement so that the debtor may solicit votes, and then hold a hearing where the disclosure statement and plan confirmation is considered all at once. § 1125(f); Rule 3017.1. The time for confirming a plan is thus presumed to be a shorter period of time. § 1129(e).

APPENDICES

A GUIDE TO BANKRUPTCY PRACTICE AND PROCEDURE

The text and chart that follows catalogues the most common types of proceedings that arise during and within a bankruptcy case, indicates the type of pleading required, by when it is due, and notes the applicable rules relating to hearing and notice.

Motions. The Bankruptcy Rules govern the procedures used in bankruptcy cases and dictate what types of documents must be filed in each of various circumstances. As a general rule, a request for an order should be made by written motion.[58] For example, a request for relief from the automatic stay is made by motion. Not all motions require a response and some can be presented on an *ex parte* basis.

Adversary Proceedings. A request to obtain certain types of orders must be made by instituting an adversary proceeding. Adversary proceedings are begun by filing a complaint, the same way civil actions are begun in federal district court. Rule 7001 lists ten types of actions which must be commenced by an adversary complaint. These include actions to avoid liens, to recover prepetition transfers, to challenge the debtor's discharge, or to challenge the dischargeability of a particular debt.

Applications. Certain requests for a court order are to be made by application.[59] The ostensible difference between a motion and an application is that an application need not be served on anyone.[60]

Proof of Claim. To participate in the bankruptcy proceeding – and possibly receive a distribution from the bankruptcy estate – a creditor must file a proof of claim. In a proof of claim, which is to be accompanied by supporting documentation, the creditor asserts how much the debtor owes to the creditor and for what.[61]

Notice. To avoid unnecessary litigation, some proposals are initiated merely by sending notice thereof to certain specified parties. If no objection is filed within a specified period, the proposed conduct is deemed authorized. If the court receives a timely objection, the court will conduct a hearing and then enter an order either

---

[58] *See* Rule 9013. *See also* Rule 9014.

[59] *See, e.g.*, Rule 2014 (request for appointment of professional persons); Rule 2016 (request for compensation or reimbursement of expenses).

In non-bankruptcy proceedings, similar requests would often be made by petition. To avoid confusion, the Bankruptcy Code and Rules limit the term "petition" to the pleading which initiates a bankruptcy case.

[60] *But cf.* Rule 9013, indicating that some motions need not be served.

[61] *See* Official Form 10.

authorizing or declining to authorize the proposed conduct. Matters handled in this manner include proposals by the trustee to use, sell, or lease property of the estate outside the ordinary course of business,[62] or to abandon property of the estate.[63]

Objections. Objections are used to challenge proposals initiated by motion.[64] They are also used to seek court review of other pleadings that, unless challenged, will be summarily approved. In particular, objections are used to challenge a creditor's claim[65] or an exemption claimed by the debtor.[66]

---

[62] *See* Rules 6004(a), 2002(c)(1).

[63] *See* Rule 6007(a). In contrast, a request by someone else for the trustee to abandon property is to be made by motion. *See* Rule 6007(b).

[64] *See* Rule 6004(b) (concerning challenges to proposed sale of property of the estate).

[65] *See* Rule 3007.

[66] *See* Rule 4003(b).

Type of Proceeding	Code Section	Bankruptcy Rule	Type of Pleading	When Pleading Due	Must Opportunity for Hearing Be Afforded?
Request for Consolidation or Joint Administration	§ 302	1015, 9013, 9014	Motion		Yes
Response to Involuntary Petition	§ 303	1010, 1011	Answer or motion	Within 20 days after service of summons.	Yes
Request for Appointment of Trustee in Involuntary Chapter 7 Case Prior to Entry of Order for Relief	§ 303(g)	2001	Motion		Yes
Dismissal of Involuntary Petition	§ 303(j)	2002(a)(5), 1017	Motion or stipulation among debtor and petitioners.		Yes
Request to Remove Trustee	§ 324	9013	Motion		Yes
Request for Court Approval of Trustee's Employment of Professionals	§§ 327, 1103	2014	Application		No, review may be obtained when the professional files for compensation.
Statement of Payments by Debtor to Debtor's Attorney	§ 329	2016, 2017	Statement	Within 15 days after order for relief.	Yes
Request for Compensation for Services and Expenses	§ 330	2016	Application		Yes
Request for Interim Compensation	§ 331	2016(a)	Application	Not more frequently than every 120 days.	Yes

Type of Proceeding	Code Section	Bankruptcy Rule	Type of Pleading	When Pleading Due	Must Opportunity for Hearing Be Afforded?
First Meeting of Creditors	§ 341	2002(a)(1), 2003	None. Scheduling of meeting triggered by entry of order for relief.	Not less than 20 nor more than 40 days after order for relief.	Mandatory meeting
Request to Compel Debtor to Attend an Examination	§ 343	2005	Motion		*See* R. 2005.
Request for Relief from Automatic Stay	§ 362(d)	4001(a), 9014	Motion		Yes
Request to Use, Sell, or Lease Property of the Estate	§ 363	2002, 6004	Notice	If action proposed is outside the ordinary course of debtor's business, clerk must distribute notice at least 20 days before proposed use, sale or lease.	No, if the business of the debtor is authorized to be operated and if the proposed sale, use or lease is in the ordinary course, otherwise notice is required.
Request to Sell Property Free of Co-Owner's Interest	§ 363(h)	7001	Complaint		Yes
Request for Approval to Obtain Credit Not in Ordinary Course	§ 364	9013	Motion		Yes

Type of Proceeding	Code Section	Bankruptcy Rule	Type of Pleading	When Pleading Due	Must Opportunity for Hearing Be Afforded?
Request to Assume or Reject Executory Contracts & Unexpired Lease	§ 365	6006	Motion or plan	In Chapter 7 cases, contracts and leases (other than of nonresidential realty) are deemed rejected if not accepted within 60 days after order for relief.	Yes
Proof of Claim	§ 501	3001, 3002, 3004–3008	Proof of Claim	In Chapter 7, 12 & 13 cases, within 90 days after first date set for creditors' meeting. In other cases, as the court directs.	No, unless objection to claim is filed. See § 502(a).
Objection to Proof of Claim	§ 502(b) or (d)	3007	Objection		Yes
Reconsideration of Determination on Proof of Claim	§ 502(j)	3008	Motion	See R. 9024.	Yes
Withdrawal of Proof of Claim		3006	Notice of withdrawal is adequate in some circumstances while motion for withdrawal is required in others.		If a motion is required, a hearing is required.

Type of Proceeding	Code Section	Bankruptcy Rule	Type of Pleading	When Pleading Due	Must Opportunity for Hearing Be Afforded?
Request for Allowance of Administrative Expenses	§ 503	Cf. 2016	Application		Yes
Request for Valuation of Secured Claim	§ 506(a)	3012	Motion		Yes
Request to Recover Expenses of Preserving Collateral	§ 506(c)	7001	Complaint		Yes
Avoidance of Lien Under § 506	§ 506(d)	7001	Complaint		Yes
Request to Subordinate Claim	§ 510(c)		Complaint		Yes
Filing of Schedules	§ 521	1007(a), (c) 1019(1)	Schedules	With the petition in a voluntary case; within 15 days after the order for relief in an involuntary case; or within 15 days after the order converting the case to Chapter 7.	No
Request by Debtor to Amend Schedules	§ 521	1009	Amendment		No
Request by Party Other Than Debtor to Amend Schedules	§ 521	1009	Motion		Yes

Type of Proceeding	Code Section	Bankruptcy Rule	Type of Pleading	When Pleading Due	Must Opportunity for Hearing Be Afforded?
Objection to Debtor's Claimed Exemptions	§ 522	4003	Objection	Within 30 days after the creditors' meeting or the filing of amended schedules, unless the court grants more time.	Yes
Avoidance of Lien Under § 522(f)	§ 522(f)	4003(d)	Motion		Yes
Complaint Seeking and Exception to Discharge (*i.e.*, and acknowledgment of nondischargeability)	§ 523	2002(f)(6), 4007	Complaint	If under § 523(c), within 60 days after first date set for creditors' meeting. Otherwise anytime, even after case.	Yes
Request for Approval of Reaffirmation	§ 524(c), (d)	4008, 9013	Possibly a Motion		See § 524(c)
Request for Turnover of Property to Estate	§ 542(a)	7001	Complaint or possibly a motion		Yes
Request for Payment of Debt Owed to Estate	§ 542(b)	7001	Complaint or possibly a motion		Yes
Avoidance Under § 544 ("Strong Arm" Clause)	§ 544	7001	Complaint	Under § 546(a), within 2 years after trustee's appointment.	Yes

Type of Proceeding	Code Section	Bankruptcy Rule	Type of Pleading	When Pleading Due	Must Opportunity for Hearing Be Afforded?
Avoidance Under § 545 (Statutory Liens)	§ 545	7001	Complaint	Under § 546(a), within 2 years after trustee's appointment.	Yes
Avoidance Under § 547(b), (Preferences)	§ 547(b)	7001	Complaint	Under § 546(a), within 2 years after trustee's appointment.	Yes
Avoidance Under § 548 (Fraudulent Transfers)	§ 548	7001	Complaint	Under § 546(a), within 2 years after trustee's appointment.	Yes
Avoidance Under § 549 (Postpetition Transfers)	§ 549	6001, 7001	Complaint	Under § 549(d), within two years after transfer.	Yes
Recovery Under § 550 (Transferee's Liability)	§ 550	7001	Complaint	Under § 550(e), within one year after avoidance of transfer.	Yes
Request to Restrict Prepetition Security Interest from Attaching to Postpetition Property	§ 552(b)	9013	Motion		Yes

Type of Proceeding	Code Section	Bankruptcy Rule	Type of Pleading	When Pleading Due	Must Opportunity for Hearing Be Afforded?
Request for Approval of Abandonment of Estate Property	§ 554	6007, 9013	Notice, if filed by debtor or trustee. Motion, if filed by any other party.		Yes, if a party other than the trustee or debtor filed the notice. Otherwise, only if an objection is filed within 15 days of the mailing of the notice.
Notice of Report and Account of Trustee in a Chapter 7 Case	§ 704(a)(9)	2002(f)(8)	Notice		No
Request for Conversion from a Chapter 7 Case	§ 706	1017(f)	Motion		Yes
Request for Dismissal of a Chapter 7 Case	§ 707	1017(f)	Motion		Yes
Request to Redeem Property	§ 722	6008	Motion		Yes
Avoidance Under § 724(a) (To Avoid Liens Securing Punitive Damages)	§ 724(a)	7001	Complaint		Yes
Request to Extend Time to File Claims Against Surplus of Estate of Chapter 7 Debtor	§ 726	2002(a)(4), 3002(c)(6)	Notice		No

Type of Proceeding	Code Section	Bankruptcy Rule	Type of Pleading	When Pleading Due	Must Opportunity for Hearing Be Afforded?
Objection to Discharge in a Chapter 7 Case	§ 727	4004, 4005	Complaint	No more than 60 days after the first date set for the creditors' meeting.	Yes
Request to Revoke Discharge in Chapter 7 Case	§ 727(d), (e)	7001	Complaint	Generally, within one year of the granting of the discharge.	Yes
Request for Appointment of Additional Committees	§ 1102(a)(2)	9013	Motion		
Request for Appointment of Trustee in a Chapter 11 Case	§ 1104	9013	Motion		Yes
Appointment of Examiner in a Chapter 11 Case	§ 1104(b)		Motion	Before confirmation of a plan.	Yes
Request for Termination of Trustee's Services in a Chapter 11 Case	§ 1105	9013	Motion		Yes
Request that Trustee or Debtor Not Continue to Operate Business in a Chapter 11 Case	§ 1108	9013, 9014	Motion		Yes
Election Under § 1111(b)(2) on Non-Recourse Debts	§ 1111(b)(2)	3014	Ballot	Prior to the conclusion of the hearing on the disclosure statement.	No

B

Type of Proceeding	Code Section	Bankruptcy Rule	Type of Pleading	When Pleading Due	Must Opportunity for Hearing Be Afforded?
Request for Conversion from a Chapter 11 Case	§ 1112	1017(f)	Motion		Yes
Request for Dismissal of a Chapter 11 Case	§ 1112(b)	1017(f)	Motion		Yes
Request to Assume or Reject Collective Bargaining Agreement (Chapter 11)	§ 1113(a)		Application		Yes, hearing must be scheduled no more than 14 days after filing of application (unless additional 7 days authorized).
Filing of Plan (Chapter 11)	§ 1121	3016	Plan	Debtor has exclusive right to file for 120 days order for relief.	No leave of court required to file a plan.
Request to Extend or Reduce 120 and 180 Day Limits for Filing Plan (Chapter 11)	§ 1121(d)	9013	Motion		Yes
Request for Approval of Disclosure Statement	§ 1125(b)	3016(c), 3017(a), (b)	None other than the disclosure statement itself, although arguably a motion may be needed.	With the plan, or within a time fixed by the court.	Yes

Type of Proceeding	Code Section	Bankruptcy Rule	Type of Pleading	When Pleading Due	Must Opportunity for Hearing Be Afforded?
Request for Provisional Allowance of Claim for Purposes of Voting on Plan, Notwithstanding Pending Objection to Claim		3018(a), 9013	Motion		Yes
Acceptances or Rejections of Plan (Chapter 11)	§ 1126	3017	Ballot (acceptance or rejection)		No, but a confirmation hearing will be held.
Request to Change or Withdraw Vote on Plan (Chapter 11)		3018(a), 9013	Motion		Yes
Request to Disallow an Entity's Vote on Plan (Chapter 11)	§ 1126(e)	9013	Motion		Yes
Request to Modify Plan (Chapter 11) After Acceptance but Prior to Confirmation	§ 1127(a)	3019	Motion		Yes
Request to Modify Plan (Chapter 11) After Confirmation	§ 1127(b)	9013	Motion	Before substantial consummation of the plan.	Yes
Request for Confirmation of Plan (Chapter 11)	§ 1128	3020	Possibly a motion.		Mandatory, § 1128(a)

Type of Proceeding	Code Section	Bankruptcy Rule	Type of Pleading	When Pleading Due	Must Opportunity for Hearing Be Afforded?
Objection to Discharge in a Chapter 11 Case	§ 1141(d)	4004, 4005	Complaint	No later than the first date set for the confirmation hearing.	Yes
Request to Revoke Confirmation of Plan (Chapter 11)	§ 1144	7001	Complaint	Within 180 days after order confirming plan.	Yes
Request for Relief from Stay as to Co-Debtor in Chapter 13	§ 1301	4001	Motion		Yes
Request by Debtor for Conversion from a Chapter 13 Case	§ 1307(a)	1017(f)(3)	Notice		No, notice constitutes order.
Request by Debtor for Dismissal of a Chapter 13 Case	§ 1307(b)	1017(f)	Motion		Yes
Request by Non-debtor for Conversion from or Dismissal of a Chapter 13 Case	§ 1307(c)	1017(f)	Motion		Yes
Filing of Plan (Chapter 13)	§ 1321	3015	Plan	Within 15 days after filing of petition.	No leave of court required to file plan.
Request to Extend Duration of Plan (Chapter 13)	§§ 1322(c), 1329(c)	9013	Motion		Yes

Type of Proceeding	Code Section	Bankruptcy Rule	Type of Pleading	When Pleading Due	Must Opportunity for Hearing Be Afforded?
Objection to Confirmation of Plan (Chapter 13)	§ 1324		Objection		Yes, objections heard at confirmation hearing.
Request for Hardship Discharge in a Chapter 13 Case	§ 1328(b)	4007(d)	Motion		Yes
Request to Revoke Discharge in a Chapter 13 Case	§ 1328(e)	7001	Complaint	Within one year after order granting discharge.	Yes
Request to Modify Plan (Chapter 13) After Confirmation	§ 1329	9013	Motion	Before payments under plan are completed.	Yes
Request to Revoke Confirmation of Plan (Chapter 13)	§ 1330	7001	Complaint	Within 180 days after order confirming plan.	Yes
Request to Pay Filing Fee in Installments	28 U.S.C. § 1930(a)	1006	Application		No
Determination of Whether a Matter is a Core Proceeding	28 U.S.C. § 157(b)(3)		Motion by party in interest or sua sponte by the court.		Yes
Examination of Any Entity		2004	Motion		No, at least if the subject of the order is the debtor.

Type of Proceeding	Code Section	Bankruptcy Rule	Type of Pleading	When Pleading Due	Must Opportunity for Hearing Be Afforded?
Request for Reduction or Enlargement of Time		9006(b), (c)	With or without motion prior to the expiration of the period; by motion if the period has expired.		No, unless the court directs otherwise if the period has not yet expired; notice on opposing party if the period has expired, R.9013 or R.9014.
Request for Approval of Compromise or Settlement		2002(a)(3), 9019	Motion		Yes
Appeal from a Final Order of Bankruptcy Court	28 U.S.C. § 158	8002	Notice of Appeal	Within 10 days after entry of final order.	No

SELECTED MEANS TEST DATA

National Standards Based on Gross Monthly Income
For Cases Filed on or After February 13, 2006

[amounts listed combine allowances for food, housing supplies,
apparel & services, personal care products and services, and miscellaneous]

	< $833	$833 to $1,249	$1,250 to $1,666	$1,667 to $2,499	$2,500 to $3,333	$3,334 to $4,166	$4,167 to $5,833	≥ $5,834
One Person	$367	$409	$461	$498	$556	$621	$703	$916
Two People	$578	$595	$627	$679	$744	$825	$904	$1,306
Three People	$802	$808	$812	$819	$924	$937	$1,017	$1,368
Four People	$856	$890	$936	$941	$1,042	$1,063	$1,203	$1,546
Each Additional Person	$138	$149	$160	$171	$182	$193	$204	$216

Maximum Additional Amount Computed as 5% of Food and Clothing

	< $833	$833 to $1,249	$1,250 to $1,666	$1,667 to $2,499	$2,500 to $3,333	$3,334 to $4,166	$4,167 to $5,833	≥ $5,834
One Person	$11	$13	$15	$16	$19	$22	$26	$35
Two People	$19	$20	$21	$23	$26	$29	$33	$50
Three People	$28	$28	$28	$29	$32	$33	$37	$52
Four People	$29	$30	$33	$33	$37	$38	$44	$59
Each Additional Person	$5	$5	$6	$6	$7	$7	$8	$8

Local Housing and Utilities Standards
For Cases Filed on or After February 13, 2006

WASHINGTON
[Selected Counties]

	Family Size and Expense Type					
	1 or 2 Person		3 Person		4 or More Persons	
	Non-Mortgage	Mortgage /Rent	Non-Mortgage	Mortgage /Rent	Non-Mortgage	Mortgage /Rent
Garfield County	$361	$388	$425	$457	$489	$525
King County	$376	$1,205	$442	$1,419	$508	$1,632
Kitsap County	$348	$952	$409	$1,121	$471	$1,288
San Juan County	$430	$1,004	$506	$1,181	$582	$1,357
Snohomish County	$335	$1,159	$394	$1,364	$454	$1,567
Spokane County	$303	$747	$356	$879	$410	$1,011
Walla Walla County	$344	$680	$405	$799	$466	$919
Yakima County	$339	$694	$399	$817	$459	$939

Local Transportation Standards
For Cases Filed on or After February 13, 2006

Operating Costs & Public Transportation Costs

	No Car	One Car	Two Cars
West Census Region	$252	$338	$420

Ownership Costs

	First Car	Second Car
National	$471	$332

Schedule of Actual Administrative Expenses
of Administering a Chapter 13 Plan
For Cases Filed on or After February 13, 2006

Eastern District of Washington	Western District of Washington
6%	8.8%

Median Family Income by Family Size
For Cases Filed on or After February 13, 2006

WASHINGTON

Family Size				
One Earner	Two People	Three People	Four People	More than Four People
$43,891	$54,044	$59,732	$73,259	$6300 more per person over 4

MODEL CHAPTER 13 PLAN
FOR THE EASTERN DISTRICT OF WASHINGTON

———————

UNITED STATES BANKRUPTCY COURT
EASTERN DISTRICT OF WASHINGTON

In re:_____   Case No._____
          Debtor(s)

NOTICE

The following plan proposed by the debtor contains provisions which may significantly affect your rights. If you need additional information to determine how your rights might be affected, you may attend the meeting of creditors, obtain copies of schedules and statement of affairs from the court's website at www.waeb.uscourts.gov, or seek the advice of an attorney.

A creditor who wishes to oppose the plan may do so by filing a timely objection to the plan. Any objection must be in writing, filed with the court and served upon the debtor, debtor's counsel (if any), and the Chapter 13 Trustee within twenty-five (25) days following service of the plan or within five (5) days following the conclusion of the meeting of creditors, whichever is later. The provisions of the confirmed plan will bind the debtor and each creditor, whether or not they have filed a proof of claim.

A proof of claim must be filed by or on behalf of each creditor, including secured creditors, in order for the creditor to be eligible to be paid by the Trustee. The Trustee will treat the amount stated on the filed proof of claim as the amount of a creditor's claim unless otherwise determined by order of the court. See the notice of commencement of case for the claims bar date, the date by which a proof of claim must be filed in order to be treated as timely filed.

Certain pre-confirmation distributions are authorized to be made by the Trustee based on provisions in the plan. Once the plan is confirmed, the Trustee will make payments based only on the proof of claim. Where no proof of claim is filed, no further distributions will be made.

CHAPTER 13 PLAN

Debtor proposes the following ☐ ORIGINAL   ☐ ____ (Seq. #) AMENDED Chapter 13 Plan.

I.   FUTURE EARNINGS, INCOME AND ASSETS COMMITTED TO TRUSTEE FOR FUNDING OF PLAN

A.   Debtor shall pay the Trustee as follows:

$_____ each month for first _____ months, commencing not later than 30 days after the date of the filing of the plan or the order for relief, whichever is earlier.

$_____ each month for next months, commencing _____

$_____ each month for next months, commencing _____

B.   Debtor ☐ COMMITS   ☐ DOES NOT COMMIT all tax refunds to funding of the plan, except to the extent otherwise subject by law to setoff, recoupment, or alternative disposition.

C.   Debtor commits the following other income and assets to funding of the plan.

DATE   SOURCE   AMOUNT

D.   This plan is a: ☐ 100% Plan   ☐ Base Plan/Base Amount $_____.
[For "base plan", the base amount is the total sum of payments to be made to the Trustee over the entire plan. If the base amount is ultimately insufficient to pay those creditors required to be paid in full under the plan, (i.e. administrative expenses and/or secured, executory contract/unexpired lease, arrearage/default, priority and separate classification claims) the base amount will be increased to the extent necessary to fund the plan.]

II.   DURATION OF PLAN

Payments shall be made over a period of not less than 36 months nor more than 60 months, unless debtor pays all creditors in full in less than 36 months. Estimated length of plan is___ months.

III.   DISBURSEMENTS, COSTS OF ADMINISTRATION, AND CLAIMS

A.   DISBURSEMENTS MADE BY TRUSTEE

From funds received, the Trustee shall make disbursements in the sequence set forth below (sections III.A.1 through III.A.9) except as provided in section VII. (If the Trustee has insufficient funds on hand to make disbursements to all classes, the funds will be distributed as provided to the extent funds are available. Claims within a particular class which cannot be paid the proposed disbursements shall be paid a pro rata share of the funds available, except as set forth in section III.A.2.) A monthly payment of less than $15.00 on any particular claim need not be distributed, but may be accumulated and distributed each time the aggregate amount of accumulated funds is $15.00 or more. For each distribution period, the Trustee is permitted to hold back, in the same manner as set out for distribution, estimated or applied for attorney's fees as projected costs of administration.

Pre-Confirmation Payments: Prior to confirmation of the plan, the Trustee is authorized to make monthly pre-confirmation payments to creditors in the amount of the monthly disbursement set forth in sections III.A.2, III.A.3, and III.A.4. Pre-confirmation payments shall be made in the sequence set forth below.

Post-Confirmation Payments: A proof of claim must be filed by or on behalf of a creditor, including secured creditors, in order for that creditor to be eligible to be paid by the Trustee pursuant to the terms of the plan. The Trustee will treat the amount stated on the filed proof of claim as the amount of a creditor's claim unless otherwise determined by order of the court or agreement of the parties.

1. **COSTS OF ADMINISTRATION**

    a. To the standing trustee, the percentage fee fixed under 28 U.S.C. § 586(e)(1)(B).

    b. To the debtor's attorney:

        ☐ A flat fee of $_____, based on the flat fee agreement between the debtor and the attorney in accordance with LBR 2016-1(d) and of which $___ shall be paid by the Trustee as set forth below in section III.A.1.c.

        ☐ Estimated fees of $____, and of which $____ shall be paid by the Trustee as set forth below in section III.A.1.c. Estimated fees shall be withheld from plan disbursements and paid by the Trustee only as allowed by the court after separate application and order in accordance with LBR 2016-1 (a), (b), and (c).

    c. Payment of Attorney Fees by Trustee from plan payments:

        The debtor's attorney will be paid all allowed fees in full before any priority, separate classification, general unsecured or post-petition creditors receive any money; but after payment of continuing, executory contract/ unexpired lease, secured, and arrearage/default creditors, except as set forth below:

        ☐ $_____ per month to the debtor's attorney for allowed fees before any priority, separate classification, general unsecured or postpetition creditors receive any money; but after payment of continuing, executory contract/unexpired lease, secured and arrearage/default creditors.

☐ $\underline{\hspace{2cm}}$ per month to the debtor's attorney for allowed fees before any arrearage/ default, priority, separate classification, general unsecured or post-petition creditors receive any money; but after payment of continuing, executory contract/unexpired lease, and secured creditors.

☐ Other:$\underline{\hspace{8cm}}$

$\underline{\hspace{10cm}}$

Nothing herein shall bar a creditor from requesting relief from stay, dismissal of the case, conversion to another chapter, or other appropriate relief if the debtor does not make payment to the Trustee as proposed by the plan.

2. **CONTINUING CLAIMS**

Available funds shall be disbursed to each creditor in full in the order set forth below.

a. Post-Petition Domestic Support Obligations:

To creditors having post-petition claims for domestic support obligations, which are not being collected directly from the debtor(s), regular periodic payments accruing post-petition on such obligations will be paid to such creditor by Trustee as set forth below. Arrearage will be paid as set forth in section III.A.6 (Priority Claims):

CREDITOR	**MONTHLY PAYMENT AMOUNT**	**MONTHLY PAYMENT COMMENCES**

b. Long Term Debts:

To creditors to whom the last payments are due beyond the term of the plan, payments shall be maintained according to the terms of the original obligation as set forth below. In the event any obligation is paid in full before the plan is complete, future funds previously devoted to such creditor will be disbursed to other creditors under the plan.

1. Regular periodic payments accruing post-petition on real property obligations that were current as of the date of petition filing will be paid directly to such creditor by debtor as set forth in section III.B (Disbursements Made By Debtor).

2. Regular periodic payments accruing post-petition on real property obligations that were delinquent as of the date of petition filing will be paid to such creditor by Trustee as set forth below. Arrearage will be paid as set forth in section III.A5 (Arrearage/Defaults).

3. Regular periodic payments accruing post-petition on personal property obligations will be paid to such creditors by the Trustee as set forth below.

CREDITOR	DESCRIPTION OF PROPERTY/CLAIM	MONTHLY PAYMENT	MONTHLY PYMT COMMENCES

3. EXECUTORY CONTRACTS AND UNEXPIRED LEASES

a. ASSUMPTIONS

Debtor assumes the following executory contracts and/or unexpired leases. Adequate assurance of future performance will be provided by the contract or lease payments being made according to the terms of the original obligation, and will be paid to such creditor by Trustee as set forth below. Any defaults/pecuniary losses will be paid as set forth in section III.A.5 (Arrearage/Defaults).

CREDITOR	TYPE OF AGREEMENT	DESCRIPTION OF PROPERTY/CLAIM	MONTHLY PAYMENT	MONTHLY PYMT COMMENCES

b. REJECTIONS

Debtor rejects the following executory contracts and/or unexpired leases and surrenders the property. Any allowed unsecured claim for damages resulting from such rejection shall be paid as provided in section III.A.8 (Unsecured Claims). The entry of the order confirming the plan shall terminate the automatic stay of 11 U.S.C. § 362(a) as to the property surrendered, thereby allowing recovery and disposition of such property according to applicable non-bankruptcy law.

CREDITOR	TYPE OF AGREEMENT	DESCRIPTION OF PROPERTY/CLAIM

4. SECURED CLAIMS

    a. To creditors whose allowed secured claims will be paid within the term of the plan, each creditor shall be paid the amount of its secured claim plus interest from the date of petition filing as calculated by the Trustee at the interest rate and monthly payment set forth below. The amount of a creditor's secured claim shall be the amount stated as secured on a proof of claim filed by or on behalf of the creditor unless the court orders or the parties agree otherwise. To the extent that the amount of a creditor's allowed secured claim is determined to be less than the amount of its total claim, any portion of the claim in excess of the amount of its allowed secured claim will be treated as an unsecured claim and paid as provided in section III.A.6 (Priority Claims), if entitled to priority under 11 U.S.C. § 507, or if not, as provided in section III.A.8 (Unsecured Claims) below:

CREDITOR	DATE DEBT INCURRED	DESCRIPTION OF PROPERTY	TOTAL CLAIM	COLLATERAL VALUE	INTEREST RATE	MONTHLY PAYMENT	MONTHLY PYMT BEGINS

    b. Debtor surrenders the collateral securing the claims of the following creditors in satisfaction of the secured portion of such creditor's claim. To the extent the collateral does not satisfy such creditor's claim, the creditor shall be treated as the holder of an unsecured claim and paid as provided in section III.A.6 (Priority Claims), if entitled to priority under 11 U.S.C § 507, or if not, as provided in section III.A.8 (Unsecured Claims). The entry of the order confirming the plan shall terminate the automatic stay of 11 U.S.C. § 362(a) as to the collateral surrendered, thereby allowing recovery and disposition of such property according to applicable non-bankruptcy law.

CREDITOR	DESCRIPTION OF PROPERTY	TOTAL CLAIM	COLLATERAL VALUE

    c. Debtor shall file a separate motion under 11 U.S.C. § 522(f) to avoid the following judicial liens or nonpossessory, non-purchase money security interests. Any claim on which the lien is avoided shall be treated as an unsecured claim not entitled to priority and paid as provided in section III.A.8 (Unsecured Claims).

CREDITOR	DESCRIPTION OF INTEREST	EXEMPTION IMPAIRED

5.   **ARREARAGE/DEFAULTS**

     a.   To creditors to whom the last payments are due beyond the term of the plan, arrearage shall be cured at the interest rate and monthly payment set forth below.

CREDITOR	DESCRIPTION OF PROPERTY/CLAIM	AMOUNT OF ARREARAGE	INTEREST RATE	MONTHLY PAYMENT

     b.   To creditors whose executory contracts and/or unexpired leases have been assumed, debtor will cure any default and compensate the other party to such contract and/or unexpired lease for any actual pecuniary loss at the interest rate and monthly payment set forth below.

CREDITOR	DESCRIPTION OF PROPERTY/CLAIM	AMOUNT OF ARREARAGE	INTEREST RATE	MONTHLY PAYMENT

6.   **PRIORITY CLAIMS (OTHER THAN COSTS OF ADMINISTRATION)**

Unsecured creditors entitled to priority as defined in 11 U.S.C. § 507, who file a proof of claim within 90 days after the first date set for the meeting of creditors called pursuant to 11 U.S.C. § 341(a) [or before 180 days after the date of the order for relief in the case of governmental units], shall be paid as provided in this section. Unsecured creditors entitled to priority in a class superior to those in a junior class, as determined by 11 U.S.C. § 507(a), shall be paid in full before creditors in the junior class begin receiving payments. Priority creditors within the same class shall be paid pro rata. Unsecured creditors entitled to priority, who fail to file a proof of claim within the time set forth above, shall be paid as provided in section III.A.8 (Unsecured Claims) below.

     a.   To all unsecured priority creditors, except those provided for in section III.A.6.b below, payments in full in deferred cash payments over the term of the plan as follows, unless the holder of a particular claim agrees to a different treatment.

CREDITOR	DESCRIPTION OF CLAIM	AMOUNT OF CLAIM

b.   To the following unsecured priority creditors provided for in 11 U.S.C. § 507(a)(1)(B), where the debtor has proposed a 60-month plan, payments in deferred cash payments over the term of the plan to the extent of the funds remaining after payment of administrative expenses, continuing, executory contract/unexpired lease, secured, arrearage/default, priority claims set forth in section III.A.6.a.

CREDITOR   **DESCRIPTION OF CLAIM**   **AMOUNT OF CLAIM**

7.   **SEPARATE CLASSIFICATIONS OF UNSECURED CLAIMS**

To unsecured creditors not entitled to priority, separately classified pursuant to 11 U.S.C § 1322(b)(1), a dividend over the term of the plan pro rata as follows. (Debtor has filed with the plan an affidavit stating the basis for each separate classification.)

CREDITOR   **DESCRIPTION OF CLAIM**   **AMOUNT OF CLAIM**

8.   **UNSECURED CLAIMS**

a.   TIMELY FILED

To unsecured creditors not entitled to priority, who file a proof of claim within 90 days after the first date set for the meeting of creditors called pursuant to 11 U.S.C. § 341(a) [or before 180 days after the date of the order for relief in the case of governmental units], a dividend over the term of plan pro rata as follows:

☐ Base Plan: Payment of their allowed claims to the extent of the funds remaining after payment of administrative expenses, continuing, secured, executory contract/unexpired lease, secured, arrearage/default, priority and separate classification claims.

☐ 100% Plan: Full payment of their allowed claims.

☐ 100% Plan: Full payment of their allowed claims. After full payment of unsecured allowed claims, then allowed unsecured claims that are non-dischargeable under 11 U.S.C. § 1328(a) shall receive pro rata payments for interest to the extent funds are available in the plan at the interest rate set forth below.

CREDITOR	STATUTORY BASIS FOR **INTEREST**	**CLAIM** AMOUNT	**INTEREST** RATE

b. TARDILY FILED

To unsecured creditors, who fail to file a proof of claim within 90 days after the first date set for the meeting of creditors called pursuant to 11 U.S.C. § 341(a) [or before 180 days after the date of the order for relief in the case of governmental units], a dividend over the term of plan pro rata as follows:

SUCH CLAIMS SHALL BE TREATED AS ALLOWED CLAIMS, UNLESS DISALLOWED BY ORDER OF THE COURT, BUT SHALL BE SUBORDINATED TO TIMELY FILED CLAIMS AND PAID PRO RATA ONLY AFTER FULL PAYMENT OF TIMELY FILED CLAIMS TO THE EXTENT NECESSARY FOR THE PLAN TO COMPLY WITH 11 U.S.C. § 1325(a)(4) AND 11 U.S.C. § 1325(b)(1)(B).

9. **POST-PETITION CLAIMS**

Claims filed under 11 U.S.C § 1305 shall be treated as follows:

a. Claims for taxes that become payable to a governmental unit while the case is pending shall be treated as priority claims and paid as provided in section III.A.6 (Priority Claims) above.

b. Claims for consumer debt that arise after the date of petition filing, and that are for property or services necessary for the debtor's performance under the plan, shall be treated as timely filed unsecured claims and paid as provided in section III.A.8 (Unsecured Claims), but only if the specific claim is provided for in a modification of the plan. The claim shall be disallowed if the creditor knew or should have known that prior approval by the Trustee of the debtor's incurring the obligation was practicable and was not obtained.

B. **DISBURSEMENTS MADE BY DEBTOR**

Debtor shall make disbursement directly to creditors as follows:

1. To creditors secured by real property whose rights are not being modified pursuant to 11 U.S.C. § 1322(b)(2) and are not otherwise impaired, the secured claim of each shall be paid directly by the debtor according to the terms of the original obligation at the interest rate and monthly payment set forth below. [A secured claim is not being modified and is not impaired if all payments were current as of the date of petition

filing, none of the terms of the debtor's agreement with the creditor are being changed, and the collateral had a value as of the date of petition filing equal to or greater than the net amount due.]

CREDITOR	ADDRESS & PARCEL NUMBER	TOTAL CLAIM	PROPERTY VALUE	INTEREST RATE	MONTHLY PAYMENT	FINAL PYMT DATE

2. To creditors holding claims defined as domestic support obligations:

CREDITOR	TOTAL MONTHLY PAYMENT

IV. INSURANCE

Debtor shall keep any collateral continuously insured in accordance with the terms of the original obligation with the creditor until the amount of its secured claim is paid.

V. TAX RETURNS

A. ☐ All tax returns and tax reports due pre-petition have been filed.

☐ The following tax returns and tax reports due as of the date of petition filing have not been filed:

TAX AGENCY	KIND OF TAX	TAX PERIOD	DATE WHEN RETURN WILL BE FILED

B. Debtor shall file all post-petition tax returns/tax reports and pay all post-petition taxes as they come due.

VI. COMPARISON WITH CHAPTER 7

The value, as of the date of petition filing, of property to be distributed under the plan on account of each allowed unsecured claim is not less than the amount that would be paid on such claim if the estate of the debtor were liquidated under Chapter 7 of the Code on such date.

VII. **SPECIAL PROVISIONS**

The plan includes the following special provisions:

VII. **REVESTMENT OF PROPERTY**

Property of the estate shall revest in the debtor upon confirmation of the plan, or at a later time or in another entity as follows:

☐   Dismissal or discharge only.

☐   _____

In the event the case is converted to Chapter 7, 11 or 12, property of the estate shall vest in accordance with the applicable law. Debtor shall be responsible for the preservation and protection of all property of the estate.

IX. **RETENTION OF LIENS**

Each creditor shall retain its lien or other interest in property vesting in the debtor until payment in full of the underlying debt or discharge under 11 U.S.C. § 1328.

X. **CERTIFICATE OF COMPLIANCE WITH LAW AND LOCAL FORM 2083**

The debtor's attorney (or the debtor if no attorney) hereby certifies under penalty of perjury that:
A.   This plan is a duplicate of the plan provided for by Local Rule 2083.
B.   This plan has been proposed in good faith and not by any means forbidden by law.
C.   This plan complies with the provisions of Chapter 13, with the other applicable provisions of Title 11, United States Code, and with all applicable national and local bankruptcy rules.

DATED:_____   Debtor:_____

Attorney for Debtor:_____   Debtor:_____

Attorney Address:_____

_____

Attorney Telephone:_____

PROJECTS RELATED TO BANKRUPTCY PRACTICE

The projects below are designed to provide students with some experience in the practice of bankruptcy. Each can be done in isolation or in conjunction with one or more of the others. They can be assigned at the end of the book chapter to which they relate, in the middle of that chapter immediately following coverage of the related material, or at the end of the course.

Project One

Assume you are getting ready to file for bankruptcy protection. An attorney has helped you complete the petition, *see* Official Form 1, and has given you blank copies of Schedules A, B, I and J of Official Form 6, which call for a list of your assets, income, and expenses. Complete those schedules fully. A copy of the schedules can be obtained at the following web site: http://www.uscourts.gov/bkforms/index.html. If you prefer, you may interview a friend or family member and, using the information that person provides you, complete the schedules for that person.

In connection with Schedule J, be sure to list (on Line 17) the prorated amount of any expenses that you pay less frequently than each month (*e.g.*, $1/12$ of any annual expense). In doing so, consider what expenses you have that are not already provided for on the form.

Project Two

Schedule J, Line 4 requires that the debtor identify the amount spent on food each month by the debtor's household. Estimate that amount for your household. Then, to test the accuracy of that estimate, have everyone in your household – family members only, not roommates – keep detailed records of all amounts spent for food for 30 consecutive days. This includes amount spent at restaurants, coffee shops or carts, and grocery stores. Note, make sure not to count amounts spend at supermarkets for things than food (*e.g,*, cleaning and hygiene products; medicines).

Project Three

Assume you are getting ready to file for bankruptcy protection. An attorney has helped you complete the petition, *see* Official Form 1, and has given you blank copies of Schedule C of Official Form 6, which calls for a list of your assets that you could claim as exempt. Assume that the law governing your exemptions is the law of the jurisdiction in which you currently reside, which may or may not have "opted out" of the federal exemptions. *See* § 522(b)(2). Determine which of your assets you may exempt and to what extent, and then complete the schedule. A copy of the schedule can be obtained at the following web site: http://www.uscourts.gov/bkforms/index.html. If you prefer, you may interview a friend or family member and, using the information that person provides you, complete the schedule for that person.

Project Four

Fourteen months ago, Dumont was run over by a car driven by Negligent. Dumont hired you to sue Negligent and signed a written contingent fee agreement entitling you to one-third of any recovery. While the case was pending, Dumont was unable to work and fell deeply in debt. Last week, Dumont filed for Chapter 7 bankruptcy protection and claimed the cause of action against Negligent as exempt. Yesterday, you received a check for $21,000 pursuant to a settlement reached shortly before the bankruptcy petition was filed. Dumont is demanding that you turn over the entire amount to him and the bankruptcy trustee is demanding that you turn over the entire amount to her.

A. Research the law in your state about whether and when an attorney acquires a common-law or statutory lien on client recoveries.

B. Given your analysis in Part A, prepare a memorandum analyzing what you should do now. How much of the settlement funds must you turn over and to whom? What arguments can you make to support your right to retain one-third of the recovery? *See In re Miglia*, 345 B.R. 919 (Bankr. N.D. Iowa 2006).

C. Given your analysis in Part B, is there a way to restructure or rephrase your fee agreements to avoid this problem in the future or to otherwise ensure that you will not end up having to disgorge all settlement proceeds and file an unsecured claim?

Project Five

Dupont filed for Chapter 7 bankruptcy protection last week. Among the assets listed on Dupont's schedules is a commercial building that Dupont rents out to two different tenants. Tenant One has two years left on a lease calling for payments of $1,800 per month. Tenant Two has one year left on a lease calling for payments of $1,400 per month. The building secures a debt to Lender that, as of the petition date, totaled approximately $425,000. Interest is accruing on the debt at a variable rate adjusted semiannually. That rate was recently increased to 8.6% (yielding interest of approximately $100 per day) and is likely to continue to rise in accordance with the prevailing trend in market interest rates. Dupont's Schedule A lists the property with a value of $485,000 but Lender thinks it is worth substantially less, probably somewhere in the $395,000–$415,000 range. The debtor stopped making payments about three months ago.

At Lender's request, you prepared and filed a motion for relief from the stay under § 362(d)(2). You now need to plan for the hearing on that motion. Prepare a memorandum to the file detailing precisely what you need to prove and how you plan to prove it. Be specific as to what documentary evidence you will seek to admit, who you will call to testify, and what testimony you will seek to elicit.

Project Six

Assume you are getting ready to file for bankruptcy protection. An attorney has helped you complete the petition, *see* Official Form 1, and has given you blank copies of Schedules D, E, and F of Official Form 6, which calls for a list of your secured, unsecured, and priority debts. Complete those schedules fully. A copy of the schedules can be obtained at: http://www.uscourts.gov/bkforms/index.html. If you prefer, you may interview a friend or family member and, using the information that person provides you, complete the schedules for that person.

Project Seven

On June 1, 2005, Tony and Natalie Delvecchio completed an application for a $40,000 home improvement loan from Neighborhood Bank. The Delvecchios submitted accurate earnings statements and current bank statements with their loan application. On June 15, 2005, the Delvecchios met with Bank's loan officer, Lucy Olson, to execute the loan documents. During the conference, Natalie expressed reservations about signing the completed loan documents because the information contained in the final loan application, which was retyped by Bank from the original loan application, included old bank account balances that were now substantially inaccurate. In addition, the final loan agreement contained provisions indicating that "all loan proceeds are to be used exclusively for the acquisition of materials to be affixed to the property," and that "the written agreement represents the entire and integrated agreement between the parties and supersedes any prior negotiations, representations, or agreements, either written or oral, and represents the complete and final agreement." The Delvecchios advised Ms. Olson that they intended to purchase some new kitchen appliances, including a refrigerator, with part of the loan proceeds. Ms. Olson advised the Delvecchios that the documents needed to be executed in their current form, and assured them it was proper and acceptable to do so for the project proposed. The Delvecchios reluctantly agreed and executed the loan documents and mortgage securing the loan. They received a check and used the entire proceeds to remodel their kitchen, including buying a new refrigerator.

On January 16, 2006, Tony Delvecchio was terminated from his job. Mrs. Delvecchio's income was insufficient to make all their payments to Bank and other Creditors. On September 20, 2006, Bank foreclosed judicially its mortgage against the Delvecchios' home, leaving a $23,000 deficiency claim due and owing Bank. The Delvecchios used their credit card with Bank, charging $2,500.00 between December 15, 2006 and January 15, 2007 for living expenses and Christmas gifts.

On February 1, 2007, the Delvecchios filed a joint petition for Chapter 7 bankruptcy relief. At the § 341 Meeting of Creditors, conducted on March 2, 2007, the Delvecchios disclosed to the trustee that they had inadvertently failed to disclose in their bankruptcy schedules a 1991 20-foot boat and trailer stored at home of Tony's brother since September 2005. The attorney for the Delvecchios advised the trustee that the Delvecchios intended to amend their Schedule B, to disclose the asset, and their Schedule C, to claim the asset as exempt in full.

Bank wants you to advise it whether to bring an adversary proceeding objecting to the Delvecchios' discharge under § 727 and challenging the dischargeability of its claim under § 523(a).

A. Prepare the complaint.

B. Prepare a memorandum of law to the file that, for each of the two claims, outlines what you must prove to be successful, identifies the evidence you will seek to admit, and analyzes the merits of the claim.